A History of
The Expansion of Christianity

Volume VII
ADVANCE THROUGH STORM
A.D. 1914 AND AFTER,
WITH CONCLUDING GENERALIZATIONS

A History of

THE EXPANSION OF CHRISTIANITY

(Volume VII)

ADVANCE THROUGH STORM

STORM

A.D. 1914 AND AFTER,
WITH CONCLUDING GENERALIZATIONS

By
KENNETH SCOTT LATOURETTE
*D. Willis James Professor of Missions
and Oriental History in Yale University*

HARPER & BROTHERS PUBLISHERS
New York and London

In memory of

HARLAN PAGE BEACH

1854-1933

ACKNOWLEDGEMENTS

In prelude to this final stage in our long pilgrimage, gratitude must first be expressed for the assistance which has been so generously given by institutions and individuals in the preparation of this particular volume. As in the preceding number in the series, the author has had the advantage of access to the library of the Congregation for the Propagation of the Faith, in Rome, to the British Museum, to the Wason collection (now in Cornell University), to the Morrison library on China (now in Tokyo), to the library of the North China Branch of the Royal Asiatic Society, in Shanghai, to the library of New College, Edinburgh, to the Missionary Research Library, in New York City, and, above all, to the libraries of Yale University, especially the Day Missions Library. To the staffs of each of these collections the author is most deeply indebted, not only for the ready permission to avail himself of the resources of which they have been faithful custodians, but also for the unfailing courtesy which brightened the long days of research. More even than in any preceding volume, the author has taken toll of many minds. They have been from all the continents and from several of the islands of the sea. They have been from most of the great branches of the Church and many of them have had an active part in the events and movements which the following pages record. They are far too numerous to catalogue, but as these lines are written memories come flooding back of conversations on steamers, in railroad trains, in quiet universities, in remote mission stations, in great cities in the Orient and the Occident, in libraries with their musty tang of books so familiar to the scholar, in crowded conferences and conventions, in the interstices of time in meetings of committees and boards, in hotels, in offices, and in leisurely walks across green countrysides. The unquestioning hospitality, the kindly, understanding faces, the quick and thoughtful response to questions, the penetrating comments, the frank honesty and unselfish objectivity of appraisal, even of projects, institutions, and persons dearer than life itself, and the ungrudging courtesies to the inquiring and peripatetic stranger from a quite different branch of the Church have been rich reward, entirely beyond the author's deserving, for all the labour entailed in travel, research, and writing.

This is as well the opportunity to acknowledge the debt for the multifarious assistance without which not only this concluding volume but also the entire work would have been impossible. Here detailed acknowledgement is even more out of the question. One cannot, however, allow these pages to pass into print without mention of a few of the many who have been particularly helpful. Although use has been made of collections in several widely separated parts of the world, the author's chief reliance has been upon the Day Missions Library. The author, therefore, is peculiarly indebted to the late Professor George Edward Day who began the assembling of the books and whose bequest, supplemented by that of his wife, Olivia H. Day, made provision for the continuation and enlargement of the library which bears their name. The late Professor Harlan Page Beach was long in charge of the library and to him it owes its arrangement and much of its later dimensions. The present librarian, Professor Raymond Philip Morris, has built worthily on the foundations so ably laid and by his unfailing interest has been of more help than he knows. The generosity, nearly a generation since, of Mrs. Ellen S. James and Arthur Curtiss James, endowed the chair which has made possible for the author the freedom from financial care so necessary to a task of the dimensions which these volumes have assumed. Mrs. Charles T. Lincoln has turned into seemly and accurate typescript the original manuscript, often a sore trial of patience, of the entire work, and has made detailed suggestions which have been invaluable in the final revision. Over the span of a quarter of a century successive annual instalments of students have sat through the lectures in which the material in these volumes was brought into orderly form and by their interest and questions have quickened their instructor's mind and deepened his insight. To the American publishers, Harper and Brothers, and especially to their manufacturing department, and to Eyre and Spottiswoode Publishers, Limited, of London, the author is under peculiar obligation for undertaking the formidable task of making the volumes available to the public and in so admirable a format. That they did this, most of it during the stress of a world war, is no mean achievement, and the author cannot forbear expressing the thanks which he so deeply feels.

The author must also, in this formal fashion, record his gratitude for the millions, the vast majority of them now unknown, who spent themselves that the Gospel of Christ might be known and in whom it was incarnate. It is not because without them there would have been no story to tell that the author would chiefly express his thanks, but because of what they wrought for their own and succeeding generations. Many of them of the present century have been familiar and dear friends. Others, of earlier centuries, have, through the author's glimpses of them through the fragmentary traces of their lives, seemed also to have deigned to permit themselves to be accounted as friends. Because of them the author, like millions of others, is forever the richer. As he recalls them, there comes to his mind the familiar line, so eminently fitting for them and their lives:

"The glorious company of the Apostles praise Thee."

It is as a small and quite unworthy supplement to that age-long chorus of adoration and thanksgiving that the author would dedicate this and its sister volumes.

Contents

Chapter I

Chapter II

Chapter III

Chapter IV

Chapter V

Chapter VI

Chapter VII

Chapter VIII

Chapter IX

MAPS (in rear of volume).

A History of
The Expansion of Christianity

Volume VII

ADVANCE THROUGH STORM

A.D. 1914 AND AFTER,
WITH CONCLUDING GENERALIZATIONS

Chapter I

BY WAY OF INTRODUCTION

W E NOW come to what, for the time being, must be the final volume of our story. In it we must attempt two main tasks. First we must describe the course of the expansion of Christianity in the years from 1914 to 1944, the date when, from the necessities of the author and the publisher, this work is being brought to its conclusion. Second, we must look back over the course of the entire narrative, from the inception of Christianity to A.D. 1944, and endeavour to discover and summarize such general conclusions as seem to arise from it.

The tasks are ones of peculiar difficulty. The period which seems to have begun in A.D. 1914 did not end in 1944. We have been viewing the other eras of the spread of Christianity from the perspective of time. While an age seldom begins or concludes with a precise day or year, we have been able to give approximate dates for their inception and termination. We have looked back upon them as completed and have surveyed the well-rounded whole. We cannot do that with the era which commenced in 1914. Obviously in 1944 it was still unfinished. We cannot view the entire scroll because it was not then completely unrolled. So, too, with our attempt to draw generalizations from the history of the expansion of Christianity. That story has not been ended. Indeed, in spite of its nearly nineteen and a half centuries, in 1944 it seemed to be only in its early stages. Not until the nineteenth and twentieth centuries did Christianity become really world-wide in its geographic extent. Even then among many peoples, some of them the most numerous on the globe, it was merely beginning to have a marked influence. Those who for centuries had professed adherence to it were by no means fully conformed to it. It is tantalizing to be compelled to pause at a semi-colon, but we have no other option.

Moreover, as one attempts to summarize the course of Christianity thus far he becomes painfully aware of the imperfections and superficialities of the historian's craft. From the standpoint of Christian affirmation, the most important "effects of Christianity on its environment" lie "beyond history." The environment with which Christianity primarily deals is human lives, and these, so Christians have always confidently declared, have only barely begun this

1

side of what men call death and have their finest fruitage the other side of the grave. "If in this life only we have hope in Christ," they insist, "we are of all men most miserable." Into that life "beyond the river" the historian cannot reach. Only the poet dares venture there, and he on the wings of faith. He can report merely in terms of inadequate imagery what he has glimpsed. Even this side of the grave, as we have again and again said, the answers to many of the most important questions largely elude us. We cannot always be sure, for instance, why Christianity spread or why in certain areas and lands it failed to spread and even declined. We can only infrequently measure with exactness the effect of Christianity on its environment and of the environment on Christianity. At best we must usually content ourselves with approximations. We cannot know satisfactorily the effect of Christianity upon any one individual this side of death, even when we have for him voluminous autobiographical and biographical material. We cannot penetrate fully into his inner life nor record all the forces which have made him. Still less can we know intimately the millions of individuals who have called themselves Christians or determine precisely the extent and the manner in which their faith has moulded them.

Yet, difficult though the task of this volume is, there is in it much of exciting challenge. The story of which we are to write is one in which we live and are participants. What is happening affects us and those who shall come after us, perhaps critically. To some slight degree we can hope to modify the course of events. We are watching unfold an important act in a great drama. We are both spectators and actors. But what we are in is more than a play. Great issues are at stake, for us as individuals, for nations, for cultures, and for mankind and civilization as a whole. We are dealing with basic problems of human history. They have to do with the ultimate meaning of life. They are of major concern to us all.

Moreover, while it is brief when measured in terms of man's presence on this planet, the past course of Christianity has been long enough to permit some positive conclusions, to enable us to formulate definite questions, and to offer answers, even though some of them be only tentative. The task is one which we must not seek to evade because it is hard. We must attempt it, even when we recognize our inability adequately to perform it.

We will first address ourselves to the era which began in 1914. At the outset we will seek to discover the forces chiefly at work in it, and particularly those peculiar to it and which gave it the characteristics that separated it from its predecessors. We will recount the main course and the new movements in Christianity. We will speak of modifications in the processes by which Christianity spread. Then we will circle the globe, depicting, region by region, the expansion or the recession of Christianity. In this we shall be dealing with the now familiar categories of what it was that spread, the reasons for the spread or the contraction, the processes of the spread, and the effects on the environment and of the environment. On the basis of this survey we will seek to discover whether, measured by the criteria we have applied to other eras, the period was one of advance or recession.

The title chosen for the volume both anticipates and summarizes our conclusion. The three decades were ones of advance, but of advance through storm. The advance was not as rapid as in "the great century" from 1800 to 1914. There were what appeared to be startling losses. Yet in the main in 1944 Christianity found itself in a stronger position than in 1914. Indeed, if one views, as one must, the world-wide story as a whole, it becomes clear that the thirty years which followed 1914 constituted one of the greatest eras in the history of Christianity.

In this portion of the volume the author has had the advantage of having lived through the period, and in his mature years. He has known personally many of those who loom most prominently in the narrative, chiefly among Protestants but also, although to a more limited extent, among Roman Catholics. He has visited a number of the countries covered and has seen with his own eyes much of what is described. He has participated in several of the movements and gatherings which helped to shape the Christianity of these years. In part, therefore, this portion of the volume is the first-hand account of an eye witness. Much of the rest is based upon the reports, oral and written, of actual participants.

The title, "advance through storm," is also appropriate for the second part of the volume. In this we will attempt to look over the entire story so far as it has gone, from the beginning to the present. Here we must first have a brief chronological summary, by periods. We will seek light through a comparison of the expansion of Christianity with that of other religions. Then we must attempt to formulate answers to the major questions with which we have concerned ourselves. Only now we must view the nineteen and a half centuries as an entirety and mankind as a unit. Finally, we will endeavour to formulate such insight into the meaning of human history as our story has seemed to disclose. Again our title anticipates part of our conclusion. From its beginning the expansion of Christianity has been against opposition and through perils which have threatened the very existence of the faith. Yet the course has been one of advance. Measured by geographic extent and seen against the background of the globe and the entire human race, it has been not decline and fall, but expansion. This has been true both of the years since 1914 and of the centuries since Calvary.

This does not necessarily mean that the world is by progressive steps to conform completely to Christian ideals. Here is no unqualified endorsement of the doctrine of progress. Measured by its influence upon the race as a whole, Christianity has unquestionably played a larger and larger part in human history. However, its standards are so far beyond both individuals and society that neither can fully attain them "within history." Even the greatest of Christian saints have not been perfect as their "heavenly Father is perfect,"[1] nor have they been "filled unto all the fulness of God."[2] Yet these are the goals which the New Testament sets before the Christian. If exceptional individuals cannot reach them this side of death, how much less can human society as a whole be expected to do so. Moreover, in the very areas where Christian influence has been strongest, some of the collective ills of mankind have assumed their largest dimensions. This was true of Negro slavery and of war. Our survey, in other words, does not entitle us to an easy-going optimism of the achievement of Christian perfection within those realms with which the historian deals. However, the implication is by no means one of despair nor is the history of Christianity one of Sisyphean labours. If mankind never reaches the goal set by the Sermon on the Mount and if some evils swell to their most colossal stature in regions and among peoples longest under the impact of Christianity, it has been primarily through Christianity that some of these evils have been eliminated and that the most hopeful battles have been waged against the others. Through Christianity some of the chronic handicaps of mankind, such as illiteracy and disease, have been more effectively attacked on a world-wide scale than through any other force or combination of forces. Moreover, increasing millions have been introduced to a life of growing approximation to New Testament ideals. The resolution of these seeming paradoxes is beyond the office of the historian. To the problems presented by them, however, we shall return in our closing chapters.

[1] Matt. v, 48.
[2] Eph. iii, 19.

Chapter II

THE MOVEMENTS WHICH GAVE THE AGE ITS DISTINCTIVE CHARACTER

AT THE outset of the attempt to narrate the course of Christianity in the post-1914 world we must seek to describe the main features which gave to the age its chief characteristics. Only by seeing the setting can we hope to understand the recessions and the advances registered by the faith.

The task is both challenging and baffling. The endeavour to discover the forces which mould the lives of men can never fail to be inviting. It is peculiarly alluring when, as here, it has to do with those movements which have shaped the days of our immediate parents and of ourselves. It is baffling because of the complexity of the scene and of the lack of perspective which our own proximity to the events entails. Yet it must be essayed.

It seems clear that with the fateful events of the summer of 1914 mankind was ushered into a new age and that with it another era began in the spread of Christianity. Seldom does one period end sharply and a new one begin with abruptness. Usually some features of each era persist into its successor. That was true of the pre-1914 and the post-1914 sections of human history. The post-1914 world was the child of the nineteenth century and many of the distinguishing marks of the parent were seen in the offspring. Yet the outbreak of the world war which began in 1914 was obviously the transition from one epoch to another.

Some of the forces which had given its form to the nineteenth century ran on into the post-1914 years. Indeed, they then came into riper fruition. The development of science and the attendant mastery by man of his physical environment had been prominent in the nineteenth century. They became even more so in the twentieth century. Machinery played an ever-increasing part in the life of mankind. Inventions became more numerous. Steamships, railroads, motor cars, and factories, already present, multiplied. Through them Western Europe, the United States, and Japan were still further industrialized. Industrialization began or proceeded apace in other lands, notably in Russia. To the mechanical devices familiar to the closing years of the pre-1914 age were added others, among them the airplane and the radio. Through them the globe continued to shrink in time-distances. A world culture was emerging characterized chiefly by the use of science and of the machines and appliances developed through science. The members of the human race were brought ever more closely into physical proximity with one another. Increasingly the world was becoming a neighbourhood. Nationalism and racial friction were making that neighbourhood extremely quarrelsome. Nationalism in an intense form was a nineteenth century phenomenon. It was associated with democracy, although not always or inseparably, and democracy was another striking feature of the nineteenth century which carried over into the post-1914 world. Other social theories which after 1914 attained widespread and prominent application had been given their determinating formulation in the nineteenth century. That was true of Marxian socialism.

Yet commencing with the fateful summer of 1914 the world became palpably different. The most immediate contrast was the coming of world wars. Wars involving more than one continent were not a new phenomenon. The Mongol irruption in the thirteenth century had affected almost all civilized mankind. The series of conflicts which had upset the Occident in the eighteenth century had spread to all five continents. However, the wars which began in 1914 engrossed all of mankind to a degree attained by none of their predecessors. It was not entirely lack of perspective or egoistic exaggeration of the importance of its own affairs which led the generation which spanned the first four decades of the twentieth century to label the struggle of 1914-1918 World War I and that which assumed larger dimensions in September, 1939, World War II. Although not every nation was drawn into formal belligerency, in these two wars all the major powers were active participants and those countries which legally remained neutral were profoundly disturbed. World War II was a continuation of World War I. The years between the two conflicts were an uneasy truce, feverish and with problems left unresolved by the first stage of the conflict. The second phase of the struggle was ushered in by the Japanese adventure in China. This began in 1931 in Manchuria and by successive steps spread to all of East Asia and the Pacific Ocean. In persisting in her programme in Manchuria Japan challenged the structure for the maintenance of peace which had been set up after the war of 1914-1918 in the League of Nations and in the agreements reached at the Washington Conference in 1921-1922. Her initial successes and the seeming impotence of her critics prepared the way for an Italian invasion of Ethiopia, the German disregard of the Treaty of Versailles, a thinly veiled Italian and German intervention in a Spanish civil war, and the daring German expansion in Europe. The titanic struggle which in 1937 embroiled all China, which in 1939 engulfed Europe and its colonies, which late in 1941 brought the United States into active belligerency, and which then drew in some of the Latin American countries, was in effect one war with that which broke out in August, 1914, and which had seemed to end in November, 1918.

The contrast between the wars that began in 1914 and the comparative peace of the century which followed Waterloo was tragically striking. The decades between 1815 and 1914 saw many wars, but none involved even all Europe and none remotely approached the dimensions either of the Napoleonic conflicts or of the struggles ushered in by 1914.

Into the reasons for the relative peace of the nineteenth century we need not go in any detail. They were associated with the British control of the seas and the related British priority in the industrial revolution and British dominance in industry and commerce. Great Britain had led in the development of the new machinery and the factory system and long enjoyed a virtual monopoly of these devices. Her control of the seas, confirmed by her defeat of Napoleon and strengthened by her industrial might, facilitated the growth of her domains in all four quarters of the globe. To keep open the communications with this far-flung empire and for her commerce she held key positions on most of the world's main arteries of ocean travel and could prevent any local quarrel from becoming world-wide.

When, as was almost inevitable, other peoples acquired the tools of the new age, Great Britain's position was challenged. An industrialized Germany, with a growing population, did not view with equanimity Great Britain's control of the sea approaches to North-western Europe. A Japan dependent upon foreign markets for the output of her growing factories was not content with the privileged position of Great Britain in the Far East. The economic factor was by no means the sole cause of the gigantic wars of the first half of the twentieth century, but it was important.

The spreading use of the new mechanical appliances made the wars, as they broke out, world-wide in their scope and very destructive. Until mankind could learn fresh habits and develop new institutions which would reduce the frequency and extent of wars, the tools presented to it by the advance of science would threaten civilization. So long as the new machines were concentrated chiefly in Great Britain relative peace could be maintained, for it was to the interest of British trade to keep the sea lanes open to the ships of all nations. In the construction of the British Empire many wars were fought but most of the more severe ones were before the nineteenth century. As, in the nineteenth century, Great Britain developed the new tools and enjoyed a monopoly of them, she won most of her armed contests with relatively slight effort. Some of them were severe, notably that in the Crimea and the one with the Boers, but they were localized. When the British monopoly ceased and numbers of other nations equipped themselves with the appliances of the new age, wars multiplied and became more widespread and intense.

Revolutions marked the new age. Usually they came in consequence of defeat or over-strain in war. Some of them were precipitated by the world-wide economic depression which followed, after an eleven year interval, the conflict of 1914-1918. Most of them embodied social programmes and philosophies which were formulated in the nineteenth century. Indeed, the revolutions were as much in basic ideas as in political, economic, and social structures. Systems of thought which had heretofore been largely limited to minorities now became the guide of large masses. Some of them challenged the basic convictions of the Christian faith, even where these had been woven into the fabric of culture. Western Europe could no longer, as it had for a thousand years or more, be termed Christendom. Never had it been fully Christian but officially it had been committed to that faith. Now, by some European nations and by large elements in other European peoples Christianity was openly repudiated, conceptions of the universe and of man which were contradictory to it were aggressively avowed and followed, and its adherents were persecuted. The situation was made more serious by the fact that these anti-Christian programmes and attitudes issued from trends long present in Western society and which had been growing in the nineteenth century. Much of what had come out of the rationalism of the Renaissance and the eighteenth century and the tendency of the scientific and machine age challenged fundamental Christian postulates. In a certain sense this was not new. Always, even in what some, with nostalgic distortion, looked back upon as "the ages of faith," there had been much of scepticism and of practical rejection of Christian standards. Now, however, that repudiation was more openly articulate and systematized and was much more effectively organized.

In the course of the nineteenth century, chiefly in the two or three decades which immediately preceded 1914, the aggressive impact of the Occident had brought to many peoples the beginning of cultural disintegration. Non-Western peoples could not stand against the incursion of the Occident, equipped as it was with the new machinery. After an attempt at armed resistance, usually brief and futile, they acquiesced in the coming of the white man and sought to adopt some or all of his ways. In the post-1914 years these cultural revolutions among non-European peoples continued and were intensified. They were particularly marked in Africa south of the Sahara, in Turkey, in Iran, in India, and in China. Japan was also in revolution. By her promptness in accepting the Occident and entering into treaty relations with the powers, she had avoided open military defeat, but she had been constrained to accept extra-territoriality and tariffs fixed by conventions with Western governments. To assume the leadership to which her ambition called her, she had adopted and adapted much of Occidental culture. Her inherited institutions were not as fundamentally altered as were those of some other peoples, but superficially the changes were startling. A revolution which brought into power the more extreme elements in her armed services followed the world-wide economic depression of the late 1920's and early 1930's. Moreover, even Occidental nations which had not been defeated in war and which were the source of the ideas and machines which were working such profound changes among other peoples were themselves displaying rapid cultural reshaping. In their case the alterations were usually not so spectacular as elsewhere, but they were exten-sive. For instance, after 1918 both Great Britain and the United States expe-rienced cultural change.

The wars of the 1930's and 1940's which culminated and coalesced in what was often called World War II were accompanied and succeeded by revolu-tions and the intensification of revolutions already in progress. These were especially marked in France, Italy, Germany, and some of the smaller peoples of Europe. European society as a whole was more deeply altered than by the war of 1914-1918 or by any series of events since the French Revolution and the wars of Napoleon. The accelerated revolutions were also striking in Japan, China, India, and the peoples of South-eastern Asia. No land completely escaped them.

The inherited institutions and thought of mankind as a whole were more kaleidoscopic than in any previous period of which history gives a clear record. Particular portions of the human race and segments of the globe had in earlier times been as greatly or even more greatly altered and in as brief a space of time. However, never before had all of mankind been so dramatically on the march. The rate varied with the nation, but for all the race one age was giving way to another.

Closely associated with the wars and the cultural revolutions was another set of changes: the non-white peoples were in revolt, actual or incipient, against white domination. During the preceding four centuries the peoples of Europe, and particularly Western Europe, had been expanding and had imposed their rule or their culture or both upon a large proportion of the rest of mankind. In the nineteenth century, equipped with the appliances provided by the science which they had developed, they had rapidly enlarged that dominion. In 1914 almost all of mankind felt it in one form or another. Non-white peoples had never been happy under it. They now began to hope to free themselves from it. The wars which commenced in 1914, while eventually global in their extent, were chiefly, except that which broke out in 1931 and in which Japan took the initiative, between Western peoples. In effect they were civil strife in the Occident into which, because of the domination of the Occident, the rest of the world was drawn. The Occident was, therefore, the chief sufferer. Because it was weakened, the Occident might be compelled to relax its grip. Western ideas of democracy and nationalism spread with the extension of Occidental culture and intensified existing desires for freedom. "Self-determination" by peoples of their own form of government was a slogan in the war of 1914-1918. It was coined in the Occident and was an avowed objective of the victorious powers. War-time propaganda gave it wide currency and quickened hope among subject peoples. Japan asked equality for herself and posed as a champion of Asiatic peoples against the white races. In land after land ruled by Western peoples demands were made for an increased share in government or for full independence. Since most of the leading colonial powers were on the victorious side of the war of 1914-1918 and by their professed aims in the struggle had committed themselves to democracy and self-determination, they felt themselves under obligation to take measures in their political dependencies which would be consonant with their pronouncements. Indeed, even before 1914 some of them, notably Great Britain and the United States, had colonial policies which looked in that direction. The years following 1914 saw the pace towards self government of dependent peoples considerably accelerated. This was especially marked in the Philippines, India, Burma, and the Netherlands East Indies, but it was also seen elsewhere. Usually concessions by the ruling power stimulated a hunger for more and were not given rapidly enough to satisfy the radical elements in either the subject or the governing peoples. Yet they were being made.

Countries which had technically maintained their political independence but had compromised it in their treaties with Western powers insisted on regaining full autonomy. This was notably the case in Turkey, Iran, Thailand, and China. The very names of Iran and Thailand, substituted for the earlier Persia and Siam, were evidence of augmented nationalism. In Latin America, notably in Mexico, where they were in the majority, the Indian elements in the population were restive under the white domination and were seeking greater privileges.

The renewal of the wars on a world-wide scale in 1939 and 1941 gave new impetus to the movement towards independence from white rule. Liberal and radical voices in the Occident joined with nationalist voices in the Orient in insisting upon it. In their conflict with Japan, Great Britain, the United States, and the Netherlands felt themselves constrained, if for no other motive than diplomatic strategy, to promise to hasten the steps towards a greater degree of self government or outright independence for the peoples subject to them in the South and to the East of Asia and to abandon some of the legal and treaty provisions which had seemed to the Chinese "unequal." Japan had been proclaiming herself the liberator of Asia from the Occident and was loudly announcing measures to attest her good faith. Her enemies in the West could do no less. The ferment of nationalism and democracy was at work. It did not immediately end the colonial system, but it was tending in that direction.

What would be the fate of Christianity in this rapidly changing world? Once again, as so often in its history, Christianity was having to face a new age and movements which challenged its very existence. Now, however, they were world-wide and not regional. In the ten decades of comparative peace between 1815 and 1914 it had enjoyed the greatest century of its expansion and, taking mankind as a whole, the largest influence it had ever exerted. In spite of many adverse features in its environment, it had come to 1914 on a rising tide. That nineteenth century world had now receded into the past. In place of peace had come the most extensive wars that the human race had ever known. Wars brought disruption of communication between the younger and the founding churches. They cut off many missionaries from their constituencies and led to the interning, as enemy aliens, of numbers of representatives of the churches of the West. In much of Europe church buildings were destroyed and the ranks of the clergy were depleted by compulsory service in the armed forces and by the draining of the student bodies of the theological faculties and seminaries in which the clergy were trained. Vast shifts in population, some of them involuntary, to centres of war industries suddenly presented the churches with fresh and gigantic problems. In much of Asia, notably in China, in great areas church organizations were disrupted and Christian schools and hospitals were discontinued. War, too, by its very temper, the hatred and revenge which it engendered, was directly counter to the message and the ideals of the Christian faith. Revolutions simultaneously or in quick succession destroyed much of that nineteenth century order which Christianity had known. As we suggested a few paragraphs above, some of the revolutions were in part the product and the expression of systems of thought which by tradition and their very nature were hostile to Christianity. That was true in Russia, in Germany, and in Italy. Russia was the home of the strongest member of the Orthodox churches. Germany had been the birthplace of the Protestant Reformation. Italy contained the administrative centre of the Roman Catholic Church. All three of the major wings of Christianity were thus menaced in their traditional strongholds. The intense nationalism which had impelled Japan to her adventure in East Asia had at its core a religion, *Shinto*, which deified her Emperor, her heroes, and the nation itself and which could not logically brook Christianity. For the time being the new regimes in these four states might feel constrained for prudential reasons to temporize with Christianity, but by the essence of the ideologies which animated them they were incompatible with it. In non-Occidental lands the revolutions were affected by those revolutions in the West in which anti-Christian systems of thought had become dominant. The trend in revolutions, among both European and non-European peoples, was away from Christianity. The growing effective resentment against Occidental domination at times regarded Christianity and the nineteenth century missions which had spread it as adjuncts of the hated Western imperialism. As non-Western peoples freed themselves from the chains of Western political and economic control they might be inclined either to raise fresh opposition to the Christian missionary and his converts or to undertake to strangle the incipient Christian communities in their midst.

To be sure, the outcome of the war of 1914-1918 was a triumph for those nations, Great Britain, the United States, and France, in connexion with which Christianity had had its great extension in the nineteenth century. World War II was also apparently to be in their favour. In the second conflict three of the regimes most hostile to Christianity, those of Nazi Germany, Fascist Italy, and Shintoist Japan, were supposedly to be swept into the discard and in the stress of the struggle the Communist Union of Socialist Soviet Republics had felt itself constrained to grant an added measure of toleration to Christianity.

However, France had suffered terribly in the two wars and no longer held even the degree of prominence which it enjoyed in the nineteenth century; Great Britain was showing the strain and could not hope for the undisputed mastery of the seas, commerce, industry, and finance which had been hers in that halcyon age; and Soviet Russia, which could not be expected to assist the spread of Christianity, was coming out of the second war with a prestige and a power which its Tzarist predecessor had never possessed.

Moreover, much of the trend in the victorious powers was against conditions in connexion with which Christianity had had its phenomenal nineteenth century expansion. The strong tendency was away from *laissez faire* and individual initiative towards control and direction by the state. It had been in the atmosphere of freedom for the individual and of encouragement for individual creativity that nineteenth century missions had flourished. The missionary enterprise of that period had been staffed by those who had volunteered for that purpose and had been financed by the gifts of hundreds of thousands of private citizens. It had owed less to the assistance of the state than had the spread of Christianity in any age since Constantine. The United States Government, although not unfriendly, could scarcely be expected to underwrite and man the Christian missionary enterprise even if the churches, as was quite unlikely, would permit it to do so. Nor would the situation be any different with the British Government, and that in spite of strong remnants of official ties between Church and state in England and Scotland. Wars and the added costs of governments which were assuming more and more functions led to high taxes. These impinged with peculiar weight upon the upper and middle income strata of the population, the elements from which much of the gifts to the churches and the missionary societies were drawn. Presumably the budgets of these bodies would suffer. Then, too, even in the British Isles, the British Dominions, and the United States, where the churches were strong, there was much religious scepticism. The intellectual currents of the eighteenth and nineteenth centuries which undercut Christian beliefs persisted and in many circles were very potent. Even more sobering were the preoccupation with war and war industries and the vast shifts of population induced by the changes in the economies of these lands. Millions were uprooted from habits of thought and once familiar surroundings in which church membership and attendance were easy and were transplanted to mental and physical surroundings where they were difficult or impossible.

The enhanced power of the state seemed peculiarly adverse to Christianity. It was no fresh experience for Christianity to be confronted with absolute political power. That faith had won its first great victories in an empire in which the trend was towards increasing centralization and minute control of the individual by an autocratic government and in which, for most of the first three centuries, the state was hostile. In the sixteenth, seventeenth, and eighteenth centuries Christianity had been confronted by absolute monarchies in the major part of Europe. However, in the days of Christianity's birth and first victories the Roman Empire had allowed much latitude to local customs in the culturally and racially diverse region which it ruled. Not until Christianity had become well established and had given rise to a strong empire-wide church had the centralizing processes reached an extreme. It was the third and fourth centuries before the state made its most determined efforts at general persecutions, and the two first of these, those of Decius and Valerian, were brought to early ends by the deaths of the Emperors who had ordered them. Beginning with Constantine, except for the brief reaction under Julian, the Roman state was increasingly co-operative. The absolute monarchies of the Europe of the sixteenth, seventeenth, and eighteenth centuries were friendly to the Church and for their own purposes aided it both at home and in their colonies. This was true of the Orthodox Church in Russia, of the Roman Catholic Church in Austria, France, Spain, and Portugal, of the Lutheran churches in Prussia and Scandinavia, and of the Church of England in Tudor and Stuart England. In contrast, the leading totalitarian states of the twentieth century were either openly or covertly hostile to Christianity, and most of the states, whether totalitarian or democratic, deprived the churches of some of the traditional functions through which they had perpetuated themselves by directly or indirectly curtailing or abolishing their control over marriage and the education and organization of youth.

Then, too, there was abroad in the Occident a pessimism and a lack of faith in those forces which had made the nineteenth century. In the nineteenth century, optimism had characterized Western nations, and especially Great Britain and the United States. The territories, the population, and the wealth of these countries were rapidly expanding. Progress was believed to be automatic and of the very nature of the universe. Under these conditions movements for the spread of Christianity were implemented by abounding hope. Now, in the post-1914 world, doubt, and at times extreme pessimism and despair, swept across the peoples of the Occident. In Europe the post-1918 years were clouded by unrest, financial crisis, uncertainty, and the fear of renewed armed conflict. The fair hopes for enduring peace which had been cherished during the war of 1914-1918 seemed shattered by the failure of much of the international machinery which had been set up after that conflict and by the threat and then the renewal of war on a vastly enlarged scale. Instead of adventuring on new undertakings, the peoples of states which had been the ostensible victors in the first round of the world wars made slogans of safety for themselves as nations and for their individual citizens. Systems were set up for "social security." The "four freedoms" which were widely proclaimed as goals in the second series of world wars were emancipation from certain dangers. For many they were indicative more of fatigue or lethargy than of an urge towards perilous fresh undertakings. To be sure, in some areas the pulses of new life were bounding with daring confidence, but these were mainly Germany, Italy, Japan, and especially Russia, lands whose regimes were more or less openly avowed enemies of Christianity. In Italy, Germany, and Japan the fierce optimism was fleeting and among some thoughtful souls was always shadowed by apprehension. For many it was to be succeeded by bleak despair, sullen resentment, or stormy outbursts of retaliation. In Great

Britain, the United States, and France, from which the chief expansion of Christianity had come in the nineteenth century, the temper seemed to be one of holding to what had already been won. The rate of growth of the population was declining in Western Europe and the United States. Indeed, populations here were on the way to becoming stationary. Enveloped by this atmosphere, the Christianity of these lands was handicapped. A sad acquiescence in evil infected some ecclesiastical and theological circles. The climate of the environment was one of defense, of seeking to conserve what had been won in a previous age. Under these conditions enterprises for the expansion of Christianity could be expected to suffer.

All the main divisions of Christianity were affected by the adverse conditions. In the Near East the Nestorian and Armenian communities, for centuries attacked by recurring persecutions and already sadly dwindled, were reduced by massacres and deportations associated with the war of 1914-1918. In Egypt the Copts, long a minority on the defensive against the encircling Islam, lost thousands to the Moslems. The ancient Ethiopian Church was distraught by the Italian invasion. Nationalist Turkey, seeking racial and cultural unity, by deportation and other measures dealt blows to the Armenians and Greek Orthodox within its borders. The Œcumenical Patriarchate of the Greek Orthodox Church, while still with its seat in Constantinople, found the faithful who were directly supervised by it greatly shrunken in numbers. The German and Italian invasions of Greece and the Balkans in the 1940's brought distress to the Orthodox Church in that region. In Russia the Orthodox Church reached a lower ebb than at any time in its long history. In North-western Europe the Protestant churches were dealt staggering blows by the Nazi regime, first in Germany itself and then in the lands occupied by the Nazi armies. In the main centres of its nineteenth century strength, Great Britain, the United States, and the British Dominions of Canada, Australia, New Zealand, and South Africa, Protestantism was much less disturbed than on the continent of Europe, but it could not fail to be affected by the times. The Roman Catholic Church found itself on the defensive against the new regimes in Fascist Italy, Nazi Germany, and Communist Russia and could not but share in the disasters which war brought to Western and Central Europe, particularly in Germany, Austria, Poland, Czecho-Slovakia, France, Italy, and Spain.

In these adversities Protestantism for a time suffered more severely than did Roman Catholicism. In the nineteenth century, as we saw in the last three volumes, both had expanded but the former had spread more rapidly than had the latter. Until then the chief extension of Christianity had been through the Roman Catholic Church. In the sixteenth, seventeenth, and eighteenth centuries Protestantism had been a minority movement limited to North-west Europe and a few colonies. In these same centuries Roman Catholic Christianity had been carried to all the continents and had become particularly strong in the Americas. In the nineteenth century, in contrast, the main stream of Christianity seemed to be flowing through what in its broadest sense was loosely, if incorrectly, termed Protestantism. It was from Protestantism that most of the new Christian revivals had sprung. It was through Protestantism that the majority of the movements to influence human society which stemmed from Christianity had their rise. Protestantism was chiefly responsible, for instance, for the abolition of Negro slavery, the inception of the peace societies, the reduction of languages to writing, and the creation of educational institutions on the frontiers of Occidental settlement and empire. Protestantism had been closely associated with democracy, a *laissez faire* economic structure, and the dominance of Great Britain. As these were menaced or disappeared, it, too, was jeopardized. Relative to their comparative strength in the nineteenth century, after 1914 Roman Catholicism made greater advances than Protestantism. Occidental foreign missionary staffs of the Roman Catholics markedly increased while those of Protestants, after a brave surge in the years immediately following 1918, remained nearly stationary or declined.[1] The advantages of Roman Catholicism were several. Its temper was more totalitarian than democratic and the post-1914 trend towards authority favoured it. Added support to its missions came from Belgium, Germany (before the Nazi regime), and the United States. In the United States the Roman Catholic Church had profited by the immigration of the nineteenth century and the descendants of that immigration were growing in wealth.

Yet the gains of Roman Catholicism were only relative. Protestant Christianity was still advancing[2] and, in general, was continuing to display more new movements and to exert a greater influence upon mankind as a whole than was the Roman Catholic Church. Moreover, after 1939, when the new world war engulfed almost all Europe, the Roman Catholic forces suffered severely. More than Protestantism, Roman Catholic missions drew personnel and money from the continent of Europe. As the war spread, many German and Italian missionaries were interned in British colonial territories, missionaries were cut off from their supporting constituencies, and few reinforcements could be sent. In contrast, the main bases of Protestant missions could still

[1] Beach and St. John, *World Statistics of Christian Missions,* pp. 59, 103, 104; Parker, *Interpretative Statistical Survey of the World Mission of the Christian Church,* pp. 17, 33-35, 262-264.
[2] *Ibid.*

function. Then, too, numerically Protestantism was winning many more converts from the Roman Catholic Church than was the latter from Protestantism. This was not in Europe nor in Anglo-Saxon lands but in Latin America and the Philippines. Here, from nominal Roman Catholics, large accessions were coming to Protestantism.

One of the thought-provoking features of the age was the fashion in which the upheavals had been most severe in the regions in which Christianity had long had the chief centres of its strength. For more than a thousand years, from the sixth through the nineteenth century, the main expansion of Christianity had been from Europe, and especially from Western and Southern Europe. It was in Western Europe and in the new nations which had arisen from its colonies that Christianity had freest course and its most profound effects. Now, beginning in 1914, Europe was the main centre of the wars and the revolutions which were threatening the existing order and, apparently, civilization itself. It was here that Christianity was being dealt its most telling blows. Had Christianity failed? If, as from time to time we have suggested, it was at least one of the sources and perhaps the chief original inspiration of the science and the intellectual, social, and political ideas which were making Western Europe so potent in the affairs of men and therefore of the explosive movements which were shaking all mankind and threatening Christianity itself, did Christianity carry within itself the seeds of its own destruction and of the death of the cultures to which it had given rise? It had failed to safeguard the Roman Empire after that state had yielded professed allegiance to it. It had not preserved the structure of the medieval Europe which it had done so much to shape. Clearly it was not now saving the culture of the nineteenth century which it helped to form and in that failure was having its own existence threatened.

Indeed, part of what had seemed strength in the nineteenth century was now a source of weakness. In the nineteenth century one of the trends of Christianity, both Roman Catholic and Protestant, was away from the group or mass conversion which had been the process by which the faith had effected its chief geographic gains since the third century. Instead, the churches had been, in general, raising their standards of membership. They were more stringent in their requirements for admission to full membership and asked more from their members in conduct and religious observances. This was especially the case on the newer frontiers among non-European peoples, but it was also a tendency in Europe and parts of the Americas. The trend was hastened by the open antagonism to Christianity and the Church which had been one of the features of the nineteenth century Occident and which had been greatly accentuated after 1914. To this there were exceptions. Mass movements were still occurring. The rising percentage of church membership in the United States, India, and some parts of the Netherlands Indies and Africa was a continuation of the earlier pattern. More and more, however, Christianity was moving away from the status of a territorial faith to a faith represented by minority communities which were consciously set against much of the drift in the surrounding world.

This phase of the picture, seemingly so adverse to Christianity, was only one angle of the whole. It was not necessarily the function of Christianity to protect an age or a culture against disintegration. By its very nature Christianity was revolutionary, combatting elements which were contrary to its teachings and seeking to inculcate and achieve conformity to its standards. Christianity had never been intimately associated with any culture which even roughly approximated to its ethical and spiritual ideals. To preserve a civilization which was in many aspects a contradiction of the genius of Christianity would be a prostitution of the faith. Christians, if they were to be true to their profession, could not rest content with any of the cultures in which they found themselves, but must be seeking to transform them. In that endeavour they might strive for gradual transition, rather than acquiesce in the crude violence which was usually a feature of the transition from one age to another. Indeed, they would bear their witness against much of that violence and, if they consented to it or assisted it, would do so sadly. Yet they could not be loyal to their principles and seek to preserve, unaltered, the *status quo*.

The violence came from elements both in the dying and the nascent culture which were contradictory to Christianity. Its existence was witness to the fact that Christianity had not fully transformed either the old or the new and so might be said to testify to the failure of the faith. However, this seeming failure must be seen against the total span of history and of mankind.

Contrasted with the millenniums which mankind had been on the earth and even with the twelve to five millenniums which composed the history of civilization, Christianity was a recent arrival and was still young. Each time that a culture with which it had been intimately associated and which it had helped to mould had collapsed, after the period of decline which had followed the catastrophe a new age ensued in which, when the globe was viewed as a whole, it became apparent that Christianity was exerting a greater influence upon the human race than in the preceding era of its prosperity.

That was true after the fall of the Roman Empire and the disintegration of Græco-Roman culture. Several centuries followed in which Christianity seemed to be in process of vanishing from the human scene. Yet in the very period of presumed decay it was registering fresh territorial advances in northern and western Europe and in Asia. Out of those in western Europe came a culture, that of the European Middle Ages, which Christianity had a larger share in shaping than it had had in that of the Græco-Roman world. By the fourteenth century Christianity was more widely spread than it had been when the Roman Empire had begun to dwindle and its effects were more profound and more striking.

So, too, it was with the transition from the thirteenth and fourteenth centuries to the era which dawned at the end of the fifteenth century. For a time the geographical boundaries which embraced the Christian communities shrank. In extensive areas Christianity disappeared. In western Europe the culture which Christianity had done so much to inspire passed into desuetude. That culture had never been fully Christian. Many features of it were patently anti-Christian. Yet the peoples who had developed it called themselves Christians and in most of its aspects Christian elements were present. The vigorous new age which followed seemed to be ushering Christianity off the scene. Much of the Renaissance, while rendering lip service to the avowed faith of western Europe, ignored and by its temper and achievements contradicted it. The official church was first weak and divided and then was both corrupt and, at headquarters, captured by the Renaissance. Early in the fifteenth century the Protestant revolt still further divided the forces of organized Christianity. The new absolute monarchies were demoting the Church from the proud dominance which it had held in the Middle Ages. Yet great awakenings came in Christianity and in some respects the faith left its impress upon western Europe of the sixteenth and seventeenth centuries more deeply than it had upon that of the Middle Ages. In its spread in the two and a half centuries after A.D. 1500 Christianity accompanied and even exceeded the political and commercial expansion of Europe and profoundly affected for good the impact of European upon non-European peoples. By A.D. 1750 Christianity was having an influence upon mankind as a whole far greater than at any previous time.

In the transition from the eighteenth to the nineteenth century Christianity again seemed threatened. Some of the forces which inaugurated and shaped the new century were hostile to the faith. Many intelligent observers predicted that the latter could not survive. However, in contrast with the sombre initial outlook, Christianity experienced striking revivals and entered upon what, up to that time, was its "great century," the era of its widest expansion and of its largest effect upon the human race.

Christianity had in part been responsible for the new forces which had disrupted the western Europe of the Middle Ages, the era which began in the fourteenth and fifteenth centuries, the three centuries which followed A.D. 1500, and the world of the nineteenth century. It was not only the source of the Protestantism which had finally terminated the unity of the ecclesiastical structure which had held together western Europe since the disintegration of the Roman Empire in that region: it was probably also one of the impulses which gave rise to the Renaissance and was certainly a determining incentive to the vast explorations, settlements, and conquests by European peoples which began in the fifteenth century. Christianity seems to have been to some extent accountable for the intellectual discipline and daring which made possible the scientific method and the rapid advance in the knowledge and mastery of his physical environment achieved by man in the nineteenth and twentieth centuries and for the idealism which was the creative force in democracy and socialism. Yet it was these which helped first to form and then to destroy the age which culminated in the eighteenth century and that which was spanned by the nineteenth century.

In other words, there was in Christianity a propulsive vigour which would not permit mankind to remain content with past attainments but which urged it on. Christianity was forever giving rise to something new. It could not guarantee that its contributions would remain unmixed with other and contradictory elements. More than one of the movements of which it was a source was diverted to quite un-Christian purposes and wrought harm rather than good. Yet in Christianity was a vital force which in impelling man to fresh endeavours towards the "high calling of God" to be "filled with all the fullness of God" was destroying old cultural patterns and creating new ones. Other and evil factors might and often did pervert, to man's sore hurt, something of what was accomplished, but by no means always was this the case. The movements inspired by Christianity also to a high degree made for man's good.

Very similar was the part of Christianity in the act in the human drama which was being enacted after 1914. Christianity was one of the formative causes of the forces which brought the nineteenth century to an end and which ushered in the terrifying but thrilling age of the twentieth century. It had been a chief source of the dream of human progress and of the high value of the individual which were among the major ingredients of the social theories to which appeal was made in the revolutions of the post-1914 world. It had been a factor, albeit only one in many, in the rise of nationalism, for nationalism stemmed in part from the pride and sense of ownership of millions of individual citizens, who were stimulated in turn by visions, even though clouded and distorted, of the dignity and breath-taking destiny of man. Nationalism was one of the main causes of the wars which racked the post-1914 age. As a source of science and therefore of the machine, Christianity contributed to the shattering of time-distances, the shrinking of the globe, and the destructive magnitude of the wars which marked the end of one era and were among the characteristics of the new age.

Yet, as in other periods when one culture with which Christianity had been intimately associated was violently disrupted and a new age eventually emerged in which Christianity displayed enhanced influence, so in the new world whose outlines began to be apparent after 1914 Christianity had a greater effect upon mankind as a whole than it had had in the nineteenth century. In our survey of the course of Christianity we have measured the progress and recession of the faith in the human scene by the three criteria of geographic extent, new movements emerging from the Christian stream, and the effects upon mankind. When the Christianity of the post-1914 world is appraised by these standards, in spite of obstacles and some serious reverses, it is seen to have registered an advance. Indeed, each of the three taken independently shows it to have displayed gains during these momentous years.

Subsequently to 1914, geographically the adherents of Christianity became distributed more nearly evenly over the earth's surface than at any previous time. Since the fifteenth century Christianity had been found more widely throughout the globe than had ever any religion professed by man. It had, however, centred primarily in Europe and in the new nations which had emerged across the oceans through the migration of Europeans. After 1914 it was still predominantly Occidental in its adherents. Numerically it gained in some lands of the Occident. In the United States the proportion of church members in the population, which had mounted through most of the nineteenth century, continued to grow. By the natural increase of population the totals of church membership rose in the United States, Canada, Australia, and New Zealand, and possibly in Latin America and Scandinavia. However, the major percentage increases were in non-Occidental lands. They were particularly striking in Africa south of the Sahara, in India, the Netherlands Indies, and China. In all these countries except some sections of Africa and the East Indies Christians were still only small minorities, but in proportion to the population as a whole these minorities were rapidly expanding.

Moreover, as a significant phase of the world-wide extension of the faith, it was becoming clear that Christianity was taking root among non-Occidental peoples. No longer were the Christian communities among others than Europeans so dependent upon their fellow Christians of the Occident for leadership and financial assistance as they had been in the nineteenth century. They had then seemed to be enclaves of a kind of Western ecclesiastical imperialism, planted, sustained, and controlled by the churches of the Occident. This dependence did not immediately disappear. Much of it long persisted. Yet after 1914 striking progress was achieved towards a status of equality with the founding bodies. This was seen in both Roman Catholic and Protestant circles. An indigenous leadership was being rapidly developed.

Roman Catholics were placing great emphasis upon the rearing of a native clergy led by an episcopate from its own ranks. The indigenous priesthood was multiplying. In several non-Occidental lands, among them Japan, China, Indo-China, India, and Africa, the Roman Catholic Church was consecrating bishops who were from the peoples of the soil. In most of these regions a native episcopate had not existed in the nineteenth century. The new trend was spectacularly demonstrated when on one day set aside as "missions Sunday," in 1939, the Pope consecrated twelve missionary bishops, the number being deliberately symbolic of the Twelve Apostles and the universal programme of the Church. They included one African, from Uganda, one Malagasy, from Madagascar, one Chinese, and one Indian.[3] By the autumn of 1939 in India seven dioceses were in charge of the indigenous clergy. In Indo-China three, in Africa one, in Japan two, and in China twenty-three had similarly been transferred.[4] In 1933 it was estimated that sixty per cent. of the Roman Catholics in Asia were under indigenous clergy and twenty per cent. under indigenous bishops.[5] Between 1918 and 1923 there was said to have been an increase of 102 per cent. in preparatory seminaries, of 6.6 per cent. in major seminaries, of 74.4 per cent. in native brothers, of 50.4 per cent. in native sisters, and of 12.8 per cent. in native priests.[6] Never before, when measured in terms of the wide racial spread of its hierarchy, had the Church of Rome come so near to the realization of its dream of universality implied in its proud designation of Catholic.

Protestant missionaries were also developing a native leadership and turning over to it the administration of their churches and educational and philanthropic institutions. In raising up an indigenous clergy Protestants were not so obviously successful as were Roman Catholics. They had not laid so much stress upon bringing the Church into being as had the latter. Relatively they had placed more emphasis upon schools, hospitals, and other philanthropic agencies for influencing culture as a whole and for meeting this-worldly needs. Moreover, the traditional forms of the Protestant clergy were less adapted to the constituency of non-Occidental Christianity than was the Roman Catholic

[3] *Fides News Service*, Oct. 21 and Oct. 28, 1939.
[4] *Fides News Service*, Sept. 30, 1939, Oct. 28, 1939.
[5] *The International Review of Missions*, Vol. XXIII, p. 99.
[6] Streit, *Catholic Missions in Figures and Symbols*, p. 118.

type of clergy. The latter was celibate and could be supported with slight financial outlay. It could, therefore, be maintained by the poor and the humble who made up much of the Roman Catholic non-Occidental communities. In contrast, the Protestant clergy were by tradition married and in their functions and training were adapted to the middle class society in which so much of Occidental Protestant Christianity had its chief strength. In most non-Western countries Protestants drew mainly from low income groups who could not support that kind of clergy. To this Japan was an exception. Here Protestants were largely from the urban middle class and there was no dearth of clergy nor serious difficulty in finding their support from Japanese sources. Protestants were not unaware of the problem.[7] Nor had they completely failed in meeting it. Protestant clergy were emerging and were rapidly growing in numbers[8] and in ability. In Protestant bodies which were episcopally organized, bishops from the indigenous membership were being consecrated. Administrative posts such as the headships of schools and colleges and the secretaryships of boards and committees were more and more being transferred to what were termed, to avoid the word "native" with its somewhat opprobrious associations, "nationals."

This shift of authority to indigenous leadership was due in part to the pressure of nationalism. The younger churches were sensitive to the charge that they were subject to foreigners and were therefore tools of Western imperialism. Even without the criticism they were eager for full independence. Yet long before nationalism had taken the acute forms displayed after 1914 missionaries had been working for the day when the younger churches could be staffed by their own members.[9] Indeed, for years the objective of "self-supporting, self-governing, and self-propagating churches" had been so much stressed in Protestant missionary circles as to have become almost a *cliché*. It was due to the foundations laid over many years in recruiting and in schools that when the demand came from the nationals, personnel was at hand to take over the places vacated by foreigners. Many of the nationals were of outstanding ability and compared favourably with their colleagues of the West.[10] In Protestantism the process was not limited to the substitution of native for foreign leadership

[7] See, for instance, *The Madras Series*, Vol. 17, pp. 186 ff.

[8] Parker, *Interpretative Statistical Survey of the World Mission of the Christian Church*, pp. 17, 244.

[9] For a valuable historical treatment of the development in several missions see Daniel Johnson Fleming, *Devolution in Mission Administration: As Exemplified by the Legislative History of Five American Missionary Societies in India* (Chicago, Fleming H. Revell Co., 1916, pp. 310), *passim*.

[10] See a testimony to this in Van Dusen, *For the Healing of the Nations*, pp. 184-186.

but also meant the transfer of ecclesiastical authority and administration to indigenous organizations.[11]

To a lesser degree the rootage of Christianity in non-Western environments was showing itself in the adaptation to Christian purposes of indigenous forms of expression in painting, architecture, symbolism, and worship, Christianity was beginning to divest itself of some of the dress which it had acquired in the Occident and to assume native garbs. Of this we are to say more in subsequent chapters.

Appraised by the criterion of new movements arising from pulsing vigour, in the three decades and more after 1914 Christianity gave evidence of unabated vitality. Confronted with the disorders which were disrupting the world of which it had been an integral part and in which it had made such striking advances, Christianity, far from going to pieces, created movements which would help it meet the new conditions and rise triumphantly above them. This was true of both Roman Catholicism and Protestantism, those forms of the faith which had been most responsible for the maintenance and spread of the faith in the preceding era.

The Roman Catholic Church displayed this vigour in part through the traditional channels of new orders and societies. For a thousand years or more revivals in the Roman Catholic fold had given birth to new monastic orders. Souls which had been brought through them to full devotion had kindled other spirits and had founded orders and congregations. In such fashion the Benedictines, the Cistercians, the Franciscans, the Dominicans, and the Salesians had come into being—to mention only a few. Or Roman Catholic revivals had given rise to associations of those who had not fully left the world and to societies for the achievement of particular objectives. Such movements continued to emerge after 1914. There were also revivals in existing orders. For instance, in that most venerable of all the orders of the West, the Benedictines, a renewal of life was taking the form of a return to the original rules and ideals of the founder. It was too early to know whether any of the new orders and congregations would attain the dimensions of some of the older ones, but many sprang into being. It is significant of the world-wide extension of the Roman Catholic Church that many of these were in non-European lands.[12] What was known as Catholic Action, chiefly for enlisting and directing the energies of laymen, became very widely spread. Among other achievements, in Japan it organized a settlement among the poor of Tokyo, in Korea it

---

[11] Fleming, *op. cit., passim.*

[12] For examples see Planchet, *Les Missions de Chine et du Japon,* 1929, p. 580; *Fides News Service,* Apr. 1939.

inaugurated vigorous efforts to spread the faith, in China it stimulated the preparation of text-books, in India it had the inclusive aim of bringing private and public life into harmony with Catholic standards, and in South Africa, where the tensions between whites and blacks were especially acute, it stood in its own membership for an absence of racial discrimination.[13] Great Eucharistic congresses in various parts of the world both witnessed to and quickened the devotion of clergy and laity.[14] The movement had begun in the last decade of the nineteenth century, but after 1914 it took on increased dimensions. There was also vigour in theological thinking, a return in some intellectual quarters to Roman Catholic theology, and a continued rise in the interest in the great formulations of the faith by Thomas Aquinas. Scholars were emerging among clergy and laity who, aroused by the terrifying challenge of the age, were presenting with clarity and cogency the Catholic world-view against the systems which so blatantly denied it.[15]

It was indicative of its vigour in spreading Christianity that in the Roman Catholic Church the years after 1914 witnessed the inauguration of many new societies and other organizations for the propagation of the faith. In slightly over a decade beginning in 1914 more than sixty such came into being in Europe alone.[16] Of some of these we are to speak more in detail in the next chapter. We shall see still others in our country by country survey.

Protestantism also put forth fresh shoots. Some were new denominations, but of these, none attained enough prominence to warrant description in as brief a survey as ours must necessarily be. A movement which for a time attracted attention was what styled itself the Oxford Groups and for a period on the eve of the world war of 1939 and after the outbreak of that struggle made much of what it called moral rearmament. It had as its originator and leader Frank N. D. Buchman, from Pennsylvania. It addressed itself especially but by no means exclusively to those of education, wealth, and social prominence. It strove to deepen the moral cleansing and devotion of those already bearing the Christian name, to win others to the Christian faith, and to bring about "personal, social, racial, national, and supernational change." It enlisted adherents from many different denominations and in many countries, both in the Occident and elsewhere.[17] Its novel methods won for it publicity, some of

[13] *The International Review of Missions*, Vol. XXIII, p. 103.

[14] On the early developments see *The Catholic Encyclopedia*, Vol. V, pp. 592-594.

[15] For a brief summary, by a Protestant, but objective, see Horton, *Contemporary Continental Theology*, pp. 46 ff.

[16] Arens, *Handbuch der katholischen Missionen* (1925 edition), pp. 308-331.

[17] On this movement a large bibliography could be compiled. For a brief summary by Buchman see *Who's Who in America* (Chicago, The A. N. Marquis Co., 1942, pp. 2578), p. 422. For a critical appraisal, see H. P. Van Dusen in *The Atlantic Monthly*, Vol. CLIV, pp. 1-16, 240-252.

it critical. Through George F. MacLeod, a clergyman of the Church of Scotland, a movement was inaugurated with its centre at Iona, the island from which, more than a thousand years before, much of the conversion of Scotland had proceeded. It sought, through a form of community, to bring about a quickening of the religious life of Scotland, to reach the un-churched masses, and to seek a new and better social order.[18]

More widespread was a strong theological trend. It was in part a reaction from the liberalism of the nineteenth century and a return towards earlier Protestant orthodoxy, especially towards Calvin. To some degree it was a product of the environment. As the earlier liberalism had reflected the optimism, humanism, and scientific attitudes of the nineteenth century, so this "neo-orthodoxy," "theology of crisis," or "dialectical theology," while it had nineteenth century forerunners, notably the Dane Kierkegaard, to no small degree arose from the pessimism, the distrust of man's abilities, and the despair begotten of the terrors of the post-1914 world with their threat to Western civilization. It was also new and creative, although some of its exponents would probably have denied either adjective. It emphasized man's sinfulness and his inability, unaided, to discover God or to extricate himself from the horrors brought by his depravity, and stressed the "otherness" of God, the gulf between God and man, unbridgeable except by divine act, and the grace of God in overcoming that gulf through the Word of God and God as Reconciler and Redeemer. In Europe it had its chief spokesman in Karl Barth.[19] In the United States the most vocal figure, but by no means a slavish adherent to the Barthian precedent, was Reinhold Niebuhr.[20] There were, as well, other theological currents[21] which showed that the creative intellectual urge in Protestantism, far from being moribund, was displaying fresh life.

What was probably the most striking of the new movements issuing from Protestantism was that to which was given the title Ecumenical. In its most inclusive form it embraced all the various channels and organizations through which Protestants were co-operating across confessional lines, not only within but also beyond Protestantism.

[18] See the official publication of the movement, *The Coracle* (Iona and Glasgow, 1938 ff.).

[19] The literature is vast. For a brief summary of the subject see Horton, *Contemporary Continental Theology*, pp. 85 ff.

[20] The book of Niebuhr's which first attracted widespread attention was *Moral Man and Immoral Society* (New York, Charles Scribner's Sons, 1932, pp. xxv, 284). His most formidable work was *The Nature and Destiny of Man* (New York, Charles Scribner's Sons, 2 vols., 1941-1943).

[21] For a brief summary see Horton, *Contemporary Continental Theology*, pp. 127 ff.; Horton, *Contemporary English Theology, passim.*

The Ecumenical Movement was most remarkable. By its nature Protestanism tended towards individualism and fissiparousness. Prominent in the origin and nature of Protestantism was salvation by faith with the corollaries of the priesthood of all believers and the right and obligation of individual judgment. Obviously this made for seemingly endless division. Yet in the nineteenth century and the first decade of the twentieth century a trend had already become apparent towards co-operation.[22] This was multiform and in many lands. It was most prominent on the newer geographic frontiers of Christianity, notably the United States, the British Dominions, and the non-Occidental lands such as India, China, and Japan, where missionaries from a number of different denominations were labouring. By the year 1914 it was rapidly mounting. It was represented by such organizations as the World's Evangelical Alliance (although this had lost in relative prominence since the days in the second half of the nineteenth century when it had been a major centre for unity among Protestants), the World's Student Christian Federation, the Federal Council of the Churches of Christ in America, the Foreign Missions Conference of North America, the World's Alliance of the Young Men's Christian Associations, the World's Young Women's Christian Association, the World's Christian Endeavour Union, the World's Sunday School Association, and the Conference of Missionary Societies of Great Britain and Ireland. Notable for their inclusive character and for what stemmed from them was the series of missionary conferences which began in 1854 and 1860 in New York and Liverpool respectively and which culminated, so far as the pre-1914 era was concerned, in the World Missionary Conference in Edinburgh in 1910. Particularly significant was the World's Student Christian Federation and the student Christian movements which it embraced, for from them came much of the leadership for the chief organizations through which post-1914 Protestantism was being brought together. It was the vision and the training of the impressionable years of youth which had their fruition in the later larger enterprises.

After 1914 the trend towards co-operation took on added momentum. One of its phases was actual unions of previously disparate ecclesiastical bodies, but for the most part it left denominations intact.

The reasons for the marked growth of co-operation and union were many. They sprang in part from the urgent sense of a common task which could be better accomplished by working together than by working separately. This was true of many efforts for social and moral reform, such as temperance, anti-slavery, and peace. Societies with these objectives were organized which included thousands of individuals from many denominations. In addressing themselves

[22] See a partial list in Vol. IV, pp. 102-106.

to the spread of their faith in new situations in the Occident or upon fresh geographic and social frontiers in the Occident and outside the Occident, Protestants found it wise to approach their problems unitedly. Thus the Young Men's and Young Women's Christian Associations flourished because of the need for common effort in enlisting youth in the colleges and universities and in the cities. The attempt to bring the Christian Gospel to non-Occidental peoples was particularly potent in bringing Protestants together. The era ushered in by the world war of 1914-1918, terrifying in its gigantic revolutions and in its menace to civilization, challenged Christians to rise above the historic differences which separated them and through united planning and action to make Christian ideals more effective in life. The threat to Christianity brought by the forces of the new age engendered in some the conviction that if Christianity was to survive, the adherents of the faith, no matter of what communion, must labour together to meet the common danger. The Ecumenical Movement had its origin and most of its leadership in English-speaking lands. This was partly because it was in these countries that Protestantism had been most vigorous in the nineteenth and twentieth centuries and because from them it had had its greatest expansion. It was also in part because of the variety which Protestantism displayed in these countries and the growing tendency to place all the churches on the same legal basis. In the British Isles there were still churches which enjoyed a special affiliation with the state and the prestige and privilege which accrued from that relationship. However, in most other English-speaking lands ecclesiastical establishments, if they had ever existed, had ceased to be, and in the various political entities in the British Isles the tie between the state and a particular church had either been severed or was becoming tenuous. Since no one church could effectively claim an exclusive legal position and since many different communions were found in a particular country, the trend towards co-operation on the basis of equality assumed growing strength. It might have been supposed to arise from religious indifferentism, the feeling on the part of the rank and file of the membership that all churches were about equally true and perhaps equally false, had it not been for the fact that the efforts for co-operation and the Ecumenical Movement came not primarily from the laity but from the clergy. On the part of the leadership there may have been something of the element of fear, both of a defection of the laity if co-operation was not achieved and of destruction by the common foe if a united front was not presented. To one who knew the movement intimately, however, it was clear that these factors, if present, were relatively minor. The primary urge was far different. It was one of conviction that followers of a common master, Jesus Christ, if they were true to his spirit, would achieve unity, of urgency in community-wide, nation-wide, and world-wide tasks to be performed, and from a belief that in a world which was becoming a neighbourhood but was so palpably a quarrelsome neighbourhood, the Christian Church, because of its nature and its world-wide extent, could provide a common bond and could constitute a moral and spiritual basis of a world culture. The chief motives were ones of achievement and the dominant spirit one of fresh adventure.

Of the many organizations, local, regional, national, and international, which were the fruits of this movement towards co-operation and union,[23] the International Missionary Council was the earliest which was based upon bodies controlled by the churches to develop a comprehensive, nearly world-wide organization with a secretariat giving full time. It came into being in 1921.[24] It was the direct sequel of the World Missionary Conference which had been held at Edinburgh in 1910. John R. Mott, its chief organizer and first chairman, had come up through the Young Men's Christian Association, the Student Volunteer Movement, and the World's Student Christian Federation, all of which drew their membership from many different communions. Solid, with a vision and an acquaintance world-wide in scope, and with a genius for promotion and administration, Mott was one of the ablest leaders which the Church had ever produced. The first two secretaries of the International Missionary Council, J. H. Oldham and A. L. Warnshuis, had also had long experience in organizations which overpassed denominational lines. The membership was composed of regional and national organizations in various parts of the world which in turn were representative of missionary societies and churches. In 1944 the constituent bodies numbered twenty-six, one of which was in the United States and Canada, nine in Europe and the British Isles, four in Latin America, seven in Asia and adjacent regions and islands, three in Africa, and two in Australasia. Two of the twenty-six were individual societies, the sole representatives of particular countries.[25] Notable meetings of the International Missionary Council, held in Jerusalem in 1928[26] and on the outskirts of Madras in 1938[27] were important symbols of interdenominational

[23] On a list and brief history and description of the co-operative enterprises in missions, see Charles H. Fahs and Helen E. Davis, *Conspectus of Coöperative Missionary Enterprises* (New York, International Missionary Council, 1935, pp. v, 252).

[24] Frank Lenwood in *The International Review of Missions*, Vol. XI, pp. 30-42.

[25] The letterhead of the International Missionary Council, 1944.

[26] See the official report in *The Jerusalem Meeting of the International Missionary Council, March 24–April 8, 1928* (New York and London, International Missionary Council, 7 vols., 1928).

[27] See the official report in *"The Madras Series," Presenting Papers Based upon the Meeting of the International Missionary Council, at Tambaram, Madras, India, Decem-

fellowship and means of co-operative planning. It was significant of the fashion in which Protestantism was becoming rooted among non-Occidental peoples that at the successive conferences of 1910, 1928, and 1938 the proportion of non-Occidentals progressively increased. The gathering at Edinburgh in 1910 was overwhelmingly one of Occidentals who were conducting missions in non-Western lands. Only a few of non-Western blood were present. In 1928 a substantial minority were in the latter category. In 1938 approximately half of the regular delegates were in that classification and the gathering was directed primarily to the strengthening of the "younger churches."

Even more comprehensive in its projected scope was the World Council of Churches. This had its immediate source in two organizations known as the World Conference on Faith and Order and the Universal Christian Council for Life and Work.

The World Conference on Faith and Order arose in part from the World Missionary Conference held at Edinburgh in 1910. It became clear that at the latter gathering the basic questions of faith and order which had historically separated the churches were not being faced. With the purpose of obtaining the fullest possible co-operation those concerned with the expansion of Christianity were consciously avoiding the issues which had been traditional sources of division and were seeking to rise above them in meeting together the tasks which all had in common. Yet these issues remained and prevented the full achievement of a united front. Questions of fundamental beliefs concerning the Christian faith, the Holy Communion or Lord's Supper, the nature of the ministry, the ordination of the ministry, and the organization of the Church would not down. It was felt that representatives of the churches should frankly face them together. If for the moment no way appeared of reconciling the historic differences, sympathetic understanding might be achieved by each of the communions of the reasons why members of other communions believed as they did. It might be that through this understanding the desire for comprehensive union would be awakened and strengthened and a way, as yet unforeseeable, would be found for attaining the apparently impossible. An early leader was Charles H. Brent, a bishop of the Protestant Episcopal Church in the United States of America, who had been present at Edinburgh. A preliminary meeting convened at Geneva, Switzerland, in 1920[28] and full meetings were

---

ber 12th to 29th, 1938 (New York and London, International Missionary Council, 7 vols., 1939).

[28] *World Conference on Faith and Order. Report of the Preliminary Meeting at Geneva, Switzerland, August 12-20, 1920* (The Continuation Committee, no place or date, pp. 95).

held at Lausanne in 1927[29] and at Edinburgh in 1937.[30] There was also a continuing organization.[31]

The Universal Christian Council for Life and Work did not come into being until after 1914, but it had its roots in movements which antedated that fateful year. In the years immediately preceding 1914, increasing tension in the international situation stimulated earnest Christians in Europe and America to arouse the churches to efforts on behalf of peace. The recently formed Federal Council of the Churches of Christ in America was active and gave support to the Church Peace Union. The latter undertook a conference which met in Switzerland on August 1, 1914, when war was breaking out. The gathering failed of its immediate objective. However, the Church Peace Union did not despair, but continued as the World Alliance for International Friendship through the Churches and with an endowment from Andrew Carnegie. In November, 1914, Nathan Soederblom, Archbishop of Upsala, stimulated by the tragedy of that summer, sent out an appeal in an effort to obtain a united voice from Christians in behalf of peace. Attempts to bring about a gathering of churchmen from belligerent and neutral countries during the war failed, but in the autumn of 1919 a meeting of the World Alliance for International Friendship through the Churches convened in Holland and the following year a conference was held in Geneva which called itself "the preliminary meeting to consider a Universal Conference of the Church of Christ on Life and Work." The conference was held in Stockholm in 1925. Out of it came a continuation committee and the Universal Christian Council for Life and Work.[32] It addressed itself to the task of creating a better social, economic, political, and international order in the world. A conference, memorable for the careful

[29] *Faith and Order. Proceedings of the World Conference, Lausanne, August 3-21, 1927,* edited by H. N. Bate (Garden City, Doubleday, Doran & Company, 1928, pp. xxiii, 541), *passim.*

[30] *The Second World Conference on Faith and Order, held at Edinburgh, August 3-18, 1937,* edited by Leonard Hodgson (New York, The Macmillan Company, 1938, pp. ix, 386), *passim.*

[31] *World Conference on Faith and Order. The 1939 Meeting of the Continuation Committee, held at St. George's School, Clarens, Switzerland, August 21-23, 1939* (Oxford and New York, the Committee, pp. 82).

[32] Charles S. MacFarland, *Steps Toward the World Council. Origins of the Ecumenical Movement as Expressed in the Universal Christian Council for Life and Work* (New York, Fleming H. Revell Company, 1938, pp. 128), *passim*; *The Stockholm Conference, 1925. The Official Report of the Universal Christian Conference on Life and Work held in Stockholm, 19-30 August, 1925,* edited by G. K. A. Bell (Oxford University Press, 1926, pp. xv, 791), *passim*; Edward Shillito, *Life and Work. The Universal Christian Conference on Life and Work held in Stockholm, 1925* (New York, Longmans, Green and Co., 1926, pp. vii, 104).

preparation which preceded it and for its widely representative membership,
assembled in Oxford in the summer of 1937.[33]

Since both movements, Faith and Order and Life and Work, held their
meetings in Great Britain in the summer of 1937 and many delegates to the one
went also to the other, it was not unnatural that there should have been an
effort to bring the two together in an organization more inclusive than either.
There came, therefore, the proposal for a World Council of Churches. At
Utrecht, in Holland, in May, 1938, there convened, at the invitation of a committee arising from the two conferences, about eighty delegates from the
churches which had been represented at Oxford and Edinburgh who drafted a
constitution for the World Council of Churches. This document provided for
an Assembly meeting every five years and a smaller Central Committee. Observers from other world Christian organizations were invited to the Utrecht
gathering and provision was made in the constitution for bringing these bodies
into co-operation with the World Council of Churches. The chairman of the
provisional organization was William Temple, then Archbishop of York and
later Archbishop of Canterbury. One of the first three secretaries was William
Paton, who was also a secretary of the International Missionary Council and
prominent in the organization of the British Council of Churches. Another
was W. A. Visser 't Hooft, who had been a secretary of the World's Student
Christian Federation, and the third was Henry S. Leiper, formerly a missionary
in China and later associated with co-operative enterprises in the United States.
The outbreak of another world war in 1939 delayed the initial meeting of the
Assembly and the completion of the organization, but in the interval more
than eighty different churches in nearly thirty different countries gave their
adherence and through offices in New York, London, and Geneva, the World
Council of Churches, while officially described as "in process of formation," was
actually functioning, and across warring lines. Its membership embraced
churches from all the great ecclesiastical families of the Protestant world,
including several of the Anglican, Lutheran, Presbyterian, Reformed, Methodist, Congregational, and Baptist bodies. It had in it such diverse groups as
the General Convention of the New Jerusalem in the U.S.A. (followers of
Emanuel Swedenborg), the Salvation Army, and the Friends. It also contained
some of the smaller Orthodox and Old Catholic churches, the Mar Thoma
Syrian Church of Malabar, and the Nestorians. The membership was not
purely Occidental. It was in all five continents, the East and West Indies, Aus-

---

[33] J. H. Oldham, *The Oxford Conference (Official Report)* (Chicago, Willett, Clark &
Company, 1937, pp. xvi, 290).

tralia, and New Zealand.[34] Although the World Council of Churches was primarily Protestant, it was reaching out to other than Protestant churches. Nor was this with any thought of making these churches Protestant. Here was an organization more inclusive ecclesiastically than any other which the Christian Church had ever known.

Protestants formed many federations and councils of churches, local, regional, and national. These brought together different denominations, but not for "organic" union. The movement began before 1914 but was accelerated after that year. It was to be found in a number of lands but was particularly strong in English-speaking countries.[35]

The Protestant movement towards co-operation and unity had as one of its phases the actual union of ecclesiastical bodies. Many of these were of different branches of the same ecclesiastical family. For instance, in 1917 and 1918 the United Lutheran Church of America was constituted by the General Synod, the General Council, and the United Synod of the South.[36] In 1917 three bodies came together to form the Norwegian Lutheran Church of America, and in 1931 three other Lutheran bodies joined in the American Lutheran Church.[37] In 1929 the Church of Scotland and the United Free Church of Scotland healed the breach which had existed since the Disruption, in 1843.[38] In 1932 the largest groups of English Methodism consummated complete corporate union.[39] In 1939 the Methodist Episcopal Church, the Methodist Episcopal Church South, and the Methodist Protestant Church joined in constituting the Methodist Churches in the United States.[40] These were only a few of such unions.[41] There were also unions of bodies which were originally of different families. Notable among them were the United Church of Canada, formed in 1925 by Methodists, Congregationalists, and Presbyterians;[42] the Church of Christ in China, constituted in 1927 by Presbyterians and embracing many former Congregationalists, Baptists, Methodists, and United Brethren;[43] and the Church of Christ in Japan,

---

[34] *We have Dared and God has Justified Our Daring* (New York, World Council of Churches, 1943, pp. 25), *passim*; *The World Council Courier*, *passim*. For an autobiographical account by a leading participant in the movement for world-wide Christian unity, see Brown, *A Teacher and His Times*, pp. 335-365.

[35] See a brief account and an incomplete list in Slosser, *Christian Unity*, pp. 279 ff.

[36] Slosser, *op. cit.*, p. 299; Douglass, *Church Unity Movements in the United States*, p. 51.

[37] Douglass, *op. cit.*, p. 51.

[38] Slosser, *op. cit.*, p. 303; Douglass, *A Decade of Objective Progress in Church Unity, 1927-1936*, pp. 106-111.

[39] Douglass, *A Decade of Objective Progress in Church Unity, 1927-1936*, p. 89.

[40] *The International Review of Missions*, Vol. XXIX, pp. 103, 104.

[41] See a partial list in Douglass, *op. cit.*, pp. 89 ff.

[42] Silcox, *Church Union in Canada*, pp. 107-109.

[43] A. R. Kepler, a leader of the new body, in *The China Christian Year Book*, 1928, pp. 84-86.

which brought together in 1941 the overwhelming majority of Protestant Christians in Japan, including Presbyterians, *Kumiai* (Congregationalists), Reformed, Methodists, Baptists, and Lutherans, embracing forty-one bodies in all,[44] and which later also drew in most of the Anglicans.

Protestants were not content with co-operation and union within their own ranks. In a variety of ways they reached out to Christians of other communions. In the aspects which we are to mention in the next few lines this was not with the purpose of winning converts to Protestantism. Rather it was with the objective of enlarging Christian understanding and fellowship to embrace as many as possible of those who bore the Christian name or to induce all Christians to join in action for particular social or moral goals. Some Jews were also brought in. Several of the Old Catholic and of the Orthodox and other Eastern churches, as we saw in the third paragraph above, became members of the World Council of Churches. In the United States the Religious Education Association, founded by Protestants near the outset of the twentieth century and predominantly Protestant in membership, included some Jews and Roman Catholics.[45] The National Conference of Jews and Christians, later called the National Conference of Christians and Jews, formed in the United States in the 1930's and at Protestant initiative, had as its chief purpose the cultivation of understanding and tolerance among Protestants, Roman Catholics, and Jews.[46]

The trend towards co-operation and unity was not without opposition from within Protestant ranks. Many, notably among Lutherans, Anglo-Catholics, and extreme conservatives among Baptists and Presbyterians distrusted it. Indeed, one of the movements of the period which gained considerably headway and which was present in a number of denominations, especially in the United States, was Fundamentalism. It stressed what it deemed the basic convictions essential to any true Christianity and its adherents were distrustful of all who did not fully subscribe to its tenets. To most of them, and to some others, such organizations as the Federal Council of Churches of Christ in America and the World Council of Churches were anathema. However, after 1914 the movement represented by the latter bodies continued to gather momentum and its manifestations and achievements multiplied. Even Fundamentalists felt themselves constrained to come together across denominational and organizational barriers.[47] In the world war of 1914-1918 co-operation was

---

[44] C. W. Iglehart in *The International Review of Missions*, Vol. XXX, pp. 493-502.
[45] Clinchy, *All in the Name of God*, p. 141.
[46] Clinchy, *op. cit.*, p. 140.
[47] In 1917, for instance, interdenominational "faith missions," by whom most of the denominational agencies were stigmatized as "modernist," formed the Interdenominational

only beginning, but some of its aspects spanned the warring lines. In the world war which broke out in 1939 it was much stronger and continued to gain in vigour during that conflict.

Here was an amazing phenomenon, new in Christian history. The Catholic Church constituted in the first centuries of the Christian era had succeeded by the close of the third century in bringing into one fellowship the majority of professed Christians. Since the fourth century, however, the drift had been towards further division. Now, in the nineteenth century and especially after 1914, the trend was reversed. Christians were coming together. This was not the triumph of one church over its rivals, as had been true in the victory, albeit incomplete, of the Catholic Church of the Roman Empire. Nor was it furthered, as had been the growth of the Catholic Church of the first few centuries, by political unity in its environment. It was coming into being in a day when the nations of the world were pulling apart and in the midst of the most world-shaking wars which the human race had ever experienced. It arose from within Protestantism, by tradition and apparently by nature the most divided of the main great types of Christianity. It had organization, but it was not producing uniformity. Its chief emphasis was upon a unity of spirit. That spirit was more and more clothing itself in an inclusive fellowship, in part institutional and in part for common action, but it was primarily a temper of mind, an attitude, and a loyalty, which found their common centre in Jesus Christ.

If in its geographic spread and rootage and in the new movements which emerged from it, Christianity was advancing in the turbulent post-1914 world, so also it was growing in its effect upon mankind as a whole. Much of this we are to see more in detail as we pass from country to country in our geographic pilgrimage in later chapters. Here we can only give a brief preview of what we are later to note more at length.

In some areas Christianity seemed to have lost ground. That appeared to be notably the case in much of Europe where anti-Christian philosophies threatened Christianity and where, in the violence of war and revolution, a ruthlessness and a stark cruelty prevailed which at times gloated over the infliction of pain.

Yet even in Europe Christianity was by no means without influence. In the storm of the world war of 1914-1918 it contributed potently to the dream of an

---

Foreign Mission Association of North America as a counterpart to the older Foreign Missions Conference of North America. By 1930 fifteen organizations had joined.—*Faith Missions. Interdenominational Foreign Mission Association of North America* (New York, The Gibbs Press, 1930, pp. 19), *passim.* In the 1940's some of the extreme conservatives in the United States formed a council as a counterpart to the Federal Council of Churches.

international government to enforce peace. In the interval between the world wars it was probably the determinative factor in the emergence of the League of Nations. But for Woodrow Wilson the League would presumably never have come into being. Wilson was from a line of Presbyterian clergymen on both sides of his house and was himself a devout Christian. His faith seems to have been the main source of the idealism and the courage which inspired and nerved him in his struggle to bring the League to birth and make it effective. The League of Nations failed in the critical test of preventing war, but in all the experience of the human race it was the most daring and comprehensive attempt which came to formal implementation to insure justice and peace on a world-wide scale. But for the Christian faith it probably would never have been. When, in the second world war of the twentieth century, Europe appeared to be under the heel of a callous conqueror, the churches displayed more power of resistance than did any other set of institutions, spoke out against exploitation of the weak and the Jews, and kept alive conscience and hope.

Moreover, it must be noted that Christianity had much to do with moulding the ideals and to some extent the policies of two of the great powers, Great Britain and the United States, who were victors in the first of world wars and who appeared to be winning in the second of the world conflicts. This does not necessarily mean that it was responsible for the victories. It does mean that through the victories it had a part in forming the post-war world. The world war of 1914-1918 was ostensibly fought "to make the world safe for democracy." In the world war which broke out in 1939 there was much talk of "freedom-loving peoples" and, in the United States, of the "four freedoms." There were efforts in the United States and Great Britain to construct an international organization in which all peoples would have a place and no one race or nation would dominate the others. Backward peoples, so this dream declared, were ultimately to have their freedom and in the meantime the powers who controlled them were not to exploit them but to regard their dominance as a trust for the subject peoples and for mankind. Much of this idealism, perhaps most of it, stemmed from Christian sources and especially from Anglo-Saxon Protestantism.

The Institute of Pacific Relations, formed in the mid-1920's, originally sprang from the Young Men's Christian Associations. It soon became a purely secular organization for promoting understanding and co-operation among the peoples of the Pacific area, but its original impulse was from Christianity.[48]

Protestantism, and particularly the Protestantism of Great Britain and the

[48] Conversation of the author with the organizing secretary, J. Merle Davis, Dec. 18, 1938.

United States, had made much, as a corollary of salvation by faith and the priesthood of all believers, of the rights of every individual and had been the major source of democracy. This kind of Christianity was now becoming an integral although not the dominant factor in shaping the new world order which Great Britain and the United States were professedly wishing to build. Especially in the second world war the Protestant churches of the United States and Great Britain were uniting in formulating and giving wide circulation to plans which involved international government, international agreement on matters of economics, the adaptation of the treaty structure to changing conditions, the progress of subject peoples towards self-government, the international control of armed power, and religious and intellectual liberty for individuals.[49]

In Japan, through figures like Kagawa, Christianity exerted greater influence after 1914 than before that year. In China under the Republic which counted October 10, 1911 as its birthday, Christianity had effects all out of proportion to its numerical strength. In India after 1914 Christianity made itself more felt than before. It contributed to the movements among the outcastes for emancipation, to an improving status of women, and, through its share in shaping the ideals and methods of Gandhi, to the form and the strength of the programme of the Indian National Congress. Not only in these three major lands of Asia, but also in some of the smaller countries, Christianity was a mounting force. It was increasingly to be reckoned with in Africa south of the Sahara. It was of growing moment in the East Indies, particularly among the peoples of animistic background. While in most lands it was still a minor factor, if mankind be viewed as a whole Christianity was more potent after 1914 than ever it had been before that year.

From this survey of the main characteristics of the post-1914 world we are to turn, after a sketch of the organization and methods employed for the expansion of the faith, to a more detailed account, region by region, of the recession and the spread of Christianity in that era. In many ways the age was a mingling of the sombre and the lurid. Throughout the globe old patterns of life were disintegrating under the pressure of gigantic forces. Several of these forces were the antithesis of Christianity. The hearts of many were failing

[49] See, among other documents, *A Just and Durable Peace. Statement of Guiding Principles, Adopted by the Federal Council of Churches, December 11, 1942, Prepared by the Commission to Study the Bases of a Just and Durable Peace* (New York, 1942, pp. 6); *A Christian Basis for Reconstruction: A Statement signed by fourteen British Church Leaders, including the Archbishops of Canterbury and York and the Moderator of the Church of Scotland* (New York, Federal Council of the Churches of Christ in America, 1943, pp. 13).

them for fear. The very existence of Christianity was menaced. To some it seemed that such advance as the Christian faith made in geographic extent and in influence was because of momentum gained in the century of relative peace and prosperity between 1815 and 1914. As the nineteenth century faded more and more into the past and that momentum was lost, so it was gloomily declared, Christianity would also recede. Similar discouraging analyses and predictions might have been made at the time of the disintegration of the Roman Empire, but only to be disproved by the event. Christianity then displayed an inner vitality which provided it with renewed and even greater momentum. Before three decades had elapsed after the decisive events of 1914 it began to be clear that this experience was to be repeated. While in the storms of that turbulent era Christianity did not register such rapid gains as it had in the preceding ten decades, it was still advancing, and in some lands at an accelerated pace. Here was one of the great eras of the Christian faith.

Chapter III

THE PROCESSES BY WHICH CHRISTIANITY SPREAD. MODIFICATIONS AND DEVELOPMENTS IN ORGANIZATION AND METHODS

IN THE period after 1914 the processes by which Christianity spread were in large part a continuation of those which had characterized the nineteenth century. In the methods employed there was no basic revolution and not even any striking innovation. As in the nineteenth century,[1] very little assistance came from the state, but the agencies were non-political societies, orders, and congregations supported by the gifts of millions of individual Christians and staffed by the voluntary offering of lives. Women played, as before, a large part, both in raising funds and in contributing personnel. High standards were still set for admission to the Church. In some areas, notably in India and Africa, mass movements towards Christianity occurred, but the stress remained very largely upon the conversion of individuals. Emphasis continued to be placed by Protestants upon the permeation of all culture by Christian ideals. However, as time passed Protestants began to give somewhat more attention to the building of the Church. This persistence of nineteenth century processes and methods was to be expected, for the forces, both Roman Catholic and Protestant, which had made chiefly for the spread of the faith in that age continued after 1914.

One important modification of emphasis, common to both great branches of Christianity, was hinted at in the preceding chapter: more than before 1914 the effort was made to train an indigenous leadership and to transfer administration to it. Yet even this was by no means new. In theory both Roman Catholics and Protestants had had this as a principle throughout the nineteenth century. Indeed, their success in effecting the transition from Occidental to local leadership was largely possible because of the foundations which had been consciously laid in the ten or more decades before 1914.

One important change in the processes by which Christianity spread as between the pre-1914 and the post-1914 years was referred to in the preceding chapter—the practical disappearance of advance on the part of the Eastern churches. In the first three centuries the gains of Christianity had been most

[1] For a description of the nineteenth century characteristics, see Vol. IV, pp. 47 ff.

striking in western Asia. In subsequent centuries one or another of the Eastern forms of Christianity had displayed a vast territorial expansion. Greek Orthodox Christianity had won most of the Balkan Peninsula and Russia. For centuries the Nestorians were widely distributed in Asia, although in most areas as small minorities. Monophysites were strong in western Asia, Egypt, up the Nile, and in Ethiopia. However, by slow degrees the chief achievements in the propagation of the faith were increasingly by western European peoples. This trend had begun in the first five centuries. It continued through the next thousand years and became especially marked after 1500. After A.D. 1500 most of the territorial advances were by western Christianity, Roman Catholic and Protestant. Yet even in the nineteenth century what was then the strongest of the Eastern churches, that of Russia, was making geographic gains in the Russian Empire and had a few missions beyond the Russian borders. After 1914, with the exception of the Western Hemisphere, recession characterized the Eastern churches. Massacres which accompanied the World War of 1914-1918 greatly reduced the numbers of Armenian and Nestorian Christians. The post-war events in Turkey dealt further blows to the Eastern churches in that country. The revolution in Russia threatened the existence of the Church in that vast empire and the small Russian Orthodox missions in China and Japan languished. In Egypt the slow assimilation of the Coptic Christians to Islam, in process for many centuries, continued. The Italian invasion of Ethiopia brought difficult days to the ancient and decrepit church of that land. Only in the Western Hemisphere, chiefly in the United States, were the Eastern churches free to expand. Here their growth was mostly by the natural increase of their constituencies, for they had almost no converts and the flood of immigration by which they had been recruited dwindled to a trickle. After 1914, as in no previous time, the expansion of Christianity was solely by its western forms, Roman Catholicism and Protestantism.

In the Roman Catholic Church the main burden of missions continued to be carried by the organizations which had borne it in the nineteenth century, or even earlier. In 1930, for example, those orders and societies having the largest numbers of missionaries were, first, the Society of Jesus, then the Société des Missions Étrangères of Paris, and then the Franciscans.[2] The Society for the Propagation of the Faith was still the chief general agency for the raising of funds.

However, a number of new organizations and institutions came into being to

[2] *The International Review of Missions,* Vol. XX, p. 71.

further missions. Although some new varieties appeared, these were, in general, of the same type as those of pre-1914 years. Their inauguration was not an indication of fresh methods but rather of vitality in the Roman Catholic Church. In 1917 there was instituted in Italy the Missionary Union of the Clergy.[3] It had as its founder Paolo Manna, the superior general of the Milan seminary for foreign missions. Its purpose was the enlistment of the clergy in the cause of missions. It was to accomplish this by educational means. It was organized by countries and each national council was to have a head appointed by the Propaganda. By 1936 it had spread to 22 countries and counted a membership of more than 145,000, mostly among the secular clergy.[4] In 1930 the Society of St. Patrick for Foreign Missions was organized in Ireland and sent an initial contingent of seven priests to Calabar, in Africa.[5] In 1922 a new project, the Apostleship of the Sea, received papal approval. It was quickly extended to a large number of lands and took as its field Roman Catholic seafarers, providing for them port chaplains, clubs, and service centres.[6] In 1922 a group was formed in Würzburg by Christopher Becker, there to found a medical missionary institute to train nurses, to give certain types of preparation to physicians who wished to go as missionaries, and with medical courses for missionary priests.[7] In 1931 there was completed in Vichy, in France, the *Maison du Missionnaire*, for the care of invalid missionaries.[8] In 1927 the Propaganda created the *Fides* agency to collect missionary news and to distribute it through the press.[9] In the 1920's "Aucam," the *Association Universitaire Catholique d'Aide aux Missions*, came into being, a student organization.[10] The year 1923 saw the inception of the Association of the Friends of Missions, which had as its object the spreading of information in France concerning French missions.[11] We hear of international student missionary congresses, of a French national missionary congress,[12] and of missions weeks held yearly at Louvain for the study of missionary methods.[13] We also read of a proposed new seminary in Portugal for foreign missions.[14] In 1925 there was founded in Washington, D.C., a society

[3] Lesourd, *L'Année Missionnaire, 1931*, pp. 314-317.

[4] *Fides News Service*, March 21, 1936. See also *Priester und Mission*, 1929, pp. 99-102, for somewhat earlier developments.

[5] *The International Review of Missions*, Vol. XX, p. 71.

[6] *Fides News Service*, May 19, 1934, Sept. 28, 1935.

[7] Berg, *Die katholische Heidenmission als Kulturträger*, Vol. III, pp. 138-146; *Fides News Service*, Apr. 10, 1937.

[8] Watthé, *La Belle Vie du Missionnaire en Chine*, pp. 211-223.

[9] Lesourd, *op. cit.*, 1931, p. 313.

[10] *The International Review of Missions*, Vol. XX, p. 76.

[11] Lesourd, *op. cit.*, pp. 318-321.

[12] *The International Review of Missions*, Vol. XXIII, p. 105.

[13] A conversation, Apr. 30, 1934, with the real organizer of this week, Pierre Charles.

[14] Lesourd, *op. cit.*, p. 566.

of medical missionaries, composed of women physicians and nurses who had as their chief purpose the care of Moslem women.[15] In 1939, in spite of the disruption of normal life due to the exhausting civil war in their country, the Spanish Dominicans decided to inaugurate a training college for members of their order preparing for Latin America.[16] In 1927 *Miva* (*Missions-Verkehr-Arbeitsgemeinschaft*) was founded in Germany to provide missionaries with modern means of transport, such as automobiles, motor-boats, and airplanes.[17] In 1918 there was formed at Scarboro Bluffs, Ontario, a foreign mission society as a centre for the missionary interest of English-speaking Canadian Roman Catholics.[18] This is only an incomplete and random list, but it is some indication of the striking growth of interest among Occidental Roman Catholics in missions to the non-Occident.

A marked increase occurred in Roman Catholic activity in medical missions. In addition to the two movements noted in the last paragraph, there were several other organizations for assisting and training for this branch of the Church's activity.[19] In spite of the fact that priests were supposed to be too busy with their special functions to practice medicine or surgery,[20] some short courses were arranged for them. Most of the burden, however, was carried by women and lay brothers.[21]

The rise in interest in missions was unevenly distributed by countries. Proportionately France began to recede from the position of leadership which she had held in the nineteenth century. In 1900 about seventy per cent. of Roman Catholic missionaries were from France. By 1930 less than half were of French nationality.[22] However, France still led. Indeed, in 1935 it was said that Alsace was then the world's greatest nursery of Roman Catholic missionaries.[23] In 1934 the Société des Missions Étrangères of Paris had over a thousand foreign missionaries and was responsible for Roman Catholic effort in one-fifth of the non-Christian population of the world. While some of the orders, notably the Jesuits, had more missionaries, the Paris society was the largest of the institutes

---

[15] Williams, *The Catholic Church in Action*, p. 242.

[16] *Fides News Service*, March 11, 1939.

[17] *The International Review of Missions*, Vol. XX, p. 71. See also Paul Schulte, *The Flying Missionary,* translated from the German (New York, Benziger Brothers, 1936, pp. x, 257), *passim.*

[18] *Fides News Service*, Nov. 18, 1939.

[19] Lesourd, *op. cit.*, pp. 351-358; *Fides News Service*, Jan. 21, 1939.

[20] Berg, *op. cit.*, Vol. III, pp. 91-94.

[21] On the part of women in medical missions, see Arlette Butavand, *Les Femmes Médecins Missionnaires* (Louvain, Éditions de l'Aucam, 1933, pp. 142), pp. 89 ff.

[22] Hayes, *France, A Nation of Patriots*, p. 105.

[23] *Fides News Service*, March 23, 1935.

of the church devoted exclusively to foreign missions.[24] In 1930 there were reported to be 7,754 French priests, lay brothers, and sisters serving in foreign missions. Next among Occidental lands was Italy, with 2,876, then, in order, Germany, with 2,807, Holland, with 2,503, Belgium, with 2,175, Ireland, with 1,719, Spain, with 1,404, Canada, with 816, the United States, with 728, England, with 571, South America, with 336, Switzerland, with 293, Austria, with 229, Poland, with 139, Portugal, with 137, little Malta, with 102, Luxemberg, with 58, Czechoslovakia, with 45, Scotland, with 42, Hungary, with 36, Jugoslavia, with 24, Bulgaria, with 10, and Lithuania, with 5.[25] These figures may not be entirely accurate, for it is said that in 1936 5,163 Dutch were serving as missionaries, or one for every 580 Roman Catholics in Holland.[26] From some of the countries the numbers of recruits continued to mount. Thus between November, 1934 and November, 1935, 176 priests, brothers, and sisters left Ireland for the missions[27] and in 1936 the total was 174,[28] or accessions in two years of more than a fifth of the Irish mission staff of 1930.

The diminished place of France in the Roman Catholic missionary enterprise was not due alone to a decline in the religious zeal, the resources, and the position in international affairs of that country, although these were contributory factors. It was also and probably primarily the result of a rising missionary interest among Roman Catholics in other lands. The increase was notable in Germany, Italy, Holland, Belgium, and Ireland. Even Spain, in spite of poverty and civil strife, continued prominent, although with a position far behind that which she had held in her great days in the sixteenth and seventeenth centuries. In 1929 her activity was both stimulated and made vivid by a missionary exposition. At that time it was said that there were 1,973 Spanish priests, brothers, and nuns in foreign missions in Asia, Africa, the Americas, and Oceania, caring for 2,379,042 Roman Catholics and 68,270 catechumens.[29] These figures, it will be noted, are slightly above those given earlier in this paragraph. In addition, in the late 1920's 2,955 Spanish regulars were reported to be serving abroad, most of them in Spanish America, but several hundred in the United States and the Philippines and a few in Europe.[30] The civil commotion of the 1930's cut tragically into Spain's financial contributions, but in 1938 those to the Society for the Propagation of the Faith were still approximately half of what they had been before the war.[31]

[24] *Fides News Service,* May 19, 1934.
[25] *Testo-Atlante Illustrato delle Missioni,* p. 100.
[26] *Fides News Service,* May 2, 1936.
[27] *Fides News Service,* Feb., 1936.
[28] *Fides News Service,* Jan. 9, 1937.
[29] *Revista de la Exposición Misional Española,* pp. 458-461.
[30] *Revista de la Exposición Misional Española,* pp. 728, 729.
[31] *Fides News Service,* May 13, 1939.

Of great promise for the future was the rapidly growing part which Roman Catholics in the United States were taking in supplying funds and personnel for the foreign missions of their church. Until 1914 the Roman Catholics of the great republic had their energies almost completely absorbed in caring for the immigrants of their faith who were pouring into that land from Europe. Most of these were from the lower income levels and in the New World became unskilled labourers. For them churches and schools had to be built and clergy trained. The achievement, as we have seen,[32] was magnificent, but it left little energy for other lands. After 1914 the situation rapidly changed. In that year the world war brought a halt to most of the immigration. Restrictive legislation enacted not long afterwards kept it at a mere fraction of its former volume. Roman Catholic forces in the United States began to have leisure and resources for other tasks than the ones forced upon them by the new arrivals. Moreover, as they were longer in the United States, Roman Catholics shared increasingly in the prosperity of their adopted land, and, rising in the economic scale, were better able to participate in the world-wide enterprise of their church. Earlier successes in planting and nourishing their church bore their fruit in loyalty and sacrifice for overseas tasks.

The result of this combination of factors was a marked acceleration in the American share in Roman Catholic foreign missions. Prominent in this development was the Catholic Foreign Mission Society of America—better known by the name of its headquarters, Maryknoll. It was founded in 1911, with very modest beginnings. When, approximately a quarter of a century later, in 1936, James A. Walsh, its co-founder and superior-general, died, it had 550 members, including priests, lay brothers, and students, and the associated Foreign Mission Sisters of St. Dominic numbered 525.[33] In 1941 or 1942 the number of priests and brothers from the United States serving as missionaries in other lands was said to be 1,489, and of sisters 1,250, a total of 2,739. The largest number were in China, about 45 per cent. of the whole, with the West Indies next, followed, in order, by Oceania, the Philippine Islands, South America, and Africa, with smaller numbers in eight other sections and countries.[34] This was a striking increase over the 728 reported in 1930,[35] only a little more than a decade earlier. However, the latter figure may be in error, for in 1934 the total was said to have been 1,498.[36] The missionaries were by no means all from one society or

[32] Vol. IV, pp. 224 ff.

[33] *Fides News Service*, Apr. 18, 1936. On Walsh see Daniel Sargent, *All the Day Long. James Anthony Walsh, Cofounder of Maryknoll* (New York, Longmans Green & Company, 1941, pp. 259).

[34] Considine, *Across a World*, pp. 386-390.

[35] *Testo-Atlante Illustrato delle Missioni*, p. 100.

[36] *Fides News Service*, Sept. 15, 1934.

congregation. In 1942 not far from 40 organizations were listed as sending them. Most of these were American provinces of orders or societies of European origin, such as the Franciscans, the Jesuits, and the Society of the Divine Word.[37] Giving mounted, not only directly to these organizations, but also through other bodies, notably the Society for the Propagation of the Faith. During seven years from 1922 into 1929 American contributions to that society rose from $350,000 to $1,400,000, or a four-fold advance.[38]

It was fortunate for the Roman Catholic missionary enterprise that the faithful in the United States were so rapidly assuming much of the responsibility for it. The Nazi regime in Germany bore hard upon the missions from that land. Then, after war broke out in 1939, the tides of the conflict engulfed France, Germany, Italy, Holland, and Belgium, the lands from which had come the large majority of the missionaries in the quarter of a century before that conflict. Many of the priests and seminarians were called to the colours.[39] The home organization was crippled and contacts between the supporting constituencies and the fields were either cut off or rendered difficult. The growth of American missions in part compensated for the loss, and that in spite of the fact that approximately half of the American missionary staff was in Japan and in areas overwhelmed by the Japanese armies.

After 1914 various new methods for the prosecution or assistance of Roman Catholic missions were either inaugurated or largely expanded. For instance, there was an extensive movement to promote continuous prayer for particular areas by the houses of the contemplative orders, such as the Trappists and the Carmelites. Scores of such territories were thus "adopted" by communities in various lands of the Occident.[40] One Sunday in the year was set aside by the church for the offering of prayers and alms for the Society for the Propagation of the Faith.[41] The use of the cinema for missions seems to have begun in 1930.[42] Chairs of what was known as missiology were introduced in some of the Roman Catholic universities, notably the Gregoriana, staffed by the Jesuits, in Rome.[43]

Attempts were also made to meet the demands of the rising tide of non-Occidental nationalism and racial feeling which resented white domination.

[37] *The Official Catholic Directory, 1942* (New York, P. J. Kenedy & Sons), Part II, pp. 868-872.
[38] *The International Review of Missions*, Vol. XX, p. 70.
[39] *Fides News Service*, Nov. 11, 25, 1939.
[40] *The International Review of Missions*, Vol. XX, p. 71.
[41] *Fides News Service*, Oct. 12, 1935.
[42] Lesourd, *L'Année Missionnaire, 1931*, pp. 531-538.
[43] Information given the author in April, 1934, by members of the Faculty of Missiology in the Gregoriana.

We saw in the last chapter that marked emphasis was placed upon an indigenous priesthood and episcopate. In 1917 Benedict XV, out of respect for the susceptibilities of the eastern uniate bodies, detached from the Congregation for the Propagation of the Faith the section on Oriental rites and created for it an independent congregation, the Sacred Congregation for the Oriental Church, with the Pope himself as the prefect.[44] Efforts were made to encourage ecclesiastical art and architecture which would incorporate indigenous traditions.[45] Costantini, the first resident Apostolic Delegate to China and later secretary to the Propaganda, was an ardent advocate of this policy.[46] The Propaganda also insisted that only those native customs should be forbidden which were counter to good morals and religion: the others were to be left undisturbed.[47]

The remarkable expansion of Roman Catholic Christianity in the post-1914 period could not be ascribed to any one man or group of men. It arose from vigorous life within the church. However, it was given impetus and guidance by men in high position. One of these was Willem van Rossum, a Dutch Redemptorist of marked piety and administrative gifts, who as cardinal and head of the Propaganda in the crucial years immediately following the world war of 1914-1918 had much to do with the great growth of missions in that period.[48] Pius XI, who came to the papal throne in 1922, was a prodigious worker, a very able administrator, and because of his interest in that phase of the church's enterprise was known as the "missionary Pope." In the year of his accession he made an official pronouncement on missions.[49] That year, too, he transferred the headquarters of the Society for the Propagation of the Faith to Rome and placed the organization more directly under the supervision of the Holy See.[50] There was a feeling that the society had been too exclusively French in control and that this held back the giving through it from other lands. The step now taken seems to have been justified, for the total gifts through the society doubled between 1923 and 1928.[51] This rise, however, may have been

---

[44] Baudrillart in Descamps, *Histoire Générale Comparée des Missions*, p. 517; Lesourd, *op. cit.*, p. 37.

[45] As an illustration of this trend, the entire issue of *Arte Christiana* (Milan, 1913 ff.), for February, 1934 (Vol. XXII, No. 2) was devoted to "missionary art," with illustrations of adaptations to indigenous styles.

[46] Costantini in *Arte Christiana*, Vol. XXII, pp. 33-64; *Dossiers de la Commission Synodale*, May, 1932, pp. 410-412.

[47] *Dossiers de la Commission Synodale*, May, 1932, pp. 408, 409.

[48] *Fides News Service*, May 13, 1939.

[49] Tragella, *Pio XI, Papa Missionario*, p. 9.

[50] Baudrillart in Descamps, *Histoire Générale Comparée des Missions*, p. 518.

[51] Lesourd, *L'Année Missionnaire, 1931*, p. 303.

due to a general increase of interest in missions throughout the Roman Catholic world. The receipts of the Association of the Holy Infancy more than doubled during the same period.[52] In 1922 Pius XI created an apostolic delegation for China and one also for South Africa.[53] In 1923 he erected in India the first native diocese of the Latin rite and instituted the hierarchy of the Malabar church. In 1924 a plenary council convened in China, a national council in Japan, and a council-general in South Africa.[54] In 1925 a missionary exposition was held in Rome which attracted much attention.[55] In 1926, following up the pronouncement of his predecessor, Benedict XV, in *Maximum Illud* (1919), which encouraged the multiplication of missions and a native clergy and episcopate, Pius XI, in *Rerum Ecclesiae*, placed great stress upon the training of an indigenous clergy.[56] He also encouraged other education.[57] He sought to induce all provinces or all orders and congregations to undertake missions.[58]

The striking growth in Roman Catholic missions in the interval between the two world wars was not without its reverses. The world-wide economic depression which began in 1929 seriously affected the contributions of the faithful. Between 1929 and 1933 the income of the Society for the Propagation of the Faith declined about forty-five per cent.[59] The decrease was particularly marked in the United States. Dwindling totals were seen in some other societies.[60] However, in 1934, as the depression began to lift, giving once more gained and the improvement continued to the eve of the next world war.[61]

The outbreak of the new and more extensive world war dealt Roman Catholic missions more severe blows than did the earlier conflict of 1914-1918. However, by that time the participation of Roman Catholics of the United States had reached substantial dimensions and was not at once adversely affected. It was, therefore, able in part to relieve the shock.

In general, the three decades which followed 1914, while marked by few new missionary ideals or methods, were halcyon ones for the spread and increased rootage of the Roman Catholic Church in non-Occidental lands. In 1939, the

[52] Lesourd, *op. cit.*, p. 308.
[53] Tragella, *op. cit.*, pp. 20, 21.
[54] Tragella, *op. cit.*, p. 25.
[55] Tragella, *op. cit.*, pp. 41 ff.
[56] *The International Review of Missions*, Vol. XXI, pp. 364, 365.
[57] Kandel, *Educational Yearbook of the International Institute of Teachers College*, 1933, p. 566.
[58] J. J. Considine, in conversation with the author, Apr. 18, 1934.
[59] *Fides News Service*, Oct. 21, 1934.
[60] *Fides News Service*, May 4, 1934.
[61] *Fides News Service*, May 9, 1936, Apr. 1, 1939, July 22, 1939.

very year of the coming of the new war, ten new ecclesiastical districts were erected in the areas under the jurisdiction of the Propaganda.[62]

In Protestant as in Roman Catholic circles the main features of the processes by which Christianity spread in the nineteenth century continued. Some new societies came into being, but for the most part these followed the organizational patterns and the methods of those already in existence. None of the new societies, except those which were mergers or reorganizations of older ones, attained the dimensions of those which had been constituted before 1914. The principal burden of the propagation of Protestant Christianity continued to be carried by the bodies which were bearing it before 1914. The methods by which Protestants had accomplished the remarkable spread of their branch of the faith in the nineteenth century were those which were chiefly followed in the post-1914 years. The processes still fell into the time-honoured divisions of evangelism, with the nurturing of churches, education, the preparation and distribution of literature, medical care, and various projects for social betterment. The translation and circulation of the Bible continued with marked initiative and efficiency. The Christian Scriptures were put into new tongues and improved revised editions were made of existing versions: their sales increased.[63]

Yet, even more than in the propagation of Roman Catholic Christianity, new currents and altered emphases appeared. This was probably to a large degree because, by its very nature, Protestantism was less inflexible and more responsive to its environment than was Roman Catholicism. In part, too, it was an indication of vigour within Protestantism. It is to the modifications in the processes by which Protestant Christianity spread after 1914 that we must now address ourselves. They were important in affecting the rate of growth and the nature of Protestantism on its geographic frontiers.

In the preceding chapter we called attention to the development of indigenous leadership and the transfer of authority to it. As in succeeding chapters we pursue our pilgrimage around the globe we shall find this to be characteristic of most of the areas in which Protestantism was newly planted. More than in the Roman Catholic Church this trend was in the direction of full autonomy. Because of the character of its structure, the Roman Catholic Church could not give full independence to the churches fostered by its missions. In every land and among every people that church was kept under the direction of Rome.

[62] *Fides News Service*, Jan. 14, 1939.
[63] See a useful summary in North, *The Book of a Thousand Tongues, passim.*

The Pope surrendered none of his powers and the supervision of the entire church was still by the papal curia. Protestants, however, had no central autocratic authority. By nature and tradition they were divided into many different, reciprocally independent bodies. Progressively, therefore, full autonomy was granted by the parent bodies to the younger churches. More and more, the missions of the "older" churches were in the form of assistance to the "younger" churches. Missionary personnel and funds were increasingly placed under the partial or complete control of the latter bodies. This was true in the newer communities of Occidental peoples. It was also although sometimes more tardily the case among non-Occidental peoples.

We have already summarized in the preceding chapter the striking trend towards co-operation and unity among Protestants, a trend which had local, regional, national, and global expressions. Older and younger churches were being knit into a fellowship which respected the autonomy of the individual bodies and allowed and even encouraged diversity, but which was more and more effective in promoting a sense of unity and common thought and action. We are to see this in detail as we pass from land to land.

Integral to this effort to evoke indigenous leadership and to build a worldwide Christian community were the attempts to make of Christian missions a movement from the non-Occident to the Occident as well as from the Occident to the non-Occident. It was felt that there should be no purely "sending" church, but that all churches should be "receiving" as well as "sending."[64] Thus a Mission of Help came from the churches of India to those of Great Britain, the World Student's Christian Federation had secretaries of Asiatic birth and rearing who travelled in the Occident, and a distinguished Japanese Christian, Kagawa, made tours in the United States which assembled large audiences.

Also as a corollary to the transfer of leadership to those of indigenous origin and to the encouragement of variety and the rooting of Christianity in many lands and cultures, Protestants were developing expressions of their faith in music, painting, architecture, forms of worship, and organization which would adapt national traditions to Christian purposes.[65] This was partly in response to the rising tide of nationalism and of resentment of non-white peoples at white domination. If Christianity was to prevail among non-white peoples, it

[64] As an example of this attitude see Edward Shillito, *Craftsmen All. Fellow-Workers in the Younger Churches* (London, Edinburgh House Press, 1932, pp. 142), *passim*.

[65] For examples of this in art see Fleming, *The Heritage of Beauty: Pictorial Studies of Modern Christian Architecture in Asia and Africa. Illustrating the Influence of Indigenous Cultures, passim*; Fleming, *Each with his Own Brush; Contemporary Christian Art in Asia and Africa, passim*; Fleming, *Christian Symbolism in a World Community, passim*. For an interesting experiment in education in utilizing indigenous conceptions, see Shaw, *God's Candlelights, an Educational Venture in Northern Rhodesia, passim*.

must, so far as possible, divest itself of its Occidental dress. The trend also arose from the desire on the part of both missionaries and nationals to plant their faith more deeply in other lands and cultures. It was paralleled, as we saw a few paragraphs above, by a similar movement among Roman Catholics. To a large degree, it was initiated and promoted by missionaries and to that extent was artificial. Some of the nationals opposed adopting indigenous forms of architecture on the ground that even when modified, these were associated with non-Christian traditions and so would compromise the Christian faith. To a great degree, however, the movement took rootage and even sprang spontaneously from the soil. It was most significant in prayers,[66] an indication that their faith was so real that the Christians were voicing it not in forms learned from the missionary but in their own terminology.

Somewhat related to the movement towards the acclimatizing of Christianity to non-Occidental environments, but with quite different expressions, was the growing awareness in the supporting constituencies of Protestant missions of the values in non-Occidental cultures and non-Christian religions. With this went a questioning of the validity of the missionary enterprise and a tolerance of other religious traditions which insisted that, if Christian missions be continued, they be on a different basis than in the past. There was a feeling that all religions, including Christianity, arose from man's search for truth, that each had in it elements of truth, and that all had in them something of error. Ultimate truth would be attained, if ever, by the sharing of the results of these many quests. Christian missions, so it was held, should be the endeavour to contribute to other peoples and cultures whatever of good Christianity might contain, but with a humility alien to the aggressive temper prevailing in the nineteenth century Occident. This was to be conjoined with a willingness to learn from other faiths and cultures. The attitude arose from a variety of sources. Among many traditionally Christian there was a religious illiteracy with only the most superficial knowledge of Christianity and an ever greater ignorance of other religions, but with a vague and often dogmatic belief that all religions were about equally true and equally false. Some sensitive spirits, condemnatory of Western imperialism, regarded Christian missions as one phase of Western aggression. Many, reinforced by some schools of anthropology, deplored the disruption brought to non-European cultures by Westerners, including especially, as they saw it, missionaries. A well informed and thoughtful minority, well grounded in the Christian faith and with an expert knowledge of other religions, wished for a reciprocal tolerance and willingness to learn. The trend

---

[66] See an admirable and comprehensive collection of these prayers in Fleming, *The World at One in Prayer, passim.*

was particularly vocal in the United States, perhaps because with the numerous varieties of Christianity represented in that land, the presence of Judaism, and the absence of a state church, many had been accustomed to tolerance and the appreciation of excellencies in other expressions of religion than their own.

The manifestations of the trend were legion.[67] The one which attracted the most attention arose from the Laymen's Foreign Missions Inquiry.[68] This was initiated in 1930 by American business men, generous supporters of missions, who were convinced that the situation confronting the enterprise demanded a thorough study of past achievements and current programmes and, presumably, drastic changes. Some of them were disturbed, too, by the lack of interest among their own children in Christian missions and were eager to know whether alterations would not win their allegiance. A survey was, accordingly, undertaken of the missions of their denominations in India, Burma, China, and Japan. Several of the group had earlier backed the Laymen's Missionary Movement, which had arisen in the decade before 1914 in an attempt to obtain the funds for "the evangelization of the world in this generation." The Laymen's Foreign Missions Inquiry was in part a critical examination of what the Laymen's Missionary Movement had helped to make possible. The contrast in titles was indicative of a change in attitude which was symptomatic of many earnest Christians of the day. As a first stage in the inquiry corps of "fact-finders" were sent to make careful examinations and assemble data. They compiled a survey which was at once the most comprehensive and detailed which had ever been made of any large segment of the enterprise for the spread of Christianity.[69] There then went, in 1931-1932, a much smaller group, a commission of appraisal, composed of eminent Protestant Christians from the United States, all of them sympathetic with missions, which visited the various areas studied and, on the basis of their own observations and of the material accumulated by the fact-finders, made their report. The report, published under

[67] For an interpretation of the function of the Christian missionary from this point of view, see Archibald G. Baker, *Christian Missions and a New World Culture* (Chicago, Willett, Clark & Company, 1934, pp. xv, 322), *passim*. A form of this conviction is by a former secretary of the London Missionary Society, Frank Lenwood, in *Jesus, Lord or Leader?* (London, Constable & Company, 1930, pp. ix, 351). Lenwood resigned from the society before writing the book, fearing that his views would embarrass that organization. An objective study pointing out various kinds of approaches, including this one, is Daniel Johnson Fleming, *Ways of Sharing with Other Faiths* (New York, Association Press, 1929, pp. xii, 268).

[68] For a brief sketch of the history and purpose of the Inquiry, see Hocking, *Re-thinking Missions*, pp. ix ff.

[69] The published portions, only a fraction of the whole, are *Laymen's Foreign Missions Inquiry. Regional Reports of the Commission of Appraisal*, Orville A. Petty, editor (New York, Harper & Brothers, 7 vols., 1933).

the title *Re-thinking Missions*,[70] attracted wide attention. In general, its position was one of endorsement but with suggestions for resolute changes in programme. The section which provoked the greatest discussion, some of it acrimonious, was that termed *General Principles*. It took an appreciative attitude towards non-Christian faiths which to many missionaries and officials of churches and mission boards seemed to destroy the motive for missions.[71] The chairman of the commission, William E. Hocking, of Harvard, later elaborated the philosophical position of *Re-thinking Missions* over his own signature.[72] A Movement for World Christianity, as it was officially called and which proved short-lived (it was organized in 1934 and was terminated in 1939), endeavoured to promote the ideals set forth in *Re-thinking Missions*.[73] It had a following among some liberal intellectuals, but the brevity of its career testified to the lack of enthusiasm for it among the rank and file of those from whom most of the financial support for the Protestant missionary enterprise was derived.

Many of the most earnest of the constituency of the missionary enterprise cherished convictions which were quite the opposite of those represented by *Re-thinking Missions*. These rejected completely the attitude that Christianity, like other religions, arose from mankind's search for truth. To them Christianity originated in the self-revelation of God in Christ and the other religions were the outgrowth of sinful man's beclouded groping for God. This set of convictions was cogently expressed in a volume, *The Christian Message in a Non-Christian World*,[74] written at the request of the Committee of the International Missionary Council in preparation for its meeting at Madras in 1938. It was also that of the Fundamentalists, of conservative groups who supported the so-called "faith missions," and of such small and intensely earnest bodies as the Seventh Day Adventists and the Christian and Missionary Alliance. The position found some of its most aggressive' advocates in the United States and Great Britain, but it also prevailed among most of the constituency of missions

[70] *Re-thinking Missions. A Laymen's Inquiry after One Hundred Years. By the Commission of Appraisal, William Ernest Hocking, Chairman* (New York, Harper & Brothers, 1932, pp. xv, 349).

[71] See articles by K. S. Latourette and John A. Mackay in *The International Review of Missions*, Vol. XXII, pp. 153-188, and by Robert E. Speer in *The Missionary Review of the World*, Vol. LVI, pp. 7-27. See also *The Missionary Review of the World*, Vol. LVI, pp. 43-45.

[72] William Ernest Hocking, *Living Religions and a World Faith* (New York, The Macmillan Company, 1940, pp. 291).

[73] The official organ was *World Christianity, a Digest* (Chicago, 1937-1939). See also *The Christian Century*, Vol. LI, p. 716; *Modern Missions Movement, an Announcement* (Chicago, The Executive Committee of the Modern Missions Movement, 1934, pp. 19).

[74] H. Kramer, *The Christian Message in a Non-Christian World* (New York, Harper & Brothers, 1938, pp. xvi, 455).

on the continent of Europe and was reinforced by the neo-orthodoxy of the crisis or dialectical theology.

In addition to the traditional emphases upon evangelism, education, literature, and medicine, much stress was placed upon meeting the needs of the rural populations. Since the large majority of mankind, especially those outside the Occident, lived in rural communities,[75] it was felt that the Christian missionary must pay particular attention to their problems. Towards the close of the nineteenth century and in the fore part of the twentieth century several missionaries were appointed who were specialists in rural conditions.[76] However, in 1932 or 1933 there were said to be less than four hundred who could be described as agricultural missionaries sent out by the North American societies,[77] the bodies presumably most responsive to the new trend. The Jerusalem meeting of the International Missionary Council (1928) gave special attention to the rural field.[78] Largely in consequence of it, Kenyon Leech Butterfield, a prominent American expert in agriculture, made extended and unhurried tours of Africa and several countries of Asia which brought stimulus to the movement and helped in the formulation of concrete plans.[79] Near the close of 1931 there came into being the Agricultural Missions Foundation to co-ordinate and encourage efforts on behalf of rural populations.[80] The years after 1914 and especially after 1928 saw marked growth in such specialized activities.[81]

Out of the Jerusalem meeting of the International Missionary Council also came (1930) the Department of Social and Industrial Research and Counsel of that organization.[82] Under its first head, John Merle Davis, important studies were conducted of the labour situation in the copper mines in Northern

---

[75] Carson, *Agricultural Missions*, p. 1.

[76] Hunnicutt and Reid, *The Story of Agricultural Missions*, pp. 16-18.

[77] Carson, *op. cit.*, p. 7.

[78] *The Jerusalem Meeting of the International Missionary Council, March 24-April 8, 1928.* Volume VI, *The Christian Mission in Relation to Rural Problems* (New York, International Missionary Council, 1928, pp. ix, 272).

[79] Two of the studies which emerged as a result of these visits were Kenyon Leech Butterfield, *The Christian Mission in Rural India. Report and Recommendations* (New York, International Missionary Council, 1930, pp. vi, 162), and Kenyon Leech Butterfield, *The Rural Mission of the Church in Eastern Asia: Report and Recommendations* (New York, International Missionary Council, 1931, pp. 222).

[80] *Quarterly Notes, Being the Bulletin of the International Missionary Council*, p. 4, in *The International Review of Missions*, July, 1932.

[81] Oral report given in the presence of the author by K. L. Butterfield, Oct. 29, 1931. As one example see *The Tungchow Rural Institute. A Report of the North China Institute for Supervisors of Rural Work held under the Auspices of the North China Christian Rural Service Union . . . Tung Hsien, Hopei, China, March 20-April 3, 1935*, p. 90.

[82] *Annual Report of the International Missionary Council to the Foreign Missions Conference of North America, 1932; Quarterly Notes . . . Bulletin of the International Missionary Council*, Apr., 1931, p. 1.

Rhodesia and the Belgian Congo,[83] of the production of wholesale moving pictures for Africans,[84] and of the economic bases of the Church in various places in Asia, Latin America, and the West Indies.[85]

A large proportion of the personnel and money provided by the churches of the Occident went into schools. In the 1930's about one-half of these were said to be thus assigned.[86] To assist in the co-ordination and most effective use of these resources various commissions were sent to particular countries, some of them interdenominational[87] and one or more by an independent foundation with strong religious interests.[88] It was felt that the churches of the West were spreading their available means too thinly and that better results could be obtained by greater concentration.[89]

A phase of missionary effort which received added emphasis was religious education. The Jerusalem meeting of the International Missionary Council made it one of its main subjects,[90] and conventions of the World's Sunday School Association, held in centres which for the majority of Protestants were regarded as foreign mission fields, helped to strengthen this aspect of the Church's activities.[91]

The clashes between races and the resentment of non-white peoples against white domination and discrimination which were accentuated after the world war of 1914-1918 helped to call forth attempts at Christian solutions of the tensions.[92]

The colossal physical suffering of civilians which accompanied the world wars of the period stimulated the Christian conscience to works of relief. Two

[83] John Merle Davis, *Modern Industry and the African* (London, Macmillan and Co., 1933, pp. xviii, 425).

[84] *The International Review of Missions*, Vol. XXV, p. 89.

[85] Among these studies see *The Madras Series*, Vol. V; and John Merle Davis, *The Church in the New Jamaica* (New York, The International Missionary Council, 1942, pp. x, 100).

[86] *Report of the Commission of Appraisal of the Laymen's Foreign Missions Inquiry*, Chap. 6, p. 4.

[87] Among these were those reported in Daniel Johnson Fleming, *Schools with a Message in India* (Oxford University Press, 1921, pp. 209); *Christian Education in Japan* (New York, The International Missionary Council, 1932, pp. xi, 247); *The Christian College in India* (Oxford University Press, 1931, pp. xiii, 388); *Christian Education in China* (New York, Committee of Reference and Counsel, 1922, pp. xv, 430).

[88] *Education in East Africa* (New York, Phelps-Stokes Fund, 1925, pp. xxviii, 416).

[89] Galen Fisher, oral report in the hearing of the author, Oct. 17, 1931.

[90] *The Jerusalem Meeting of the International Missionary Council, March 24-April 8, 1928*. Vol. II, *Religious Education* (New York, International Missionary Council, 1928, pp. viii, 225).

[91] *Quarterly Notes*, No. 37, p. 22 in *The International Review of Missions*, Jan., 1933.

[92] For examples see *The Jerusalem Meeting of the International Missionary Council*, Vol. IV, *The Christian Mission in the Light of Race Conflict* (New York, International Missionary Council, 1928, pp. vii, 208).

major organizations which arose out of Protestant effort were Near East Relief[93] and the American Friends Service Committee.[94] These were not for the formal spread of Christianity in the sense of making converts, but they were attempts to meet concrete physical and spiritual needs. The former was associated with the first of the world wars. The latter, beginning in 1917 and helping in the first war and its aftermath, assumed its largest proportions during the second of these struggles. Although under the aegis of the Friends, it drew both personnel and funds from members of many different Christian communions.

We must also note the world-wide activities of the Rockefeller Foundation on behalf of public health and of education. They were not under ecclesiastical auspices nor were they even in the Christian name. However, the funds and the vision which made them possible were from Protestant sources and from motives of distinctly Christian origin.

In all this multiplicity of activities for human betterment, Protestants did not lose sight of the fact that if Christianity were to continue it must be through organized Christian communities, the Church in one or another of its manifestations. Now that the day of white domination in the non-Occidental world was so clearly passing, it became particularly imperative that strong, continuing Christian bodies should be nourished in every land. It was significant, therefore, that the Tambaram (Madras) meeting of the International Missionary Council centred its emphasis on the Church.[95] More attention, too, was being paid to theological education. This involved not only the preparation of leadership for the younger churches, but also the study of what types of leadership were best fitted for the situation in which the Church found itself in particular countries. It was recognized that the problem would not be met by the reproduction of the training prevailing in theological faculties in the West, but that adaptations must be made and, in places, completely new approaches and methods devised.[96] Symptomatic of the trend was the World Dominion Movement, an independent foundation which had as its primary purpose the encouragement of churches which would be rooted in the soil, self-supporting and self-propagating, the chief agencies for spreading the faith.[97]

The variety of tasks to which Protestant missionaries devoted themselves

[93] Barton, *The Story of Near East Relief (1915-1930)*, *passim*.

[94] For an account of earlier stages of this organization, see Lester Martin Jones, *Quakers in Action* (New York, The Macmillan Company, 1929, pp. xviii, 226), *passim*.

[95] This was made abundantly clear by the programme and the discussions preserved in the official report, "*The Madras Series.*"

[96] As an example of this see "*The Madras Series,*" Vol. IV, pp. 187-235.

[97] Vol. IV, p. 100; A. McLeish in *The International Review of Missions*, Vol. XXIII, pp. 215-224; Strong and Warnshuis, *Directory of Foreign Missions*, p. 35.

continued to be multiform and, if anything, increased. In addition to the ones we have mentioned, there were many others, of which those that follow are only specimens. As before 1914, there were leper colonies.[98] There were attempts at improving the conditions of labourers in the great mining centre in Johannesburg, in South Africa.[99] Summer camps were held for young people, physical education was furthered, projects were undertaken for the improvement of the condition of women, and efforts were made through education for better homes.[100]

There was much talk about what was called "world service." The inclusiveness and wide scope of the plans were matched only by their daring and the seeming audacity of the projects for implementing them with the small staffs available. With a total communicant body in 1925 of about three and a half millions and in 1938 of about six millions, with a "native" staff in 1938 of perhaps two hundred thousand, and with a foreign personnel which seems never to have exceeded thirty thousand (all these spread over Asia, Latin America, and among the non-white peoples of Africa and the islands of the Pacific),[101] Protestants were endeavouring to propagate their faith throughout the non-Occidental world, to plant continuing churches, to minister wholesomely to clamant human needs, and to remake whole cultures. What Protestants were essaying in non-Occidental lands they were also undertaking in Occidental countries where their numbers were larger.

Not all Protestants were committed to so wide-ranging a programme. Those endorsing it were found chiefly in what were termed Anglo-Saxon lands: even here by no means all official Protestant bodies had so extensive a vision. Among the adherents of the organizations which formally sponsored such plans, the majority were lukewarm. Yet even though supported by only a minority of Protestants, and these in some lands only an infinitesimal percentage of the entire population, the programme had outstanding achievements to its credit. Some of these we are to see in succeeding chapters.

The clear-eyed among the proponents of the programme did not expect the organized Christian forces by themselves to accomplish all the tasks to which they had set their hands. They hoped by their pioneering to stimulate other agencies with larger resources in funds and personnel to undertake on a more

[98] *The International Review of Missions*, Vol. XXI, pp. 264-271; Tinling, *Hope for the Leper, passim.*
[99] Phillips, *The Bantu are Coming*, pp. 115 ff.
[100] *International Survey of the Young Men's and Young Women's Christian Associations*, pp. 177-185, 194-198; Burton, *World Coöperation of the Young Women's Christian Association of the United States of America*, p. 9.
[101] Parker, *Interpretative Statistical Survey of the World Mission of the Christian Church*, p. 17.

extensive scale that which had thus been shown to be feasible and necessary. In a number of important instances they were not disappointed. Two in the field of education were outstanding examples. During the world war of 1914-1918 Y. C. James Yen, a Chinese Christian then studying at Yale, interrupted his university course to serve, under the Young Men's Christian Association, the Chinese coolies who had been brought to France as labourers behind the warring lines. While in France, Yen worked out a device for teaching these illiterate fellow-countrymen to read. It proved so successful that, when the war was over, he proceeded to apply it in China. At first, as in France, he pursued the plan in co-operation with the Young Men's Christian Association.[102] Later, as the effort assumed national proportions, he felt it wise to act independently of that organization through the National Association of the Mass Education Movement which he called into being for that purpose.[103] In the 1930's Frank Charles Laubach, since 1915 a representative in the Philippines of the American Board of Commissioners for Foreign Missions, devised a simple form of writing through Roman letters for the Moros, Moslems among whom he was living, and through it and a method which he evolved, began teaching adults to read. Later he carried the idea into other parts of the Philippines, through Southern Asia, especially India, and to Latin America.[104] His enthusiasm and devotion attracted many outside Protestant circles. Several of the Latin American governments officially adopted his method.[105]

It remained to be seen whether Protestants, by spreading their energies over so many different kinds of activities in the non-Occidental world where their numbers were comparatively small, could build continuing movements which would persist as avowedly Christian fellowships or churches after the day of Western leadership, apparently rapidly drawing to its close, should have ended. It was this sobering prospect which gave stimulus to the efforts to strengthen the churches and their leadership. The churches continued to grow and, taken the non-Occidental world over, the numbers and the quality of the indigenous leadership mounted. As yet, however, the institutions and movements which Protestants from the Occident had initiated, financed, and staffed were beyond the resources of the younger churches fully to maintain. As some of these institutions, including schools and hospitals, passed out of the control of the

---

[102] Y. C. James Yen in *The China Mission Year Book*, 1923, pp. 205-215.

[103] Y. C. James Yen, *The Mass Education Movement in China* (Shanghai, The Commercial Press, Ltd., 1925, pp. ii, 25), *passim*.

[104] Frank C. Laubach, *The Silent Billion Speak* (New York, Friendship Press, 1943, pp. vi, 201), *passim*.

[105] *Quarterly Notes . . . of the International Missionary Council*, Oct., 1943, p. iii.

Occidental missionaries who had founded them, numbers of them drew their support and their direction primarily from governmental or other non-Christian sources.

This did not necessarily mean that Protestantism was a waning force in these lands. Indeed, part of the genius of Protestantism in the countries in the Occident where it was the most vigorous had been to call into being institutions and movements which, as they gained in popularity, ceased to think of themselves as Christian or at most retained only a formal connexion with the churches. Yet this did not prove that Protestantism was dwindling. Certainly as a world-wide fellowship of churches Protestantism was displaying increased strength and was making some of its most spectacular gains in non-Occidental lands.

In the undergirding of its enterprises Protestantism experienced startling fluctuations of financial support, personnel, and apparent conviction. At times these seemed to augur ill for the future of that branch of Christianity. Yet in spite of them, when one took into consideration the entire span of the years and not simply a decade, a persistent vitality was evident. The situation varied from country to country and no generalizations can be made which accurately cover the history of all the main centres of Protestantism.

The world war of 1914-1918 and its aftermath obviously bore heavily on Germany. During the war the home constituency was largely cut off from its missionaries. Many of the latter, in British territories, were interned or repatriated. As a result of the war, the German colonies, major fields of some German societies, were transferred to other countries, with here and there embarrassment to German missions. The extreme inflation which followed the war was a severe blow. Yet in 1932 the income of the German societies was only 27 per cent. less than in 1913 and in the fields which remained to them the German missions had a foreign personnel three-fourths as numerous as that of 1914.[106] German missions suffered from continued economic distress, from the attitude of the Nazi regime, and from the crisis theology which in some of its aspects condemned all attempts to propagate the faith.[107] The world war of 1939 cut off the German churches even more effectively from

---

[106] *The International Review of Missions*, Vol. XXI, pp. 349, 350.

[107] *The International Review of Missions*, Vol. XXI, p. 350. In an effort to conserve foreign exchange, the National Socialist regime cut down on the amount of money which could be sent abroad to missionaries. Swedes, Dutch, Americans, and English came to the assistance of the distressed German missions.—*Quarterly Notes*, pp. vi, viii, in *The International Review of Missions*, April, 1935; *The International Review of Missions*, Vol. XXV, p. 93. However, German missions continued. For a picture of them on the eve of the second world war, see Julius Richter, editor, *Das Buch der deutschen Weltmission* (Gotha, Leopold Klotz, 1935, pp. 331, 64).

their missions than did the earlier struggle. Yet money continued to be raised by the societies in the hope that sometime it could be sent abroad.[108] Thanks in part to representations to the proper British authorities by the International Missionary Council, not all German missionaries in British territories were immediately interned in the second of the world wars.[109] As that struggle proceeded the policy of the British Government and of the Dutch administration in the Netherlands East Indies stiffened.[110] Yet in British territories some German missionaries were permitted to continue at their normal tasks.[111]

For the British societies the first world war effected a slight decrease in foreign staffs[112] but for some societies was marked by an increase in incomes.[113] The same war dealt severe blows to both personnel and income of French Protestant missions.[114] For neutral European countries, however, the incomes and the missionary staffs increased.[115] In the interval between the two wars, in spite of the difficult financial situation, British societies about held their own in giving[116] and in some of the smaller European countries advances were registered.[117] The second of the world wars brought much more severe dislocation to the missionary activities of French,[118] Dutch, and Scandinavian Protestants. The German occupation of France, Holland, Belgium, Denmark, and Norway largely cut off the home constituencies from their missions. Yet in an amazing fashion giving continued and, in Holland, the preparation of missionary candidates.[119] Moreover, as evidence of the growing ecumenical spirit and in part through the activity of the International Missionary Council, assistance came from across national and denominational lines to what were termed the "orphaned missions." Thanks largely to that aid, so far as could be ascertained no enterprise maintained by continental European societies in non-Occidental lands was discontinued for lack of funds and every case of need was met.[120]

In the United States the record was very different from that of Europe.

[108] *The International Review of Missions*, Vol. XXXII, p. 68.
[109] *The International Review of Missions*, Vol. XXIX, p. 110.
[110] *The International Review of Missions*, Vol. XXX, pp. 105-107.
[111] *The International Review of Missions*, Vol. XXXI, p. 89.
[112] *The International Review of Missions*, Vol. VIII, p. 480.
[113] *The International Review of Missions*, Vol. IV, pp. 62, 63, Vol. V, p. 179, Vol. VI, p. 179.
[114] *The International Review of Missions*, Vol. IV, p. 62, Vol. VIII, p. 481.
[115] *The International Review of Missions*, Vol. V, p. 183, Vol. VIII, p. 481.
[116] *The International Review of Missions*, Vol. XXI, p. 354.
[117] *The International Review of Missions*, Vol. XXI, pp. 350-352.
[118] In the first few months of the war approximately half the French missionaries were called to the colours.—*The International Review of Missions*, Vol. XXIX, p. 117.
[119] *The International Review of Missions*, Vol. XXXII, pp. 67-69.
[120] *Christian World Facts*, 1943-1944, pp. 26, 27.

Here a great increase in giving and in personnel sent abroad was accomplished during and immediately after the first of the world wars. That increase continued through 1920. The causes were many. They had to do mostly with the temper of the country. Americans had entered the war partly in the spirit of a crusade "to make the world safe for democracy" and "to end war." Many church leaders felt that if this aim was to be achieved the growth of the Christian Church around the world must be greatly accelerated. To accomplish this purpose several of the larger denominations inaugurated movements, among them those bearing the significant titles of the New Era[121] and the New World[122] which served as slogans and indicated the announced objectives. These sought to raise vast funds for the enterprises of the denominations at home and abroad. Local congregations undertook to build new and enlarged physical plants. These, in turn, meant more staff and required greater budgets. The Interchurch World Movement, which came into being as a result of a meeting held in December, 1918, endeavoured to draw together the various denominations in a programme for giving which would enlist the "friendly citizens" who normally had not contributed largely to the churches but who had given lavishly to various benevolent objects connected with the war. Far from bringing added incomes to the proposed beneficiaries, the Interchurch World Movement collapsed, leaving a huge deficit in its expense account to be met by the co-operating denominations.[123] From this feverish effort with its grandiose dreams a reaction began and the giving of churches to causes, whether domestic or foreign, outside the local parishes and communities fell off sharply,[124] and that in spite of frantic efforts of denominational officials to

[121] *The Eighty-Third Annual Report of the Board of Foreign Missions of the Presbyterian Church in the United States of America* (1920), p. 6.

[122] *The New World Movement of the Northern Baptist Convention* (The General Board of Promotion of the Northern Baptist Convention, 1919, pp. 112).

[123] For a brief account of the inception, see *American Baptist Foreign Mission Society, 1919, One-hundred-fifth Annual Report*, pp. 22, 23.

For volumes showing the scope of the enterprises envisioned, see *World Survey by the Interchurch World Movement of North America* (New York City, Interchurch Press, 2 vols., 1920). Vol. I dealt with America, Vol. II with foreign missions and statistical tables.

For the collapse and the way it affected one of the co-operating denominations, see *American Baptist Foreign Mission Society, 1921, One-hundred-seventh Annual Report*, pp. 41, 42.

[124] C. H. Fahs in *The International Review of Missions*, Vol. XVIII, pp. 539-544. Committee of Reference and Counsel of the Foreign Mission Conference of North America. *Brief Survey of Trends in Missionary Finances* (manuscript, mimeographed, September, 1932), *passim*. In spite of the decline from the peak years in the early 1920's, for six of the major foreign mission societies between 1919 and 1929 there was a total increase of 44 percent. in net income.—*Laymen's Foreign Missions Inquiry. Fact-Finders Reports*, Vol. VII, *Supplementary Series*, Part II, pp. 67, 68.

stem the retreat. The decline was ascribed to various factors.[125] Probably the constituency had been pushed beyond its normal convictions. Then, too, not so many from the "lost generation" which had come to maturity during and immediately after the war were committed to world-wide Christianity as from that of their fathers and older brothers.[126] On top of these losses came the financial depression of 1929 with still further decrease in giving.[127] Yet the sobering years which followed 1929, shadowed as they were by economic crisis and impending war, brought a resurgence of conviction, even though only among minorities. In the second of the world wars the decline in giving ceased and slight increases were recorded.[128] It must be noted that, largely as a result of the experiences in and after the first of the world wars, new methods of raising money were devised. No longer, as a rule, did the foreign and the home societies of a denomination go out independently to appeal for funds. The trend was for each denomination to raise its budget as a whole for all its organizations.[129] Whether this made for more giving or for less was a matter of debate. The fluctuations in the United States, much greater than in Great Britain or even than in most of the countries of Europe, were particularly momentous, since half or more of the income of the Protestant foreign missions of the world came from that country.[130]

The slowing down of the rate of increase in giving for the spread of Christianity which in some instances became a decline had the greater effect because of the rise in prices in various parts of the world. Inflation in varying degrees followed the onset of the wars, especially the second of the world wars. Inflation meant increased costs. The incomes of the benevolent societies of the Occident, even when these were augmented, were seldom sufficient to keep pace.

Stationary or declining incomes were accompanied by a reduction of reinforcements. The offering of life for service abroad fell off. Especially was there a shrinkage in the numbers of those enlisted through the Student Volunteer

[125] C. H. Fahs in *The International Review of Missions*, Vol. XVI, pp. 405-414.

[126] This seems also to have been true in Great Britain. See J. R. Mott in *The International Review of Missions*, Vol. XX, p. 93.

[127] See graphs for several of the major American boards in *Journal of the Annual Meeting of the Board of Foreign Missions of the Methodist Episcopal Church*, 1933, pp. 130 ff. From 1928 to 1938 the income of American foreign mission societies dropped 30 per cent.—Leslie B. Moss in release from Foreign Missions Conference of North America (mimeographed).

[128] *Quarterly Notes . . . of the International Missionary Council*, July, 1943, p. iv.

[129] *Laymen's Foreign Missions Inquiry. Fact-Finders Reports. Home Base and Missionary Personnel.* Vol. VII, *Supplementary Series*, Part II, p. 123; Drach, *Our Church Abroad*, p. 250; Garrison, *Religion Follows the Frontier*, p. 293.

[130] *Ibid.; Quarterly Notes . . . of the International Missionary Council*, Oct., 1932, p. iv.

Movement for Foreign Missions,[131] the agency which had made so striking an appeal in the three decades before 1914. It was noted, too, that at least among American missionaries there seemed to be a decrease in the sense of a distinct vocation for work abroad.[132] This was in part a consequence of the spiritual deadening which seemed to follow the war and which in the 1920's had marked repercussions upon students. The lowering of spiritual temperature in student circles was also noted in the British Isles.[133] Partly because of the pressure placed on the recruits to maintain existing enterprises with diminished reinforcements, a large proportion of the new missionaries were not allowed time to obtain an adequate knowledge of the language.[134] However, in 1930 more than half of the North American foreign missions boards were able to obtain all the men and women whom their incomes permitted them to send and were of the opinion that the quality of their candidates was better than in previous years.[135] Moreover, in the 1930's and 1940's something of an increase of interest was noted among students in the world-wide outreach of the Church. The adverse effects of the first of the world wars were beginning to be overcome when the second of the cataclysms overtook the Christian forces. Then, too, in spite of all the difficulties, in 1938 the numbers of Protestant missionaries in non-Occidental or Roman Catholic lands were about half again as large as in 1911 and were only slightly less than in 1925, when the great decline in American giving had only begun to take effect.[136]

The stationary or declining assistance in personnel and funds from the older churches did not prove as severe a handicap to the younger churches as might have been anticipated. Here and there were losses and a slowing down of advance, but in many regions the newly planted Christianity proved to have enough vitality to rise to the challenge. In the younger churches in Latin America[137] and Asia[138] an increased effort towards self support was seen and an access of spiritual life accompanied the improvement in self reliance.[139]

Moreover, not all the organizations for the spread of Protestant Christianity

[131] C. H. Fahs in *Laymen's Foreign Missions Inquiry. Fact-Finders Reports.* Vol. VII, *Supplementary Series*, Part II, p. 17.

[132] F. P. Turner in *Laymen's Foreign Missions Inquiry. Fact-Finders Reports.* Vol. VII, *Supplementary Series*, Part II, pp. 168, 169.

[133] Tatlow, *The Story of the Student Christian Movement*, p. 643.

[134] F. P. Turner in *Laymen's Foreign Missions Inquiry. Fact-Finders Reports.* Vol. VII, *Supplementary Series*, Part II, p. 163.

[135] *Foreign Missions Conference of North America. The Present Situation in the Mission Boards* (Jan., 1931, mimeographed).

[136] Parker, *Interpretative Statistical Survey of the World Mission of the Christian Church*, p. 17.

[137] *The International Review of Missions*, Vol. XXIII, p. 82.

[138] *The International Review of Missions*, Vol. XXIII, pp. 84, 85.

[139] Davis, *Mission Finance Policies and the Younger Churches*, p. 92.

were affected as markedly by the adversities of the post-1914 era as were the majority. A striking exception was the Seventh Day Adventists. Before 1914, as we have repeatedly seen in the last two volumes, that denomination, of American origin, had been planted in many different countries. After 1914 it continued its phenomenal expansion. Numerically it remained one of the smaller ecclesiastical bodies. In 1933 it had a world membership of less than 400,000. Yet by the close of the year it was in 295 lands, used 504 languages, and had 22,254 "evangelistic and institutional labourers." Its income for propagating its type of Christianity was $8,642,652, or $22.50 per capita of its membership.[140] In 1940 its members were giving more to foreign missions than were those of any other one American Protestant denomination.[114] Presumably this phenomenal growth was due in part to the conviction of the imminent return of Christ, a conviction reinforced by the calamities of the age.

Before we move on to a geographic pilgrimage to trace the course of Christianity in the post-1914 era, it may be well to summarize this chapter according to our now familiar categories.

The Christianity which spread in this period was almost exclusively Roman Catholic and Protestant. The Eastern churches, most of them sufferers for centuries from overwhelmingly adverse environments, had been dealt severe blows by the events which began in 1914. They lost rather than gained ground. Now, for the first time in history, they ceased to participate in the expansion of the faith. Relative to Protestant Christianity, Roman Catholic Christianity had a somewhat greater share in the propagation of the faith than in the nineteenth century. It was less dependent upon France for its spread among non-Occidental peoples than it had been in the preceding hundred years. Roman Catholics from other countries, partly from the continent of Europe but most notably from the United States, were assuming a larger part of the burden. This was probably wholesome, for it argued a broader base less subject to local vicissitudes. Protestant Christianity was still spreading. It showed the effects of the new age, an age which in many respects was a contradiction of that nineteenth century in which Protestantism had its amazing expansion. Yet it was displaying vigour, some of it in fresh ways, and was probably still, as in the nineteenth century, the channel through which the Christian stream was coursing the most strongly. As in the nineteenth century, it was mainly Anglo-

[140] *The Chinese Recorder*, Vol. LXVI, p. 68.
[141] *Report of the Committee of Reference and Counsel . . . to the Foreign Missions Conference of North America*, 1940, pp. 40, 41.

Saxon Protestantism which spread. Because of the damage wrought by war to the continent of Europe, the propagation of that form of the faith was even more than before from the British Isles, the United States, and the British Dominions.

The reasons for the spread of Christianity were chiefly a continuation of those which operated in the nineteenth century. They were associated with the expansion and the domination of European peoples. The acceptance of Christianity was made possible by the impinging of Western civilization upon non-Occidental tribes and nations and by the migration of European peoples. The disintegration of non-Western cultures under the impact of the West and the prestige of the civilization with which Christianity seemed to be affiliated made for a certain degree of open-mindedness to the Christian missionary and his message. This was the more so because frequently the missionary, from a desire to help bewildered and needy peoples, was the purveyor of much from the Occident which non-Europeans wanted, particularly in education and medicine. To be sure, after 1914 the white man suffered in prestige and white conquest and migration slowed down. Yet many aspects of the culture which had its origin in the Occident were even more eagerly sought for than before 1914, since their acquisition appeared to be a means of obtaining political and economic emancipation from the white man. As before 1914, moreover, the spread of Christianity was chiefly dependent upon the vigour of the faith of the churches of the West. It was from the vitality of that faith that the funds, the missionaries, the vision, the devotion, and the daring issued which after 1914 as before that year were the mainspring of the Christian missionary enterprise. More than before 1914, however, the faith of Westerners was reinforced and supplemented by that of the churches which were arising in non-Western lands.

The processes by which Christianity spread after 1914 were substantially those of the nineteenth century. It was by voluntary agencies, financed, not by governments, but by the gifts of many hundreds of thousands of individuals, the vast majority of whom had no ulterior political or economic aim, that the Christian propaganda was maintained. Women continued to have a large share in contributing both money and personnel. Mass movements towards Christianity occurred, notably in India and Africa, but, as compared with some of the pre-nineteenth century periods, the standards for baptism and communicant membership were high, a fact which partly accounted for the small percentage of Christians among non-Occidental peoples. All these processes were characteristic of both Roman Catholic and Protestant activities on the geographic frontiers of the faith. Roman Catholics continued to stress the Church and its sacraments and directed their higher education chiefly towards the preparation of priests and catechists. As in the nineteenth century, Protestants divided their energies among a number of different types of activities. They were interested in bringing Christian communities into being and in training leadership for them. In this they had growing success. They sought through various forms of what was termed evangelism to broadcast a knowledge of the Christian faith. They made much of the translation and circulation of the Scriptures. They also gave a great deal of attention to education, medicine, and various forms of social service which they felt would be of use to the community as a whole and sought to shape changing cultures in ways which seemed to them whole-some.

Both Roman Catholic and Protestant Christianity showed the effect of the storms of the age. Both suffered, in some lands most grievously. However, as we pursue our journey around the globe, we shall see that although in some areas both branches of the faith experienced losses, their gains were even more widespread. In spite of the tempests amid which they were constrained to operate, when the earth was viewed as a whole they are seen to have registered an amazing advance.

Chapter IV

EUROPE

THE FIRST WORLD WAR: RUSSIA: ITALY: GERMANY: THE NATIONAL SOCIALISTS AND THE JEWS: THE SECOND WORLD WAR: EFFECT ON THE ENVIRONMENT: EFFECT OF THE ENVIRONMENT

IN NONE of the other continents did the era inaugurated by 1914 see such striking and comprehensive revolutions as in Europe. All the continents experienced changes. In China the revolution which was in progress on the eve of 1914 continued after that year with accelerated pace and was even more thoroughgoing than that in Europe. Other lands of Asia witnessed alterations which in some instances assumed revolutionary proportions. In Africa south of the Sahara the old forms of native life were rapidly disintegrating. The Americas did not stand still. Yet in none of the other continents, taken as a whole, unless it may have been Africa, was the order which existed at the beginning of 1914 so shattered by the events of the following four decades as in Europe.

The passing of the old structure of European life proceeded with quickened pace. Never since the outbreak of the French Revolution, in 1789, could Europe have been called static. In the nineteenth century, politically, socially, economically, religiously, and intellectually the life of much of the continent had been greatly altered. In the four decades before 1914, however, the tempo of change had seemed to slow down. Except for the threats of seething nationalisms in Central Europe and the Balkans and for rumblings in Russia which broke to the surface in an abortive revolution in 1905 after the existing regime had been discredited by an exhausting war with Japan, at the dawn of 1914 Europe appeared fairly stable. The war of 1914-1918 was followed by revolutions. The Hapsburg empire was broken up. Poland and some smaller countries reappeared or appeared for the first time as independent entities. The Hohenzollerns were expelled from Germany and were followed by what was variously known as the Weimar Republic and the Second Reich. Revolution in Russia deposed the Romanoffs, ended the centuries old Tsardom, and, after

66

transition and civil strife, was captured by the Communist Bolsheviki and issued in the Union of Soviet Socialist Republics with a fairly thoroughgoing erasure of the old political, social, and economic regime and the construction of a new order. In Italy the Fascists created a totalitarian state. In Germany, after uneasy and at times stormy years, the Weimar Republic was swept aside and replaced by the Nazis and their Third Reich. There was revolution and wasting civil strife in Spain. The new world war which broke out in 1939 centred in Europe, as had its precursor of 1914-1918. It engulfed even more of Europe and was accompanied by greater destruction of the inherited structure of society than was its predecessor. Not since the slow downfall of the Roman Empire and the centuries of the barbarian invasions had so much of Europe been so profoundly disrupted. With the speeding up of events by the machine, the generation which succeeded 1914 witnessed more sweeping changes over the wide range of the continent than had any of its predecessors. Probably not even the invasions of the fifth century and the capture of Rome by the Goths had so reshaped the face of as much of Europe as had the events of the thirty years subsequent to 1914.

For Christianity the passing of the pre-1914 Europe was of particular moment. Here for at least a millennium and a half that faith had had its chief stronghold. From here most of its expansion in that fifteen centuries had proceeded. Thanks to the remarkable spread since A.D. 1500 and especially since A.D. 1800, great centres of the faith had been established elsewhere, chiefly in the Americas and Australasia and most notably in the United States. Because of this fact the developments of the post-1914 era were not as disastrous for Christianity as they would otherwise have been. They were, however, serious enough. The major new regimes established in Germany and Russia, the leading states on the European continent, were, in general, hostile to Christianity. There was something sinister for Christianity in the near-synchronization of the emergence of totalitarian governments. Here were movements appearing in the two major and one of the other strong states of continental Europe not far from the same time which sought to control all of human life and for purely secular ends. They might out of necessity, as in Italy, make their peace with the Church, but by their very nature they could tolerate it only through expedient compromise. In their essence they were new religions which could not brook the competition of the older and largely contradictory faith. Even had the totalitarian regimes not been unfriendly, the success of Christianity in earlier periods and its consequent association with the culture which it had helped to create would have handicapped it in meeting the new day. Christianity seemed to be fighting a rear-guard action. It appeared to be a survival of an outmoded and discarded age, perhaps the hardiest feature of an era which was passing, but doomed.

Yet Christianity in Europe displayed amazing vitality. By 1945 it was still too early to be certain that this would ensure a revival which would make Christianity as potent, or, possibly, more potent than in the past or whether it would simply postpone the demise of the faith in its erstwhile citadel. That vitality was there could not be questioned. For a time Christianity had seemed to be all but finished in Russia, but by 1945 it became obvious that it was still very much alive. If this was its case in a land where in the nineteenth century, much more than in western Europe, in some of its phases it had seemed palsied and almost moribund, the presumption would seem to be that it would not only survive but go on to fresh strength in much of western Europe. That, however, was prophecy. Here we are concerned with history.

To that history we must now turn, seeking in what must necessarily be a brief summary to give the main outlines of what at best is a kaleidoscopic scene. We shall first sketch the changes in the first world war and the immediate aftermath in western Europe, then recount the developments in Russia, go on to the adjustment to the Fascist regime in Italy, picture the fate of Christianity in Germany under the Nazis, attempt to summarize what came in consequence of the second of the world wars, endeavour to appraise the effect of Christianity upon its turbulent environment, and, finally, essay some comments on the effect of the environment on Christianity. In general we can say that while in 1945 organizationally Christianity in Europe was weaker than in 1914 and while it had fewer formal adherents, as a force in the contemporary life of the continent it was probably more potent than at the beginning of the period.

The world war of 1914-1918 had profound effects upon the religious life of Europe. The most revolutionary phase of its immediate aftermath was in Russia. To that we are to devote a special section. In other parts of Europe the results were not at once so spectacular as were some of the later developments. Yet they could not fail to be grave. War has seldom if ever been friendly to Christian practice and ideals. The lowering of morals and the disruption of families attendant upon war worked adversely to the faith of many, particularly of youth. Numbers of the clergy lost their lives in the battles fighting. Many church buildings were destroyed. There were some dislocations of populations, with removal from accustomed religious settings. The inflation which accompanied and followed the war impaired some endowments and wiped out others and thus crippled charitable institutions and theological schools. It bore with particular rigour upon the classes from which much of the giving came to the various missionary societies, and was therefore hard on those agencies, such as the *Inner Mission*, which strove to keep the faith alive in religiously underprivileged communities.[1] As a result of the war a number of churches were either fully disestablished or had their revenues from the state curtailed. This happened, for instance, to Protestant and Roman Catholic churches in Germany and Transylvania.[2] The shifting of boundaries and the creation of new political entities brought problems to other groups of Christians, for they made necessary either fresh ecclesiastical structures or the modification of existing ones. This was true of Germans in Czechoslovakia, of Russian Orthodox in predominantly Roman Catholic Poland, and of Roman Catholics, Orthodox, and Protestants in Latvia, Esthonia, and Lithuania.[3] In the British Isles the spiritual temperature, notably among youth, was lowered by the war.[4] These are only examples which could be multiplied indefinitely.

Yet Christianity displayed a remarkable vitality in meeting the problems brought by the war. Never before had Christian philanthropy been poured out on so vast a scale for the relief of a particular emergency. This was especially from Great Britain and the United States, most notably from the latter. American Christian agencies carried on extensive works of relief and for troops and prisoners of war. The American Young Men's Christian Associations raised more than $150,000,000 by voluntary subscriptions and served more than twenty million soldiers and over five million prisoners of war. It was active on all five continents.[5] Out of these efforts came continuing national organizations of the Young Men's Christian Associations in such lands as Czechoslovakia, Esthonia, Latvia, Poland, and Rumania, and associations of an American type in Italy.[6] American Methodists[7] and Baptists[8] gave relief, expanded existing activities, and entered new areas. There was, for instance, a growing but persecuted Bap-

---

[1] Keller and Stewart, *Protestant Europe*, pp. 23-27.

[2] Keller and Stewart, *op. cit.*, p. 21.

[3] Keller and Stewart, *op. cit.*, p. 23.

[4] Tatlow, *The Story of the Student Christian Movement*, p. 643.

[5] *Service with Fighting Men. An Account of the Work of the American Young Men's Christian Associations in the World War* (New York, Association Press, 2 vols., 1924).

[6] *International Survey of the Young Men's and Young Women's Christian Associations*, pp. 277 ff.

[7] *Annual Report of the Board of Foreign Missions of the Methodist Episcopal Church for the Year 1919*, p. 387.

[8] *Seventy-Sixth Annual Report of the Foreign Mission Board of the Southern Baptist Convention*, 1921, pp. 213, 214; Taylor, *Baptists in Sunny Italy*, pp. 250-252; *American Baptist Foreign Mission Society, 1923*, pp. 184-187.

tist movement among Rumanian peasants.[9] Beginning with service for Belgians during the war came the Belgian Gospel Mission, Protestant and American in its leadership.[10] British and American Christian students gave relief to European students.[11] In Sweden Archbishop Söderblom by his energy and liberalism won for the Church of Sweden the confidence of leading radicals and progressives who had regarded the Church as reactionary.[12] In Hungary beginning in 1937, as a result of a deputation of pastors from Finland who told what was being done in their country, popular universities for peasants were begun by Protestant initiative and under Protestant auspices, with religious instruction as part of the curriculum.[13] In England there were those who continued to give themselves to the poor in the name of Christ.[14] Not far from 1937 it was said that of the potential Protestant constituency in England only about 14 per cent. were communicant members of churches, that only 5 or 10 per cent. of the population were regular attendants at church, and that scarcely one-fourth of the population went to church as often as once in three months.[15] Whether this was an increase or a decrease would have been hard to determine. Of the new movements in Germany we are to hear later in the chapter. The developments in Protestant thought, including the crisis theology, were evidences of vigour. To be sure, that theology was a symptom of the times, in part an effect of the environment, for it represented the loss of confidence in rationalistic liberalism and the despair of human reason which were born of the catastrophes of the era. However, it was also an indication of life. Except possibly for the "social gospel" (and that had German antecedents) the chief creative currents in Protestant theology, as so generally in the past, continued to stem from the Continent of Europe rather than from the British Isles or America. The Protestantism of the latter lands found its outstanding expressions in "activism," in organization, and in practical piety, rather than in original and profound theological thought. *Copec,* the abbreviated name given to the Conference on Christian Politics, Economics, and Citizenship, held in Great Britain in 1924, was typical of an important aspect of Anglo-Saxon Protestantism, an indication of a direction in which the life of that branch of Protestant Christianity tended.[16]

[9] Gill, *Europe and the Gospel,* pp. 68 ff.
[10] Edith F. Norton, *Ralph Norton and The Belgian Gospel Mission* (New York, Fleming H. Revell Company, 1935, pp. 253), pp. 93 ff.
[11] Tatlow, *op. cit.,* p. 711.
[12] Gunnar Westin in *Christendom,* Vol. V, pp. 514-523.
[13] *International Christian Press and Information Service,* No. 18, May, 1941.
[14] As an example see Desmond Morse-Boycott, *Ten Years in a London Slum. Being the Adventures of a Clerical Micawber* (London, Skeffington & Son, no date, pp. 128).
[15] E. Shilitto in *The Christian Century,* Vol. LVIII, p. 665.
[16] *The Proceedings of C.O.P.E.C. Being a Report of the Meetings of the Conference on*

The Roman Catholic Church experienced a notable revival. Benedict XV, the Pope whose reign spanned the war of 1914-1918, attempted to persuade the belligerents to settle their disputes through peaceful means. He used the resources of his church to alleviate the sufferings entailed by the war through negotiating the exchange of civilians and prisoners in occupied countries, assisting the hospitalization of the sick in neutral lands, facilitating the correspondence of prisoners of war with their families, the repatriation of prisoners, the relief of the inhabitants of devastated areas, the securing of truces to bury the dead, and the obtaining of Sunday as a day of rest for prisoners.[17] In France some of the outstanding intellectuals gave the Roman Catholic Church their devoted allegiance.[18] Youth were attracted. In 1925 the Catholic Youth International was organized.[19] There were also, for youth, the pacifist International Catholic Alliance and the *Pax Romana*.[20] In the years immediately after the war the numbers of episcopal sees increased[21] and there was a growth in monastic, educational, and charitable institutions. The Apostolate of Saints Cyril and Methodius, organized in the 1880's, in 1916 founded a mission institute in which priests were trained for work among Poles and Jugoslavs.[22] The Eucharistic movement and liturgical reform were symptoms and channels of renewed life.[23] The practice of frequent communion, growing before 1914, took on added momentum,[24] and that in spite of the ominous fact that after the war, in some industrial sections, the reception of the sacraments declined.[25]

For the resurgence of European Roman Catholicism after the first of the world wars a number of reasons were given. Disillusionment with an intellectual agnosticism and liberalism which had failed to prevent the cataclysm accounted for part of it. Many thoughtful spirits believed that these trends had ended in disaster and that greater evils were to be avoided only by a return to the faith which had been the spiritual basis of European culture. Insecurity and terror in the changes of the time impelled some to seek haven in a venerable institution which claimed to hold the keys to time and eternity. The

Christian Politics, Economics, and Citizenship, held in Birmingham, April 5-12, 1924 (London, Longmans, Green, and Co., 1924, pp. xi, 295).

[17] Eckhardt, *The Papacy and World Affairs*, p. 260.

[18] Horton, *Contemporary Continental Theology*, pp. 48 ff.; Iswolsky, *Light before Dusk*, pp. 11 ff.

[19] Keller and Stewart, *op. cit.*, p. 62.

[20] Keller and Stewart, *op. cit.*, pp. 62, 63.

[21] Keller and Stewart, *op. cit.*, p. 169.

[22] *Priester und Mission*, 1929, p. 59.

[23] Keller and Stewart, *op. cit.*, pp. 168, 170-172; Day in Guilday, *The Catholic Church in Contemporary Europe, 1919-1931*, Vol. II, pp. 14, 15.

[24] Day in Guilday, *op. cit.*, Vol. II, p. 14.

[25] Day in Guilday, *op. cit.*, Vol. II, pp. 42, 43.

heroism of many of the priests, especially the French priests, who had served in the war had impressed many.[26] The emergence of Poland, a predominantly Roman Catholic country, as an independent power strengthened the forces of that church. Although Poland's new constitution guaranteed freedom of conscience and religion, it declared that "the Roman Catholic creed . . . shall have a preponderating authority in the state."[27] New concordats between Rome and European governments reinforced the position of the Roman Catholic Church.[28] Belgium, a predominantly Roman Catholic country, came out of the war with enhanced prestige, a gain which was reflected in the church as personified in the figure of its primate, Mercier. In the states which emerged from the break-up of the Hapsburg Empire—Austria, Hungary, Czechoslovakia, Yugoslavia, and the enlarged Rumania—the status of the Roman Catholic Church was bettered.[29] In France the relations between Church and state, made unfriendly by the anti-clerical policy of the latter which had culminated in a drastic law in 1905, became less strained.[30] Under the Weimar Republic the legal and civic position of the Roman Catholic Church in Germany improved.[31]

This did not mean that in the agelong competition between Protestantism and Roman Catholicism the latter was now gaining at the expense of the former. Each won converts from the other's ranks. The aggregate of the accessions of neither was very impressive numerically. It was a matter of dispute as to which had the more.[32]

The Orthodox churches in the Balkans, European Turkey, and Greece could not escape the effects of a war which actively engaged their constituencies and led to profound changes in their environment. In Constantinople the Œcumenical Patriarchate, by tradition the ranking see in Eastern Orthodoxy, suffered severely. After the war much of its remaining constituency was depleted by the expulsion of the Greeks from Turkey under the euphemism of an exchange of populations between that country and Greece.[33] Yet there were new currents of life in Orthodoxy in the Balkans. The *Zoe* movement enlisted and inspired a number of select souls in Greece.[34] In

[26] Souvay in Guilday, *op. cit.*, Vol. II, pp. 88, 89.
[27] Strahkovsky in Guilday, *op. cit.*, Vol. II, pp. 201 ff.
[28] Keller and Stewart, *op. cit.*, pp. 158 ff.
[29] Guilday, *op. cit.*, Vol. II, p. viii.
[30] Souvay in Guilday, *op. cit.*, Vol. II, pp. 90 ff.
[31] Betten in Guilday, *op. cit.*, Vol. II, p. 105.
[32] Keller and Stewart, *op. cit.*, pp. 159-161.
[33] S. A. Morrison in *The International Review of Missions*, Vol. XXIV, p. 456; M. Spinka, address to American Society of Church History, Dec. 28, 1934.
[34] Bratsiotis in *World Dominion*, Vol. XVI, pp. 416-421.

Rumania the Orthodox Church took on increased vigour, partly through lay initiative.[35] In Bulgaria the government improved the theological education out of which came the priesthood for its Orthodox Church. There was more reading of the Bible than formerly.[36] Several thousands of Carpathian Uniates returned to the Orthodoxy of their fathers.[37]

Far more striking than the developments in the religious life in central and western Europe during the war of 1914-1918 and the years of its immediate aftermath were the changes in Russia. It is one of the thrilling commonplaces of the history of these crowded years that in Russia the Tsarist regime was overthrown (1917-1918) and, after a brief interval of bewildering transition, was succeeded by Communism. We must not take the space for even the main outlines of the political and economic developments which ensued. The new order was established by ruthless violence which was directed against all forms of opposition, whether from the old aristocracy, the bourgeoisie, or the more prosperous peasants. It successfully met the armies which were raised by the opposition, even when these were assisted from abroad. It set about making a clean sweep of the old. The atmosphere was one of innovation and abounding achievement for the benefit of the masses. For years the cherished dream was world revolution. As the old had been Holy Russia, the champion of Orthodox Christianity, so the new would espouse the cause of the proletariat throughout the world, oppressed by the capitalists, and bring in justice and opportunity for the masses. Eventually the purpose of actively fostering world revolution was subordinated to that of building the ideals of Communism into a Russia whose success should be so obvious that it would awaken enough admiration among other peoples to carry through the revolution with little or no active assistance from Moscow. Nationalism prevailed as against revolutionary internationalism. In the meantime, Russians were isolated from the rest of the world. In every other land the entrenched interests feared them. Other governments might enter into diplomatic intercourse with that of Russia, although some were slow to do so, but these relations, while usually technically correct, were seldom cordial and were marked by much plain speaking, particularly by the Russians. The Union of Socialist Soviet Republics was an unashamed Ishmael among governments, with its hand set against all and their hands against it. Not until the German attack on Russia in the second of the

[35] D. A. Davis in talk with author, June 6, 1934.
[36] *Ibid*; Visser t'Hooft, *Anglo-Catholicism and Orthodoxy*, pp. 84, 85.
[37] Bolshakoff, *The Foreign Missions of the Russian Orthodox Church*, pp. 104, 105.

world wars and the common cause of what were hopefully called the United Nations against the Axis, did relations between Russia on the one hand and Great Britain and the United States on the other approach cordiality.

Under these circumstances the lot of Christianity in Russia could not but be hard. All religion, especially Christianity, was looked upon as an integral part of the despised and hated order from which Communism was emancipating mankind. Karl Marx's phrase which stigmatized religion as "the opium of the people" was often quoted.[38] Religion was deemed a convenient instrument of the exploiting classes for the maintenance of their privileged position. By it the proletariat was induced, so it was held, to endure misery and injustice in this life in the hope of consolation beyond the grave. Lenin, the hero of the Communist regime, was a convinced atheist and a hater of religion. He was particularly distrustful of a Christianity which sought social reform.[39] Obviously the Russian Orthodox Church would be in disfavour. It had been intimately bound to the Tsarist regime. Since the time of Peter the Great it had been an instrument of the state and as recently as the latter part of the nineteenth century its administrative head, Pobiedonostsev, the Procurator of the Holy Synod, had used it as a means of curbing what he deemed the pernicious liberal and radical ideas from western Europe. Its priests were a kind of extra police who were supposed to report the words of their parishioners to the civil authorities.[40] It was enormously wealthy and was, therefore, regarded as allied with those who were exploiting the poor. It was looked upon as nourishing superstition and obscurantism in an age which should be controlled by science. Nor would those Christian groups which dissented from the official church be treated more leniently. Whether Old Believers, Stundists, Lutherans, Roman Catholics, Armenians, or one of the other Christian movements which existed in the decades immediately preceding 1917, they were thought of as inimical to the kind of culture and society which Communism was attempting to set up. Particularly must they be kept from perpetuating themselves by educating their youth.

Into the measures taken by the Communists, now dominant, against Christianity we have not the space to go in detail. We must, however, attempt to give some of their main features. They were the most thoroughgoing attempts to uproot Christianity which had been made over so wide an area since the great persecutions of the third and fourth centuries of the Roman Empire.

Not even Islam had been so resolutely hostile in the centuries and lands

[38] Berdyaev, *The Origin of Russian Communism*, p. 192; Anderson, *People, Church and State in Modern Russia*, p. 58.
[39] Berdyaev, *op. cit.*, p. 194.
[40] Pares in *Foreign Affairs*, Vol. XXI, p. 636.

in which it was slowly strangling once flourishing Christian churches. It is interesting to compare the fate of Christianity in lands with Moslem governments with a Russia in which the state was Communist. Christianity suffered more under the former and experienced greater losses than it did under the latter. This was in part because Islam maintained the worship of one God and promised some of the goods beyond this present life which Christianity offered, but with a simpler creed and less exacting ethical demands. With this it coupled the lure of emancipation from social and economic disabilities under which the non-Moslems laboured and the stern prohibition, ruthlessly enforced, of defection from Islam. Communism could not assure to its adherents the other-worldly benefits which Christianity had to give: it could only deny their reality. Nor could it substitute one kind of worship of God and of mystical experience for another, as did Islam: it was able merely fiercely to declare that God does not exist. While it could promise the material goods which twentieth century man sought, it could not offer to meet the ineradicable demand of the human spirit for dependence on God, awe in His presence, and humble fellowship with Him. As compared with Islam, therefore, Communism was at a disadvantage in its contest with Christianity. It was, however, more drastic in its treatment of that faith than was Fascism or than was Naziism in the years of peace.

Not long after the Communists came to power (November, 1917) they began their measures against the Church. In December, 1917, church property and the schools were nationalized and civil marriage and the civil registration of births were instituted.[41] In January, 1918, the Church was officially declared separated from the state and the school. Financial aid was withdrawn from the Church. Freedom of conscience was ostensibly granted, with liberty to hold any religious belief or none. Religious rites might be performed so long as they did not interfere with public order. Religious vows and oaths were abrogated. No religious instruction was permitted in state schools or in private schools where general subjects were taught, but citizens might give or receive religious instruction in private. No ecclesiastical or religious body was permitted to possess property, but buildings and objects appointed for the purposes of worship, although confiscated to the state, might, in accordance with governmental regulations, be turned over, free of charge, to responsible religious associations.[42]

Large elements within the Russian Orthodox Church took vigorous exception to these regulations. Tikhon, newly elected to the revived Patriarchate,

[41] Emhardt, *Religion in Soviet Russia*, p. 19.
[42] Emhardt, *op. cit.*, pp. 19, 20; Spinka, *Christianity Confronts Communism*, pp. 53-55.

joined in the denunciation.[43] *Émigrés* held a church council in Yugoslavia which demanded the restoration of the Romanoff dynasty.[44]

Since the Communist regime was fighting for its life against both foreign and domestic foes, it is not strange that it retaliated and sought to eliminate so dangerous an opponent. Beginning in the summer of 1918 still more drastic action was taken.[45] Priests and bishops were classed with idiots and other persons deemed non-productive and were disfranchised. Education for the priesthood was made almost impossible. Divisions in the church were fomented and fostered and by torture and pressure on their families some priests were induced to serve as spies on their fellow clergy. The clergy were ridiculed.[46] About a thousand priests and forty bishops perished in the civil war.[47] Anti-religious propaganda was permitted but religious instruction to youths under eighteen years of age was forbidden in groups of more than four. When ministers of religion violated the law against religious education, they were prosecuted.[48] In 1922 church articles, although theoretically not those used for sacred purposes, were confiscated for the ostensible purpose of famine relief.[49] In a famous trial a Roman Catholic archbishop was condemned to death and one of his clergy was actually executed.[50] Societies for the propagation of atheism sprang up, a Union of the Godless was organized, and periodicals for the anti-religious movement were published.[51] In its attempt to eradicate all remnants of bourgeois life and what it deemed the exploiting classes, the Communist party, which was dominant in the state, espoused anti-religious propaganda.[52]

In 1929 even harder blows began to be directed against religion. A five-year plan was adopted for the purpose of carrying out more thoroughly the conversion of Russia into a Communist state. This involved quickening the pace of industrialization and of the collectivization of the farms. It also entailed, on the cultural front, the moulding of public opinion, and particularly that of the younger generation, to Communist ideology. The five year programme could scarcely be accomplished without great initial hardship upon many of the

[43] Emhardt, *op. cit.*, pp. 21, 22; Anderson, *People, Church and State in Modern Russia*, pp. 65 ff.

[44] Spinka, *op. cit.*, p. 57.

[45] Emhardt, *op. cit.*, pp. 25-27.

[46] Spinka, *op. cit.*, pp. 57-60.

[47] Pares in *Foreign Affairs*, Vol. XXI, p. 638.

[48] *Ibid.*

[49] Emhardt, *op. cit.*, pp. 43 ff.; Anderson, *op. cit.*, pp. 74, 75.

[50] Emhardt, *op. cit.*, pp. 181 ff.; McCullagh, *The Bolshevik Persecution of Christianity*, pp. 99 ff.

[51] Hecker, *Religion and Communism*, pp. 215-217.

[52] See documents translated in Hecker, *op. cit.*, pp. 275 ff.

population. The peasants especially suffered, and in 1932-1933 in the fertile Ukraine and the northern Caucasus a severe famine ensued.[53] The immediate sacrifices with the "liquidation" of obstructive elements was held to be the best even if a drastic way to the larger good of the nation. As part of the procedure for carrying out the plan, more severe measures were taken against religion.[54] Religion was still permitted, but religious societies must petition the proper state bodies for registration and that permission might be denied. Full lists of members of such societies had to be given to the appropriate government authority, a requirement which, presumably, might allow unfriendly officials to institute persecution and also deter the timorous from declaring their religious faith. The printing of religious books by the Church was made difficult if not impossible. Religious societies were not permitted to organize co-operative organizations or mutual credit associations, to conduct sanatoriums, to organize medical care, to give material aid to their members, or to bring together children, young people, or women for meetings of any kind, for Biblical instruction, or for recreation. Only such books as were necessary for the purposes of the cult were to be kept in buildings used for worship. The teaching of religion in any school, public or private, was strictly forbidden. Religious instruction was allowed only in special theological courses for which permission had been expressly given by the designated state bodies. Presumably to estop missionary efforts, the work of ministers of religion was confined to the area in which the members of their religious societies resided. Regional or national religious gatherings were tolerated, but only with the consent of specified government departments. The officers of such regional or national bodies were not to collect any kind of central fund, to own religious property, or to conclude contracts. Buildings used for religious purposes were still to remain government property. No religious service could be held in any state, public, co-operative, or private institution. Religious processions were permitted, but only under certain conditions. In other words, restricted religious freedom was preserved, but legally conditioned in such fashion that unfriendly officials could nullify it. Presumably it was to be only for the older generation who were too wedded to their traditional faith to be divorced from it. The instruction of the rising generation in religion was made so difficult as to be almost impossible.

In harmony with this policy, no believer in religion was permitted to teach in a Soviet school. Indeed, the schools became anti-religious. As systematically

[53] Spinka, *op. cit.*, pp. 81 ff.
[54] See a translation of the regulations of 1929 in Guilday, *The Catholic Church in Contemporary Europe, 1919-1931*, Vol. II, pp. 270 ff.

as possible, youth was indoctrinated with Communism and with its attitude of scorn for religion.[55]

The legislation of 1929 seems to have had in mind the dissenters from the Russian Orthodox body as much as it did what had once been the official church. The disestablishment of the latter had indirectly favoured the dissenters. The disorders of the years following 1917, including the famine of 1920-1921, had made the ground fertile for the growth of the sects, especially the Baptists and Evangelicals. Travelling preachers, some of them going barefoot and bareheaded, had won many to these forms of the faith.[56] At times some of the Communist authorities, including Lenin himself, tolerated and even encouraged the meetings held by these preachers.[57] Now the attitude of the state changed. The portion of the legislation of 1929 which confined the labours of ministers of religion to the area in which their members resided seems to have been directed against these itinerants. The prohibition of religious propaganda appears to have had the same purpose. Many Evangelicals were put in concentration camps and in December, 1936, the position of the sects was made more difficult by a decree which permitted the holding of religious services only in places licensed for that purpose.[58]

In the enforcement of the new laws stern measures were employed. Religion, and especially the attempt to spread religion, were regarded as counter-revolutionary and hence intolerable. Many Russian Orthodox, Roman Catholic, and Protestant clergymen and Russian Orthodox monks were arrested. Scores of them were sentenced to hard physical labour in lumber camps and farms in Northern Russia and Siberia.[59] Many church buildings were turned into moving picture houses. Families were separated and property confiscated. Often amid great suffering, thousands of Protestants migrated, among them Mennonites whose ancestors had been induced to come to Russia by tempting offers of economic independence and religious liberty. Some of them went to Germany and others to Canada and South America.[60] Difficulties, at times insuperable, were set up by the authorities to prevent the leasing of buildings for worship. Excessive taxes were placed on priests. Many priests were expelled from their villages and, since they did not have economic or political rights, they could not obtain employment and were doomed to beggary and slow

---

[55] Spinka, *op. cit.*, pp. 91, 92; Anderson, *People, Church and State in Modern Russia*, pp. 102 ff.

[56] Müller in *World Dominion*, Vol. XVII, pp. 20-29; Spinka, *op. cit.*, p. 95.

[57] Prokhanoff, *The Cauldron of Russia*, pp. 175-177.

[58] Müller in *World Dominion*, Vol. XVII, pp. 20-29.

[59] Carlo von Kügelgen, *The Whited Sepulchre*, pp. 36 ff.

[60] *Central Bureau for Relief of the Evangelical Churches of Europe. A Report on the Christian Refugee Problem at Harbin, China* (New York, 1931, pp. 8), *passim.*

starvation. It is said that 28 bishops, 1,219 priests, and thousands of lay believers perished during the destructive period of the revolution.[61] Lay members of congregations were discriminated against by the loss of employment and the expulsion of their children from school. A five-day and then a six-day week were substituted for the seven-day week, and thus Sunday worship was made difficult and for many impossible. The holy days of the Church also suffered. Many churches were closed by the simple expedient of placing on the congregations unbearable burdens for repairs, taxes, insurance, and rental. It is said that in the first year of the new five-year plan about two thousand churches were closed, or approximately the number which had been liquidated in the preceding eleven years.[62] Children, so it is declared, were taught to defame religion, to march in anti-religious processions on holy days, and to defile the cross and ikons.[63]

At the same time, anti-religious propaganda was intensified. The great cathedral in Kazan and a cathedral in Leningrad were turned into museums of religion which in effect were anti-religious.[64] Numbers of other museums were set up for the purpose of combatting religion and promoting science. In them the stories of the Bible were held up to ridicule, the miracles of the Church and its saints were denounced as fraudulent, and the churches were labeled as opposing education, science, and measures for public health, and as encouraging drunkenness and war. The Union of Militant Atheists had as its motto "the fight against religion is the fight for socialism." Anti-religious books, periodicals, motion pictures, plays, lectures, and radio broadcasts were largely employed and in some schools there were special anti-religious departments.[65] By May, 1932, the Godless Union is said to have numbered 80,000 cells, with 7,000,000 members besides 1,500,000 children classified as Godless.[66]

The anti-religious campaign was assisted by the growth of the urban population. As a result of the rapid industrialization of the country, there was a marked increase in the size of the cities. In this new environment, where churches were few or non-existent, the trend was towards the disappearance of religious faith. It was in the rural districts, where the older patterns of life more nearly persisted, that Christianity proved hardest to eradicate. In this respect conditions in Russia were not unlike those in other countries.

[61] Sorokin in *Religion in Life*, Vol. XIII, p. 12.
[62] Spinka, *Christianity Confronts Communism*, pp. 102-107.
[63] Brian-Chaninov, *The Russian Church*, pp. 179, 180.
[64] Spinka, *op. cit.*, p. 107.
[65] Corliss Lamont, *Soviet Russia and Religion* (New York, International Pamphlets, 1936, pp. 23), p. 11; Anderson, *People, Church and State in Modern Russia*, pp. 114 ff.
[66] Bolshakoff, *The Christian Church and the Soviet State,* p. 45. But see slightly smaller figures in Anderson, *op. cit.*, p. 115.

In some respects the restrictions against Christianity were lightened after 1935. The constitution of 1936 recognized freedom of both religious worship and anti-religious propaganda. In 1936 bell-ringing and the collection of funds for churches were allowed. In 1938 the showing of anti-Christian films and plays and the anti-Christmas and anti-Easter carnivals were forbidden. Workers were not penalized for absences during the Christmas and Easter festivals. In 1940 the seven-day week was restored and Sunday was made a compulsory holiday. Yet in 1938 several bishops were shot as spies. By the device of raising the rent, in 1937 numbers of churches, Orthodox, Roman Catholic, and Lutheran, as well as some mosques and synagogues, were closed.[67]

Under the impact of these blows, dealt over a period of a quarter of a century, organized Christianity suffered.

Its chief expression, the Russian Orthodox Church, entered the new era under a handicap. In addition to its intimate connexion with a discredited and extinct regime, in the twilight of the Tsars it had been embarrassed by a strange figure, Gregori Efimovich Rasputin, of peasant stock, who rose to prominence in the early years of the twentieth century.[68] He seems to have been a mixture of bestiality and mysticism. In spite of the suspicions of some of the ecclesiastical authorities, he gained a reputation as a holy man. He won the full confidence of the Tsarina and soon after 1914 on the strength of his influence with her became the most powerful figure in the state church. He was able to place his protégés in high ecclesiastical positions and was a force to be reckoned with in politics. His assassination, in December, 1916, freed the church of his incubus, but not before he had brought grave discredit upon it at a time when it could ill afford such a liability. It may have been that the state church had been losing ground in the nineteenth century. Certainly, by 1914, a very large proportion of the intelligentsia had ceased to be held by it.[69] Traditional weaknesses were not remedied as the years passed—the huge size of the dioceses, the frequent transfers of bishops from one to another with the resulting inadequate episcopal supervision, some venality in ecclesiastical circles, the gulf between the higher and lower clergy, the drunkenness and disorderliness of students in the ecclesiastical academies where men were prepared for the higher offices of the church, the hereditary character of the village priesthood entailing, among other evils, a cleavage between the priest and his peasant flock, the burdens placed upon the priests by the government, and the me-

[67] Bolshakoff, *op. cit.*, pp. 55, 56.

[68] Curtiss, *Church and State in Russia*, pp. 366 ff.; René Fölüp-Miller, *Rasputin, the Holy Devil*, translated from the German by F. S. Flint and D. F. Tait (New York, The Viking Press, 1928, pp. xii, 386), *passim*.

[69] Curtiss, *op. cit.*, p 79.

chanical nature of much of the formal observances of religion.[70] In the decade before 1914, moreover, in spite of a small number of sympathetic priests, the official structure of the state church had run true to form and had, in general, opposed such beginnings of political liberalism as had followed the Russo-Japanese war.[71] The Russian Orthodox Church had never set itself to the transformation of society. It was not without an ethical message, but its stress was upon liturgy, mysticism, and otherworldliness. In contrast with Roman Catholicism and Protestantism, it had largely eschewed attempts to remake society. When the Communists sought to confine religion to religious services they were, although in an exaggerated way, but taking the Russian Orthodox Church at its word. One would have expected that a church, tied so closely to the old order and with so many palpable weaknesses, would have collapsed with the disappearance of the Tsarist regime and would have been quickly and easily swept into the discard.

There can be no doubt that the Russian Orthodox Church lost in organizational strength and in whatever influence it may once have enjoyed with large numbers of the population. It made efforts to maintain itself in the new order. In 1917, during the throes of the revolution, a national church council was convened. Even while the Red army was fighting for the control of Moscow, the council revived the Patriarchate which had been abolished by Peter the Great and placed the supreme authority in a *sobor* or council composed of bishops, priests, and laymen. As Patriarch there was elected Tikhon, the Metropolitan of Moscow, a kindly, humble, and pious prelate, although lacking the forcefulness of character demanded by the emergency.[72] The church was thus attempting to re-assert its independence and prepare itself for the new day. However, it remained in the control of conservative elements which were far from sympathetic with the changes envisaged by the Communists. Tikhon and his colleagues set themselves against the Bolsheviki. Tikhon formally anathematized the Bolshevik acts against the church and the latter became the centre of the opposition to the new regime.[73] The opposition of Tikhon and his subordinates to the governmental order of 1922 for the sale of superfluous church treasures to help relieve the famine of that time led to the arrest of thousands of laymen, priests, and bishops, among them Tikhon himself,[74]

[70] Curtiss, *op. cit.*, pp. 35 ff.; Anderson, *People, Church and State in Modern Russia*, pp. 32-40.
[71] Curtiss, *op. cit.*, pp. 197 ff.
[72] Emhardt, *Religion in Soviet Russia*, pp. 3-8; Spinka, *Christianity Confronts Communism*, pp. 50-52.
[73] Spinka, *op. cit.*, pp. 55, 56.
[74] Spinka, *op. cit.*, pp. 60, 61.

and to the execution of at least forty-five churchmen and long-term imprison-
ments for about two hundred and fifty.[75]

What seemed to be the Patriarch's refusal to aid in meeting the famine
emergency precipitated a revolt against him among the clergy. It was in part a
declaration of independence of the parish priests, the so-called "white" clergy,
against the control of the church by the monks, the "black" clergy, from whose
ranks the episcopate was traditionally recruited. The dissidents formed what
was termed the Living Church, more in sympathy with the government and its
measures than was the organization headed by Tikhon.[76] With the co-operation
of some of the bishops of the old church, bishops were consecrated from the
ranks of the married or "white" clergy. This Living Church attempted to make
its peace with the state and condemned Tikhon as an apostate and traitor.
Many of the old bishops were expelled from their sees and partisans of the
new movement were substituted for them. Tikhon, released, denounced the
acts of his critics. Thus arose a schism in the ranks of the church which further
weakened a sorely beleaguered body.[77]

To this division were added others. In 1921, because of nationalistic feeling
in the Ukraine, an autonomous church for that region was constituted by
clerical and lay delegates and without episcopal permission or co-operation
elected and consecrated bishops. The new body stressed the vernacular, permitted a married episcopacy, and gave to laymen an extensive share in the
administration. Fissures soon appeared in the Ukrainian church and through
them several independent ecclesiastical bodies arose.[78] In Georgia the Orthodox
Church declared its independence of that of Russia.[79] The death of Tikhon, in
1925, was followed by further dissensions. Peter, who succeeded Tikhon, was
exiled to Siberia, a development which precipitated an additional schism.
Sergius, whom Peter designated as his successor, added to the confusion by
making his peace with the government, ordering loyalty to the state and
prayers for its rulers. Many bishops and congregations refused to follow him.
Sergius did not have the title of Patriarch, but only that of Metropolitan of
Moscow and Primate of Russia.[80] In Poland, Finland, and the young Baltic
republics Orthodox churches declared their autonomy and became independent

[75] Hecker, *Religion and Communism*, p. 209.

[76] Hecker, *op. cit.*, pp. 209-211.

[77] Hecker, *op. cit.*, pp. 210-214; Spinka, *op. cit.*, pp. 63-66; Anderson, *People, Church and
State in Modern Russia*, pp. 83 ff.

[78] Spinka, *op. cit.*, pp. 67-70; McCullagh, *The Bolshevik Persecution of Christianity*,
pp. 290, 291.

[79] Spinka, *op. cit.*, p. 70.

[80] Spinka, *op. cit.*, pp. 71-74.

of the Russian church.[81] Other splits in the Orthodox body appeared in the émigré organizations in central and western Europe and in the Russian churches in America.[82]

A church weakened by internal dissensions was clearly handicapped in its attempts to survive in its struggle with a powerful, hostile, and ruthless state. It was a church thus hampered which was forced to face the more drastic new legislation of 1929.

What seem to have been official figures of the Russian Government asserted that in 1940 the number of Orthodox churches in use and the number of priests had declined 90 per cent. since 1917, the total of deacons about 80 per cent., and the bishops 75 per cent. Orthodox monasteries were declared to have decreased from 1,026 in 1914 to 37 in 1941. Between 1937 and 1940 religious associations were reported to have fallen from 33,000 to 30,000.[83] In Moscow the number of Orthodox parishes was said still to be declining between 1937 and 1939.[84]

Other Christian bodies also suffered. In 1935 there were said to be only 73 Roman Catholic priests in Russia and of these 14 were in prison.[85] In 1937 there were reported to be only 10 Roman Catholic priests serving in the country, but the territorial acquisitions in Poland, Lithuania, and Latvia after the outbreak of the second of the world wars in 1939 brought several millions of Roman Catholics under Russian control.[86] In 1940 six was given as the total of Armenian parishes in the entire country.[87] The number of Evangelical congregations may have dwindled by two-thirds between 1933 and 1940.[88] It is said that in 1935 there were 85 Evangelical ministers in the country, of whom 47 were in exile, and that in 1939 none was at liberty to serve his congregation. By 1935 the central organization of the Baptists had been practically dissolved.[89]

It is one of the amazing facts of Christian history that a church which entered the new day so handicapped and which as the era proceeded suffered from internal divisions as well as from the hostility of a powerful and implacable enemy should have survived. That it did so is evidence that Christianity had

[81] Brian-Chaninov, *The Russian Church*, p. 169.

[82] Spinka, *op. cit.*, pp. 75-77.

[83] Bolshakoff, *The Christian Church and the Soviet State*, p. 59, citing *Soviet War News*, August 22, 1941, published by the Soviet Press Bureau in London. In 1934 it was said that of the 30,000 Russian Orthodox churches of Tsarist times, from 8,000 to 15,000 were still open and that 100 of the former 600 churches in Moscow were in use.—Sherwood Eddy, mimeographed letter, Aug. 11, 1934. See also Anderson, *op. cit.*, pp. 159, 160.

[84] Bolshakoff, *op. cit.*, p. 57.

[85] Paul Anderson in "*The Madras Series*," Vol. VI, p. 244.

[86] Bolshakoff, *op. cit.*, pp. 60, 61.

[87] Bolshakoff, *op. cit.*, p. 61.

[88] Bolshakoff, *op. cit.*, p. 60.

[89] Paul Anderson in "*The Madras Series*," Vol. VI, pp. 244, 245.

penetrated the Russian soul so deeply that it endured in spite of the weaknesses of the former official church. It kept that organization alive, even though in divided forms, and also displayed itself in bodies and individuals outside the fellowship of the Orthodox churches. Presumably, too, the persistence of Christianity is evidence of the fashion in which that faith appeals to the human spirit and of the inability of even so potent a set of ideas as that embodied in Communism to meet some of the deepest of human needs.

That Christianity continued is clear. Whether the adversities through which it had passed had weakened or intensified its share in Russian life is impossible to measure with any degree of accuracy. That in its organizational expressions it was less strong in 1945 than in 1914 is obvious. That fewer Russians had a formal connexion with the Church in one of its several forms is also beyond cavil. What cannot be determined it whether Christianity as a moulding factor in the life and spirit of Russia had declined or grown.

The evidence of the persistence of Christianity, whether in organizations or as a consciously recognized factor in individual conviction and living, is multiform. The fashion in which Russia was isolated from the outside world prevented the acquisition of a complete picture by those beyond the borders of the country. Possibly no one within the country, unless it may be some one in the inner circles of the government who had access to the files of the secret police, had anything approaching full knowledge. Yet from time to time fragments of information were to be obtained which gave some inkling of what a well rounded description would presumably present. In the late 1920's after a decade of restrictions, there were priests, some of whom had been deprived of their parishes, who as spiritual guides and father-confessors had wide influence. There were, too, many who selflessly spread the Christian message with no thought of safety for themselves.[90] After 1932 the organized Godless movement began to decline. The circulation of its periodical publications fell off and, in spite of repeated efforts to put new life into the enterprise, interest waned. The change was said to be due to the passing of the older generation to whom the Church was an abomination and to the rise of a generation reared under the new regime, somewhat indifferent to religion, but passionately Russian. To them the Church was a relic of Russia's past and so was to be preserved. When hostile to religion they were much less emphatically so than were their elders.[91] In February, 1941, a publication of the League of Militant Godless declared sadly that many who doubted the existence of God preserved their ikons and that every one knew about Jesus, as a good man who

[90] Emhardt, *Religion in Soviet Russia*, pp. 296, 297.
[91] Bolshakoff, *op. cit.*, p. 47.

lived long ago and thought and acted justly.[92] In 1940 the monthly periodical of the League estimated that about two-thirds of the urban population over sixteen years of age called themselves atheists and that in the villages about two-thirds believed in God.[93] Many children, so the League reported, attended church on Christmas Day and during Lent.[94] A special investigation in 1935 showed that in two provinces, one of them Moscow, more than half the children went to church and prayed at home.[95] The rising generation was by no means entirely lost to the faith. Some teachers and even some members of the Communist party participated in church ceremonies.[96] In 1939 the official journal of the League of Militant Godless lamented the reappearance of ikons in homes of collective farmers and that religious practices were being revived.[97] Not far from the same time it was said that theological training was being secretly given and that hidden houses of prayer existed.[98] In 1942 it was reported that few signs of deep-seated hostility to the Church were to be seen and that in spite of a widespread ignorance of Christianity among the youth a much larger proportion of Russians than had been supposed preserved an attachment for the Orthodox Church.[99] We hear of a priest who, although banished, secretly travelled widely, confirming the faith of believers. It was reported that numbers of women missionaries memorized the New Testament and the main parts of the prayer book and then went from home to home baptizing the children, instructing the faithful, and reciting the communion service.[100] Many who had been indifferent turned to the Church, possibly out of opposition to the Communist regime. Some who knew little of God went to church secretly at the risk of their lives.[101] In 1942 what seems to have been an attempt at an objective appraisal reported that while a small minority were engaged in attacking the Church and another and somewhat larger minority had lost all understanding of religion and had no belief in God, the large majority, particularly in the rural districts, although having been shaken out of their confidence in religious customs, still cherished much of Christian faith.[102] There were said to be numbers of secret monasteries.[103] There was a

[92] *International Christian Press and Information Service,* No. 14, Apr. 1941.

[93] Timasheff, *Religion in Soviet Russia,* p. 65.

[94] Timasheff, *op. cit.,* p. 67.

[95] Timasheff, *op. cit.,* p. 69.

[96] Timasheff, *op. cit.,* pp. 70, 71.

[97] Timasheff, *op. cit.,* p. 75.

[98] *International Christian Press and Information Service,* No. 37, Oct., 1941.

[99] *The Christian News-Letter,* Apr. 1, 1942.

[100] *The Christian News-Letter,* March 13, 1940.

[101] *International Christian Press and Information Service, Information Series,* No. 12, March, 1943.

[102] *International Christian Press and Information Service. Information Series.* No. 35.

[103] Timasheff, *op. cit.,* p. 80.

report, too, of young men who while living in the world had secretly taken monastic vows and who found inspiration in the liturgy of the Church.[104] In 1939 the Russian Government began to order a check on anti-religious activities.[105] Priests were given the right to vote, previously denied them. Christian faith had ceased to be a bar to official position in the state.[106] In 1943, moreover, the government permitted the Orthodox Church to elect a Patriarch.[107]

Concerning the so-called sectarian movements information was much more scanty. Evangelical groups, some of them akin to the Baptists in belief and practice, had flourished on the eve of 1914. They continued to grow in the first years of the Communist regime. Indeed, the Communists seem to have welcomed them as a possible means of weakening the Orthodox Church. They were said at one time to total about fifteen millions and to have doubled or even trebled their strength as against the period immediately before the Revolution.[108] The movement was reinforced by men returning from camps for prisoners of war where they had become converts.[109] Some financial assistance came from Protestants in the United States and Great Britain.[110] Among the city poor, Baptists and different varieties of Brethren won many by their moral preaching and the strictness of their personal lives.[111] In the 1920's various groups, such as Spiritual Christians and Seventh Day Adventists, together with Baptists and those known as Evangelicals, had large accretions of members. Some Communist leaders were hopeful of winning their co-operation and were disposed to treat them leniently.[112] While after 1929 the government became severe with the "sects" as well as with the Orthodox Church, the movements continued, and their registered membership was not the measure of their strength.[113] In spite of persecution, Baptists made so many converts as to arouse the alarm of the official press.[114] In 1940 Baptists were said to number about five millions.[115] Another report, in 1943, declared that Baptists and Evangelicals

[104] Fedotov in *Christianity and Crisis*, Apr. 6, 1942.
[105] Timasheff, *op. cit.*, pp. 112 ff.
[106] Pares in *Foreign Affairs*, Vol. VI, p. 643.
[107] *The New York Times*, Sept. 19, 1943.
[108] Spinka, *Christianity Confronts Communism*, p. 70.
[109] Blumit, *Sentenced to Siberia*, pp. 123-129; Müller in *World Dominion*, Vol. XVII, pp. 20-29.
[110] McCullagh, *The Bolshevik Persecution of Christianity*, pp. 298, 299; Blumit, *op. cit.*, pp. 123, 124.
[111] Emhardt, *Religion in Soviet Russia*, p. 295.
[112] Emhardt, *op. cit.*, pp. 267, 268.
[113] Paul Anderson in "*The Madras Series*," Vol. VI, p. 245.
[114] Pares in *Foreign Affairs*, Vol. XXI, p. 640.
[115] Fedotov in *Christianity and Crisis*, Apr. 6, 1942.

totalled four millions, that they were disposed to keep aloof from political debate, and that the government was encouraging them.[116]

Persecution, moreover, led members of differing Christian groups to assist one another and partly erased their reciprocal intolerances. Orthodox and Jews aided one another in keeping open their places of worship and Baptists contributed to the maintenance of Orthodox parishes.[117] Baptists, Old Believers, and even Moslems were said to pray in the same churches, but at different times.[118]

The Roman Catholic Church suffered severely under the Communist regime. This was in part because of the opposition of that church to Communism. It was also because, through the independence of Poland after the world war of 1914-1915, most of Tsarist Russia's Roman Catholics were outside the Russian boundaries, for the large majority of Russia's Roman Catholics had been Poles. Since Poles were disliked in Russia, the Roman Catholic Church shared in their unpopularity. Rome apparently hoped that their distresses might win over the Orthodox to it. Some conversions there were from among the *émigrés*, but there was no marked Rome-ward movement in Russia itself. In the 1920's, a Papal Relief Mission gave extensive physical assistance to destitute Orthodox as well as to Roman Catholics, but it was viewed with suspicion by the Communists as a forerunner of proselytism.[119] The strain on the official relations between Poland and Russia also made difficult the situation of the Roman Catholics within Soviet territories.[120] We noted a few paragraphs above the notorious trial of Roman Catholic clergy. The world war which broke out in 1939 for a time brought more Roman Catholics under Russian control. The Russian treatment of them in Lithuania, Latvia, Esthonia, and Poland was sometimes harsh.[121] Uniates in Galicia seem to have experienced more leniency.[122] As the German tide rolled into Russia and then the slow Russian counter advance regained ground, the situation again changed. Yet, although a small minority, Roman Catholics survived within the Communist borders.

While, then, in its organized and visible aspects Christianity had spectacularly lost ground in Russia under the rule of the Communists, it had persisted. Even organizationally it had showed more vitality than any other phase of the old

[116] J. H. Rushbrooke, *Baptists in the U.S.S.R.* (Nashville, Boardman Press, 1943), cited in *Information Service*, Jan. 8, 1944.
[117] Pares in *Foreign Affairs*, Vol. XXI, p. 641.
[118] *The Christian News-Letter*, March 13, 1940.
[119] McCullagh, *op. cit.*, pp. 303 ff.
[120] Bolshakoff, *The Christian Church and the Soviet State*, pp. 71, 72.
[121] Bolshakoff, *op. cit.*, p. 72.
[122] *Ibid.*

regime. As a force in the lives of a large proportion of the population, in 1945 it was still to be reckoned with. The campaign against it seemed to be dying and here and there Christianity appeared to be regaining ground.

Moreover, it must be remembered that in its share in shaping Communism, in its tillage of the Russian soil for that ideology, and in its influence on some of the Soviet leaders Christianity was making an indirect contribution to the new Russia. How great that was could not be accurately appraised. We have seen[123] that the Marxist form of Communism, the type which was taken as standard in Russia, was indebted somewhat to Christianity, partly through Hegel and the latter's semi-theological view of history, and, possibly, through Marx's Christian family connexions. Marx thought of himself as anti-Christian, but his confidence in the triumph of the proletariat and of the coming of an ideal society had something of the predetermined and automatic about it which resembled some kinds of Christian millenarianism and Jewish-Christian apocalypticism and eschatology. The acceptance of his system by Russia may have been facilitated by the preparation which Christianity had given to the Russian soul. Certainly among some Russians Christianity had reinforced or perhaps even created a regard for the lowly, a belief that the universe was against injustice to the poor, and the conviction that eventually the oppressed and underprivileged majority would be emancipated. Stalin, the dominant leader of Communist Russia, although not the son of a priest, had some of his formal education in a theological seminary.[124] How far that training shaped him it is impossible to say. While in the seminary he was brought in contact with radical literature which had been smuggled in and became a revolutionist, but whether his rebellion was unconsciously stimulated by Christianity against much that was a contradiction of Christianity probably not even he would have known. Apparently, too, the messianic attitude engendered by Christianity by which Russia had regarded herself as the "third Rome" and as such the divinely appointed guardian of true Christianity after Rome had succumbed to the "Latin heresy" and Constantinople, the second Rome, had fallen to the Turks, helped to reinforce the Russian devotion to Communism, and, now that official allegiance had been shifted from Christ to Marx, to inspire the Russians to regard themselves as the exemplars and champions of the Communist message for the salvation of mankind.[125] In this there was possibly something akin to the contribution that Christianity seems to have made to

[123] Vol. IV, p. 159.

[124] Spinka, *Christianity Confronts Communism*, p. 26.

[125] Nicolas Berdyaev, *The Origin of Russian Communism*, translated from the Russian by R. M. French (London, Geoffrey Bles: the Centenary Press, 1937, pp. 239), *passim* and especially p. 228.

the French Revolution a century and a quarter earlier.[126] In Russia as in France Christianity appears to have helped to shape an attitude which looked expectantly towards an age in which opportunity for an abundant life would be open to all, especially to the hitherto underprivileged. In both Russia and France were movements, only on a gigantic scale, similar to those which we have seen in many different parts of the globe[127] in which Christianity was an inspiration to attempts at revolution which in many of their aspects were a negation of Christianity.

Russian Christianity also survived in exile. Thousands of the adherents of the old regime, largely of the aristocrats, the intellectuals, and the middle class, took refuge in other countries. Many of these carried with them the Russian Orthodox faith. Others, in the trials to which their changed lot subjected them, now found significance to life and support in their tribulations in a discovery of what the Christian faith could mean. Probably, too, some gave their allegiance to the Russian Orthodox Church or had it strengthened because that church was Russian and as such was a familiar and welcome representative of what they had known at home and in an age now passed. Of the exiles between 150,000 and 300,000 became domiciled in France, about half of them in and around Paris. There a vigorous life displayed itself in the Orthodox Church. A theological seminary was founded in Paris. Financial assistance for it came from the American Young Men's Christian Association and the British Russian Clergy and Church Aid Fund. On the teaching staff of the seminary were some distinguished theologians, among them N. Berdyaev and S. Bulgakoff, both at one time Marxian intellectuals but now convinced Christians. The churches became the centres of the Russian community life, from time to time new parishes were developed, and *Action Orthodoxe* was founded as an agency for spreading the faith.[128] Paris was the seat of a metropolitan whose diocese, that of western Europe, included most of the European countries except Russia, Poland, the Balkans, and the Baltic republics. In 1938 the diocese embraced, in addition to the theological school, several religious houses and about a hundred parishes. Many of the parishes constituted the main centres of community life for the *émigrés*, with camps for boys and girls, libraries, lectures, meals for the unemployed, and hostels for the aged and infirm.[129] For a time there was also a synod of Russian bishops with headquarters at Karlovtsy, in Jugoslavia. It supported the candidacy of one of the

[126] See Vol. III, p. 391.
[127] See Vol. III, pp. 388, 389, Vol. V, pp. 183, 268, 269, Vol. VI, pp. 182, 361, 363.
[128] P. E. Widdrington in *Christendom*, Vol. II, pp. 74-83; Sorokin in *Religion in Life,* Vol. XIII, p. 14.
[129] N. Zernov in *World Dominion*, Vol. XVI, pp. 358-363.

grand dukes for the vacant Tsarist throne.[130] In 1923 the Russian Student Christian Movement had its rise in a conference in Czechoslovakia. It succeeded in drawing to its platform Russians from several parties in the Orthodox Church.[131] Many Christians who did not conform to the Orthodox Church also found refuge abroad. Some of these were in the Baltic states and the Balkans. Others went to America. There were Baptist and Evangelical communities among the Russian exiles in Harbin, Mukden, Dairen, Tientsin, and Shanghai.[132] By 1923 about twenty-three thousand Mennonites are said to have gone to Canada.[133]

In Italy the Fascist regime did not work such damage to the organized church as did Communism in Russia. Indeed, in some respects the Roman Catholic Church achieved a stronger position under Fascism than it had held under the preceding form of government. However, there was conflict. Fascism was frankly totalitarian and sought to dominate the entire life of the nation. Especially did it wish to monopolize the training of the young. Inevitably there was friction between Fascism and the church. Probably in essence the two were incompatible. Yet the latter, in the two decades of Fascist rule, gained ground. Except for numerically insignificant minorities of Protestants and a few Jews, Roman Catholicism was the nominal faith of the Italian people. The course of Christianity in Italy was practically identified with it.

The Roman Catholic Church entered the era which was opened by 1914 in a somewhat paradoxical position. On the one hand it had the professed adherence of the Italian people and had the headquarters of its world-wide administration in Rome, a city which was at once the seat of the Pope and the capital of the Kingdom of Italy. For more than three centuries all the Popes had been Italians and in 1914 approximately half of the cardinals were of that nationality. Yet there was much of anti-clericalism, especially in the cities and the government, the Masonic movement, traditionally anti-clerical in Latin lands, was potent in the chief political circles, and the Pope chose to think of himself as a prisoner in the Vatican. The formation of the new Italian kingdom through the *risorgimento* in the second and third quarters of the nineteenth century had brought conflict over the question of whether the Papal States should be incorporated in the civil state. They were absorbed, the culminating act being the entrance of the troops of the new Italy into Rome in 1870 and

[130] Brian-Chaninov, *The Russian Church*, pp. 170, 171.
[131] Tatlow, *The Story of the Student Christian Movement*, p. 667.
[132] Müller in *World Dominion*, Vol. XVII, pp. 20-29.
[133] O. L. Miller in *Fellowship*, Vol. II, p. 8.

the moving of the political capital to that city. To this obliteration of its long cherished temporal power the Papacy would not submit. It and the Kingdom of Italy did not, therefore, have official relations with each other. The Popes believed that they could not accede to the new situation without jeopardizing their dignity and that of the church and, possibly, sacrificing their autonomy.[134]

In the three decades after 1914 the Roman Catholic Church entered into formal relations with the state and thereby buttressed its power. The *rapprochement* was chiefly the work of two remarkable men, Pope Pius XI and Mussolini. The way had been preparing for the reconciliation, but it was they who brought it about. When, in 1922, Cardinal Ratti became Pius XI, his initial blessing *urbi et orbi* was given from the front balcony of St. Peter's, breaking the precedent of his immediate predecessors who, since 1870, had given it within the Vatican. Thus, at the inception of his reign, he began to come out of the Papal seclusion. Mussolini, like Pius XI, was courageous and a man of action. While not deeply religious and not orthodox in his views, he deemed it prudent to achieve friendly relations with the most powerful single institution in Italy and one through which Italy had a world-wide outreach. In 1929 two documents were signed between the Papacy and the Italian state. By one of them, the Treaty of the Vatican, the Papal temporal power was restored through the creation of the State of Vatican City, a small domain of 109 acres centring about St. Peter's but giving the Pope status as a sovereign prince. An indemnity was paid the Vatican for the loss of revenues resulting from its deprivation of taxes from its former domains. By the other, a concordat, the relations between Church and state were regulated. The former law which called for a civil marriage before the religious ceremony was replaced by the recognition of the religious ceremony as effective in civil law. The teaching of the Roman Catholic faith was made obligatory in secondary education, carrying further the introduction (in 1923) of religious instruction in primary education. Other features of the concordat reinforced the position of the Roman Catholic Church. The clergy were accorded special privileges. In return the state was given a voice in the appointment of the clergy to benefices. Dioceses were to have their boundaries redefined to make them correspond as nearly as possible with those of the civil provinces.[135]

Yet scarcely was the ink dry on these documents when conflict arose over education. Mussolini wished the Fascist state to have full authority over the training of youth. He ordered the church organizations of boys and girls absorbed into the Fascist structure. In 1931 he followed this with the dissolution

---

[134] Binchy, *Church and State in Fascist Italy*, pp. 3-70.
[135] Binchy, *op. cit.*, pp. 71 ff.

of the young men's organizations which were connected with Catholic Action. The Pope meanwhile (May 15, 1931) had claimed the right in the encyclical *Quadragesimo Anno* to give authoritative answers to social and economic questions. Pius XI had been furthering Catholic Action in Italy, a movement for the religious instruction and growth of its members, fellowship among the faithful, and the exerting of influence upon society. Obviously such an organization would be regarded with unfriendly eye by a totalitarian ruler such as Mussolini. The Fascist state, too, endeavoured, not unsuccessfully, to extend its control over the schools maintained by the church. Pius XI declared his intransigency on the issues at stake, but on Catholic Action he acquiesced in a compromise by which the Fascists agreed to the restoration of the Catholic youth organizations and the Papacy to limitations upon the functions of these bodies. Many in the church believed much of the education given in the state schools to be contrary to Christian faith.[136] Both church and Fascist state wished full control of the shaping of youth. Neither could fully achieve it and tension was unavoidable. Moreover, between Fascism and the Christian faith there was a basic incompatibility which leading Roman Catholics and Fascists recognized.[137] Any peace between the church and the Fascist state could only be an uneasy compromise, a truce dictated by expediency.

Protestantism was so negligible a factor in the life of Italy, both numerically and in its influence, that we must not give it the space for more than passing mention. Under the Kingdom of Italy all cults were legally on the same footing. Indeed, it was complained that the state, while controlling and so restricting the Roman Catholic Church, gave full liberty to its rivals.[138] Fascist legislation in 1929 and 1930, while assuring toleration to "admitted cults other than the Catholic Roman and Apostolic Religion" which did not "profess principles and practice rites contrary to public order or good morals," placed them under the rigid control of the state. Indeed, one denomination, the Pentecostals, propagated from the United States, was suppressed. Legally the Roman Catholic Church was accorded precedence—a position it had not previously held under the Kingdom of Italy. Yet, in spite of Papal protests, Protestant missionary efforts among Roman Catholics were permitted.[139] These were chiefly by American Methodists, English Wesleyans, American Baptists, and the Plymouth Brethren.[140] Protestant efforts were largely financed from abroad. That was true

---

[136] Binchy, *op. cit.*, pp. 434 ff.
[137] Binchy, *op. cit.*, pp. 319 ff.
[138] Binchy, *op. cit.*, pp. 582, 583.
[139] Binchy, *op. cit.*, pp. 586-596.
[140] Dexter G. Whittinghill, *Italy and Baptist Missions* (Rome, "Bilychnis" Publication House, c. 1930, pp. 45), p. 16.

even of the Waldensees, the only Protestant denomination which could claim to be indigenous in Italy (and it by tradition had been French-using and had its chief strength in Alpine valleys in the extreme north).[141] Protestantism was, therefore, suspect by the Fascists as a possible foothold of alien and subversive tendencies. It was, moreover, branded by Mussolini as a threat to religious and therefore to national unity.[142] Increasing difficulties were experienced by foreign societies in their relations wtih the Fascist state.[143] Restrictions were placed even upon the Waldensees in the acquisition of new property for churches.[144] The embarrassment of Protestantism was enhanced by the declining receipts from the United States. Yet Protestant churches for Italians existed almost under the shadow of St. Peter's and it was said that Protestantism had exerted an influence in the wider reading of the Bible in the vernacular, in more preaching in the mother tongue, and in movements against profanity and the use of liquor.[145]

Far more serious than Fascism in its adverse effects upon Christianity was the National Socialist or Nazi regime in Germany and in the other lands which were brought within the Nazi orbit. While not so openly anti-Christian as Russian Communism, in its essence it was fully as incompatible with that faith. Because of the strength of the churches in Germany and the other lands under its sway, it was at first constrained to compromise with those bodies, but from almost the beginning it sought to constrict them or bring them under its full control and, if possible, denature them. Later, particularly under the stress of war conditions, it became increasingly intransigent towards the faith and its organized expressions. It did not yield as much in compromise as did Fascism. If it was less immediately open in its attack on Christianity and if it was less successful in reducing the strength of the faith than was Russian Communism, that was probably because of the greater vigour of the faith in Germany. In the end, however, it dealt more severe blows to Christianity in western Europe than had been suffered there by that faith since the initial conversion of the region. Both Protestant and Roman Catholic Christianity were affected. The trial was more acute for the former. Protestants were almost twice as numerous as Roman Catholics.[146] Germany was, too, the home of the Reformation and

[141] Information given the author by Waldensian leaders in Italy in 1934; Goodman, *Glimpses of the Story of the Waldensians*, p. 20.

[142] Information given the author by Protestant leaders in Italy in 1934.

[143] *Journal of the Annual Meeting of the Board of Foreign Missions of the Methodist Episcopal Church*, 1939, pp. 81-86.

[144] Information from a Waldensian in Italy, 1934.

[145] Information from a Protestant leader in Italy, 1934.

[146] By the census of 1933 62.7 per cent. were declared to be Protestants and 32.5 per cent. Roman Catholics.—*The Statesman's Year Book*, 1935, p. 951.

had long been a source of leading movements in Protestant life and thought. Indeed, some of the most important intellectual developments in Protestantism in the nineteenth and twentieth centuries had been in Germany. Germany was, in contrast, somewhat on the periphery of Roman Catholic Europe.

One of the unanswered questions of history was why the land which had so long been prominent in Protestant thought should also be the scene of the greatest organized threat which Christianity had faced in western Europe since the barbarian invasions. A superficial and facile answer would be that the one had been the cause of the other. Yet Hitler was not a Protestant but technically a Roman Catholic. Moreover, the question was akin to the paradox of western Europe—that from the area in which Christianity had longest exercised its most potent influence there arose in their most colossal forms such evils as global war and crass secularism.

When, in 1933, National Socialism, led by Adolf Hitler, came to the top in Germany, Christianity, and especially Protestant Christianity, was deemed to be in a serious crisis in that land. From the beginning, German Lutheranism had encouraged the power of the state and had reinforced nationalism. It was, therefore, a contributary force to the development of the extreme totalitarianism and nationalism which culminated in the Nazi state. It had, moreover, tended to eschew all efforts at the thoroughgoing transformation of society. We must remind ourselves, however, that this was not necessarily an essential feature of Lutheranism. In Scandinavia, much more nearly solidly Lutheran than was Germany, these trends, if present, were not so potent. There, indeed, from Lutheranism had sprung movements for the remaking of the structure of national life, as in Grundtvig,[147] and, as we saw in the preceding chapter, from the Primate of the Church of Sweden, staunchly Lutheran, came the initial leadership of the Universal Christian Council for Life and Work, which had as its goal the application of Christian principles to all society. It would be both interesting and important to know the reasons for the difference between German and Scandinavian Lutheranism. Perhaps it is to be found in the experience of Germany in the Thirty Years War (1618-1648), when so much of Germany was laid waste, and sensitive and devoted Lutheran Christians, in their reaction from the colossal evils of the time, took refuge in a Pietism which nourished the inner life and stimulated philanthropy to those suffering from social ills, but despaired of being able to remake society as a whole. Certainly it was from Pietism that, beginning with the later decades of the seventeenth century, there issued most of the vigour of German Lutheranism. Apparently, too, Pietism encouraged submission to the state as part of its asceticism. Bis-

[147] Vol. IV, pp. 157, 167, 272, 277.

marck, who was much influenced by it, did not feel it to be inconsistent with his political role in furthering nationalism and autocracy. Whatever the reason, German Lutheranism had acquiesced in absolutism on the part of the state and in extreme nationalism. It had, moreover, not opposed capitalism.[148] The Reformed churches in Germany, although by the genius of their Calvinism far less subject to civil authorities, had by the end of the nineteenth century largely acceded to the dominance of the state.[149]

German Protestantism entered the new age sadly disunited. The division was in part between Lutheran and Reformed and some smaller confessions. There were also, as elsewhere in Protestantism, disagreements between conservatives who resisted the scientific and scholarly trends of the nineteenth century and liberals who sought to reconcile them with the Christian faith. Very significant, too, was the fragmentation through political boundaries. Each of the Protestant states of Germany had its church, allied with the state and supported by public taxation. These lines had not been erased by the new German Empire which came into being in the second half of the nineteenth century. Nor, in spite of the fact that under it in theory Church and state were separate, did the Weimar Republic terminate them. After 1918 there had been an effort to bring together these *Landeskirchen*, as the state churches were called, and in 1921-1922 there was constituted the German Evangelical Church Federation. This was not a union but simply a federation of twenty-eight churches of as many different states, plus the Moravians.[150] German Protestantism remained divided and tied to the state.

This Protestantism, handicapped by outmoded state barriers in the midst of a rising nationalism, was attacked by those who wished a German religion and who, if they held to Christianity at all, wished to free it from what they deemed its Jewish integuments. As one ingredient of the revolt there was a frank rebellion against Christianity. It had been growing in the nineteenth century and was identified with such names as Schopenhauer, Richard Wagner, Eduard von Hartmann, Paul de Lagarde, and Friedrich Nietzsche.[151] To it were added the secularism of the age, the disruption of society by Germany's defeat in the world war of 1914-1918, and economic difficulties, including extreme inflation. The torture through which the German soul was passing, compounded with nationalism and various pre-1914 trends, issued in a number of movements in

[148] For aspects of this see Means, *Things that are Caesar's*, pp. 1-17. For a stimulating analysis by a German Protestant, see Paul Tillich, *The Religious Situation*, translated by H. R. Niebuhr (New York, Henry Holt and Company, 1932, pp. xxv, 182), pp. 153 ff.

[149] Means, *op. cit.*, pp. 9-13.

[150] Keller and Stewart, *Protestant Europe*, pp. 204, 205; Macfarland, *The New Church in the New Germany*, pp. 21-23.

[151] Means, *op. cit.*, pp. 56 ff.

the days of the Weimar Republic, some of them holding to Christianity and others of them departing boldly from it, but all of them intensely German and seeking for a spiritual rebirth of the nation.[152] In a sense they were an effect of the environment on Christianity. They came from Protestantism rather than from Roman Catholicism, partly because Protestantism already more reflected the German *milieu* and partly because by its nature and organization it was less resistant to the changing scene.

Roman Catholic Christianity was in slightly better case than were its Protestant rivals. It had not given so many hostages to the absolute state and the dominant nationalism and in the Pope it had a centre of authority and stability to which nineteenth century ultramontanism had knitted it more firmly than at any previous time. Moreover, in its political expression, the Centre Party, German Roman Catholicism could offer a fairly solid front. Under the Weimar Republic the Centre Party, with its social policy, became a force to be reckoned with. The Roman Catholic Church had, moreover, several societies for workers and youth which had been formed in the nineteenth century and which, with social programmes that sought to meet the needs of the new day, enjoyed a striking growth in the years immediately following the world war of 1914-1918.[153] The passing of the Hohenzollerns and the coming of the Weimar Republic gave the Roman Catholic Church more freedom. It was now of national importance and not limited, as heretofore, to Bavaria and the Rhine. The appointment of a Papal Nuncio brought further prestige and influence, particularly since the first to hold the post was the very able Pacelli, later Pope Pius XII.[154] The Roman Catholic Church, like Protestantism, felt the onslaught of the accumulated anti-Christian drive which culminated in the National Socialist regime, but it was in a somewhat more favourable condition to meet it.

Hitler did not directly disavow Christianity. He attacked those parties which called themselves Christian, especially the Centre Party.[155] He also believed that Christianity was waning and that the numerical gains made by its missions in Asia and Africa did not compensate for the losses in Europe.[156] However, he admired what he deemed the intransigency by which Christianity had won in the Roman Empire and the strict adherence of the Roman Catholic Church to its dogmas, a trait which he held had made that church stand firmer than ever in the contemporary scene.[157] The programme of his party, which he

---

[152] For some of these see Douglass, *God among the Germans*, pp. 61-63. See also Frey, *Cross and Swastika*, pp. 102 ff.

[153] Teeling, *Crisis for Christianity*, pp. 70-97; Shuster, *Like a Mighty Army*, pp. 175 ff.

[154] Duncan-Jones, *The Struggle for Religious Freedom in Germany*, pp. 155, 156.

[155] Hitler, *Mein Kampf*, pp. 364-368.

[156] Hitler, *op. cit.*, p. 365.

[157] Hitler, *op. cit.*, pp. 487, 675, 682.

staunchly defended, professed "the viewpoint of positive Christianity," a phrase which he earlier interpreted as inculcating respect for the churches, but which after 1933 he regarded as meaning a different kind of Christianity from that of his opponents among the ecclesiastical leaders.[158]

An early colleague of Hitler was Alfred Rosenberg who denounced what he deemed the Jewish corruptions of Christianity. He stressed what he esteemed as the German soul and a kind of German mysticism.[159] He fitted in with trends which found partial expression in National Socialism.

The coming of the National Socialists to power, with their emphasis upon the German *volk*, brought a fresh access of strength to those movements which would make Christianity conform to the German spirit. Some of their leaders were actuated by the conviction that the new Germany, to be effective, must have a religious foundation. Obviously the organizations and schools of thought which advocated a German religion, whether by the accommodation of Christianity to the German genius or by the frank adoption of a revived pre-Christian German paganism, would forge to the fore. Obviously, too, there would be an attempt to weld the Protestant churches together into a well articulated national body and thus end the anachronism of the *Landeskirchen*, embodying as they did the political fissiparousness of a bygone age which was so repugnant to the ardent nationalist.

Representative of the movement for a German religion was Jacob Wilhelm Hauer. He was originally from the missionary training school at Basel, then for five years was a missionary in India, later was a pastor in Germany, and eventually was a professor of comparative religion in the University of Tübingen.[160] His spiritual pilgrimage took him completely outside Christianity. He was a persuasive spokesman for the German Faith Movement. That movement, launched in 1933, was frankly co-ordinated with the formation of the Third Reich. It professed to be an "eruption from the biological and spiritual depths of the German nation," an emancipation from Christianity, and a return to the German spirit of pre-Christian times.[161] The German Faith Movement attracted other groups which wished a religion that would be at once an incarnation of the German spirit and a release from non-German Christianity. Among these were the German Faith Community, the Society for the Advancement of the Nordic Religion, the League of Free Religious Congregations, and the Association of Free Religious Congregations. The latter two had their roots

[158] Hitler, *op. cit.*, p. 694.
[159] Douglass, *God among the Germans*, pp. 30-46; Means, *Things that are Caesar's*, pp. 169 ff.
[160] Scott-Craig and Davis, *Germany's New Religion*, pp. 22, 23.
[161] Hauer in Scott-Craig and Davies, *op. cit.*, pp. 27 ff.

in nineteenth century efforts to devise a rationalistic Christianity and had enjoyed a striking growth in the stormy years after 1918. In 1934 the diverse elements were welded more firmly together under the leadership of Hauer. In spite of the latter's outstanding position in it, the German Faith Movement still gave evidence of the many elements which had entered into its composition. In general it was made up of those who desired a religion but who were dissatisfied with what they found in the Christian churches, whether Roman Catholic or Protestant: some completely disavowed Christianity, but others, while rejecting the churches, revered Jesus. It disclaimed any desire to revive the cult of the old German gods and clearly bore the imprint of the Christian background of its members. It permitted in an associate membership those who continued affiliation with other religious bodies, but full members could not belong to the Christian Church. Nor were those admitted who had Jewish or coloured blood.[162] Here was a body, led in part by intellectuals, which was against historic Christianity but which, far from being aggressively opposed to all religion, as was the Union of Militant Atheists in Russia, warmly espoused religion and preserved something of what had come from the Christian heritage. Within a few years Hauer turned his back on the movement which he had done so much to evoke, and as an organization it disintegrated.[163]

During the war of 1914-1918 there began a development which in the 1920's flowered in the League of the German Church. With it coalesced other organizations of somewhat similar aim. In the main the purpose of the German Church was to work for the invigoration of the Church and the Christian life through bringing into them elements from the proposals for a German religion. It sought to remain Christian but to purge the faith of what it regarded as Jewish accretions and to adjust the Christian message to the German mind.[164]

More closely allied with National Socialism were the German Christians. They were an expression of the demand for a German religion and became a religious phase of National Socialism. The name "German Christians" was given them by Hitler himself. The German Christians crystallized formally in March, 1932, at first under the leadership of a Berlin pastor, Joachim Hossenfelder. Hossenfelder had joined the National Socialists in 1929 and cherished the purpose of making the Kingdom of God the soul of the Third Reich. He wished to bring the revived Germany to a consciousness of the Church and to make its religion Christ. The German Christians were to be of Aryan descent and were to belong to no Masonic lodge. Their organization was

---

[162] Frey, *Cross and Swastika*, pp. 80-101; Douglass, *op. cit.*, pp. 58-71; Means, *op. cit.*, pp. 178, 179.

[163] Frey, *op. cit.*, p. 102.

[164] Douglass, *op. cit.*, pp. 72-79.

carefully articulated and endeavoured to have a unit in each parish. It wished
to make of the Church one unified body which would parallel the Nationalist
Socialist state. Sharing the Nazi horror of the Communists, it denounced
Communist atheism and was for positive Christianity as it believed it saw it
in the German spirit and in Luther. It would support foreign missions, but
would have the converts hold to the racial allegiance and character of their
ancestors. It attracted a number of diverse elements, among them several of
Germany's theologians. Some of the members were drawn by self-interest—by
the desire to retain their offices and, if pastors, to continue the performance
of their clerical functions.[165]

It was this Faith Movement of German Christians which had the support of
Hitler in his effort to unify the Protestant forces into a church which would
reinforce the National Socialist state. The test came in the spring and summer
of 1933 and led to a bitter conflict whose echoes were long in dying. The
details are so confusing that we must not attempt to go into them. Only part
of the main outline of the struggle can be given room in our pages.

Fearing an attempt to unify the Protestant churches through the dictation
of the state, the German Evangelical Church Federation essayed the task and
worked out a rough draft for a structure in which both Lutherans and Reformed should be combined under a Lutheran Reichbishop. As bishop there
was elected Friedrich von Bodelschwingh, head of a famous Inner Mission
institution at Bielefeld. This choice angered the German Christians. In July,
1933, came a state ordinance commanding all churches to display the Nazi
flag and ordering all pastors in their church services to give thanks for the
Nazi regime and pray for its prosperity. Most of the pastors obeyed but some
were defiant. In Prussia the Nazi state dismissed all the officers of the church
government, a step which did not make for peace. Karl Barth came out in
July, 1933, with a blast against the German Christians and the changes which
were being forced upon the Church by the state. Nevertheless, through the co-
operation of a committee of the German Evangelical Church Federation, a new
constitution was worked out for the German Evangelical Church and received
the approval of Hitler. It brought together in one centralized organization the
Lutheran and Reformed churches under a Reichbishop. In the ensuing church
elections the German Christians were overwhelmingly successful and one of
their number, Ludwig Müller, an ardent supporter of Hitler, was chosen
bishop.[166]

[165] Macfarland, *The New Church and the New Germany*, p. 27; Douglass, *op. cit.*, p.
87; Nygren, *The Church Controversy in Germany*, pp. 33 ff.

[166] Means, *op. cit.*, pp. 214-239; Douglass, *op. cit.*, pp. 176-216; Andreas Duhm, *Der
Kampf um die deutsche Kirche. Eine Kirchengeschichte des Jahres 1933/34 dargestellt*

Against this domination of the German Christians opposition groups arose, notably one of about two thousand of the clergy, the Pastors' Emergency Federation, headed by Bodelschwingh. The attempt of the German Christians to confine membership in the Church to Aryans provoked revolt. In November, 1933, a speech of a leader of the German Christians insisting that there should be a second German reformation in which the Old Testament and the Pauline theology should be eliminated aroused another storm. Official Nazi support of the German Christians was withdrawn and the movement began to disintegrate. However, Müller remained in office and became even more dictatorial. Early in 1934 a number of protesting pastors had been placed in concentration camps and the Evangelical Youth Associations were absorbed into the Hitler Youth.[167]

Outstanding in the opposition was Martin Niemöller. The son of a Lutheran pastor, Niemöller had served as an officer in submarines during the world war of 1914-1918. The war over, after a period of readjustment he went into the ministry and became one of the leading preachers in Germany. From his pulpit in a fashionable Berlin parish he fearlessly opposed Hitler's church programme and became a symbol of the resistance of the Protestants to the Nazis.[168]

Those who would not accede to Müller and the full Nazi programme for the Protestant churches began to organize on a nation-wide scale. In the fore part of 1934 they began forming, at first chiefly among the Reformed churches, for these had been used to such procedures, what were known as Confessional Synods. The latter were in several parts of the country and continued in spite of some interference by the secret police. In April a national conference of the Confessional leaders was held and inaugurated what it called the Evangelical Church of Germany. In May a national synod of this church was convened. Representatives of Lutheran, Reformed, and United (Lutheran and Reformed) churches were present.[169] Thus was the gauntlet thrown down to the Nazi-inspired national church.

The struggle was now further intensified. The death of Hindenburg, the President of the Reich, in August, 1934, removed a moderating influence, for

---

für das evangelische Volk (Gotha, Leopold Klotz, no date, pp. 361), *passim*; Nygren, *op. cit.*, pp. 21-32.

[167] Means, *op. cit.*, pp. 239-255; Douglass, *op. cit.*, 216-240; Nygren, *op. cit.*, pp. 54 ff.

[168] Martin Niemöller, *From U-Boat to Pulpit* (Chicago, Willett, Clark & Company, 1937, pp. viii, 223); Martin Niemöller, *"God is My Fuehrer"* (New York, Philosophical Library and Alliance Book Corporation, 1941, pp. 294); Miller, *Martin Niemoeller, passim*; Leo Stein, *I was in Hell with Niemoeller* (New York, Fleming H. Revell Company, 1942, pp. 253).

[169] Nygren, *op. cit.*, pp. 71 ff.; Douglass, *op. cit.*, pp. 240 ff.; Frey, *Cross and Swastika*, pp. 137 ff.; Duncan-Jones, *The Struggle for Religious Freedom in Germany*, pp. 74 ff.

the aged statesman had been unhappy over the controversy and had sought to restrain Müller and some of the extremists among the German Christians.[170] Jäger, who had been appointed in the spring as a member of the ministry and who was also on the Nazi Supreme Council, became the real power in the German Evangelical Church[171] and Müller, although formally installed in September as Reichbishop,[172] tended to fade into the background. In Bavaria and Württemberg the Protestant bishops, adamant against the new German Evangelical Church and backed by constituencies which traditionally were inclined to be hostile to orders from Prussia, were removed from office by Jäger.[173] In October, 1934, the Confessional Synod, meeting at Dahlmen, set up an ecclesiastical structure for the entire Reich.

In October, 1934, Jäger resigned, presumably because by failing to heal the breach in the church he had lost the confidence of Hitler. Hitler, moreover, received in audience the bishops of Bavaria and Württemberg, now released from arrest. Yet the Confessional leaders, not satisfied that they had won the battle, continued the organization of their church. The Confessional church had the support of the majority of the pastors. Müller persisted in his refusal to resign, but by March, 1935, he had ceased to be an effective force.[174]

This, however, was only a lull before the renewal of the storm. The Confessional leaders were alarmed by the apparent movement of the state towards a German paganism and issued a manifesto against it. The document was read by many pastors from their pulpits. The government retaliated by placing under arrest about seven hundred of the offending clergy.[175] The names of the imprisoned were given publicity from Confessional pulpits and more arrests followed. The state took steps to alter the legal position of the Church, to the latter's hurt. This deepened a cleavage in the Confessional camp, already apparent, between Lutherans and Reformed. In July, 1935, a Reich Ministry for Church Affairs was created and Kerrl, a Nazi of long standing, was appointed to head it. In September Kerrl obtained dictatorial power over the Church. He attempted to solve the ecclesiastical problem by setting up church committees. The Confessionals kept their organization intact and Kerrl re-

[170] Henry Smith Leiper, *The Church-State Struggle in Germany. A personal view based on two months' intimate contact with the situation in Europe during August and September, 1934* (New York, American Section, Universal Christian Council for Life and Work, pp. 32), p. 3.

[171] Duncan-Jones, *op. cit.*, p. 78.

[172] Duncan-Jones, *op. cit.*, pp. 87, 88.

[173] Duncan-Jones, *op. cit.*, pp. 84, 85, 88, 89.

[174] Duncan-Jones, *op. cit.*, pp. 91-99.

[175] On some of the imprisoned, see Charles S. Macfarland, *"I Was in Prison"* . . . *The Suppressed Letters of Imprisoned German Pastors* (New York, Fleming H. Revell Company, 1939, pp. 112).

solved on its destruction. He succeeded in widening the rift in the Confessional ranks between Lutherans and Reformed, for the former were by tradition more ready to submit to the state than were the latter. The Confessional leaders appealed to Hitler himself against the paganizing tendencies of some of his subordinates but received no reply. More and more the state insisted upon the control of the youth. Rosenberg was prominent in utterances in behalf of a German religion. Many persons of prominence ostentatiously renounced church membership. Pastors were placed financially under complete state control (July, 1937), and collections were forbidden which might be used for the support of Confessional pastors or of wives and children of imprisoned pastors. Confessional colleges were suppressed, Confessional funds were seized, and Confessional leaders were incarcerated.[176] In July, 1937, Niemöller, the chief pulpit spokesman for the Confessional movement, was arrested. Although in the following March, after a famous trial, he was released by the court with a comparatively small fine, the secret police seized him and whisked him off to a concentration camp.[177] The Nazis seemed to be winning.

In the meantime, what had been the fate of the Roman Catholic Church? Hitler had been reared in that branch of the faith and had never openly repudiated it. The then reigning Pope, Pius XI, had a deeply seated distrust of Communism and might be expected, at least at the outset, to turn a friendly eye towards a party so openly anti-Communist as the National Socialists.[178] However, the Nazis would not tolerate the presence of the strong Centre Party, their most formidable organized rival for political power, and that party was predominantly Roman Catholic.[179] Indeed, German Lutheranism, being traditionally more submissive to the state, was at the beginning regarded by the Nazis with less hostility than was Roman Catholicism.[180] The Centre Party voluntarily disbanded in the summer of 1933,[181] but the National Socialists were still distrustful of Catholic Action, fearing that it was the Centre Party in another guise.[182]

In view of these antagonisms, potential and actual, it seemed a surprisingly happy augury when the Third Reich and the Vatican entered into a concordat, signed July 20 and ratified September 10, 1933, which appeared on its face to be favourable to the Roman Catholic Church. By it, among other provisions, that church was guaranteed freedom of faith and the public exercise of its

[176] Duncan-Jones, *op. cit.*, pp. 109-148.
[177] Duncan-Jones, *op. cit.*, pp. 149-152.
[178] Duncan-Jones, *op. cit.*, pp. 157, 158.
[179] Micklem, *National Socialism and the Roman Catholic Church*, p. 53.
[180] Duncan-Jones, *op. cit.*, p. 157.
[181] Harcourt, *The German Catholics*, pp. 97, 98.
[182] Micklem, *op. cit.*, pp. 55, 56.

religion. The Pope and the bishops were assured liberty of communicating with the faithful and of publishing such documents as pastoral letters; a Papal Nuncio was to reside at the German capital and a German Ambassador was to be accredited to the Holy See; in their spiritual activities the clergy were to enjoy the protection of the state; the secrecy of the confessional was confirmed; the church was given the right to appoint to all its offices and benefices without the co-operation of state or civil communities, except as might have been specified in existing concordats with Prussia, Bavaria, and Baden, and except that all those holding ecclesiastical offices in Germany were to be German citizens, were to have been matriculated from a German secondary school, and were to have studied theology either in Germany or in a Papal college in Rome, and bishops were to take an oath of loyalty to the state; Roman Catholic theological faculties in state universities were to be maintained; religious orders and congregations were not to be subject to special restrictions by the state; religious instruction in the schools according to Roman Catholic principles was to be maintained as a regular part of the curriculum; the retention of Roman Catholic denominational schools and the establishment of new ones were guaranteed and in them only Roman Catholics were to be employed as teachers; religious orders and congregations were allowed to establish and conduct private schools; ecclesiastical marriage was to precede the civil ceremony; and Roman Catholic societies for purely charitable, cultural, and religious ends were to be protected in their activities and institutions.[183] It appeared as though the most essential claims of the Roman Catholic Church had been made secure.

The hopes awakened by the document in large part proved illusory. The concordat gave the Roman Catholic Church nothing but what it had in theory enjoyed under the preceding regime. It might seem to indicate that there would be no new *Kulturkampf*, no attempt such as that made by the First Reich to curb the church. Yet in some of its provisions it hinted ominously at what could be constraint and where it made settlement of moot points contingent upon both church and state the latter might demur. Moreover, it was scarcely to be expected that the National Socialists, any more than any other regime which aspired to totalitarian rule, would be content to share with the church the moulding of youth.

The struggle began in earnest in 1935 when in Bavaria, predominantly Roman Catholic, the Nazis endeavoured to bring all children into schools in which both Protestants and Roman Catholics would be given the world view

[183] See a translation of the text in *The Persecution of the Catholic Church in the Third Reich*, pp. 516-522.

of the dominant party. Soon several Roman Catholic teachers' training colleges for women were suppressed.[184] The movement to substitute state for denominational schools spread to other parts of Germany. Nazi-indoctrinated school children were used to spy on parents and teachers.[185] The National Socialists, too, disregarding the concordat, sought to discourage the Roman Catholic as they had the Protestant church organizations for youth. However, many of the Roman Catholic youth held to their societies and became more zealous than ever in the practice of their religious duties.[186] The law passed in 1934 for the sterilization of persons supposed by the state to be unfit to reproduce their kind ran counter to Papal teaching.[187] There were, moreover, efforts to curb the freedom of the Roman Catholic as well as of the Protestant pulpit, especially in criticism of the state.[188] Beginning in 1934 attempts were made to break up Roman Catholic labour organizations by making it impossible to belong both to them and to the German Labour Front. Membership in the latter was important in obtaining work.[189] Under the guise of excluding the church from politics, repressive measures against the Roman Catholic press were taken.[190] Efforts were made to defame the church. One of these was in March, 1935, when Roman Catholic religious houses were accused of being centres of currency smuggling. In the following weeks hundreds of their members were imprisoned.[191] Charges of sexual irregularity were also brought against members of religious communities.[192]

The officials of the Roman Catholic Church did not tamely submit to the measures directed against their communion. In 1936 the bishops at their meeting at Fulda pronounced against the war on the denominational schools.[193] From Oldenburg came a popular protest, led by the bishop, against the removal of the crucifix from public buildings.[194]

The annexation of Austria by the Nazis further complicated relations with the Roman Catholic Church. Austria was overwhelmingly Roman Catholic

[184] Duncan-Jones, *op. cit.*, p. 169.

[185] Micklem, *op. cit.*, 145-154; *The Persecution of the Catholic Church in the Third Reich*, pp. 115-162.

[186] Duncan-Jones, *op. cit.*, pp. 171, 172, 177; Micklem, *op. cit.*, pp. 123-125; *The Persecution of the Catholic Church in the Third Reich*, pp. 82 ff.

[187] Duncan-Jones, *op. cit.*, pp. 173-175.

[188] Duncan-Jones, *op. cit.*, pp. 175, 176.

[189] Duncan-Jones, *op. cit.*, p. 178; *The Persecution of the Catholic Church in the Third Reich*, pp. 353 ff.

[190] Duncan-Jones, *op. cit.*, pp. 184-186.

[191] Duncan-Jones, *op. cit.*, pp. 192-194; Micklem, *op. cit.*, pp. 119-122.

[192] Duncan-Jones, *op. cit.*, pp. 198-202; Micklem, *op. cit.*, pp. 158-161; *The Persecution of the Catholic Church in the Third Reich*, pp. 298 ff.

[193] Duncan-Jones, *op. cit.*, pp. 206-208.

[194] Duncan-Jones, *op. cit.*, pp. 217, 218.

and in its government the bishops had been influential.[195] Beginning in 1933, under Dollfuss, who wished to be loyally Roman Catholic, there was an attempt to bring into being a German Co-operative Christian State. The assassination of Dollfuss, in 1934, brought one stage of the experiment to a tragic end.[196] In 1938 came the annexation by Germany. The Austrian bishops, led by Cardinal Innitzer, seemed to welcome the *Anschluss*. Yet the Vatican was not enthusiastic and the Austrian bishops attempted to insist that their church be assured that youth would be reared in their faith.[197] In Austria, now the Ostmark, as in the rest of the Third Reich, the Roman Catholic Church was to face difficult days. In the Ostmark it was spared some of the indignities which had been visited upon it in Germany before the *Anschluss*, for by 1938 that particular stage of the persecution had passed. Yet most of the schools were secularized, others of the church schools were closed, many ecclesiastical properties were taken over by the state, there was sequestration of funds, some Roman Catholic organizations were closed down, several monasteries and theological seminaries were dissolved, numbers of priests were imprisoned, insults to the church and the priesthood by Nazi youth were common, and within a few months not far from fifty thousand Austrians had renounced the church. In some ways the church suffered more severely than in the rest of the Reich.[198]

In spite of the measures taken against Christianity and the churches in the Third Reich by the National Socialist regime and by some of the extremists connected with it, the faith continued. A large proportion of the youth were caught up in Nazi organizations and were taught to distrust and even to contemn the churches and historic Christianity. Many of the populace, particularly of the youth, were indoctrinated with a religion in which some remnants of Christianity were to be found but which was a racial and national cult, a kind of neo-paganism. However, the churches persisted. Their membership had shrunk, many of their activities had been disrupted or forcibly curtailed, but the more faithful spirits had had their loyalty heightened by persecution. More than any other set of pre-Nazi institutions of any kind, secular or religious, the churches went on as a continuing feature of German life. It is said that in the very time when Hitler was consolidating his power in Germany, from 1933 to 1938, each year the sales of the Bible outstripped those of his own widely promoted book, *Mein Kampf*, by more than 200,000, and that the sales of the Bible in Germany rose from 830,000 copies in 1930 to 1,120,000

[195] Teeling, *Crisis for Christianity*, pp. 268 ff.
[196] Power, *Religion in the Reich*, pp. 162-164.
[197] Duncan-Jones, *op. cit.*, pp. 235-242; Power, *op. cit.*, pp. 165 ff.
[198] Power, *op. cit.*, pp. 159 ff.; McLeish, *Churches under Trial*, p. 23.

in 1939. For large numbers of Germans, Christianity was more consciously vital than it had been before the advent of Hitler.

One phase of the relations of the National Socialist movement which cannot be passed over was the treatment of the Jews. This would lie outside the proper field of a history of the expansion of Christianity were it not for the fact that Christians, including leaders of the churches, both Protestant and Roman Catholic, were prominent in denouncing the anti-Jewish measures and in relieving some of the misery of the members of the unhappy race. Obviously we cannot go into the full history of the anti-Semitism of the Nazis and their allies. We can take time merely to hint at some of the actions taken by Christians in criticism and relief.

Hitler crystallized and augmented the rising anti-Semitism of Germany.[199] This came partly from the attempt to find a scapegoat for German misfortunes and partly from the strong racialism which was basic in National Socialism. The measures against the Jews and those with Jewish blood were fairly steadily intensified and, even before 1939, led to the greatest sufferings which the Jews had experienced since the time of their expulsion from Spain (1492) and Portugal (1497)[200] or, possibly, under the Tsarist regime in Russia in the second half of the nineteenth century.[201] The Jews were victims of anti-Semitic measures by the White armies who opposed the Reds in the opening years of the Communist era in Russia, but, in general, while hostile to their religion, the Soviets sought to liberate the Jews from racial discrimination.[202] The measures adopted by the National Socialists, however, were progressively more thoroughgoing, in their attempts to exterminate the race, than any in Spain, Portugal, or Russia, or, indeed, than any others of which we have record. In 1938, with the increasing collaboration between Hitler and Mussolini, the latter shifted from his earlier tolerance of Jews to pronounced anti-Semitism.[203]

This anti-Semitism came in a Europe in which Christian missions to the Jews were continuing much as they had been before 1914. Soon after 1918 in some countries there was a movement of Jews into the Church, notably in Hungary, Austria, Poland, and even Russia, but this seems to have been from mixed motives.[204] In Germany a few score Jews a year were won to Protestant-

[199] Hitler, *Mein Kampf*, pp. 66 ff., 312 ff.
[200] Vol. II, pp. 220, 221.
[201] Vol. IV, pp. 117, 118.
[202] Avrahm Yarmolinsky, *The Jews and Other Minor Nationalities under the Soviets* (New York, Vanguard Press, 1928, pp. xiii, 193), pp. 48 ff.
[203] Binchy, *Church and State in Fascist Italy*, pp. 606 ff.
[204] Schonfield, *The History of Jewish Christianity*, pp. 237, 238.

ism.[205] The International Missionary Council held conferences on the Jewish problem and appointed a special secretary to promote activities for them.[206] There continued to be conversions to Roman Catholicism in several European lands, especially Poland.[207]

One of the early effects of the anti-Jewish measures of the Third Reich was to slow down conversions in that land.[208] Obviously the Nazis would look upon them with unfriendly eye. The headquarters of one of the great German missionary societies for the Jews was moved from Leipzig to Vienna[209] and then to London,[210] and another similar organization was discontinued at the request of the government.[211] Yet as late as 1939 Bible study groups for Jews were meeting privately and a Swedish mission for the Jews was permitted to continue in Vienna.[212]

In Germany, churches as organizations were slow to speak out in behalf of the Jews.[213] Indeed, as late as 1935 some of the clergy in Poland and Rumania encouraged anti-Semitism[214] and in 1939 two of the Protestant churches of Germany excluded Jews from membership.[215] Still, the churches by refusing to divest themselves of the Old Testament or to eliminate what some of their Nazi opponents denounced as the Jewish elements of Christianity, were clearly not joining the Nazi anti-Jewish programme. The Roman Catholic bishops declined to separate from their fellowship Christians of Jewish blood.[216] Some individual Christians in Germany approved the anti-Semitic measures of the state. Some others acquiesced in them. But at least one Protestant church leader came out publicly for tolerance of the Jews and numbers of pastors and ecclesiastical officers helped to obtain the release of Jewish prisoners and in other ways gave succour to members of the unfortunate race.[217] This was the more noteworthy since by doing so they might bring upon themselves added displeasure from a state which was already hostile. Many Protestants publicly

---

[205] Ruppin, *The Jews in the Modern World*, pp. 329 ff.

[206] *The Christian Approach to the Jew. Being a Report of the Conferences on the Subject Held at Budapest and Warsaw in April, 1927* (London, Edinburgh House Press, 1927, pp. vii, 208).

[207] *The International Review of Missions*, Vol. XXV, p. 134.

[208] *The International Review of Missions*, Vol. XXII, pp. 345-352.

[209] *The International Review of Missions*, Vol. XXV, p. 86.

[210] *The International Review of Missions*, Vol. XXIX, p. 103.

[211] *Minutes of the International Committee on the Christian Approach to the Jews. British and European Sections. Kasteel Hemmen*, Holland, Apr. 28, 29, 1936 (London, International Missionary Council, 1936), *passim.*

[212] *The International Review of Missions*, Vol. XXIX, p. 102.

[213] Micklem, *National Socialism and the Roman Catholic Church*, p. 9.

[214] Information given privately to the author from an unimpeachable source.

[215] *The International Review of Missions*, Vol. XXIX, p. 98.

[216] Macfarland, *The New Church in the New Germany*, p. 85.

[217] Macfarland, *op. cit.*, pp. 76-80.

dissociated themselves from actions intended to bring racial discrimination into their churches.[218] Pius XI lost no time in putting himself publicly and squarely against the philosophy of racialism which underlay the Fascist anti-Semitic measures of 1938. This brought down on his head a storm of Fascist denunciation. Some of the Italian clergy and even one of the bishops were said to be more in accord with Fascism on this issue than with the Pope. Yet the head of the church had spoken and several Italian bishops followed his example.[219] Many leading Christians in both Germany and Italy were further placing in jeopardy their already precarious position by opposing measures against a race most of whose members were of a faith which had a long record of resistance to Christianity.

In September, 1939, came the outbreak of the European war which eventually joined with an earlier one in the Far East and became even more world-embracing than was the struggle of 1914-1918. Through this second of the world wars Christianity in Europe was more profoundly affected than by its predecessor or by the events of the intervening decades.

In general, the effects of the war on Christianity were adverse for that faith. War in itself carries much that is destructive to Christian morals and to the orderly processes of civilization with which the organized expressions of Christianity have normally been connected. In this particular conflict the earlier stages were accompanied by an intensification of the measures of the National Socialists against the churches in Germany and by actions against the churches in the lands which were overrun by German armies. Then, too, vast dislocations of population accompanied the war. By them millions were removed from their accustomed church connexions and the churches found difficulty in following them. The supply of clergy was badly depleted by the great reduction, through required war service, of the student bodies in theological faculties.[220] Hundreds, probably thousands, of church buildings were destroyed, many by bombing from the air and others by the competing armies. In Poland both Roman Catholic and Protestant churches suffered severely under the German occupation. Church buildings were pillaged and it is said that 7 bishops and 90 per cent. of the Roman Catholic clergy, a total of 2,700, were imprisoned or exiled. Numbers of the clergy were killed. In the Protestant churches the Polish pastors were deported and much ecclesiastical

[218] Macfarland, *op. cit.*, pp. 69 ff.
[219] Binchy, *op. cit.*, pp. 614 ff.
[220] *World Council of Churches, Second Memorandum on the Reconstruction of Christian Institutions in Europe.*

property was destroyed.[221] In France all Catholic Action associations were suppressed. In Czechoslovakia hundreds of priests and pastors were placed in concentration camps. In Latvia, Esthonia, and Lithuania the churches, whether Protestant, Roman Catholic, or Orthodox, suffered from the Russian occupation.[222] In Croatia the Orthodox Church lost at the expense of the Roman Catholic Church.[223] The structure of organized Christianity in much of Europe became weaker than in any time in centuries—possibly since the low ebb not far from A.D. 950.

In the face of these dismaying conditions, Christianity displayed striking vitality. In Germany and in the countries occupied by Germany it was the source of the chief expressions of resistance to the totalitarian regime of the National Socialists. It was the well-spring of many works of mercy for the sick, the wounded, the starving, and the prisoners of war. For instance, through an Ecumenical Commission for the Chaplaincy Service to Prisoners of War, spiritual ministrations were maintained for many held captive in Germany. In connexion with it large quantities of Bible and other religious literature were distributed.[224] The Christian faith heartened thousands in courageous and hopeful endurance of overwhelming evils. In lands where that was possible, notably in Great Britain, Christianity aroused churches to follow and serve the great movements of population brought by war conditions. It also stimulated dreams and action for a better world.

It is to an amplification, necessarily also brief, of the fashion in which Christianity was affected by this most devastating of European wars and of the manner in which it rose to the emergency that we must now turn. Many features of the story still lie hidden from us. Yet some of the facts we can know. It is doubtful, indeed, whether the general outlines which can be sketched even now will later be substantially altered by newly emerging details. It is an amazing record and no superlatives can do it justice. Still less can the measured and compact language of the sober historian give more than vague hints of what really occurred.

In Spain, where several years before the outbreak of the general European war civil strife gave opportunity for German and Italian aid in a kind of dress rehearsal for the larger conflict, the triumph of Franco seemed to strengthen

[221] *The Christian News-Letter*, No. 161.

[222] McLeish, *Churches under Trial*, pp. 39 ff.; *International Christian Press and Information Service, Information Series*, No. 14, Apr., 1941; H. Perlitz, *The Fate of Religion and Church under Soviet Rule in Estonia, 1940-1941* (New York, World Association of Estonians, 1944, pp. 29-56), *passim*.

[223] *International Christian Press and Information Service*, No. 11, March, 1942.

[224] *International Christian Press and Information Service, Information Series*, Jan., 1943.

the Roman Catholic Church. Although not all the clergy had been on his side and in the fighting there was destruction of ecclesiastical as well as other property, Franco and his supporters declared that the order over which he presided must be based upon the Roman Catholic faith and the power of that church was reinforced.[225] Under these circumstances Protestantism, never strong, was curbed and weakened.[226]

In Germany the war gave occasion for an intensification of the attacks on the churches and Christianity. Some of the National Socialists came out even more frankly than before with the assertion that the convictions of their party and Christianity were irreconcilable, that the Christian ideal of a universal church could not be tolerated, and that German religion must displace both Protestantism and Roman Catholicism.[227] In 1941 several pastors of the Confessional Church were imprisoned and tried for giving theological examinations to candidates for the ministry.[228] Pastors and lay Christians were being arrested for protesting against the euthanasia of the aged and infirm, for criticizing the harsh treatment accorded the Jews, for objecting to the glorification of the unmarried mother, and for preaching or circulating sermons hostile to the government.[229] Ostensibly because of the shortage of paper produced by war conditions, church publications were either greatly curtailed or entirely prohibited, while ample paper was found for purposes which the government favoured.[230] Some smaller Christian sects were suppressed.[231] The buildings of Young Men's Christian Associations and of numbers of monasteries were expropriated.[232] Further difficulties were placed in the way of giving religious instruction to children and youths.[233]

Added to these overt measures of restriction were other blows to the churches in Germany which came as concomitants of war. Some of these were unavoidable. Others may have been accentuated by the policies of the state. Church buildings were destroyed or damaged by enemy bombing.[234] Church bells were melted down to provide needed munitions.[235] Many of the clergy were

[225] *International Christian Press and Information Service, Information Series*, No. 6; Keller, *Christian Europe Today*, p. 106.

[226] Keller, *op. cit.*, pp. 106, 107.

[227] Van Dusen, *What IS the Church Doing?*, pp. 33-35; *The World Council Courier*, March, 1942.

[228] *The Spiritual Issues of the War*, No. 153.

[229] *Ibid.*

[230] *Ibid.*; Herman, *It's Your Souls We Want*, pp. 218, 219, 221.

[231] Herman, *op. cit.*, pp. 219, 220.

[232] Herman, *op. cit.*, pp. 219, 222.

[233] Van Dusen, *op. cit.*, pp. 32, 33.

[234] Herman, *op. cit.*, pp. 215, 216.

[235] Herman, *op. cit.*, p. 213.

mobilized. It is said that about 85 per cent. of the pastors of the Confessional Church were taken into the armies.[236] Shortage of coal for the heating of buildings reduced the frequency of church services.[237] Thousands of children were evacuated from cities which might be subject to air raids and the complaint was heard that the attempt was being made by the authorities to use their separation from their accustomed family and church environment to wean them from religion.[238]

In spite of these and other difficulties Christianity persisted in Germany, through the heroism both of its spokesmen and of the rank and file of its lay adherents. The Confessional Church continued to function and numbers of the former moderates in other Protestant churches who earlier had been inclined to co-operate with the government, seeing to what anti-Christian extremes the Nazi policy was leading, joined hands with it.[239] The Protestant churches were active in spreading their faith and did something for prisoners of war, especially Russians. They endeavoured to keep alive in their constituency the ideals of the Ecumenical Movement, with its fellowship with Christians of other lands.[240] Many of the Roman Catholic clergy stood out against the anti-Christian tendencies of the state. These included some of the bishops as well as many of the parish priests. In 1942 the Roman Catholic bishops spoke out collectively in a pastoral letter against the violations of the concordat by the Nazi power.[241] The churches were not intent merely on preserving their own existence: they also set themselves against much of the Nazi ideology and of the attack of the government upon Christianity and Christian ethics.[242] For instance, the pastoral letter of the German Roman Catholic bishops issued March 22, 1942, not only protested the departure of the government from the concordat: it likewise raised its voice against restrictions on personal freedom and the euthanasia of the insane and incurables.[243] The churches were the only organizations which dared to come out thus boldly in criticism of the state. The common peril drew Protestants and Roman Catholics more nearly together than at any time since the historic division at the Reformation. They co-operated in resistance to the Nazis. It is said that Roman Catholic

---

[236] *The Spiritual Issues of the War*, No. 176.

[237] Herman, *op. cit.*, pp. 211, 212.

[238] Herman, *op. cit.*, pp. 217, 218.

[239] *The Spiritual Issues of the War*, No. 176; *The World Council Courier*, Vol. II, No. 4.

[240] *The Christian News-Letter*, No. 192.

[241] Van Dusen, *op. cit.*, pp. 35-39.

[242] Herman, *op. cit.*, pp. 221, 222; *International Christian Press and Information Service, Information Series*, No. 46, December, 1943.

[243] See the text, translated, in Herman, *op. cit.*, pp. 301-306.

priests preached from Protestant pulpits, that some Protestant pastors expelled from their parishes by the political authorities were enabled to subsist by funds from the Roman Catholic Church, and that in at least one instance a Protestant church allowed Roman Catholics, bombed out of their own sanctuary, to use its buildings for early service.[244] Numerically the churches in Germany were weaker than in 1914. As an active force in German life, aware of the anti-Christian trend of life about them and in open opposition to it, they were undoubtedly more potent than in that year. In 1944 church attendance was increasing. Thousands, becoming aware of the emptiness of the Nazi ideology, were turning wistfully to Christianity. Effective church membership was probably stronger in 1944 than before the Nazi storm.[245]

In the lands overrun by the Germans in Western Europe, the churches constituted the chief centres of open opposition to the conquerors. They were not organizing nuclei of violent sabotage or insurrection. However, they became rallying points of popular intransigence and of spiritual and moral resistance. They protested the attempts of the invaders at regimentation and, not content with seeking to preserve their own existence and the national life, several of them through their official spokesmen risked the further wrath of the Nazi masters by denouncing the measures against the Jews.

The opposition in lands occupied by Germany was especially spectacular in Norway. When, in 1940, the Germans effected their conquest of Norway, they sought to set up a government which would co-operate with them and bring the land into conformity with the ideals of National Socialism. The Norwegian Church was in the forefront of opposition to this programme. The Germans wished, among other things, that the church would endorse the war against Russia as a crusade against atheistic Communism. A small minority of the pastors submitted, but the overwhelming majority of the clergy, led by their bishops and their primate, Eyvind Berggrav, were recalcitrant. Berggrav was imprisoned, but the church continued its opposition and in this had the support of the majority of the nation. It insisted upon being free from the Nazi state and protested against the Nazi attempt to monopolize the education of youth.[246]

---

[244] Arvid Fredborg in *Behind the Steel Wall*, summarized in *The Reader's Digest* (Jan., 1944), Vol. XLIV, p. 138: *International Christian Press and Information Service*, Jan., 1944.

[245] See the *Herald-Tribune* (New York), Jan. 2, 1944. *International Christian Press and Information Service*, May, 1944.

[246] Bjarne Höye and Trygve M. Ager, *The Fight of the Norwegian Church against Nazism* (New York, The Macmillan Company, 1943, pp. 180), *passim*; *The Spiritual Issues of the War*, No. 153.

Since Denmark had voluntarily admitted the Germans, it was not immediately treated as a conquered country. However, the Danish Church clearly sympathized with its sister Lutheran body in Norway. It, too, declined to endorse the German war with Russia. It experienced something of a revival, with fresh emphasis upon the teachings of Grundtvig, the clergyman in whom, in an earlier crisis, the nation had found a leader in its regeneration.[247]

In the Netherlands the Reformed churches awoke to a reinvigorated life under the adverse conditions brought by the German occupation. Their leaders denounced the anti-Jewish measures of the Nazis. Indeed, the Student Christian Movement voluntarily passed out of existence rather than consent to the exclusion from its membership of those of non-Aryan blood. Pastors continued public prayers for the exiled Queen. The churches resisted the Nazi attempts to de-Christianize society. In the parishes, too, there was increased lay activity in teaching the Bible and in winning others to a deeper Christian faith. All this was in spite of the imprisonment or confinement in concentration camps of some of the clerical organizers of the opposition.[248] The bishops and clergy of the Roman Catholics, although the latter were a minority of the population, boldly stood with the German bishops against the Nazi policy towards their church.[249] Jointly with the Protestants they publicly opposed the Nazi treatment of the Jews and the National Socialist conception of life and of the world.[250] Roman Catholic and Protestant churches also protested together the enforced deportation of Dutch labourers to Germany, the National Socialist education in so far as that interfered with freedom of teaching in Christian schools, the execution of hostages, and the harsh imprisonment of many men, including church officials.[251] Many Jews in the Netherlands joined the church, although this did not obtain for them better treatment by the Germans.[252] As a result of a nation-wide evangelistic campaign, church attendance increased among those not customarily of that habit. Parishes were mobilized in anticipation of their post-war responsibilities.[253]

In Belgium the Roman Catholic majority found a leader in their spiritual resistance in their primate, Van Roey. He forbade his clergy to give communion to those in German uniforms or to say masses for those killed as

[247] Van Dusen, op. cit., pp. 13-15. On Grundtvig see Vol. IV, p. 157.
[248] Keller, Christian Europe Today, pp. 98, 143, 174, 175; Van Dusen, op. cit., pp. 42-50; International Christian Press and Information Service, Information Series, No. 35.
[249] Van Dusen, op. cit., pp. 45, 46.
[250] The Spiritual Issues of the War, No. 179; The Christian News-Letter. No. 181.
[251] Ibid.
[252] International Christian Press and Information Service, Information Series, Jan., 1943.
[253] International Christian Press and Information Service, Information Series, Dec., 1943.

traitors to their country. He ordered the schools and universities of the church closed rather than have them taken over by the Nazi authorities.[254]

In France the two main Protestant churches had been reunited in 1939, on the eve of the war. The new body displayed a remarkable resilience in maintaining its congregations, clergy, and missions. Roman Catholics and Protestants came out boldly against the anti-Jewish policies of the regime which was co-operating with the Germans.[255] The French Protestant Federation publicly criticized the deportation of labourers.[256] Both French and foreign Christian organizations did much to alleviate the hard lot of Christian refugees in France.[257] The French Protestant Federation formed a committee to serve repatriated French Protestant prisoners of war.[258]

In Greece the Metropolitan of Athens protested, at the risk of his life, the German hostage system, with its disintegration of families and its attendant famine.[259]

In Serbia the Patriarch of the Orthodox Church opposed the Nazis, and while a church organization subservient to the Germans was set up, at least one of the bishops, deposed by the German regime, cast in his lot with anti-German guerillas.[260] A congress of the Orthodox Church urged the support by the clergy of the army of liberation.[261]

In Czechoslovakia the churches became centres of spiritual reinforcement of the hope of liberation from the German yoke.[262]

In some of the lands which co-operated with Germany the churches continued to show vigour. Thus in Hungary the leaders of the Reformed and Lutheran bodies, stimulated by a representative of the World Council of Churches, in July, 1943, formed an Ecumenical Council.[263] The churches were able to maintain their youth organizations and their missions to Jews: they conformed to neither the National Socialist youth programme nor anti-semitism.[264] Indeed, the Hungarian churches organized a committee to aid

[254] Van Dusen, *op. cit.*, pp. 17, 18.

[255] Van Dusen, *op. cit.*, pp. 19-24.

[256] *International Christian Press and Information Service*, No. 9, May, 1943.

[257] *War Conditions in the European Churches* (No. 10) (New York, Central Bureau for the Relief of the Evangelical Churches in Europe, Sept., 1942), p. 9.

[258] *International Christian Press and Information Service, Information Series*, No. 42, Nov., 1943.

[259] *International Christian Press and Information Service*, No. 12, June, 1943.

[260] Van Dusen, *op. cit.*, pp. 29, 30.

[261] *International Christian Press and Information Service, Information Series*, Jan., 1943.

[262] Van Dusen, *op. cit.*, p. 31.

[263] *World Council of Churches. Report on Activities during the Period July, 1942—July, 1043* (mimeographed).

[264] *International Christian Press and Information Service, Information Series*, Feb., 1943.

non-Aryan Christians who were suffering from racial discrimination.[265] At an inter-faith conference Roman Catholics and Protestants discussed Hungarian social problems.[266]

In the brief period in which the German arms surged forward into Russia, in parts of the occupied area there seemed to be something of a return to Christianity, especially by the older generation. In portions of the territory the Rumanian Church, taking advantage of the co-operation of the Rumanian armies with Germany, sent in a large staff of priests. Through them there were many baptisms, local congregations were provided with the physical equipment for worship, and a faculty of Orthodox theology was opened in Odessa.[267] Obviously, as the Russian armies regained the lost regions, this Rumanian effort, associated as it was with the endeavour to assimilate the population to Rumanian rule, proved ephemeral.

Among the Russians taken prisoners by the Finns there was a desire for the Christian sacraments, and at least one Finnish Lutheran pastor sought to meet the need.[268]

In Great Britain, so prominent in the spread of Protestant Christianity in the nineteenth and twentieth centuries, the second of the world wars brought grave difficulties to the churches. The churches entered the war with an effective hold upon only a minority of the population. It was said that not more than 5 to 10 per cent. of the population regularly attended church and that perhaps a quarter of the population went every three months. Of the potential Protestant church membership it was estimated that only 14 per cent. were communicants.[269] There were vast movements of population to new areas. These were partly because of the evacuation to avoid the aerial bombings, and partly because of the shifts due to war industries. Moreover, large numbers of the civilian population were so engrossed with activities connected with the war, even on Sundays, that they had little time for the Church. While some increase in church attendance was reported in some communities, in more localities church-going declined.[270] Many church buildings were destroyed by the enemy bombings. The future supply of clergy was threatened by the great reduction in the enrolment in theological colleges brought by the draft. There

[265] *International Christian Press and Information Service, Information Series,* Sept., 1943.
[266] *Ibid.*
[267] *International Christian Press and Information Service, Information Series,* No. 38, Nov., 1942.
[268] *Ibid.*
[269] Shillito in *The Christian Century,* Vol. LVIII, p. 665.
[270] *Christian News-Letter.* Supplement to No. 172.

was, too, the sag in morals which has been the normal accompaniment of war.[271]

Yet Christianity in Great Britain was giving evidence of marked vigour and the churches were grappling valiantly with the problems brought by the emergency. A few examples, drawn almost at random, will help to make vivid what a more detailed survey would merely elaborate. In 1942 the British Council of Churches came into being and drew into its co-operative fellowship the Church of England, the Church of Scotland, and most of the nonconformist churches.[272] In many cities and towns the Protestant churches co-operated in a united approach to the entire community in what was known as a Religion and Life Week.[273] Chaplains, deaconesses, and lay workers were assigned to care for labourers in war factories.[274] In Scotland numbers of churches and halls were erected to meet the needs of the migrants to new areas.[275] Through their primate, Cardinal Hinsley, Roman Catholics co-operated more with Protestants than they ever before had done in Great Britain.[276] They had, too, their Sword of the Spirit movement, a new development. Much assistance was given by Christian organizations to refugees from the continent.[277] Plans were made for better religious education of the youth through the schools. Funds were raised to erect new churches, partly to take the places of those destroyed by enemy action and partly to meet the needs of new communities.[278] Under the leadership of William Temple, Archbishop of York and then of Canterbury, the Christian forces endorsed plans for extensive social reconstruction which would ensure greater opportunity to the hitherto underprivileged masses.[279] British Christianity was very much alive.

The appraisal of the effect of Christianity upon Europe in the stormy decades which followed 1914 is peculiarly difficult. It is tantalizing, for it is of great importance yet defies accurate measurement. Was Christianity a declining or a growing factor in Europe after 1914? We cannot clearly know. Obviously it was being openly challenged as it had not been since the radical

[271] World Dominion, Vol. XXI, pp. 154-157.

[272] The Church in the World. The Bulletin of the British Council of Churches, New Series, No. 1, Nov., 1942.

[273] Ibid.

[274] Ibid.; The Spiritual Issues of the War, No. 174.

[275] International Christian Press and Information Service, Information Series, No. 12, March, 1943.

[276] International Christian Press and Information Service, No. 7, Apr., 1943.

[277] The International Review of Missions, Vol. XXVIII, p. 85.

[278] International Christian Press and Information Service, No. 19, May, 1941.

[279] The Spiritual Issues of the War, No. 152.

stages of the French Revolution and more widely than it had then been. Not
quite so obviously and yet certainly Christianity was a potent factor in post-
1914 Europe. Much of this must be apparent from what we have pointed out
earlier in this and the preceding two chapters. Christianity had influence upon
the moral ideals of Europe. Some would regard that as waning, the fading
remnant of an earlier formative participation. At times, too, official spokesmen
for Christianity seemed to be following the nationalistic tide rather than questioning or opposing it. Or they became ardent partisans of a cause to which
the attraction seems to have been the self-interest of an ecclesiastical organization. Thus the Italian clergy applauded the invasion of Ethiopia by Mussolini's
forces and Pope Pius XI supported the cause of Franco in Spain.[280]

In some respects, however, Christianity was making contributions to the
collective life of Europe which were fresh and not a carry-over from an earlier
age. As an impelling source of works of relief to mitigate the sufferings
brought by war and revolution it operated on a larger scale than ever before.
In its important and probably determinative share in bringing into being the
League of Nations it was at least partly responsible for the most ambitious
attempt ever implemented for the reduction of the frequency of war in Europe
and throughout the world and the placing of intercourse between nations on
the basis of law rather than of unregulated force. That the League of Nations
did not succeed in averting the second of the world wars of the period does
not make less impressive the daring of the attempt, nor does it prove it to have
been a complete failure. It is possible that the League will later be seen to
mark a significant step in man's successful endeavour to eliminate war. In the
Ecumenical Movement fissiparous Protestantism was being drawn together in
a fellowship which transcended national lines and reached out to the Orthodox
churches and in some aspects, still limited, to the Roman Catholics. The
Ecumenical Movement grew in the interval between the two world wars and
even during the throes of the second of these cataclysms. In a Europe which
was being torn apart by national and racial hatreds it was a force, feeble as
yet, but increasing, which was making for reconciliation. Through it Christians of the British Isles and of the United States were planning to assist their
fellow Christians of the continent of Europe, regardless of denomination, in
the spiritual and material rebuilding of their lands when once the storm of
war had passed. In an attempt to meet some of the urgent contemporary
issues, in the Universal Christian Council for Life and Work Protestantism

---

[280] See an excellent summary in Sherman S. Hayden, *Foreign Policy of the Vatican,*
in *Foreign Policy Reports* (New York, Foreign Policy Association), Vol. XIX, No. 21,
Jan. 15, 1944, pp. 281, 282.

had developed an agency, European in its initiative and in much of its leadership, which dealt courageously with social, economic, and political problems. Other movements, not so inclusive internationally, had sprung from British Christianity, and still others from the Roman Catholic Church, in an endeavour to bring Christian principles to bear upon the economic and political situation. Successive Popes in their appeals, among them a notable one at Christmas, 1943, sought to call Europe and mankind as a whole to the observance of Christian principles in international relations and made pronouncements on urgent social and economic problems. They could not but win a respectful hearing from many millions and have some influence, even though not determinative, upon the course of events. Christian churches, moreover, were the main centres of internal resistance to the totalitarian regimes which strove to impose non-Christian ideologies upon Europe. In other words, Christianity was displaying vitality in putting forth movements, some of them new, to meet the most pressing issues of the Europe of the day. It was seeking to deal with the problem of international anarchy, it was endeavouring to create a healing fellowship in the midst of a Europe and a world of hate, it was grappling with the economic and social problems which threatened the livelihood and well-being of underprivileged millions, and it was combatting systems of thought and of community and state which were counter to its basic convictions. In these efforts Christianity was by no means entirely successful. However, no other force was as potent in these respects throughout the length and breadth of Europe. Other factors might be more successful in limited areas in the achievement of some of these objectives. None other was making such headway in all of them in so much of the continent.

Moreover, as usual in its history, Christianity was bringing transformation of life to millions of individuals. In their faith countless Christians were finding, in varying degrees, moral empowerment and strength to meet triumphantly not only the ordinary vicissitudes of life but also the extraordinary ones which characterized the thrilling and terrifying age.

The impress upon Christianity of the environment of Europe in the post-1914 age was also profound. Here, too, we need simply to summarize what has been said more at length in the preceding pages of this volume.

One of the most obvious effects was to place Christians and the Church in more striking contrast with their environment than at any time since the official conversion of Europe. Christianity can never be completely at home in a world which does not and probably cannot ever fully conform to its standards. Yet through the mass accessions to the Church during the centuries of the formal conversion of Europe the tradition had been established that Christianity was the community religion of most of the continent. For centuries Europe was Christendom. In most European countries the overwhelming majority had been baptized and confirmed in the Church. Western European peoples, while never attaining to Christian ideals, had been profoundly influenced by them. In the eighteenth and nineteenth centuries a progressive open defection had begun. After 1914 it was greatly accentuated. Millions either ignored Christianity and the Church or frankly dissociated themselves from them. New ideologies, some of them avowedly anti-Christian, became popular. The Church and those intelligently loyal to it were, therefore, minorities. In some lands these minorities were persecuted and there was the saying that the Church had once more been driven into the catacombs. In other lands, such as Norway and the Netherlands, the Church became the rallying centre of national opposition to an alien invader. In still other countries, among them Great Britain and Ireland, Switzerland, Sweden, and Hungary, the Church and Christianity remained accepted parts of society, in some instances still officially connected with the state. Here it faced indifference on the part of a minority which in some lands was a majority, but not overt hostility. In general, however, because of the trends of the age, Christians were more nearly conscious than they had been for centuries of the contrast between the demands of their faith and the standards of the society about them. They were more aware of being in a world which was a contradiction of much which they held most precious. Some Christians gave over any thought of transforming the world but believed that their faith taught that the wheat and tares would grow together until God, by direct act, would bring the age to an end in destructive judgment and Christ would visibly return to set up his rule. Others, while perhaps realizing that human society could never fully attain Christian standards, still struggled to permeate all of civilization with Christian ideals and strove to bring mankind to a nearer approximation to them.

It was partly in consequence of the terrors of the times that some so despaired of man's reason and ability that they stressed the complete otherness of Christianity. Man by his searching, so it was held, could never find God. He was too corrupted by sin to do so. God must reveal himself and this he had done through Christ. This was not a new note in Christianity. It had been present even in the optimistic nineteenth century. Now, however, it became more prominent. What was known as the crisis or Barthian theology was obviously in some degree a product of the times, the result of the struggle of earnest souls with the spiritual and moral problems presented by Europe's agony.

So, too, the attempts to combine Christianity with nationalism and racialism which gave rise to the German Christian movement were in large degree an outgrowth of the environment. The endeavour of many Germans to achieve a new birth of their nation after the humiliation of 1918 and the sufferings which followed defeat coalesced with currents which had been present before 1914 to produce faiths which either sought to conjoin some elements of historic Christianity with the German spirit or were frankly and entirely German and pagan.

Still another effect of the environment was to enrich the faith and experience of many. The intense sufferings of these decades, particularly the years of the second of the world wars, drove thousands to delve deeply into the resources of Christianity. As the familiar world dissolved about them and as ruthless power and stark cruelty operating on a gigantic scale seemed to mock the individual and all the values which the Christian faith had placed upon human personality, some were constrained to enter more fully and with larger insight into a faith which had as its symbol a cross, but a cross succeeded by the resurrection and a new and infinitely enriched and enlarged life. Because there was in the Christian Gospel that which responded and more than responded to their deep need, there followed, among a choice minority, a revival of Christianity such as had not been known on the continent in the comparatively easygoing nineteenth century.

It is not easy to summarize briefly and successfully the course of Christianity in Europe in the three decades after 1914.

In the thirty years which followed 1914 most of Europe was shaken to its foundations. Sweeping revolutions and two world wars which had their centres in Europe destroyed much of the familiar fabric, not only of the nineteenth century but also of a millennium. In this destruction Christianity, which had been woven so closely into the warp and woof of European life, could not hope to survive unscathed. It was in danger of being cast into the discard with remnants of an age which had now passed. Numerically and in organized strength Christianity suffered sorely. In some lands, such as Russia and Germany, the churches lost in numbers and physical equipment. In several other lands, such as Great Britain and Ireland, Sweden, Switzerland, Italy, and Hungary, the losses were not so marked. Yet in no country did Christianity entirely escape the trials of the time. Some of the new ideologies, powerfully supported by great states, more or less openly challenged Christianity. In every land the secularism and the growth of the state which were among the features of the age were a menace. The one seemed to make Christianity irrelevant and would by-pass it when it did not openly attack it. The other would seek the complete control of youth and of the life of the community in disregard of the claims of the Church. All branches of the Church were affected. The Eastern Orthodox Churches were especially hard hit. More than in 1914 Christianity was represented in 1945 by Protestantism and the Roman Catholic Church.

In some respects, however, Christianity was stronger in 1945 than it had been in 1914 and was more of a force in the life of Europe. In no land had it been blotted out. The ideas which, clothing themselves in social and political systems, had seemed its most threatening enemies were to some degree an outgrowth from it and were partial if tragically garbled attempts to obtain for the rank and file of mankind the opportunity and the dignity which the Christian Gospel had been inculcating for more than a thousand years. It was no accident that Communism and National Socialism arose within Christendom rather than in India, in the Moslem East, or in China. Christianity gave birth to the most valiant attempts which mankind had ever known to rid the world of war and to the most extensive endeavours in history to alleviate the sufferings brought by war. In the Ecumenical Movement Protestantism was beginning to transcend national and confessional barriers to form a bond of unity in what appeared to be a hopelessly divided Europe. Christianity stimulated programmes for the elimination of poverty and the giving to all men opportunity for education, livelihood, and a secure old age. In Germany and in lands occupied by Germany in the second of the world wars the churches were the main nuclei of spiritual resistance to the dominant Nazi power. Urged on by the tragedies of the time and by its faith, the Christian mind formulated fresh statements of theology. Moreover, and more important still, thousands were discovering in Christianity the resources to meet the untold sufferings of the era and were finding strength not only to help them to endure but also to minister to the needs of others. Now, as in all the centuries since Jesus of Nazareth, there were Christians who because of their faith were the light of the world and the salt of the earth.

Chapter V

THE UNITED STATES OF AMERICA

THE CHANGING SCENE: THE IMMIGRANTS: THE INDIANS:
THE NEGROES: SHIFTING POPULATIONS AND NEW SOCIAL
CONDITIONS: EFFECT ON THE ENVIRONMENT: EFFECT
OF THE ENVIRONMENT

THE United States of America was much less affected by the changes that
followed 1914 than was Europe. It by no means escaped them. It was a
participant in both world wars. Some of the economic forces which moulded
Europe were felt within its borders. Indeed, it was the centre in which in 1929
what proved to be a world-wide financial crisis first broke and from which
it spread. Its government assumed greatly enhanced functions. Industrialization
proceeded apace and with it the growth of cities. There were vast shifts in
population, some of them due to industrialization, some in consequence of
an extensive drought in the west central states in the 1930's, and others because
of the war industries of the second world conflict. The new intellectual currents
of the time were also felt within its borders. Both Communism and National
Socialism, especially the former, had their sympathizers. Yet the pre-1914 structure of life continued with much less revolutionary alteration than in Europe.
The new age brought no such sharp break as in some European lands. Indeed,
the changes were not as revolutionary as they were in the British Isles.

One aspect of the era made developments in the United States of larger im-
port than they had been in the nineteenth century: the United States was much
more prominent in world affairs than previously. This was partly because of
the growing wealth and population of the country. It was also because of the
impoverishment of Europe through war and revolution. The United States
rather than England was becoming the main financial centre of the globe. In
military, naval, and air power the United States was more potent in the second
of the world wars than it had been before. It was increasingly a major factor
in the international scene.

The prominence of the United States was also in the realm of religion.
The United States had a growing share in both the Protestant and Roman

Catholic forms of Christianity and even in the Eastern churches, small minorities though they were in that land. It loomed more largely in the financing and personnel of both Protestant and Roman Catholic missions in non-Occidental countries and it provided a mounting proportion of administrative leadership in world-wide Protestantism. Most of the creative theological thought was still in Europe, but several American Protestant scholars were taken seriously on the other side of the Atlantic, a fairly novel phenomenon.

Some problems which had been outstanding in the expansion of Christianity in the United States before 1914 receded after that year. The Western frontier had practically faded out before 1914, although here and there the older frontier conditions persisted in small and usually isolated pockets. These were in the mountains in the South and in mining and lumber camps and cattle ranches in the West. The flood of immigration had dwindled to a trickle. The first of the world wars of the period cut it off from Europe. When that conflict had passed, legislation reduced the numbers admitted to a small fraction of their former dimensions. The immigrants who had arrived before 1914 constituted, together with their children, a continuing problem, but that was waning. The upheavals in Europe, that in Russia after the first world war and especially those which were brought by National Socialism in the 1930's and 1940's, particularly the anti-Semitic measures of the Nazis and their sympathizers, presented the United States and American Christians with perplexities of admitting and caring for refugees. The treatment of Japanese, especially in the second world war, confronted the churches with acute issues. However, in numbers none of these immigrant groups approached in magnitude those which had swarmed across the seas in the century preceding 1914. The Indians were still present, but with the growth of the white population they more and more receded from public attention and were small although not necessarily fading minorities. The Negroes continued numerous and of major importance. To them the churches devoted much attention. Very serious from the standpoint of Christianity were the great migrations within the country. These were of several kinds. There was the drift towards the cities, a movement which had been in progress before 1914 but which assumed enlarging proportions with the growth of manufactures and the increasing application of machinery to agriculture. The automobile brought marked changes to rural life, to small towns, and to the cities. It led to movements of populations, some of them to the suburbs and to towns on the edges of cities and some away from earlier villages. There were extensive migrations of Negroes to Northern cities. Tens of thousands of farmers moved from the "dust bowl," the lands of marginal rainfall in the West, to communities of presumably greater economic opportunity. Poverty-stricken and transient, they tended to lose whatever church connexions they might once have had. The second of the world wars affected the United States much more than the first. The millions of men and women in the armed services and distributed over a large proportion of the earth's surface presented a problem to the organized Christian forces. Millions more moved into towns and cities in which industries that supplied munitions, aircraft, and ships were developed. A large proportion of them were without church affiliations in their new communities. Added to these migrations were the problems brought by the changing climate of opinion. The "movies" and the radio affected all but very small minorities and helped to mould attitudes and convictions. The scientific frame of mind was widespread and while only superficially understood by the majority, it directly or indirectly shaped the thinking of almost every one. The family progressively disintegrated. Of the decay in this basic social institution the mounting divorce rate was both a symptom and a cause. In consequence, the family, which could formerly be counted upon as a major means of religious instruction, more and more abdicated that function. Life in the United States was not as spectacularly revolutionized as was that in Europe, but it was being profoundly altered.[1]

Protestants and Roman Catholics still addressed themselves to the task of spreading their faith and serving the community. For instance, in the fore part of the 1930's Protestants were spending about $27,500,000 a year on what they called home missions. In this connexion they had nearly 30,000 different enterprises with a staff of over 22,000. Most of this effort was concentrated in the South and the far West.[2] There was a growing feeling that it needed redistribution and that too much of it contributed to competing churches in small communities and to assisting congregations which were not making a reasonable attempt to attain self support.[3] However, there was no thought of discontinuing home missions, but merely of altering the emphases. The churches were gaining numerically. What may be called the mass conversion of the country which had been in progress during the nineteenth century was still going on. The percentage of the population having church membership, which was said to be 6.9 per cent. in 1800, 15.5 per cent. in 1850, and 43.5 per cent. in 1910,[4] was reported to be a little over 50 per cent. in 1941-1942.[5] Whether

---

[1] For pictures of one American city, objective in purpose although slightly anti-religious in bias, see Lynd, *Middletown, passim,* especially pp. 321-403, and Lynd, *Middletown in Transition,* pp. 29 ff.

[2] Morse, *Home Missions Today and Tomorrow,* pp. 12, 22.

[3] Morse, *op. cit.,* p. 239.

[4] Vol. IV, p. 385.

[5] The membership of religious bodies in 1941-1942 was said to be 68,501,186.— *Information Service,* Jan. 1, 1944. The census of 1940 gave the total population of the United States as 131,669,275.

that meant an enhanced permeation of the life of the United States by Christianity could be debated. There were indications that the increasing proportion of church membership was paralleled by a growing religious illiteracy among a majority of those owning to this connexion. As church membership became more and more a social convention, an accepted feature of American life, its distinctive significance tended to decline. That is what had happened earlier in other lands: presumably the United States was no exception. Yet by 1945 there were indications that for a growing minority the Christian faith was more intelligently held and given a more thoroughgoing commitment than had been true two decades earlier.

In general, after 1914 the denominational complexion of Christianity in the United States was about as it had been before that year. No new major religious bodies appeared on the scene, either by indigenous development or by importation. The relative strength of the various denominations experienced alterations. Co-operation mounted. Here and there the sharp lines of distinction between the various divisions of Christians were more blurred than earlier. In a few instances they were accentuated. The environment increasingly placed its impress upon what had come from the Old World.

We must now go somewhat more in detail into the story thus briefly outlined. Even so we can give only a few glimpses of what a full picture would reveal and round out slightly the bare outlines sketched in this introductory preview.

While the frontier had passed, it still left traces of its presence in the extent to which the population had church connexions. In the older states the proportion of church membership was higher than in the newer states, and it became progressively smaller from east to west. In 1926 it was 62 and 63 per cent. on the Atlantic seaboard, 51 and 52 per cent. in the central states, 44 per cent. in the Rocky Mountain states, and 35 per cent. on the Pacific Coast.[6] There was some variation from state to state,[7] but in general it was states which had most recently been the frontier and in which frontier conditions most nearly persisted which had the smallest proportion of adult church membership. The churches had been strikingly successful in dealing with the frontier, but they had not entirely caught up with it. Although the frontier, properly socalled, had all but disappeared, there was still a westward movement of population and the churches were not fully keeping pace with it.[8]

[6] Fry, *The United States Looks at Its Churches,* p. 10.
[7] Fry, *op. cit.,* p. 13.
[8] Kolb and Brunner, *A Study of Rural Society,* p. 468.

The reduction of the stream of immigration from Europe brought profound alterations to the Rome Catholic Church in the United States. For a century or more and particularly for the past two generations the chief problem of the Roman Catholic Church had been to hold to the faith the millions of immigrants who were traditionally of its constituency, to provide them with spiritual care, and to knit them into a national structure which would be at once a part of the life of the United States and an organic member of the world-wide Roman Catholic fellowship. For this purpose it had erected thousands of churches, had developed a great system of schools, and had trained a large body of clergy. It had done this with some help from Europe but chiefly through the support of the immigrants and their children who out of their poverty had given to the perpetuation of their church. The achievement had been among the most striking in the history of Christianity.[9]

The dwindling immigration meant that the Roman Catholic Church was able to catch up with its task. An immediate consequence was that it loomed larger in the American scene. Its constituency had now been long enough in the United States to have shared in the prosperity of that land. The wealth both of the constituency and of the church increased. Additional buildings for churches and schools were erected and in progressively better architectural style.[10] Roman Catholic colleges and universities had a growing part in the higher education of the nation. The bishops and clergy became more prominent in their respective communities and were not so palpably foreign. From being an alien intrusion into a land predominantly Protestant in background, the Roman Catholic Church became more and more an integral element of the country's life. In proportion to their membership Roman Catholics still ranked far behind the major Protestant denominations, even those of such proletarian constituency as the Methodists, in the number of outstanding individuals in the various phases of the nation's activities.[11] In the emotional stress which accompanied and followed the first world war there was a recrudescence of the anti-Roman Catholic feeling which had been very marked in the second half of the preceding century, and a Democratic candidate for the Presidency, Alfred E. Smith, was defeated (1928) in part because he was of that church. The fact that he could be nominated, however, was an indication that those of his faith were being accepted as they had not been before.

The sharp decline in immigration meant that the main source of growth of

[9] Vol. IV, pp. 229 ff.

[10] See a picture of this rapid growth in the life of Mundelein, who became Archbishop of the Chicago area in 1916, in Martin, *The First Cardinal of the West, passim,* especially pp. 66, 72.

[11] Moore, *Will America Become Catholic?,* pp. 216-236.

the Roman Catholic Church was now cut off. There were some converts from non-Catholics. Roman Catholic forces expended a good deal of energy in endeavouring to win them. Through the Paulist Fathers, the Catholic Unity League, the National Converts League, the Catholic Missionary Union, the League for Prayer for the Conversion of America, the Friars of the Atonement, by contacts through their numerous hospitals and schools, and by other measures Roman Catholics were striving to bring into their fold their "separated brethren" and the frankly non-Christian. Through the marriage of Roman Catholics to non-Roman Catholics some of the latter became converts. Yet, according to official figures, in 1928 the number of accessions from outside the fold was only about 40,000.[12] These were probably about offset, and perhaps more than offset, by losses to Protestantism, to schism, and to religious indifferentism. The leakage was said to be one of the major problems of the church in the United States.[13] Some members slipped away through marriage outside the church. There were group defections. We have already noted one of the latter, the Polish National Catholic Church of America (1904).[14] Although in 1923 or 1924 the Holy See gave the Ruthenian Uniates in the United States a bishop of their own,[15] this did not prevent the secession of several congregations, who among other grievances resented the efforts to enforce celibacy upon a clergy to whom marriage had hitherto been permitted. The Ukrainian Orthodox Church of America was the result.[16] Moreover, Protestant missions to Roman Catholic immigrants brought about the formation of numbers of Italian and Spanish Protestant congregations.[17] Many former Roman Catholics joined existing Protestant congregations which did not have a special racial or national complexion. Because it had been recruited chiefly from immigrants who had come as labourers in the rapidly growing mines and industries, in the United States the Roman Catholic Church was predominantly urban.[18] That meant a declining birth rate. In spite of the numbers of children born to the first generation of immigrants and the hostility of the ecclesiastical officials to artificial measures for birth control, by the second and third generations the average size of families dwindled sharply. Among the Irish, who had settled more extensively in the cities than had the Germans and who, with the Germans, had been the earliest large stream of Roman Catholic immigration

[12] Moore, *op. cit.*, pp. 154-184. See also O'Brein, *The Priesthood in a Changing World,* p. 96, which declares that in 1927 the number of converts was about 35,000.
[13] O'Brien, *op. cit.*, p. 177.
[14] Vol. IV, p. 254.
[15] Attwater, *The Catholic Eastern Churches,* p. 94.
[16] Halich, *Ukrainians in the United States,* p. 103.
[17] Moore, *op. cit.*, pp. 137-153.
[18] Moore, *op. cit.*, pp. 61, 62, 70, 71.

and had provided a substantial part of the leadership of the church, this tendency was particularly marked.[19]

The drying up of immigration, the failure of accessions to overbalance leakages, and the decline of the birth rate might be ominous for the far future, but for the time being the Roman Catholic Church was gaining in position. Moreover, American Roman Catholics were more and more prominent in the world-wide work of their church. After the first of the world wars they became the chief source of the revenues of the Holy See.[20] They were having a rapidly growing part in providing personnel and funds for the missions of their church in non-Occidental lands. Not only did the indigenous Catholic Foreign Mission Society of America, which came into being in 1911, have a phenomenal expansion,[21] but orders of European origin through their American provinces also strengthened the staffs and finances of their missions in Asia and Africa and either bolstered or augmented enterprises previously dependent upon a now impoverished and distraught Europe or began new ones. What in 1914 had still been an immigrant church straining every nerve to hold and assimilate the flood of newcomers, unprecedented in size in human history, was now becoming a normal part of the American scene and was beginning to take an outstanding share in the life of its world-wide communion.

Here and there were modifications in the racial composition of the immigrant problem which confronted the Roman Catholic Church. Many Italians, nominally Roman Catholic, had been lukewarm towards the church. This was said to be in part because of the anti-clericalism of Italian nationalism. The concordat between Mussolini and the Pope of which we spoke in the preceding chapter is said to have been followed by a greater cordiality of Italian Americans towards the church.[22] The large Mexican immigration in the South-west was usually from regions where the church was strong, but much of it in the new environment tended to become indifferent or to go over to Protestantism.[23]

The dwindling of the immigrant tide did not mean that the Protestant forces quickly turned to other problems. After 1914 there were millions of first generation immigrants. They and their children presented a situation which the Protestant churches could not ignore. Those traditionally Protestant were

---

[19] Moore, *op. cit.*, pp. 121-136.

[20] Binchy, *Church and State in Fascist Italy*, p. 308.

[21] George C. Powers, *The Maryknoll Movement* (Maryknoll, The Catholic Foreign Mission Society of America, 1926, pp. xix, 167), *passim*.

[22] Abel, *Protestant Home Missions and Catholic Immigrants*, p. 48.

[23] Gamio, *Mexican Immigration to the United States*, p. 116.

largely served by denominations with which the immigrant had been affiliated in the mother country. The latter were centres of community life, especially for the first generation, partly because they were the institutions which most reminded them of their native lands. They succeeded, too, in holding many of the second and third generations.[24] The Protestant denominations which were primarily those of the older American stock of British antecedents put forth extensive efforts for the immigrants from the continent of Europe, whether Roman Catholic, Protestant, or Orthodox. In these Northern Presbyterians, Northern Baptists, and Northern Methodists were the most prominent.[25] In general their programmes for them were two-fold. By various means, including community centres, they sought to serve them in social and educational ways and to further their assimilation to American life. In this they were fairly successful.[26] They also endeavoured to win them to church membership in their respective church bodies. For them they brought into existence special congregations for particular nationalities—among them Slavs, Italians, Magyars, and Spanish-Americans. In this their numerical progress was relatively slight. In the 1930's it was reported that in the special churches for immigrants there were less than 60,000 converts from Roman Catholicism.[27] In rural districts English-using Protestant churches set up especially for the immigrants by bodies of Anglo-Saxon provenance were said to have much less success than those bodies identified with the national background of the immigrants.[28] There were many more accessions from second and third generation descendants of immigrants who in the process of assimilation joined Protestant congregations which were not specifically for immigrants but which were predominantly of the older American stock.

After 1914 large numbers of Mexicans came as labourers to the South-west. By 1926 these numbered not far from 900,000. Most of them were uneducated and poverty-stricken and many were migratory, going back and forth across the border at frequent intervals.[29] In Texas the Apostolic Faith, with its highly emotional appeal and its recourse to prayer for physical healing, made some headway.[30] Several of the major Protestant denominations also had missions among them.[31] Schools and social centres were inaugurated. Here and there

---

[24] Vol. IV, pp. 261 ff.; Brunner, *Immigrant Farmers and their Children*, pp. 121-124.
[25] Abel, *op. cit.*, p. ix.
[26] Abel, *op. cit.*, pp. 79, 81.
[27] Abel, *op. cit.*, pp. 33-39.
[28] Brunner, *op. cit.*, pp. 116 ff.
[29] Gamio, *op. cit.*, p. 229.
[30] Gamio, *op. cit.*, p. 223.
[31] *Survey of Service, Disciples of Christ*, pp. 120-130.

flourishing congregations arose, but the percentage of Mexicans who became Protestants was negligible.[32]

The Jews were a challenge. Their numbers were rapidly growing. They are said to have increased from a little less than three millions in 1914 to nearly four and a quarter millions in 1927. The total was augmented by refugees from the European anti-Semitism of the 1930's and 1940's. A few Protestant denominations put forth special efforts to reach them, but these were never on a large scale. Most of the Protestant missions to the Jews were small, professedly undenominational, staunchly conservative, usually operating in special halls. They made little appeal to the highly educated Jews and won relatively few converts.[33] There were scores of cities where not even this kind of effort was made. In the meantime thousands of Jews had joined the Church of Christ Scientist. Why Christian Science attracted them is not entirely clear. It was said that it was because they were not required by it to subscribe to the divinity of Christ, because they found no racial discrimination in the Christian Science churches, and because many were chronically in a state of alarm about their health.[34]

Japanese constituted a peculiar problem. They were not numerous. In continental United States they did not exceed 100,000. In Hawaii in 1920 they numbered 132,000 and were slightly more than half the population. Elsewhere they were a small minority. However, fear that they might swamp the West Coast and their competition in some types of agriculture and horticulture led to state legislation against them, especially in California. In 1942, after the Japanese attack on the United States at Pearl Harbour and Manila in the preceding December, the large majority of those in the continental United States, whether born in Japan or in the United States, were taken from their homes and placed in special camps. Only gradually were some of them allowed to resume participation in the normal life of the nation.

Protestants had more missions among the Japanese than among any other of the immigrants from the Far East.[35] Several church groups in California, the Home Missions Council, the Federal Council of Churches, and a number of other Protestant organizations opposed the discriminatory legislation by the Federal Government which in 1924 abrogated the Gentlemen's Agreement

[32] Jay S. Stowell, *A Study of Mexicans and Spanish Americans in the United States* (New York, Home Missions Council and the Council of Women for Home Missions, 1920, pp. 78), *passim*.

[33] C. H. Fahs, *A Study of Jewish Experience in Relation to Christianity and the Church* (in preparation for a conference on the Christian approach to the Jews held by the International Missionary Council, 1931, pp. 61, 102), *passim*.

[34] Conversation with an expert on missions to the Jews, June, 1932.

[35] Morse, *Home Missions Today and Tomorrow*, p. 157.

by which Japanese immigration had been regulated for more than a decade.[36] When, in 1942, the Japanese were placed in what were known euphemistically as relocation centres, the Protestant churches ministered to them and in a variety of ways sought to alleviate their lot. There were numbers of baptisms among them.[37]

The Eastern churches were not greatly helped by immigration and continued to have a minority role in American life. Not many of the Armenians who were driven out of their homes by the Turks during the first of the world wars were able to make their way to the United States.[38] Accordingly the numbers of the ancient Gregorian Church (or Church of Armenia) were not markedly swelled. Indeed, they seemed to have suffered a decline.[39] The dissensions in the Russian Orthodox Church in the mother country were in part reflected in the branches of that body in the United States. There was division between those sympathetic with Communism and those not sympathetic. The latter constituted a majority. Ecclesiastically they became fully independent of the church in Russia.[40] Following 1914 various national groups from the Balkans, formerly under the structure of the Russian Orthodox Church in the United States, set up separate Orthodox bodies in this country. Some of these retained an ecclesiastical connexion with the corresponding church in Europe. Others were fully autonomous. The new ones were the Albanian Orthodox Church; the Bulgarian Orthodox Church, after 1922 under the Bulgarian Orthodox Mission to America and Canada, which in turn was under the state synod of Bulgaria; the Greek Orthodox Church (Hellenic), organized in 1922 under authority of the Ecumenical Patriarch of Constantinople, but troubled by the question of the connexion with the church in Greece; the Rumanian Orthodox Church, soon after 1914 staffed by priests from Rumania and under the archbishop of that country, but after 1929 organizationally autonomous; the Serbian Orthodox Church, under a diocese inaugurated in 1921; and the Ukrainian Orthodox Church, with a bishopric formed in 1931-1932. There were also some small bodies formed after 1914 which under one title or another

---

[36] Eleanor Tupper and George E. McReynolds, *Japan in American Public Opinion* (New York, The Macmillan Company, 1937, pp. xiii, 465), p. 194.

[37] C. W. Iglehart, *Japanese-American Resettlement* (New York, Foreign Missions Conference, Committee on East Asia, May 6, 1943, mimeographed), *passim*; S. E. Evans, *Board of Missions and Church Extension of the Methodist Church,* mimeographed, no date.

[38] M. Vartan Malcom, *The Armenians in America* (Boston, the Pilgrim Press, 1919, pp. xxvi, 142), p. 65.

[39] Department of Commerce, Bureau of the Census, *Religious Bodies,* 1936, Vol. II, p. 378.

[40] Department of Commerce, Bureau of the Census, *op. cit.,* Vol. II, p. 590; Emhardt, *Religion in Soviet Russia,* pp. 195 ff.

took the Orthodox name.[41] However, the movement was not entirely fissiparous. In the 1940's a federation of orthodox churches was formed which included the Syrian, Russian, Serbian, Ukrainian, Carpatho-Russian, and Rumanian churches in America.[42]

With the emergence of other problems of greater numerical magnitude, after 1914 the Indian did not occupy so large a place in the consciousness of the whites of the United States as he had during the eighteenth and much of the nineteenth century. The 360,000 who in the 1940's were counted as Indians were an inconsiderable minority of the population. Only in limited areas, in Oklahoma and on reservations in various other states, were they prominent.

To the winning of the Indians to the Christian faith and to attempts to serve them through schools, hospitals, and other social agencies, the churches had devoted much effort. As a result, in 1914 between a third and a half of the Indians were either professed Christians or were under Christian influence.[43] About half of these were Protestants and about half Roman Catholics.

In the three decades which followed 1914 both Protestants and Roman Catholics continued to devote attention to the Indians, and that in spite of the fact that the latter were now much more on the periphery of the interest of the missionary forces of the country than they had once been. Protestants spent more per capita on the Indians than they did on any other racial group.[44]

In some respects the conditions under which Christian missions to the Indians operated became more difficult as the years proceeded. In 1933 the programme for the Indians followed by the United States Government was radically altered. For decades the efforts of the administration had largely been directed towards the assimilation of the Indians to the culture of the whites. Now the policy was adopted of preserving as much of Indian culture as possible and encouraging the maintenance of tribal unity and organization.[45] The bouleversement brought embarrassment to the missionaries. This was partly because by encouraging Indian culture the new programme seemed to reinforce the indigenous Indian religions and to discourage conversion to Christianity.[46]

[41] Department of Commerce, Bureau of the Census, op. cit., Vol. II, pp. 553 ff. On the Rumanian Orthodox Church see also Christian Avghi Galitzi, A Study of Assimilation among the Roumanians in the United States (New York, Columbia University Press, 1929, pp. 282), pp. 95-98.

[42] International Christian Press and Information Service, April, 1944.

[43] Vol. IV, pp. 299-324.

[44] Morse, op. cit., pp. 23-25.

[45] J. Collier in Loram and McIlwraith, The North American Indian Today, pp. 140-151.

[46] The Navajo Indian Problem, pp. 107-110.

There were also chronic difficulties which had been present before as well as after 1914. Among these were the many tribal units, some of them small, their scattered habitats, and the multiplicity of languages. Another was found in the large numbers of Protestant denominations, frequently more than one of them within one tribe, and the differing policies of the denominations.[47] Among Protestants, with a few notable exceptions, the missionaries were said to be narrow-minded, bigoted, and ill-prepared to deal with the difficulties presented by the situation.[48] Protestants, moreover, had largely failed to raise up an adequate Indian leadership.[49]

In spite of obstacles and deficiencies, progress was being recorded. By 1939, approximately 200,000, or nearly three-fifths, of the Indians were said to be Christians, about half of them Protestants and about half Roman Catholics.[50] There was some co-operative action by Protestants, partly through the Joint Indian Committee of the Home Missions Council and the Council of Women for Home Missions.[51] Some Protestant missions confined their activities to an emotional appeal for conversion and to purely religious instruction and worship,[52] but others sought to minister as well to the Indians' physical needs through hospitals, wholesome recreation, the marketing of Indian products, and assistance in obtaining water for irrigation.[53] In 1939 Roman Catholics were active on about 81 reservations, maintained 408 chapels, had about 150 priests giving full time and at least 75 more giving part time to Indians, and had as well 527 nuns, 85 brothers, 38 lay teachers, and 169 Indian catechists.[54] Some of the missionaries were aiding their parishioners in obtaining land and marketing produce.[55] In spite of the greatly enhanced financial resources made available by the Federal Government for its schools and the falling off of mission funds because of the financial depression which began in 1929, both Protestants and Roman Catholics continued to maintain educational institutions for Indians. The proportion of professed Christians among the Indians was growing and was not far from that which was found in the white population.

The Negroes continued to be an important element in the population and to present a conundrum to themselves and to the nation as a whole which the

---

[47] *The Navajo Indian Problem*, pp. 94-102.
[48] M. A. Dawber in Loram and McIlwraith, *op. cit.,* p. 101.
[49] M. A. Dawber in Loram and McIlwraith, *op. cit.,* pp. 102, 103.
[50] M. A. Dawber in Loram and McIlwraith, *op. cit.,* p. 98.
[51] Meriam and Hinman, *Facing the Future in Indian Missions*, pp. 173, 174.
[52] *The Navajo Indian Problem*, p. 105.
[53] Meriam and Hinman, *op. cit.,* pp. 105, 169.
[54] J. B. Tennelly in Loram and McIlwraith, *op. cit.,* pp. 87, 88.
[55] Meriam and Hinman, *op. cit.,* p. 105.

churches could not and did not ignore. Although their gross number had increased from 9,827,763 in 1910 to 12,865,518 in 1940, in 1940 they were a slightly smaller proportion of the total population than in 1910, 9.8 per cent. in the later as against 10.7 per cent. in the earlier year. Their death rate, although in the 1930's almost half again as large as that of the whites, was declining, and their general position, economic and educational, while low, was improving.[56] They were moving from the farms to the cities. While they still were more numerous in the rural than in the urban sections, in both South and North the percentage on the farms was declining and that in the cities was increasing.[57] They were also migrating from the South to the North and from the old South to the South-west. Some of the states in the Old South, such as Virginia, Georgia, and South Carolina, actually showed a decrease in their Negro population.[58] The northward movement was from a number of factors, among them the increased demand for labour due to the drying up of the stream which had come from Europe, the blow dealt to cotton, the chief crop of the Negro farmer, by the boll weevil, and the greater discrimination against the Negro in the South than in the North.[59] This was in spite of the fact that in the South the per capita expenditure for the education of Negro children had increased proportionately more rapidly than for white children.[60]

The major effort by Christians for the Negroes continued to be by Protestants. This was by both white and Negro churches. In 1932 white Protestant denominations spent more than $2,000,000 on Negroes, or more than double the amount which they expended on any other one group of the population, and by means of it supported a staff of more than 3,000. Of the latter nearly half were teachers, for it was through schools that the white churches continued to give the larger part of their assistance, about two-fifths were pastors, and a small sprinkling were physicians, nurses, and community workers.[61] Church co-operation across racial lines was still limited.[62] Not far from 1930 about 644,000 Negroes were members of denominations which were predominantly white,[63] but most of these were in Negro congregations. In the Northern cities Negroes usually moved into sections which the whites were

[56] Morse, *Home Missions Today and Tomorrow,* pp. 162-164.
[57] T. J. Woofter, Jr., *Negro Problems in Cities* (Garden City, Doubleday, Doran & Company, 1928, pp. 284), pp. 26 ff.
[58] Morse, *op. cit.,* pp. 162-164.
[59] Mays and Nicholson, *The Negro's Church,* pp. 94 ff.
[60] Morse, *op. cit.,* p. 166.
[61] Morse, *op. cit.,* p. 170.
[62] Mays and Nicholson, *op. cit.,* p. 158.
[63] Work, *Negro Year Book, 1931-1932,* p. 261.

abandoning and often bought church buildings which had once served whites. This sometimes led to tension, for the Negroes were inclined to believe that their white creditors were too harsh and the white churches regarded the Negroes as financially undependable and faithless to their obligations.[64]

By far the largest part of the burden of maintaining churches among the Negroes and of reaching the unchurched was carried by the Negroes themselves. Early in the 1930's Negro churches spent $350,000 a year on home missions and maintained over 200 home missionaries and assisted about 350 churches.[65] In addition and chiefly, they financed their own congregations and ministry. Nine out of ten of their churches were reported to be self-supporting.[66] It was said that nearly three-fourths of the Negro churches were in debt[67] and that the Negroes were trying to carry on more churches than they could maintain in a healthy condition.[68] Yet they were managing to keep them going. The urban congregations were larger[69] and had better trained clergy[70] than the rural churches. Only about a fifth of the clergy were college graduates.[71] Revivals and protracted meetings, long prominent in Negro church life, particularly as a means of winning non-Christians, made less appeal than formerly.[72] In this the experience of the Negro was paralleling that of the white churches. More than two-thirds of the Negro church members were Baptists and not quite one-fourth were Methodists.[73] In 1926 73 per cent. of the Negro women and only 46 per cent. of the Negro men were church members. The disparity between the sexes was greater than among the white churches, for 62 per cent. of the white women and 49 per cent. of the white males were members of churches.[74] The proportion of the Negro population in the churches was slightly larger than that among the whites. One set of figures seemed to indicate that the Negro churches held their student and professional classes somewhat more effectively than they did the race as a whole.[75] As before 1914, the Negro churches constituted an important phase of Negro life. They provided an opportunity for members of different social strata to

[64] Mays and Nicholson, *op. cit.,* pp. 181-183.
[65] Work, *op. cit.,* p. 258.
[66] Mays and Nicholson, *op. cit.,* pp. 192, 280.
[67] Mays and Nicholson, *op. cit.,* p. 278.
[68] Mays and Nicholson, *op. cit.,* p. 225.
[69] Mays and Nicholson, *op. cit.,* pp. 15-17.
[70] Mays and Nicholson, *op. cit.,* pp. 249-251.
[71] Mays and Nicholson, *op. cit.,* pp. 15-17.
[72] Mays and Nicholson, *op. cit.,* p. 253.
[73] Department of Commerce, Bureau of the Census, *Religious Bodies,* 1936, Vol. I, p. 851.
[74] Fry, *The U. S. Looks at Its Churches,* p. 8.
[75] Mays and Nicholson, *op. cit.,* p. 287.

mingle.[76] They were a medium of the advertisement of Negro business.[77] While the sermons were said on the whole to emphasize other-worldly themes rather than to deal with such social problems as juvenile delinquency,[78] the clergy did much to encourage the members of their congregations to sacrifice that their children might be educated and so better their lot. The belief cherished by many Negro parents that education was the panacea for their ills appears largely to have come from their pastors.[79] The most extensive institutionalized recreation for Negro youth was through the Young Men's and Young Women's Christian Associations. Often these had interracial boards.[80] Moreover, we hear of a council of Negro churches which appealed to its members to demand political, social, and economic justice for their race.[81]

Roman Catholics still had very slight hold upon the Negroes. Precisely how many Negro Roman Catholics there were we do not know. The Bureau of the Census of the United States Government reported the totals as 51,688 in 1916, 124,324 in 1926, and 137,684 in 1936.[82] Official Roman Catholic figures gave them in 1928 as 203,986[83] and in 1940 as 296,998.[84] Both sets of statistics indicate an increase, but the latter makes it much more marked in the later years of the period than does the former. Even if the larger official Roman Catholic figure for 1940 is taken, only between 5 and 6 per cent. of the Negro church members were Roman Catholics, for the 1936 figures of the Bureau of the Census put the total Negro church membership at 5,660,618.[85]

However, whether by government reckoning or that of the Roman Catholic Church, Negro Roman Catholics were increasing proportionately more rapidly than Protestants. They were predominantly in the cities.[86] They were both in congregations which were exclusively for Negroes and in ones in which there were white and coloured. The increase reflected the fact that Roman Catholics were giving more and more attention to the Negroes. Between 1928 and 1941 mission units for the race nearly doubled: the number of resident units with one or more priests grew 89 per cent. They were most numerous in the South,

---

[76] *Ibid.*
[77] Mays and Nicholson, *op. cit.*, p. 285.
[78] Mays and Nicholson, *op. cit.*, p. 278.
[79] Mays and Nicholson, *op. cit.*, p. 285.
[80] Johnson, *The Negro in American Civilization*, p. 309.
[81] *The Christian Century*, Vol. LII, pp. 1134, 1135.
[82] Gillard, *Colored Catholics in the United States*, pp. 107-109; Department of Commerce, Bureau of the Census, *Religious Bodies, 1936*, Vol. I, pp. 852, 853.
[83] Gillard, *The Catholic Church and the American Negro*, p. 49.
[84] Gillard, *Colored Catholics in the United States*, p. 141.
[85] Department of Commerce, Bureau of the Census, *Religious Bodies, 1936*, Vol. I, p. 901.
[86] Department of Commerce, Bureau of the Census, *Religious Bodies, 1936*, Vol. I, pp. 852, 853.

particularly in Louisiana, long the chief centre of Negro Roman Catholics, but they were also in the North.[87] In 1941 486 priests were giving full time to the Negroes, an increase of 148 per cent. as against 1928. Only about a seventh of these were diocesan clergy. They were from a number of orders and societies, but more than half were from the Society of St. Joseph (Mill Hill), the Society of the Divine Word, and the Holy Ghost Fathers.[88] A beginning had been made towards training Negroes for the priesthood and in 1941 there were 23 coloured priests.[89] Schools and teaching nuns constituted the backbone of the Roman Catholic missionary effort. In 1941 there were 1,670 sisters of 72 different religious communities giving their entire time to Negroes. Of these, 1,068, or more than two-thirds, were teaching, and the remainder were in various forms of social service.[90] The schools ranged all the way from those of primary grade through colleges and a university and about one-third of their pupils were not Roman Catholics.[91] There were various welfare agencies and activities and a Catholic Interracial Council of both white and coloured for the promotion of better relations between the races.[92] Roman Catholics were making decided gains among what had previously been a Protestant constituency. This was in spite of leakages through migration, losses due to the fact that in moving, especially from one section to another, the Negro was no longer in touch with the particular priest whom he knew and might not make contact with another.[93]

Here and there non-Christian cults won adherents among the Negroes. In several cities there were groups of Negroes who claimed to be Moslems,[94] and in at least one city congregations were to be found who called themselves Jews.[95] However, none of these appealed to more than small minorities. So far as they had any religious affiliation, the overwhelming majority of Negroes were Christians.

The proportion of Negroes who were in one or another of the Christian churches seems slightly to have increased after 1914. If the figures of the Bureau of the Census are reliable, the membership was 3,691,844 in 1906, 4,602,805 in 1916, 5,203,487 in 1926, and 5,660,618 in 1936.[96] This would mean

[87] Gillard, *Colored Catholics in the United States*, p. 128.
[88] Gillard, *op. cit.*, pp. 180, 181.
[89] Gillard, *op. cit.*, pp. 187, 188.
[90] Gillard, *op. cit.*, p. 190.
[91] Gillard, *op. cit.*, pp. 196 ff.
[92] Gillard, *op. cit.*, pp. 220 ff.
[93] Gillard, *op. cit.*, pp. 152 ff.
[94] Work, *Negro Year Book*, 1931-1932, p. 258.
[95] *Ibid.*
[96] Department of Commerce, Bureau of the Census, *Religious Bodies*, 1936, Vol. I, p. 901

that in 1906 about 40 per cent. of the Negroes were church members, and that in 1916, 1926, and 1936 the percentage was 45 and slightly above. There was only a small percentage increase after 1916.

The vast migrations which we mentioned in the introductory section of the chapter confronted Christianity with grave situations. These were closely associated with economic developments which brought altered conditions to large segments of the nation. Would Christianity be able to retain such hold as it possessed upon those who were uprooted from their accustomed habitat? Could it increase its participation in the life of the community under the new conditions? Could it contribute to meeting the urgent problems brought by economic, mechanical, and social developments?

A movement which affected almost every part of the nation was the shift of population from the rural district to the urban centres. This had begun long before 1914 but it was accelerated after that year. From being overwhelmingly rural, as it was at the dawn of the nineteenth century, by 1945 the United States had become predominantly urban. Moreover, in both rural and urban communities population was moving. Changes in methods of transportation and other factors led to the abandonment of some farms and rural villages and to the development of others and brought millions from the hearts of the cities to the suburbs.

It had been popularly supposed that the stronghold of Christianity in the United States, and especially of Protestantism, was in the farming and rural village communities. However, the first census, that of 1926, which made possible reasonably accurate comprehensive statistics as between city and country seemed to indicate that about 52 per cent. of the rural population were members of churches as against 58 per cent. in the cities.[97] In the rural districts the status of the churches reflected to a large degree the economic and population trends. In more prosperous communities the churches were growing.[98] For instance, in some counties in California in which irrigation had led to a rapid development of agriculture, churches were thriving and were sending many of their young people into the full time service of these bodies.[99] In communities where population and prosperity were dwindling the churches were

[97] Fry, *The U. S. Looks at Its Churches*, p. 15.
[98] Fry, *Diagnosing the Rural Church*, pp. 226 ff.
[99] Edmund deS. and Mary V. Brunner, *Irrigation and Religion. A Study of Religious and Social Conditions in Two California Counties* (New York, George H. Doran Company, 1922, pp. 128), p. 101.

losing ground.[100] There was some indication that the proportion of church members attending church had declined.[101] In rural villages the churches were stronger than in the country-side. A larger proportion of them had resident pastors. There the churches, with the schools, were the chief foci of community life.[102] In both the country-side and the villages many of the Protestant churches were aided financially by home mission organizations, but the proportion of the assisted in the former was considerably larger than in the latter.[103] In the villages there was much of what may be described as over-churching; that is to say, several different denominations were represented and a constituency was divided which would have been sufficient for only one properly staffed and equipped congregation.[104] The same was true in some country-sides: here, notably in the South, there were often too many churches, inadequately housed and poorly financed.[105] The multiplication was accentuated by aid from home mission agencies, but sometimes that assistance made for greater effectiveness, for it rendered competition keener and promoted abler clerical leadership. However, interdenominational rivalry contributed to the neglect of religiously destitute areas.[106] In villages in the West the division of the Christian forces was enhanced by the appearance of new denominations using highly emotional methods.[107]

As the years passed, the churches in the country-side tended to die out and more and more of the farming community had membership in village churches.[108] This was made possible by the improvement in roads and the ubiquity of the automobile. It was a trend which was seen in other phases of rural life, for the crossroads store was passing and "consolidated" graded village schools drawing from the country-side by means of buses were being substituted for the one-room country schools.[109] Yet the proportion of folk in the country-side having church membership was much smaller than that in the villages.[110] The growth of village churches at the expense of the country churches was not necessarily accompanied by a more effective approach to the

[100] Fry, *Diagnosing the Rural Church,* pp. 226 ff.

[101] Fry, *op. cit.,* p. 231.

[102] Brunner, Hughes, and Patten, *American Agricultural Villages,* pp. 172, 173.

[103] Brunner, Hughes, and Patten, *op. cit.,* p. 174.

[104] Brunner, Hughes, and Patten, *op. cit.,* pp. 174-178; Kolb and Brunner, *A Study of Rural Society,* p. 462.

[105] Jesse Marvin Ormond, *The Country Church in North Carolina* (Durham, Duke University Press, 1931, pp. xv, 369), *passim.*

[106] Brunner, Hughes, and Patten, *op. cit.,* p. 176.

[107] Brunner, Hughes, and Patten, *op. cit.,* pp. 186-188.

[108] Brunner, Hughes, and Patten, *op. cit.,* pp. 180-182.

[109] Kolb and Brunner, *op. cit.,* p. 465.

[110] Brunner, Hughes, and Patten, *op. cit.,* pp. 183-186.

farming communities. Protestant leaders were alarmed and were declaring that the town and country churches were dying and that the financial depression of the 1930's was speeding the end.[111] In the mid-1930's it was estimated that there were thirteen million children and young people of school age in the rural communities who were receiving no Christian instruction.[112] The economic depression of the 1930's brought a decline in the already low salaries of the village clergy and made still more difficult the problem of adequate leadership.[113] In the 1930's, moreover, village churches were giving a much smaller proportion of their incomes than formerly to objects outside themselves.[114] It was as yet too early to say whether these disheartening trends were only temporary and would be reversed as economic conditions improved.

The churches were not supinely accepting adverse conditions as being irremediable. Their initiative in devising and applying new methods was an indication of vigour. In many sections there was a trend towards enlarging the programme of the churches to include a wider range of interests, towards making the churches more and more centres of community life, towards increasing the professional staffs with experts on social and charitable activities, towards using daily vacation Bible schools, towards making more of wholesome recreation, and towards combining the efforts of different denominations in approaching together particular rural communities either by the actual union of congregations or by what was known as the "larger parish" with a staff employed by the several churches but diversified in its training and functions.[115] Provisions were developed for special training for clergymen to fit them to serve in rural areas. In many different parts of the nation rural communities could be found in which the Church had adapted itself to the new conditions and was taking a growing part in the neighbourhood.[116]

Certain phases of the rural situation presented the Christian forces with special problems. One of these was that of share-croppers in the South. They were the unfortunate heirs of the plantation with its concentration on cotton and the ensuing deterioration of the soil. Their unhappy lot was enhanced by the competition of other countries in the growth of cotton for the world's factories and by the advent of the boll weevil. They were both white and

[111] Morse, *Home Missions Today and Tomorrow*, p. 107.

[112] Morse, *op. cit.*, p. 266. For some neglected rural districts in Oklahoma, see Morse, *op. cit.*, p. 98.

[113] Kolb and Brunner, *op. cit.*, p. 475.

[114] Kolb and Brunner, *op. cit.*, p. 477.

[115] Morse, *op. cit.*, p. 59.

[116] Edmund deS. Brunner, editor, *Churches of Distinction in Town and Country* (New York, George H. Doran Company, 1923, pp. 198), *passim*.

Negro and were condemned by the system in which they were involuntarily caught to poverty, illiteracy, malnutrition, disease, insecurity, and migratory habits. Something was done for them by the government, especially in the 1930's and 1940's. Most of them, so far as they had contacts with organized religion, were Protestant by tradition. The churches were not unmindful of them and sought to relieve their physical as well as their spiritual lot. Here and there were individuals who, moved by their Christian faith, undertook measures in their behalf, often at great cost.[117] In several other parts of the nation the tenant farmer, usually semi-migratory, was a problem. There were, too, the growing numbers of migrant rural labourers. Some of these were unmarried. Others had families. Many were seasonal, in the grain fields and orchards and on the berry farms. Their numbers were swelled by the droughts which had made the marginal lands in the West into the "dust bowl" and had sent thousands of former farm-owners, penniless, in search of a livelihood elsewhere. For them the churches were attempting to make provision, usually through separate denominational efforts, but sometimes co-operatively. The churches not only provided religious services but also ministered to physical and social needs.[118] The churches were becoming aware of peculiarly underprivileged rural districts—sparsely settled mountain areas in the South in the Appalachians and the Ozarks, cut off by poor roads and poorer soil from the currents and opportunities of the plains, hill regions in New England with dwindling populations, logged-over lands left with scanty and religiously neglected settlers, grazing regions and dry-farming areas where in the nature of the situation the population was sparse and not to be reached in traditional ways. The problems were being studied and efforts made to solve them.[119]

Roman Catholics were also addressing themselves to the rural districts. The religious affiliations of the country-side and the rural villages were overwhelmingly Protestant, but there were millions who were untouched. By 1945 the Roman Catholics were becoming aware of the situation. They were beginning to realize that five-sixths of their membership in the United States was urban, that declining birth rates in the cities threatened their church with slow numerical decline, and that the rural regions with their larger birth rates presented an opportunity. They were bestirring themselves to take

[117] *Missions,* Vol. XXXI, pp. 201, 202; Cedric Belfrage, *South of God* (New York, Modern Age Books, 1941, pp. 346), *passim.*

[118] *Annual Report . . . Home Missions Council,* 1936, pp. 63-67, 1939, p. 105.

[119] Elizabeth R. Hooker, *Hinterlands of the Church* (New York, Institute of Social and Religious Research, 1931, pp. xvi, 314), pp. 202 ff.

advantage of it, partly in caring for the portions of the rural population which were traditionally of their faith and partly by reaching out to the unchurched and the Protestants.[120]

The growth of cities continued to challenge Christianity. Many city dwellers had come from rural districts or from other cities and tended to drop whatever church connexions had once been theirs. Numbers of them were unattached individuals, a large proportion of them men. Rooming houses and apartment houses multiplied in the older city centres and the affiliation with community institutions, including the churches, of those who used them for dwellings declined. Occupants of rooming and apartment houses were largely deracinated and many of them shifted too rapidly to be able to put down roots in any kind of organized life. As a city expanded, the older American stock, mainly Protestant by tradition, flocked to the suburbs. With the automobile, additional suburbs developed. Within a generation a family of the middle or upper income group, the kind which usually owned its own home and established church connexions, might move at least twice. The city was an enemy of the family. Divorce rates were higher there than in the rural districts. Churches, especially Protestant churches, which were adapted to the family, found their constituencies slipping away from them and the type of life about them changing. They were forced to go out of existence, to develop new kinds of programmes to fit their altered neighbourhood, or to follow their members to the suburbs. On the whole, Roman Catholics were somewhat more successful in meeting the situation than were Protestants. The latter, however, by no means completely failed. Some of the Protestant churches which remained in their old locations devised new methods to meet the changing needs. Many of those which went to the suburbs found the resources to erect even larger physical plants than had previously been theirs and developed programmes suited to suburban conditions. Church activities became more varied and less stereotyped. Numbers of the Young Men's and Young Women's Christian Associations, which had arisen to meet the urban problem, built new and enlarged plants. Although Protestant in origin, the Associations included many Roman Catholics and Jews. City-wide Protestant organizations were developed. Some of them were by individual denominations which drew from the central chests of their respective religious bodies to maintain their activities. Increasingly interdenominational councils of churches assumed responsibilities. The latter had the purpose of bringing all the Protestant forces to bear upon a comprehensive ap-

[120] National Catholic Rural Life Conference, *Manifesto on Rural Life* (Milwaukee, The Bruce Publishing Company, 1939, pp. x, 222), *passim*.

proach to the city. Their ambitious goal was never entirely attained, but some advances were made.[121]

The shifts of population brought by the second of the world wars were on a much vaster scale than those of its predecessor. The armed forces were much larger. For them chaplains were provided by the government, but with the co-operation of the churches. Millions of labourers were in what were popularly known as "defense" industries. Many existing communities were swollen by additions and new communities came into being. To meet the religious needs of these workers action had quickly to be taken and on an extensive scale. Some of this was by individual denominations, some by the Christian Commission for Camp and Defense Communities, and some by local councils of churches. There were attempts at interdenominational planning by the co-operative assignment of the different areas to particular denominations, thereby to prevent duplication of effort in some and neglect in others. Pastors and social workers were appointed, Sunday Schools organized, and chaplains brought into industrial plants.[122]

The student bodies in colleges and universities grew rapidly after 1914. In many institutions of higher learning the atmosphere, both intellectual and social, was discouraging to Christian faith. The Student Volunteer Movement for Foreign Missions continued to hold its quadrennial conventions, but the numbers whom it enrolled for service abroad markedly declined. The Young Men's and Young Women's Christian Associations, which had been a chief means of reaching the campuses religiously in the third of a century before 1914, lost ground among the students. They by no means entirely disappeared. Indeed, they remained vigorous and altered their programmes radically to meet new conditions. However, they were not so prominent as formerly. Denominational agencies especially designed for students, with the (Methodist) Wesley Foundations as outstanding pioneers, rapidly grew in importance. Numbers of institutions officially took more responsibility for the religious life of their students. Increasingly chairs and departments of religion were instituted, both in connexion with state, tax-supported colleges and universities and in colleges which

[121] Samuel C. Kincheloe, *The American City and Its Church* (New York, Friendship Press, 1938, pp. xiv, 177), *passim*; Wilbur C. Hallenbeck, *Urban Organization of Protestantism* (New York, Harper & Brothers, 1934, pp. xii, 285), *passim*; H. Paul Douglass, *The Changing Church in the Changing City. Case Studies Illustrating Adaptation* (New York, George H. Doran Company, 1927, pp. 453), *passim*; H. Paul Douglass, *The Springfield Church Survey* (New York, George H. Doran Company, 1926, pp. 445), *passim*; H. Paul Douglass, *The St. Louis Church Survey* (New York, George H. Doran Company, 1924, pp. 327), *passim*. On the Young Men's Christian Associations see a summary of a self-survey, *The Y.M.C.A. Constituency after One Hundred Years* (New York, Association Press, 1943) in *Information Service*, Nov. 6, 1943.

[122] *Federal Council Bulletin*, October, 1943, pp. 13, 14, November, 1943, pp. 10, 11.

were historically related to denominations and professedly Christian. For a time in the 1920's there seemed to be something of a decline in the religious life of students, but in the 1930's and 1940's the tide began turning in the direction of greater commitment to the Christian faith.[123]

The appraisal of the effect of Christianity upon the United States in the three decades after 1914 is peculiarly difficult. The time was so brief and the national life so complex that to determine whether Christianity was a growing or a declining force was all but impossible. So many currents and cross-currents confused the scene and so many trends appeared which might, from the perspective of another hundred or even fifty years, prove only ephemeral that generalizations concerning the impression of Christianity upon its American environment could be essayed only with the greatest caution. A number of results can be determined with rough accuracy, but whether they added up to an increase or a decrease as compared with the pre-1914 period none but the rash would have the temerity to say.

If one were to go through the "secular" literature of the period, namely that which was not written by Christians for specifically religious purposes, one would probably conclude that Christianity was a waning factor or had, indeed, been already ushered out of the life of the United States. Christianity was not so much criticized as ignored.[124] Yet in the 1940's some books built around Christian themes were among the "best sellers," an indication of widespread popular interest.

Some aspects of the scene, however, indicated that the effect of Christianity was mounting. The percentage of church members in the total population was apparently rising. In 1910 it was said to be 43.4, which was the highest thus far on record, in 1920 it was reported still to be 43.4,[125] but in 1940 it seems to have risen to 47.1.[126] Figures also appeared to show that whereas the population of the country as a whole had been augmented by 7.2 per cent. in the decade 1931-

[123] The bibliography is chiefly in the form of articles in periodicals and of brochures and is very large. No one comprehensive study exists. An excellent summary, but primarily of student Young Men's and Young Women's Christian Associations and only for the years 1915-1934, is in Clarence P. Shedd, *Two Centuries of Student Christian Movements* (New York, Association Press, 1934, pp. xxii, 466), pp. 375-422.

[124] See two admirable surveys, by a convinced Christian—Halford E. Luccock, *Contemporary American Literature and Religion* (Chicago, Willett, Clark & Company, 1934, pp. 300), *passim*, and Halford E. Luccock, *American Mirror. Social, Ethical, and Religious Aspects of American Literature, 1930-1940* (New York, The Macmillan Company, 1940, pp. vi, 300), pp. 236 ff.

[125] Weber, *Year Book of the American Churches*, 1933, p. 299.

[126] From figures in Landis, *1941 Yearbook of American Churches*, p. 135.

1940, in the same years the membership of the churches had grown by 7.86 per cent., or more rapidly by nearly a tenth.[127] A careful study gave as its conclusion that between 1926 and 1941-1942, while the population increased 14.3 per cent., the church membership had multiplied by 25.5 per cent. A number of small denominations made striking gains, but other small ones rapidly declined. Forty-three Protestant denominations, each with more than 50,000 members, had a rate of gain of 23.8 per cent., which was slightly larger than that of the Roman Catholics, 23.3 per cent.[128] The church figures were confessedly incomplete. Moreover, those for some denominations did not include children. In addition there were unknown numbers, probably several millions, who at one time or another had held church membership but had been dropped from the rolls, usually because they had become inactive.

As we suggested a few pages above, something like a mass conversion of the United States was in progress. This becomes the more apparent when we recall the figures given several paragraphs back which indicate that in the longer settled portions of the country the proportion of church members was higher than in the newer sections. As American society became older, membership in one or another of the churches tended to become normal rather than as earlier, the exception. This made of it more a social convention than a deep and progressively transforming spiritual and moral experience. The presumption would be that under such circumstances the average quality of the lives of professed Christians was declining. There was evidence which appeared to support this generalization. In Protestant circles in one city in the Middle West, for instance, the custom of grace at meals was less common than formerly, the mid-week prayer service was waning, and church attendance seemed to have fallen off.[129] In these respects this city was fairly typical. However, the opposite might be true, and the mass conversion might be accomplished by an increasing permeation of society by Christian ideals. Either conclusion would be difficult to substantiate conclusively.

The movement was almost the opposite of what was occurring in Europe, where the trend was in the direction of Christians becoming a minority, although a large minority, diametrically opposed to some of the prevailing currents. It was, too, in contrast with the original genus of some of the denominations which had attained the greatest dimensions in the United States. Both in 1926 and in 1941-1942 the Baptists were the largest group of Protestant denominations and were followed fairly closely by the Methodist bodies. Baptists

[127] Landis, *op. cit.*, p. 137.
[128] B. Y. Landis in *Information Service*, Jan. 1, 1944. See also on church membership growth in 1937, *Information Service*, Jan. 14th, 1939.
[129] Lynd, *Middletown*, pp. 334, 339, 359.

and Methodists together were only about ten per cent. less than the Roman Catholics and were probably more than the latter if Baptist children were counted (for Baptists did not baptize infants as did the latter and therefore did not include them in their statistics of membership). They were five times more numerous than the Lutherans, seven times more numerous than the Presbyterians, and ten times more numerous than the Protestant Episcopalians.[130] In other words, these two groups of Protestants, by tradition dependent upon individual conversion and complete dedication for their membership and at their inception in contrast with state churches in the Old World which in theory included all in a particular political unit, were larger than any of the Protestant bodies which on the other side of the Atlantic were state and community organizations and together were only slightly if at all smaller than Roman Catholicism, which in much of Europe had traditionally enjoyed the powerful endorsement of the government.

A method much employed among Protestants for deepening the intelligent commitment of their membership was summer conferences. Here were assembled minorities, usually select minorities, for a period of worship, fellowship, and study. They were often by age groups. They at once provided leadership for the rank and file and helped to create among a few an informed devotion to that Christian faith which was so superficially accepted by the majority. They corresponded roughly to the "retreats" employed by the Roman Catholics.

By church membership the United States continued to be predominantly Protestant. Now that the main source of Roman Catholic growth had been reduced through the dwindling of the immigrant stream, Roman Catholic membership seemed to be increasing less rapidly than that of the Protestant bodies. Between 1906 and 1926 the former is said to have grown by 25 per cent. and the latter by 46 per cent.[131] and between 1926 and 1941-1942 the former is reported to have gained 23.3 per cent. as against a gain in the total church membership of the country, Roman Catholics, Eastern churches, Jews, and Protestants, of 25.5 per cent. Since in that fifteen years the increase of the Jews, the only large non-Roman Catholic or non-Protestant segment, was only 13.7 per cent., the excess of the 25.5 per cent. over the Roman Catholic 23.3 per cent. was chiefly Protestant. The 43 major Protestant bodies increased 23.8 per cent. as against the Roman Catholic 23.3 per cent.[132] In positions of leadership in the various phases of national life, as we saw a few pages above, Protestants were still preponderant, although Roman Catholics were making gains.[133]

[130] B. Y. Landis in *Information Service.* Jan. 1, 1944.
[131] Morse, *Home Missions Today and Tomorrow,* p. 35.
[132] B. Y. Landis in *Information Service,* Jan. 1, 1944.
[133] Fry in Weber, *Year Book of American Churches,* 1933, pp. 311-316.

In the traditional ways Christianity continued to have an effect upon American life. It was a means of moral education and a source of ideals for a large proportion of the population. It maintained numerous charitable enterprises. Roman Catholics, for instance, in at least one large archdiocese co-operated in the support of their institutions through the Associated Catholic Charities.[134] The churches aided schools. Among Protestants these were mostly theological seminaries, colleges, and universities with a sprinkling of secondary schools and a few primary schools.[135] Roman Catholics had a system which was a pyramid broadly based upon parish schools and culminating in colleges, universities, and seminaries.[136] In 1942 Roman Catholics reported 203 theological seminaries with 17,545 students, 140 colleges for men, 669 colleges and academies for girls, and 1,468 high schools, with an enrolment in the last three categories of 501,088 students, and 7,701 parish schools with 2,065,198 pupils. They also recorded 300 orphan asylums with 31,263 orphans, 179 homes for the aged, and 721 hospitals. Since 1932 there had been a slight decrease in some categories of students but in several categories a marked increase.[137] The Roman Catholics attempted to co-ordinate many of their educational, social, and welfare activities through the formation, in 1919, of the National Catholic Welfare Conference.[138] Many of the Protestant activities in the social field were brought together under various departments of the Federal Council of the Churches of Christ in America.

There was some question as to whether the Protestant clergy were not losing ground. It was declared that the educational level of the Protestant ministry had been falling during a time of phenomenal increase in that of the general population,[139] that the pastor, until late in the nineteenth century usually better educated than any one else in the community and often the leading citizen, had lost this position, and that lawyers, physicians, and business men had displaced him.[140] Among the causes adduced to account for this decline was the undue multiplication of local churches with the corresponding inability of all but the largest to pay a salary which would warrant a high degree of formal training for the pastor.[141] The average salary of the ministry was decidedly below that of teachers in kindergartens or elementary schools.[142] A very large

[134] Martin, *The First Cardinal of the West*, pp. 145-147.
[135] For a list of Protestant theological seminaries, colleges, and universities, see Landis, *Year Book of American Churches, 1941*, pp. 110-117.
[136] See a picture of one archdiocese in Martin, *op. cit.*, p. 66.
[137] *The Official Catholic Directory, 1942*, p. 1224.
[138] *The Official Catholic Directory, 1942*, pp. 808, 809.
[139] *The Education of American Ministers*, Vol. II, p. 34.
[140] *The Education of American Ministers*, Vol. I, p. 6.
[141] *The Education of American Ministers*, Vol. II, pp. 114-116.
[142] *The Education of American Ministers*, Vol. II, pp. 103-108.

proportion of the clergy were from rural disticts[143] and from families of the lower income levels[144] and a decreasing number came from the older Eastern colleges and the state universities.[145] Yet they were from homes whose educational level was distinctly above the average,[146] and a larger proportion of students in the theological schools were from the professional classes and followed the calling of their fathers than was true in schools of law and medicine.[147] In spite of offsetting favourable features, it would seem that the Protestant churches were not as well equipped to lead in community and national affairs as formerly.

This, however, did not necessarily follow. It might mean that as education permeated the rank and file of the membership those impelled by Christian motives would exert a larger influence than before. Certainly the voice and the effect of Christianity were evident in a number of important phases of the nation's life.

As we saw earlier,[148] it was the Christian conscience, and primarily the conscience of Protestantism, which fought the sale and use of alcoholic beverages and in 1919 wrote the prohibition amendment into the constitution of the United States.[149] While that amendment was soon annulled, first by popular practice and then by another amendment, by 1945 the tide had again begun to swing towards prohibition.

On the issue of war, so tragically clamant after 1914, Christianity was making itself felt. During the first of the wars American philanthropy, in large part led by the Protestant forces, poured out its gifts of life and money in a fashion unprecedented in magnitude in an attempt to relieve the suffering brought by war, for prisoners of war, and, partly through the churches and related agencies, chiefly the Young Men's Christian Associations, for the men in the armed services. Much was done, too, to maintain the religious life of the soldiers and sailors, both in the army and navy of the United States and in the armies of the other belligerents.[150] In the first of the world wars organized Christianity tended in general to endorse the cause of the Allies against the Central Powers, to support the participation of the United States, and to regard the war as

[143] *The Education of American Ministers*, Vol. I, p. 110.

[144] *Ibid.*

[145] *The Education of American Ministers*, Vol. I, p. 69.

[146] *The Education of American Ministers*, Vol. I, p. 110.

[147] *The Education of American Ministers*, Vol. III, p. 283.

[148] Vol. IV, pp. 394-396.

[149] E. H. Cherrington, *The Evolution of Prohibition in the United States of America* (Westerville, The American Issue Press, 1920, pp. 384), pp. 317 ff.

[150] As examples, see Mathews, *John R. Mott*, pp. 270 ff.; Brown, *A Teacher and His Times*, pp. 223 ff.; *Service with Fighting Men: an Account of the Work of the American Young Men's Christian Associations in the World War* (New York, Association Press, 2 vols., 1924), *passim*.

righteous.[151] However, there were those who refused, on the ground of Christian conscience, to be enrolled in the armed forces, and that in spite of severe measures which were sometimes taken against them.[152] Their Christian faith led many men and women to labour resolutely and hopefully to prevent a recurrence of the catastrophe. Outstanding was the part of President Woodrow Wilson, who was largely actuated by a vigorous Christian purpose, in calling into being the League of Nations. The Institute of Pacific Relations, as we hinted earlier, was begun by American Protestants as a Christian enterprise.[153] In the interval between the two world wars, denominations in their official gatherings and other Christian bodies came out with formal pronouncements declaring that churches should no longer bless war and advocating specific measures to reduce armaments and end war.[154] Some of the denominations, including especially the Methodists, undertook to educate their constituencies on ways of achieving peace. As the sky again darkened and the storm of the second of the world wars began to break, Christians were still active. It was churches through their missionary education who had done most to familiarize Americans with the Far East and to create a sympathy for China, the sufferer from the Japanese advance.[155] Many Christians, by opposing the sale of scrap iron to Japan in an effort at "non-participation in Japanese aggression,"[156] contributed to the mounting feeling against the Japanese programme and so to the outbreak of war between Japan and the United States. That, however, was by no means the major cause of that conflict: presumably hostilities would have come without it. In the second of the world wars, organized Christian opinion obtained somewhat more lenient treatment of conscientious objectors than in the first war, and a larger number, although still an infinitesimal minority,[157] enrolled themselves in that category. Official church bodies did not, as in the earlier of the struggles, endorse the war as a righteous crusade. The general attitude was of sorrowful but grimly determined participation in what was re-

[151] Allen, *The Fight for Peace*, pp. 39-42.

[152] Wright, *Conscientious Objectors in the Civil War*, pp. 220-245; Wenger, *History of the Mennonites of the Franconia Conference*, pp. 65-74; Harold Studley Gray, edited by Kenneth Irving Brown, *Character "Bad." The Story of a Conscientious Objector* (New York, Harper & Brothers, 1934, pp. ix, 258).

[153] From personal knowledge and from the oral narrative of the first chief secretary, J. Merle Davis.

[154] Among many possible references are Van Kirk, *Religion Renounces War, passim*, and Allen, *op. cit.*, p. 47. On the part of the Federal Council of the Churches of Christ in America in this movement, see Hutchison, *We are not Divided*, pp. 163 ff.

[155] Stimson, *The Far Eastern Crisis*, pp. 153-156.

[156] For an instance see *Missions*, Vol. XXXI, p. 217.

[157] For news of the conscientious objectors see the files of *Fellowship* (New York, 1935 ff.).

garded as an unavoidable conflict.[158] Through a commission appointed by the Federal Council of Churches there was widespread study of what were termed "the bases of a just and durable peace." More maturity of thought and more informed opinion were evident in the churches than in the war of 1914-1918. There were in the Christian faith a purpose and a power which were impelling those who held it, as did no other factor in the life of America or the world as a whole, to work hopefully and resolutely to rid civilization of the greatest single menace of the age.

In a variety of ways, sometimes through ecclesiastical agencies, Christians were seeking to bring the principles of their faith to bear upon the clamant economic and social conditions of their day. Problems of labour, industry, agriculture, distribution, housing, and race, to mention only a few, were wrestled with by Christian individuals and groups.[159] It was said that almost all radical leaders of consequence in the struggle for economic and social justice were originally inspired by religious conviction—even though later they may have broken with organized Christianity.[160] There were efforts to improve the moral quality of the moving pictures which had attained great dimensions as a popular recreation.[161]

In none of these international and social measures did Christians have their full way. Not always did they agree among themselves. Frequently they ignored important phases of the situation about them. In some urgent social situations in which they were set by the quick growth of industrial towns the churches seemed to have only an other-worldly message or to confine their ethical teachings to phases of morals which did not meet the fundamental economic factors which were jeopardizing their constituencies.[162] When they were aware of problems and sought to meet them they had many adversaries. Yet the Christian

---

[158] See a mimeographed study by R. H. Bainton, *The Churches and the War* (1943).

[159] A few instances are Hunting, *The Adventures of Mr. Friend*, pp. 98-106; *The Christian Century*, Vol. LVII, pp. 667-669; and the oral report by J. G. K. McClure, Jr., Oct., 1932, of his organization of farmers' co-operatives in North Carolina. For the work of the Federal Council of the Churches of Christ in America in these areas, see Hutchison, *op. cit.*, pp. 99 ff.

[160] Reinhold Niebuhr in *The Christian Century*, Vol. LI, pp. 491, 492, giving concrete instances. See as one example Henry A. Wallace (prominent under President Franklin D. Roosevelt as Secretary of Agriculture and then as Vice President), *Statesmanship and Religion* (New York, Round Table Press, 1934, pp. 139), *passim*.

[161] For instance, the Roman Catholics, stimulated by an encyclical of Pope Pius XI, through their National Legion of Decency issued approved lists of pictures.—Weber, *Yearbook of American Churches*, 1937, p. 152.

[162] See the situation depicted in Liston Pope, *Millhands & Preachers. A Study of Gastonia* (Yale University Press, 1942, pp. xii, 369). Yet the author was a clergyman, active in the life of the Church and seeking to arouse it and direct its energies to correct the ills which he described.

forces were sometimes important in shaping policies and events. Christianity continued to be an element to be reckoned with in the life of the United States.

Always, moreover, as in the past, Christianity bore its characteristic fruits in the lives of countless individuals. In some these were marked. In others they were faint. But they were there and in varying degrees were potent not only in the lives of the individuals, but, through them, in the society of which they were a part.

In the effect of the environment of the United States upon Christianity there was chiefly a continuation of those trends which had been present before 1914.

There was still the multiplicity of organized expressions of Christianity which because of importation through immigration embraced almost all the kinds to be found anywhere else in the world and to which a few indigenous additions had been made.

After 1914 several new denominations appeared, but none of them attained the numerical dimensions of such earlier American creations as the Church of Jesus Christ of Latter Day Saints (Mormons), the Disciples of Christ, the Christian Scientists, or the Seventh Day Adventists. After 1914 some of these native bodies had a striking growth. That was true of all four of the denominations mentioned. Several of the smaller denominations of American birth, chiefly those which emphasized a highly emotional religious experience and strictness of personal morals and which appealed largely to the lower income groups of the older American stock, added rapidly to their numbers.[163] They were due in part to dissatisfaction with the departure of some of the larger denominations from the earlier separateness from the world and were attempts at more exacting Christian living. Several of them were offshoots of Methodism.

The great body of church membership, however, was in the denominations in which it was to be found in 1914. The dwindling of immigration had worked changes, but these we have already noted in this chapter. In general the denominational complexion of the Christianity of the United States had not been basically altered in the new era. Moreover, the denominational alignment still reflected the different periods and sources of origin of immigration. The older American stock, whether white or Negro, belonged mainly (except for Lutherans and some of the Reformed) to denominations of British provenance. Lutherans and Reformed were divided between those of pre-nineteenth cen-

---

[163] Landis in *Information Service*, Jan. 1, 1944; Elmer T. Clark, *The Small Sects in America* (Nashville, Cokesbury Press, 1937, pp. 311), *passim*.

tury and nineteenth century arrival. As before, Lutherans grouped themselves ecclesiastically largely according to nationality.

A trend which had begun to be prominent before 1914 continued with accelerated pace. This was the movement towards co-operation, union, and the interpenetration of almost all bodies by the others. Living together in fairly close intimacy and none of them enjoying a privileged legal position, the various religious bodies more and more accommodated themselves to one another, took over the others' methods, worked together at common tasks, and in some instances united. As was to be expected, the bodies longer in the United States and those closer to one another ecclesiastically were most affected. Few if any, however, failed to give evidence of this feature of the American environment. The movement was so multiform that we can take the space for only a few examples and generalizations. Between 1900 and 1934 twenty-three denominations were merged into ten and these by re-merger were reduced to eight.[164] Usually the unions were of units of the same denominational families, like that which in 1918 brought together into the United Lutheran Church the General Council, the General Synod, and the United Synod, South,[165] that which culminated (1930) in the American Lutheran Church, made up of the former synods of Buffalo, Iowa, and Ohio,[166] and the very large one which in 1939 constituted the Methodist Church out of the Methodist Episcopal Church, the Methodist Episcopal Church, South, and the Methodist Protestant Church.[167] Sometimes they were of those of common racial origin, such as that which in 1934 fused two bodies of German background, the Evangelical Synod of North America and the Reformed Church in the United States.[168] Never were the unions of such diverse bodies as those which we are to meet later in this volume in Canada, Japan, and China. The Federal Council of the Churches of Christ in America, formed in 1908, grew in membership and influence. More than any other organization it was the voice of American Protestantism.[169] State home missions councils, for interdenominational co-operation, multiplied. In 1934 there were twenty-two of them, three-fifths of them formed within the preceding decade.[170] There were also state and city federations or councils of churches.[171] The National Conference of Christians and Jews brought

[164] Douglass, *Church Unity Movements in the United States*, p. 50.

[165] *The Lutheran World Almanac*, 1921, pp. 71-84.

[166] *The Lutheran World Almanac*, 1932, p. 53.

[167] Landis, *1941 Yearbook of American Churches*, p. 59.

[168] Douglass, *A Decade of Objective Progress in Church Unity, 1927-1936*, p. 98.

[169] Hutchison, *We are not Divided*, passim.

[170] Morse, *Home Missions Today and Tomorrow*, p. 41.

[171] Morse, *op. cit.*, p. 43; H. Paul Douglass, *Church Comity. A Study of Coöperation in American Cities* (Garden City, Doubleday, Doran & Company, 1929, pp. vii, 181), passim.

Protestants, Roman Catholics, and Jews together for reciprocal understanding.[172] In 1943, moreover, leading members and officials of these three fellowships joined in a statement advocating seven points for international organization and world peace,[173] the first time that they had spoken so emphatically with a common voice. Some were declaring that an American religion was emerging in which elements from all these historic bodies were being incorporated.[174] There was no indication of an early fusion into an organic or uniform whole of the diverse religious traditions represented in the United States, but there was increasing reciprocal tolerance. It may have been that the absence of extensive missions to the Jews by most of the Christian denominations was in part due to the feeling, under the accommodating influence of the American environment, that the difference between Judaism and Christianity was not great enough to warrant efforts to win adherents of the one to the other.

Active resistance developed to the movement towards Christian unity. Some of it, as we saw earlier, was by Fundamentalists, an element present in several denominations. Fundamentalism was in part a resistance to the attempts to reach agreement between Christian faith and modern science. It maintained the infallibility of the Bible, denounced the evolutionary hypothesis, held to the authenticity of all the miracles recorded in the Scriptures, including the virgin birth and the physical resurrection of Jesus, and taught the substitutionary theory of the atonement and the visible second coming of Christ. To it such institutions as the Federal Council of the Churches of Christ in America and the World Council of Churches were anathema, for they were led by those whom it dubbed "modernist" and "compromised" with Catholics, whether these were Roman or Eastern. Fundamentalism became very vigorous soon after the first of the world wars and had a recrudescence during the second of the world struggles.

There seemed to be something of a correlation between trends in business and in the rate of accessions to churches. When the movement in the economic sphere was towards prosperity, additions to the churches slowed down. They increased when adversity overtook business.[175] The correlation was somewhat uncertain and by no means precise, but it was close enough to be interesting.

Another and somewhat different trend which seemed to reflect the environment was the growth of ritualism in traditionally non-liturgical churches. The use of vestments by choirs and ministers, more written prayers, and a growing

---

[172] See a summary of progress by R. A. Ashworth, one of the secretaries of the Conference, in Landis, *op. cit.*, pp. 142-150.

[173] *The New York Times*, Oct. 7, 1943, p. 15.

[174] The comment of a leading Jewish scholar to the author.

[175] Weber, *Yearbook of American Churches*, 1933, p. 307.

dignity and order in public worship appeared in churches which earlier had spurned such usages as part of what they deemed the corruption of pure Christianity by the Roman Catholic Church. Presumably the change was due in some degree to the growing maturity of the country. It was most apparent in the older sections and in the cities and was least common in the South, the West, and in rural districts, or, in other words, in communities where the older America more nearly persisted.

In spite of these accommodations to its environment, the Christianity of the United States was by no means a passive reflection of its *milieu*. Its very ability to adjust itself to the changing times was evidence of vigour. Moreover, as elsewhere, it and the culture in which it was immersed interacted on each other. It helped to mould its surroundings probably fully as much as it was moulded by them. Different though the Christianity of the United States was from that of the lands from which it was derived, the contrasts were not sufficiently great to estop Christians from those churches which most responded to the American environment from taking a leading part in bringing into being the Ecumenical Movement. The leadership of that movement was in large degree from the United States and to a surprising extent from those very denominations which had been longest in the land and from the wings of those bodies which had proved the most flexible. The gulf, if one existed, between American and European Christianity was not too wide to be bridged. In other words, American Christianity had not so far conformed to its environment that it had severed its connexion with its historic roots. Indeed, the striking role which American Protestant churchmen assumed in the Ecumenical Movement was in some degree evidence that their environment had prepared them to help pioneer in the life of the world-wide Church. Moreover, through the Ecumenical Movement the Protestantism of the United States, especially that of the older stock which had seemed to depart furthest from historic Christianity, was being made vividly and appreciatively aware of the values in the older Christian bodies. The situation in the United States was in some respects a microcosm of that in the earth as a whole. In both there were many branches of the Church all of which were on the basis of legal equality in the eyes of any inclusive political authority. Their experience in their own country had prepared American Christians to participate in the Church on a global scale.

As one attempts to summarize the course of Christianity in the United States in the three decades which followed 1914 he is aware that neither the opening date nor the one which closes our narrative marks a sharp or revolutionary transition. The United States was altered by both the first and the second of the world wars and by the movements which were accelerated by these cataclysms. It was not changed as profoundly as was Europe or as were some other parts of the world. Most of the forces which affected Christianity in the United States were in operation before 1914. The events which were inaugurated by that year simply quickened their pace or intensified their effects. The prominence of the United States in world affairs which came after 1914 was then clearly in the offing and was merely hastened and accentuated by the events of the succeeding decades. Even the restrictions on immigration which began so abruptly in 1914 had been foreshadowed. The fevered prosperity of the 1920's and the depression of 1929 were probably given exaggerated proportions by the war, but they bore a family resemblance to what the country had previously experienced in its business cycles. The movement of population from country to city was already under way. The intellectual currents were largely a continuation of pre-1914 years. Nor did the second of the world wars immediately bring such major changes in the religious life as it did in much of the rest of the world. Presumably it would ultimately prove momentous. Larger numbers were drawn into the armed forces than in the earlier war and for longer periods. The divorce from normal surroundings and customary church associations was therefore more extensive. War industries, too, dislocated a much greater percentage of the civilian population than had the previous global struggle. In 1945, however, the effects of these shifts of population had only begun to appear.

The major problems which Christianity faced in its spread in the United States after 1914 were, then, for the most part what they had been on the eve of that year. The frontier had all but disappeared in the 1890's, but its aftermath was seen in the decreased proportion of the population which had church membership as one moved from the older to the younger portions of the country. The sharp reduction of immigration brought first by the outbreak of war in Europe in 1914 and then made continuing by legislation partly relieved the churches of an urgent set of problems. It gave the Roman Catholic Church the opportunity to catch up with its task of assimilation and hastened its participation in the spread of Christianity outside the country. The reduction of immigration, however, made it fairly certain that Roman Catholic Christianity would remain a minority faith, for conversions probably no more than offset losses, as predominantly urban it had to face a declining birth rate, and the source of its rapid growth was now cut off. Protestants made some numerical gains from the non-Protestant pre-1914 immigrants and their children, but more in the course of assimilation to a culture which was by tradition of their complexion than because of organized missions. Ecclesiastical lines still reflected the sources of the pre-1914 immigration. The progress of Christianity among the Indians continued. The proportion of church members among the Negroes also persisted in its rise, and that in spite of the northward and cityward movements of the race. As heretofore, the large majority of the Negro Christians were Baptists or Methodists. The rural districts were for the most part still Protestant, but country churches seemed to be losing ground at the expense of village and town churches. Protestants had not met the problem of the city with as much apparent success as had Roman Catholics, but both branches of the faith were displaying ingenuity and vigour as they addressed themselves to it. Christianity continued to exert an influence upon its environment, partly in traditional ways and partly by seeking to solve the complicated situations forced on the country by international relations and the changing economic, industrial, and social scene. It also, as previously, reflected its environment, and partly in consequence the movement towards Christian unity prospered. Whether Christianity was less or more a factor in American life in 1945 than in 1914 would be impossible to determine with accuracy. It had met serious challenges, sometimes without an appreciation of their importance and unsuccessfully, sometimes with only indifferent success, but on occasion with marked achievement. In the majority of the population it was a factor with which to reckon and for uncounted thousands it was a source of transforming and invigorating life.

Chapter VI

BRITISH, DANISH, AND DUTCH TERRITORIES IN THE AMERICAS

THE territories in the Western Hemisphere which constituted parts of the empires of the European powers which were traditionally Protestant must be passed over hurriedly. Like the United States, in general they were less profoundly affected by the events of the three decades which followed 1914 than were Europe and a number of other parts of the globe. For them, as for the United States, the second of the world wars brought much greater changes than did the earlier struggle, but, as in the case of their great neighbour, by 1945 these alterations had not yet become fully apparent.

By far the largest of the territories was the Dominion of Canada. In spite of its huge extent, its population, even after an increase of over 50 per cent. between 1914 and 1941, was less than a tenth of that of the United States.

The problems with which Canada confronted Christianity in the three decades after 1914 were not unlike those before that year. There were the growth of communities in the West, the expansion of the urban population, and the small enclaves of Indians and Eskimos. Immigration was still a factor, but it declined: it was mostly from Great Britain and the United States.[1] The second of the world wars brought greater problems than its predecessor, but by 1945 there was insufficient perspective on them adequately to appraise them.

In these decades in Canada one of the features of the religious scene was the growth in numbers and in vigour of the Roman Catholic Church. According to the returns of the government census, those who reported themselves as Roman Catholics were approximately 40 per cent. of the population in 1911, 1921, and 1931, but about 43.8 per cent. in 1941.[2] In the decade between 1931 and 1941 population increased 10.5 per cent., but Roman Catholics added to their numbers by over 16 per cent.[3] As heretofore, for historic reasons they dominated

[1] See figures in *The Statesman's Year-Book*, 1924, p. 273, 1935, p. 296, 1943, p. 307.
[2] *The Statesman's Year-Book*, 1915, p. 278, 1924, p. 274; *Christendom*, Vol. VIII, p. 434.
[3] *Christendom*, Vol. VIII, pp. 434, 435.

the province of Quebec, where in 1941 they were 87 per cent. of the population. In 1941 they were about half the population in New Brunswick, about a third in Nova Scotia, nearly a fourth in Ontario, where their proportion had risen from about a fifth ten years before, a little more than a fourth in the prairie provinces, and about a seventh in British Columbia, as against a ninth in that province a decade earlier.[4] Between 1931 and 1941 the rate of increase was much larger than that of any of the major Protestant denominations.[5] This seems to have been due not to conversions but to a high birth rate. Nearly two-thirds of the Roman Catholics were of French descent, and their church was, along with the French language, the symbol and the tie of their French particularism. While about half the population of the Dominion was urban,[6] the French were predominantly a rural folk. This helped to make for large families as against the cities. The other main Roman Catholic element was Irish, from the nineteenth century immigration.[7] In the United States the lower birth rates in the cities as compared with the rural districts militated against the Roman Catholics, for they were overwhelmingly urban. In Canada, in contrast, it favoured the Roman Catholics, for there they were mainly rural and the Protestants largely city-dwellers.

To the Roman Catholic Church in Canada there came some assistance from Europe. For instance, in 1927 Capuchins from the Belgian province of that order arrived to care for Flemish and Dutch immigrants.[8]

However, except for such specialized tasks the Canadian Roman Catholics were providing their own staff. They were continuing active missions on the frontiers to the Indians and the Eskimos.[9] Some of these were expanding.[10] Roman Catholic missionaries were pioneers in carrying the cultivation of cereals into the arctic and used the airplane in covering their posts in the sparsely peopled North.[11] In the regions of white population new parishes and dioceses were being created.[12] Several new parishes were formed on the frontier through the initiative of a priest who organized migration to new dis-

---

[4] *Christendom*, Vol. VIII, p. 435. For the 1931 figures see *The Statesman's Year-Book*, 1943, pp. 305, 307.

[5] *Christendom*, Vol. VIII, p. 435.

[6] *The Statesman's Year-Book*, 1943, p. 306.

[7] *Le Canada Ecclesiastique*, 1921, pp. viii-x.

[8] *Le Canada Ecclesiastique*, 1932, p. 611.

[9] *Missiones Catholicae Cura S. Congregationis de Propaganda Fide*, 1927, pp. 298, 299, 312, 313; Pierre Duchaussois, *Hidden Apostles. Our Lay Brother Missionaries* (London, Geo. E. J. Coldwell, Ltd., 1937, pp. 222), *passim*; Lecompte, *Les Missions Modernes de la Compagnie de Jésus au Canada (1842-1924)* (Montreal, Imprimerie du Messager, 1925, pp. 72), *passim*.

[10] *Le Canada Ecclesiastique*, 1932, p. 140.

[11] V. Stefansson in *Foreign Affairs*, Vol. XVII, pp. 518, 519

[12] *Le Canada Ecclesiastique*, 1921, pp. viii-x.

tricts.[13] Canadian Roman Catholics were also taking an increased part in the foreign missions of their church. In 1921, for example, *La Société des Missions Étrangères de la Province de Quebec* was founded to train and send secular priests to missions abroad.[14] In 1931 more than two hundred Canadian Roman Catholic missionaries sailed for other countries, principally to China, Japan, and South Africa.[15] There were attempts to meet domestic problems. A *Semaine sociale*, an annual gathering, the first being held in 1920, had as its purpose the meeting of social and labour issues.[16] In 1920 a conference was convened which decided to inaugurate a national confederation of Catholic labourers.[17] The liturgical movement which sought the improvement of the public services of the church also reached Canada.[18]

Those listed in the census as having Greek Orthodox affiliation showed strange fluctuations in their totals—88,507 in 1911,[19] 169,822 in 1921,[20] 102,389 in 1931, and 139,629 in 1941.[21] At most, however, they were only a small percentage of the population. Doukhobors, dissenters from the Russian Orthodox Church who had found refuge in Canada before 1914, experienced interesting developments after that year, but remained only a few thousand.[22]

The major Protestant denominations continued, as before, to be those of British provenance—Anglicans, Presbyterians, Methodists, and Baptists. Lutherans, of continental European background, formed about the same proportion of the Protestant constituency as in the United States, but they were increasing less rapidly than most of the other major groups.[23] A striking event was the consummation, in 1925, of the merger of Methodists, Congregationalists, and a large proportion of the Presbyterians into the United Church of Canada.[24] Since not all the Presbyterians entered and the Congregationalists were a small denomination, the Methodists constituted a majority in the new church. The United Church of Canada was in part an effect of the environment, for one of the primary urges back of its formation was the pressure to avoid duplication

---

[13] Canadian National Railways, *Canada. Atlantic to Pacific* (no place or date of publication, pp. 256), p. 97.

[14] *Le Canada Ecclesiastique*, 1932, p. 626.

[15] *Le Canada Ecclesiastique*, 1932, p. 139.

[16] *Le Canada Ecclesiastique*, 1921, pp. xiv, xv, 1932, p. 130.

[17] *Le Canada Ecclesiastique*, 1921, pp. xiv, xv.

[18] *Le Canada Ecclesiastique*, 1932, p. 131.

[19] *The Statesman's Year-Book*, 1918, p. 271.

[20] *The Statesman's Year-Book*, 1921, p. 274.

[21] *Christendom*, Vol. VIII, p. 434.

[22] J. F. C. Wright, *Slava Bohu. The Story of the Dukhobors* (New York, Farrar & Rinehart, Inc., 1940, pp. x, 438), *passim*.

[23] *Christendom*, Vol. VIII, pp. 434, 435.

[24] Claris Edwin Silcox, *Church Union in Canada* (New York, Institute of Social and Religious Research, 1933, pp. xvii, 493), *passim*.

of organized Christian effort in meeting the religious needs of the rapidly grow-ing West. It was also a symptom of the movement towards Christian unity which was so characteristic of the age. Nowhere else in the world was there any other organic union of such diverse denominations on so large a numerical scale. This was partly because the Protestant portion of Canada was still close to pioneer conditions and hence socially more nearly fluid and more prepared to experiment and to break with inherited traditions than an older society, even one so slightly older as that of the United States would have been. In the United Church of Canada the strong Methodist influence made for the advocacy of social reform. The new body erected a large number of church buildings and manses, especially in the West. It pressed its efforts to reach with the Christian message immigrants, Indians, and new communities of white stock, and to solve the problems presented by the growing cities. In 1930 it had about 1,700 home missionaries and was giving its message within the Dominion in 25 different languages.[25] It was by far the largest Protestant denomination in Canada and held a position more outstanding in that country than did any one denomination in the United States. Between 1931 and 1941 those who claimed some kind of affiliation with it increased proportionately more rapidly than did the Anglicans, but less rapidly than the Roman Catholics or the population as a whole.[26]

The Church of England in Canada, to which a larger number professed at-tachment than to any other non-Roman Catholic body except the United Church of Canada, also pursued its mission in the Dominion. It was interested in both the regions of older settlement and the West and North, including the Indians and the Eskimos. Aid to Anglican effort continued to come from the British Isles. The Society for the Propagation of the Gospel in Foreign Parts gave assistance, as it had for generations, and the new Bible Churchmen's Missionary Society sent representatives. The Cowley Fathers were active in opening new parishes and erecting churches in frontier regions.[27] The Church Missionary Society ceased its subventions in 1920 and thus withdrew from labours for Canadian aborigines in which it had long been prominent.[28]

Of the immigration movements, one of the most interesting was that of Mennonites. In the 1920's, in an effort to escape from Communism and the

[25] J. Stauffer in Stelzle, *The New Handbook of the Churches*, 1931, pp. 26-30; *Finishing the First Decade, 1925-1935* (Toronto, Board of Home Missions, The United Church of Canada), *passim.*

[26] *Christendom*, Vol. VIII, pp. 434, 435.

[27] *"Rejoicing in Hope." Triennial Report of the Board of Management M.S.C.C. to the General Synod* (1937), pp. 83 ff.

[28] T. B. R. Westgate in Loram and McIlwraith, *The North American Indian Today*, pp. 110-122.

measures of the Soviet state, thousands of Mennonites left Russia. About twenty thousand came to Canada. They were aided by fellow Mennonites, by other friends, and by the Canadian Pacific Railway. Most of them found homes in the Western provinces, but some settled in Ontario.[29] By 1941 the number in Canada reporting Mennonite affiliation was 111,380. This made the Mennonites, next to the Lutherans, the largest of the Protestant groups in Canada of non-British origin.[30] Overwhelmingly rural, they presumably had a high birth rate and hence a rapid increase even without accessions from the outside.

The movement in Canada towards Christian unity and co-operation showed itself not only in the formation of the United Church of Canada, but also in the coming into being of a number of interdenominational committees and councils for particular phases of the Christian enterprise. Eventually there was proposed a Canadian Council of Churches. By the beginning of 1944 this was winning the endorsement of the two largest Protestant bodies, the United Church of Canada and the Church of England in Canada, and of the Baptists of the Maritime Provinces.[31] It was formally organized later in 1944.

Canadian Christianity came to 1945 as it had been in 1914, vigorous, expanding within its own borders, and taking a part in the spread of Christianity in other parts of the world.

Newfoundland and Labrador, it will be recalled, were not in the Dominion of Canada, but constituted a separate unit of the British Empire. Population increased by approximately a fifth between 1914 and 1940, being about 300,000 in the latter year in Newfoundland and not far from 4,700 in Labrador. As in Canada, the overwhelming majority claimed attachment to one form or another of the Christian Church. The proportions associated with the chief denominations had not greatly altered in the three decades. About a third were Anglicans and another third Roman Catholics, with the latter slightly in excess of the former. Approximately a fourth claimed connexion with the United Church of Canada. In Newfoundland that body was made up almost entirely of former Methodists, for the Presbyterians, comparatively few in number, had most of them remained outside the merger. A traveller, deeply interested in the Christian faith, reported favourably upon the conditions of the three major churches and noted especially the peaceful relations between Protestants and Roman Catholics, the seasonal missions conducted for the latter by their

[29] Yoder, *For Conscience Sake*, pp. 131-140.
[30] *Christendom*, Vol. VIII, p. 434.
[31] *Federal Council Bulletin*, Vol. XXVII, pp. 7, 8.

clergy, and the general growth in strength of the Anglicans.[32] The Salvation Army numbered 6 per cent. of the population in 1940, a striking increase from 4 per cent. in 1911.[33] Its prominence may have reflected the stern economic conditions and the rough life which were the lot of a large part of the population.

Of Greenland, with its sparse population clinging precariously to the southern fringes of the ice-capped island and under Danish rule, little need be said. The religious condition had not substantially altered between 1914 and 1940 and by 1945 it was as yet too early to know what continuing effect the occupation by American forces would have.

As we pass from the North to the Caribbean we come to a very different world. Here the islands in the possession of the British and the Dutch had a predominantly Negro population. The largest, Jamaica, was more overwhelmingly Negro in blood than any of the West Indies except Haiti. The whites were in control. On some islands, notably in Trinidad, there were enclaves of labourers originally introduced from India. Those having a mixture of white and Negro blood were in varying proportion on the different islands. The masses of the Negro population were extremely poor. Poverty was not from any single cause. Nor did it necessarily imply overpopulation. On Jamaica there was unutilized land and much of that already under cultivation could readily have been made to yield more. Part of the difficulty was the unwillingness of the Negroes to work more than a low minimum of hours and part was chronic ignorance.[34]

As we saw in an earlier volume,[35] the Christian faith had been actively propagated, chiefly by Protestants and mostly from the British Isles. Some missionaries were from the United States and Canada. In the Dutch and Danish possessions and in Jamaica Moravians were prominent. The large majority of the population claimed some kind of affiliation with one or another of the denominations. The communicant membership, however, was much smaller.[36] In the British islands, as was to be expected, the leading denominations were those which were outstanding in Great Britain—Anglican, Methodist, Presbyterian, and Baptist.

[32] J. Edwin Orr, *Times of Refreshing* (London, Marshall, Morgan & Scott, Ltd., 1936, pp. 127), pp. 20, 21.
[33] For statistics see *The Statesman's Year-Book*, 1916, pp. 325, 326, 1943, p. 274.
[34] Davis, *The Church in the New Jamaica*, pp. 24 ff.
[35] Vol. V, pp. 48-61.
[36] Davis, *op. cit.*, p. 14.

Among many, Christianity was an active force, but it had by no means raised the Negroes, still only about a hundred years out of slavery, to its standards. It had been a major factor, probably the chief factor, in bringing emancipation. Yet it had not thereby fully solved the problem posed by the involuntary Negro migration to the islands. In Jamaica transmitted African religious practices, Obeah and Myalism, persisted,[37] and from 1928 to 1937 more than 70 per cent. of the births were illegitimate. Illegitimacy arose from a variety of causes, but was evidence of the weakness of the family among the majority and of the incompleteness of the permeation of social life and standards by the Christian faith.[38] Yet among at least a minority, and in some islands possibly a majority, Christianity was potent.[39] It was through the churches that a large proportion of the schools were conducted. The family, where it existed, and it was effective among a substantial minority, was chiefly the product of Christian teaching and example. The Christian hope gave meaning to thousands of lives which otherwise would have been drab. The Christian faith impelled many to labour for better conditions.

One of the striking features of the religious scene, in part a development after 1914, was the presence of a large number of small bodies, mainly by contact with the United States. Some flourished for a season and then dwindled or died out, to be followed by others of an ephemeral or semi-ephemeral character. These groups were especially multitudinous in Jamaica.[40]

The movement for greater co-operation among Protestants had repercussions in the West Indies. In 1941 a Christian Council was formed in Jamaica and in several other islands similar councils followed.[41] By these common planning and action were furthered.

The second of the world wars brought dislocation to the West Indies as elsewhere. The building of the naval bases leased to the United States involved the concentration of fairly large numbers of labourers, with corresponding disruption of church life, augmented moral problems, and accentuated need for social and religious services.[42]

[37] Davis, op. cit., pp. 44-46. See also Joseph J. Williams, a Jesuit missionary in Jamaica, in Whisperings of the Caribbean. Reflections of a Missionary (New York, Benziger Brothers, 1925, pp. 252), pp. 192 ff.

[38] Davis, op. cit., p. 32.

[39] See sketches in F. Deaville Walker, The Call of the West Indies (London, The Cargate Press, no date, pp. 190), pp. 103 ff.; J. E. Henderson, A Visit to the West Indies (London, The Cargate Press, 1939, pp. 104); John Levo, The Romantic Isles. A Sketch of the Church in the West Indies (London, S.P.G. and S.P.C.K., no date, pp. 88), pp. 50 ff.

[40] Hickman Johnson in The International Review of Missions, Vol. XXIV, pp. 344-348; Smith, Conquests of Christ in the West Indies, pp. 75, 86, 89.

[41] The International Review of Missions, Vol. XXXII, p. 59.

[42] The International Review of Missions, Vol. XXXII, p. 58.

In 1940 a West Indian Royal Commission proposed the expenditure by the British Government of £1,000,000 a year for twenty years in an endeavour to improve economic, educational, housing, health, labour, and moral conditions.[43] Presumably the programme would assist the churches in many of their tasks.

In British Guiana and (Dutch) Surinam the world-wide economic depression of the 1930's followed by the second of the world wars brought difficulties, but Christianity persisted and as against 1914 here and there gained ground.[44] In Surinam, for instance, the Moravians registered some progress among the labourers from British India and the Javanese who had been brought in to work the plantations.[45] Roman Catholics were represented by Redemptorists, Franciscans of Mary, Franciscan Sisters of the Oudenbosch Congregation, and Sisters of Mercy of Tilberg. Progress was slow, and in 1938 slightly less than a fifth of the population were of that branch of the faith.[46]

For none of the portions of the British and Dutch empires in the Western hemisphere or for Danish Greenland did the decades which immediately followed 1914 work such marked contrasts as in Europe. The spread of Christianity went on much as it had immediately preceding that year. Here and there were changes. Such episodes as the drought in the 1930's in the western prairies of Canada, the deterioration of the market for sugar, a chief crop of the West Indies, the transfer of the Danish West Indies to the United States (1917), and the incidence of the world-wide economic crisis which followed 1929 had effects, but did not work revolutions or fundamental modifications in the progress of the Christian faith. The second of the world wars brought more acute problems, but for the most part they had not, by 1945, shaken society or altered the course of Christianity as greatly as had events in Europe, Asia, and Africa.

[43] *The International Review of Missions,* Vol. XXX, p. 80.
[44] *The International Review of Missions,* Vol. XXIV, p. 85, Vol. XXIX, p. 89, Vol. XXX, p. 82.
[45] Schulze, *200 Jahre Brüdermission,* Vol. II, pp. 321-335; P. M. Legene, *Wie is uw Naaste? een Vraag aan Protestantsch Nederland* (The Hague, De Algemeene Boekhandel voor Inwendige en Uitwendige Zending, no date, pp. 64), *passim.*
[46] *Fides News Service,* Apr. 23, 1938.

Chapter VII

LATIN AMERICA

GENERAL FEATURES, ROMAN CATHOLIC, PROTESTANT: PUERTO RICO: CUBA: MEXICO: BRAZIL: OTHER COUNTRIES

THE vast portion of the Western Hemisphere which, because of the controlling element in its population and culture, was described collectively as Latin America was probably even less affected than were the United States and Canada by the convulsions which shook so much of the rest of the world after 1914. Several of its republics were technically belligerents in one or both of the world wars of the period, but none took a very active part in the actual fighting. The social movements and the ideologies which were working revolution in Europe could not but have their repercussions in a region whose cultural ties were still strongly with the Latin lands of that continent. Communism and Fascism, the latter chiefly in its Spanish phase, the Falangists, had many sympathizers, although in opposite camps. The one stirred some of the underprivileged masses and those who wished to better their lot. The other had advocates among the wealthy and conservative elements who most nearly perpetuated the special privileges of the colonial era. Here and there were rumblings which possibly might swell into upheavals of the exploited majority. In Mexico such an upsurge was actually under way. Closely tied to the economic structure of the United States and Western Europe, sending to them its exports of food, wool, minerals, and other raw materials, and drawing from them most of the manufactures and much of the capital which it needed, Latin America shared both in the fevered prosperity of the 1920's and in the back-wash from the first world war and that gilded decade in the depression of the 1930's. The second of the world wars disturbed its economy. The colossus of the North loomed ever larger on its borders. Puerto Rico was a possession of the United States. Cuba and Panama were satellites. Mexico, Haiti, Santo Domingo, Central America, and Venezuela were more and more penetrated by its business interests. In its struggles to shake off the ensuing bonds, Mexico periodically suffered from strained relations with its huge neighbour. Gradually, particularly after 1929 and especially after 1933, the United States developed what it called a "good neighbour" policy. This was greatly extended under the pressure of the second of the world wars. It made for closer ties between the United States and Latin America. The United States Government poured millions of dollars into the republics on its south, partly in the construction of naval bases. Through the subsidized Pan American Airways it had a dominant share in the rapidly growing air traffic of the region. In an effort at better understanding and to offset the traditional intellectual ties between Latin America and Europe it developed cultural interchange. It sought to avoid procedures which would provoke resentment among Latin American peoples. This was the environment in which Christianity found itself after 1914.

It will be recalled that Roman Catholic Christianity had been widely propagated in the colonial era, but in such fashion that it was passive and relied upon Spain and Portugal for leadership and control.[1] Political independence had dealt it severe blows from which by 1914 it had only begun to recover. In the nineteenth century Protestantism had been introduced, mainly by immigration from Germany and by missions from Great Britain and the United States. There were small enclaves, through immigrants, of Eastern Christianity.[2]

When the region is taken as a whole, Christianity gained in Latin America after 1914. This it did in both its Roman Catholic and its Protestant form. The course of Christianity could not be expected to be uniform throughout so large an area. It varied from section to section. Not always did the two great branches of the faith prosper in the same region or at the same time. Each, particularly the Roman Catholic Church, suffered occasional reverses. Yet in general the Christianity of each of these major divisions was more vigorous and influential by 1945 than it had been three decades earlier.

The second of the world wars led adherents of both branches of the faith from outside Latin America to direct more of their missionary efforts to that region. Some of their major fields became difficult of access or were completely closed. Obstacles to travel slowed the sending of reinforcements to Africa and much of Asia. The Japanese advance in the East of Asia and the adjacent islands first discouraged the dispatching of missionaries to that part of the world and then completely blocked access to great areas and forced numbers of the staff home. With many of its accustomed outlets closed, Christian missionary effort sought enlarged opportunities in Latin America. Many of the staff brought back from the Far East were sent south and additional personnel was recruited. This was done by both Roman Catholics and Prot-

[1] Vol. III, pp. 83-167.
[2] Vol. IV, pp. 68-129.

estants. Some of the new Protestant missionaries were from the British Isles, but the major part of the reinforcements for both Roman Catholics and Protestants were from the United States.

Difficulties were encountered in augmenting the foreign representatives of both branches of the faith. Local nationalisms sometimes resented the enhanced activities of aliens. This was especially the case in Mexico, as we shall see in a few moments, and even before the mounting of the missionary tide which accompanied the second world war. During that conflict the government of the United States was at times reluctant to grant passports to its citizens who wished to go south as missionaries. This was presumably from fear that a large missionary invasion would provoke ill will and so jeopardize its good neighbour policy. Protestants complained bitterly that they were being discriminated against in favour of Roman Catholics, but Roman Catholics also felt aggrieved. Some North American Roman Catholics, claiming that Latin America was of that faith, objected to Protestant missionaries as an unwarranted intrusion and productive of irritation.[3] Yet missionaries continued to be sent by both Roman Catholics and Protestants.

In the three decades following 1914 there was a substantial expansion of Roman Catholic effort for the non-Christian Indians in Latin America. Several millions of the aborigines were still in that category. This was notably true of the Amazon Valley and the Andes, both of them regions difficult of access for the white man and only imperfectly penetrated by Western civilization. Many other Indians on the frontiers, moreover, although nominally Christian, were without adequate spiritual oversight and presented an appealing field. The Roman Catholic Church in Latin America, handicapped by the lack of initiative inherited from colonial days and from the fashion in which the Church had then been planted and supervised, and not yet fully recovered from the blows dealt it in the years in which the Latin American countries were achieving their independence,[4] displayed very little enterprise in extending its borders in these neglected areas. To meet the challenge missionaries of several orders came from Europe and the United States.

A few examples may indicate something of what a complete narrative would disclose. In the 1930's Italian Salesians were placed in charge of the Prefecture Apostolic of the Upper Orinoco, the scene of important missions in colonial days and where many of the population were professedly Christian but had long been without clergy.[5] In 1919 a Servite was made bishop

[3] J. A. Mackay in *Christian World Facts*, 1943-1944, p. 16.
[4] See Vol. V, pp. 68 ff.
[5] *Fides News Service*, May 18, 1940.

in an area on the borders of Peru and Bolivia and in 1920 entered with a group of missionaries.[6] In 1936 and 1940 Servites came to Brazil and Argentina.[7] In 1918 Discalced Carmelites from Spanish Navarre inaugurated a mission among Indians in the northern part of Colombia. Before many years they had a village centre with a boarding school for boys, a model farm, and an industrial training school. By 1939 most of the population in the prefecture apostolic, about thirty thousand in all, had been baptized.[8] In 1926 some islands belonging to Colombia were assigned to Spanish Capuchins from Valencia.[9] In 1930 Spanish Capuchins also penetrated for the first time to two pagan Indian tribes in the southern part of Venezuela and within a few years could report encouraging progress.[10] In the 1930's a Spanish Franciscan while seeking to make contacts with roving tribes celebrated what he believed to be the first mass in a region in the south-eastern part of Ecuador.[11] In 1923 there came to Colombia the first contingent from St. Francis Xavier's College (known locally as the *Colegio de Ultramer*) of Burgos, which had been founded in 1899 by Gerard Villota to train priests from Spanish-speaking America.[12]

In the 1920's a comprehensive survey showed scores of foreign priests, lay brothers, and sisters at work in Central America, Colombia, Bolivia, Brazil, Chile, Peru, and Venezuela, with schools, hospitals, and leper asylums. Among the orders and congregations represented were Jesuits from the United States, German Oblates of Mary Immaculate, Spanish Sons of Mary Immaculate, Belgian Sisters of Providence, and German Capuchins.[13] Capuchins from the United States were assigned territories in Nicaragua and Puerto Rico.[14] In 1942, the Catholic Foreign Mission Society of America, seeking additional fields now that war had curtailed its enterprises in the Far East, the area to which it had primarily directed its energies, sent an initial contingent of priests to Bolivia. By mid-1944 it had fifteen groups scattered from Central America to Chile.[15] In Latin America, exclusive of the West Indies, the numbers of Christians in regions classified as missionary showed an increase from

[6] *The Servite* (Chicago), Dec., 1943.
[7] *Ibid.*
[8] *Fides News Service*, Apr. 8, 1939.
[9] *Revista de la Exposición Misional Española*, pp. 699-706.
[10] *Fides News Service*, Aug. 14, 1936.
[11] *Fides News Service*, Oct. 19, 1935.
[12] *Fides News Service*, Dec. 30, 1939.
[13] *Missiones Catholicae Cura S. Cong. de Prop. Fide*, 1927, pp. 298 ff.
[14] *1944 Mission Annual of the Seraphic Mass Association*, Sept. 10, 1943, pp. 26, 27.
[15] *The New York Times*, Apr. 7, 1942; *Maryknoll. The Field Afar*, June, 1944, pp. 7, 8.

472,000 in 1911 to 1,675,000 in 1925 and to 1,940,000 in 1938.[16] Presumably many of the additions were converts.

In a number of other ways the Roman Catholic form of Christianity achieved gains in some sections of Latin America. Illustrations gathered somewhat at random will help to make the generalization concrete. In Brazil Roman Catholic missionaries were labouring among the Japanese immigrants. In 1935 they had recently started a school to train Japanese youths for the priesthood. Japanese were accepting the Roman Catholic faith as part of the process of becoming Brazilians, but often retained many pre-Christian customs.[17] In 1928 the episcopate of Argentina approved the transformation of the *Union Popular Católica Argentina* into *La Acción Católica Argentina*. In 1930 the Argentine Government also gave its assent. In the new organization were included a national association of Catholic men, a league of Catholic women, a federation of Catholic youth, and a league of Catholic young men.[18] *Acción Católica* sought to permeate with Roman Catholic faith and morals culture, science, philosophy, politics, and the economic and social phases of life.[19] Among other issues it addressed itself to the situation created by the cinema, especially the films imported from the United States.[20] Associations of Roman Catholics were formed for various nationalities, notably the Germans and the Irish, for social and religious purposes.[21] The Neo-Thomist movement, with its revival of emphasis upon Thomas Aquinas, had followers in Latin America. It was, for example, potent in Argentina[22] and Mexico.[23] Although not indigenous, but an overflow from Europe, where it had been on a rising tide late in the nineteenth and in the twentieth century, it attracted attention and won adherence from many of Latin America's intellectuals and helped to win respect for Christianity among some of the educated who previously had despised the faith as outmoded and obscurantist. Moreover, a number of the intelligentsia who had been reared as Roman Catholics but who had drifted completely away from the church, or at best had preserved only tenuous relations with it, seemed to be turning to Christ and cherished a warm and reverent admiration for

[16] Bates, *Data on the Distribution of the Missionary Enterprise*, p. 5.

[17] *The International Review of Missions*, Vol. XXV, p. 98; a Protestant missionary to Brazil to the author, Jan. 7, 1935.

[18] *Anuario Católico Argentino*, 1932, pp. 124, 125.

[19] *Anuario Católico Argentino*, 1933, pp. 48-68.

[20] *Anuario Católico Argentino*, 1932, pp. 120-122.

[21] *Anuario Católico Argentino*, 1933, pp. 344-346, 467-469.

[22] Mackay, *The Other Spanish Christ*, pp. 84-87.

[23] F. S. C. Northrop, after a visit to Mexico, which brought him, a philosopher, in touch with Mexican philosophers, in conversation with the author, June 16, 1943.

him.[24] We hear of a Roman Catholic missionary congress held in Rio de Janeiro in 1926 which among other objectives sought to interest both clergy and laity in making better provision for the religious needs of Brazil. Here and there sons from the better families were entering the Brazilian priesthood.[25] In Chile, where in the second half of the nineteenth century it had suffered a marked limitation on its functions[26] and where in 1925 the union between Church and state was dissolved,[27] the Roman Catholic Church developed notable leaders, some of whom applied themselves to remedying the deplorable social and economic lot of the masses. Sisterhoods and other organizations gave themselves to charitable enterprises for the poor and progress was made in self-support.[28] Unlike several others of the Latin American republics, the clergy were largely native born and many were from wealthy and socially prominent families. In Peru, possibly because of Protestant competition, the Archbishop of Lima ordered more preaching in the churches.[29] In the 1930's a movement called *Hispanidad* became prominent. It was strengthened by the existence of the Franco government in Spain. Pan Hispanian, it sought a return to the Hispanic ideals of the sixteenth and seventeenth centuries before the mother country had been affected by anti-clericalism and liberalism. It attained a wide vogue among the conservative classes. Since it was rooted partly in Roman Catholicism, it bolstered that branch of the Christian faith.[30] It was clear, too, that in the past two decades Roman Catholic Christianity had here and there made gains among the intellectuals. This it had done partly through universities and partly as a reaction against Protestant Christianity.[31]

This did not mean that the Roman Catholic Church had completely purged itself of the abuses or fully repaired the weaknesses from which it had chronically suffered in Latin America. One of the Brazilian bishops publicly lamented the dearth of priests and the neglect of catechetical instruction in his diocese. An archbishop, also in Brazil, in seeking to stimulate vocations for the priesthood declared that the number of young men entering the seminaries had been declining and that it was only the presence of members of foreign religious

[24] Mackay, *op. cit.*, pp. 206-230; Ricardo Rojas, *The Invisible Christ*, translated by W. E. Browning (Cincinnati, The Abingdon Press, 1931, pp. 336), *passim*.

[25] Braga and Grubb, *The Republic of Brazil*, p. 36; a Protestant missionary to Brazil to the author, Jan. 7, 1935.

[26] Vol. V, p. 82.

[27] Herring, *Good Neighbors*, p. 220.

[28] *Ibid.*; Browning, Ritchie, and Grubb, *The West Coast Republics of South America*, pp. 26, 43.

[29] Browning, Ritchie, and Grubb, *op. cit.*, pp. 71 ff.

[30] From confidential information—although the movement was quite well known.

[31] L. A. Sanchez in *Christendom*, Vol. IX, pp. 47, 48.

orders which kept some parishes from being entirely without clergy.[32] The church still derived much of its support from members of landed families who were trying to preserve their privileged position and among the ignorant and poverty-stricken masses. Its hold was mainly on the women. Those affected by the new currents of thought and movements for social justice tended to hold aloof from it and to regard it as an obstacle to human betterment. The church had not remedied the abject poverty of the underprivileged majority, the sexual irregularities, the extensive illegitimacy, or the political corruption which characterized the life of much of the region.[33] There was much of superstition.

Although some of them recognized extenuating circumstances, Protestants were disposed to pillory these conditions as a mark of a congenital weakness in the Roman Catholic Church.[34] The causes were not so simple. Very similar conditions existed in some of the British West Indies, as we saw in the preceding chapter, where Protestant Christianity had enjoyed dominance for several generations. The source of the unhappy situation was rather to be sought in a social and economic structure, some of which in the pre-Columbian civilized portions of the region went back to the days before the Spanish conquest. The Roman Catholic Church had not succeeded in remedying the evils, but, as was true in Protestant Jamaica, their Christian faith was stimulating some of the choicest spirits to a courageous and hopeful struggle with them.

Yet in several of the republics a very large proportion even of the clergy who cared for the Christian population, as well as most of the missionaries to the non-Christian Indians mentioned above, came from Europe, especially from Spain and Italy. In Colombia in 1944 several of the bishops were foreign born. In Brazil, Argentina, and Peru, the law required the episcopate to be native born, but a high percentage of the lower clergy were foreign.[35] The Roman Catholic Church of Latin America did not possess vitality enough to provide sufficient priests to care for those who were Christians by heredity. It was not strange, therefore, that it did little to present the faith to non-Christians in its own area and in other parts of the world.

The growth of Protestantism in Latin America was much more marked after 1914 than was that of the Roman Catholic Church. The gain in Protestant

---

[32] Braga and Grubb, *op. cit.*, p. 36.
[33] Rycroft, *On This Foundation*, pp. 64, 65.
[34] L. Mann in *Religion in Life*, Vol. XII, pp. 514-523.
[35] From a well informed, widely travelled Argentine citizen, in personal conversation, Feb., 1944.

communicants in churches affiliated with missions from other lands in continental Latin America, that is, Latin America except for the West Indies, was from 139,000 in 1911 to 164,000 in 1923 and to 424,000 in 1936.[36] Missionaries from outside Latin America totalled (again with the exception of the West Indies) 1,306 in 1911, 2,300 in 1923, and 2,300 in 1936.[37] Although, presumably because of the financial depression in the United States, the source of most of the missionaries, the figures for the latter had been stationary between 1925 and 1938, in continental Latin America the "national workers," that is, the native-born in the employ of the churches, rose from 342 in 1911 to 605 in 1923 and to 1,540 in 1936.[38]

A feature in the advance of Protestantism was the development of co-operation among some of the major Protestant bodies represented in Latin America. This was a phase of the increase of co-operation among Protestants which characterized the post-1914 period elsewhere in the world. It was given impetus in Latin America by the criticism leveled at Protestants in that area that in contrast with the impressive façade of unity presented by the Roman Catholic Church (no matter how great and numerous its internal jealousies and rivalries) Protestants were patently divided.[39] Because of the opposition of some of the Germans and the Anglicans, who insisted that because it was a Christian region it did not fall within its purview, the World Missionary Conference which met at Edinburgh in 1910 did not include Latin America in its programme. Many from the United States were unhappy over the omission. In consequence, in 1913 there was held in New York City, under the auspices of the Committee of Reference and Counsel of the Foreign Missions Conference of North America, a conference on missions in Latin America at which were represented societies of the United States and Canada.[40] Out of this meeting came a continuing organization, the Committee on Co-operation in Latin America. It achieved a prominent place in promoting and co-ordinating Protestant efforts.[41] In 1916 there was convened at Panama a conference on Protestant missions in which a number of societies joined.[42] Following it, after the pattern of the Edinburgh conference, seven regional

[36] Bates, *Data on the Distribution of the Missionary Enterprise*, p. 5.

[37] Bates, *op. cit.*, p. 6.

[38] Bates, *op. cit.*, p. 7.

[39] A distinguished Mexican Protestant to the author, June, 1932.

[40] See the report in *Conference on Missions in Latin America* (New York, 1913).

[41] *Christian Work in Latin America*, Vol. I, pp. 9-11. See also the annual reports of the Committee on Co-operation in Latin America.

[42] See the report in *Christian Work in Latin America* (New York, The Missionary Education Movement, 3 vols., 1917. Back title, *Panama Congress, 1916*).

conferences were held.[43] Further congresses on Christian work in Latin America met at Montevideo in 1925[44] and Havana in 1929.[45] These gave additional impetus to joint effort.

Co-operation in more limited regions followed. A committee on co-operation in Mexico was constituted in 1927 in the form of the National Christian Council. In 1930 this was succeeded by the National Council of Evangelical Churches of Mexico.[46] From this, however, some of the strongest Protestant bodies held aloof. In 1930, too, the two Methodist churches which grew out of the missions of the northern and southern bodies in Mexico were united and a new church, independent of the parent bodies, was formed.[47] In Brazil, soon after the Panama conference of 1916, a committee on co-operation was organized. In the 1930's this was succeeded by a federation of Evangelical churches.[48] In Brazil also by the 1930's there were a Federation of Evangelical Schools, the Cayuá Indian Mission in which Presbyterians and Methodists joined, a Methodist and Presbyterian mission to the Japanese, and an institute in which several groups collaborated in the preparation of theological students.[49] National councils of Protestants also came into being in Argentina, Cuba, and Peru.[50] In Santo Domingo there was a Board of Christian Work which was a union of Methodists, Presbyterians, and United Brethren, with a church, a hospital, schools, and community service.[51]

The movement for co-operation did not entirely prevent friction. Several "faith" missions, usually theologically conservative and undenominational, entered areas where other Protestant groups were represented. This occasionally produced unhappiness among the latter.[52]

Its rapid growth in Latin America did not mean that Protestantism had become fully acclimatized or that opposition to it had died out. In the 1930's an outstanding Latin American Protestant could declare that Protestantism was still exotic and was under suspicion as a possible agency for the advance-

---

[43] See the reports in *Regional Conferences in Latin America* (New York, The Missionary Education Movement, 1917).

[44] See the report in *Christian Work in South America* (New York, Fleming H. Revell Company, 2 vols., 1925).

[45] Rycroft, *On This Foundation*, p. 93.

[46] *The International Review of Missions*, Vol. XX, p. 61.

[47] *Ibid.*; *The Methodist Church of Mexico (La Iglesia Metodista de Mexico). The Report of the Joint Commission on Unification in Mexico . . . July 7-8, 1930* (Issued by the authority of the Commission, pp. 46), *passim.*

[48] Braga and Grubb, *The Republic of Brazil*, p. 92.

[49] Braga and Grubb, *op. cit.*, pp. 80-82.

[50] Rycroft, *On This Foundation*, p. 92.

[51] Conversation with the head of the mission, B. N. Morgan, Oct. 17, 1931; *The Evangelical Handbook of Latin America*, 1937, p. 64.

[52] Braga and Grubb, *op. cit.*, pp. 69-71.

ment of the influence of the United States south of the Rio Grande. A Roman Catholic youth movement vigorously denounced it on much the same grounds —that it was alien to the Latin spirit and was a precursor to foreign domination.[53]

As a consequence of the Russian revolution, several tens of thousands of Orthodox Russians, Ukrainians, and Esthonians migrated to South America. They settled in Brazil, Argentina, Uruguay, Paraguay, Chile, and Peru. For their supervision the Russian Synod Abroad appointed (1934) a bishop, Theodosius, transferred from Detroit. He made his headquarters in São Paulo, Brazil. Constantin Israstzov, who had come to Buenos Aires in the 1880's and whose energy and organizing ability were mainly responsible for the erection of new buildings and the gathering of congregations, was made Protopresbyter and was left in charge of Argentina.[54]

It may help to give particularity to the picture to turn briefly from these generalizations to some of the individual islands and countries.

Puerto Rico was unique among the larger islands of the West Indies in being the territory of the United States, a position which it had held since 1898. Like several of its neighbours, it had a dense and growing population, was predominantly rural and agricultural, depended mainly on one crop, sugar, which it exported, and imported a large proportion of its food. There was much chronic under-nourishment. Approximately three-fourths of the population were white and one-fourth Negro. The connexion with the United States had brought a system of state schools of the same general pattern of that in the dominant power, with a university as its capstone, and, latterly, numerous projects which had as their purpose the cultural and economic transformation of the island. The overwhelming majority of the population were Roman Catholics. More than half of these seem to have been fairly regular attendants at church. In general the condition of the Roman Catholic Church appeared to be improving. Aid came from continental United States. In 1929, for instance, American Capuchins were assigned two stations on the island.[55] After 1898 Protestantism was vigorously propagated from the United

[53] Address made in presence of the author, June, 1932: Mackay, *The Other Spanish Christ,* pp. 79-81.
[54] Bolshakoff, *The Foreign Missions of the Russian Orthodox Church,* pp. 93-95.
[55] *1944 Mission Annual of the Seraphic Mass Association,* Sept. 10, 1943.

States. The main denominations were the Baptists, the Disciples, the Episcopalians, the Congregationalists, the United Brethren, the Methodists, the
Presbyterians, the United Lutherans, the Pentecostals, and the Seventh Day
Adventists. Among most of these there was much co-operation and division of
territory. In 1941 there were 319 organized Protestant churches with a membership of 32,122 and a constituency estimated at 81,854. Five denominations united
in a theological seminary. The Roman Catholic Church was in part supported
by endowments in lands. Protestant churches reproduced in large measure
the organization of that branch of the faith in the mainland of the United
States, where a quite different type of society existed. The Pentecostal and
Seventh Day Adventist congregations were chiefly self-supporting, but the
others depended heavily upon financial assistance from the missionary societies
of the United States. In a land which was prevailingly rural the Protestant
churches were predominantly urban.[56]

Cuba, the largest of the West Indies, also had sugar as its chief crop. Its
economy was subject, therefore, to the price of that commodity in the world
market. Since the price suffered great fluctuations during the post-1914 years,
Cuba knew alternately feverish prosperity and unnerving depression. Employment on the sugar plantations and in the sugar mills was seasonal. This
condition made for idleness for the population during the larger proportion of
the year and entailed poverty and moral disintegration. Most of the capital was
foreign, a circumstance which encouraged economic dependence and stifled
initiative.[57] More than two-thirds of the population were white and about a
fourth Negro. Roman Catholic Christianity was nominally the religion of the
overwhelming majority, but the island had never been as well supplied with
churches as had been some other parts of Latin America—much less than the
neighbouring Mexico, for instance. The Roman Catholic Church had suffered
in the transition to political independence, for, as in the rest of Latin America,
it had tended to be the stronghold of those who held to the older order and
the liberals, now dominant, had largely been alienated from it. It did not fully
supply its own clergy and nuns but drew many of these from Spain. It was,
therefore, in part an alien institution.[58] In the religious vacuum which followed,
various movements, some of them non-Christian, gained wide acceptance.
Christian Science, theosophy, and spiritualism of at least three kinds had

[56] J. Merle Davis, *The Church in Puerto Rico's Dilemma* (New York, International
Missionary Council, 1942, pp. viii, 80), *passim*; Morse, *Home Missions Today and Tomorrow*, pp. 215-220.
[57] Davis, *The Cuban Church in a Sugar Economy*, pp. 16-41.
[58] Davis, *op. cit.*, pp. 14, 15, 49, 50.

extensive followings. In the rural districts the cruder forms of spiritualism were popular. Among the Negroes cults flourished of which at least one, *ñáñigos*, was in part a survival of African fetishmen with an admixture of Christian ceremonies and phrases.[59] Protestant Christianity was introduced mainly from the United States and by denominations which were of such standard Anglo-Saxon origin as the Presbyterians, Baptists, Methodists, Episcopalians, Friends, and Seventh Day Adventists. Most of these bodies began operations between 1898, the date of active intervention by the United States on behalf of Cuba's freedom, and 1914. By the close of 1941 those won by these societies numbered about 35,000, if actual church members were counted, or about 150,000 if children and those thinking of themselves as Evangelicals (Protestants) were included. They were mainly in the towns and cities and from the lower middle class. In 1941 the majority of the churches were still financially dependent upon aid from the founding societies. Protestants stressed schools and the winning of converts.[60]

For Mexico the year 1911 rather than 1914 was the dividing line of an era. It was marked by a revolution which shook existing society more profoundly than did any other in a major Latin American land in the three decades after 1914. It was not new. It was the continuation of a struggle which had been intermittent during much of the nineteenth century. We must not take the space for the details of the conflict. Basically it was an attempt of the underprivileged majority to achieve a more favourable position. It was complicated by strong personalities, their rivalries and ambitions. Ideas of socialist and Communist provenance were prominent, but none of them succeeded in fully remaking society after its pattern. One of the most striking features was the attempt to halt the concentration of land in great estates and to reverse the trend to peonage with its half free status. The ideal was to bring about a redistribution of the land into smaller holdings. Some of this was accomplished, although the tenure of the larger part of the acreage of the country remained unaltered.[61] The revolution sought, too, better educational opportunities for the masses and strove for better educational procedures under the direction of the state. It made great strides in the education of the rural Indian population.[62] It endeavoured to curb foreign capital and to bring in better conditions

[59] Davis, *op. cit.*, pp. 50, 51.

[60] Davis, *op. cit.*, p. 62. On the American Baptist Foreign Mission Society and the progress of self support, see Detweiler, *The Waiting Isles*, pp. 74-87.

[61] Frank Tannenbaum, *The Mexican Agrarian Revolution* (Washington, The Brookings Institution, 1930, pp. xvi, 543), *passim*.

[62] Cameron Duncan Ebaugh, *The National System of Education in Mexico* (Baltimore, The Johns Hopkins Press, 1931, pp. ix, 149), *passim*.

for the labourers in industries and mines.[63] There was an attempt to reduce alcoholism.[64]

Deeply involved in this political and social upheaval, the churches and the Christianity of which they were the vehicle were vitally affected.

The Roman Catholic Church suffered reverses. It had been extremely powerful in colonial times and had then acquired vast landed estates. It had possessed a practical monopoly of education. Conflicts between civil and ecclesiastical dignitaries had punctuated the annals of colonial Mexico. Although some of the clergy had favoured independence and liberal movements, the main weight of the hierarchy and of clergy had been thrown against independence from Spain. Then, when independence had been achieved, the official structure of the Roman Catholic Church became a bulwark of what remained of the old social and economic order and was an active obstacle to liberal political and social trends. It had the support of wealthy landlords and sought by political means to ensure the continuation of its privileged status. In the 1850's the triumph of the liberals, temporary as it proved, made legal religious liberty, by refusing to acknowledge the Roman Catholic faith as that of the country tended to demote that form of Christianity from its privileged position, secularized the public schools, nationalized much of the property of the church, and sought to curb the religious orders. Church lands were confiscated as part of a general programme which had as its objective the division among small individual farmers of the great estates, whether ecclesiastical or secular.[65] Into the troubled decades which followed the 1850's and the swing of the pendulum for and against the church we need not go. In the process, most of the radical measures to curb the church were nullified. Under the regime of Porfirio Diaz, which spanned the quarter of a century from 1886 to 1911, the church gradually strengthened its hold. Church schools were increasing, ecclesiastical charitable institutions were acquiring lands, and stock companies under clerical control for dealing in real estate and mortgages were being formed.[66] The church was, moreover, becoming active in some phases of social reform. It was advocating work for all labourers, forming societies for labourers, fighting drunkenness, and recommending better housing and health measures.[67]

On the coming of the new revolution a Catholic party sprang into being

[63] Ross, *The Social Revolution in Mexico*, pp. 100-133; Camargo and Grubb, *Religion in the Republic of Mexico*, pp. 38-42.

[64] Camargo and Grubb, *op. cit.*, pp. 53, 54.

[65] Wilfrid Hardy Callcott, *Church and State in Mexico 1822-1857* (Duke University Press, pp. 357), *passim*.

[66] Callcott, *Liberalism in Mexico 1857-1929*, pp. 181-184.

[67] Callcott, *op. cit.*, pp. 178-181.

(1911) and was influential. However, some of the Roman Catholics insisted that their church as such and the clergy were not active in politics.[68]

The constitution framed in 1917 went further towards curbing the church than had any of its predecessors. It repeated some of the restrictions of earlier legislation and added to them. It forbade any religious corporation or minister of religion to inaugurate or direct primary schools, it prohibited the establishment of religious orders, it placed all public worship under the supervision of the government, it made state property even the buildings used for worship, it declared marriage to be a civil contract, it debarred clergymen from voting or holding office, it permitted only native Mexicans to be ministers of any faith, it allowed the state legislatures to determine the number of ministers in any locality, it estopped religious periodicals from dealing with affairs of state, and it banned all political organizations whose titles included any word implying religious belief.[69]

The Mexican bishops denounced the document. For several years it was not strictly enforced. The church countered, too, by fostering new organizations of its members, among them a National Catholic Confederation of Labour. Yet the church was suffering from a lack of clergy brought about by the closing of theological seminaries during the political upheavals. Spiritualism and to a less extent theosophy flourished.[70]

In 1926 the storm broke in intensified form. Under President Calles[71] the restrictive articles of the constitution were applied. The hierarchy hit back by suspending religious services, hoping thus to bring popular pressure on the government. The agitation spread to the Roman Catholics of the United States. The hierarchy of the northern republic publicly protested some of the acts of the Mexican state. Some Roman Catholics of the United States pressed for intervention by their government. In Mexico active revolt in behalf of the church broke out under the name of *Cristero*. However, the church lost in influence. The revolt was suppressed.[72] Foreign clergy were being expelled: for example, in 1926 twenty-eight Spanish Capuchins were deported and their churches, schools, and residences were closed.[73]

In 1929 an agreement was reached between state and church in which each

---

[68] Callcott, *op. cit.*, pp. 214-217.
[69] Callcott, *op. cit.*, pp. 274-279.
[70] Callcott, *op. cit.*, pp. 292, 293.
[71] See a presentation of his case by Calles in *Mexico before the World. Public Documents and Addresses of Plutarco Elias Calles*, translated from the Spanish and edited by Robert Hammond Murray (New York, The Academy Press, 1927, pp. 244), pp. 116-132.
[72] Callcott, *op. cit.*, pp. 351-373.
[73] *Capucins Missionnaires. Missions Françaises*, p. 74.

made concessions. The church then resumed its services.[74] Nuns were allowed (1930) to re-enter the country on their promise to observe the laws against convent and community life.[75] Exiled bishops returned. Catholic Action began achieving rapid progress in reaching, enlisting, and instructing the laity. Catholic student organizations were formed.[76]

In 1931 the conflict was again resumed. In spite of Papal protests and in part because of them, the state took more extreme measures. The renewed movement was not merely anti-clerical: some of it was openly anti-Christian, with scurrilous attacks on religion.[77] In one state a law was passed forbidding teachers to attend mass. There was a schismatic movement, short-lived as it proved, which sought to form a Catholic church independent of Rome which would support the revolution.[78] In 1935 it was said that there were seven states without either Roman Catholic or Protestant clergy and that in the entire country less than two hundred Roman Catholic priests had complied with the government regulations and registered.[79] By 1935 fourteen states had forbidden priests and made saying mass or giving the sacraments a criminal offense. In other states about twenty-five hundred priests were said to be unrecognized by the government and therefore without means of support. Many of those who in disobedience to the law remained by their flocks were imprisoned. Numbers of church buildings were put to secular uses.[80] In October, 1932, Pope Pius XI issued an encyclical to the archbishops and bishops of Mexico in which he rehearsed the story of the persecution and declared the purpose of the government to be the destruction of the Catholic Church. He permitted priests to ask for state licenses to officiate, but enjoined continued protests against the measures taken by the government. The encyclical intensified the storm, for radicals declared it to be foreign intervention in the affairs of the nation. The Apostolic Delegate was deported.[81] In the following two years efforts were made to impose upon the private schools the teaching of socialism. This was abhorrent to the teachers, most of whom were nuns in lay garb. Classes for teaching the catechism were violently stopped. Further restrictions were placed on the clergy in some of the states, in part through heavy professional taxes.[82]

[74] Callcott, *op. cit.*, p. 378; Macfarland, *Chaos in Mexico*, p. 73.
[75] *The International Review of Missions*, Vol. XX, pp. 60, 61.
[76] Parsons, *Mexican Martyrdom*, pp. 142-150.
[77] Macfarland, *op. cit.*, pp. 272-275.
[78] *The International Review of Missions*, Vol. XXIII, p. 98.
[79] K. G. Grubb in *The International Review of Missions*, Vol. XXIV, pp. 524-530.
[80] Parsons, *op. cit.*, pp. 174-177.
[81] Parsons, *op. cit.*, pp. 198-203.
[82] Parsons, *op. cit.*, pp. 228-234; Camargo and Grubb, *Religion in the Republic of Mexico*, pp. 82-84.

In at least some of the public schools the teaching was openly anti-religious and atheistic.[83]

The very violence of the attack on religion drew attention to Christianity and aroused active discussion.[84] Something of a reaction set in. By 1940 aggressive atheism had largely subsided.[85] By 1945 the church was once more having, in practice, a voice in the schools.

The hold of the Roman Catholic Church had been shaken and the Christianity which it had transmitted had been weakened. However, the church had not been destroyed. At least a minority had proved loyal to it in the face of persecution. Much of the Christian inheritance survived.

Protestantism could not escape the storm which shook the Roman Catholic Church. In principle and to a large extent in practice the measures taken by the state were applied impartially to all forms of Christianity. Protestant pastors could not teach in the schools. Foreigners could not be pastors. In some places, as in the state of Tobasco, the anti-religious persecution was directed against Protestants as well as against Roman Catholics. For a time in Tobasco all outward traces of Protestantism disappeared.[86] However, Protestantism displayed enough vitality to adapt itself to the new conditions and to grow.[87] The government census showed Protestants to be 68,839 in 1910, 73,951 in 1921, and 130,322 in 1930. To every 100,000 of the population in 1910 there were 454 Protestants, in 1921 516, and in 1930 787.[88] These figures included foreign residents but presumably showed a growth of native Mexicans of that faith. Protestants were largely in the cities and towns rather than in the rural districts and were most numerous in the regions bordering on the United States and in the central plateau.[89] Several areas saw a marked growth of Protestantism after 1920, some of it by purely Mexican initiative.[90] Here and there, as among the Huastecas of San Louis Potosi and the Mayas of Yucatan, there was notable expansion among the rural Indian population.[91] In part because of the pressure from the government, Mexicans came rapidly into positions of lead-

---

[83] Davis, *The Economic Basis of the Evangelical Church in Mexico*, pp. 27, 28.

[84] Camargo and Grubb, *op. cit.*, pp. 84, 85.

[85] *The International Review of Missions*, Vol. XXVIII, p. 71.

[86] Davis, *op. cit.*, p. 29.

[87] See among other evidences *Religious Education in the Methodist Church of Mexico* (Chicago, Joint Committee of Religious Education, 1937, pp. 100), *passim*. For the growth of the mission of the Pilgrim Holiness Church, begun after 1914, see Mrs. F. H. Soltero, *The Romance of Pilgrim Missions in Mexico* (Indianapolis, Pilgrim Publishing House, no date, pp. 95), *passim*.

[88] Camargo and Grubb, *op. cit.*, p. 103.

[89] Camargo and Grubb, *op. cit.*, pp. 93-98.

[90] Camargo and Grubb, *op. cit.*, pp. 97, 98.

[91] Davis, *op. cit.*, pp. 78-87.

ership in the Protestant churches. For instance, in 1930 and 1931 respectively the Methodists and Anglicans raised a Mexican to the episcopate.[92] Some mission schools were discontinued and some were transformed into centres for social service and hostels.[93] There was rapid growth in co-operation among the various denominations.[94] In general, Protestantism was exerting an influence quite out of proportion to its numbers.[95] In the 1930's it was said to be the most vital religious force in the land.[96]

In spite of the endurance shown by the Roman Catholic Church and the growth of Protestantism, in contrast with much of Latin America Christianity probably declined in strength in Mexico in the three decades after 1914.

The loss was sobering and perhaps significant. Mexico had been one of the two strongest centres of Latin American colonial Christianity. That Christianity had not been able sufficiently to adapt itself to the new conditions of the nineteenth and twentieth centuries to hold its own. It was clearly losing ground. This might have been ominous for the future of Christianity elsewhere in Latin America were it not for the fact that in some other Latin American lands the adjustment was apparently being made, although belatedly, and the Roman Catholic Church was registering some advances.

In Brazil, the largest of the Latin American states, the situation was different. Here in the three decades after 1914 Christianity was clearly gaining. In the colonial era and in the nineteenth century it had been weaker than in Mexico or Peru. The Roman Catholic Church, through which it had then been represented, although active politically, was still, after 1914, far from enlisting the hearty allegiance of more than a minority or from providing enough priests to minister to the religious needs of the masses. The vast majority, while nominally Roman Catholics, were not "practising Catholics." Into the void thus created had come spiritualism, theosophy, and positivism, all of which, although introduced earlier, were growing after 1914.[97] However, since its disestablishment, in 1890, the Roman Catholic Church had augmented the number of its dioceses and the efficiency of its clergy.[98] Moreover, Protestantism was rapidly increasing. Introduced from abroad by missionaries from Great Britain and the United States, chiefly from the latter country, and by a large immigration, mainly from Germany, it was becoming rooted in the soil and by 1945 was

[92] *The International Review of Missions*, Vol. XXI, p. 319.
[93] S. G. Inman in *Christian World Facts*, No. 16, Oct. 1935.
[94] Camargo and Grubb, *op. cit.*, pp. 104-107.
[95] K. G. Grubb in *The International Review of Missions*, Vol. XXIV, pp. 529, 530.
[96] H. E. Davis in *Christendom*, Vol. II, pp. 266, 270.
[97] Braga and Grubb, *The Republic of Brazil*, pp. 43, 44.
[98] Braga and Grubb, *op. cit.*, pp. 42, 43.

spreading spontaneously through the Brazilians themselves. Not far from 1930 the total Protestant community was estimated as being about 700,000.[99] The number of organized churches was rapidly mounting. It more than trebled between 1910 and 1930.[100] The 1930's saw most of the Protestants in denominations organized nationally and autonomously, although assistance still came from missionaries.[101] In 1930, for example, the Methodist Church of Brazil was constituted and elected its own bishop.[102] Brazilian Protestants were more and more spreading their faith on their own initiative. Large numbers of congregations, especially of the Presbyterians, Congregationalists, Pentecostals, and Seventh Day Adventists, were entirely self-supporting. In the 1940's there was a striking growth through the migration of Protestants to new frontiers and from the rural communities to the cities. The country, much of it raw and pioneering, was in a state of flux, with an eager sense of rapid development, and populations were shifting. As they moved to new "backwoods" regions and from rural districts to urban areas, Protestants were witnessing to their faith and were forming new congregations. They were doing this largely through lay initiative.[103] The majority of the Protestants were in the southern states, but that branch of the faith was also strong in the extreme north-eastern "bulge."[104] Most Protestants were from the lower classes and, except in some of the larger cities, were very little from the middle classes. Yet out of these underprivileged groups Protestantism, through its schools, its ideals of self-discipline, and its standards for morals and personality, was creating a middle class.[105]

Eastern Christianity was represented by a few Arabic-speaking Syrian Orthodox and by Russian refugees from Communism. A Russian bishop, as we saw a few pages above, had his seat at São Paulo.[106]

Partly through the Roman Catholic Church but chiefly through Protestantism, in Brazil Christianity was becoming more of a force to be reckoned with.

The other countries of Latin America must not long detain us. We can take

---

[99] Braga and Grubb, *op. cit.*, p. 140.

[100] Braga and Grubb, *op. cit.*, p. 84. For a picture of some Presbyterian missions see W. Reginald Wheeler *et alii*, *Modern Missions in Chile and Brazil* (Philadelphia, The Westminster Press, 1926, pp. xviii, 434), pp. 173 ff.

[101] Braga and Grubb, *op. cit.*, p. 85.

[102] Braga and Grubb, *op. cit.*, pp. 90, 91.

[103] *The International Review of Missions*, Vol. XXXII, p. 57, quoting J. Merle Davis. J. Merle Davis, after a visit of investigation in Brazil, to the author in the autumn of 1942.

[104] See the map in Braga and Grubb, *op. cit.*, opposite p. 96.

[105] J. Merle Davis to the author, autumn, 1942.

[106] Braga and Grubb, *op. cit.*, p. 43; Bolshakoff, *The Foreign Missions of the Russian Orthodox Church*, p. 94.

the space for only a few illustrations, somewhat scattered, to indicate what was happening. These will have to do with Protestantism, for it was that branch of the faith which was making the chief gains in this period. A few hundred Mennonites, some of them from Russia, some from Poland, and some from Canada, found new homes on tracts in Latin America—in Mexico, Brazil, and Paraguay.[107] Protestants, like Roman Catholics, were reaching out towards non-Christian Indian tribes in the interior. They were doing this largely through undenominational "faith missions."[108] The Bible, in whole or in part, was being translated and circulated in additional Indian tongues.[109] Numbers of new enterprises were undertaken by Protestant bodies. For instance, in 1918 the Protestant Episcopal Church of the United States entered two centres in Santo Domingo and in 1920 the Plymouth Brethren opened another centre in that republic.[110] In 1925, after the occupation of Haiti by armed forces of the United States, the American Baptist Home Mission Society sent a representative to that country who reinforced and encouraged existing Baptist efforts and soon saw many conversions, among them those of voodoo priests.[111] In 1920, in response to a plea from a layman of that land, the Evangelical Synod inaugurated a mission in Honduras.[112] There was a Pan-Lutheran Society for Latin America formed by individuals from various Lutheran synods in the United States. To Argentina there came in 1918 the United Lutherans, in 1927 the Missouri Synod (Lutheran), and in 1928 the New Testament Missionary Union.[113] In Argentina, among the groups of foreign immigrants, there were Armenian Congregationalists, Danish Lutherans, Dutch Reformed, French Protestants, German Congregationalists, German Evangelicals, Hebrew Christians, Hungarian Lutherans, Swedish Lutherans, Norwegian Lutherans, Scottish Presbyterians, Ukrainian Evangelicals, and Waldensians.[114] In Bolivia there arrived in 1920 the initial contingents of the Bolivian Friends Holiness

[107] Yoder, *For Conscience Sake*, pp. 103-111, 170-188.

[108] *The International Review of Missions*, Vol. XX, pp. 228-240, Vol. XXV, p. 77; Mackay, *The Other Spanish Christ*, pp. 242, 243; Strong and Warnshuis, *Directory of Foreign Missions*, p. 55; Walters, *Charles T. Studd*, p. 121; K. G. Grubb, *The Lowland Indians of Amazonia* (London, World Dominion Press, 1927, pp. 159), *passim*; W. F. Jordan, *Central American Indians and the Bible* (New York, Fleming H. Revell Company, 1926, pp. 91), pp. 78 ff.; *The Journals of Ernest George Fenton Hall* (London, Worldwide Evangelisation Crusade and Heart of Amazonia Mission, 1926, pp. 150, xvii), *passim*; A. R. Hay, *The Indians of South America and the Gospel* (New York, Fleming H. Revell Company, 1928, pp. 167), *passim*.

[109] *The International Review of Missions*, Vol. XXXIII, p. 68.

[110] Smith, *Conquests for Christ in the West Indies*, p. 101.

[111] Detweiler, *The Waiting Isles*, pp. 108-114.

[112] Edith Moulton Melick, *Seed Sowing in Honduras* (St. Louis, Eden Publishing House, 1927, pp. 166), *passim*.

[113] *The Evangelical Handbook of Latin America*, 1937 edition, p. 27.

[114] *The Evangelical Handbook of Latin America*, 1937 edition, p. 20.

Mission, in 1921 of the Plymouth Brethren, in 1927 of the Inland South American Missionary Union.[115] Brazil saw the inauguration of effort in 1914 by the Inland South American Missionary Union and the Örebro Missionary Society, in 1922 by the Salvation Army, and in 1924 by the Unevangelized Fields Mission.[116] The Southern Baptist Convention sent its first representatives to Chile in 1917 and the Young Men's and Young Women's Christian Associations in 1920 and 1921 respectively.[117] To Colombia there came after 1914 the Christian and Missionary Alliance, the World-wide Evangelization Crusade, the Assemblies of God, and the Inland South American Missionary Union.[118] In 1921 Costa Rica became a field of the Latin American Evangelization Campaign.[119] The Christian and Missionary Alliance arrived in force in Ecuador, beginning in 1922,[120] and in Peru in 1926.[121] This list of new undertakings gives evidence of the prominence of the "faith missions." The Methodist Episcopal Church, which had long functioned in Latin America, began several fresh types of enterprises. It sent two Negro nurses to South America;[122] it developed a large farm in Chile as a means of giving opportunities to unemployed and underprivileged urban dwellers;[123] and it made possible in many centres lectures on Christianity to the intelligentsia by a peculiarly gifted Argentinian of North American descent.[124] Protestant schools continued to be prominent.[125] Moreover, Protestantism was beginning to show initiative in its own propagation, especially in Brazil. Through the International Missionary Council, the World's Student Christian Federation, and the World Council of Churches it was beginning to be drawn into a worldwide fellowship.

In its numerical strength and internal vigour Protestantism was still very unevenly distributed. As before 1914, it was strongest in Mexico and Brazil. In some other nations, as in Argentina, it was relatively weak. Everywhere it was a minority movement, but it was making contributions through its new types of schools, its physical culture, its hospitals, its distribution of the Bible,

[115] *The Evangelical Handbook of Latin America*, 1937 edition, p. 32.
[116] *The Evangelical Handbook of Latin America*, 1937 edition, p. 46.
[117] *The Evangelical Handbook of Latin America*, 1937 edition, p. 51.
[118] *The Evangelical Handbook of Latin America*, 1937 edition, p. 55.
[119] *The Evangelical Handbook of Latin America*, 1937 edition, p. 58.
[120] *The Evangelical Handbook of Latin America*, 1937 edition, p. 69.
[121] *The Evangelical Handbook of Latin America*, 1937 edition, p. 103.
[122] Diffendorfer, *A Voyage of Discovery*, p. 6.
[123] Diffendorfer, *op. cit.*, pp. 18-35.
[124] George Parkinson Howard, *A Spiritual Adventure in South America* (New York, Committee on Cooperation in Latin America, 1943, pp. 68), *passim*.
[125] Committee on Cooperation in Latin America, Annual Report 1931, pp. 3-5.

its emphasis upon spiritual and moral transformation, and its stimulus, through competition, to the Roman Catholic Church.[126]

In spite of losses in Mexico through the blows dealt the Roman Catholic Church, in the three decades after 1914 Christianity was gaining in Latin America. It was doing this in part through accessions of vigour to the Roman Catholic Church, through immigration, and, especially, through the rapid growth of Protestantism. It was making contributions to the life of the area through education, through some of its charities and social services, and through its religious message. However, Latin American Christianity was still, as it had been in the past, passive. It did not display sufficient vitality to initiate missons to other countries. It gave but scanty assistance in personnel and funds to the great missionary agencies of the Roman Catholic Church.[127] It still relied for much of its personnel upon the churches of other lands. It showed almost no enterprise in carrying the Christian message to non-Christian Indians within its own borders. A large proportion of the upper classes maintained at most a formal connexion with it. Its outstanding representative, the Roman Catholic Church, seemed to many of the finest spirits obscurantist, allied to the exploiting classes, a bulwark of superstition, and a political rather than a moral force. Yet there were signs of improvement and it was possibly an augury of the future that in the land where Protestantism was the strongest numerically, Brazil, the native-born adherents of that branch of the faith were beginning to be spontaneously active in its propagation. Christianity seemed to be slowly emerging from the nadir to which it had been forced by the political revolutions of the fore part of the nineteenth century.

[126] On instances of its stimulus to the Roman Catholic Church see Sanchez in *Christendom*, Vol. IX, pp. 42, 45, 47, 49.

[127] Not far from 1930 only 336 Roman Catholic missionaries were listed as from South America. Only 55 of these were priests and only 66 lay brothers. 199, or nearly two-thirds, were sisters. This was less than half the total provided by Canada, whose Roman Catholic population was less than a tenth of that of South America.—*Testo-Atlante Illustrato delle Missioni*, p. 100.

Chapter VIII

THE LANDS IN THE PACIFIC
AUSTRALIA: NEW ZEALAND: THE PACIFIC ISLANDS: THE
EAST INDIES: THE PHILIPPINES

TO THE lands and islands which were enclosed by the Pacific Ocean the three decades which succeeded 1914 brought varying degrees of changes and at different times. In some the first of the world wars wrought an alteration in sovereignty. The islands and areas which in 1914 were in the possession of Germany were transferred to the victorious nations, north of the equator to Japan and south of that line to Australia or New Zealand. This was done under the guise of mandates supervised by the League of Nations, but the mandatory power was substantially in full control. The Marianas (except for Guam, which belonged to the United States), the Caroline, and the Marshall Islands went to Japan, the north-eastern section of New Guinea, New Britain, New Ireland, the Admiralty Islands, the northern Solomons and several adjacent groups to Australia, and the German portion of Samoa to New Zealand. Obviously the shifts in political allegiance would be followed by modifications of the religious situation. The Philippines moved rapidly towards independence. More halting steps towards self-government were taken in the Netherlands East Indies.

The second of the world wars was accompanied by striking developments in almost all the region. Australia and New Zealand were even more deeply involved than in the earlier conflict. The Japanese conquered the Philippines, the East Indies (except for the Portuguese portion of Timor, and this they controlled), and several of the groups which had been under Great Britain and Australia. The islands in the possession of France were cut off from that country. In the counter operations through which the British, the Australians, the New Zealanders, and the Americans drove back the Japanese many of the islanders were brought more intimately in touch with Westerners and their civilization than ever before. For the most part, then, the peoples of the Pacific were more profoundly affected by the events which came with the second world war and particularly following the extension of that war to the Pacific following the attack of Japan upon Pearl Harbour on December 7, 1941, than they had been by the first of the world wars and its immediate aftermath. By 1945 it was still too early to see clearly what the consequences would be for Christianity, especially in the regions occupied by the Japanese. For most of the territory embraced in this chapter the little more than two and a half decades which intervened between 1914 and the full engulfment of the Pacific in the second of the world wars were a continuation, without a sharp break, of the years which immediately preceded 1914. The course of Christianity can, therefore, be dealt with rather more briefly than if the earlier part of the era had been more revolutionary.

In Australia the proportion of those professing to have a connexion with the Church in some of its many forms or a preference for one of them declined after 1914. In 1921 the percentage of those not acknowledging either connexion or preference was 3.1,[1] while in 1933 the percentage not specifying such a relationship explicitly was about 13.[2] This seems to indicate a rapid increase in those having too little attachment to Christianity to feel an interest in any branch of the Church. The difference may, however, have been in the method of taking the census. Among the religious bodies, in 1933 the Church of England led in size, with about a fourth of the population, the Roman Catholics were next with a little over a sixth, and the Methodists and Presbyterians followed, with a little over a tenth each. The others were much smaller.[3] Between 1921 and 1933 the Greek Catholics more than doubled, but in the latter year they still numbered only 11,911. Next in proportionate increase were the Seventh Day Adventists, with an addition of about 24 per cent. in these years, but in 1933 they were only 13,965. Of the larger denominations, in the twelve year period Presbyterians grew about 11 per cent., Methodists about 8 per cent., the Church of England about 6 per cent., and those specifically labelling themselves Roman Catholics only about 2.5 per cent. However, those classifying themselves as Catholics, without indicating whether this meant Roman or Anglican, more than doubled. If, as is probable, most of them were Roman Catholics, the Roman Catholic increase was about 10 per cent. Next to the four leading denominations, but far behind them, were the Baptists and the Congregationalists. In the twelve year interval between the two censuses the former barely held their own and the latter lost about 12.5 per cent.[4] Denominationally the Christianity of Australia clearly was still largely that of the British Isles.

[1] Wilson, *Official Year Book of the Commonwealth of Australia*, No. 32, 1939, p. 381.
[2] *Ibid.*
[3] *Ibid.*
[4] *Ibid.*

Such groups of non-British origin as the Seventh Day Adventists, the Church of Christ, and the Lutherans were very small minorities: none of them attracted as many as one per cent. of the population.[5] No indigenous denomination of any size emerged.

The movement towards union on a national scale of similar denominations continued.[6] The Church of England, which had formed an Australian-wide general synod in 1872, after 1914 began the steps to sever the legal tie which bound it to the Church of England in the mother country and which made it an autonomous member of the Anglican communion.[7] Because of the German origin of most of the membership, legal and popular restrictions were placed on some of the Lutheran activities during the first of the world wars. However, these did not entail any great loss to Lutheranism. The pre-1914 movement towards bringing together the several Lutheran bodies continued and in 1921 reached an important milestone in the formation of the United Evangelical Lutheran Church in Australia. This included 54 per cent. of the Lutherans of the Commonwealth. The other 46 per cent. were in the Evangelical Lutheran Synod in Australia, closely allied with the Missouri Synod in the United States.[8]

Co-operation between religious bodies was increasing. In 1926 there was held in Melbourne, under the chairmanship of John R. Mott, a meeting of the missionary societies of various denominations which issued, in 1927, in the formation of the National Missionary Council of Australia.[9]

A movement was under way for a comprehensive Protestant church for all Australia. Serious proposals were made for the union of Presbyterians, Methodists, and Congregationalists, somewhat akin to what had been achieved in the sister commonwealth, the Dominion of Canada.[10]

Participation in the International Missionary Council through the National Missionary Council and the early adherence of the Church of England in Australia and the Presbyterian Church of Australia to the nascent World

[5] *Ibid.*

[6] For its earlier stages see Vol. V, pp. 173, 174.

[7] R. A. Giles, *The Constitutional History of the Australian Church* (London, Skeffington & Son, Ltd., 1929, pp. 320), pp. 168 ff.; *The Official Year-Book of the National Assembly of the Church of England*, 1933, p. 621.

[8] Th. Hebart, *The United Evangelical Lutheran Church in Australia (U.E.L.C.A.)* (North Adelaide, Lutheran Book Depot, 1938, pp. 336), *passim*. For a history of one branch of the United Evangelical Lutheran Church in Australia see F. Otto Theile, *One Hundred Years of the Lutheran Church in Queensland* (Publication Committee of the Queensland District, United Evangelical Lutheran Church in Australia, 1938, pp. 290).

[9] *The International Review of Missions*, Vol. XXI, p. 352; *Australia Facing the Non-Christian World. Report of Australian Missionary Conference . . . April, 1926* (Melbourne, Alpha Printing Company, pp. 139), *passim*.

[10] Macdonald, *One Hundred Years of Presbyterianism in Victoria*, pp. 149 ff.

Council of Churches drew the majority of Australian Christians into the world-wide family of non-Roman Catholic Christianity.

Australian Christianity was still receiving aid from the mother country, at least in the form of personnel.[11] However, it was more and more reaching out to meet the needs of its own continent and to propagate its faith in other lands and islands. For instance, in Victoria the number of Presbyterian charges increased from 192 in 1904 to 228 in 1920 and to 246 in 1936, and the presbyteries from 14 to 17 and then to 20 in these successive years. In 1936 the Presbyterian Home Mission Committee of Victoria was assisting 85 mission stations.[12] After the formation of the United Evangelical Lutheran Church in Australia (1921), the Lutherans associated with it showed augmented activity in home missions, particularly since an increasing number of young pastors were available who could use both German and English.[13] The churches continued to bear a large part of the burden of education, especially of secondary and higher schools.[14] They also persisted in their efforts to win the aborigines and to protect them from the disintegrating influences of the impact of white civilization. In 1926 the various Protestant bodies had 72 missionaries among the aborigines. It was estimated that there were then 29 mission stations, of which 5 were Roman Catholic, and that about 10,000 of the approximately 73,000 aborigines in the continent were in touch with missionaries.[15] It was said that while on the government reservations the death rate exceeded the birth rate, in the settlements maintained by the missions the birth rate was greater than the death rate.[16] The Roman Catholic missions had been chiefly in the hands of non-Australians, but in the 1930's it was reported that Australian Roman Catholics were taking an increasing interest in the conversion of the aborigines.[17] In 1926 Protestants

[11] Information given the author by a leading Scottish churchman (July, 1936) about personnel from Scotland for the Australian ministry.

[12] Macdonald, *op. cit.*, pp. 67, 68.

[13] Theile, *op. cit.*, pp. 126, 127.

[14] Macdonald, *op. cit.*, pp. 82-85; *Twenty-Seventh Annual Report 1929 and Syllabus for 1930. Catholic Schools, Archdiocese of Sydney*, p. 1; Watson A. Steel, *The History of All Saints' College Bathurst 1873-1934* (Australia, Angus & Robertson, Ltd., 1936, pp. 217), *passim.*

[15] *Australia Facing the Non-Christian World*, pp. 6, 11, 12; *The International Review of Missions*, Vol. XXVIII, p. 81, Vol. XXXII, pp. 196-200, 301-310; Daisy Bates, *The Passing of the Aborigines. A Lifetime Spent among the Natives of Australia* (London, John Murray, 1938, pp. xviii, 258); J. S. Needham, *White and Black in Australia* (London, The Society for Promoting Christian Knowledge, 1935, pp. 174); Patrick H. Ritchie, *North of the Never Never* (London, Burns, Oates & Washbourne, Ltd., 1935, pp. xii, 227). See also *Ernabella News Letter* concerning a mission of the Presbyterian Church of Australia among the aborigines in South Australia, opened in 1936.

[16] *Australia Facing the Non-Christian World*, p. 17.

[17] *Fides News Service*, March 7, 1936.

were maintaining ten missionaries among the Chinese in Australia.[18] Australian Protestants were, moreover, lifting their horizons to include other parts of the world. They supported missionaries in a number of the adjacent islands in the Pacific, especially those under Australian rule. They also had them in several sections of Asia. These were not only in India, for which as a member of the British Empire they might feel a peculiar responsibility, but also in the Far East beyond the borders of British territory.[19]

While the three decades after 1914 had witnessed no revolutionary developments, Christianity was becoming increasingly an integral element in the life of Australia. Australian Christianity was still to some degree colonial, depending to a certain extent upon the mother country for leadership in personnel and even more for its thought. As yet it was making few if any original contributions to the Church Universal. However, it was fairly steadily becoming less dependent upon the founding churches in the British Isles. More and more it was taking the responsibility for the Australian Continent and was sharing in the spread of the faith in the Eastern Hemisphere. Moreover, by its connexions with the International Missionary Council, the incipient World Council of Churches, and other phases of the Ecumenical Movement, Australian Protestantism was being brought into the life of the world Church.

In New Zealand, as we saw earlier,[20] the aborigines were of a very different race from those in Australia. They were Maoris, Polynesians, sturdier and more persistent in the face of the white man than were the primitive folk of Australia. The fact that, unlike Australia, the initial contacts of the white man with the native peoples were chiefly through missionaries may also have enabled the Maoris better to survive the irruption of Western culture and more quickly to make their adjustment to it. By the middle of the nineteenth century almost all Maoris regarded themselves as Christians, even though only a small proportion were communicants of a Christian church. In the government census of 1926 only about 5 per cent. refused to acknowledge a religious preference.[21] In the decades following 1914 the trend was towards an enhanced race consciousness and desire for religious autonomy. The largest proportion to adhere to any religious fellowship, approximately a third in 1926, counted themselves as Anglicans.[22] Some time after 1914 the Maori Anglicans de-

---

[18] *Australia Facing the Non-Christian World*, p. 6.
[19] *Ibid.*
[20] Vol. V, pp. 177-185.
[21] Keesing, *The Changing Maori*, pp. 143, 144.
[22] *Ibid.*

manded that instead of being distributed among various dioceses they have an organization of their own, with one of their number as bishop. This was accomplished, and a Maori clergyman was consecrated as a suffragan.[23] In 1926, next to the Anglicans the largest proportion of Maoris, between a fifth and a sixth, were in the Ratana Church. This body had come into being as the result of a movement led by a Maori, Tahu Wiremu Ratana. Beginning in 1920, Ratana challenged his people to turn from their superstitions to God and promised that if they complied God would send his angels to minister to them. He attracted much attention by his claim to heal diseases by faith. At one stage he declared that the Japanese were coming to right the wrongs of the Maoris. He was said at one time to have had the following of about two-thirds of the Maoris. In 1925 a separate church was formed for his adherents. It developed an intricate organization with a bank, town-planning, and an economic and political emphasis. Ratana himself faded into the background.[24] Another Maori leader, Rua, preached that in 1927 Christ would return and that all would be destroyed who did not take refuge in a designated mountain stronghold.[25] From the Maoris, then, movements were continuing to emerge, partly Christian in background, somewhat akin to the earlier Hau Hau and other prophet-led sects,[26] and not unlike many others which had appeared from time to time in various countries.

New Zealand's white population, which was not far from a million and a half in 1936, was more nearly committed to Christianity than was that of Australia. This may have been because of the absence of the convict element in the foundations of the dominion which played so large a part in Australia and because of the strong religious factors in the planting of the two large centres of Christchurch and Dunedin.[27] Certainly the proportion of those who in the census of 1936 declined to state any church preference, a little short of 6 per cent., was less than half of that in Australia.[28] The distribution of the population among the major denominations did not change much with the years. Anglicans and Presbyterians loomed larger than in Australia, with about two-fifths and a quarter of the whole respectively. Roman Catholics, with about 13 per cent., and Methodists with slightly over 8 per cent., were smaller elements than in Australia. Presbyterians and Roman Catholics were increasing slightly in proportion to the population and Anglicans less than proportionately. In

[23] Keesing, op. cit., p. 151.
[24] Keesing, op. cit., pp. 149, 150; Pinfold, Fifty Years in Maoriland, pp. 124, 125.
[25] Keesing, op. cit., p. 146.
[26] Vol. V, p. 183.
[27] Vol. V, pp. 185-196.
[28] The Statesman's Year-Book, 1943, p. 411.

the ten years before 1936 Methodists lost in numbers. Between the 1880's and 1936 Congregationalists and Baptists, always small minorities, had markedly decreased in their percentages of the whole, the former by nearly two-thirds and the latter by about a half.[29] Even more than in Australia, the white population was sprung from Britain and the churches were from that land. The high income level, much above that of the British Isles, made possible the generous financial support of the churches and of their overseas mission efforts.[30] The rapid growth of cities and the shift of the centre of population from the South to the North Island made necessary much new building of churches and parsonages. This was accomplished and home mission aid was given to weaker parishes, an evidence of the inherent strength of New Zealand Christianity.[31] Missions were also maintained in several of the islands of the Pacific and in India and the Far East.[32] The churches had an important share in education. Several colleges were opened after 1914.[33] Some of the churches were active in the advocacy of temperance and marriage legislation.[34] During the second of the world wars the leading churches supported a Campaign for Christian Order. This was in part an outgrowth of the Oxford Life and Work Conference on Church, Community, and State of 1937 and of later movements in Great Britain and the United States.[35] Through the National Missionary Council of New Zealand there was connexion with the International Missionary Council.[36] The two main churches, the Anglican Church of the Province of New Zealand and the Presbyterian Church of New Zealand, were among the bodies which early gave adherence to the World Council of Churches. As in so many other countries and regions of nineteenth century planting, after 1914 the Christianity of New Zealand grew in vigour and became increasingly a conscious part of a world-wide Christian fellowship.

There is neither space nor occasion for a detailed account of the vicissitudes of Christianity in the three decades following 1914 in all of the many islands and groups of islands which stud the Pacific. We have earlier described the introduction and growth of Christianity, one of the most thrilling chapters

[29] Elder, *The History of the Presbyterian Church of New Zealand*, p. 187.
[30] Elder, *op. cit.*, p. 193.
[31] Elder, *op. cit.*, pp. 179 ff.
[32] Elder, *op. cit.*, pp. 269-309; Parker, *Directory of World Missions*, pp. 5-7.
[33] Elder, *op. cit.*, pp. 363-366.
[34] Elder, *op. cit.*, pp. 346 ff.
[35] *The Spiritual Issues of the War*, Nov. 12, 1942.
[36] Parker, *op. cit.*, p. 92.

in the story of the spread of the faith.[37] Before 1914 the populations of a number of the island groups, especially those which were Polynesian, had moved *en masse* into the Christian Church and had sent missionaries to other islands. In most of the others Christianity had been planted. In the three decades after 1914 self government and self support increased among the churches of the islands which were already Christian.[38] The faith continued to gain converts among the populations which had not yet fully adhered to it. For instance, in the Gilbert Islands between 1920 and 1930 the churches mounted from 96 to 116, the ordained Gilbertese from 16 to 42, and the church members from 3,737 to 5,489.[39]

However, even before the second of the world wars the airplane and commerce were bringing the islands and their populations more and more into the currents of the world's life and the disintegration of the older structure of society went on apace. The second of the world wars accelerated the process.

Something of a problem still existed in achieving financial self-support by the churches. Protestant missionaries tended to build institutions on a scale to which they had become accustomed at home but whose maintenance was quite beyond the reach of the more limited economy of the islanders. Roman Catholic missions drew heavily from endowments and contributions in the lands from which their personnel came and in some instances engaged in commerce and cultivated plantations to augment their incomes.[40] Christians and Christian pastors were becoming more racially self conscious and were objecting to being called "natives," a term which to them carried a tinge of opprobrium. Increasing emphasis was placed by Protestants upon the training of an indigenous ministry.[41] In 1929 and 1931 the London Missionary Society put into operation a plan of organization which gave a much larger degree of control in ecclesiastical matters to the Samoan churches which had arisen out of its efforts.[42] In the 1920's these churches bore the entire cost of the white missionaries and contributed in men and money to missions on the Gilbert and Ellice Islands and in New Guinea.[43]

A general trend, especially in the islands which had been longest subject

[37] Vol. V, pp. 198-263.
[38] *The International Review of Missions*, Vol. XXVIII, pp. 76, 77.
[39] *The Hundred and Thirty-Sixth Report of the London Missionary Society*, p. 168.
[40] Burton, *Missionary Survey of the Pacific Islands*, pp. 19-21.
[41] Burton, *op. cit.*, p. 22.
[42] Felix M. Keesing, *Modern Samoa. Its Government and Changing Life* (London, George Allen & Unwin, Ltd., pp. 506), p. 406; Cecil Northcott, *Southward Ho!* (London, Livingstone Press, no date, pp. 98), pp. 84, 85.
[43] *The Hundred and Thirty-Sixth Report of the London Missionary Society*, p. 166.

to white government, was the passing of education from the missions to the colonial administration. Yet the process was by no means completed by 1945.[44]

The churches of Australia and New Zealand carried a larger proportion of the responsibility for the Protestant missions in the area than did those of other countries. That share was augmented by the outcome of the first of the world wars and the increase in territory under the control of those two commonwealths.

The Fiji Islands presented an acute problem to the Christian forces. Primarily through Methodist missions in the second half of the nineteenth century most of the population had become Christians. However, between 1879 and 1916 about 60,000 Indians were introduced as indentured labourers on the plantations. Two-thirds of these were from the United and Central Provinces and about a third from South India. The indenture system carried with it abuses which were a challenge to the Christian conscience. After 1916 these were partially remedied. Most of the Indians remained in Fiji after their contracts expired. A large proportion became peasant cultivators of the soil. They leased fertile tracts from the Fijians, pushing the latter onto the less fertile hills. Their rate of natural increase was much greater than that of the Fijians and by 1936 they were almost as numerous as the latter. Some attempt was made by the Methodists to help the Fijians to better methods of cultivation and marketing, but the native population was in danger of losing out.[45] The Indians were Moslems, Hindus, or Sikhs. Although there were Anglican, Methodist, and Roman Catholic missions among them, converts were slow in coming.[46] Yet it was estimated that in the mid-1930's about an eighth of the Indians professed to be Christians.[47] In 1939 a Fiji-born Indian, a convert from Hinduism, was ordained an Anglican priest.[48]

Hawaii presented, as before 1914, a mixture of diverse races, the most numerous, the Japanese, non-Christian by tradition. After 1914 immigration, except from the Philippines and the mainland of the United States, largely ceased. Amalgamation proceeded apace. Christianity continued to make progress

[44] Goodall in *The International Review of Missions*, Vol. XXXII, p. 400. The increase of government as against mission schools was marked in Fiji.—Mann, *Education in Fiji*, p. 26.

[45] John Wesley Coulter, *Fiji. Little India of the Pacific* (University of Chicago Press, 1942, pp. xiii, 156), pp. 17, 42, 81.

[46] W. J. Hands, *Polynesia* (Westminster, Society for the Propagation of the Gospel in Foreign Parts, 1929, pp. 54), pp. 42-45; C. W. W. Aston, *Levuka Days* (Westminster, Society for the Propagation of the Gospel in Foreign Parts, 1936, pp. 95), pp. 72-77.

[47] Mann, *Education in Fiji*, p. 73.

[48] *The International Review of Missions*, Vol. XXIX, p. 95.

among the non-Christians. The remarkable approach to amity in the relations between the races was to no small degree due to the Christian faith.[49]

The shifts of territory which accompanied the first of the world wars brought changes in the ecclesiastical map. These were often followed by continued gains in the spread of Christianity. The Japanese acquisition of the Mariana, Caroline, and Marshall Islands had as an early sequel the compulsory withdrawal of the German missionaries. The Roman Catholics were largely Capuchins, representatives of the Hiltrup house of the Holy Heart of Jesus, and Protestants were associated with the Liebenzell Mission.[50] The missionaries of the American Board of Commissioners for Foreign Missions continued, as before, on the Marshall group. At the instance of the Japanese administration the *Kumiai* (Congregational) churches of Japan formed the *Nanyo Dendo San* (South Sea Mission) and with the aid of a government subsidy sent out a small staff (1920). In 1932 this mission took over the enterprise of the American Board. In 1927 the German Liebenzell missionaries were permitted to resume. Beginning in 1921 the Spanish Capuchins revived the Roman Catholic cause. Under the new order Christians in the Japanese mandated islands increased both in total numbers and in proportion to the population. In 1926 they were said to be 54 per cent. and in 1936 78 per cent. of the population. Protestants were slightly in excess of Roman Catholics. It was declared that Christianity, and particularly Protestant Christianity, had broken down the old forms of religion, had reduced the frequency of polygamy, drinking, and smoking, had curbed the native dances, had reduced the languages to writing, and had inculcated industry, improved sanitation, and restrained tribal warfare.[51]

The passing of the northern of the Gilbert Islands from German to British control as the result of the first of the world wars precipitated a step which had long been contemplated, the transfer of the activities in that area from the American Board of Commissioners for Foreign Missions to the London Missionary Society.[52] The two societies were so closely related in background and constituency that the change was made with a minimum of disturbance to the continuing Protestant community. Moreover, the London Missionary

---

[49] Sidney L. Gulick, *Mixing the Races in Hawaii* (Honolulu, The Hawaiian Board Book Rooms, 1937, pp. xiii, 220), *passim*, especially pp. 27-33, 72-76, 99-116, 127-137, 142-165; *Handbooks on the Missions of the Episcopal Church*, No. VIII. *Hawaiian Islands* (New York, The National Council of the Protestant Episcopal Church, Department of Missions, 1927, pp. 95), pp. 87-91.

[50] Vol. V, pp. 257, 258.

[51] Tadao Yanaihara, *Pacific Islands under Japanese Mandate* (Shanghai, Kelly and Walsh, Ltd., 1939, pp. x, 312), pp. 233, 234; W. B. Harris in *Foreign Affairs*, Vol. X, pp. 691-697; P. H. Clyde in *Contemporary Japan*, Vol. III, pp. 425-436.

[52] *The One Hundredth and Seventh Report of the American Board of Commissioners for Foreign Missions*, p. 221.

Society had been in the southern Gilberts since 1899. Between 1920 and 1930, as we saw a few paragraphs above, that society counted an advance from 3,737 to 5,489 church members and from 16 to 42 Gilbertese ordained ministers.[53]

In the Solomons the transfer of the northern islands from Germany to Australian mandate did not work any marked change in the missionary situation. The Marists made progress.[54] In 1930 a new vicariate was created and an American Marist was appointed vicar apostolic.[55] The same Protestant societies were present as before 1914,[56] except that in 1922 the Australian Methodists transferred their undertaking to the Methodists of New Zealand.[57] Advance continued, with successful approaches to new tribes and villages, an increase in numbers of Christians, and the translation of parts of the Bible into fresh tongues.[58] Christianity was both partly fitting into the earlier pattern of native life and working changes in it.[59] The natives were beginning to take more and more responsibility. Among the Anglicans an indigenous brotherhood and a native sisterhood arose.[60]

The change in the north-eastern section of New Guinea from German rule to Australian mandate which came as a result of the first world war worked alterations in the missionary situation but did not markedly retard the Christian advance. Some embarrassment was brought to the Roman Catholic enterprise. This was represented by the Society of the Divine Word. The fact that it had been largely self-supporting through an extensive plantation system kept it from suffering greatly financially from the first of the world wars and the attendant interruption of contact with the home constituency. However, the Australians placed difficulties in the way of bringing reinforcements from Germany, even after the treaty of peace. Not until 1922 did additions to the foreign personnel begin to arrive. They were chiefly from Holland, Austria, and Germany. In spite of the hiatus, the number of Roman Catholics increased. Financial aid was given by the American branch of the society.[61] An interesting

[53] *The Hundred and Thirty-Sixth Report of the London Missionary Society*, p. 168.

[54] Mary Rose, *Saving the Solomons* (Boston, The Society for the Propagation of the Faith, 1942, pp. 297), pp. 123 ff.

[55] Lesourd, *L'Année Missionnaire*, 1931, p. 558.

[56] Vol. V, pp. 237, 238.

[57] Burton, *Missionary Survey of the Pacific Islands*, p. 53.

[58] Burton, *op. cit.*, pp. 53, 116, 117; R. C. Nicholson, *The Son of a Savage. The Story of Daniel Bula* (New York, The Abingdon Press, no date, pp. 127), *passim*.

[59] H. Ian Hogbin, *Experiments in Civilization. The Effects of European Culture on a Native Community of the Solomon Islands* (London, George Routledge & Sons, Ltd., 1939, pp. xvii, 268), pp. 173 ff.

[60] Stuart W. Artless, *The Church in Melanesia* (Westminster, Melanesian Mission, no date, pp. 106), pp. 53 ff., 103.

[61] Hagspiel, *Along the Mission Trail*, Vol. III, pp. 125-131; Johannes Thauren, *Die Missionen der Gesellschaft des Göttl. Wortes in den Heidenländern. Die Missionen in Neu Guinea* (Steyl, Missionsdruckerei, 1931, pp. 40), *passim*.

accompaniment of the Roman Catholic mission was a marked increase in the birth rate in the areas under its influence.[62] Before 1914 the Protestants had been represented by the Rhenish and Neuendettelsau missions, both German. The first of the world wars cut off their communications with Germany. The Australian Lutherans who later merged in the United Evangelical Lutheran Church came to the rescue. So also did the Iowa Synod of the United States, a body which had been assisting before the war.[63] The Rhenish and the Neuendettelsau enterprises later coalesced. The number of Christians grew rapidly, partly because the native Christians were themselves active in propagating their faith.[64] In 1932 the American Lutheran Church, into which, in 1930, the Iowa Synod merged, formally took over part of the Neuendettelsau field. In 1936 the United Evangelical Lutheran Synod of Australia assumed responsibility for a section.[65] The Melanesian Mission (Anglican) also extended its operations to the region.

In the south-eastern portion of New Guinea, or Papua as it was officially known, the pre-1914 Protestant missions, which were British and Australian, penetrated more and more of the interior and had increasing numerical success.[66]

Although in consequence of the first of the world wars New Britain and New Ireland and the adjacent smaller islands passed from German hands to the British Empire under a mandate to Australia, no great alteration was made in the missionary complexion of the region. The Australian Methodists continued the enterprise which they had begun before 1914. To it was added the Melanesian Mission (Anglican).[67] The Roman Catholics were still represented by the Congregation of the Holy Heart of Jesus.[68]

Between the first and the second of the world wars Christianity continued

---

[62] Berg, *Die katholische Heidenmission als Kulturträger,* Vol. I, p. 231.

[63] Drach, *Our Church Abroad,* pp. 201-220; Richter, *Die evangelische Mission in Fern- und Südost Asien, Australien, Amerika,* pp. 278-296; Joh. Frierl, *1886-1936. Eine kurze Denkschrift* (no place or date of publication, pp. 93), pp. 53 ff.; Johann Frierl, *Gottes Wort in den Urwäldern von Neu Guinea* (Verlag des Missionshauses Neuendettelsau, 1929, pp. 172), pp. 85 ff.; Joh. Frierl, *Christ in New Guinea* (Tanunda, South Australia, Auricht's Printing Office, 1932, pp. 207), *passim*; Christian Keysser, *Gottes Weg ins Hubeland* (Dresden, C. Ludwig Ungelenk, 1936, pp. 63).

[64] Burton, *op. cit.,* p. 55; *The Madras Series,* Vol. III, pp. 292 ff.

[65] Mimeographed memorandum, *Orphaned Missions* (New York, International Missionary Council, Feb., 1944).

[66] *The International Review of Missions,* Vol. XXIX, p. 95; William E. Bromilow, *Twenty Years among Primitive Papuans* (London, The Epworth Press, 1929, pp. 316), pp. 244 ff.; John Wear Burton, *Our Task in Papua* (London, The Epworth Press, 1926, pp. 124), pp. 89 ff.

[67] Burton, *Missionary Survey of the Pacific Islands,* pp. 56, 57.

[68] Hagspiel, *op. cit.,* Vol. III, p. 231.

to make progress in the large groupings of islands which were classified under Polynesia, Melanesia, and Micronesia. No such spectacular developments were witnessed as in the nineteenth century. Western governments had brought order in most of the islands and the days of tribal wars and unregulated exploitation by white traders had largely passed. The striking mass conversion of entire populations belonged in the earlier period. By 1914 Polynesia was largely Christian in name. It was, therefore, chiefly in Melanesia and Micronesia that the post-1914 numerical advance was seen. Here it was marked. Between 1911 and 1936 Protestant communicants in Polynesia, Melanesia, and Micronesia are reported to have risen from 93,000 to 166,000, Roman Catholics from 158,000 in 1925 to 276,000 in 1933, Protestant missionaries from 417 in 1911 to 682 in 1936, and ordained natives from 549 in 1911 to 851 in 1936.[69] Protestant and Roman Catholic totals are not entirely comparable since the former included only communicants and the latter all the baptized. A Roman Catholic estimate of about the year 1931 reported 325,465 of its faith as against 365,111 Protestants.[70] These totals must be viewed together with the somewhat different ones from Protestant sources. Not far from 1930 these gave the number of Protestants as about 375,000 and of Roman Catholics as approximately 250,000.[71] It was clear that by either count Protestants, as before 1914, were more numerous than Roman Catholics. The Bible was being translated into additional tongues.[72] In spite of the disintegrating inroads of some forms of Western culture and disease, the Church was growing throughout almost the entire broad area.[73]

Upon this vast expanse of island-studded water the second of the world wars broke with progressively increasing force. The shrinking dimensions of the globe were appallingly demonstrated by the fashion in which this region, so remote from Europe, became much more intimately involved in the second of the struggles than it had in the first. The Christianity of the region was affected. In the first years of the conflict German and then French missionaries were cut off from their home constituencies. Numbers of German missionaries in New Guinea were interned.[74] Financial assistance came to Protestant missions from Great Britain and the United States, in part through the Orphaned Missions Fund of the International Missionary Council. So far as was known, no German or French enterprise had to be discontinued for lack of funds.

[69] Bates, *Data on the Distribution of the Missionary Enterprise*, pp. 5-7.
[70] *Testo-Atlante illustrato delle Missioni*, p. 39.
[71] Burton, *Missionary Survey of the Pacific Islands*, p. 91.
[72] Burton, *op. cit.*, pp. 116, 117.
[73] *The International Review of Missions*, Vol. XXIX, pp. 94, 95.
[74] Mimeographed memorandum, *Orphaned Missions* (New York, International Missionary Council, Feb., 1944).

The dearth of shipping and the loss of much of the European market for copra brought financial distress to some of the islands with a consequent falling off of native contributions[75] and, on at least Samoa, an increase in illegitimacy due to the inability of couples desiring marriage to pay the wedding fees.[76] Yet gains continued to be made even in these difficult years, with the opening of new stations in Papua, improved native leadership in Fiji, and the spread of Christianity to the previously uninhabited Phoenix Islands by government-aided migration from the Gilbert Islands.[77] With the rapid extension of hostilities in the Pacific late in 1941 and in the following months, missionaries and the churches were more deeply disturbed. As the Japanese advanced southward, they interned some of the missionaries. Thus the Capuchins on Guam were taken to Kobe for that purpose.[78] On New Britain Methodist missionaries were interned.[79] In Papua several missionaries lost their lives. There was much destruction of mission and church property. Some of the islands, notably Tonga, New Caledonia, the New Hebrides, and the Fijis, experienced a greatly augmented impact of Western civilization through the presence of the armed forces of the allies.[80] Yet as the Japanese tide was pushed backward missionaries resumed operations in areas from which they had been excluded. The advance of Christianity seemed to be arrested only temporarily if at all.

In the varied populations in the huge areas and the hundreds of large and small islands which comprised the East Indies the progress of Christianity which had been so marked in the century before 1914[81] continued, in several areas with augmented momentum. The East Indies could not escape some of the repercussions of the first of the world wars and the developments which succeeded it. Yet in the first of the wars both Holland and Portugal were neutral and the sections under British rule did not become scenes of actual combat. It was not until the second of the world wars that the course of Christianity experienced serious interruptions.

The first of the world wars brought difficulties to the extensive German missions. The Dutch and particularly the German societies suffered from a dearth of reinforcements, but mass movements towards Christianity in the

[75] *The International Review of Missions,* Vol. XXXI, p. 77.
[76] *N.C.W.C. News Service,* Jan. 5, 1942.
[77] *The International Review of Missions,* Vol. XXX, p. 87, Vol. XXXI, pp. 78, 79.
[78] *1944 Mission Annual of the Seraphic Mass Association,* p. 2.
[79] *The International Review of Missions,* Vol. XXXII, p. 62.
[80] *The International Review of Missions,* Vol. XXXIII, pp. 70-73.
[81] Vol. V, pp. 275-300.

German fields in Sumatra and Nias which had been in progress before 1914 persisted.[82] The aftermath of the war with the destructive inflation in Germany brought added financial embarrassment to the Rhenish Missionary Society. The Dutch colonial administration made it annual grants for a number of years beginning in 1920, and in 1925 the Basel Mission enabled the Rhenish society better to concentrate its efforts upon Sumatra and Nias by taking over its field in Borneo.[83]

The years immediately following the first of the world wars witnessed an augmented nationalism among the educated of the Javanese. This was accompanied by something of a renewal in Islam, the dominant religion of Java. The Moslem revival had begun before 1914.[84] The movement had anti-Christian aspects. There were repercussions of the Moslem awakenings, brief-lived as it proved, issuing from Mecca and Cairo, which temporarily strengthened the Islam of Java. Moslem missionaries came from India, one of whom professed to be moved by a purpose to "stop Christianity." Most of these efforts subsided rather quickly, but an indigenous Moslem association, the *Muhammadiya,* which began in 1912 in Java, owed its origin to a desire to demonstrate that Islam could render disinterested service as effectively as could Christianity, and founded schools, hospitals, and orphanages, published literature, and engaged in preaching. It was paying Christian missions the sincere flattery of imitation and was in part a result of the Christian faith.[85]

The spirit of nationalism, augmented throughout the world during and after the first of the world wars and often expressing itself in restlessness against the domination of the white man, had other effects in the East Indies than the quickening of Islam. It also contributed to greater self reliance among Christians, more financial self support, and increased initiative in spreading the faith. Here, as in many other non-Occidental lands, partly because of the stimulus of nationalism and partly because of its own inner vitality, Christianity was sending down roots into the soil. It was ceasing to be dependent for its existence exclusively upon the support of the founding churches.

The nationalistic temper in these various manifestations was marked among the Bataks, in Sumatra. By 1939 approximately a third of that vigorous people had been won to the Christian faith.[86] About seventy-five of the Batak congregations, a minority of the whole, broke away from association with the missionaries and set up a training school with a Negro from Surinam as the

[82] *The International Review of Missions,* Vol. VI, p. 24, Vol. VII, p. 22.
[83] *The International Review of Missions,* Vol. XXI, pp. 161, 162.
[84] N. Adriani in *The International Review of Missions,* Vol. VII, pp. 113-125.
[85] Kraemer in Rauws et alii, *The Netherlands Indies,* pp. 91-93, 104-106.
[86] Davis in *The Madras Series,* Vol. V, p. 391.

principal.[87] In the 1920's the Batak Protestant Church was organized with a framework which gave to the Bataks more voice in ecclesiastical administration. In 1931 it was recognized by the government as an independent body. White missionaries still had a share in the church and the latter was not fully independent of them.[88] Missionaries, however, were too few to take much part in local affairs but concerned themselves chiefly with supervision and the spiritual nurture of the Batak leaders. The Bataks contributed freely to the financial aid of weaker congregations, to the support of schools, to foreign missions, to the building of new church edifices, and to the maintenance of their own congregations. No financial assistance came from the missionaries to the Batak Protestant Church. The latter, too, had its own missionary society which supported missionaries among non-Christian Bataks. The numbers of Christian Bataks were increasing year by year. This was at the expense of animism. It was a race between Islam and Christianity for the allegiance of the Bataks, and instances were known in which Islam had won some of the Christians.[89]

There was also a movement which led to greatly increased autonomy in the East Indian Church. This church had arisen from the activities of the East India Company and the clergy appointed and supported by it. When the East India Company passed out of existence the colonial government succeeded to its ecclesiastical functions and maintained them through the nineteenth and the fore part of the twentieth century. Until 1935, the ministers of the East Indian Church were appointed by the Crown. The church received financial assistance from the government and until 1927 it was the only Protestant organization recognized as such by the state. Since 1847 the Roman Catholic Church had also received state financial aid but with little limitation on its freedom. The change in status of the Protestant body came in part through the agitation of East Indian nationalists. The government, for the purpose of increasing political self government, had inaugurated the Volksraad, a beginning of a representative assembly. At the very first meeting of the Volksraad, an Indonesian member criticized the close association of Church and state. It was, indeed, something of an anomaly in a region where the overwhelming majority were Moslems and no subsidy was given by the state to Islam. In 1919, at the instance of an Indonesian member, a resolution was passed expressing the desire for an early separation of Church and state. A similar motion was passed in 1932. In 1920 the Church Board acquiesced in principle. In 1935 adminis-

---

[87] Rauws, *op. cit.*, p. 121.
[88] Rauws, *op. cit.*, pp. 121-123.
[89] Davis in *The Madras Series*, Vol. V, pp. 395-429.

trative separation was effected, but financial assistance still came from the state for the support of several scores of ministers, both European and Indonesian. The resulting ecclesiastical body bore the name of the Protestant Church in the Netherlands Indies. It was a federation and some of its members, especially those in Minahassa (in the northern peninsula of Celebes) and the Moluccas, assumed a large degree of autonomy.[90] This was mainly because the Indonesian Christians were restive under the control of the white clergy and the alien colonial government.[91]

Autonomy was achieved by several other bodies. In 1923 the oldest Christian community in Eastern Java was given that status and in 1931 the Church of Eastern Java was constituted with only a tenth of the controlling synod Europeans.[92] The Chinese Christian Church of East Java was formed in 1934 by the union of two groups. In that same year the Church of West Java came into being, in large part out of the congregations which had arisen from the efforts of the Netherlands Missionary Society.[93] In 1935 the independent Dayak Church was constituted.[94] The first general synod of an autonomous church in the island of Nias convened in 1936.[95]

The attainment of autonomy was usually accompanied or followed by an increased zeal of the new bodies in propagating the Christian faith. Thus the Church of Eastern Java not only had missions to non-Christians in its own immediate neighbourhood: it also sent missionaries to the adjacent island of Bali.[96] The church in Amboina undertook missions in Dutch New Guinea and some other islands.[97] Amboinese Christians, like the Batak Christians, held to their faith when they migrated to other parts of the Indies and here and there spread it among non-Christians.[98]

Provision was made for the co-operative training of Indonesian clergy. In 1934 a union theological seminary was inaugurated near Batavia and in 1936 was brought to Batavia itself.[99]

The distress through which Europe passed following the first of the world

[90] Amry Vandenbosch, *The Dutch East Indies* (University of California Press, 3d ed., 1942, pp. viii, 458), pp. 41-44; Slotemaker de Bruine in *The International Review of Missions*, Vol. XXIV, p. 134; Kraemer, *De Huidige Stand van het Christendom in Nederlandsch-Indië*, pp. 69 ff.

[91] Crommelin in *The International Review of Missions*, Vol. XXIII, pp. 372, 373.

[92] Crommelin in *The International Review of Missions*, Vol. XXIII, p. 373.

[93] Rauws, *op. cit.*, p. 167.

[94] Kraemer, *op. cit.*, p. 26.

[95] *The International Review of Missions*, Vol. XXVI, p. 28.

[96] Rauws, *op. cit.*, p. 167.

[97] *The International Review of Missions*, Vol. XXV, p. 31.

[98] Crommelin in *The International Review of Missions*, Vol. XXIII, p. 376.

[99] *The International Review of Missions*, Vol. XXVI, p. 28.

wars accelerated the movement towards autonomy of the East Indian churches. War and the ensuing inflation meant scarcity of funds and difficulties in reinforcing the staffs of the Rhenish Missionary Society. This encouraged the assumption by the Batak Christians of more responsibility for their churches.[100]

The world-wide economic depression which began in 1929 embarrassed the government and led to a reduction in its subsidies to the Protestant Church in the Netherlands Indies.[101] Thus forced to more financial self reliance, in at least some parts of the islands the church rose to its task. Obviously the financial difficulties were not in themselves enough to account for the healthful fashion in which they were met. But for an inward vigour in the churches their effect would have been disastrous.

A feature of the insurgency against the white man's dominance was the emergence of a large and growing number of small Christian bodies independent of white control and even of fellowship with white Christians. Their rapid rise and multiplication and their irregularities puzzled and annoyed the Dutch missionary forces.[102]

After 1914 the large majority of the missionaries were from those societies, Dutch and German, which had established themselves in the East Indies before that year. There came, however, representatives from several societies, most of them British or American, which had heretofore not been in the region. In 1929 the Christian and Missionary Alliance received the permission of the government to enter. It soon won several hundreds of Dayaks in Borneo. It also began operations in Bali, the island which was Hindu by faith.[103] There it had made a few converts when the state stepped in and forbade all missionary effort on the island. The government pled as justification for its action the culturally disruptive effect of Christian missions in a society which was integrated with other religious conceptions.[104] The Pentecostal Movement was officially registered in 1924. In 1931 similar recognition was given the Indian Advent Mission.[105] These, the Salvation Army, and the Seventh Day Adventists, previously present, brought variety and at times spelled perplexity for the older agencies.[106]

[100] Rauws, *op. cit.,* p. 121; *The International Review of Missions,* Vol. XXI, p. 161.

[101] Slotemaker de Bruine in *The International Review of Missions,* Vol. XXIV, p. 134.

[102] The Missions Consul, Steven Cornelis Graaf van Randwijck, December, 1938, in the presence of the author; Richter, *Die evangelische Mission in Niederländisch-Indien,* p. 151.

[103] Rauws, *op. cit.,* p. 126.

[104] A. Vandenbosch in *The International Review of Missions,* Vol. XXIII, pp. 205-214.

[105] Rauws, *op. cit.,* p. 128.

[106] J. Rauws, *Overzicht van het Zendingswerk in Nederlandsch Oost-en West-Indië (October, 1935-1936)* (Oegstgeest, Zendings Bureau, 1936, pp. 62.), p. 36.

In spite of the growing number of societies and of fissiparous native churches, in general co-operation increased and the Protestantism of the islands was more and more brought into the fellowship of the Ecumenical Movement. The Netherlands Indies were represented in the International Missionary Council. The Protestant Church in the Netherlands Indies had membership in the incipient World Council of Churches.

The numerical advance of Protestant Christianity continued to be striking. In 1936 the number of indigenous Protestant Christians was reported by the government to be 1,610,533. To this were to be added about 115,000 Europeans.[107] As before 1914, Protestants were most numerous in the north of Sumatra (among the Bataks), in the northern portion of Celebes (where the Minahassian tribes were fairly solidly Christian), in the centre of Celebes (where the progress of the faith was very rapid), and in the Moluccas and the Sangi and Talaud Islands. Most of the gains were at the expense of a disappearing animism. In Java, the island which held the majority of the population, the dominance of Islam retarded the growth. Yet even here there were more than 50,000 native Christians.[108] The Protestant Christians who were such because of the labours of the missionary societies in the nineteenth and twentieth centuries (this was exclusive of the state church) are said to have totalled 403,000 in 1910,[109] 751,000 in 1924,[110] and 883,000 in 1936.[111] In 1931 the number of baptized native Christians in the East Indian Church which was associated with the government was reported to be 494,142.[112]

A few examples will give some indication of what a complete account would reveal. For many years the Dutch portion of New Guinea had been an unfruitful field for Christian missions. However, by the 1930's the number of converts was multiplying. It was said that each year in spite of the paucity of missionaries from 8,000 to 10,000 were being baptized.[113] In the face of declining subsidies from the state, the East Indian Church made gains. In 1927 in the western part of the island of Ceram thirteen new congregations were begun and fourteen new schools were opened. Not far from the same time there was also a mass movement in the eastern part of that island and many animists flocked to baptism.[114] In the 1920's on one of the islands not far from Timor

[107] H. Kraemer in Parker, *Interpretative Statistical Survey of the World Mission of the Christian Church*, pp. 282-284.

[108] *Ibid.*

[109] Dennis, Beach, and Fahs, *World Atlas of Christian Missions*, p. 88.

[110] Beach and Fahs, *World Missionary Atlas*, p. 101.

[111] Parker, *op. cit.*, p. 52.

[112] *Indisch Verslag*, 1931, pp. 116, 117.

[113] Kraemer, *De Huidige Stand van het Christendom in Nederlandsch-Indië*, p. 28; *The International Review of Missions*, Vol. XXVIII, p. 24.

[114] Richter, *Die evangelische Mission in Niederländisch-Indien*, p. 129.

there was another mass movement towards the Church and several thousand were baptized.[115] The decade after 1926 saw the number of Christians in Borneo associated with the Basel Mission approximately doubled.[116] In 1916 a mass movement towards Christianity began on Nias, an island off the north-west coast of Sumatra. From about 17,000 at the beginning of the movement, by 1932 the numbers of Christians on the island had grown to approximately 84,000.[117] By 1934 church membership on the island had risen to 102,000.[118] In the 1930's Christianity was successfully planted on the resistant Bali and by 1940 that island had about 1,000 adherents to the faith.[119]

Marked as was the growth of Protestantism in the Netherlands Indies in the three decades after 1914, proportionately that of Roman Catholic Christianity was even greater. In 1940 Protestants still decidedly outnumbered Roman Catholics, but the gains of the latter had been more striking. During much of the nineteenth century the Roman Catholic Church received financial assistance from the state, but in 1913 the Netherlands Indies had only 35,336 Europeans and 46,950 "coloured" of that branch of the faith.[120] In 1927 there were reported to be 66,413 European and 192,397 non-European Roman Catholics.[121] Another set of statistics declared that in 1923 the total number of Roman Catholics was 122,143, in 1933 237,587, and in 1937 493,932.[122] The figures in the last sentence seem to have included only non-Europeans. Most of the increase was among the Indonesians, but part of it was among the Europeans, for in 1935 there were 77,898 of the latter of that faith.[123] The single vicariate apostolic of 1900 had grown by 1938 to seven vicariates and seven prefectures apostolic.[124]

The rapid growth of the Roman Catholic Church in the Netherlands East Indies was in part a reflection of the prosperity of that communion in Holland. It is said that in 1784 there were in the latter country only 350 parishes and 400 priests.[125] In 1929 there were 1,234 parishes and 2,820 diocesan priests, and Roman Catholics numbered 2,563,650,[126] or about a third of the population.

The increase of the Roman Catholic population in Holland was clearly

[115] Richter, op. cit., p. 130.
[116] Rauws, et alii, The Netherlands Indies, p. 123.
[117] The International Review of Missions, Vol. XXI, p. 162; Rauws, op. cit., p. 122.
[118] Rauws, op. cit., p. 122.
[119] The International Review of Missions, Vol. XXX, p. 27.
[120] Schwager in Zeitschrift für Missionswissenschaft, Vol. III, p. 315.
[121] De R. K. Kerk in Nederlandsch Indië Missie Almanak, 1929, p. 34.
[122] Fides Service, March 26, 1938.
[123] Fides Service, Apr. 6, 1935.
[124] Fides Service, March 26, 1938.
[125] Rauws, op. cit., p. 132.
[126] Streit, Catholic World-Atlas, table XIII.

responsible for the rapid growth of the missionary staff of the Roman Catholic Church in the Netherlands East Indies. Here was the largest Dutch colonial possession. It is not strange that Dutch Roman Catholic missionary interest sought an outlet there or that the Roman Catholic missionary personnel in the Indies, whether priests, lay brothers, or sisters, was overwhelmingly Dutch.[127]

More than half of the Roman Catholics in the Netherlands East Indies in 1931 were in the Vicariate Apostolic of the Sunda Islands. This was in care of the Society of the Divine Word.[128] It was only as recently as 1913 that the area had been entrusted to that society. The Jesuits had preceded it, but had too small a staff to man that and the populous island of Java for which they were chiefly responsible. The assignment of the Society of the Divine Word did not at first include the island of Flores, but this, too, was transferred to them in 1914. The representatives of the society found as a result of the labours of the Jesuits about 30,000 Roman Catholics.[129] In 1931 the vicariate counted 169,699 Roman Catholics.[130] Something of a mass movement towards the Roman Catholic Church was in progress. In 1934 about 10,000 adult conversions were recorded, or approximately 70 per cent. of the total that year in the entire Netherlands East Indies.[131] There was, too, a corresponding growth in schools under the control of the mission. In 1914 elementary schools in the vicariate totalled 25 and pupils 2,371. In 1937 they were 244 and 27,490 respectively.[132]

Next to the Vicariate Apostolic of the Sunda Islands in numbers of Roman Catholics and of conversions was the Vicariate of Batavia. In 1937 it had 55,879 Roman Catholics[133] and in 1934 it reported 2,268 conversions.[134] An increasing number of its clergy were devoting themselves to the Chinese.[135] Of the total figure of Roman Catholics in the vicariate the large majority seem to have been Europeans and less than a fourth non-Europeans.[136]

For Roman Catholics as for Protestants, the Dutch portion of New Guinea was becoming a promising field. In 1933, 29,126 Roman Catholics were reported in that area.[137]

[127] *Missiones Catholicae Cura S. Congregationis de Propaganda Fide,* 1927, pp. 360, 361.
[128] *Testo-Atlante illustrato delle Missioni,* p. 110.
[129] Hagspiel, *Along the Mission Trail,* Vol. II, pp. 74-78.
[130] *Testo-Atlante illustrato delle Missioni,* p. 110.
[131] *Fides Service,* Apr. 6, 1935.
[132] *Fides Service,* Feb. 13, 1937.
[133] *Fides Service,* May 15, 1937.
[134] *Fides Service,* Apr. 6, 1935.
[135] *Fides Service,* Aug. 6, 1938.
[136] *Indisch Verslag,* 1931, p. 110.
[137] *De Katholieke Missie in Nederlandsch Oost-Indië,* 1933, pp. 215-217.

Most of the Roman Catholic staff in the Indies were still European, but a beginning had been made towards an indigenous personnel. In 1933 there were reported to be 6 native priests, 9 native brothers, and 40 native sisters, but there were 179 natives in preparation for the priesthood.[138]

Roman Catholics were declared to be largely from the middle ranks of society.[139] They, like the Protestants, were having their conversions chiefly from folk of animistic cults.

Earlier the rule of the government had been that Protestants and Roman Catholics were not to conduct missions in the same territory. The Roman Catholics were restive under this restriction, partly because they felt under obligation to proclaim their faith everywhere, regardless of what other form of Christianity was represented, and partly because, being late in developing missions in the Netherlands East Indies, they found some of the most attractive areas pre-empted by Protestants. By 1935 the government had ceased to enforce this principle. If in any instance Roman Catholics believed themselves discriminated against they brought pressure, usually effectively, upon the home government.[140]

In the British portion of the East Indies, the territories which stretched along the north coast of Borneo—Sarawak, Labuan, Brunei, and British North Borneo—there was a fairly steady growth of Christianity after 1914 until the storm of the Japanese invasion in the second of the world wars swept over the land. The Anglicans, organized in the Diocese of Sarawak and Labuan, increased their staff through the addition of Chinese and Dayak priests. The European staff showed a slight decline.[141] In 1937 the diocese counted about 12,500 baptized.[142] The American Methodists, who had entered in so interesting a fashion with a colony of Chinese immigrants,[143] reached out (in 1939) among the Dayaks in a river valley in Sarawak.[144] The missionaries of the Basel Society were constrained to leave British North Borneo during the first of the world wars and could not return until 1924. By 1927 they had a self-

---

[138] *Ibid.*

[139] *Missiones Catholicae Cura S. Congregationis de Propaganda Fide,* 1927, pp. 344-353.

[140] A Dutch colonial administrator from the Netherlands Indies in conversation with the author, March 29, 1935.

[141] *Borneo Mission Association Annual Reports,* 1914, and 1940; L. E. Currey, *Borneo* (Westminster, The Society for the Propagation of the Gospel in Foreign Parts, 1933, pp. 96), pp. 72-81; Ruth Henrich, *No Richer Harvest. The Story of the Church in Borneo* (Westminster, Society for Promoting Christian Knowledge, 1934, pp. 71), *passim.*

[142] Parker, *Interpretative Statistical Survey of the World Mission of the Christian Church,* p. 53.

[143] Vol. V, p. 297.

[144] *Journal of the Annual Meeting of the Board of Foreign Missions of the Methodist Episcopal Church,* 1939, p. 106.

supporting independent church.[145] The Roman Catholic Church was represented by Mill Hill contingents. They had two prefectures apostolic, created in
1927,[146] and not far from 1930 counted about 12,000 Christians, or approximately the total of the Anglicans.[147]

The second of the world wars brought profound changes to the Netherlands
East Indies and to the Christian missions and churches of the islands. Indeed,
these were the most revolutionary which Christianity in the islands had faced
since the Dutch conquest in the seventeenth century. Not all of them could be
known until after the curtain of war had been lifted and connexions reestablished between the Christian communities and the founding bodies. The
first effect of the outbreak of hostilities in Europe was to cut off the German
Protestant missionaries from their supporting constituencies. Then came, in the
spring of 1940, the invasion of Holland by Germany. The Netherlands East
Indies were loyal to the exiled queen. The German missionaries were interned.
Funds could no longer come from Holland to the Dutch missionaries. The
Dutch Protestant missions and the Protestant churches rose to meet the crisis
and co-operated in an emergency board. The government placed them in
charge of the fields of the German missions. They redistributed their forces
to care for the areas thus left vacant.[148] The indigenous Christians were faced
with both the opportunity and the necessity of assuming more responsibility
for the administration and support of their churches. This posed problems for
the Batak Christians. In spite of partial autonomy, they had still been to some
degree under the paternalistic direction of the German missionaries and the
funds for their central administration were largely from Germany. The Batak
church now became more nearly self-governing and self-supporting. It adopted
measures for raising the necessary budgets. In 1940 the first three Batak ministers were ordained. Independence brought its difficulties, for there were
revivals of native dances and the beating of the *gondang*, forbidden by the
missionaries and objected to by some of the Batak Christians because of their
association with paganism. Secessions from the Batak church appeared, made
on the basis of race. The relations between church and mission still proved
troublesome and were complicated by the relation of church and school.[149]
In general, throughout the islands Christians, both European and non-European, responded remarkably well. They contributed generously in money. The

[145] *The International Review of Missions*, Vol. XXI, p. 159.
[146] Streit, *Catholic World-Atlas*, table XXVIII.
[147] *Testo-Atlante illustrato delle Missioni*, p. 110.
[148] *Netherlands East Indies. Missions Emergency Board* (Batavia, Oct. 3, 1940, pp.
15. Mimeographed), *passim*.
[149] Gramberg in *The International Review of Missions*, Vol. XXXI, pp. 322-328.

government gave added grants to mission schools.[150] Financial assistance
came from Christians of other lands and communions through the Orphaned
Missions Fund of the International Missionary Council.[151] Here and there in
the face of the hard conditions advances were being made. For instance, the
1941 synod of the Dayak Church in South Borneo drew plans for an increased
spread of the faith through the individual witness of every church member
and house-to-house visitation. A new translation into Timorese of two books
of the New Testament was published.[152]

Roman Catholic missions, with their Dutch personnel, did not have to face
the critical situation presented to Protestants with their extensive German contingents by the internment of a large proportion of the foreign personnel. The
occupation of Holland by Germany, however, made difficult the reinforcement
of the staff and confronted Roman Catholic enterprises with the problem of
support. Fortunately the emphasis upon the training of an indigenous clergy
was beginning to bring results on an increased scale. In January, 1941, for
instance, there were ordained priests, as members of the Society of the Divine
Word, two natives, the first of their race to be so honoured within the field of
that society.[153] A Javanese Jesuit was raised to the episcopate and made the
head of one of the vicariates apostolic. The laity came to the rescue financially.
A central committee was formed and funds were raised which helped to meet
some of the most urgent needs.[154]

The Japanese conquest brought new perplexities, particularly since all
Dutch, British, and American missionaries, namely those upon whom the
missions were mainly dependent, were regarded as enemy aliens by the occupying regime. Yet from the meagre information which was transmitted across
the warring lines it seemed clear that Christianity was not being stamped out.
Protestant activities were going on fairly normally. As we shall discover to
have been the case in some of the other areas under Japanese occupation,
Japanese Christians were coming, with the consent of the fighting services,
and were making contacts with the churches. Presumably the Japanese authorities allowed this in the hope of obtaining the co-operation of the churches.
Much the same procedures were enforced as were being witnessed in Japan
and the Japanese-held portions of China: all the Protestant bodies in a particular
area were brought together into one united organization independent of Eu-

[150] *The International Review of Missions*, Vol. XXXI, p. 21.
[151] Information given to the author by a secretary of the International Missionary
Council.
[152] *The Christian Family and Our Missions*, July, 1941, p. 250.
[153] *The International Review of Missions*, Vol. XXXII, p. 15.
[154] *Lumen Service*, March 22, 1941.

ropean administrative control or financial aid.[155] In what had been the British portions of Borneo the Anglican bishop and some of the clergy and women missionaries remained at their stations,[156] but they were later interned.[157]

Up to the time of the Japanese conquest, then, Christianity in the East Indies, whether in the Dutch or British portions, was going forward fairly steadily in numbers and, among the Protestants, in the self reliance and autonomy of the indigenous churches. Native leadership was multiplying among Protestants and Roman Catholics. The advances of both great wings of the Christian forces were mainly among the animistic minorities of the islands, but a few thousand were being won in Java from the Moslem majority. Such large accessions to Christianity from Islam, coming as they did without pressure from the state, were unique in the twentieth century. Christianity was in an increasingly favourable position to meet the crisis brought by the Japanese conquest.

For the Philippine Islands the year 1914 bore no revolutionary significance. For them the outstanding years in their recent history were 1898, with the coming of the Americans, 1935, when the Commonwealth government, with its autonomy in internal affairs, was set up, and 1941 and 1942, which saw the Japanese conquest. Of these dates, the ones which marked the most abrupt transitions were the first and the last. From 1898 to 1942 the course of Filipino history had been one whose patterns had been set by the American occupation. The years had witnessed the introduction and growth of government and culture after the fashion of the United States. The change had been from the idealism and institutions of Spain to those of the United States. Under both regimes the islands had experienced an imperialism in which benevolence sprung chiefly from Christian sources was mixed with the desire for exploitation in the interests of a limited number of individuals and groups of the occupying power. Spanish times witnessed the conversion of the majority of the population to the Roman Catholic form of Christianity and the closely associated introduction and spread of the Spanish version of Western civilization. Spanish rule had been paternalistic: in Church and state the Spaniard had continued dominant. After the first flush of conquest the life of the islands had been one of isolation and somnolence towards the close of the nineteenth century disturbed slightly by the liberalism of Latin Europe. The connexion with the

[155] *The International Review of Missions,* Vol. XXXII, p. 15, Vol. XXXIII, p. 26.
[156] *Borneo Mission Association, Annual Report,* 1941, p. 3.
[157] *The International Review of Missions,* Vol. XXXIII, p. 26.

United States brought Protestantism in the forms which prevailed among the older stock of that country, rapid nurture in self government in forms which had developed in large measure in conjunction with Anglo-Saxon Protestantism, education of the kind which prevailed in the United States, and a close integration of the economic life of the islands with that of the United States. Under American rule the islands prospered. Between 1918 and 1939 population increased from 10,314,310 to 16,000,303.[158] There was an atmosphere of hopeful and vigorous nationalism.

Religiously, as we saw earlier,[159] the American period saw the extensive nationalistic secession from the Roman Catholic Church associated with the name of Aglipay, the introduction and rapid growth of Protestantism, and the attempt to revitalize and refurbish the Roman Catholic Church to meet the competition of these two movements and the other factors of the new day. The islands remained overwhelmingly Christian by profession. In 1939 approximately nine-tenths avowed connexion with one or another of the branches of that faith. The Philippines continued to contain more Christians than all the rest of the Far East and, indeed, constituted a larger Christian enclave than was to be found in any one country in Asia. Of the non-Christian minority, the largest proportion, a little less than half, were Moslems. Christianity continued to make headway among the non-Christians, notably the animists of primitive culture. Here Roman Catholics through the Congregation of the Immaculate Heart of Mary (Scheutveld) and the Protestant Episcopalians and United Brethren were active.[160]

In the years between 1914 and 1942 these religious developments continued. The Filipino Independent Church, headed by Aglipay, and, after his death, by Santiago A. Fonacier, tended to languish. Its numbers increased slightly, presumably by an excess of births over deaths, but its proportion of the total population declined from about 13.7 per cent. in 1918[161] to about 9.8 per cent. in 1939. It lacked a sufficient supply of educated clergy and was kept alive more by inertia and nationalism than by inward religious vitality. It was liberal theologically but in its public services held to much of the ritual which it had inherited from the Roman Catholic Church. Some of its members were active in local and national politics and Aglipay polled about 14 per cent. of the votes when he was a candidate in the first election for the presidency of the Commonwealth.[162]

[158] *The Statesman's Year-Book*, 1940, p. 665, 1943, p. 665.
[159] Vol. V, pp. 267-274.
[160] Felix M. Keesing and Marie Keesing, *Taming Philippine Headhunters* (London, George Allen & Unwin, Ltd., 1934, pp. 288), p. 226.
[161] Hayden, *The Philippines*, pp. 572, 573.
[162] Hayden, *op. cit.*, p. 573.

In contrast, Protestantism had a very rapid growth. Not far from 1910 it counted 36,571 communicants and 167 missionaries,[163] in 1924 64,184 communicants and 287 missionaries,[164] and in 1936 193,608 communicants and 295 missionaries.[165] According to the government census the percentage of Protestants rose from 1.3 in 1918 to 2.4 in 1939.[166] This was in part by the excess of births over deaths in the Protestant constituency, but largely by conversions. The latter were predominantly from nominal Roman Catholics. Some may have been attracted by the connexion with the United States, for the Protestant missionaries were from that country. Many, too, were drawn by the appeal of the Protestant form of Christianity to those who, thinking of themselves as Christians by heredity, were not happy with what they found in the dominant church and felt that they had in Protestantism a more satisfying faith. Almost none of the Protestants were from the small group of families in which most of the wealth and the political power of the islands were concentrated. They were, rather, largely from the rapidly growing middle class which had been educated in the public schools of the American regime. As in Latin America, Protestantism contributed to the growth of the middle class.[167] While the Protestant movement was active in the towns and cities, it also had strong rural congregations. One of these particularly through its lay leadership was reaching out into the surrounding area and was entirely self-supporting.[168] Nationalism was rampant and was demanding political independence. It also led to a demand for Filipino control in the churches founded by the missions. In several instances it gave rise to schism and the emergence of new, fully autonomous groups. Nationalism combined with the necessity of presenting a common front to the Roman Catholic Church and the general trend in the Protestant world towards unity brought together much of Filipino Protestantism under indigenous leadership. In 1929 the United Evangelical Church of the Philippines was constituted by a fusion of the Presbyterians, Congregationalists, and United Brethren and elected a Filipino as it first Moderator. In 1932 eleven groups which had broken away from the standard denominations in earlier years came together as the *Iglesia Evangelica Unida en Islas Filipinas*.[169] In 1929, as a result of a visit of John R. Mott, a National Christian Council was

[163] Dennis, Beach, and Fahs, *World Atlas of Christian Missions*, p. 167.

[164] Beach and Fahs, *World Missionary Atlas*, pp. 76, 77.

[165] Parker, *Interpretative Statistical Survey of the World Mission of the Christian Church*, pp. 19, 21.

[166] Hayden, *op. cit.*, p. 572.

[167] Hayden, *op. cit.*, p. 578.

[168] Butterfield in *The Rural Mission of the Church in Eastern Asia*, pp. 169-172; E. K. Higdon in *The International Review of Missions*, Vol. XXXIII, pp. 422-429.

[169] *The International Review of Missions*, Vol. XXI, p. 333.

formed which became the local unit of the International Missionary Council.[170] In 1939 this became the Philippine Federation of Evangelical Churches.[171] Protestants continued to be active in education: only a minority of their number remained illiterate. It was while a missionary in the Philippines that Frank C. Laubach worked out a method of removing illiteracy (he devised it as an approach to the Moslems) which he later taught in several other parts of the world.[172]

The Roman Catholic Church made remarkable progress in these decades in adjusting itself to the new conditions and faced the Japanese occupation in a much stronger position and with more vigour than it had displayed at the time of the American annexation. As we saw in a preceding volume,[173] clergy came from the United States and new orders entered from European countries other than Spain. These continued after 1914.[174] The Roman Catholic Church, too, made progress in raising up a Filipino clergy and in placing them in parishes and in the hierarchy. By 1936 the majority of the parishes were in charge of Filipino priests. In that year, moreover, of the ten bishops seven were Filipino, two Americans, and only one a Spaniard. In 1934 a Filipino was made Archbishop of Manila, the highest ecclesiastical post in the islands.[175] The Roman Catholic Church was thus meeting the nationalistic demand which had earlier proved the decisive factor in the secession of the Aglipayans. In 1937 Filipino pride was flattered by the choice of Manila as the meeting place of an international Eucharistic Congress.[176] Under the Commonwealth progress was made towards the removal of a source of friction of long standing through the purchase by the government of some of the *haciendas*, great landed estates, which belonged to the church.[177] However, the Roman Catholic Church, while in a much better position and healthier than in most of the Latin American countries, did not dominate the Commonwealth regime. There was no clerical political party. In the system of public schools children might, on request from their parents, be given religious instruction by priests or their representatives, but the teachers employed by the state were forbidden to be propagandists

[170] Archie Lowell Ryan, *Religious Education in the Philippines* (Manila, The Methodist Publishing House, 1930, pp. xiv, 205), p. 56.
[171] *The International Review of Missions,* Vol. XXVIII, p. 81.
[172] F. C. Laubach in *The International Review of Missions,* Vol. XXV, pp. 235-249.
[173] Vol. V, pp. 272, 273.
[174] For illustrations see Thomas J. Feeney, *The Padre of the Press, Recollections of Rev. John J. Monahan, S. J.* (New York, Jesuit Mission Press, 1931, pp. 161), *passim*; Hagspiel, *Along the Mission Trail,* Vol. I, pp. 90 ff.; E. J. Edwards, *Thy People. My People* (Milwaukee, The Bruce Publishing Company, 1941, pp. ix, 251), *passim*.
[175] Hayden, *The Philippines,* p. 563.
[176] Hayden, *op. cit.,* p. 564.
[177] Hayden, *op. cit.,* p. 570.

either against religion or for any particular church.[178] The Roman Catholic Church maintained schools, but they enrolled only about a sixteenth as many as did the public system of education.[179]

Upon the Philippine Islands and the growing strength of Christianity broke the Japanese storm. Launching their attack on December 8, 1941, coincidently with their exploit at Pearl Harbour, within the next few months the Japanese effected the reduction of the islands. Since they wished the co-operation of the Filipinos and the latter, by an overwhelming majority, were Christians, they felt it wise to cultivate the friendship of the churches and not to deal over-harshly with the missionaries, even when the latter were enemy aliens. Their armies had a section of experts on religion which included some Christians. For a time after initial restrictions in the first wave of conquest many missionaries were allowed to continue some of their normal activities.[180] Eventually greater limitations were imposed and more of the missionaries were interned. Under the auspices of the Japanese armed forces and presumably because of pressure from them, a Japanese Roman Catholic bishop and scores of Japanese Roman Catholic priests went to the Philippines,[181] probably to induce their fellow churchmen to acquiesce in the new regime, Christianity was not suffering persecution.

The three decades which began with the year 1914 saw, in general, a continuation of the progress of Christianity in the lands in the Pacific which had been one of the outstanding features of the history of the region in the preceding century. In most islands the advance was neither so rapid nor so spectacular as it had been. This did not necessarily indicate any decrease in vigour on the part of the faith. It was chiefly and perhaps entirely because the pioneer days of settlement by the whites in Australia and New Zealand and the initial impact of Western civilization upon the non-Europeans of the vast region had passed. In Australia and New Zealand the churches for the whites became less dependent on the churches in the mother country than they had been and were accepted features of the life of their respective lands. Among the non-Europeans who had been converted before 1914 the churches were more nearly self supporting financially and were increasing in self government and in indigenous leadership. Conversions continued to be more from the non-Christians, especially in New Guinea and in the Netherlands East Indies. The missions still had

[178] Hayden, *op. cit.*, pp. 563, 564.
[179] Feeney, *op. cit.*, p. 75.
[180] *The International Review of Missions*, Vol. XXXII, pp. 63, 64.
[181] *Les Missions Franciscaines*, Sept., Oct., 1943.

a large share in education. In some islands, however, this was decreasing in the face of the state schools. The Bible was being put into more tongues. The Protestant churches were progressively knit into the world-wide fellowship of the Ecumenical Movement. The first of the world wars brought important alterations in only a few of the islands and even there did not greatly retard the spread of the faith. The second of the world wars entailed more marked changes, particularly in the islands which were overwhelmed by the Japanese. By 1945, however, in few if any of these had Christianity suffered serious reverses.

Chapter IX

MADAGASCAR. AFRICA SOUTH OF THE SAHARA
GENERAL CHANGES; REGIONAL SURVEY; EFFECT ON THE
ENVIRONMENT; EFFECT OF THE ENVIRONMENT

IN THAT largest congeries of peoples of primitive cultures, on the island
of Madagascar and in Africa south of the Sahara, the three decades following the year 1914 wrought great changes. They were due primarily to the penetration of the white man's culture. This had been in process before 1914 but it
was now accelerated.

The first of the world wars of the period quickened the pace, particularly
because hostilities extended to some of the territories held by the Germans at
the outbreak of the conflict and because thousands of Malagasy and Africans
were enrolled in the Allied forces in Europe, North Africa, and Western Asia
and brought back with them first hand impressions of the white man's world.

As the decades passed, the white man more and more dominated the life of
the region and made it ancillary to his economy. Africa became for him increasingly a source of raw materials. He continued to develop the gold mines
and the diamond diggings in the South. He exploited the rich copper deposits
in Northern Rhodesia and the southern part of the Belgian Congo. He exported
the tropical woods. He stimulated the growth of plantations for cacao, tobacco,
and rubber. From Africa he drew a substantial proportion of the chrome ore,
manganese, platinum, asbestos, graphite, palm oil, and sisal which he used. For
all of these labour was required. That labour was native. Through these contacts
blacks were introduced to the white man's ways. By his railways, steam-boats,
automobiles, and airplanes the white man greatly facilitated travel and made
possible quick and convenient access to regions which a half century before
could be reached, if at all, only by slow, toilsome, and dangerous journeys. The
money economy which followed and which was reinforced by the methods of
taxation of the colonial governments effected other alterations. The goods
from the factories of the outside world, some from the West and some from
Japan, increased the influence of the outer world. The inconveniences which accompanied the world-wide financial depression of 1929 and the 1930's demonstrated the dependence of Africa upon Europe and the United States. The

second of the world wars still further intensified the impact of the white man's civilization. Malagasy and Africans again served their European masters away from their native habitats. Great new airways brought hitherto remote parts of Africa within a few hours of America and Europe. White armed forces, including some from the United States, were seen in increased numbers.

This impact of the white man meant the progressive and rapid disintegration of the old patterns of African life.[1] The tribal structure with its traditional customs and forms of social control and education was passing. Thousands of Africans, deracinated individuals, were cast adrift. Colonial governments and administrators wrestled with the problems thus presented. The changes proceeded at unequal pace in various parts of the vast area. In some regions, notably in much of the Union of South Africa, Rhodesia, parts of the Belgian Congo, and along the coast of the Gulf of Guinea, they were very marked. In some other areas they had barely begun.

It was this *milieu* in which Christianity and Christian missionaries were placed. Earlier they had been pioneers of the white man's penetration. They had fought the initial crude exploitation of the blacks by the less conscientious of the white men. By reducing languages to writing, inaugurating schools, introducing improved medical care, and bringing a fresh and powerful spiritual and moral dynamic they had begun the preparation of the black folk for the momentous transition. Now their task of helping the Malagasy and the Africans to adjust themselves to the new environment was vastly augmented. In some ways the Malagasy and the Africans were much more accessible and were more responsive to the Christian message than before. Yet there were aspects of its task which the Church found more difficult. It was not only reaching individuals and groups with the Christian message and bringing into being Christian communities with indigenous leadership. It was also providing the spiritual basis of a fresh society on the ruins of the old. The old was vanishing so rapidly that there was all too little time to build the new.

The populations involved were large. That of Madagascar was only about 3,500,000, but that of Africa south of the Sahara was probably somewhere between 135,000,000 and 165,000,000.[2] Vital statistics were so unreliable that it was impossible to know whether the total was increasing or declining. In some areas population was clearly dwindling; in others it was increasing. Migration had much to do with both trends.[3]

---

[1] See vivid and accurate pictures of some of the localities in which the changes were most marked in Davis, *Modern Industry and the African, passim*; Phillips, *The Bantu in the City, passim*. For a more comprehensive study see Hailey, *An African Survey, passim*.

[2] Hailey, *op. cit.*, p. 107.

[3] Hailey, *op. cit.*, pp. 109 ff.

In this scene in the three decades after 1914 Christianity had a striking numerical increase. The advance was most marked in the belt which included the Belgian Congo, the adjoining Belgian mandated territory, and the British possessions, protectorates, and mandate which lay to the east and south of Belgian Africa. Yet it was pronounced in some other areas and there were few regions which did not experience it. Roman Catholicism showed a greater proportionate growth than did Protestantism. In Africa south of the Sahara, Protestant communicants were estimated as 556,000 in 1911, in 1924 as 996,000, and in 1936 as 2,131,000, or a multiplication in a quarter of a century of a little less than four-fold. Roman Catholics (and their figures included not only communicants but also all baptized) were said to be 724,000 in 1911, 2,294,000 in 1925, and 4,613,000 in 1933, or a nearly seven-fold advance. In Africa south of the Sahara the increase in Roman Catholic missionaries was also greater than that of Protestants. In 1924 the total for the former was 7,006 and in 1936 10,384, as against 5,556 and 7,514 respectively for the latter.[4] The totals of the missionary force, when brought together, are impressive, but actually the foreign staff, distributed over the huge continent, was pitifully small for the colossal and complicated task committed to it.

Madagascar, to which we come first on our journey westward from the Pacific, racially belonged more to Asia, the East Indies, Polynesia, and Melanesia, than to Africa.

We have seen how in the nineteenth century Christianity made phenomenal gains, especially among the Hòva, the people who dwelt in the high interior and who were more nearly civilized than any of the other groups of the island.[5] Both Protestants and Roman Catholics were active.

After 1914 both branches of Christianity continued to grow numerically. In 1923 or 1924 baptized Protestants were said to total about 268,000,[6] and Roman Catholics were reported to have about 409,000 in 1927 or 1928.[7] Not far from 1936 baptized Protestants were reported to be 212,481 and in 1933 Roman

---

[4] Bates, *Data on the Distribution of the Missionary Enterprise*, pp. 5, 6. The total of baptized Protestants in 1936 was about three and a third millions—Parker, *Interpretative Statistical Survey of the World Mission of the Christian Church*, pp. 18, 19. This represented more than a three-fold advance from 1914 or 1915 when baptized Protestants totalled slightly over a million—Beach and St. John, *World Statistics of Christian Missions*, p. 59.

[5] Vol. V, pp. 301-314.

[6] Beach and Fahs, *World Missionary Atlas*, p. 77. In 1914 or 1915 they were less than 90,000—Beach and St. John. *op. cit.*, p. 59.

[7] Streit, *Catholic World Atlas*, table XLII.

Catholics to be 516,226.[8] In 1938 Roman Catholics were said to total 588,812.[9] This meant that in the latter year Christians were approximately one-fourth of the population. They were proportionately even more influential than this percentage would indicate, for the Hòva were very largely Christian and were the most vigorous and prominent of the Malagasy. The Hòva were predominantly Protestant.

Protestantism was represented after 1914 by seven societies. All but one of them, and that with the smallest constituency, the Seventh Day Adventists, had been active before that year. Six had been holding joint missionary conferences at irregular and long intervals since 1913 and had allocated territory in such fashion as to cover the island and prevent what might seem to be needless overlapping. Yet often Roman Catholics and Protestants were in the same town or city. In 1934 the majority of the societies agreed to have the congregations connected with them bear the common designation "The United Protestant Church of Madagascar," but with each denominational branch preserving its identity and form of ecclesiastical government.[10] For some of the denominations there was an easy interchange of membership as Christians moved from the territory of one to that of another. The Hòva were active as missionaries. There was also an organization through which Christians of more than one denomination co-operated in the spread of their faith. Hundreds of the Malagasy were among the clergy and other hundreds were lay preachers.[11] Malagasy women were active as deacons, lay preachers, and evangelists. In the decade following 1922 religious awakenings swept through parts of the islands.[12] There were some discouraging features. It was said that the Hòva Christians tended to hold themselves aloof from peoples of other tribes.[13] When, in the 1930's, be-

---

[8] Parker, *Interpretative Statistical Survey of the World Mission of the Christian Church*, p. 74. The 1936 Protestant figures do not include baptized non-communicants connected with the London Missionary Society and so are misleading for purposes of comparison with earlier figures, for these include them. Protestant communicants, however, seem to have decreased slightly between 1924 and 1936.

[9] *Fides News Service,* May 14, 1939.

[10] Harold A. Ridgwell, *The Great Island. Madagascar: Past and Present* (London, The Livingstone Press, 1937, pp. 110), pp. 63, 64.

[11] A. M. Chirgwin in *The International Review of Missions,* Vol. XXVII, pp. 94-104. See also A. M. Chirgwin, *On the Road to Madagascar* (London, Student Christian Movement Press, 1933, pp. 159), *passim;* Jean Vernier, *A Madagascar. La Vie d'un District Missionnaire Diégo-Suarez* (Paris, Société des Missions Évangéliques, 1929, pp. 58), pp. 27 ff.; H. Rusillon, *Un Petit Continent. Madagascar* (Paris, Société des Missions Évangéliques, 1933, pp. viii, 414), pp. 353 ff.; William Kendall Gale, *Church Planting in Madagascar* (London, The World Dominion Press, 1937, pp. 88), *passim;* A. N. Webster, *Madagascar* (Westminster, The Society for the Propagation of the Gospel in Foreign Parts, 1932, pp. 71), pp. 47 ff.

[12] *The International Review of Missions,* Vol. XXI, p. 243.

[13] A leader in the Société des Missions Évangéliques to the author, June, 1934.

cause of the financial depression, funds from Europe and America declined and fewer Malagasy assistants could be employed, a recrudescence of witchcraft and sorcery was seen in some of the rural districts.[14] However, Malagasy Christians were rising, a least in part, to the added responsibilities placed upon them, and additional clergy were being ordained.[15]

As may be gathered from the statistics of their numbers, Roman Catholics were making progress. For a time in the 1920's there was a disheartening paucity of Malagasy priests. Yet candidates for training for that vocation were increasing, and there were several flourishing organizations for lay folk of various age groups.[16] In 1925 nine Malagasy were ordained priests. The enthusiasm aroused by this step was tempered by the fact that, of the nine, three soon died.[17] In 1937 a translation of the complete Bible into Malagasy by the Jesuits was issued.[18] In 1939 a newly created vicariate apostolic was entrusted to Malagasy clergy and as its head one of their number was consecrated bishop.[19]

The second of the world wars brought embarrassment to the Christian forces in Madagascar. The occupation of their respective countries by the Germans largely cut off the Norwegian and French missionaries from their supporting constituencies. Some assistance came to Protestant missions through the International Missionary Council. Moreover, the Malagasy themselves rallied to meet the emergency. Christians among Malagasy troops serving overseas witnessed to the vitality of their faith by spontaneously forming congregations and holding services.[20] The occupation by the Allied forces brought slightly better contacts between the home organizations and their missionaries. In face of the common problem co-operation between Protestant missions went forward. Then, too, the government introduced religious instruction in the state schools. Churches and missions took responsibility for it, thus enlarging their contacts with youth.[21] In 1939 a small group of representatives of the London Missionary Society were permitted by the government to return to the island.[22] Christianity seemed not to be losing but rather gaining because of the distresses of the time.

[14] *The International Review of Missions,* Vol. XXIV, p. 82, Vol. XXV, p. 75.

[15] *The International Review of Missions,* Vol. XXIII, p. 77, Vol. XXIV, p. 82.

[16] Lesourd, *L'Année Missionnaire,* 1931, pp. 173-175.

[17] Léon Derville, *Madagascar-Betsiléo. Ils sont que Quarante. Les Jesuites chez les Betsiléos* (Paris, Dillen et Cie, 1930, pp. 126), pp. 76-81; Hubert Nicol, *Premiers Prêtres de la Terre Malgache* (Paris, no date, pp. 51), *passim.*

[18] *Fides Service,* Dec. 12, 1936.

[19] *Fides News Service,* June 2, 1939.

[20] *The International Review of Missions,* Vol. XXX, p. 70.

[21] *The International Review of Missions,* Vol. XXXIII, p. 64.

[22] *International Missionary Council Bulletin* #15, Feb., 1944 (mimeographed).

To Christianity in Africa south of the Sahara the first of the world wars inevitably brought difficulties and fresh problems. In so vast a region these varied from colony to colony and according to the complexion of the ruling power. In some of the territories which in 1914 were under German rule, notably East Africa, there was actual fighting. From several of the colonies troops were recruited. A large proportion of the Africans were aware that fighting was in progress in Europe. Many missionary staffs were depleted by the lack of reinforcements or the calling of some of the younger men to the colours.[23] Communications with supporting constituencies were slowed down or interrupted. Many Africans, if not in the armies, served as labourers in connexion with the armies and, if Christians, were away from their normal church environment. Numbers were puzzled by the spectacle of peoples whom they deemed Christians fighting among themselves.[24] During the war German missionaries in British territories suffered some inconvenience. After the armistice and even after the signing of the Treaty of Versailles, many Germans, including missionaries, were deported from British possessions.[25] The German Reich lost its territories in Africa and, as a rule, German missionaries in these areas were expelled.[26] In 1924 the British ban was removed and German missionaries began to return: by 1932 German missions were permitted to resume operations in all British territories. By that time, however, some of the area served by the German organizations had been transferred to other bodies. Even then German missionaries were excluded from the portion of Cameroon which had become a French mandate and from Ruanda-Urundi, formerly part of German East Africa and now a Belgian mandate.[27]

Yet during the war years some advance was registered. The Church Missionary Society reported that in 1914 it had 11,000 baptisms in Nigeria, the largest total it had ever had in any one year in any of its missions.[28] As we have earlier noted,[29] from 1913 into 1915 an African, William Wadé Harris, came

---

[23] *The International Review of Missions,* Vol. IV, p. 40, Vol. V, p. 63, Vol. VII, pp. 45, 47.

[24] Agnes R. Fraser, *Donald Fraser of Livingstonia* (London, Hodder and Stoughton, 1934, pp. ix, 325), pp. 226-237. For the death of an African Christian due indirectly to the war, see Donald Fraser, *The Autobiography of an African . . . Daniel Mtusu* (London, Seeley, Service & Co., Limited, 1925, pp. 210), pp. 205-210.

[25] Richter, *Geschichte der evangelischen Mission in Afrika,* pp. 515-518.

[26] Schmidlin, *Das deutsche Missionswerk der Gegenwart,* p. 30; Jones, *Education in East Africa,* p. 292; Heinrich Driessler, *Die Rheinische Mission in Südwestafrika* (Gütersloh, C. Bertelsmann, 1932, pp. viii, 318), *passim.*

[27] *The International Review of Missions,* Vol. XXI, p. 237.

[28] *The International Review of Missions,* Vol. V, p. 61.

[29] Vol. V, p. 449.

from Liberia to the Ivory Coast, preaching. He felt himself impelled by the New Testament command to go, make disciples, baptize, and teach.[30] He was an impressive figure, tall, garbed in a robe and stole, wearing a cross, and bearing a high cross and a Bible. He knew the latter thoroughly. He exhorted the Africans to burn their fetishes, to observe Sunday, to eschew alcohol, thieving, and adultery, and to believe in one God. He baptized those who accepted his message. His preaching was attended by extreme emotional manifestations and he had a following which numbered thousands. He would not accept money, except to give to the poor, and he had no political aspirations. He told his adherents to wait for the coming of white missionaries. He resembled other African prophets of whom we are to hear more a few paragraphs below. All of them combined Christianity and African lore, but in him was more of the Christian tradition than in some of the others. The French authorities, fearing unrest from the vast throngs, required him to leave their territory. He won some among the primitive folk in Sierre Leone. Great crowds in the Gold Coast heeded him. On his encouragement, his adherents erected buildings for worship. They sang hymns, badly garbled from their European originals. Several years after the movement began, English Wesleyan missionaries learned of it, and, through their efforts, about 45,000 from it were gathered into their churches.[31] The war years also saw advances in some other portions of Africa.[32]

Unrest in various sections of Africa followed the first of the world wars. It was akin to the global intensification of nationalism in these years and was part of the general restlessness of non-white peoples against the white man's rule. It took many forms. We shall meet some of them in the ensuing pages. In general, in so far as they directly affected Christianity, they issued in prophets and their followings, in churches independent of white control, and in a hastening of black participation in those churches which were associated with white missions.[33]

Except for the dislocation of German missions and the substitution of those of the victorious nations for some of them, the missionary map of Africa after 1918 was mostly an expansion of that before 1914. Protestant missionaries were chiefly from the British Isles and the continent of Europe. A few new societies entered and several already represented greatly enlarged their enterprises. Thus

[30] Matt. xxviii, 19, 20.

[31] Platt, *An African Prophet,* pp. 31 ff.; Platt, *From Fetish to Faith,* pp. 86 ff.; F. Deaville Walker, *The Story of the Ivory Coast* (London, The Cargate Press, 1926, pp. 82), *passim*; Cooksey and McLeish, *Religion and Civilization in West Africa,* pp. 58 ff.

[32] *The International Review of Missions,* Vol. VI, p. 44, Vol. VII, p. 42.

[33] For some of these movements in South Africa see D.D.T. Jabavu in *The International Review of Missions,* Vol. XI, pp. 249 ff.

the Salvation Army grew rapidly,[34] and the Seventh Day Adventists sought access to many areas. The major loads were still carried by the bodies upon whom they had rested in 1914. Roman Catholic missionaries were predominantly from the continent of Europe, mainly from France and Belgium. For the missionary forces of the United States Africa was still a very secondary interest. American missions concerned themselves chiefly with the Far East, India, and Western Asia. Roman Catholics rapidly expanded their staffs and their organization, much more so than did Protestants.[35] The foreign personnel of the former totalled 7,006 in 1924 and 10,384 in 1936 as against 4,102 of the latter in 1910, 5,556 in 1924, and 7,514 in 1933.[36] For the better supervision of its growing enterprises, in the 1920's the Holy See created two Apostolic Delegations for Africa south of the Sahara.[37] Protestants were more and more working together co-operatively for Africa south of the Sahara and in 1926 held a noteworthy conference for joint and comprehensive planning for the region.[38]

The second of the world wars, like the first, wrought changes. These were probably more marked than those which accompanied the earlier ones. By 1945, however, sufficient perspective could not be had to appraise them comprehensively. Since no German possessions remained after the first of the conflicts, the region south of the Sahara saw but little fighting. However, the economic and social phases of its life were probably more affected than in the earlier struggle. Most German missionaries were interned, but they were only a minority of the missionary body. Many Protestant and Roman Catholic missionaries were cut off from their supporting constituencies. Although financial support was found for them—for the Protestants largely through the Orphaned Missions Fund[39] —reinforcements could not be had. Even for missions not so separated from their home churches, additions to the staffs could be sent only with difficulty and were few.

Yet even under these circumstances, seemingly adverse, the war years witnessed advances of Christianity. Of these it was possible to gain a few glimpses which, presumably, were fairly typical. In the year preceding June 30, 1942, Roman Catholics in the Belgian Congo and Ruanda-Urundi increased 249,899,

[34] Arthur Copping, *Banners in Africa* (London, Hodder and Stoughton, 1933, pp. 152), *passim*, gives a survey in the form of a travelogue.

[35] For an interesting travelogue by a Jesuit, covering much of Roman Catholic missions in Africa, see T. Gavan Duffy, *Let's Go* (London, Sheed and Ward, 1928, pp. 511).

[36] Bates, *Data on the Distribution of the Missionary Enterprise*, p. 6.

[37] *Testo-Atlante illustrato delle Missioni*, p. 82.

[38] Edwin W. Smith, *The Christian Mission in Africa. A Study based on the work of the International Conference at Le Zoute, Belgium, September 14th to 21st, 1926* (London, The International Missionary Council, 1926, pp. viii, 192).

[39] *The International Review of Missions*, Vol. XXXIII, p. 58.

or about 13 per cent.[40] Between June 30, 1939 and June 30, 1941 the Christians in charge of the White Fathers mounted from 1,587,558 to 1,827,518, catechumens from 400,917 to 590,491, and stations from 309 to 318. Of European missionaries connected with the White Fathers, in the same two year period the number of priests had grown from 910 to 985, but that of lay brothers had declined from 269 to 242 and that of sisters from 721 to 684. The increase in the African staff, however, more than made up the difference, for in that interval priests rose from 171 to 221, brothers from 99 to 154, and sisters from 546 to 689.[41] This growth in the missions of the White Fathers was especially significant because of the large proportion of Africa which was in their charge. In Uganda by 1944 the Mill Hill Fathers had opened six new stations since the beginning of the war.[42] The mounting death rate among the Holy Ghost Fathers, however, showed the toll of the war years on another of the orders serving large areas in Africa.[43]

Among Protestant missions we hear of the assumption by the African Christians of additional financial responsibility for their churches, of advances into fresh territories on the Ivory Coast, and of the opening of a new secondary school for girls in Southern Nigeria.[44]

It may assist in obtaining a picture of the developments in Christianity in Africa south of the Sahara if we follow the procedure of an earlier volume and recount our story according to the political divisions. We shall follow the order of the nineteenth century narrative and begin in the South, journeying northward and then westward. We shall, unfortunately, need even more relentlessly to condense our account than we did that of the preceding period. The chapter[45] which we devoted to the nineteenth century story of Christianity in Africa was of necessity one of rigid compression. Yet, although most of it was devoted to the five or six decades before 1914, we gave to it approximately four times the space which we can assign to the three decades after that year. In these three decades, moreover, the Christian enterprise assumed much larger dimensions than it had before 1914. At best, therefore, we can only select a few

---

[40] *Delegato Apostolica in Congo Belgico et Ruanda Urundi. Resumé des Statistiques des Missions du Congo Belge et du Ruanda-Urundi, au 30 Juin, 1942.*

[41] Letter of J. D. Murphy, of the White Fathers, Nov. 27, 1943, to J. J. Considine (Ms).

[42] *The International Review of Missions*, Vol. XXXIII, p. 85.

[43] *Circular letter Number 14. May 4, 1943* [apparently from the Africa missions of the Holy Ghost Fathers] gives a total of 40 deaths in 1939, 45 in 1940, 53 in 1941, and 54 in 1942.

[44] *The International Review of Missions*, Vol. XXXIII, pp. 52, 53, 59.

[45] Vol. V, Chap. XI.

salient events and movements and trust them to yield some inkling of what a detailed narrative would reveal.

We begin our African pilgrimage, then, with the Union of South Africa, the protectorates, Basutoland, Swaziland, and Bechuanaland, which were geographically associated with it, and Southwest Africa, before the first world war German, but now become a mandate of the Union.

In population the Union of South Africa nearly doubled in the quarter of a century between 1911 and 1936. That of European blood rose from 1,276,242 in the former to 2,003,857 in the latter year. The non-European population, the vast majority of it Bantus of varying tribal stocks, increased in the same interval from 4,697,152 to 7,586,041.[46] Non-Europeans, therefore, outnumbered the whites between three and four to one and were increasing proportionately slightly more rapidly than the latter. The whites were determined to remain in control, politically, economically, and socially. The result was discrimination and acute and chronic inter-racial tensions which, next to the anti-Semitism of the Third German Reich, were the most serious on the planet.[47] They were aggravated by the progressive disintegration of the inherited tribal structure and economic life of the blacks and the cityward movement of a deracinated indigenous, usually poverty-stricken and landless proletariat.[48] They were further complicated by the presence of large "poor white" elements and by racial minorities in which "coloured" and Indians were especially an irritant.

Of those in the Union of South Africa of European descent a larger proportion (if Jews are excepted) professed a connexion with some branch of the Christian Church than either in Australia or New Zealand. In 1936 those without a membership or a preference were less than one per cent. of the white population. By denominations the proportions altered slightly between the census taken in 1911 and that of 1936. In both, those of the Dutch Reformed churches were about 54 per cent. of the whole, but Anglicans decreased from 20 per cent. to 17.26 per cent., Presbyterians from 4.6 per cent. to 4.1 per cent., Lutherans from 1.8 per cent. to 1.29 per cent., and Baptists from 1.2 per cent. to 1. per cent. Between the same years, on the other hand, Methodists rose from 6.3 per cent. to 7.08 per cent., Congregationalists from 1.05 per cent. to 1.07 per cent., and Roman Catholics from 4.4 per cent. to 4.6 per cent.[49] Roman Catholics, it may be noted, constituted a smaller proportion of the population than in any of the three other major dominions of the British Empire—Canada, Australia, and New Zealand.

[46] *The Statesman's Year-Book,* 1943, p. 437.
[47] See Brookes, *The Colour Problems of South Africa, passim.*
[48] Phillips, *The Bantu in the City, passim.*
[49] *The Statesman's Year-Book,* 1919, p. 210, 1943, p. 437.

Among the non-Europeans, mostly Bantus, of the Union, in the twenty-five year interval between 1911 and 1936 those claiming the Christian name rose from about one-third to more than one-half of the population. Among the various Christian bodies the increase was most marked among what were known as the native separatist churches, of which we are to say more in a moment and which in 1936 numbered about 14 per cent. of the non-European population, and among the Roman Catholics, who mounted from about .8 per cent of the non-European population in 1911 to about 3.6 per cent. in 1933. In terms of percentages of all non-Europeans, between 1911 and 1936 those connected with the Dutch Reformed bodies rose from 4.4 to 5, Anglicans from 5.9 to 7.5, Methodists from 9.7 to 11.2, and Lutherans from 4.2 to 4.9, while Congregationalists declined from 3.7 to 1.9 and Presbyterians from 1.8 to 1.5.[50] The decrease in the percentage of the last two communions presumably was due to losses to the native Christian bodies. To those familiar with the earlier history of Christianity in South Africa[51] it will be obvious that most of the religious groups which had been responsible for the planting and nourishing of Christianity among the blacks continued to share in the growth of the faith and in proportions not far from those of the pre-1914 period. The marked exceptions were the Roman Catholics, the independent native churches, and the Congregationalists and Presbyterians. It must also be clear that Christianity was rapidly becoming the faith of the non-European population. There were small communities of Hindus, Buddhists, Confucianists, and Moslems, descendants of immigrants from Asia, the East Indies, and the east coast of Africa, but in 1936 they constituted only about 3.2 per cent. of the non-European population and in proportion to the whole they were declining.[52] The vast majority had been animists and their faith, together with the inherited fabric of their life, was crumbling, and Christianity, when earnestly propagated, made rapid gains.[53]

The remarkable growth of the Roman Catholics was unequally distributed. In 1936 Roman Catholics were an inconsiderable fraction of the population of the Cape Province and of the Transvaal, but were much more numerous than before, both actually and relatively, in Natal, and in Basutoland constituted about a fifth of the whole.[54] A Roman Catholic community of not far from 2,500 had been built up among the Indians, a portion of the population rather difficult to reach with the faith.[55] In the thirty years after 1914 additional vicariates and

[50] *Ibid.*
[51] See Vol. V, pp. 336-378.
[52] *The Statesman's Year-Book,* 1919, p. 210, 1943, p. 437.
[53] *Union of South Africa. Report of Native Churches Commission,* pp. 19-22.
[54] *Fides News Service,* Jan. 23, 1937.
[55] *Fides News Service,* June 12, 1937.

prefectures apostolic were created. Between 1914 and 1931 these increased from eight to nineteen.[56] In 1922 Rome instituted an Apostolic Delegation for the better supervision of South Africa and the more effective propagation of the faith.[57] An outstanding feature of the years was the record of Bernard Huss, of the Trappist enterprise at Mariannhill, in Natal. Huss had striking success in promoting Catholic Action, particularly in the form of co-operative credit societies and farm schools among the blacks.[58] In 1923, moreover, the Catholic Union of South Africa was inaugurated with the purpose of combating Communism, of promoting the spiritual, economic, physical, social, and intellectual welfare of the natives, and of furthering fellowship between Bantus and Europeans.[59] However, in 1944, Roman Catholics, while growing,[60] were still only a small portion of the non-European population, proportionately less even than of the European stock.

The native separatist churches constituted one of the outstanding phenomena of Christianity in South Africa after 1914. They had begun before 1914 and were akin to what was being found in several other parts of Africa[61] and in other portions of the non-Occidental world, especially where Protestant Christianity came in touch with folk of primitive cultures. To some degree they were an effect of Protestant Christianity on the environment and also a phase of the effect of the environment on Christianity. In no other region of the world in this era was there so extensive a proliferation of sects as in South Africa. In 1906 there were said to be fifteen or more, in 1922 sixty-five, and in 1932 over three hundred.[62] In 1936 they were reported by the census to have slightly over one million adherents.[63] The sources of their origin and multiplication were many. Probably the chief was the desire of the Bantu to manage his own affairs. This was reinforced by the restlessness, common through much of the world, under white domination, and accentuated in South Africa by the peculiarly inflamed inter-racial situation. The tribe was disintegrating and the Church was growing. The white man had control of economic and political life. Under these conditions, the Church in its Protestant forms gave the Bantu one of his best opportunities for self-expression. Indeed, ecclesiastical autonomy had been

---

[56] Streit, *Catholic World Atlas*, table XVII; *Testo-Atlante illustrato delle Missioni*, p. 150.

[57] *Catholic Directory of South Africa*, 1934, pp. 18, 19.

[58] Davis, *Modern Industry and the African*, p. 335; *Fides Service*, June 2, 1934.

[59] *Fides News Service*, Feb. 13, 1937.

[60] For a picture of Roman Catholic missions in South Africa in the early part of the 1930's, see Martindale, *African Angelus*, pp. 1-209.

[61] Wrong, *Africa and the Making of Books*, p. 13.

[62] R. H. W. Shepard in *The International Review of Missions*, Vol. XXVI, pp. 453 ff.

[63] *The Statesman's Year-Book*, 1943, p. 437.

encouraged by some of the Protestant missions, notably those from the British Isles and of Congregational and Presbyterian constituencies. There seemed to be very little anti-white racial feeling in these bodies, but, rather, a desire for independence. Occasionally there also entered into the causes of division resentment over moral discipline by missionaries, disillusionment with the moral corruption witnessed among whites in the cities, and the influence of American Negro churches. The tribal factor made its contribution. The Bantus, being accustomed to the organization of society by numerous tribes, were inclined to regard denominations as belonging to that pattern and were not disturbed by the existence of sects. In general, the separatist churches tended to have lower ethical standards, to be more tolerant of polygamy, and to have a more poorly trained ministry than did the churches connected with white missions.[64] They were a symptom of the times, a local manifestation of the trend towards rooting Christianity in the soil and making it less exclusively Occidental.

In the face of this multiplication of ecclesiastical divisions and in view of the gulfs which separated white and black, Boers and British, and Indian and non-Indian, attempts to bring about in South Africa the kind of co-operation among the Protestant forces which was growing rapidly in other parts of the world found heavy going. A Christian Council of South Africa was formed and had membership in the International Missionary Council, but its course was stormy. In contrast with Australia, New Zealand, and Canada, the major denominations of South Africa were slow in associating themselves with the World Council of Churches. Yet in spite of difficulties, the Christian Council of South Africa was inaugurated and was kept functioning and (1931) several of the Methodist bodies achieved union.[65] Formal negotiations were also begun looking towards merging Congregationalists, Presbyterians, and Methodists.[66] These, however, were between churches of British origin and complexion. The deeper cleavage between Boer and Briton was still to be closed.

Although the churches were growing rapidly, there were indications of a decline of the hold of Christianity upon the Bantus in the great urban areas on the Witwatersrand, the region which was supplying the world with a large proportion of its gold. Here mission organizations were finding the road increasingly difficult and some of the educated African Christians declared that

[64] Allen Lea, *The Native Separatist Church Movement in South Africa* (Cape Town, Juta & Co., Ltd., 1926, pp. 84), *passim*; R. H. W. Shepard in *The International Review of Missions*, Vol. XXVI, pp. 453 ff.; *Union of South Africa. Report of Native Churches Commission*, pp. 22-36; *Union of South Africa Official Year Book*, No. 9, 1926-1927, p. 963; Eiselen in Schapera, *Western Civilization and the Natives of South Africa*, pp. 75, 76.

[65] Allen Lea, *The Story of Methodist Union in South Africa* (Cape Town, The Methodist Book Depot and Publishing House, no date, pp. 96), *passim*.

[66] Douglass, *A Decade of Objective Progress in Church Unity, 1927-1936*, pp. 38-41.

the Church was actually losing ground. The causes of the decline were laid to the incredibly adverse economic conditions of the Bantu Christians, the evil example of Europeans, the colour bar in Church and state, a lack of concern of the churches for the physical needs of their constituencies, the ignorance of the clergy, the imperfections of the church members, and anti-Christian Communist propaganda.[67]

Here and there, moreover, were complaints that the existing Christianity was deteriorating. It was declared that reliance upon magic was increasing among Christians and that there were Christian witch-doctors, at least one of whom alleged Biblical support for the occupation.[68] The assertion was also made that second and third generation Christians were often inferior in moral stamina to the converts of the first generation and that their faith did not effectively offset the moral decay which followed upon the disintegration of the inherited *mores* through the impact of European civilization.[69] It would, indeed, have been amazing if Christianity had been able immediately to solve all the problems brought by the contact of cultures, the rapid dissolution of the native social and economic life, and the exploitation of the blacks by the whites.

In spite of discouragements and the colossal nature and complexity of the situation, Christians were grappling with the problems involved and in some phases and areas were registering progress. The whites of South Africa were becoming more active in missions to the blacks.[70] The Dutch Reformed Church was taking a greater interest in them. Each of its four synods had a society which was conducting missions both within and outside its borders. This was particularly notable in the three northern provinces of the Union, for here, because of early experiences with missionaries, there had long been a prejudice against them.[71] Many whites were engaging in religious activities, such as teaching in Sunday Schools, which brought them in touch with blacks.[72] Through opening to them teaching posts in its schools and the clerical profession the church afforded most of the few outlets for educated blacks.[73] Mission "reserves" of land provided opportunities for progressive individual blacks who wished to carry on improved methods of agriculture unhampered by conservative chiefs.[74] Most of the schools for blacks were conducted by missions, although

[67] Phillips, *The Bantu in the City,* pp. 258-279.
[68] G. Callaway in *The International Review of Missions,* Vol. XXV, pp. 223-225.
[69] William Eiselen, quoted in *The International Review of Missions,* Vol. XXIV, p. 214.
[70] *The International Review of Missions,* Vol. XXVIII, p. 64.
[71] J. Reyneke, General Mission Secretary of the Dutch Reformed Church of South Africa, in conversation with the author, Oct. 23, 1937.
[72] Noble, *The Black Trek,* p. 115.
[73] Macmillan, *Complex South Africa,* pp. 136, 198 ff.
[74] Macmillan, *op. cit.,* p. 136.

with inspection and financial aid by the state.[75] There were white Christians who though not in the employ of church or mission laboured manfully for greater opportunities for the Bantus and for more friendly relations between the races.[76] In the 1920's the majority of the churches of South Africa joined in a campaign for more inter-racial harmony.[77] In the extraordinarily baffling array of difficulties presented by Johannesburg and other cities on the Witwatersrand, Christian forces, including chiefly churches and missions, were striving for a more wholesome religious, moral, intellectual, and recreational life for the underprivileged blacks who crowded the festering slums.[78] In 1930 a joint student Christian conference was held composed of Bantus and Europeans in an attempt to face together in the light of their faith the common life of the races in South Africa.[79] Non-white preachers were invited to the pulpit of at least one fashionable white church.[80] In 1925 Christian leaders from both English-speaking and Dutch-speaking communities raised their voices against the Colour Bar Bill.[81] In an attempt to banish drunkenness and its demoralization of Bantu life, churches and missions fought intemperance and stood for total abstinence.[82]

Not all of South African Christianity was in the cities, the crucial points of conflict between the races and the old and the new cultures. Missions continued to labour in the *hinterland* and to push forward the geographical frontiers of the faith. For example, the Paris Evangelical Missionary Society pursued its highly successful enterprise in Basutoland and, in accord with the temper of the times, increased trained indigenous leadership, gave the local church more of a united organization, and provided for Basuto participation in it.[83]

[75] Brookes, *Native Education in South Africa*, p. 103; Chirgwin, *An African Pilgrimage*, pp. 69-92; *Report of the Special Committee on Education in Relation to Evangelism, 1932-1933*, London Missionary Society, p. 12; *The International Review of Missions*, Vol. XXIX, p. 82; Oldham and Gibson, *The Remaking of Man in Africa*, pp. 123, 170, 171; Gottfried Gevers, *Die Kulturarbeit der deutschen evangelischen Missionen in Südafrika* (Göttingen, 1929, pp. ix, 79), pp. 11, 78.

[76] Howard Pim, *A Transkei Enquiry, 1933* (Lovedale Press, no date, pp. xiii, 82), pp. iii-vi; Phillips, *The Bantu in the City*, p. 304.

[77] Fraser, *Donald Fraser*, pp. 258-266.

[78] Phillips, *The Bantu in the City*, pp. 300-304; Phillips, *The Bantu are Coming*, pp. 43, 106-152.

[79] *Christian Students and Modern South Africa. A Report of the Bantu-European Student Christian Conference, Fort Hare, June 27th-July 3d, 1930* (Fort Hare, Student Christian Union, 1930, pp. xii, 243), *passim*.

[80] Brookes, *The Colour Problems of South Africa*, p. 165.

[81] *Ibid.*

[82] Chirgwin, *An African Pilgrimage*, p. 37; Lennox, *The Story of Our Missions in South Africa*, p. 68.

[83] V. Ellenberger, *Un Siècle de Mission au Lessouto (1833-1933)* (Paris, Société des Missions Évangéliques, no date, pp. 447), pp. 371 ff.; V. Ellenberger, *Sur les Hauts-Plateaux du Lessouto. Notes et Souvenirs de Voyage* (Paris, Société des Missions Évangéliques, 1930, pp. 234), *passim*.

The second of the world wars brought no marked revolution in South African Christianity. The large number of Germans in their missionary body—twice that of any other nationality[84]—presented Roman Catholics with a serious situation, but Roman Catholics were only a small minority. In spite of the heightened Afrikaans nationalism which had repercussions in the Dutch Reformed churches, for these were in part an expression and embodiment of that spirit, some contact was had between the Christian Council of South Africa and the newly constituted Federal Council of Dutch Reformed Churches.[85] Under the Christian Council of South Africa a conference was held in 1942 which, after the pattern of what was being done in Great Britain, formulated ideals for a more nearly Christian social order in the post war years, with improved livelihood for all, including Bantus, and with better relations between the races. Quiet advance was registered in several phases of the work of the churches during these years.[86]

Marked as was the numerical growth of Christianity in the Union of South Africa in the three decades after 1914, proportionately that in the Rhodesias, Southern and Northern, was even greater. In 1924 the number of baptized Protestants in the Rhodesias was about 30,000.[87] In 1936 it was about 134,000.[88] In other words, it had more than quadrupled in less than a decade and a half. In 1933 the number of Roman Catholics was not far from 100,000.[89] This was an increase from about 89,000 in 1931.[90] In some parts of Rhodesia missions had preceded the extension of British political authority. From the beginning of the latter, missions and colonial administrators had co-operated amicably and, in characteristic British fashion, the colonial regime had utilized the missions in its educational programme and had subsidized their schools. From mission schools came clerks and interpreters for government offices and teachers for the normal schools maintained by the state.[91] In general, the policy of the government towards the natives was one of benevolent paternalism.

The development of copper mines in Northern Rhodesia brought together black labourers from various areas and confronted the Christian forces with acute problems. These included higher prices, the draining off of artisans, and

---

[84] *Testo-Atlante illustrato delle Missioni,* p. 81.
[85] *The International Review of Missions,* Vol. XXXIII, p. 61.
[86] *The International Review of Missions,* Vol. XXXII, pp. 50-53, Vol. XXXIII, pp. 60-30.
[87] Beach and Fahs, *World Missionary Atlas,* p. 77.
[88] Parker, *Interpretative Statistical Survey of the World Mission of the Christian Church,* p. 71. For a picture of one of the Protestant missions, see E. M. Jakeman, *Pioneering in Northern Rhodesia* (London, Morgan & Scott, Ltd., no date, pp. 63).
[89] Parker, *op. cit.,* p. 33.
[90] *Testo-Atlante illustrato delle Missioni,* p. 122.
[91] Davis, *Modern Industry and the African,* pp. 292, 346.

the organization of new sects by ambitious native leaders.[92] However, the Protestant forces co-operated. Largely on the initiative of the African Christians a union church was formed, and the mining companies assisted by providing suitable buildings. The Roman Catholics, too, were active.[93] Staffs for the welfare enterprises of the mining companies were recruited in large part from missionaries.[94]

The Roman Catholic forces were augmented by the arrival of Irish Capuchins, with a field in Barotseland, and Italian Conventuals. They relieved the pressure on the Polish Jesuits, who had been attempting to cover most of Northern Rhodesia.[95] The White Fathers were still responsible for the North-east. There were, as well, a few priests and brothers from Mariannhill.[96]

For the co-ordination of the Christian forces there existed the General Missionary Conference of Southern Rhodesia, in which both Protestant and Roman Catholic missionaries had membership,[97] and the General Missionary Conference of Northern Rhodesia, which held its first meeting in 1914 and in which all the missions, including the Protestants, the Jesuits, and the White Fathers, were represented.[98] These were interesting examples of co-operation between Protestants and Roman Catholics. They were somewhat exceptional, but in the three decades after 1914 they had parallels of growing frequency in various parts of the world and in several forms.

A disturbing element entered Rhodesia in the form of the Watch Tower Movement. This, an American outgrowth of Protestantism,[99] known also under the name of Jehovah's Witnesses, seems to have come to Rhodesia by way of South Africa. It was self-supporting and under indigenous leaders. The latter were often men of forceful character and marked gifts of oratory. They taught the imminent second coming of Christ with the destruction of human society and the setting up of a new order in which the formerly underprivileged would sit in judgment on their erstwhile rulers and oppressors. It also encouraged "speaking with tongues" and belief in the avenging power of the spirits of the ancestors. It denounced government, both white and black, and missions, whether Protestant or Roman Catholic. It found fertile soil in an Africa restive under the rapid penetration and domination of the white man. In the 1930's it

[92] Davis, *op. cit.,* pp. 282-285.
[93] Davis, *op. cit.,* pp. 293-295.
[94] Davis, *op. cit.,* p. 310.
[95] Martindale, *African Angelus,* p. 265.
[96] Smith, *The Way of the White Fields,* pp. 56, 80, 81.
[97] Smith, *op. cit.,* p. 71.
[98] Smith, *op. cit.,* pp. 97, 98.
[99] Vol. IV, pp. 443, 444.

contributed to violent disturbances and the state and the chiefs took steps to suppress it. Yet it persisted.[100]

In Nyasaland the striking spread of Christianity which had begun before 1914[101] continued. No missions which attained large proportions entered after that year. Those previously represented, however, experienced great accessions of members. Not far from 1924 baptized Protestants totalled about 66,000[102] and in 1936 approximately 174,000.[103] Not far from 1928 Roman Catholics were said to number about 41,000[104] and five years later slightly over 100,000.[105] Protestants were still the more numerous. In 1924 a step towards union and self government was taken when the Church of Central Africa, Presbyterian, was constituted, originally by the Christians connected with missions of the United Free Church and the Church of Scotland.[106] It later also included those which arose out of the missions of the Dutch Reformed Church of South Africa. In 1942 the Nyasaland Christian Council was formed.[107]

The great Portuguese possessions of Angola and Mozambique (Portuguese East Africa) were, as earlier, fields for both Roman Catholics and Protestants.[108] In Angola Roman Catholic enterprises suffered during the first of the world wars, but had a marked revival later, with the addition of many missionaries, some of them Alsatians. Much literature was prepared in the vernaculars.[109] In the 1930's Roman Catholics in Angola multiplied nearly four-fold.[110] The Portuguese Government, while in theory granting religious toleration and permitting Protestant missions in its possessions, accorded special financial assistance to Roman Catholic undertakings. A decree of October, 1926, gave added encouragement to Roman Catholic missions.[111] To the bodies already represented were added, in Portuguese East Africa, the Fathers of Mary of Montfort, in 1922, and the Consolate Fathers, in 1925.[112] A concordat of 1940 between the Vatican and Portugal provided for further co-operation between the Holy See

[100] Q. Quick in *The International Review of Missions,* Vol. XXIX, pp. 216-226.

[101] Vol. V, pp. 390-397.

[102] Beach and Fahs, *World Missionary Atlas,* p. 77.

[103] Parker, *Interpretative Statistical Survey of the World Mission of the Christian Church,* p. 19.

[104] Streit, *Catholic World Atlas,* table XLII.

[105] Parker, *op. cit.,* p. 33.

[106] Wm. J. W. Roome, *A Great Emancipation. A Missionary Survey of Nyasaland* (London, World Dominion Press, 1926, pp. 64), pp. 46, 47.

[107] *The International Review of Missions,* Vol. XXXII, p. 48.

[108] For pre-1914 missions see Vol. V, pp. 397-403.

[109] Tucker, *Angola,* pp. 34, 35.

[110] Tucker, *op. cit.,* p. 143.

[111] *Testo-Atlante illustrato delle Missioni,* p. 71; Moreira, *Portuguese East Africa,* pp. 83 ff.

[112] Moreira, *op. cit.,* p. 18.

and the Portuguese Government in the latter's colonies. Roman Catholic dioceses and missions were to receive state subsidies.[113]

The Portuguese were critical of Protestant efforts on the ground that they wrought a breach in the religious unity of the colonies, that they taught in the vernacular, thus impeding the spread of the Portuguese language and assimilation to Portuguese culture, and that in subtle ways they undermined Portuguese rule.[114] Protestant missionaries felt that they were suffering from increasing discrimination against them.[115] Yet Protestant missions persevered and had a growth in membership. In 1926, too, those in Portuguese East Africa constituted an Evangelical Missionary Association, thus giving evidence of the effect of the world-wide trend towards co-operation.[116] In Angola, in the decades after the first of the world wars, something of a mass movement was seen towards the churches nourished by the United Church of Canada and the American Board of Commissioners for Foreign Missions.[117] Protestantism spread to some extent among Portuguese settlers.[118] There was much spontaneous propagation of Protestantism by Africans.[119] Protestant missionaries were, of course, active in reaching non-Christian Africans.[120]

By the census of 1940 Angola was said to have 741,000 Roman Catholics and 286,000 Protestants. This meant that nearly 30 per cent. of the population were Christians. The Ovimbundu were the leading people among the natives and owed this position in part to the effect of the missions of the American Board and the United Church of Canada.[121]

In what before 1914 had been German East Africa and what after the first of the world wars was mostly included in a British mandate under the name of Tanganyika, there had been extensive missions, both Protestant and Roman Catholic.[122] The war of 1914-1918 brought some changes. The territory suffered from the fighting. Some of the tribes were scattered and disease and famine were rife. Moreover, all the Germans, including Protestant and Roman

---

[113] *The International Review of Missions,* Vol. XXX, p. 72.

[114] Moreira, *op. cit.,* p. 62.

[115] *The International Review of Missions,* Vol. XXXI, p. 58.

[116] *The International Review of Missions,* Vol. XXI, p. 227. For a sketch of one of the Protestant missions in Portuguese East Africa, see Henri Guye, *Beira, Une Porte Ouverte* (Lausanne, Mission Suisse dans l'Afrique du Sud, 1938, pp. 38), *passim.*

[117] F. F. Goodsell, after a visit to Angola, in the presence of the author, Sept., 1935. See also Tucker, *op. cit.,* p. 53.

[118] Tucker, *op. cit.,* pp. 116 ff.

[119] Tucker, *op. cit.,* pp. 76-81, 133.

[120] For an illustration see John C. Wengatz, *Miracles in Black, Missionary Experiences in the Wilds of Africa* (New York, Fleming H. Revell Company, 1938, pp. 177), *passim.*

[121] *The International Review of Missions,* Vol. XXXIII, pp. 55, 56.

[122] Vol. V, pp. 403-409.

Catholic missionaries of that nationality, were imprisoned or repatriated.[123] However, under British administration the population seems to have increased by about a fourth, from 4,063,000 in 1913 and 4,107,000 in 1921 to 5,138,000 in 1936.[124] Roads and railways were built.[125] In pursuance of the mandatory principle, with its emphasis upon preparing the Africans for self government, what was known as indirect administration was developed, with the placing of as much responsibility as possible upon the native chiefs.[126] In the 1920's German missionaries were permitted to return.[127]

The main organizations, Protestant and Roman Catholic, British and German, which carried the chief portion of the responsibility for spreading the Christian faith before 1914 continued to bear it in the three decades after that year. Thanks in part to the principles elaborated by Bruno Gutmann for the utilization of the Bantu social structure in the development of the indigenous church,[128] under his society, that bearing the name of Leipzig, there was developed in its field in the foothills of Kilimanjaro a native church which held its first synod in 1930.[129] Both Protestants and Roman Catholics multiplied amazingly, the latter even more than the former.[130] By 1936 the former counted 133,000 baptized,[131] and by 1933 the latter totalled 255,000.[132] Together they were then, with the adherents and catechumens which must be added to the preceding figures, more than ten per cent. of the population. Islam was also spreading, and, after 1918, had a fairly actively organized propaganda with schools, travelling missionaries, and groups of dervishes. In some areas Islam, traditionally strong in the adjacent Zanzibar, was making much more striking advances than was Christianity.[133] Among the animistic population there was a race between Islam and Christianity.

[123] Richter, *Tanganyika and Its Future,* pp. 7, 8.

[124] Hailey, *An African Survey,* pp. 108, 113.

[125] Richter, *op. cit.,* p. 10.

[126] Hailey, *op. cit.,* pp. 434-443.

[127] For the life of one after his return, see Johanssen, *Führung und Erfahrung in 40 jährigem Missionsdienst* (Bethel bei Bielefeld, Anstalt Bethel, 3 vols., no date), Vol. III, *passim.*

[128] Bruno Gutmann, *Gemeinde aufbau aus dem Evangelium Grundsätzliches für Mission und Heimatkirche* (Leipzig, Evang. luth. Mission, 1925, pp. 214), *passim.*

[129] Richter, *op. cit.,* p. 21. For sketches of the mission and its environment see Bruno Gutmann, *Unter dem Trutzbaum* (Leipzig, Evang. luth. Mission, no date, pp. 134), *passim.*

[130] On Roman Catholic mission schools see Franz Solan Schäppi, *Die katholische Missionsschule im ehemaligen Deutsch-Ostafrika* (Paderborn, Ferdinand Schöningh, 1937, pp. 399), pp. 233 ff.

[131] Parker, *Interpretative Statistical Survey of the World Mission of the Christian Church,* p. 19.

[132] Parker, *op. cit.,* p. 33.

[133] Richter, *op. cit.,* pp. 55, 56.

The second of the world wars brought grave problems, for a large proportion of the missionaries were Germans and a few were Danes. Their missions suffered. For the Protestants, some help came from British and Swedish sources, but this was insufficient to cover all the enterprises left without white supervision. However, in an area where denominational and national differences had heretofore prevented the formation of an inclusive Protestant cooperative organization, the pressure of the war situation hastened the constituting of the Tanganyika Missionary Council. This body attempted to deal with the emergency in a comprehensive fashion.[134]

Kenya, with its population in 1936 of approximately three millions,[135] presented a situation somewhat different from that of its immediate neighbours. Because it possessed highlands, suitable for the residence of Europeans, a rare circumstance in the African tropics, a white population entered it intent upon developing its resources. Whites remained in the small minority, in 1934 only about 17,000 of whom only about 2,000 occupied land.[136] Yet their presence accelerated the permeation of the region by European culture. Moreover, while less than a tenth of the area was made available for white settlement, the consequent dislocation of native life and the problem of reserves kept for the natives in the neighbourhood presented difficulties.[137] The first of the world wars also hastened the impact of the white man's civilization upon the Africans of Kenya. Thousands were recruited as carriers for the army and were brought into contact with modern machines. Famine and influenza followed hard on the heels of war.[138] Then came the quickened pace of the white development of the country.

Under these circumstances the accessions to Christianity multiplied. The major missions, both Protestant and Roman Catholic, which had been present before 1914,[139] continued. Baptized Protestants were said to be 47,078 in 1924[140] and 77,537 in 1936.[141] The Roman Catholic population of Kenya is reported to have increased from 8,556 in 1921 to 104,833 in 1936.[142] These figures, however, may be in error, for another set places the totals of Roman Catholics

---

[134] *The International Review of Missions,* Vol. XXXII, pp. 73, 74, Vol. XXXIII, pp. 57, 58.

[135] Hailey, *An African Survey,* p. 108.

[136] Hailey, *op. cit.,* p. 383.

[137] Hailey, *op. cit.,* p. 748.

[138] Philp, *A New Day in Kenya,* pp. 32, 33.

[139] Vol. V, pp. 409-412.

[140] Beach and Fahs, *World Missionary Atlas,* p. 77.

[141] Parker, *op. cit.,* p. 19. For sketches of incidents in connexion with Africans and Christianity, see Horace R. A. Philp, *God and the African in Kenya* (London, Marshall, Morgan & Scott, Ltd., no date, pp. 189), *passim.*

[142] *Fides News Service,* July 31, 1937.

at 55,244 in 1929 and at 60,505 in 1930.[143] Roman Catholics partly adjusted their organization to the tribal structure by using elders and councils of elders to instruct catechumens, administer baptism, serve the dying, and fight the use of alcoholic drinks.[144] There was also a beginning of a native sisterhood.[145] Protestant missionaries in Kenya and missionaries and churches in Great Britain were active in defending the African against the encroachments of the white man.[146] In spite of the opposition of some of the Anglo-Catholic spokesmen outside of Kenya, measures were taken by the Church Missionary Society, the Church of Scotland Mission, the Methodist Missionary Society, and the Africa Inland Mission for closer co-operation, and in 1918 these formed the Alliance of Missions in Kenya. This was succeeded, in 1924, by the Kenya Missionary Council. In 1932 a proposal was put forward for the union of the Christians connected with the four chief Protestant agencies.[147] In 1943 the Christian Council of Kenya was constituted, in which African as well as European church leaders joined.[148]

It will be remembered that Uganda had been the scene of some of the most dramatic experiences in the spread of Christianity in Africa and that it had also been the region in which Christianity had had a spectacular growth in the four decades before 1914. In this the Church Missionary Society for the Protestants and the White Fathers and the Mill Hillers for the Roman Catholics had been the chief foreign agents.[149] The growth was not interrupted by the events subsequent to 1914 and was still mainly although not entirely through the enterprises associated with these three societies.[150] Baptized Anglicans increased from 98,477 in 1914[151] to 301,000 in 1936,[152] or more than three-fold. The Roman Catholic total mounted from about 136,000 in 1912[153] to 477,000 in 1936,[154] or proportionately even more rapidly. Since in 1936 the population was about 3,661,000,[155] in that year Christians were between a fifth and a fourth of the whole. An African clergyman of the

---

[143] *Testo-Atlante illustrato delle Missioni,* p. 122.

[144] *Fides News Service,* July 31, 1937.

[145] F. M. Dreves, *The African Chronicles of Brother Giles* (London, Sands & Co., 1929, pp. 293), pp. 26 ff.

[146] *Social and Economic News,* Apr., 1933, pp. 1-4.

[147] Philp, *op. cit.,* pp. 38-46.

[148] *The International Review of Missions,* Vol. XXXIII, p. 56.

[149] Vol. V, pp. 412-419.

[150] On the progress of the other societies see *Light and Darkness in East Africa,* pp. 32-42, 59.

[151] *Proceedings of the Church Missionary Society,* 1914-15, p. xvi.

[152] Parker, *op. cit.,* p. 73.

[153] Streit, *Atlas Hierarchicus,* p. 102.

[154] Parker, *op. cit.,* p. 33.

[155] Hailey, *op. cit.,* p. 108.

Anglican communion of Uganda in turn became a missionary to the pygmies, shy and primitive denizens of the forest.[156] Increasingly the Anglican communion in Uganda was staffed by African clergy. By the 1930's they were almost entirely responsible for the pastoral care of the Christians and for the further spread of the faith. They were also providing much of the personnel for the new diocese of the Upper Nile.[157] Among them were some who were deeply zealous, seeking to awaken their fellow Christians to more earnest and devoted living.[158] There was, however, a fear among the Anglicans, borne out by what seemed to be facts, that as Christians multiplied and the faith became hereditary the quality of Christian living would deteriorate, particularly so as European culture and secularism became more widespread.[159] Roman Catholics, like the Anglicans, were rapidly raising up a native clergy.[160] Moreover, in 1939 an African was elevated to the episcopate and was placed in charge of a new vicariate apostolic which was to be entirely in the hands of African-born seculars.[161]

In the Belgian Congo and the adjoining Belgian mandate of Ruanda-Urundi the growth of Christianity after 1914 was among the most impressive of the increases in the numerical adherents of the faith anywhere in Africa or, indeed, in the world in the three decades after 1914. As was to be expected in an area where the ruling power was predominantly Roman Catholic, the advance of that branch of the faith was much more marked than that of Protestant Christianity. In 1935-6 the population of the Belgian Congo was estimated at 11,000,000 and of Ruanda-Urundi at 3,387,180.[162] It may be noted that in the Belgian Congo the population appeared to be declining rather sharply,[163] so that the proportionate increase of Christians was even greater than that in totals of individuals. In 1912 the Roman Catholics in the area were not far from 70,000,[164] but probably above rather than below this figure. In 1927 the total was said to be 564,000,[165] although this included only the Belgian Congo. In 1935 the total in the Belgian Congo and Ruanda-Urundi was reported as

---

[156] W. J. W. Roome, *Apolo. The Apostle to the Pygmies* (London, Marshall, Morgan & Scott, Ltd., no date, pp. 95), *passim*.

[157] A. L. Kitching, *From Darkness to Light. A Study of Pioneer Missionary Work in the Diocese of the Upper Nile* (London, Society for Promoting Christian Knowledge, 1935, pp. 64), pp. 38-42.

[158] As one example see *Awake! An African Calling. The Story of Blasio Kigozi and his Vision of a Revival* (London, Church Missionary Society, 1937, pp. 56).

[159] A. R. Cook in *The International Review of Missions*, Vol. XXI, pp. 254-264.

[160] Bouniol, *The White Fathers and Their Missions*, pp. 117-121.

[161] *Fides News Service*, June 3, 1939.

[162] Hailey, *op. cit.*, pp. 108, 120-122.

[163] Hailey, *op. cit.*, pp. 120, 121; *Fides Service*, July 17, 1937.

[164] Streit, *Atlas Hierarchicus*, p. 101.

[165] *Fides News Service*, Feb. 19, 1938.

1,232,000,[166] in 1937 as 1,767,000,[167] and in 1938 as 1,994,000.[168] This meant that Roman Catholics had multiplied more than twenty-eight-fold in about a quarter of a century and nearly four-fold in the eleven years 1927-1938. In 1941 2,580,000 Roman Catholics were reported, a further gain of approximately 30 per cent. in three years.[169] In the meantime baptized Protestants had risen from about 60,000 in 1924[170] to about 281,000 in 1936,[171] or between four and five-fold. This was in spite of an appalling leakage of those who, once professedly Christian, had lost active contact with the Church.[172] A little application of mathematics will show that in the decade before 1938 Protestants were increasing proportionately at a quicker pace than were Roman Catholics, at the rate of a little less than 40 per cent. a year contrasted with the latter's slightly under 30 per cent. a year. However, the latter outnumbered the former by more than five to one. Together in 1936 they were about 13 per cent. of the population.

The rapid growth of Christianity here, as in other parts of Africa south of the Sahara and in much of the Pacific and sections of Asia, was due in part to the fact that it was among primitive peoples of animistic cults and that society was dissolving because of the corrosive penetration of white civilization. The development of mining by white companies after 1914—for copper, gold, radium, and diamonds—and the corresponding utilization of African labour hastened the passing of the old order. The multiplication of adherents was also because of the fact that the black man might well suppose Christianity to be integral in the culture which he was now seeking to adopt. It must be

[166] *Fides News Service,* Jan. 4, 1936.

[167] *Fides News Service,* Feb. 19, 1938.

[168] *Fides News Service,* Jan. 28, 1939. For pictures of sections of the Roman Catholic activity see Joseph Frässle, *Meiner Urwaldneger Denken und Handeln* (Freiburg im B., Herder & Co., 1923, pp. 234); Pia Kühn und Ignatia Engel, *Auf Gottes Saatfeld. Erlebnisse und Beobdachtungen aus der Ruandamission* (Trier, Paulinus Druckerei, 1928, pp. 143).

[169] Delegato Apostolica in Congo Belgico et Ruanda Urundi, *Resumé des Statistiques des Missions du Congo Belge et du Ruanda-Urundi, au 30 Juin, 1942.*

[170] Beach and Fahs, *World Missionary Atlas,* p. 77.

[171] Parker, *Interpretative Statistical Survey of the World Mission of the Christian Church,* p. 19. On some sections of Protestant missions see Janet Miller, *Jungles Preferred* (Boston, Houghton Mifflin Company, 1931, pp. 321); P. H. J. Lerrigo, *Omwa? Are You Awake?* (New York, Fleming H. Revell Co., 1936, pp. 175); H. L. Hemmens, *Congo Journey* (London, The Carey Press, 1938, pp. 160); E. Hodgson, *Fishing for Congo Fisher Folk* (London, Assemblies of God in Great Britain and Ireland, preface 1934, pp. 181); Mrs. Alexander Macaw, *Congo. The First Alliance Mission Field* (Harrisburg, Christian Publications, 1937, pp. 168); Julia Lake Kellersberger, *God's Ravens* (New York, Fleming H. Revell Company, 1941, pp. 207); Josef Öhrneman, *Nybygget i Kongoskogen* (Stockholm, Svenska Missionsförbundets, 1934, pp. 190); S. A. Flodén, *"Tata" Flodén Berätter-Kongominnen* (Stockholm, Svenska Missionsförbundets, 2 vols., 1933, 1935).

[172] Ross, *Building the Church in Congo Belge,* p. 8.

ascribed as well to the presence and zeal of Christian missionaries and to the belief of many Africans that in Christianity there was the highest truth, an answer to the perplexing questions of life, and freedom from the fears which had attached to their former faith.

The growth of the missionary body in the Belgian territories was marked, although proportionately not so much so as that of the body of Christians. In 1912 Roman Catholic priests were 242, lay brothers 129, and sisters 149. All of these were European and none African.[173] In 1931 there were 667 foreign and 24 native priests, 345 foreign and 18 native brothers, and 642 sisters, of whom 571 were foreign, 28 native, and 43 with origin unspecified.[174] In June, 1935, the foreign priests totalled 887 and the native 43, the foreign brothers 485 and the native 71, and the foreign sisters 1,136.[175] In June, 1942, foreign priests numbered 1,239, native priests 123, foreign brothers 586, foreign sisters 1,504, and native sisters 263.[176] Obviously the decades after 1914 and especially the 1930's had seen a very substantial augmentation of the foreign staff and the encouraging beginning of African personnel. To these figures must be added the catechists, 18,307 in 1935.[177] The Protestant personnel was not so extensive. In 1923 the foreigners totalled 653, of whom 177 were ordained men, 130 un-ordained men, 218 wives, and 128 unmarried women. The African staff was 4,528, of whom only 5 were ordained.[178] In 1936 the corresponding figures were a total of 1,079 foreigners, or less than half that of the Roman Catholics (of the 1,079, 344 were ordained men, 108 unordained men, 365 wives, and 262 unmarried women), and an African staff of 8,304 (of whom 336 were ordained).[179] Although there was complaint from missionaries that native initiative was backward,[180] some advance was being seen in African participation and in financial self-support of the churches.[181]

Protestants protested that the Belgian colonial authorities favoured Roman Catholic missions. They averred that Roman Catholic enterprises were regarded as national missions, that the government accorded substantial financial assistance and recognition to Roman Catholic schools and other institutions, that it also gave much larger grants of land to Roman Catholic than to

---

[173] Streit, *Atlas Hierarchicus*, p. 101.
[174] *Testo-Atlante illustrato delle Missioni*, p. 121.
[175] *Fides News Service*, Jan. 25, 1936.
[176] Delegato Apostolia in Congo Belgico et Ruanda Urundi, *Resumé des Statistiques des Missions du Congo Belge et du Ruanda-Urundi, au 30 Juin, 1942.*
[177] *Fides News Service*, Jan. 4, 1936.
[178] Beach and Fahs, *op. cit.*, pp. 76, 77.
[179] Parker, *op. cit.*, pp. 19, 21.
[180] Ross, *op. cit.*, p. 8.
[181] Ross, *op. cit.*, pp. 3, 4.

Protestant missions, that often there was veiled and at times open hostility of colonial officials towards Protestant missions, that Roman Catholic missionaries had been known to close Protestant schools, abuse the teachers, terrorize chiefs who inclined toward Protestantism, deny equal justice to Protestant natives, and steal away Protestant pupils. Protestants pled the Treaty of Berlin of 1884-5 and the Convention of 1919 as promising religious freedom for all sects and nationalities.[182] It seemed clear that in Belgium a vigorous Roman Catholic Church was concentrating its missionary efforts upon the great Belgian colonial possession and that in the 1920's a liberal and only mildly Roman Catholic regime was replaced by one which was ardently pro-Roman Catholic. To the latter, Protestants were non-Belgian and heretical intruders.[183] Protestants in Belgium were an infinitesimal minority and the great majority of Protestant missionaries in the Belgian Congo were non-Belgians. In contrast, most of the Roman Catholic missionaries were Belgians.[184] It is not surprising that ardent Belgian nationalists who were also zealous Roman Catholics were annoyed by the Protestant missions and gave preference to Roman Catholic missions. Indeed, the rapid Roman Catholic expansion was in part stimulated by the desire to counteract Protestant enterprise.[185] However, before 1939 the tension had relaxed and the government was less partisan.[186] Yet even in 1942 Protestants felt their schools still to be discriminated against by the state policy of granting recognition only to those of "national" (Belgian) missions, which meant in practice, with the exception of the small *Société Belge des Missions Protestants,* only Roman Catholic institutions.[187]

In a region as large as the Belgian Congo and in which so many Protestant agencies were present, some kind of co-operation among the latter was clearly imperative. Steps towards it were taken as early as 1902 in a Congo missionary conference. In 1911 the Congo Continuation Committee of the Edinburgh Conference was formed.[188] By successive stages there came into being the

---

[182] *Review of the Work of the Congo Mission of the American Baptist Foreign Mission Society and the Woman's American Baptist Foreign Mission Society* (1934, mimeographed, pp. 30), p. 17; Oldham and Gibson, *The Remaking of Man in Africa,* p. 126; Stonelake, *Congo, Past and Present,* pp. 131-136.

[183] A confidential Protestant document.

[184] *Missiones Catholicae cura S. Congregationis de Propaganda Fide,* 1927, pp. 250, 251.

[185] Alfred Corman, *Annuaire des Missions Catholiques au Congo Belge* (Brussels, Librairie Albert Dewit, 1924, pp. 228), p. 182.

[186] *The International Review of Missions,* Vol. XXVI, p. 66, Vol. XXVII, p. 68, Vol. XXXVIII, p. 58.

[187] *The International Review of Missions,* Vol. XXXIII, p. 55.

[188] Stonelake, *op. cit.,* pp. 59, 60; Stonelake in *The International Review of Missions,* Vol. VIII, p. 326.

Conseil Protestant du Congo to which joint functions of various Protestant bodies were increasingly entrusted. In the mid-1930's a common name, *l'Église du Christ au Congo*, was adopted by several of the missions, and the possibility of organic union was discussed.[189] In the Katanga copper belt, moreover, the Methodist mission acted for all the Protestant bodies in caring for the black labourers coming from areas served by the different societies.[190]

A phase of the history of the Belgian Congo in the years immediately after the first of the world wars was the emergence of "prophets" who to some extent took their inspiration from Christianity. Here as elsewhere their appearance was symptomatic of the racial and nationalistic aspirations of the era and of the share of the Christian faith in bringing them into being. Of the Congo prophets the chief was Simon Kabangu or Kimbangu. He had been a member of a church associated with the English Baptists. In 1921 he began to attract attention by his preaching and his alleged healing of the sick by faith. High emotion ensued and a large following was gathered, much of it from the Protestant and Roman Catholic churches. Other prophets arose, apparently by contagion, both in the Belgian Congo and in the adjacent sections of Portuguese territory. They professed to take the New Testament as standard but became antagonistic to the missionaries. The colonial authorities feared political rebellion, arrested Kabangu and his chief lieutenants, exiled the former, and gave prison terms to the others.[191] In the 1930's another new religious movement was reported which was a medley of Protestant, Roman Catholic, and pagan beliefs, organization, and rites, and whose adherents called themselves "the Enlightened of the Holy Ghost."[192]

The second of the world wars could not but bring embarrassment to the Christian missions in the Congo, particularly since the majority of the Roman Catholic foreign personnel were Belgian and their mother country fell into the hands of the Germans. However, operations of the Christian agencies were not disturbed as much as might have been expected. The Belgian colonial administration was not interrupted. Financial assistance to Roman Catholic missions continued to be given by the government. Protestant missionaries who were cut off from their home constituencies were accorded relief by the *Conseil Protestant du Congo*, aided by the Orphaned Missions Fund of the

---

[189] Stonelake, *Congo, Past and Present*, pp. 61-68; *The International Review of Missions*, Vol. XXXIII, p. 54.

[190] Davis, *Modern Industry and the African*, pp. 298-300.

[191] P. H. J. Lerrigo in *The International Review of Missions*, Vol. XI, pp. 270-277; R. H. Carson Graham, *Under Seven Congo Kings* (London, The Carey Press, no date, pp. xii, 293), pp. 182-194.

[192] *Fides Service*, June 9, 1934

International Missionary Council, and by gifts of missionaries, Africans, and the Governor General. A Danish mission even found it possible to advance into territory which previously it had not developed.[193]

Of French Equatorial Africa, the large area which stretched north of the Belgian Congo, we need here say very little. Its population, in 1935-1936 about 3,386,000,[194] was one of the most sparse of any of the political divisions of Africa. To it must be added the portion of Cameroon which came to the French as a mandate after the first of the world wars, with a population in 1935-1936 of about 2,341,000.[195] The German missionaries, Protestant and Roman Catholic, who were in Cameroon during the slightly over a quarter of a century of German colonial administration,[196] were not permitted to return. However, the Paris Evangelical Missionary Society succeeded to the flourishing enterprise of the Basel Mission,[197] and the American Presbyterians continued.[198] On the departure of the German Roman Catholic missionaries some defection among the Christians took place but a French order came in and progress was resumed.[199] The marked increase of Christians which was seen in most of the rest of Africa was also present here, but was not nearly so striking as in the Belgian Congo. Protestants in French Equatorial Africa seem to have multiplied about eight-fold between 1924 and 1936 and those in French Cameroon to have more than doubled, but in 1936 the total in the former was only about 24,000, and in the latter about 96,000.[200] Roman Catholics in both colonies were about 204,000 in 1928[201] and about 397,000 in 1933.[202] In the 1930's a mass movement in Cameroon towards the Roman Catholic Church was witnessed and the first native priests were ordained.[203] In 1936 Christians

---

[193] *The International Review of Missions*, Vol. XXXIII, p. 54.

[194] Hailey, *An African Survey*, p. 108.

[195] *Ibid.*

[196] Vol. V, pp. 433, 434.

[197] *The International Review of Missions*, Vol. VII, pp. 43, 44. For the French mission, see H. Nicod, *Sur les Sentiers de l'Afrique Equatoriale* (Paris, Société des Missions Évangéliques, no date, pp. 309), *passim*; Richter, *Geschichte der evangelischen Mission in Afrika*, pp. 185-189.

[198] See a description of the mission in W. Reginald Wheeler, *The Words of God in an African Forest. The Story of an American Mission in West Africa* (New York, Fleming H. Revell Company, 1931, pp. 318).

[199] *Cameroun Français. La Mission de Foumban des Prêtres du Sacré-Coeur de Saint-Quentin* (Paris, Dillen et Cie, 1931, pp. 63), *passim*.

[200] Beach and Fahs, *World Missionary Atlas*, p. 77; Parker, *Interpretative Statistical Survey of the World Mission of the Christian Church*, p. 68. For a vivid picture of the rapid movement towards Protestantism in the 1920's and 1930's, see Platt, *From Fetish to Faith*, p. 17.

[201] Streit, *Catholic World-Atlas,* table XLI.

[202] Parker, *op. cit.*, p. 33.

[203] *Fides Service*, July 14, 1934.

in both colonies taken together were about 8.6 per cent. of the population, considerably less than in the Belgian Congo. The most famous missionary figure was Albert Schweitzer, philosopher, Biblical scholar, organist, and expert on Bach, who in 1913 had come as a Protestant medical missionary to French Equatorial Africa.[204] The numerical results of his labours were probably not conspicuous, but he had large influence in thoughtful Protestant circles in Europe and America and his devoted service could not fail to make an impression on at least some of the Africans.

Had the traveller of 1944 moved westward into British territory, to the portion of Cameroon which after the first of the world wars was assigned to Great Britain as a mandate and to the much larger Nigeria, he would have been confronted by a somewhat different situation. Here was a less sparse population, amounting in 1935-6 to about 20,000,000.[205] Proportionately the number of Christians was smaller, only about 3 per cent. in 1936. Here, moreover, thanks chiefly to the extensive and well developed enterprise of the Church Missionary Society, and as was to be expected in British territory, Protestants outnumbered Roman Catholics about two to one. In 1936 the former were about 410,565[206] and in 1933 the latter about 208,170.[207] These, however, represented substantial increases, the former from 93,620 in 1924,[208] and the latter from not far from 110,000 in 1928.[209]

The Christians were mainly in the South,[210] where the population had been largely animistic and had been longer in touch with European civilization, rather than farther inland, where Islam was stronger and where Europeans and their culture had more recently arrived. As the native culture disintegrated, mass movements towards Christianity occurred.[211] In the British portion of Cameroon, too, the Basel Mission was able to resume the enterprise which had been interrupted by the first of the world wars.[212] It was in the South that during the first of the world wars an African, Garrick Sokari Braid, a Chris-

---

[204] Vol. V, p. 430. In addition to the bibliography given there, see Albert Schweitzer, *Zwischen Wasser und Urwald. Erlebnisse und Beobachtungen eines Arztes im Urwalde Äquatorialafrikas* (Munich, C. H. Beck'sche Verlagsbuchhandlung, 1926, pp. 169).

[205] Hailey, *op. cit.*, p. 108.

[206] Parker, *op. cit.*, p. 68.

[207] Parker, *op. cit.*, p. 33.

[208] Beach and Fahs, *op. cit.*, p. 77.

[209] Streit, *op. cit.*, table XLI.

[210] Walker, *Romance of the Black River*, p. 254.

[211] As an example see J. M. Welch in *The International Review of Missions*, Vol. XX, pp. 556-574.

[212] Georg Haessig, *Unter den Urwaldstämmen in Kamerun* (Stuttgart, Evang. Missionsverlag, 1933, pp. 229); Emanuel Kellerhals, *Das Volk hintern Berg. Land, Leute und Missionsarbeit in Kamerun* (Stuttgart, Evang. Missionsverlag, 1935. pp. 186).

tian, proclaimed himself to be the Prophet Elijah, professed to heal through prayer, called for repentance, denounced fetishes and alcoholic drinks, administered baptism, and headed a movement which within a few months attracted hundreds of thousands, among them many Christians. The movement had a strong racial, anti-white character, and the British authorities, already made nervous by the war, clapped Braid in prison. This did not, however, immediately disband his following.[213] To the South, too, to Calabar, came representatives of St. Patrick's Society for Foreign Missions, Irish, as may be gathered from its name, canonically erected in 1932 in response to an appeal for help in the region.[214]

The northern parts of Nigeria and Cameroon were not neglected. The societies which had entered before 1914[215] continued their labours.[216] At least one additional society began operations.[217] The principle of indirect rule maintained by the British regime made difficult the penetration of areas in which Islam was strong and the native emirs were antagonistic. However, late in the 1920's some relaxation in these restrictions was obtained.[218]

In various ways Christianity was striking root in Nigeria and the British portion of Cameroon. We hear of a prophet movement in the North from which numbers were gathered into the churches.[219] Although Africans migrating into the coast towns of the South, being no longer under their chiefs, tended to moral laxity, some of the migrants, Christians, organized societies according to the inherited tribal lines and attempted through them to maintain better standards.[220] In the British portion of Cameroon a native Roman Catholic catechist held together the mission when, during the first of the world wars, the foreign priests were constrained to leave. Moreover, he and catechists trained by him won many to the Christian faith and prepared them for bap-

---

[213] Richter, *op. cit.*, pp. 141, 142; *The Church Missionary Review*, Vol. LXVII, pp. 455-462, Vol. LXVII, pp. 142-145.

[214] *Fides News Service*, May 21, 1938.

[215] Vol. V, p. 442.

[216] See, for instance, Johanna Veenstra, *Pioneering for Christ in the Sudan* (Grand Rapids, Smitter Book Company, 1926, pp. 233); Henry Beets, *Johanna of Nigeria. Life and Labors of Johanna Veenstra, S.U.M.* (Grand Rapids, Grand Rapids Printing Company, 1937, pp. 228); Desmond W. Bittinger, *An Educational Experiment in Northern Nigeria in Its Cultural Setting* (Elgin, The Brethren Publishing House, 1941, pp. xvi, 343); Walter Miller, *Yesterday and To-morrow in Northern Nigeria* (London, Student Christian Movement Press, 1938, pp. xvi, 182).

[217] Moyer, *Missions in the Church of the Brethren*, pp. 190-195; Albert D. Helser, *Education of Primitive People* (New York, Fleming H. Revell Company, 1934, pp. 316), *passim*.

[218] *The International Review of Missions*, Vol. XX, p. 53, Vol. XXI, pp. 239, 240.

[219] Platt, *From Fetish to Faith*, p. 83.

[220] Platt, *op. cit.*, pp. 67-69.

tism.[221] The year 1930 saw the first admission of an African to one of the sister-hoods.[222] In 1933 three new Anglican bishops were consecrated for Nigeria, and of these two were Africans.[223] They were not the first Africans to be raised to the Anglican episcopate in Nigeria. In addition to the well remembered Samuel Adjai Crowther,[224] there had been assistant bishops, among them one consecrated in 1920.[225] It was a significant indication, however, of the naturalization of the Church in Africa that as many as two should be consecrated in one year.

In Nigeria as elsewhere there was growing co-operation among the Protestant forces. A Christian council was formed in Northern Nigeria in 1926. In 1930 the Christian Council of Nigeria was constituted for the southern provinces and affiliated with it was the council of missions east of the Niger.[226]

Obstacles to the progress of Christianity did not cease, and new ones were added. Islam was still a problem. The moral disintegration, especially on the coast, from the contacts of white and black cultures was so serious that some Christians from the interior, seeing it and disillusioned by the apparent power-lessness of the white man's faith to prevent it, returned to paganism.[227] Jehovah's Witnesses made their way into Nigeria as into several other parts of the continent and weaned away some of the Christians by their denunciation of missionaries as servants of the devil.[228] In spite of adversaries, Christianity continued to spread.

The strain of the second of the world wars could not but be felt in Nigeria, but advance was achieved by at least some of the missions.[229] An additional section was entrusted by the Propaganda to the White Fathers, largely English.[230]

Dahomy need not detain us on our westward journey, except to note that here, too, was an increase in the numbers of Christians. The Roman Catholic Church, the main representative of Christianity in the territory, counted 11,-440 in its fold in 1913[231] and 38,307 in 1933.[232] There was careful training of

[221] *Fides News Service*, Sept. 12, 1936.
[222] *The International Review of Missions,* Vol. XX, p. 74.
[223] *The International Review of Missions,* Vol. XXIII, p. 66.
[224] Vol. V, p. 437.
[225] Walker, *op. cit.*, pp. 192, 202.
[226] *The International Review of Missions,* Vol. XXI, p. 227.
[227] Platt, *op. cit.*, p. 124.
[228] Platt, *op. cit.*, p. 82.
[229] *The International Review of Missions,* Vol. XXXI, p. 56, Vol. XXXIII, p. 52.
[230] *Les Missions Franciscaines,* Vol. XXI, p. 250.
[231] Streit, *Atlas Hierarchicus,* p. 101.
[232] Parker, *Interpretative Statistical Survey of the World Mission of the Christian Church,* p. 33. For a description of the Roman Catholic missions see A. Boucher, *A Travers les Missions du Toga et du Dahomy* (Paris, Pierre Téqui, 1926, pp. 164).

African sisters.[233] A French possession, Dahomy did not have extensive Protestant missions. Nor did the portion of Togo which in consequence of the first of the world wars passed to France as a mandate.[234]

In the Gold Coast, British territory, Protestants were much more prominent than Roman Catholics. Here the population seems to have multiplied from possibly 2,300,000 in 1925 to perhaps 3,230,000 in 1935-1936.[235] Here late in the 1920's was raised nearly half of the world's cacao. The rapid development of its production was largely by peasant proprietors on thousands of small farms.[236] The wealth derived from this source greatly accelerated the introduction of European civilization and the passing of the old cultures.[237] Connected with the Gold Coast after the first of the world wars and under British mandate was part of Togo. British Togo shared in the prosperity which came to the Gold Coast.[238]

The first of the world wars brought changes in the complexion of the Protestant enterprise in the Gold Coast and Togo. The strong German missions were, perforce, discontinued. To care for the churches in the Gold Coast which had arisen from them the (Scottish) United Presbyterians came in. Through the latter these churches quickly became independent. So thoroughly had the Basel Mission performed its task that the resulting Presbyterian Church of the Gold Coast was both self-governing and self-supporting, with only a few missionaries on its synod.[239] It grew rapidly, more than doubling its members between 1917 and 1931.[240] So, too, in Togo what was called the Ewe Presbyterian Church was constituted and, with a majority of Africans on its synod committee, took full financial charge of the extensive schools.[241] In the 1920's German missions were permitted to resume operations, but the African Presbyterian churches continued their autonomy.

Numerically the chief mission in the Gold Coast was that of the English Wesleyans. Between 1912 and 1929 it multiplied about seven-fold.[242] The Gold Coast, too, was one of the areas where Harris, whom we mentioned a few pages above, won a large following. Other wandering African preachers appeared, possibly stimulated by his example, preached coming judgment, and urged

[233] *Deux Soeurs Noires—par une Religieuse de la Sainte-Famille du Sacré-Coeur* (Paris, Libraire Bloud et Gay, 1931, pp. 239), pp. 1-18.
[234] Cooksey and McLeish, *Religion and Civilization in West Africa*, pp. 72-77.
[235] Hailey, *An African Survey*, p. 108.
[236] Hailey, *op. cit.*, pp. 907, 908.
[237] Hartenstein, *Anibue*, pp. 9-27.
[238] Cooksey and McLeish, *op. cit.*, pp. 149-151.
[239] Cooksey and McLeish, *op. cit.*, pp. 133-137; Hartenstein, *op. cit.*, pp. 53 ff., 87-89.
[240] Hartenstein, *op. cit.*, pp. 53 ff.
[241] Cooksey and McLeish, *op. cit.*, p. 152.
[242] Cooksey and McLeish, *op. cit.*, p. 138.

repentance and amendment of life.[243] Marked ingatherings to the Wesleyans came not only through Harris and his successors, but also through a movement associated with Samson Opon, an Ashanti, who had lived a hard life, but in prison had vowed that if he were freed he would give up drink and serve Christ. He had visions with a voice which commanded him to preach against the fetishes of his people. In 1920 the awakening led by him began,[244] another of the kind with which we have become familiar.

In 1929 the Christian Council of the Gold Coast was formed to co-ordinate Protestant efforts.[245] Although only slightly over 10 per cent. of the population were baptized Christians, it was said that in 1936 the Gold Coast was no longer a pagan country, that fetish houses and small temples had largely vanished, that the sorcerer and the old wild dances were passing,[246] and that many non-Christians participated in Christian festivals, read the Bible, joined in Christian prayers, and regarded themselves as belonging to the Christian community.[247] Yet Islam was also spreading.[248] Moreover, few of the native chiefs were Christian, for their office was associated with the old order which Christianity and European civilization challenged.[249] There was danger, too, that as Christians multiplied the quality of their religious and moral life would deteriorate and such former customs as polygamy reappear.[250]

It was at Achimota, in the Gold Coast, that in the 1920's there was erected the plant of a notable higher educational institution for blacks. The funds were chiefly from the government, but the first two principals were clergymen, and instruction in the Christian faith formed an integral although voluntary part of the programme.[251] On the original staff was an extraordinarily able and attractive African Christian, J.E.K. Aggrey, whose early death was a severe blow.[252]

The Ivory Coast, a French possession, had a population slightly more than half that of the adjoining Gold Coast and economically and in the extent of the

---

[243] Hartenstein, op. cit., p. 73.

[244] Arthur E. Southon, Gold Coast Methodism. The First Hundred Years, 1835-1935 (Cape Coast, Methodist Book Depot, 1934, pp. 158), pp. 149-154.

[245] The International Review of Missions, Vol. XIX, p. iii.

[246] Hartenstein, op. cit., pp. 31 ff.

[247] Hartenstein, op. cit., p. 60.

[248] Hartenstein, op. cit., pp. 38-41.

[249] Hartenstein, op. cit., p. 61.

[250] Hartenstein, op. cit., pp. 75 ff. In 1935, for instance, the "African Universal Church" was reported, a sect which permitted polygamy.—The International Review of Missions, Vol. XXV, p. 62.

[251] Hailey, op. cit., pp. 1249, 1250; Cooksey and McLeish, op. cit., pp. 129, 130.

[252] Edwin W. Smith, Aggrey of Africa (New York, Richard R. Smith, Inc., 1930, pp. xii, 292); Wm. J. W. Roome, Aggrey, the African Teacher (London, Marshall, Morgan & Scott, Ltd., no date, pp. 94).

permeation of European culture was much more backward.[253] It was not strange, therefore, that by the second of the world wars Christianity had made very much less progress than in the other. In 1936 Christians were between 4 and 5 per cent. of the population[254] and would have been very much fewer but for the remarkable Harris movement of which we spoke earlier in this chapter. Roman Catholics were about a third more numerous than Protestants. The latter were mostly connected with the Wesleyans and were largely the fruit of Harris's preaching.[255] In 1934 Roman Catholics ordained their first native priest of the Ivory Coast,[256] what they hoped was the beginning of an indigenous clergy.

West and north of the Ivory Coast, in Liberia, Sierra Leone, French Guinea, Portuguese Guinea, Gambia, Senegal, and the French Sudan, the numbers of Christians were not impressive. There were, to be sure, the Christian enclave in and around Freetown, historically significant, the Christian groups in Liberia descended from the Afro-Americans, and some heroic missions. However, the increase in the numbers of Christians after 1914 was not as striking as in most of the other parts of Africa. Here and there were indications of progress in making the Church something more than exotic. For instance, in 1939 the Anglicans ordained their first Gambian African deacon.[257] That year also saw the appointment of an African-born priest to be head of a new prefecture apostolic in Senegal.[258] The progress of Christianity became less pronounced as one moved to the extreme West and towards the Sahara.

The effects of Christianity upon Africa south of the Sahara in the three decades after 1914 were largely a continuation and accentuation of those before that year. The notable growth in numbers we have recorded near the beginning of this chapter. Christians had multiplied more than five-fold in the three decades after 1914, and that during a period when the population of Africa had probably not increased greatly if at all.

The changes wrought in the African by the Christian faith obviously varied with the individual and to a certain extent with the mission. Roman Catholics required a period of instruction for catechumens of from one to four years.[259]

[253] Cooksey and McLeish, *op. cit.*, pp. 54 ff.
[254] Parker, *op. cit.*, pp. 33, 67.
[255] E. de Billy, *En Côte d'Ivoire. Mission Protestante d'A.O.F.* (Paris, Société des Missions Évangéliques, no date, pp. xv, 182).
[256] *Fides News Service*, June 23, 1934.
[257] *The International Review of Missions*, Vol. XXIX, p. 70.
[258] *Fides News Service*, June 3, 1939.
[259] Dubois, *Lé Repertoire Africaine*, p. 128.

Even less was there uniformity among Protestants of prerequisites for baptism. A large proportion of the accessions to Christianity, especially after 1914, were by mass movements. These made difficult careful individual instruction. That, in differing degrees, the faith of the Christians produced alterations in morals, in religion, and in spiritual outlook is unquestionable.[260] Even among non-Christians, an original belief in a Supreme Being was becoming more definite through contacts with Christian teaching.[261] Moreover, Christianity, especially in its Protestant forms, was stirring Africans to fresh spiritual life. The many movements led by Africans which we have noted in this chapter, some of them bizarre, some of them a multiplication of existing divisions, some having progressively less of historic Christianity in them, were affecting, often profoundly, thousands of Africans and bringing many of them into the Christian faith. African leadership in the standard churches was also increasing. Christianity was becoming rooted in Africa south of the Sahara.

Another effect of Christianity was in the reduction of languages to writing and the production of literature. The Bible, in whole or in part, was the chief literature translated and distributed.[262] However, although the total remained pitifully meagre, much other material was also prepared.[263] Schools and education after the European pattern continued to be predominantly through missions and the churches. Government participation was growing, but the Christian forces carried the heavy part of the load.[264]

Although colonial governments were increasing their share, Christian missions still bore a large proportion of the responsibility for the introduction and application of modern medicine to the diseases of Africa.[265] There were

[260] For examples see Mrs. D. M. Miller, *The Obedience of Faith. The Life of Mary Mozley* (London, Africa Inland Mission, 2d ed., 1932, pp. 159), pp. 94, 95; Francis Eling Fearse, *Africa on the Hilltops* (Westminster, Universities Mission to Central Africa, 2d ed., 1931, p. 64), pp. 49, 50; Miller, *Jungles Preferred*, p. 37. See a technical study in Richard C. Thurnwald, *Black and White in East Africa* (London, George Routledge and Sons, 1935, pp. xxii, 419), pp. 205 ff.

[261] *The International Review of Missions*, Vol. XXIII, p. 142.

[262] See a list in North, *The Book of a Thousand Tongues*, pp. 31-35.

[263] F. Rowling and C. E. Wilson, *Bibliography of African Christian Literature* (London, Conference of Missionary Societies of Great Britain and Ireland, 1923, pp. 135); F. Rowling and C. E. Wilson, *Supplement to Bibliography of African Christian Literature, 1923* (London, Conference of Missionary Societies of Great Britain and Ireland, 1927, pp. 35); Margaret Wrong, *Africa and the Making of Books. Being a Survey of Africa's Need of Literature* (London, International Committee on Christian Literature for Africa, 1934, pp. 56).

[264] See tables showing the numbers of mission and government schools, in Oldham and Gibson, *The Remaking of Man in Africa*, pp. 152-179; Thomas Jesse Jones, *Education in Africa* (New York, Phelps-Stokes Fund, no date, pp. xxviii, 323); Thomas Jesse Jones, *Education in East Africa* (New York, Phelps-Stokes Fund, no date, pp. xxviii, 416).

[265] Hailey, *An African Survey*, pp. 1114 ff.; Parker, *A Statistical Survey of the World Mission of the Christian Church*, pp. 35, 224-228; Dubois, *op. cit.*, pp. 142 ff.

many efforts at sex education and the nourishing of wholesome family life.[266]

Missionaries, too, continued to champion the cause of the Africans against any whites who would oppress or exploit them.

The effect of Christianity upon white merchants and colonial officials varied, but in some it was marked and showed itself in the policies which were adopted and implemented.[267]

In summarizing the effect of the environment on Christianity, it must first be noted that the latter tended to reflect, as before the year 1914, the political pattern which Europeans had imposed on Africa. In general, Roman Catholic Christianity flourished more in French, Belgian, and Portuguese possessions than did Protestantism, and in British territories Protestant Christianity usually was more prominent than the Roman Catholic Church. Thus, quite naturally, the imported Christianity reflected the religious complexion of the governing people.

However, Africa was also placing its stamp upon Christianity and was probably doing so in increasing measure. This was partly because numbers of missionaries were, more deliberately than formerly, attempting to adapt their procedures to African traditions. There was a rapidly mounting experimentation in preserving as much of the older African life as possible, in utilizing indigenous institutions and conceptions, and in making the transition from paganism to Christianity as little disruptive as possible in traditional African life. This was because of the repugnance which was quickened after 1914 among more sensitive souls in Europe and America against imposing their culture upon other races, because of the growing application of the findings of anthropology to mission methods, and from the mounting desire to see Christianity clothe itself, so far as was consistent with its revolutionary nature, in the culture patterns of the peoples among whom it was being planted. African cultures were being so rapidly broken by the impact of the white man apart from the missionaries, that the latter could probably only ease the pain and salvage from the wreck a little of what was good. Many were, however, making the effort. They were endeavouring to prevent African society from becoming atomized and to preserve something of group life. Thus some Roman Catholic

[266] James W. C. Dougall, editor, *Christianity and the Sex-Education of the African* (London, Society for Promoting Christian Knowledge, 1937, p. 128).

[267] For the life of one most of whose career was before 1914 and who had a great part in British policy in Africa, see Alex Johnston, *The Life and Letters of Sir Harry Johnston* (London, Jonathan Cape, 1929, p. 351).

missionaries, against the judgment of their more conservative colleagues, wished to adapt architecture and several other features of Roman Catholic practice to African forms.[268] In 1935 the Apostolic Delegate in the Congo strongly advocated the use of native art in church buildings, vestments, and fixtures.[269] A prominent German Protestant expert on missions, reflecting trends in his own country, advocated mission methods which would so far as possible avoid violence to the collective spirit and tradition of the Bantu folk.[270] In Bechuanaland the missionaries of the Dutch Reformed Church, although that was a conservative body, attempted to bring a tribe as a whole into the Christian faith. They Christianized the initiation ceremonies, retained in a modified form *lobolo* (the bride price) as a prerequisite to Christian marriage, and encouraged the erection of a church building with tribal funds and the offering of prayers for rain by the chief and the Christian minister. The entire tribe became Christian and the missionaries then gave themselves to deepening and improving the Christian living of the mass converts.[271] In Northern Rhodesia a school for girls under Mabel Shaw of the London Missionary Society became famous for its deliberate attempt to retain many elements of African life and bring them into conformity with Christian ideals.[272] In place of the traditional ceremonies of the Church, Christian blessing was some times given to marriage contracted according to native forms.[273] In Tanganyika a German mission was preserving, somewhat altered, the initiation rites by which from time immemorial the tribes had prepared girls for full woman-hood.[274]

Quite spontaneously, moreover, Africans were putting their own impress on Christianity. The many "prophet" movements of the post-1914 years and the emergence of numerous sects, some of which we have noted in the preceding pages, were indications that the African was making Christianity his own, even

---

[268] Dubois, *op. cit.*, p. 177.

[269] *Fides Service*, June 29, 1935.

[270] Siegfried Knak, *Zwischen Nil und Tafelbai. Eine Studie über Evangelium, Volkstum und Zivilization, am Beispiel der Missionsprobleme unter den Bantu* (Berlin, Heimat-dienst-Verlag, no date, pp. xiv, 328).

[271] Conversation of the author with J. Reyneke, General Mission Secretary of the Dutch Reformed Church, Oct. 23, 1937.

[272] Chirgwin, *An African Pilgrimage*, p. 137; Chirgwin, *Wayfaring for Christ*, pp. 84, 85; Mabel Shaw, *God's Candlelights. An Educational Venture in Northern Rhodesia* (London, Edinburgh House Press, 1932, pp. 197), *passim*.

[273] Cameron Chesterfield Alleyne, *Gold Coast at a Glance* (New York, The Hunt Printing Co., 1931, p. 143), pp. 120 ff.; J. W. Welch in *The International Review of Missions*, Vol. XXII, pp. 17-32; R. Allier in *The International Review of Missions*, Vol. II, pp. 547-565.

[274] Oldham and Gibson, *The Remaking of Man in Africa*, p. 104.

though in ways which at times gave grave concern to the missionaries. Here and there, too, were examples of African art applied to Christian themes.[275]

As one looks back over the course of the faith in Africa south of the Sahara in the three decades after 1914, even when through a survey in such compact and summary form as the preceding pages have necessarily been, it becomes clear that Christianity was rapidly spreading and taking root. In almost every political division the numbers of Christians were multiplying. The influence of Christianity was not limited to those bearing its name but was extending to millions of the non-baptized. Moreover, while co-operation between missions and colonial administrations continued[276] and gave to the spread of Christianity an aspect of white paternalism and conscious assimilation to European culture, African initiative was growing. This was seen in the increase in African leaders, both Protestant and Roman Catholic. It was also apparent in spontaneous movements, some of them enlisting thousands, evidence that the Christian faith was stirring Africans to a fresh spiritual and moral life and to assert the dignity and worth of the black man in face of white exploitation. These movements contained many non-Christian elements and some of them could scarcely be called Christian, but they were indications that Christianity was ceasing to be exotic. Here, moreover, as in most of the world, Protestants were increasingly coming together in co-operation. Roman Catholics and especially Protestants were transferring more responsibility to Africans. As they did so they were endeavouring, by knitting the African Christians into a world-wide Christian fellowship, to prevent too great a departure from historic Christianity.

Africa was clearly on the march. The old life was rapidly disappearing. The danger was utter moral and social disintegration with tragic consequences for the millions of black folk who lived south of the Sahara. Christianity was providing a force which made for a fresh integration and nobler individual and collective living. It was agony through which many millions of Africans were passing, an agony of whose causes and even of whose processes they were only partially aware. The inherited cultures, those of the largest aggregation of folk of primitive ways and faith on the face of the globe, were dissolving through the permeation of a civilization which was itself in revolution.

---

[275] Wrong, *Africa and the Making of Books*, p. 25; Julius E. Lips, *The Savage Hits Back, or the White Man through Native Eyes* (London, Lovat Dickson, 1937, pp. xxxi, 254), pp. 164-188.
[276] J. Mazé, *La Collaboration Scolaire des Gouvernements Coloniaux et des Missions* (Algiers, Maison-Carrée, 1933, pp. ix, 183), *passim*.

Totally unprepared, the Africans were being precipitated into a bewildering and bewildered age which at times appalled and disheartened even the most intelligent and the spiritually best prepared of mankind. Colonial administrators were attempting through the processes of political and economic institutions and through a secularized education to counteract impending chaos. Christian forces were at times co-operating with them, but they professed to be bringing a spiritual dynamic without which other measures would be futile. Those forces, although limited in personnel and in funds, were having increased effect. In them lay the secret of the salvation of Africa. No perfect salvation would be achieved: that would be expecting too much of history. Already, however, within the growing structure of the Christian Church a new life was appearing. Africans were being moved by it to exertions on behalf of themselves and their fellows. They acted with mixed motives and with results which were a combination of weal and woe. In the main, however, the force which was being released was constructive, both for individuals and for society as a whole.

Chapter X

THE NORTHERN SHORES OF AFRICA AND THE NEAR EAST

THE section of the globe which we think of as *par excellence* the Moslem world was the northern shore of Africa and Western Asia. Here Islam had its birth and here continued to have the main centre of its strength. Here, except for Christian minority enclaves and a few scattered Jewish communities, it was dominant.

Northern Africa and Western Asia were profoundly affected by the events of the three decades which began in 1914. The first of the world wars was accompanied and followed by striking changes in Turkey, by the establishment of French and British mandates in Syria and Palestine, and by new states in Mesopotamia and Arabia. The interval between the wars saw the further rapid penetration of the area by Western civilization, with especially spectacular transformations in Turkey and Iran, the growth of the Jewish elements in Palestine with the attendant friction with the Arabs, and the Italian conquest of Ethiopia. In the second of the world conflicts much of the area was a battle ground. That was true of most of the northern shore of Africa, of Ethiopia, of Syria, and of Iraq. In the effort of the United Nations to bring supplies from the United States and Great Britain to Russia, Iran was brought within the orbit of the operations of Russia on the one hand and of Britain and America on the other. The region was clearly on the march.

In the three decades the fortunes of Christianity fluctuated. The course of that faith was uneven and varied from section to section and almost from year to year. We can best picture it by journeying from political division to political division.

Until the second of the world wars, the history of Christianity along the northern shore of Africa was a relatively uneventful continuation of the preceding several decades. The European population was, as before, for the most part nominally Roman Catholic. Not far from the year 1928 there were approximately 800,000 Roman Catholics in northern Africa west of Egypt, most of them in Algeria and Tunisia.[1] There was an increase in them, presumably chiefly by an excess of births over deaths.[2] In Morocco, Algeria, Tunisia, and

[1] Streit, *Catholic World-Atlas*, table XLI.
[2] *Missiones Catholicae Cura S. Congregationis de Propaganda Fide*, 1927, pp. 198, 199.

Libya progress among the Moslem population was very slow. This was to be expected, even under European, non-Moslem rulers, for Islam had traditionally proved very resistant to Christianity. Roman Catholic missions registered gains, but numerically they were unimpressive. Among them were the following: in Morocco in the decade and a half after the first world war churches and chapels were renovated and increased in number;[3] in one year in the fore part of the 1930's three Moroccans, Franciscans, were admitted to minor orders, a beginning of an indigenous clergy;[4] in the Kabyle mission in Algeria the White Fathers recorded progress, although it was slow;[5] in 1933 the Little Brothers of the Sacred Heart of Jesus, a contemplative congregation, who were seeking to carry out the dream of Foucauld[6] of a special order, particularly for missions in the Sahara, established their first centre;[7] in Libya and Cyrenaica the Brothers Minor found the going difficult and in the early 1930's had only about 150 Christians from non-Europeans.[8]

Nor could Protestants point to greater success. Through the French portions of the area there were perhaps thirty Protestant churches for Europeans, but in 1930 several of these had long been without pastors.[9] Except for the Bible Churchmen's Missionary Society, few if any Protestant organizations entered the area for the first time. Those already represented continued.[10] The numbers of converts were not large. They were from Europeans, Jews, and Moslems. Moreover, the Italian regime discouraged Protestant mission effort in Libya.[11]

The second of the world wars made a battle field of large portions of the northern shore of Africa. Much of the fighting, however, was in Libya, where missions were less extensive than in some other sections of the area. Some inconveniences were suffered by the missionary organizations and the Moslems were said to be confirmed in their resistance to Christianity by the spectacle of war among peoples whom they regarded as Christian.[12]

In Egypt the three decades after 1914 brought no revolutionary changes in

---

[3] A. Freitag in *Zeitschrift für Missionswissenschaft*, Vol. XXII, p. 160.

[4] *Ibid.*

[5] A. Freitag in *op. cit.*, Vol. XXIV, p. 139.

[6] Vol. VI, p. 17.

[7] A. Freitag in *op. cit.*, Vol. XXIV, p. 139; M. M. Underhill in *The International Review of Missions*, Vol. XXVI, pp. 367-371.

[8] *Ibid.*

[9] Rusillon, *Une Énigme Missionnaire*, p. 108.

[10] See Rusillon, *op. cit.*, pp. 130, 131, for a list of the societies. See also Cooksey, *The Land of the Vanished Church*, pp. 59 ff.; Blanche A. F. Pigott, *I. Lilias Trotter . . . Founder of the Algiers Mission Band* (London, Marshall, Morgan & Scott, Ltd., no date, pp. ix, 245), pp. 153 ff.

[11] Cooksey, *op. cit.*, pp. 60, 61.

[12] *The International Review of Missions*, Vol. XXXII, p. 36, Vol. XXXIII, p. 47.

the situation of the Christian churches. The first of the world wars was accompanied and followed, as in so much of the rest of the world, by an intensification of nationalism. In the first flush of the new access of patriotism, Moslems and Copts tended to forget their differences and to fraternize. However, that stage soon passed and the traditional frictions reasserted themselves.[13] Islam was strengthened, although not to any overwhelming extent. The passing of the Caliphate and the demotion of Islam in the new Turkey increased the prominence of Egypt in the Moslem world. That and nationalism, together with the presence in Cairo of Al Azhar, the outstanding centre of Islamic education and scholarship, contributed to the conviction that Egypt should be the leader in Islam and at times to spasms of resentment against attempts to win Moslems to the Christian faith.[14] The provision in a governmental regulation of 1933 that primary education be made compulsory and that instruction in Islam be required, but with no opportunity for teaching their faith to children hereditarily Christian, brought alarm to the Christian minority.[15] The weakening of religious belief among Moslems who were in touch with the secularizing influences from the Occident did not reduce their fierce loyalty to Islam as national and Arab.[16]

There was a fairly continuous but slow leakage to Islam from the Coptic Church, the chief historic representative of Christianity. In the mid-1930's it was estimated as being about six hundred a year. This seems to have been chiefly from the pressure of Moslems upon Christians to accept Islam as a condition of employment and from a desire for divorce, a step easy in Islam but impossible in the Coptic Church.[17] Yet some of the apostate Copts, having obtained their divorces, returned to the church of their fathers, a step which the Egyptian Government allowed more readily than it did conversions from hereditary Moslems. Moreover, Copts did some preaching to Moslems and each year had a few baptisms from the latter.[18]

No striking alterations seem to have occurred among the other varieties of Christianity represented in Egypt. According to the census, Roman Catholics rose from 107,687 in 1917 to 126,581 in 1937, and Protestants from 47,481 in the former to 78,203 in the latter year.[19] This growth was due chiefly to the excess of births over deaths. The population of the country was rapidly mounting

[13] *The International Review of Missions*, Vol. XXI, p. 189.
[14] *The International Review of Missions*, Vol. XX, p. 47, Vol. XXIV, p. 65.
[15] *The International Review of Missions*, Vol. XXIV, p. 65.
[16] William Paton, mimeographed letter, Dec., 1930.
[17] S. A. Morrison in *The International Review of Missions*, Vol. XXV, pp. 310 ff.
[18] S. A. Morrison in conversation with the author, Jan. 2, 1939.
[19] *The Statesman's Year-Book*, 1921, p. 260, 1943, p. 850.

and Christians shared in it. The percentage of Christians of all varieties in the population of the land slightly increased. By the census of 1917 it was 8.03,[20] by that of 1927 8.34,[21] and by that of 1937 8.19.[22] Proportionately between 1917 and 1937 Roman Catholics grew slightly less rapidly than the population as a whole, while Protestants increased somewhat over a third more rapidly.[23] As before 1914, the strongest Protestant body was that which came out of the efforts of what was known as the American Mission (the United Presbyterians). In 1926 this body, as the Evangelical Church in Egypt, became self-governing and self-supporting and opened its own theological seminary.[24] The Church Missionary Society had a much smaller constituency, but it accomplished the baptism of about twenty Moslems each year.[25] In 1925 it founded for the congregations in its care "The Episcopal Church in Egypt in Communion with the Church of England."[26] The Young Men's Christian Association had at least four units[27] with a growing influence, even extending latterly to the state programme for boys. The American University, undenominational but frankly Christian, with Cairo as its location, was inaugurated in 1919 and 1920 and, under the leadership of its first president, Charles R. Watson, son of a pioneer of the American Mission, achieved wide and favourable recognition in official circles.[28] Cairo, with its Central Literature Bureau for Moslem Lands, the Nile Mission Press,[29] and other Protestant publishing agencies, was a chief centre of the production and distribution of literature for the entire Moslem world.[30] In the School of Oriental Studies, older than the American University, but later incorporated with it,[31] Cairo also had an important agency for preparing Occidental missionaries to Moslem lands. The Protestant forces were

---

[20] *The Statesman's Year-Book*, 1921, p. 260.

[21] *The Statesman's Year-Book*, 1940, p. 844.

[22] *The Statesman's Year-Book*, 1943, p. 850.

[23] *The Statesman's Year-Book*, 1921, p. 260, 1943, p. 850.

[24] *The International Review of Missions*, Vol. XXI, p. 195.

[25] William Paton, mimeographed letter, Dec., 1930. But see Addison, *The Christian Approach to the Moslem*, pp. 164, 165. Also on the Church Missionary Society see S. A. Morrison, *The Way of Partnership. With the C.M.S. in Egypt and Palestine* (London, The Church Missionary Society, 1936, pp. 87), pp. 51 ff.

[26] Addison, *op. cit.*, p. 161.

[27] *International Survey of the Young Men's and Young Women's Christian Associations*, pp. 264-266.

[28] Addison, *op. cit.*, pp. 157, 158; Erdman Harris, *New Learning in Old Egypt* (New York, Association Press, 1932, pp. 99), pp. 12-34.

[29] For incidents in the Near East narrated by one long on the staff of the Nile Mission Press, see Arthur T. Upson, *High Lights in the Near East. Reminiscences of Nearly 40 Years Service* (London, Marshall, Morgan & Scott, Ltd., no date, pp. 128).

[30] *The International Review of Missions*, Vol. XXI, p. 197.

[31] Addison, *op. cit.*, p. 158.

drawn more closely together by the formation of the Egypt Inter-Mission Council, in 1920.[32]

Neither the first nor the second of the world wars wrought basic changes in the Christian churches in Egypt. In spite of the trickle from the Coptic church to Islam, in 1944 Christianity seems to have been stronger and to have been exerting more influence upon the country than in 1914. It must be noted, however, that none of the indigenous churches, whether Coptic or Evangelical, showed much inclination to seek converts from Islam.[33] They were content to remain encysted minorities.

In the Anglo-Egyptian Sudan the thirty years subsequent to 1914 registered progress for Christianity. It will be recalled that the northern portion of the country was Moslem and that the British regime, fearing a recrudescence of the fanaticism which had earlier given it trouble, forbade direct efforts there for conversion from Islam.[34] In the animistic South the British permitted Christian missions, but did not allow more than one society in a district, a restriction which irked the Roman Catholics.[35] Missionaries from the Verona seminary, the Sons of the Holy Heart, bore the chief burden of the propagation of Roman Catholic Christianity. The foreign staff was fairly steadily augmented, and the numbers of converts grew, but in 1933 they were still only 17,000.[36] For the Protestants the three agencies represented before 1914, the United Presbyterians, the Church Missionary Society, and the Sudan United Mission, continued.[37] In co-operation with them were the British and Foreign Bible Society and the American Bible Society. Portions of the Bible were translated into fresh tongues.[38] Yet converts were few.[39] In 1943 the Evangelical Church in Egypt, which had several congregations in the northern Sudan composed of Egyptians, Syrians, and Ethiopians, volunteered to take charge of existing Protestant communities in that area and to maintain efforts for the non-Christians. In interesting co-operation in one centre an elementary

---

[32] Addison, *op. cit.*, pp. 164, 165.

[33] *The International Review of Missions*, Vol. XXI, p. 198.

[34] Vol. VI, p. 29.

[35] A. Freitag in *Zeitschrift für Missionswissenschaft*, Vol. XXII, p. 157.

[36] A. Freitag in *op. cit.*, Vol. XXII, pp. 157-159; Parker, *An Interpretative Statistical Survey of the World Mission of the Christian Church*, p. 33.

[37] *Light and Darkness in East Africa*, pp. 93-100. On the United Presbyterian mission see Ried F. Shields, *Behind the Garden of Allah* (Philadelphia, United Presbyterian Board of Foreign Missions, 1937, pp. 196), pp. 77 ff. On the Church Missionary Society see W. Wilson Cash, *The Changing Sudan* (London, Church Missionary Society, 1930, pp. vii, 88), pp. 20 ff.

[38] *Light and Darkness in East Africa*, pp. 101-107.

[39] *The International Review of Missions*, Vol. XXXIII, p. 45.

school was supported by Roman Catholics, Copts, and Evangelicals,[40] and in another by Copts, Greek Catholics, and Evangelicals.[41]

In Ethiopia (Abyssinia), the fore part of the three decades which succeeded 1914 passed without major incident for the Christian forces. The Roman Catholic Church had some gains in which Lazarists, Consolata missionaries of Turin, and Capuchins shared.[42] The Ethiopian Pontifical College was inaugurated in Rome in 1931.[43] Protestant efforts were augmented. The Swedish *Evangeliska Fosterlands-Stiftelsen* continued.[44] To Ethiopia came, in 1927, Germans of the Hermannsburg Mission, seeking a new field in place of the one in India of which they had been deprived through the vicissitudes of the first world war.[45] The United Presbyterians were active,[46] but one of their staff, Thomas A. Lambie, dissatisfied with the reluctance of his home board to sanction an advance into new territory, organized the Abyssinian Frontiers Mission. This merged with the Sudan Interior Mission and in 1927 the latter sent in a party which initiated an enterprise which established itself in Addis Ababa and before many years reached out to other centres.[47] The Seventh Day Adventists, the Bible Churchmen's Missionary Society, and the Swedish Bibeltrogna Vänner were also at work.[48]

Upon this scene there broke, in 1935, the storm of the Italian invasion. The Vatican remained technically neutral, but several of the Italian hierarchy, including at least one cardinal, publicly endorsed the Italian adventure.[49] The Roman Catholic Church bestirred itself to take advantage of the opportunity presented by the altered political situation. It appointed a special commission to study the problem, an Apostolic Delegation was created, and an ecclesiastical division of the land was arranged with prefectures apostolic and at least one vicariate.[50] The purpose was cherished of bringing the Abyssinian Church into

[40] *The International Review of Missions*, Vol. XXIX, p. 65.

[41] *The International Review of Missions*, Vol. XXX, p. 59.

[42] A. Freitag in *Zeitschrift für Missionswissenschaft*, Vol. XXII, pp. 155, 156, Vol. XXVI, p. 46.

[43] Williams, *The Catholic Church in Action*, p. 238.

[44] Martin Nordfeldt, *Abessiniens Guldland* (Stockholm, Evangeliska Fosterlands-Stiftelsens Bokförlag, preface, 1936, pp. 146), *passim*; Martin Nordfeldt, *Bland Abessiniens Gallaer* (Stockholm, Evangeliska Fosterlands-Stiftelsens Bokförlag, 1935, pp. 171), *passim*.

[45] W. Wickert, *Abbessinien, unser neues Missionsfeld* (Hermannsburg, Missionshandlung, 1931, pp. 91), pp. 47 ff.; Dietrich Wassmann, *Pionierdienst unter den Galla in Westabessinien* (Hermannsburg, Missionshandlung, 1938, pp. 113), *passim*.

[46] *Light and Darkness in East Africa*, pp. 160, 161.

[47] Rice, *Eclipse in Ethiopia*, pp. 17-24.

[48] *The International Review of Missions*, Vol. XXVI, p. 59.

[49] Binchy, *Church and State in Fascist Italy*, pp. 637-651, 677-679; G. Salvemini in *Christendom*, Vol. II, pp. 24-35.

[50] *Fides News Service*, July 10, 1937.

obedience to Rome.[51] In general, the regime set up by the conqueror was more intent upon promoting Italian than Roman Catholic interests. It sought to control the Abyssinian Church and to separate it from its connexion with the Coptic Church in Egypt: it endeavoured to replace non-Italian with Italian missionaries, whether Roman Catholic or Protestant,[52] but all this was primarily for political purposes. The policy proved embarrassing to the Protestant enterprises. They had suffered during the fighting. Although, after the completion of the occupation, not all were excluded, progressively restrictive action was taken against them.[53] The Waldensees attempted to come to the rescue, for as Italians they would presumably be tolerated, and sent a few representatives.[54] However, they were too small a body to carry the full load.

The British reconquest of Ethiopia in the second of the world wars, the expulsion of the Italians, and the restoration of the Emperor Haile Selassie again brought changes which, by destroying the pattern recently set up by the Italians, were disturbing to the Christian forces. The renewed indigenous regime was intensely nationalistic and insisted that no missions should be conducted without its permission. The Roman Catholic enterprise could not fail to feel the transition from the Italian rule under which it had been functioning. In general, however, the government was not unfriendly to missions and by 1944 most of the Protestant societies were resuming their operations.[55]

Christian missions in Eritrea and Italian Somaliland could not but be affected by the vicissitudes of the 1930's and 1940's. Indeed, in the 1920's and 1930's, before she ventured into Abyssinia, Italy was strangling the Swedish Protestant mission in Eritrea, presumably because it was not Italian. The Waldensians were valiantly attempting to substitute for it.[56] Eritrea and Italian Somaliland had not far from 3,000 Christians of both wings of the faith. These regions, however, must be passed over in a review as necessarily brief as ours. So, too, must British and French Somaliland. The latter had only a few hundred Christians, whether Roman Catholic or Protestant.

As in our survey of the spread of Christianity in the three decades after

[51] *The International Review of Missions*, Vol. XXVI, p. 60, quoting Cardinal Tisserand in *Gazetto del Popolo*, Oct. 22, 1936.
[52] Binchy, *op. cit.*, pp. 360, 361; *The International Review of Missions*, Vol. XXVI, p. 60.
[53] Rice, *op. cit.*, pp. 59 ff.; *The International Review of Missions*, Vol. XXVI, p. 59, Vol. XXVII, p. 63, Vol. XXVIII, p. 53. For one of the missionaries who lost his life while in ambulance service, see *John Melly of Ethiopia*, edited by Kathleen Nelson and Alan Sullivan (London, Faber & Faber, Limited, 1937, pp. 284), pp. 105 ff.
[54] *The International Review of Missions*, Vol. XXIX, p. 67, Vol. XXX, p. 60.
[55] Thomas A. Lambie, *A Doctor Carries On* (New York, Fleming H. Revell Company, 1942, pp. 173), *passim*; *The International Review of Missions*, Vol. XXXII, pp. 34, 35, Vol. XXXIII, p. 46.
[56] *The International Review of Missions*, Vol. XX, p. 48, Vol. XXI, p. 210.

1914 we pass from Africa to the western shores of Asia, we must speak first of all of Near East Relief, for this arose in connexion with the world war of 1914-1918 and was an outgrowth of American Protestant missions. It came into being in 1914 in the attempt to relieve the sufferings of the Armenians and to save as many as possible from extermination. The Armenians, an enterprising Christian minority, had long been regarded by the Turks with unfriendly eye. They were viewed in much the same fashion as Jews had traditionally been in various lands and for some of the same reasons. In the latter part of the nineteenth century they had been the objects of repeated attacks. In the unrest and excitement of the first of the world wars, a struggle in which they were belligerents and were threatened by strong neighbours, especially Russia, the Turks believed the Armenians to be an internal threat and determined to eliminate them. This was done in part by massacres by Turks and Kurds, and in part by mass deportations. The loss of life was enormous. Thousands of families were broken up and tens of thousands of children were orphaned.

The contacts of Americans with the Near East had been predominantly through Protestant missions. When the news of the Armenian tragedy reached the United States, those who had led in missions to the Near East resolved to do what they could to meet the need. While eventually Near East Relief drew in many without much missionary interest and although it was not for the purpose of spreading the Christian faith, most of its original organizers and of its leaders were from the Protestant missionary forces and it obtained a very large proportion of its funds from churches and Sunday Schools. At the outset it set as its goal the raising of $100,000. By 1930 it had received in contributions over $91,000,000 in cash from many thousands of individuals and about $25,000,000 in food and supplies from the United States Government, from railroads, and from foreign governments.

The original Armenian massacres were succeeded by other tragedies. These did not end with 1918. Tens of thousands of Russians, refugees from the Communists and from the disintegration of anti-Communist White armies, were added to the Armenians. The collapse of the Greek invasion of Turkey in 1922 led to the deportation of hundreds of thousands of Greeks from Anatolia and the coast of Asia Minor and deluged Greece with about 1,400,000 refugees. Relief activities were extended not only to Greece, but also, and earlier, to Syria, the Caucasus, and Persia. In Persia there were sufferers among the Nestorians as well as the Armenians.

Probably a million lives were saved. Relief was given in the form of food, clothing, and medical supplies. New industries were inaugurated and fresh agricultural methods with better seeds and improved breeds of cattle were introduced. Approximately 132,000 orphaned children were rescued, fed, and educated. For sheer magnitude, Near East Relief had few equals in the history of philanthropy by private agencies.[57] It was followed by the Near East Foundation, but the latter did not reach the dimensions of its predecessor.

The devotion and service represented by Near East Relief must not be allowed to obscure the fact that through the first of the world wars and its aftermath Christianity suffered enormous numerical losses in Western Asia. The deaths of the hundreds of thousands of Armenians, Nestorians, and Greek Orthodox and the striking reduction of the communities of these ancient branches of the faith could not be made good. At most Near East Relief was a palliative.

Although the achievement of Near East Relief was spectacular, the major part of it was limited to about a decade and a half. Less in the headlines, but continuous and probably with much more extensive results in culture and in human lives were the enterprises of Christian missions from Europe and the United States. We have seen[58] that these had reached large proportions before 1914.[59] They continued after that year.

In the post-1914 years both Roman Catholics and Protestants took steps towards a more comprehensive approach to the Near East. In 1917 Rome created the Congregation for Oriental Churches. It was planned that eventually all those of the Latin rite in the Near East and the Balkans would also pass from the Propaganda to its jurisdiction.[60] Thus the dignity accorded the eastern branches of the Roman Catholic Church which retained their traditional rites was enhanced, and those of the Latin rite were made to feel that they were on a par with the faithful in other regions. In 1924 Protestants organized the Near East Christian Council.[61] This sought to co-ordinate Protestant efforts and to bring them collectively into the International Missionary Council. In 1919 there was constituted a United Missionary Council of Syria and Palestine.[62]

In Palestine great changes followed the first of the world wars. The region

[57] James L. Barton, *Story of Near East Relief (1915-1930). An Interpretation* (New York, The Macmillan Company, 1930, pp. xxii, 479), *passim.*
[58] Vol. VI, pp. 35-64.
[59] For a survey showing the extent of these activities, especially of those from the United States, see Frank A. Ross, C. Luther Fry, Elbridge Sibley, *The Near East and American Philanthropy* (New York, Columbia University Press, 1929, pp. xiii, 308), *passim.*
[60] Williams, *The Catholic Church in Action*, p. 166; *The International Review of Missions*, Vol. XXVIII, p. 95.
[61] Strong and Warnshuis, *Directory of Foreign Missions*, p. 143.
[62] Strong and Warnshuis, *op. cit.*, p. 146.

became a British mandate. Under the impulse of Zionism many Jews set up their homes in the traditional land of their forefathers. Their presence brought friction with the Arab population which at times became acute violence. The Christian forces remained minorities and had only slight gains. Roman Catholics lamented the growing prominence of the Jews, a large proportion of whom had shed all religion, and the subjection of the schools maintained by their mission to the regulations of a secular state.[63] Yet they could report the conversion of at least one village across the Jordan and a fairly steady stream of Melchite clergy issuing from the seminary in Jerusalem maintained by the White Fathers.[64] Protestant efforts also made slow headway. Additional numbers of Jews were in Protestant schools. Efforts to reach Moslems were augmented, partly through the establishment of the Newman School of Missions (1928), and a few converts were won.[65] The Young Men's Christian Association erected a large building in Jerusalem.[66] In spite of the presence of the religiously tolerant British power, however, age-long emotional and social barriers and racial conflicts prevented Christianity from achieving major advances.

In consequence of the first of the world wars, Syria passed under French mandate. In Syria, as we saw earlier,[67] the proportion of Christians was much larger than in Palestine and several Christian communions were represented. After 1914 the numbers of Christians were swelled by refugees from other parts of Western Asia—Armenians, Nestorians, Christian Kurds, and Syrian Catholics.[68] In spite of the nationalist resentment and at times rebellion against French administration,[69] the latter was regarded by at least some Roman Catholics as favourable to their undertakings. Already strong, thanks in part to previous French backing, Roman Catholic forces were reinforced in the post-1914 years. They were active among the Armenian refugees from Turkey. They had, for instance, several schools for the Armenian children with an

---

[63] A. Freitag in *Zeitschrift für Missionswissenschaft*, Vol. XXVI, pp. 42, 43. See also *75 Jahre Deutscher Verein vom Heiligen Lande* (Cologne, J. P. Bachem, 1931, pp. 42), *passim*.

[64] A. Freitag in *Zeitschrift für Missionswissenschaft*, Vol. XXIII, p. 52.

[65] *The International Review of Missions*, Vol. XXI, pp. 185, 186, 346; Addison, *The Christian Approach to the Moslem*, pp. 318, 319.

[66] *International Survey of the Young Men's and Young Women's Christian Associations*, pp. 266, 267.

[67] Vol. VI, pp. 41-45.

[68] *The International Review of Missions*, Vol. XX, p. 44.

[69] For an account of some of this see Elizabeth P. MacCallum, *The Nationalist Crusade in Syria* (New York, The Foreign Policy Association, 1928, pp. xiii, 299), *passim*. See also W. E. Hocking, *The Spirit of World Politics, with Special Studies of the Near East* (New York, The Macmillan Company, 1932, pp. xiv, 571), pp. 227-334.

enrolment, at one time, of more than 2,000. The Jesuits not only continued their university at Beirut and a seminary which prepared clergy for several of the uniate bodies, but they also organized a seminary especially for the Maronites and reached out into new territory. Under the friendly French regime it was more possible to approach Moslems than formerly.[70] During the first of the world wars the Capuchins suffered a sharp decline in the enrolments in their schools, and in the post-war years did not fully make good their losses. Moreover, even after the war the numbers in their orphanages fell off almost to the vanishing point.[71] Since, however, in 1914 the Capuchin mission embraced part of what was later Turkey as well as a portion of Syria, the decline is to be ascribed as much to the disasters attendant upon the war in the former area as to the changes in the latter.

While not so numerous as Roman Catholics, Protestants in Syria more than doubled between 1924 and 1936.[72] The immigration of refugees brought accessions, especially of Armenians of that faith. In 1922 the latter formed the Armenian Evangelical Union of Syria and Lebanon.[73] In addition to what was done by Near East Relief, various Protestant agencies served the luckless migrants. Memorable were the labours of Karen Jeppe, of the *Deutsche Orient Mission*,[74] who, having been in Urfa in an orphanage of that mission, found haven in Aleppo and there ministered to Armenian girls who had been rescued from Moslem harems.[75] In 1939 the cession to Turkey of a portion of the French mandate led to a further exodus of Armenians to areas still under the French.[76] In 1933 the Near East School of Theology was opened in Beirut, an amalgamation of two earlier institutions.[77] The Syrian Protestant College was renamed the American University (1920) and expanded its resources and scope and its outreach into the region.[78] Other educational progress was regis-

---

[70] A. Freitag in *Zeitschrift für Missionswissenschaft*, Vol. XXIII, pp. 50, 51, Vol. XXVI, pp. 39-42; Luce Camuzet, *L'Œuvre de Syrie des Sœurs de St. Joseph de l'Apparation* (Paris, Éditions de *La Nation*, no date, pp. 54), pp. 44-48; *Missionnaires de Vingt Ans* (Paris, Éditions Dillen, 1931, pp. 237), *passim.*

[71] *Missionnaires Capucins au Levant Syrien Passé et Présent* (Beyrouth, Imp. Jeanne d'Arc, 1931, pp. 29), pp. 21, 25.

[72] Beach and Fahs, *World Missionary Atlas*, p. 77; Parker, *Interpretative Statistical Survey of the World Mission of the Christian Church*, p. 64.

[73] Strong and Warnshuis, *Directory of Foreign Missions*, p. 146.

[74] Vol. VI, p. 53.

[75] Jakob Künzler, *Dein Volk ist mein Volk. Das Lebensbild einer Heldin seltener Art, der Dänin Karen Jeppe* (Basel, Heinrich Majer, 1939, pp. 93); Ingeborg Maria Sick, *Karen Jeppe* (Stuttgart, J. F. Steinkopf, 1929, pp. 270).

[76] *The International Review of Missions*, Vol. XXIX, p. 53.

[77] *The International Review of Missions*, Vol. XXXIII, p. 54.

[78] Stephen B. L. Penrose, Jr., *That They May Have Life. The Story of the American University of Beirut, 1866-1941* (New York, The Trustees of the American University of

tered by Protestants.[79] Moslems became much more accessible and baptisms among them were recorded.[80] The Syrian Evangelical Church was organized into a synod (1924) and increased in autonomy.[81] During the second of the world wars, although Syria was the scene of some of the fighting, the life of the churches was not badly disrupted and here and there progress was seen.[82]

In no other part of the Near East did Christianity suffer such losses after 1914 as in Turkey. The revolutionaries who gained control shortly before 1914 and who retained it in the decades following that year had caught their inspiration primarily from the secularized nationalism of the Occident. They were intent upon building a strong, unified, Westernized Turkey. They were not pro-Moslem. Indeed, they were bent upon freeing Turkey from what they deemed the incubus of Islam and abolished the caliphate. To them, however, the Christian minorities were a distinct obstacle to the attainment of their goal. By long tradition and by law these minorities, Armenian, Greek, Roman Catholic, and Protestant, were separate entities. They were standing invitations to foreign intervention, for any measures against them, as had again and again been demonstrated, would bring protests and possibly belligerent action from one or another of the European governments. They were, moreover, not loved by the average Turk, for, as we hinted a few paragraphs above, they were better educated and more clever in business than the general run of the Moslems about them and were viewed in much the same manner in which minorities combining racial and religious differences had been in many other parts of the world. The nationalists determined to rid Turkey of them. With the same motive they would not permit the attempt to win adherents of Islam to the Christian faith, not because they esteemed one true and the other false, but because, having once reduced the Christian minorities to innocuous dimensions, they would not tolerate their expansion by fresh conversions.[83]

The immediate results in these years were the massacres of Armenians and Greeks and the expulsion of the survivors, a series of tragedies to which we referred a page or two earlier. Fortunately for the Christians, the boundaries of Turkey were greatly reduced in consequence of the first of the world wars

---

Beirut, 1941, pp. xviii, 347), pp. 147 ff.; *Annual Report of the Near East College Association*, 1930-1931, pp. 5 ff.; Hamlin, *Treasures of the Earth*, pp. 35-46; Stuart Carter Dodd, *A Controlled Experiment on Rural Hygiene in Syria* (American University of Beirut, 1934, pp. xv, 336).

[79] Addison, *The Christian Approach to the Moslem*, pp. 130, 131.

[80] Addison, *op. cit.*, pp. 133-138; *The International Review of Missions*, Vol. XXI, pp. 178, 179. On the legal problem see Davis, *Some Aspects of Religious Liberty of Nationals in the Near East*, pp. 29 ff., 55 ff.

[81] Strong and Warnshuis, *op. cit.*, p. 145.

[82] *The International Review of Missions*, Vol. XXX, p. 52, Vol. XXXIII, p. 29.

[83] Allen, *The Turkish Transformation*, pp. 69 ff.

and that realm was confined chiefly to Asia Minor, a part of Armenia, and a small bit of Europe. Within these areas and in some adjacent ones in the course of the war and its aftermath, the sufferings of the Christians were intense. Tens of thousands of Armenians[84] and Greeks perished, among them thousands of Roman Catholics[85] and hundreds of Protestants, and several missionaries died as a result of overstrain or of disease contracted while attempting to relieve the suffering.[86]

The effect was peculiarly devastating for the ancient Gregorian (Armenian) Church, for, while the other communions affected had only a small fraction of their members in Turkey, the chief centre of the Armenians had been in that state and on its border. Moreover, in such portions of Armenia as were within the Russian boundaries the policy of the Communist regime was only less disastrous for the Gregorian organization than was that of Turkey. Armenians of that faith outside of Russia were largely cut off from contact with their co-religionists in Russia, the number of monks in Russian Armenia declined, and when, in 1937, the Catholicos was assassinated, political conditions prevented the convening of a council to choose a successor.[87]

Roman Catholic and Protestant missions in Turkey were greatly reduced. Both had had their constituencies chiefly among the Greek and Armenian Christian communities. Now that these were depleted, missions were forced to find their fields mainly among the Turks. The abolition of the capitulations under whose extraterritorial protection foreign missionaries had previously laboured posed missions with a new problem.[88] While in theory religious liberty prevailed and a Moslem might become a Christian, in practice the traditional prejudices and inertia of the Turks were a sufficient obstacle and regulations prevented missionaries from giving Christian instruction to non-Christians in the schools which were a main means of contact with non-Christians.[89] Here and there a Moslem became a Christian, but usually the convert

[84] See, for instance, Johannes Lepsius, *Der Todesgang des Armenischen Volkes. Bericht über des Schicksal des Armenischen Volkes in der Türke, während des Weltkrieges* (Potsdam, Tempelverlag, 1919, pp. xxvii, 311), *passim*; Jensine Oerts Peters, *Tests and Triumphs of Armenians in Turkey and Macedonia* (Grand Rapids, Zondervan Publishing House, 1940, pp. 95), pp. 45 ff.

[85] Lemmens, *Geschichte der Franziskannermissionen*, pp. 30, 31.

[86] For examples see John Otis Barrows, *In the Land of Ararat. A Sketch of the Life of Mrs. Elizabeth Freeman Barrows Ussher, Missionary to Turkey and a Martyr of the Great War* (New York, Fleming H. Revell Company, 1916, pp. 184), pp. 157 ff.; Alice Shepard Riggs, *Shepard of Aintab* (New York, Interchurch Press, 1920, pp. xx, 200), pp. 183 ff.

[87] *International Press and Information Service,* No. 26, July, 1942.

[88] *The One Hundred and Thirteenth Annual Report of the American Board of Commissioners for Foreign Missions*, p. 51.

[89] Davis, *op. cit.*, pp. 27, 91 ff., 124 ff.; Allen, *op. cit.*, pp. 143 ff.

was subjected to persecution by minor officials and to social ostracism.[90] During the first of the world wars and the disorders which immediately succeeded it, it is said that a third of the Roman Catholic community, 8 bishops, 107 priests, and 45 Armenian sisters were killed,[91] and that by 1930 14 Roman Catholic Armenian dioceses had been abandoned or desolated.[92] In Constantinople (Istanbul) the number of Latin Roman Catholics experienced a sharp decline early in the 1920's.[93] The restriction on Christian teaching in the schools was a severe handicap.[94] Only imperfect progress had been made towards recovering the lost ground when the second of the world wars dealt blows to the support and the reinforcement of the foreign staffs. In 1914 the American Board of Commissioners for Foreign Missions was the Protestant agency most extensively represented in Asia Minor. It had found its chief opportunities among the Armenians and the Greeks. Its missionaries, therefore, often with very great heroism and cost to themselves, tried to ease the agony of these unfortunates.[95] The obliteration of the larger part of their constituencies brought the question as to whether the American Board should continue in Turkey. The decision (1923) was in the affirmative.[96] The situation was never easy. It was next to impossible for newly arrived American missionary physicians to obtain official license to practice,[97] and mission hospitals were handicapped by the further prohibition of using them as agencies for Christian religious instruction. In 1928 a mission school for girls was closed on the ground that undue influence was being exerted on the pupils to become Christians and in a famous trial a nominal penalty was imposed upon the accused missionary teachers.[98] Yet mission schools, as centres of the desired new learning, had full enrolments of Turks, and Robert College[99] and the

[90] S. A. Morrison in *The International Review of Missions*, Vol. XXIV, p. 455.

[91] Lemmens, *op. cit.*, pp. 30, 31.

[92] Lesourd, *L'Année Missionnaire*, 1931, p. 84.

[93] Lemmens, *op. cit.*, p. 36.

[94] A. Freitag in *Zeitschrift für Missionswissenschaft*, Vol. XXVI, pp. 38, 39; Allen, *op. cit.*, pp. 143 ff.

[95] For examples see Clarence D. Ussher and Grace H. Knapp, *An American Physician in Turkey* (Boston, Houghton Mifflin Company, 1917, pp. xiii, 338), pp. 191 ff.; Ethel D. Hubbard, *Mary Louise Graffam of Sivas, Turkey* (Boston, Woman's Board of Missions, no date, pp. 23), *passim*; Ernest Pye, *Charlotte R. Willard of Merzifon* (New York, Fleming H. Revell Company, 1933, pp. 211), pp. 99 ff.

[96] *The One Hundred and Thirteenth Annual Report of the American Board of Commissioners for Foreign Missions*, p. 52.

[97] *The One Hundred and Fourteenth Annual Report of the American Board of Commissioners for Foreign Missions*, pp. 67, 68. *

[98] *The International Review of Missions*, Vol. XXI, pp. 175-177.

[99] Caleb Frank Gates, *Not to Me Only* (Princeton University Press, 1940, pp. x, 340), pp. 207 ff.

Istanbul Woman's College[100] continued. Except for shortage in some of the physical accessories of life and for difficulties in communications with the United States, the second of the world wars did not immediately bring major problems to the American Board in Turkey. Indeed, the mission schools were full.[101] A new version of the Bible in Turkish issued in 1941 by the British and Foreign Bible Society had phenomenal introductory sales.[102]

Iraq was a state which emerged from the post-1914 disintegration of the Turkish Empire and embraced much of Mesopotamia and the latter's bounding plains and mountains. It was first assigned to Great Britain as a mandate. In 1927 Britain recognized its independence but the mandate did not terminate until early in the 1930's. Iraq was overwhelmingly Moslem by faith, but in it were Christian minorities of various ecclesiastical allegiance, among them Nestorians, Chaldeans (Nestorians who had submitted to Rome), Jacobites, Syrian uniates, and Protestants.[103] The first of the world wars and its aftermath brought severe suffering to a large proportion of the Christians. At the outset of that struggle, Kurds and Turks, on the plea that the Nestorians, as Christians, were potential allies of Russia and hence enemies, fell upon them, especially in the mountains between Mesopotamia and Persia, killed many, and drove others out. Numbers took refuge in Persia.[104] The plight of the Assyrian Christians, some of them Nestorians and some Chaldean uniates, continued hard. Hundreds were killed during and subsequent to the first of the world wars. The League of Nations eventually exerted itself in their behalf, but did not succeed in making satisfactory arrangements for them. Approximately a third of the Chaldean uniates are said to have perished.[105] In 1933 there was armed conflict between the Nestorians and the troops of Iraq, with fresh suffering for the unfortunate Assyrian Christians.[106] Both Roman Catholic and Protestant missions from the Occident persisted. In a newly constituted school in Mosul French Dominicans were preparing an indigenous clergy and in Baghdad early in the 1930's American Jesuits opened a higher school. The Carmelites maintained in Baghdad the mission which had long been their responsibility.[107] Before the end of the first of the world

[100] Mary Mills Patrick, *Under Five Sultans* (New York, The Century Co., 1929, pp. 357), pp. 255 ff.

[101] *The Undaunted Community. Report of the 131st Year of the Work of the American Board*, 1941, pp. 29, 30.

[102] *The International Review of Missions*, Vol. XXXII, p. 28.

[103] Vol. VI, p. 54.

[104] Rockwell, *The Pitiful Plight of the Assyrian Christians in Persia and Kurdistan*, *passim*.

[105] A. Freitag in *Zeitschrift für Missionswissenschaft*, Vol. XXVI, p. 43.

[106] *The International Review of Missions*, Vol. XXIII, p. 62.

[107] A. Freitag in *Zeitschrift für Missionswissenschaft*, Vol. XXVI, p. 44; Considine, *Across a World*, pp. 18, 19.

wars the Church Missionary Society closed out the enterprise which it had begun in the 1880's. Three somewhat closely related American bodies, the Reformed Church in the United States (German), the Reformed Church in America (Dutch), and the (Northern) Presbyterian Church in the United States of America, organized, in 1924, the United Mission in Mesopotamia, with an approach to Moslems as an avowed objective.[108] The missions were facilitated by legal provision for religious liberty and for freedom for the individual to change his religion, even if that should be from Islam to Christianity.[109] Social pressure might make such a step next to impossible, but the legal obstacles had been removed.

Persia, or Iran as the post-1914 world learned to call it, was the scene of striking changes, both politically and culturally. Nationalism combined with an energetic political regime to bring about the rapid penetration of the land by Occidental implements and ideas. Roads were built, a system of state schools was developed, and students were sent to Europe and Britain.[110] The trend was towards secularization, although in a land so long predominantly Moslem Islam could not be discarded. Secularization did not proceed as far as in Turkey. The second of the world wars hastened the penetration of the West, for Iran became a corridor through which aid passed to Russia from the United States and Great Britain.

During the first of the world wars the Nestorians in Persia in the vicinity of Urmia, including the Aissors, those who in the preceding twenty years had become affiliated with the Russian Orthodox Church, were decimated by attacks by their enemies as they were in the neighbouring mountains in the then Turkish Empire. The withdrawal early in the war of the Russian troops which had been defending them left them exposed to the Kurds and the Moslem Persians. Many took refuge in the compounds of the Roman Catholic and Protestant missions in Urmia, but hundreds of Nestorians, Orthodox Aissors, and Armenians were slaughtered.[111]

The Roman Catholic missions were not exempt from the destruction. In the neighbourhood of Lake Urmia the establishments of the Lazarists and the Sisters of St. Vincent de Paul were wiped out and the Apostolic Delegate and several other Lazarists were killed. In 1922 there were fresh disorders. For

---

[108] Addison, *The Christian Approach to the Moslem*, pp. 320, 321.

[109] Davis, *Some Aspects of Religious Liberty of Nationals in the Near East*, pp. 32, 33, 79 ff.

[110] J. H. Linton in *The International Review of Missions*, Vol. XX, pp. 84 ff.; Richards, *The Open Road in Persia*, pp. 1-14.

[111] Rockwell, *op. cit., passim*; Paul Shimmon, *Massacres of Syrian Christians in N. W. Persia and Kurdistan* (London, Wells Gardner, Darton and Co., Ltd., c. 1915, pp. 24), *passim*; Bolshakoff, *The Foreign Missions of the Russian Orthodox Church*, pp. 102, 103.

some time the government did not permit missionaries to return. Not until 1923 did the Lazarists again make their way to Urmia.[112] However, late in the 1920's and early in the 1930's the Lazarist mission was revived. In 1926 or 1927 the staff was said to contain thirteen native seculars, eleven Lazarists, one Discalced Carmelite, and twenty-six Daughters of Charity.[113] Schools were opened, including a seminary, and in 1934 two from the latter were ordained as secular priests. Several hundred converts were made. A strong school was inaugurated in Isfahan. Farther south, in Shiraz, the Dominicans began a school.[114]

Protestants were still chiefly represented by the American Northern Presbyterians and the Anglicans. Of the latter the Church Missionary Society was the most prominent, but the Bible Churchmen's Missionary Society also entered.[115] The enhanced patriotism brought fresh obstacles, for Islam was deemed the national faith and Christian missions, seeking, as they did, to wean Moslems away from that religion, were declared dangerous to the country's unity.[116] Late in the 1920's, moreover, there began to be an acute issue connected with religious instruction in mission schools. The question was resolved by an arrangement whereby the schools were not required to teach the Koran and the *shariat* (Moslem law) as had first been feared, but were prevented from placing on their regular curriculum formal instruction in the Christian religion.[117] On the whole, however, Protestant missionaries felt that the rapidly changing atmosphere with the increased Westernization made for greater open-mindedness. Converts were being won from Islam and some of them were active in the spread of their new faith.[118] Plans were being discussed for drawing together all Protestants, especially the Presbyterians and Anglicans, into one church.[119] The second of the world wars seemed not to lessen but to enlarge the opportunity.

Afghanistan, although separated from Iran by only a line, continued in its mountain fastnesses resolutely Moslem and all but impervious to Christianity. Yet one American Roman Catholic priest was there in 1930 and beginning in

---

[112] Lesourd, *L'Année Missionnaire*, 1931, p. 88; Coste, *La Congregation de la Mission*, p. 197; A. Freitag in *Zeitschrift für Missionswissenschaft*, Vol. XXVI, p. 44.

[113] *Missiones Catholicae Cura S. Congregationis de Propaganda Fide*, 1927, pp. 64, 65.

[114] A. Freitag in *Zeitschrift für Missionswissenschaft*, Vol. XVII, p. 39, Vol. XXIII, p. 53, Vol. XXVI, p. 44.

[115] Parker, *Interpretative Statistical Survey of the World Mission of the Christian Church*, p. 63.

[116] Richards, *The Open Road to Persia*, p. 31.

[117] *The International Review of Missions*, Vol. XXI, pp. 203, 204.

[118] R. W. Howard, *A Merry Mountaineer. The Story of Clifford Harris of Persia* (London, Church Missionary Society, 1932, pp. 93), *passim*.

[119] Richards, *op. cit.*, p. 61; *The International Review of Missions*, Vol. XXXII, p. 32.

1932 a Roman Catholic chaplain was attached to the Italian embassy.[120] There was some Protestant itineration from Iran, but very limited, and contact, also very restricted, through the north-west of India.[121]

In Arabia Christian missions were still very small. In the Roman Catholic vicariate apostolic which bore the name of Arabia and had its seat at Aden, but which also included British Somaliland, in 1930 there were less than a thousand of that faith and only three priests, five lay brothers, and nine sisters.[122] Protestants were somewhat more active. The largest of their missions was that of the Reformed Church in America, on the Persian Gulf from the head, through the Bahrein Islands, to Muscat.[123] More restricted in area and personnel were the Church of Scotland Arabia Mission[124] and the Danish Church Mission in Arabia.[125] There was much emphasis on the medical side of the enterprise,[126] but, as was to be expected in a land long so solidly Moslem, converts continued to be few.

As one looks back over this rapid survey of Christianity on the northern shores of Africa and in the Near East in the three decades which followed 1914 he becomes aware of at least three general developments. It was clear, in the first place, that in proportion to the total population Christians had become fewer than they had been since the second or third century. The loss was among the older, indigenous churches, and chiefly those in Turkey, Iraq, and Persia. There were leakages, but not so striking, from the Copts in Egypt, and a partial disruption, temporary as it proved, of the ancient church in Abyssinia. In the second place, it was obvious that the Christian forces from the Occident continued to be very active. The foreign staffs of the missions, both Roman Catholic and Protestant, had been reinforced, although that of the former had grown more rapidly than had that of the latter. In spite of severe losses in some areas, taken the region over both Protestants and Roman Catholics had increased among the native peoples. In the third place, it was also apparent that the influence of this Occidental Christianity was important in some aspects

---

[120] A. Freitag in *Zeitschrift für Missionswissenschaft*, Vol. XXVI, p. 44.

[121] Addison, *op. cit.*, p. 320.

[122] *Testo-Atlante illustrato delle Missioni*, p. 107.

[123] Storm, *Whither Arabia?*, pp. 66-70, 109, 110; Alfred DeWitt Mason and Frederick J. Barny, *History of the Arabian Mission* (New York, The Board of Foreign Missions of the Reformed Church in America, 1926, pp. 256), pp. 166 ff.

[124] Storm, *op. cit.*, pp. 109, 110.

[125] *Ibid.*; M. Borch-Jensen, *Sydarabien og Evangeliet* (Copenhagen, O. Lohse, 1937, pp. 201), pp. 141 ff.

[126] As an eminent example, see Paul W. Harrison, *Doctor in Arabia* (New York, The John Day Company, 1940, pp. 303), *passim*.

of the life of predominantly Moslem lands. Prominent were the relief enterprises in and immediately following the first of the world wars, the schools and hospitals, and the preparation and distribution of literature.

Whether Christianity was more or less potent in the life of the entire area in 1944 than it had been three decades earlier would probably be impossible to demonstrate. In some aspects and countries it had undoubtedly grown in its effect. In others it had lost ground. The decrease, as we have indicated, was chiefly in the diminished numbers and morale of some of the Eastern churches. The gains were mainly among the Moslems. Formal conversions from Islam were increasing but were still very few. The permeation of Islam seems clearly to have grown. The weakness of the Christian position, however, was in the circumstance that conversions and permeation were predominantly through the missionaries from the Occident and the institutions and churches established and nourished by them. They were not from the indigenous churches. With a few exceptions, even those Christian communities which had arisen as the result of missions from the Occident showed little inclination to reach out to their Moslem neighbours. In view of the traditional relations between Moslems and Christians this was understandable. However, in a world in which non-European peoples were more and more resentful of the privileged position of Occidentals and were rapidly throwing off the Western yoke, the outlook was sombre for a Christianity which was not well rooted in the soil but was dependent upon continuing infusions of life from Europe and America.

Chapter XI

INDIA

GENERAL CONDITIONS: SYRIAN CHRISTIANITY: ROMAN CATHOLIC CHRISTIANITY: PROTESTANT CHRISTIANITY: EFFECT ON THE ENVIRONMENT: EFFECT OF THE ENVIRONMENT

THE three decades which began in 1914 witnessed the progress of revolution in India. During these thirty years the alterations were not as profound as in India's great neighbour, China. The protective paternalism of
British rule, although seemingly in process of rapid liquidation, still gave outward cohesion, prevented devastating civil strife, and afforded opportunity for
progressive although stormy achievement of political and economic autonomy.
Hinduism, the faith of the majority, combining as it did religion with a social
structure which was largely independent of its political setting, remained substantially intact. Many of its educated adherents might be religiously sceptical,
but it was sufficiently elastic to continue to hold them without disintegrating.
Islam, as the religion of the largest minority, showed no signs of yielding. All
this was in striking contrast with China, where the Confucian state had
crumbled, enervating civil strife had wasted much of the land, Confucianism
itself, the dominant ideological force, had been deprived of some of the main
agencies by which it had been perpetuated, and a prolonged war with a foreign
foe on the soil of the country had wrought tragic and widespread destruction.
Yet rapid changes were under way in India, and the prophets of gloom foretold
an even more sombre fate than for China, with more acute civil strife when the
British had withdrawn or had been cast out, and with far less of a tradition of
unity to mend division. By the close of 1944, however, these jeremiads had not
yet found fulfilment.

The development which most affected the spread of Christianity in India
were the two world wars, the growth in population, the rapid and sweeping
rise of the tide of Indian nationalism, the stirrings among the depressed classes,
and the influence of Western secularism and Communism.

As a part of the British Empire, India was a participant in both of the world conflicts of the era. Hundreds of thousands of Indians were recruited for the armies and tens of thousands shared in the fighting. Each of the wars had its concomitants of rising prices which bore especially hard upon the masses, at best never far from the margin of subsistence. In the second war there was actual famine, most spectacular in Bengal in 1943.

The population of India was rapidly mounting. In 1911 it had been 315,156,000,[1] and in 1941 it was 388,197,000.[2] These totals included only the areas within the British Empire and were exclusive of the French and Portuguese possessions, which in 1941 contained not far from 900,000.[3] The rising population, due in part to the *pax Britannica* and to the additional areas which the British had brought under cultivation through irrigation, meant that in spite of the efforts of the government, standards of living for the masses, already incredibly low, were probably declining. It also carried with it the danger of greater famines than India had known since the British conquest in case, either after or before British rule should end, there were to come extensive and prolonged civil strife.

More immediately spectacular was Indian nationalism. This had as its chief organized expression the Indian National Congress[4] and as its outstanding figure Gandhi.[5] Indian nationalism was, however, too widespread to be confined to any one group or to be controlled by any single leader. Politically it issued in rapidly growing participation of Indians in the government and in demands for full autonomy. Some would have that autonomy inside and others outside the British Empire. Many of the Moslems, voicing their demands through the Moslem League, insisted upon a division of India, with a separate state, Pakistan, to be made up of those portions of the country where the followers of the Prophet were in the majority.

Christians, both Indians and missionaries, were inevitably affected by the political agitation. Increasingly the Indian Christians supported the movements for autonomy. Even more important for the spread of Christianity was the general atmosphere created by the super-heated nationalism. It meant, especially in the later years of the decade and particularly in the fevered days of the second of the world wars, increasing Indian initiative in the churches, the growth of Indian leadership, and the insistence by Indians that more of the administration be transferred to them from foreign hands. In the struggle for power between the various groups, groups in which, after the Indian fashion,

[1] *The Statesman's Year-Book*, 1914, p. 126.
[2] *The Statesman's Year-Book*, 1943, pp. xxviii, 114.
[3] *The Statesman's Year-Book*, 1943, pp. 901, 1109.
[4] Vol. VI, p. 68.
[5] Vol. VI, p. 200.

religion was closely associated, there was resentment, notably by Hindus, over attempts of Christians to win converts. Conversions would result in the shift of allegiance and, if extensive, would strengthen one group at the expense of another. They would also upset the existing social arrangements. This was not the reason publicly advanced for the objection, but it seems to have been at least one of the elements in the resolute opposition. To it Gandhi lent the weight of his name. In theory no criticism was offered of the philanthropic activities of Christian missionaries, but all attempts to use these as a means of inducing baptism, the assumption of church membership, and the destruction of the existing social structure were denounced.[6] So long as British rule prevailed, the official attitude of religious neutrality would presumably continue, but if a strongly nationalist government were to come into power, it might take formal steps to ban what the Hindu labelled as "proselyting." Up to at least 1944, however, this possibility was a fear and not an actuality.

The post-1914 India witnessed restlessness among many of the depressed classes. Constituting roughly a sixth of the population, these groups laboured under social disabilities and were usually of the lowest economic strata.[7] They were of diverse origins, were widely scattered, and were in no sense united, except in their misery. They were too ignorant and traditionally had too inbred a feeling of inferiority to organize in a formidable nation-wide manner to achieve a better status. Yet in these years there were extensive efforts to shake off their chains. Gandhi, himself of the castes, championed the cause of the untouchables, but the movement was largely from the underprivileged, and was in no small degree stimulated by the Christianity which had been propagated among them in the preceding decades.[8] In spite of the efforts of some Hindus, and especially Gandhi, on behalf of the *harijan* ("men of God") as he called them, and perhaps partly because of them and their presumed inadequacy, in October, 1935, Ambedkar, one of the few from the depressed classes to acquire an advanced education, announced his determination not to die a Hindu and summoned his fellow untouchables to follow his example. The movement spread rapidly and widely. Ambedkar did not specify a particular religion to which he intended to turn, but thousands seemed favourable to Sikhism and other thousands to Christianity.[9] In view of the unrest among the depressed, Christianity, which already had made marked progress among them,[10] might be expected to register even greater gains.

[6] See a statement by Gandhi in *Harijan*, quoted in *Fides News Service*, Dec. 7, 1935.
[7] Pickett, *Christian Mass Movements in India*, pp. 58-111.
[8] *The International Review of Missions*, Vol. XXI, pp. 67, 77, Vol. XXIII, pp. 36, 37, Vol. XXIV, p. 34, Vol. XXV, p. 34.
[9] *The International Review of Missions*, Vol. XXVI, pp. 33, 34.
[10] Vol. VI, pp. 84, 85, 153, 154, 165-167, 180-182, 206, 207.

The secularism of Western origin was also gaining and for numbers of the intellectuals was undermining religious faith. To many, Communism, with brilliant achievements in neighbouring Russia, was a lure. Secularism was not new. It had been nourished by the science and humanism of the pre-1914 years. Some of India's most brilliant younger leaders believed religion to be a curse and an impediment to Indian progress. Their conviction might weaken Hinduism and Islam as religions, but they would hold to them as social forces. Clearly both the augmented secularism and the accompanying Communism would be rivals and not aids to the spread of Christianity.[11]

In this India, involved in world wars, faced with poverty and a mounting population, moved by nationalism, troubled by mutterings among its underprivileged, influenced by the secularism and Communism of the West, and clearly in the early stages of revolution, could Christianity, represented only by small minorities and they mostly from the untouchables, make itself felt or even hold its own? Rather remarkably, it continued the striking advance of the nineteenth century. As in the century or so before 1914, so in the three decades inaugurated by that year, the growth was chiefly, although not entirely, that of Roman Catholics and Protestants, and especially of the latter. The former were still the more numerous, but they had about doubled between 1911 and 1936, whereas the latter had multiplied about two and half times in these years.[12] Not far from 1936 Roman Catholics totalled about three and a half millions,[13] and Protestants a little less than two and a half millions.[14] Christianity also increased in Indian leadership and in influence. To this story we must now turn.

We must first survey the state of that branch of Christianity longest in India, the Syrian Church. We had better say churches, for the stream which issued from this earliest of the Christian bodies of India had more than one organizational expression.

A large proportion of those who traced their spiritual ancestry through the Syrian Church were Roman Catholics.[15] As we are to see in a few moments, they were augmented by mass secessions from the Jacobites.

A small segment of the Syrian Christians were Nestorians, possibly with a continuous history of adherence to that wing of the faith which was not inter-

---

[11] See A. J. Appasamy in *The International Review of Missions*, Vol. XXII, pp. 69-80.
[12] For Roman Catholic totals in 1912 see Streit, *Atlas Hierarchicus*, p. 90. For Protestant figures see Beach and Fahs, *World Missionary Atlas*, p. 77.
[13] *Fides News Service*, Apr. 18, 1936.
[14] Parker, *Interpretative Statistical Survey of the World Mission of the Christian Church*, p. 19.
[15] Vol. III, pp. 263-265, Vol. VI, p. 77.

rupted either by the Roman Catholic stage in the seventeenth century or by the later acceptance of Jacobite allegiance. In the 1930's its head was Chaldean by race. However, it had no missionary activity and was numerically almost negligible.[16]

There was an independent Jacobite diocese, but it, too, was of small dimensions.[17]

Next to the Roman Catholic Church the Jacobites had the largest segments of the Syrian Christians. They had traditionally been under the Jacobite Patriarch of Antioch. Throughout the three decades a schism troubled them. It was one over jurisdiction rather than doctrine, but it was no less bitter.[18] In spite of it missions among non-Christians were maintained. Especially active were the Servants of the Cross, in the late 1930's a society with more than eighty stations and outstations. They had over twelve thousand converts, chiefly from the depressed classes. The *Suvisesha Sangham*, or Gospel Association, endeavoured to arouse among Jacobites an interest in spreading their faith. There was also the *Martha Mariam Samajam*, a women's missionary society. The Mount Tabor Mission was monastic in character.[19] The ancient church was obviously displaying signs of fresh life.

The Mar Thoma Church came into being in the second half of the nineteenth century as a result of the impact upon the Syrian church of Protestant Christianity, and especially that of the South India enterprise of the Church Missionary Society. Prolonged dissension and litigation between the section which wished to reform the existing church in accordance with ideas which came chiefly through the agents of the Church Missionary Society and the conservative elements which held to the old ways led finally, in the third quarter of the nineteenth century, to a completely distinct body, the Mar Thoma Church, which incorporated the innovations.[20] The new body had its stronghold in Travancore and, while less than half the size of the Jacobite church from which it had separated, seems to have had approximately 150,000 members[21] and was much more energetic in its approach to non-Christians than was the parent body. Through the Mar Thoma Syrian Christian Evangelistic Association, organized in 1888, it developed a steadily growing missionary enterprise, not

---

[16] Keay, *A History of the Syrian Church in India*, pp. 102-105. Estimates varied as to the numbers of these Nestorians. Ayyar, *Anthropology of the Syrian Christians*, p. ix (*errata*), gives it as 8,884 in 1901, 12,157 in 1911, and 1,882 in 1921. Gledstone, *South India*, p. 49, states it to be 40,000. Keay, *op. cit.*, p. 107, speaks of 6,809 in Cochin alone.

[17] Keay, *op. cit.*, p. 105.

[18] K. K. Kuruvilla in *The National Christian Council Review*, Vol. LII, pp. 302-307.

[19] Keay, *op. cit.*, pp. 91-100.

[20] Vol. VI, p. 114; Keay, *op. cit.*, pp. 78 ff.

[21] Keay, *op. cit.*, p. 107.

only in Travancore, but also in other parts of South India. In the late 1930's it counted about 6,000 converts, largely from the depressed classes, 6 ordained missionaries, and nearly 250 teachers and evangelists, and maintained several schools. Much of its work was by voluntary associates who served without salary. It stood firmly against caste distinctions in the Church and incorporated fully into membership the untouchables who adhered to it. It also held annually a great gathering, sometimes attended by 30,000 or more, for the promotion of the Christian life. A Sunday School Association, organized in 1905, encouraged the children to give to missions among the depressed classes. There were intercommunion and close co-operation with the Anglicans.[22]

An interesting educational venture, arising from contacts with Protestant missions, but entirely at Indian initiative, was the Union Christian College at Alwaye, in Travancore. It was begun in 1921 by a council made up of graduates of the Madras Christian College and was under more than one section of the Syrian Church. It enjoyed a healthy growth. The group which inaugurated it had high ideals of self-dedication which they endeavoured to transmit to their students. Not far from 1928 a high school for girls was begun, also by Syrian Christians. Although not necessarily directly for the purpose of spreading the Christian faith, these two institutions provided education for the leaders in the Syrian Church and were an indication and a means of vigorous life.[23] In connexion with the college a settlement for the depressed was operated as a means and a training for service.[24]

Strangely enough, in spite of the agonies through which the parent body was passing, the post-1914 years saw the founding of a small Russian Orthodox enterprise in Malabar. A priest established an *ashram* and was joined by another priest of his church. Contacts were primarily with Syrian Christians.[25]

In the first of the world wars, Roman Catholic missions, drawing as they did the larger proportion of their missionaries from belligerent nations on the continent of Europe, could not fail to be affected. Many of the French priests

---

[22] Keay, *op. cit.*, pp. 87-90; Philip, *Report on a Survey of Indigenous Christian Efforts in India, Burma, and Ceylon*, pp. 4, 11; Gledstone, *South India*, p. 49.

[23] P. O. Philip in Mackenzie, *The Christian Task in India*, pp. 215, 216; *The Christian College in India*, pp. 298, 299.

[24] Neill, *Out of Bondage. Christ and the Indian Village*, p. 12.

[25] Keay, *op. cit.*, p. 105; Bolshakoff, *The Foreign Missions of the Russian Orthodox Church*, p. 110.

were called to the colours: by the end of 1916 about fifty of the Société des Missions Etrangères in the South had been summoned.[26] Capuchin units in the North, dependent for their maintenance chiefly upon contributions from Europe, were hard hit financially.[27] Indeed, few missions escaped financial stringency. Prices sky-rocketted, funds from Europe dwindled, several stations had to be abandoned, and numbers of catechists were dismissed.[28]

The German missions were, for obvious reasons, the chief sufferers. These were the large Jesuit enterprise in Bombay-Poona, the Salvatorian prefecture apostolic in Assam, and the Capuchin unit (from the Tyrol) in Bettiah-Nepal. In the first few months of the war the German missionaries were not seriously disturbed by the British authorities.[29] Later, as the struggle was intensified, they were interned and in 1915 and 1916 most of those over military age were repatriated.[30] Even after the war had ended, the British, faced with an inflamed Indian nationalism and timorous about possible additions to the unrest from former enemies, refused passage to India for German missionaries and deported the majority of those held in concentration camps. In 1920, however, the government removed most of the restrictions on missionaries of non-British nationality.[31] Help to the church in the areas thus depleted came at first in personnel from bishops of other Indian dioceses and in personnel and funds from Roman Catholics in Britain and the United States.[32] After the war the Bombay-Poona region was entrusted to Jesuits of the Maryland-New York province, but they could not obtain passports and Rome substituted Spanish Jesuits of Aragon.[33] In 1925 the Germans were permitted to return. They centred their efforts at Poona, and Bombay remained a Spanish field.[34] Assam was at first assigned to the Belgian Jesuits, already responsible for part of Bengal,[35] but their personnel was too scanty to be made to stretch over the additional territory and in 1921 the Propaganda allotted the former Salvatorian field to the Italian Salesians of Don Bosco.[36] In 1919 Bettiah-Nepal, together with a portion of the diocese of Allahabad, was given to the Missouri province of the Jesuits and, after an

[26] Capuchin Mission Unit, *India and Its Missions*, p. 179.
[27] *Ibid.*
[28] Capuchin Mission Unit, *op. cit.*, p. 176.
[29] Schmidlin, *Das Deutsche Missionswerk der Gegenwart*, pp. 68 ff.
[30] Capuchin Mission Unit, *op. cit.*, pp. 174, 175. On the Jesuits in Bombay-Poona see Alfons Väth, *Die deutschen Jesuiten in Indien. Geschichte der Mission von Bombay-Puna (1854-1920)* (Regensburg, Jos. Kösel & Friedrich Pustet, 1920, pp. viii, 260), pp. 229 ff.
[31] Capuchin Mission Unit, *op. cit.*, p. 180.
[32] Capuchin Mission Unit, *op. cit.*, pp. 177, 178.
[33] Capuchin Mission Unit, *op. cit.*, p. 181.
[34] Schmidlin, *op. cit.*, pp. 68-79.
[35] Josson, *La Mission du Bengale Occidentale*, Vol. II, p. 312.
[36] Becker, *Im Stromtal des Brahmaputra*, p. 556.

annoying delay in obtaining passports, in 1921 the first contingent sailed for their new field.[37]

In spite of the war, the activities of the missions continued. For instance, the Belgian Jesuits, although their lines were stretched thin by having to add Bengal to their assignment and most of their home-land was in the hands of the enemy, were able to undertake tours among the Santals.[38] Chaplains, too, were provided for the labour corps from Chota Nagpur which served in France and Mesopotamia.[39]

The post-1914 years saw an expansion of Roman Catholic activity. This was facilitated by a progressive solution of the friction over the Portuguese padroado which had vexed the Roman Catholic enterprise in India since the seventeenth century.[40] Dissension was still to be found after 1914. For example, early in the 1920's the Paravas, whose fathers had been Christian since the sixteenth century and who were proud of being under the padroado, complained bitterly of what they deemed to be abuse and maladministration by the Toulouse Jesuits in the South. Some of their villages went over to the Protestants.[41] and in 1924 a vigorous defense of the padroado was published in the form of a history.[42] Yet in 1922 a public meeting of Roman Catholics of Bombay and the vicinity strongly advocated the termination of the padroado.[43] In 1928 a concordat between the Holy See and Portugal accomplished a fresh settlement. The double ecclesiastical jurisdiction which had existed in Bombay and some other ports was abolished; the padroado was continued, but in a greatly modified form. The Archbishop of Bombay was to be alternately of Portuguese and British nationality, and since the first incumbent under the new arrangement was Portuguese, the settlement had a favourable setting. The Portuguese Government was still to have a share in the filling of the dioceses which had been under the padroado, but the initiative was given to Rome,

---

[37] Capuchin Mission Unit, *op. cit.*, p. 181.

[38] L. Knockaert, *Four Mission Tours among the Santals (28th Nov. 1914-29th Nov. 1915)* (Calcutta, Catholic Orphan Press, 1916, pp. 149), *passim*.

[39] Josson, *op. cit.*, Vol. II, pp. 374-378.

[40] Vol. III, pp. 266-269, Vol. VI, pp. 73-77.

[41] C. A. Silveira, *An Appeal for Liberty of Worship and Freedom from Arbitrary and Unjust Injunctions of the Toulouse Mission against Religious Processions in Public Streets* (Madras, 1920, pp. 132), *passim*; *Fiat Justitia, or a Cry for Justice from the Padroado Christians Pearl Fishery Coast, South India, to Rome and Portugal by a Portuguese Missionary* (Madras, Hoe and Co., 1921, pp. 157, xxxii, 7), *passim*; *The Pastoral Visit of the Rt. Revd. A. Faisandier, S.T.D., Bishop of Trichinopoly, January, 1920* (Tuticorin, Velayudham Printing Press, pp. 23), *passim*.

[42] Jno. Godinho, *The Padroado of Portugal in the Orient (1454-1860)* (Bombay, Jno. Godinho, 1924, pp. 204), *passim*.

[43] *Proceedings of the Public General Meeting of East Indian Catholics of Bombay, Salsette, and Bassein Held at Andheri, Sunday, May 21, 1922*, pp. 101.

and Portugal had only a limited veto power.[44] The historic centre of Portuguese Christianity, Goa, produced more than enough priests to meet its needs and many Goanese clergy laboured in other dioceses of India and even in Portugal, Brazil, the Cape Verde Islands, and the Philippines.[45]

The interval between the world wars saw the coming of reinforcements to the Roman Catholic staff. The foreign contingent rose from 966 priests, about 326 lay brothers, and about 1,400 sisters in approximately 1912[46] to 1,113 priests and about 1,842 sisters, but with a decline to about 282 lay brothers in 1933.[47] This increase, while real, was not particularly impressive. It was not nearly so great either in proportion or in absolute figures as that in Africa south of the Sahara and in China. In fact, it showed a decline from the total of 1925: the advance was not fully maintained.[48] The Indian personnel mounted more strikingly—from 1,142 priests, approximately 109 lay brothers, and about 1,200 native sisters near the year 1912[49] to 2,583 priests, 328 lay brothers, and 5,762 sisters in the year 1933.[50] In the foreign personnel in 1930 in areas not under the padroado the French led in numbers, with the Irish a somewhat distant second, followed closely by Belgians and Italians, and with English, Spaniards, Dutch, Germans, Swiss, Austrians, Americans, and Canadians trailing after them in the order named.[51] In other words, the foreign personnel was still predominantly from the continent of Europe, with Ireland and England providing together less than a third, and with the United States, so prominent in Protestant missions in India and with rapidly growing contingents in Roman Catholic missions in China, having but a very small share.

The better to care for India the number of dioceses was increased. It was hoped that by making the dioceses smaller they would be more efficient. Rome, too, seemed to have the policy of placing missions of different orders and nations next to one another to induce friendly competition.[52]

Some of the new dioceses were entrusted to Indian clergy and bishops. It was said that in 1931 approximately half a million Roman Catholics were served by a clergy which was entirely indigenous except for its bishops.[53] In several of

[44] See the documents in English translation in Hull, *Bombay Mission History*, Vol. II, pp. iii-xi.

[45] *Fides Service*, Jan. 12, 1935.

[46] Streit, *Atlas Hierarchicus*, p. 90.

[47] Parker, *Interpretative Statistical Survey of the World Mission of the Christian Church*, p. 33.

[48] Bates, *Data on the Distribution of the Missionary Enterprise*, p. 6.

[49] Streit, *op. cit.*, p. 90.

[50] Parker, *op. cit.*, p. 33.

[51] *Testo-Atlante illustrato delle Missioni*, pp. 25, 26.

[52] The Roman Catholic Bishop of Hyderabad in conversation with the author, Dec. 11, 1938.

[53] Lesourd, *L'Année Missionnaire*, 1931, p. 43.

the dioceses and vicariates apostolic even the bishops were Indian.[54] An estimate declared that in 1930 27 per cent. of the Roman Catholics were in ecclesiastical units served by bishops, clergy, and sisters who were all Indian.[55]

A few new groups from abroad inaugurated enterprises. Thus Lazarist effort, once Portuguese, which had fared badly after the suppression of the religious orders in the mother country after 1833, was renewed in 1921 by Lazarists from Spain.[56]

In spite of the augmentation of the personnel, especially by recruiting and training Indians, it was said that as late as the 1930's ministry to the Christians absorbed the major part of the time of the clergy and their associates[57] and that only a comparatively small number of converts were being made yearly from among non-Christians. For instance, in the year ending in June, 1930, slightly less than 29,000 converts were won in all India, Burma, and Ceylon in territories under the Propaganda.[58] In the mid-1930's between 35,000 and 40,000 newly converted were being added yearly to the church.[59] The increase of Roman Catholics was mainly by an excess of births over deaths in the Christian portions of the population. The former were reported to be more than twice the latter in a given year.[60] It was also declared that in some areas more than 90 per cent. of the population was not being covered by the missionary efforts of the church.[61] In official ecclesiastical quarters the lament was heard that Protestants had forestalled the Roman Catholics in reaching the depressed classes and that some of the Moslems and other non-Christian movements were also reaching this section of the population ahead of Roman Catholics.

Yet in many places Roman Catholics were seeking to win those not of their faith and here and there were meeting with success. In the 1930's several thousand—about 18,000 so it was said—came into union with Rome from the Syrian Church.[62] They were led by an archbishop, Ivanios, who was a scholar of repute and had been the head of a Jacobite seminary and the organizer of a Jacobite monastic congregation of men and another of women. Rome recognized the validity of the ordination of himself and of those clergy who came with him and permitted the continuation of the Jacobite liturgy.[63] In

[54] Lesourd, *op. cit.*, p. 558; *Cinquant' Anni a Mangalore*, pp. 83-86, 91.

[55] *Testo-Atlante illustrato delle Missioni*, p. 25.

[56] Coste, *La Congregation de la Mission*, p. 210; *Revista de la Exposión Misional Española*, April, 1929, pp. 296-302.

[57] *Testo-Atlante illustrato delle Missioni*, p. 26.

[58] *Testo-Atlante illustrato delle Missioni*, p. 24.

[59] P. Andrews in *Zeitschrift für Missionswissenschaft*, Vol. XXVI, p. 203.

[60] *Testo-Atlante illustrato delle Missioni*, p. 25.

[61] *Missiones Catholicae Cura S. Congregationis de Propaganda Fide*, 1927, pp. 94-97.

[62] *Fides Service*, Oct. 20, 1934.

[63] Lesourd, *op. cit.*, pp. 468-470.

various parts of the country there were conversions from primitive jungle and hill folk and from depressed classes.[64] The 1930's saw something of the dimensions of a mass movement from the Telugus. One of the Mill Hill missionaries received about 10,000 into the church in five years.[65] In the same general area the superior of an enterprise of the Milan Foreign Mission Society reported the baptism of over 3,000 adults in a year.[66] In the 1920's Belgian Capuchins had an ingathering of approximately 30,000 in the Punjab.[67] In the 1930's a steady drift towards Christianity was reported among the depressed classes of Bengal, and that in spite of the hostility of Indian nationalists.[68] In the years 1923-1927 at least four new missions for pagans were opened in the diocese of Calicut.[69] In fourteen years subsequent to 1914 in the diocese of Mangalore a single missionary won about 6,000 Pariahs.[70] In nine years after 1919 another missionary in the same diocese baptized 2,000 pagans.[71] In 1939 the Bishop of Vizagapatam reported that about a dozen villages wished to become Christian but that because of a lack of catechists instruction of only two or three villages could be undertaken.[72] The largest mass movement to Roman Catholicism, that inaugurated in Chota Nagpur by Lievens in the 1880's,[73] was deliberately kept within dimensions which would permit of adequate supervision by such clergy as could be obtained or prepared. An elaborate system of village schools was developed. Yet with all these self-imposed restrictions, in the mid-1930's Roman Catholics in the diocese of Ranchi, in which was the Chota Nagpur area, totalled about a quarter of a million.[74] In addition to these gains among aborigines and the depressed classes, here and there some of the higher castes were won. Near Madras, for instance, following an earlier successful pattern, a village was established for Christian Brahmins.[75] While all of this seems impressive, we must recall what was said in the last paragraph about the comparatively small yearly totals which were being added through conversion.

In the three decades subsequent to 1914 no striking revolutions were effected in the instruments of Roman Catholic effort in India. Existing methods were

[64] *Fides Service*, July 28, 1934, Oct. 20, 1934, March 23, 1935.
[65] *Fides Service*, May 4, 1934.
[66] *Fides Service*, Sept. 28, 1935.
[67] *Catholic Directory of India, Ceylon, and Burma*, 1927, pp. ix-xiv.
[68] *Fides News Service*, Dec. 19, 1936.
[69] *Cinquant' Anni a Mangalore*, pp. 83-86, 91.
[70] Sequeira, *My Ramble through the Missions of the Diocese of Mangalore*, p. 23.
[71] Sequeira, *op. cit.*, pp. 38-40.
[72] *Fides News Service*, Sept. 16, 1939.
[73] Vol. VI, p. 85.
[74] *Fides News Service*, March 9, 1935; conversations of the author with two Roman Catholic experts on missiology, 1934.
[75] Kandel, *Educational Yearbook of the International Institute of Teachers College*, 1933, p. 592.

maintained and some of them were strengthened and enlarged. A few illustrations will serve to elaborate this generalization. In the preparation of their
staff, Jesuits, with their accustomed thoroughness, gave a prolonged training
which centred in an institution near Darjeeling and which combined Western
and Indian subjects and a period of apprenticeship in a mission.[76] It was a
Jesuit, Johanns, who sought to win the Hindus to Christ through their own
wisdom. Johanns declared that the books which the Hindus revered as standard
contained much truth as well as error. He attempted to show to the Hindus
that the truth partially given in these writings and for which the Hindus were
seeking was to be found in Christianity.[77] In a seminary in the south of India
the curriculum was broadened after 1914, with more than had been customary
of the history of philosophy, of ascetic and mystic theology, of Hindu religion and theology, of Sanskrit, and of the natural sciences. This was the better
to prepare the clergy to meet the Indian situation.[78] The Roman Catholic
periodical press was augmented. In 1925 there were said to be 112 periodicals,
one of them a daily and about a fifth weeklies, and about two-thirds in English
and a third in the vernaculars.[79] A new one, *Social Justice*, began publication
in 1937.[80] Another, *The Light of the East*, inaugurated in the 1920's and in
1931 boasting approximately 5,000 subscribers, dealt chiefly with philosophy,
Indian and Christian.[81] As heretofore there were hospitals, dispensaries, and
orphanages.[82] Much continued to be made of schools, from those of elementary
grade, through higher, normal, and professional schools and theological seminaries.[83] In the decade or so after the first of the world wars ten colleges were
founded by the Roman Catholics in the South, six of them by Jesuits, and nine
affiliated with the national universities.[84] In Mangalore a congregation of
Indian sisters was formed for the purpose of providing teachers for elementary
schools and for catechumens.[85] It was said that in the fore part of the 1930's
Roman Catholic schools cared for about 10 per cent. of the elementary school
enrolment in the South, and that about two-thirds of the children in the Roman
Catholic schools were non-Christians.[86] For the cultivation and deepening of

[76] Hocking, *Living Religions and a World Faith*, pp. 206, 207.
[77] Ohm, *Indien und Gott*, pp. 164-166.
[78] *History-Album of St. Joseph's Apostolic Central Seminary, Verapoly-Puthenpally-Alwaye, South India* (1932, pp. 72), pp. 51, 52.
[79] *Catholic Directory of India, Ceylon, and Burma*, 1926, p. 13.
[80] *Fides News Service*, March 6, 1937.
[81] Ohm, *op. cit.*, pp. 162, 163.
[82] *Missiones Catholicae Cura S. Congregationis de Propaganda Fide*, 1927, pp. 94-97.
[83] *Missiones Catholicae Cura S. Congregationis de Propaganda Fide*, 1927, pp. 86, 87; *Catholic Directory of India, Burma, and Ceylon*, 1926, p. 13, 1931, pp. 329 ff.
[84] Ohm, *op. cit.*, pp. 238-242.
[85] Lesourd, *op. cit.*, p. 566.
[86] *Fides Service*, May 26, 1934.

the spiritual life there were eucharistic congresses,[87] pilgrimages to Rome and the shrines of Europe,[88] passion plays,[89] and pilgrimages to Indian shrines, including the Crucifix of Kandal in the diocese of Coimbatore.[90] Catholic Action strove for the spread of the faith, the promotion of Catholic education, the spiritual and economic uplift of the masses, the succour of the poor and the suffering, and the preservation of religious liberty.[91] We hear of girls from middle class families giving time to work in the slums.[92] Organizations of many kinds existed among Roman Catholics which were thought of as a part of Catholic Action. Among them were apostleships of prayer, eucharistic leagues, burial funds, catechetical associations, temperance leagues, a number of student missionary leagues, societies for the publication and spread of Roman Catholic literature, sports clubs, and study clubs.[93] In 1934 a league of decency was inaugurated to fight immorality on stage and screen.[94] As nationalism mounted, Roman Catholics began to organize to assure themselves a voice in the government. In 1930, for instance, an all Indian conference of Roman Catholics, said to have been the first of its kind, asked for Catholic representation at the Round Table Conference in London.[95] Yet Roman Catholics strove not to form a political entity by themselves but to attach themselves to different existing political parties.[96] Roman Catholics and Protestants conferred on their common problems arising from the constitutional changes.[97]

India continued to place its stamp on Roman Catholics. Caste differences persisted and brought down on the church the criticism of at least one radical Indian group.[98] In spite of the permission and even encouragement of canon law, most Indian Roman Catholics were said to follow the Hindu tradition and to frown on the remarriage of widows.[99]

---

[87] *The Fifth Eucharistic Congress in India held at Old Goa December 4th, 5th, and 6th, 1931* (Mangalupusha, Alwaye, Jubilee Memorial Press, St. Joseph's Apostolic Seminary, pp. 168), *passim*.

[88] *Fides Service*, Nov. 3, 1934.

[89] *Fides Service*, Aug. 11, 1934.

[90] *Fides Service*, Jan. 26, 1935, May 25, 1935.

[91] *Proceedings of the Congress of Catholic Action, held at Karachi, October 18th to 21st, 1931* (pp. 181), *passim*.

[92] *Fides News Service*, May 15, 1937.

[93] *The Catholic Laymen's Directory of India, 1933*, pp. 1-100.

[94] *Fides Service*, July 21, 1934.

[95] *The International Review of Missions*, Vol. XX, p. 75.

[96] *Report of the Twenty-Eighth Annual General Meeting of the Catholic Indian Association of Southern India, held at Madras on the 29th September, 1939* (Madras, The N.M.S. Press, Vepery, 1930, pp. 56, 4, 5), p. 13.

[97] *Fides Service*, March 2, 1935.

[98] *The International Review of Missions*, Vol. XXII, p. 321, Vol. XXIII, p. 101.

[99] The Roman Catholic Bishop of Hyderabad, in conversation with the author, Dec. 11, 1938.

As we have suggested, the increase in the numbers of Roman Catholics in India was not as pronounced as in some other parts of the world. Proportionately it was more rapid than that of the population of India as a whole, but in percentages it was not nearly so great as that in Africa south of the Sahara or even as in the adjacent and turbulent China, although in the latter part of the period that in China seems not to have been quite so marked as in India.[100] In 1912 Roman Catholics in all India, including the Portuguese and French possessions, totalled about one and three quarters millions[101] and in 1918 not far from two and a half millions.[102] The corresponding figure for 1936 was about three and a half millions.[103] This meant a growth of approximately 100 per cent. in twenty-four years and about 40 per cent. in eighteen years.

As before 1914, the overwhelming majority of the Roman Catholics were south of an imaginary line from Goa to Madras. In southern India as delimited by that line they were about 5 per cent. of the population.[104] In other words, in spite of the mass movement in Chota Nagpur, Roman Catholic Christianity was still weak in the centre and north of India. It was by no means so nearly confined to Portuguese and French enclaves and to those who had been won from the Syrian Church as it had been at the dawn of the nineteenth century. It was enjoying a healthy growth. Yet even late in the 1930's, in spite of the wide extension over India, approximately a fourth, and perhaps more, of the Roman Catholics were in these traditional strongholds of their faith.

Although the Roman Catholic Church in India was developing an indigenous leadership and more and more of its dioceses were being turned over to Indian clergy and bishops, it was still dependent to a large degree upon foreign assistance in personnel and funds. In the mid-1920's about half of the financial support was from abroad. Some of it was from endowments and only in one diocese, Mangalore, was as much as 35 per cent. from current gifts and fees of the faithful in the area.[105]

Moreover, the Indian Roman Catholic constituency still was far from being a united community. It had a common tie in its faith and in the ecclesiastical structure, but it was rent by the divisions of caste, clans, race, and province which it had inherited from its environment.[106]

---

[100] *Fides News Service*, Oct. 8, 1934.

[101] Streit, *Atlas Hierarchicus*, p. 99.

[102] *Catholic Directory of India*, 1918.

[103] *Fides News Service*, Apr. 18, 1936. The totals given there, about four millions, are for both India and Ceylon.

[104] *Testo-Atlante illustrato delle Missioni*, p. 24.

[105] *Missiones Catholicae Cura S. Congregationis de Propaganda Fide*, 1927, pp. 94-98.

[106] *Proceedings of the Congress of Catholic Action held at Karachi, October 18-21, 1931,* p. 46.

Upon this Roman Catholic minority in India, growing, but still largely localized, dependent upon continuing infusions of personnel and funds from Europe and the British Isles, and far from being fully united, broke the storm of the second of the world wars and of the attendant political disturbances in India. The effects were more severe than were those of the first of the world conflicts. Europe and the British Isles, the source of all but a very few of the foreign staff and of most of the foreign funds, were more disrupted than by the earlier struggle. In 1943 on the basis of information obtained from the bishops it was estimated that the efficiency of the church in India had been reduced by about 70 per cent. Although some "enemy aliens" had been interned, about 70 per cent. of the missionaries remained at their posts. The source of supply of new missionaries was cut off and old age and illness were making inroads in the existing staff. The influx of members of the armed services into the cities and towns added to the work of the depleted missionary force. The United States was the chief hope of relief, and communications with that country were impeded and American Roman Catholics had already centred their foreign missionary efforts upon other areas.

In ecclesiastical circles it was believed that the day of the British *raj* was waning. It might not end immediately, but the government would, with some hesitation, be passed more and more into Indian hands. Indian nationalists would oppose conversion to Christianity and under the new conditions Roman Catholic schools would suffer and the church would be in a less favourable position. Some of the bishops viewed the future with foreboding; others were hopeful. They were clear that the Indianization of the church would proceed apace.[107] Roman Catholic Christianity in India had come to the second of the world wars on a rising tide and was much better prepared to meet the crisis than it would have been three decades earlier. It was stronger numerically, better equipped with Indian leadership, and somewhat less localized than in 1914. What the future had in store for it no one, however, ought confidently to have predicted.

As before the year 1914, so in the subsequent three decades, the Protestant forms of Christianity had a larger proportionate growth in India than did the Roman Catholic Church. In 1914 baptized Protestants totalled approximately one million.[108] In 1923 the aggregate of baptized Protestants had mounted to not quite two millions,[109] and in 1936 to a little short of two and a half mil-

---

[107] *N.C.W.C. News Service*, July 5, 1943.
[108] Beach and St. John, *World Statistics of Christian Missions*, p. 59.
[109] Beach and Fahs, *World Missionary Atlas*, p. 77.

lions.[110] It must be noted, however, that while in the nine years between 1914 and 1923 baptized Protestants had doubled, in the subsequent thirteen years they had increased by only a fourth. If our figures are to be trusted, the rate of growth, while still far greater than that of the population as a whole, had declined. In the twenty-two years following 1914 the percentage advance of Protestants was almost a fourth larger than that of the Roman Catholics, but in the latter part of the period it slowed down more markedly than did that of the other. The retardation of the increase of Protestants may have been associated with the size of the staff. Between 1914 and 1923 Protestant foreign missionaries rose from 5,465[111] to 5,682,[112] but sank to 5,112 in 1936.[113] The Indian staff, which was 39,555 in 1914[114] and 48,787 in 1923,[115] shrank to 17,323 in 1936.[116] The diminution in the later years seems to have been due to the falling off of foreign funds and this in turn was to be ascribed to the world-wide financial depression. That blow was peculiarly acute in the United States, from which came a very large proportion of the Protestant missionaries. Between 1929, the year in which the depression broke upon the United States, and 1936, the expenditures of North American societies (which included both the United States and Canada) in India, Burma, and Ceylon decreased from $6,927,000 to $4,523,000, or by more than a third.[117] Even before 1929 a reaction had begun from the high pressured giving during and immediately after the first world war.[118] Clearly the cut in budgets was transmitted chiefly to the Indian assistants, for it was among them that the decline was the most marked. However, it must be noted that in the period of financial distress the numbers of ordained Indian clergy increased, from 2,207 in 1923[119] to 2,400 in 1936.[120] In other words, in spite of financial embarrassments which made necessary the reduction of both the foreign and the Indian personnel, the ranks of the Indian clergy were augmented. Presumably this was an indication that Protestantism was acquiring a better trained indigenous leadership, a development paralleled in much of the rest of the non-Occidental world among both Protestants and Roman Catholics.

[110] Parker, *Interpretative Statistical Survey of the World Mission of the Christian Church*, p. 19.
[111] Beach and St. John, *op. cit.*, p. 59.
[112] Beach and Fahs, *op. cit.*, p. 76.
[113] Parker, *op. cit.*, p. 20.
[114] Beach and St. John, *op. cit.*, p. 59.
[115] Beach and Fahs, *op. cit.*, p. 76.
[116] Parker, *op. cit.*, p. 18.
[117] Bates, *Data on the Distribution of the Missionary Enterprise*, p. 9.
[118] This was seen in striking fashion in the missions of the Methodist Episcopal Church. —Harper, *The Methodist Episcopal Church in India*, pp. 152-155.
[119] Beach and Fahs, *op. cit.*, p. 77.
[120] Parker, *op. cit.*, p. 18.

The first of the world wars did not affect Protestant Christianity in India as seriously as it did Roman Catholic missions. A smaller proportion of Protestant than of Roman Catholic missionaries came from Europe. In 1914 only about one in ten of the Protestant missionary force were from that continent.[121] Of the continental European missions, however, those from Germany were by far the largest[122] and, based upon a country at war with Great Britain and India, they could not but suffer. As in the case of Roman Catholic German missionaries, Protestant German personnel were handled by the government with increasing firmness. In the first few months of the war they were first put on parole and then were forbidden to travel and were required to remain at their stations. Soon the unordained men were interned. This was followed by the internment of all missionaries of military age. In 1915 and 1916 all German and Austrian men not of military age and all German and Austrian women were repatriated. In 1916 the government discontinued its subsidies to German schools and hospitals. The Germans were, moreover, cut off from financial assistance from the fatherland. Others of the Protestant fellowship came to the rescue of the enterprises thus handicapped. Some funds were supplied from the United States and from missionaries of other nationalities and societies who contributed monthly from their own salaries to their German colleagues. The Swedish Lutherans assumed responsibility for the Leipzig mission, Anglicans aided the Gossner mission in Chota Nagpur, English Wesleyans and the National Missionary Society of India assumed charge of parts of the Basel field, a company was organized to continue the large Basel industrial undertakings and to assign the profits to the enterprises formerly under that mission, British Moravians took over the mission of their church on the Tibetan border, and American Lutherans helped with some of the other German fields.[123] As late as 1922 German societies were still excluded, but in 1926 and 1927 they were accorded official recognition[124]—except Hermannsburg, and its area was retained by the Ohio Lutherans.[125] The returning missionaries found that in the interval much autonomy had developed in the Christian communities.[126]

Non-German Protestant missions also felt the weight of the war. Reinforce-

---

[121] Beach and St. John, *op. cit.*, pp. 64, 65.

[122] Vol. VI, pp. 125-128, 180-182.

[123] Richter, *Indische Missionsgeschichte*, pp. 331-339; Drach, *Our Church Abroad*, p. 70.

[124] *The International Review of Missions*, Vol. XXI, p. 101. On the Leipzig mission during the war and its return and later history, see Paul Fleisch, *Hundert Jahre lutherischer Mission* (Leipzig, Verlag der Evangelischlutherischen Mission, 1936, pp. xiv, 480), pp. 309-342, 367-407.

[125] Drach, *op. cit.*, pp. 190-200.

[126] *The International Review of Missions*, Vol. XXI, p. 101.

ments and funds were cut down and some of the Indian staffs had to be reduced.[127]

The curtailment of foreign assistance stimulated the Indian Christians. Added incentive came from the general access of Indian nationalism and the desire of the Christians to have more of a share in the control of the churches. Indian Christians were increasingly active in the spread of their faith and assumed added responsibilities in ecclesiastical organizations.[128]

The mass movements of the depressed classes to Protestant Christianity were conspicuous in several parts of the country.[129] They had been notable before 1914. They were to become even more so in subsequent years.

Among many Indians the war placed Christianity under new handicaps. The spectacle of supposedly Christian peoples engaged in internecine strife seemed to many to discredit that faith.[130] Had it not been proved powerless to prevent the most widely spread of wars from originating in Christendom? The charge was difficult to answer.

In spite of the disadvantages entailed by the war, Protestant Christianity continued to grow and in the interval between that and the next world war it became much more deeply rooted as well as numerically stronger.

To be sure, the world-wide financial depression which began in 1929 and which was in some degree an aftermath of the first of the world wars brought difficulties to the missions and the Indian Christians. It both curtailed the income from the Occidental constituencies and lessened the contributions from the Indians. We hear, for instance, that among the seemingly remote Garos, primitive folk in the hills in the North-east, the depression led to a decline in the giving by the Christians, a smaller number of church-workers employed by them, and a consequent decrease in baptisms.[131] This, however, was relatively temporary and had been overcome by the time of the second world struggle.

In the three decades which followed 1914 for Protestants as for Roman Catholics the foreigners' share of the propagation of the Christian faith was predominantly by organizations represented before that year. In the ten years before 1932 thirty-four new Protestant societies are said to have entered

---

[127] *The International Review of Missions*, Vol. V, p. 38, Vol. VII, p. 31.
[128] *The International Review of Missions*, Vol. V, p. 40, Vol. VI, pp. 30, 31, Vol. VII, p. 29.
[129] *The International Review of Missions*, Vol. V, p. 44, Vol. VI, pp. 32, 33, Vol. VII, p. 30.
[130] Buck, *Christianity Tested*, pp. 35 ff.
[131] *Annual Report of F. W. Harvey for the year 1935* (American Baptist Foreign Mission Society, mimeographed).

India,[132] but none of them attained the dimensions of the largest of those which had come in the pre-1914 era.

Protestants were by no means content with merely holding the gains made in the pre-1914 period. They were, on the contrary, reaching out actively to the non-Christians. Early in the 1930's it was reported that political uncertainty had made for increased willingness in many quarters to listen to the Christian message.[133] It was held to be a hopeful evidence of deepening life in the churches that much of the initiative was now taken by Indian pastors[134] and that the first Indian to become an Anglican bishop, Azariah, was outstanding in organizing and stimulating the members of his diocese to reach their non-Christian neighbours. One of Azariah's achievements was to dispense with paid evangelists and to place responsibility for the spread of the faith squarely upon the voluntary efforts of the Christians.[135]

As before 1914, the influx into Protestant Christianity was largely by mass movements. It seemed natural that in a land where social cohesion counted for much there should be a tendency for a group as a whole to adopt the Christian faith. There were many of these movements after 1914 and in various parts of the country. They were largely, as heretofore, among the depressed classes and hill tribes of primitive culture. They were accelerated by the growing restlessness among the untouchables and attempts to achieve better conditions for themselves and their children.[136]

Some of the native princes opposed the conversion of their subjects from the depressed classes, fearing that with the education which would follow they would be unwilling to abide in their servile status.[137] Numbers of converts,

[132] *The Missionary Review of the World*, Vol. LV, pp. 517, 518.

[133] *The International Review of Missions*, Vol. XXIII, pp. 40, 41.

[134] Paton, *Christianity in the Eastern Conflicts*, p. 90.

[135] Paton, *op. cit.*, p. 92; *Church Missionary Society Mass Movement Surveys. India, 1927*; W. W. Cash in the presence of the author, June 5, 1936.

[136] *The International Review of Missions*, Vol. XXVIII, p. 29; *Church Missionary Society Mass Movement Surveys. India, 1927*; Pickett, *Christian Mass Movements in India*, p. 52; *Survey of the Evangelistic Work of the Punjab Mission of the Presbyterian Church in the U.S.A., 1929* (prepared by order of the India Council, pp. vii, 239), pp. 15 ff.; F. Whittaker, *The Growing Church among the Bhils*, in *The National Christian Council Review*, Vol. LIX, pp. 309-315; V. S. Azariah and Henry Whitehead, *Christ in the Indian Villages* (London, Student Christian Movement Press, 1930, pp. 115), *passim*; Stephen Neill, *Annals of an Indian Parish* (London, Church Missionary Society, 1934, pp. x, 68), *passim*; W. J. Noble, *Flood Tide in India. An Eye-Witness' Account of the Mass Movements* (London, The Cargate Press, 1937, pp. 92 ff.), *passim*; Godfrey Phillips, *The Untouchables' Quest* (London, Edinburgh House Press, 1936, pp. 95), *passim*; W. S. Hunt, *India's Outcastes. A New Era* (London, Church Missionary Society, 1924, pp. 113), *passim*. For vivid pictures of mass movement outcastes see Young, *Seen and Heard in a Punjab Village, passim*.

[137] Bisbee, *Adventures with Christ in Mystic India*, p. 63.

moreover, met with petty persecution by non-Christians, such as denial of access to wells, beatings, the molestation of their women, and payment in coarse instead of good grain.[138] Many Indian Christians, too, were severely critical of the large accessions from the lowest social strata, for they feared a decline in the literacy of the Christian groups, were apprehensive over the possible introduction of child marriage and child widows from the new converts, and were sensitive because of the sneers of non-Christians that the Christians were from the meanest elements of society.[139]

Some missionaries wished early baptism of the mass movement inquirers with careful instruction later. Others desired prolonged instruction and rather formidable requirements. Observation seemed to show, however, that more important was adequate provision for pastoral care, instruction, fellowship, and worship after baptism.[140] The reduction of available funds in the late 1920's and the 1930's with the consequent reduction of the staffs of Indian pastors and teachers led to the enforced neglect of thousands of the converts.[141]

Not all of the converts were from the lowest social levels. Something of a mass movement was witnessed among the Sudras in the Telugu country. The Sudras there constituted the bulk of the population and might be called middle class, although some were poverty-stricken. One of the reasons for their becoming Christians seems to have been the impression made upon them by the changes wrought by the faith in their neighbours of depressed stock.[142] Here and there a few came from the higher castes, Kshatriyas and Brahmins.[143] Not many Moslems became Christians and in some areas little attempt was made to reach them.[144] Yet the Henry Martyn School of Islamics, in Lahore, won for itself an enlarging place as a centre for preparing missionaries to Moslems.[145]

The motives which led non-Christians to become Christians were varied, as they had been before 1914 and as they had always been in every land. For many from the depressed groups it was a desire to be treated with more respect and to be freed from hereditary degrading occupations. Numbers wished better opportunities for their children than they themselves had en-

[138] Manikam, *The Christian College and the Christian Community*, p. 58.

[139] Pickett, *op. cit.*, pp. 315-317.

[140] Pickett, *op. cit.*, pp. 236-248.

[141] Pickett, *op. cit.*, p. 227.

[142] Azariah in *The International Review of Missions*, Vol. XXI, pp. 457-467; Pickett, *op. cit.*, pp. 294-312; *The Christian College in India*, pp. 59-61.

[143] Pickett, *op. cit.*, pp. 296, 297; Nicol Macnicol in the presence of the author, Nov. 3, 1934.

[144] Gledstone, *South India*, p. 30.

[145] *The Conference of Missionary Societies of Great Britain and Ireland. Report of the Twenty-second Annual Conference*, June 14-17, 1933, p. 49.

joyed.[146] Some were under the impression that by becoming Christians they could escape forced labour at low wages.[147] Others hoped by accepting Christian instruction to obtain financial assistance from the missionary, the payment of debts,[148] employment, or scholarship aid in school.[149] Here and there were those who wished better positions with the government and boasted that the King-Emperor was their brother in Christian faith.[150] One woman sought baptism in consequence of a dream.[151] Another woman, a Brahmin, childless, and wishing a son, vowed to dedicate the son to the Christians' God if she could have her desire, and, after the son came, kept her word and also won her husband to the faith.[152] A teacher in a college became a Christian because of the contrast between a Hindu conception that the blood of the Brahmin was different from that of the non-Brahmin and the Christian teaching that God had made of one blood all nations that dwelt on the face of the earth.[153] The sudden death of a young man soon after his baptism was known to have hindered for years the progress of the church in his village.[154] One missionary with wide experience with mass movements declared that back of each of them was usually some individual with a deep religious hunger or with a religious experience, and that he had known of converts in Travancore to remain true to their Christian faith even though their cattle died and the non-Christians declared this to be a sign of the displeasure of the gods.[155]

As we saw in our account of India in the nineteenth century,[156] Protestant missions paid much attention to education. This was in part because of the large place which missions, and particularly those of Protestants, gave to education in their programme and in part because of the financial assistance which the Government of India accorded to schools, if these maintained the standards set by it for them, whether they were Christian or non-Christian. In India, as in many other parts of the world, missions, and especially Protestant missions, were pioneers in introducing education of an Occidental type. In 1930 the Christian Church is said to have had in India 55 colleges, 346 high schools, 571 middle schools, 11,414 primary schools, 108 training schools, and

---

[146] Pickett, op. cit., pp. 136, 156-168, 235.
[147] Young, Seen and Heard in a Punjab Village, pp. 135, 138.
[148] Fleming, Ethical Issues Confronting World Christians, p. 37.
[149] Culshaw, A Missionary Looks at his Job, pp. 63 ff.
[150] Pickett, op. cit., pp. 53-57.
[151] Neill, Out of Bondage. Christ and the Indian Village, pp. 52, 53.
[152] Curtis, Civitas Dei, pp. 147-150.
[153] Jones, Christ's Alternative to Communism, p. 208.
[154] Culshaw, op. cit., p. 67.
[155] Frank Whittaker in the presence of the author, Dec. 21, 1938.
[156] Vol. VI, pp. 188-190.

203 schools of special character, or, all told, about a sixteenth of all educational institutions in the country.[157] These totals seem to have included both Roman Catholic and Protestant enterprises, but the latter appear to have stressed education even more than did the former. Another set of figures seems to indicate that 6 per cent. of all schools and of all pupils in India were under Protestant auspices, or about as large a proportion as the other group of statistics assigned to all Christian educational enterprises.[158]

Since 90 per cent. of India's rural population was illiterate, one of the chief problems of the country was that of the village schools. Here Christian missions made a striking contribution. In spite of the fact that the majority of Christians were from the lowest social strata, the literacy of Christian men was two and three-fourths that of the men in the population as a whole and of Christian women ten times that of the entire country.[159] It was also said that in the Madras Presidency Christian schools were making a steadily increasing impact upon the education of women and that in the fore part of the 1930's six out of every ten girls attending secondary schools in that political division were in Christian institutions.[160]

Yet it was also declared that by 1930 mission schools were declining in relative importance, a circumstance made vivid by the more rapid rate of increase of non-mission as against mission schools, both for boys and for girls.[161] As elsewhere in many countries Christian forces had led the way in meeting a particular set of needs for education, but when the community as a whole awoke to the urgency of the situation it was able to bring larger resources to the task and the Christian enterprise tended to fall into the background.

Some Protestant institutions, however, were still in the forefront of educational advance. Several of these in the post-1914 era won fame for the fashion in which they were training their pupils to go back into the villages and meet the concrete problems of the rural population.[162] Such names as Moga[163]

---

[157] W. Meston in *The International Review of Missions,* Vol. XIX, p. 345.

[158] L. B. Sipple in Laymen's Foreign Missions Inquiry, *Fact-Finders' Reports, India-Burma,* Vol. IV, Supplementary Series, Part 2, pp. 304-307.

[159] L. B. Sipple in *op. cit.,* p. 312.

[160] L. B. Sipple in *op. cit.,* p. 400.

[161] L. B. Sipple in *op. cit.,* pp. 308 ff. Yet in ten years ending in 1931 students in Protestant colleges rose from 11,579 to 16,018 and in Protestant high schools from 97,147 to 98,452.—*The International Review of Missions,* Vol. XXI, p. 87.

[162] McKee, *New Schools for Young India,* pp. 124-139; Laymen's Foreign Missions Inquiry, *Regional Reports of the Commission of Appraisal, India-Burma,* Vol. I, Supplementary Series, Part 1, pp. 119-122; Daniel Johnson Fleming, *Schools with a Message in India* (Oxford University Press, 1921, pp. 209), *passim.*

[163] McKee, *op. cit.,* pp. vii, viii, 140-184; Mackenzie, *The Christian Task in India,* pp. 75, 76.

and Asansol became symbols of progressive education.[164] American Methodists, to whom had come thousands of the mass movement converts, set as a goal the teaching of every Methodist to read and wished their village schools to train their pupils to meet the various problems, religious, agricultural, economic, and social, which confronted their communities.[165] There were experiments in teaching the blind to read.[166]

Moreover, Protestants were keenly alive to the necessity of re-examining their schools from time to time and of bringing them abreast of changing conditions and of newer methods. Thus in 1919 a commission on village-education with British, American, and Indian representatives made a careful survey[167] and conferences were called by the National Christian Council to study its findings.[168] In 1930-1931 a notable commission appointed by the International Missionary Council surveyed the Protestant Christian colleges and theological schools and formulated recommendations looking towards the greater usefulness of these institutions. It suggested, among other steps, that the colleges relate themselves more closely to the life of the communities about them by undertaking research into some of the latters' pressing problems, and by the extension of their activities in training teachers, in serving the Christian constituencies, in improving their own Christian character, and in increasing Indian initiative.[169] As the years passed, progress was registered in approaching the ideals set by the commission.[170]

A problem was presented to Christian schools by the "conscience clause," a government requirement that if financial grants-in-aid were to continue a school must exempt from attendance upon religious exercises and Bible classes pupils whose parents requested it. Missionaries were divided as to whether they could continue a school under such restrictions, but Indian educators were unanimous in favouring conformity.[171]

In the production and distribution of literature no startling new develop-

[164] Laymen's Foreign Missions Inquiry, *Regional Reports of the Commission of Appraisal, India-Burma*, Vol. I, Supplementary Series, Part 1, p. 44.

[165] Fisher and Foley, *Building the Indian Church*, pp. 62-65.

[166] *The Girl Who Learned to See. By One Who Loves India* (London, Church of England Zenana Missionary Society, no date, pp. vi, 90), *passim*.

[167] *Village Education in India. The Report of a Commission of Inquiry* (Oxford University Press, 1920, pp. xii, 210), *passim*.

[168] McKee, *op. cit.*, pp. 108-123.

[169] *The Christian College in India, passim,* especially pp. 85, 86, 160-177; George Anderson and Henry Whitehead, *Christian Education in India* (London, Macmillan and Company, 1932, pp. viii, 116), *passim*.

[170] Paton, *Christianity in the Eastern Conflicts*, pp. 87-89.

[171] Laymen's Foreign Missions Inquiry, *Regional Reports of the Commission of Appraisal, India-Burma*, Vol. I, Supplementary Series, Part 1, p. 159; *The International Review of Missions*, Vol. XXI, pp. 92-94.

ments were registered by the Protestant forces. Fairly extensive provision had been made before 1914 for this phase of Christian activities.[172] There were some additions in the three decades which followed 1914. In 1920 a programme of advance was adopted by the National Missionary Council and the Indian Literature Fund was established to assist its implementation. There were to be provincial literature committees and the setting apart in each main language of a secretary for writing and editorial work. A beginning was made, but the plan was not fully carried out. In the Malayalam-speaking area, a region in the South in which there were many Christians and where the literacy rate was unusually high among both Christians and non-Christians, after 1925 the main burden of publication was carried by the Malayalam Christian Literature Committee on which were representatives of seven denominations.[173]

In many parts of India Protestant mission hospitals had been pioneers in the application of Western medical science to the treatment of disease. However, as time passed, the government became active in training a medical profession and in erecting hospitals. With its larger financial resources it quite outstripped what the Christian forces could do. Moreover, private non-Christian hospitals multiplied.[174] Yet Christian hospitals continued.[175] The foreign staff seems to have declined in numbers,[176] but the Indian staff to have increased.[177] Protestant agencies were still leading in women's medical care for women. It was said that in 1930 out of about four hundred women physicians in India approximately one hundred and fifty were missionaries, that 43 per cent. of the women medical students of India were in mission hospitals, and that from 85 to 90 per cent. of the nurses of India were Christians trained in these institutions.[178] While it was complained that the hospitals were far behind other phases of missionary activity and of the government medical service in Indian-

[172] Vol. VI, pp. 190, 191.

[173] *The Madras Series*, Vol. IV, pp. 317-326.

[174] *Report of the Commission of Appraisal of the Laymen's Foreign Missions Inquiry*, Vol. IX, pp. 1-3.

[175] R. H. H. Goheen in *Third Biennial Conference on Medical Missions*, pp. 314-323; *The Ministry of Healing in India. Handbook of the Christian Medical Association in India* (Mysore, Wesleyan Mission Press, 1932, pp. viii, 230), *passim; A Survey of Medical Missions in India* (Poona, National Christian Council, pp. ii, 128), *passim;* Mrs. W. H. Hinton, *Ethel Ambrose* (London, Marshall, Morgan & Scott, Ltd., no date, pp. 255), *passim.*

[176] Compare the figures in Vol. VI, pp. 190, 191, with Parker, *Interpretative Statistical Survey of the World Mission of the Christian Church*, p. 90.

[177] Parker, *op. cit.,* p. 216.

[178] Laymen's Foreign Missions Inquiry, *Regional Reports of the Commission of Appraisal, India-Burma,* Vol. I, Supplementary Series, Pt. 1, p. 225. On a notable woman medical missionary and the medical school which she founded, see Mary Pauline Jeffery, *Dr. Ida: India. The Life Story of Ida S. Scudder* (New York, Fleming H. Revell Company, 1938, pp. 212), pp. 160 ff.

ization,[179] the importance of this step was recognized and was symbolized by the change of name (1925) of the Medical Missionary Association of India to the Christian Medical Association of India.[180]

It was in accordance with a trend in Protestant missions in several other lands that after 1914 and especially after the Jerusalem meeting of the International Missionary Council (1928) more attention was paid to the specific problems presented by the rural areas. It was recognized that 90 per cent. of India's population was rural and that 93 per cent. of Indian Protestant Christians were on the land.[181] The task was difficult, for in many of such villages as had Christians the converts were few and could not control the life of the community.[182] Moreover, the education given by Christian schools had not been planned with rural conditions in mind but had fitted its students for urban rather than village environments. The majority of the missionaries were stationed in cities.[183] When once they were educated most of the Christian youth from the villages sought the cities.[184] Yet a shift of emphasis began to be noted. The Salvation Army and the Young Men's Christian Association had been among the pioneers and the latter had assigned secretaries to the task of rural reorganization.[185] So had the American Presbyterians in Allahabad through the vision and initiative of the remarkable Sam Higginbottam.[186] In 1930 an all-India conference held under Butterfield declared that every mission should have a rural reconstruction unit. That term was used to designate a programme for a group of contiguous villages for education, health, recreation, industries, co-operative societies, and religious life.[187] This ideal was reinforced by the endorsement of the National Christian Council.[188] By 1937 a competent observer reported that in no aspect of Protestant missionary effort had there

[179] Laymen's Foreign Missions Inquiry, *Fact-Finders' Reports, India-Burma,* Vol. IV, Supplementary Series, Part 2, p. 428.

[180] *The International Review of Missions,* Vol. XXI, p. 94.

[181] Azariah in Mackenzie, *The Christian Task in India,* p. 27.

[182] B. C. Harrington and W. B. Foley, *Problems of Religious Work in Indian Villages and Cities (A Survey of Families. The Calcutta Area Survey of the Methodist Episcopal Church, 1930)* (Calcutta, 1931, pp. xvii, 100), *passim.*

[183] Butterfield, *The Christian Mission in Rural India,* p. 43.

[184] Laymen's Foreign Missions Inquiry, *Fact-Finders' Report. China,* Vol. V, Supplementary Series, Part 2, p. xix.

[185] Hunnicutt and Reid, *The Story of Agricultural Missions,* pp. 38-40; Butterfield, *op. cit.,* pp. 40, 41; D. Spencer Hatch, *Up from Poverty in Rural India, passim.* On the work of one of the secretaries of the Y.M.C.A. see Singha and Shepherd, *More Yarns on India,* pp. 18-36.

[186] Sam Higginbottam, *The Gospel and the Plow, or, the Gospel and Modern Farming in Ancient India* (New York, The Macmillan Company, 1921, pp. viii, 146), *passim.*

[187] Butterfield, *op cit.,* p. 68.

[188] *Quarterly Notes. Being the Bulletin of the International Missionary Council,* Apr., 1931, p. vi.

been more obvious advance in recent years than in seeking to meet rural problems, and that there had been wide acceptance of the principle of a coherent plan for building a Christian rural society in which church, school, credit bank, and hospital would join.[189] There were, too, enterprises of varying degrees of success for establishing Christian colonies on selected tracts of land.[190] Numerous attempts were seen on the part of missionaries to transform village life.[191]

From many angles missionaries and Indian Christians were, as heretofore, addressing themselves to the life of India and endeavouring to better it. The National Christian Council projected an India Social Hygiene Association with regional and national conferences.[192] The Young Men's Christian Association, in co-operation with leaders trained by the government, organized village games to fill wholesomely the leisure time. The Young Women's Christian Association was providing housing arrangements and social centres for young unmarried women in teaching and other professions.[193] The Young Men's Christian Association was striving to improve the recreation, health, and education among labourers in industries in some of the large cities.[194] In Madras there was social service of several kinds by a brotherhood founded by the Wesleyans and the example stimulated similar efforts.[195] In Bombay a number of Christian agencies joined in the training of social workers.[196] There was a project for improving the quality of films in the cinema.[197] The Dohnavur Fellowship sought to rescue girls from the fate of temple prostitutes and boys from the disintegrating life of musicians and actors in the temples.[198] Missionaries set themselves to the task of transforming pro-

---

[189] Paton, *Christianity in the Eastern Conflicts*, p. 87. See, too, Neill, *Out of Bondage*, pp. 58 ff.

[190] Davis, *The Economic and Social Environment of the Younger Churches*, pp. 132-149.

[191] Hatch, *op. cit., passim*; Charlotte Viall Wiser and William H. Wiser, *Behind Mud Walls* (New York, Richard R. Smith, 1930, pp. x, 180), *passim*.

[192] *Quarterly Notes. Being the Bulletin of the International Missionary Council*, July, 1931, p. ii.

[193] *The International Review of Missions*, Vol. XXVIII, p. 28.

[194] Laymen's Foreign Missions Inquiry, *Fact-Finders' Reports, India-Burma*, Vol. IV, Supplementary Series, Part 2, p. 148; *International Survey of the Young Men's and Young Women's Christian Associations*, pp. 200-202.

[195] *The International Review of Missions*, Vol. XXIV, p. 38.

[196] Laymen's Foreign Missions Inquiry, *Fact-Finders' Reports, India-Burma*, Vol. IV, Supplementary Series, Part 2, p. 482.

[197] *The International Review of Missions*, Vol. XXIV, p. 38.

[198] Godfrey Webb-Peploe, *Brothers of the Lotus Buds* (London, Society for Promoting Christian Knowledge, no date, pp. 150), *passim*; Amy Carmichael, *Gold Cord. The Story of a Fellowship* (London, Society for Promoting Christian Knowledge, 1932, pp. viii, 375), *passim*.

fessionally criminal tribes.[199] These are only samples of the multitudinous fashion in which Protestants, whether Indian or foreign, were striving to improve the life of the country.

The sweeping tides of nationalism inevitably affected profoundly the Protestant Christians and their efforts. The effects were by no means uniform. In general, Indian Christians sympathized with the nationalistic aspirations of their fellow-countrymen, but they tended to align themselves with the moderates rather than with the radicals and were troubled by some of the extreme measures of the latter.[200] While it was said that an Indian was no longer charged with having denationalized himself by becoming a Christian,[201] the progress of Christianity among the depressed aroused the apprehension of some of the Hindu members of the Indian National Congress and they seemed to concentrate their efforts on the Christians, trying to win them back to Hinduism.[202] From having been on the defensive against Christianity, Hindus, emboldened by nationalism, were wont to declare that the Christian missionary's assertion that there was no salvation apart from Christ was sprung from the arrogance of the Occident.[203] Christians, moreover, felt themselves discriminated against by governmental agencies under the influence of nationalism. They averred that in the assignment of scholarships Christians were passed over[204] and saw studied neglect in the failure to invite any Indian Christian to the third Round Table Conference or to be one of the assessors on the Joint Select Committee which was dealing with the problem of the new constitution for India.[205] Missionaries, and especially British missionaries, at times found themselves embarrassed. They felt that as non-Indians they could not take sides in the struggle between the nationalists and the British *raj*, and yet many of their Indian friends deemed their neutrality cowardice or sympathy with British imperialism.[206] Moreover, some Indian Christians, nationalistically sensitive, spoke resentfully of "missionary imperialism," meaning by that phrase that missionaries shared the attitudes of the ruling race and thereby deepened the gulf, already present, between these Christians from the West and those whom they had come to serve.[207]

[199] For examples see C. Phillips Cape, *Prisoners Released. The Redemption of a Criminal Tribe* (London, Wesleyan Methodist Missionary Society, preface 1924, pp. 143), *passim;* Verrier Elwin, *Leaves from the Jungle. Life in a Gond Village* (London, John Murray, 1936, pp. 243), *passim.*
[200] Macnicol, *India in the Dark Wood*, p. 123; *Christ and Students of the East*, pp. 40, 41.
[201] Frank Whittaker in conversation with the author, October, 1940.
[202] *The International Review of Missions*, Vol. XXIII, p. 37.
[203] Culshaw, *The Missionary Looks at his Job*, p. 73.
[204] *The International Review of Missions*, Vol. XXIII, p. 37.
[205] *The International Review of Missions*, Vol. XXIII, p. 35.
[206] John Mackenzie in *The International Review of Missions*, Vol. XVII, pp. 531, 532.
[207] Culshaw, *op. cit.*, pp. 43-48.

Partly because of nationalism, partly as the fruitage of long planning and endeavour by missionaries, and in no small degree because of the inherent vitality of Christianity, the three decades after 1914 witnessed a striking growth in Indian leadership and initiative in the Protestant forces. This was the more remarkable since the large majority of Protestant Christians were from the classes which by heredity had been accustomed to follow and who had what in the pseudo-psychological vernacular of the day was denominated an "inferiority complex." Even more surprising, in view of the abject poverty of the groups from which most Protestant Christians were sprung, was a growth in financial self-support. The indications of these trends were too numerous to permit any doubt of their being real and progressively characteristic of Indian Christianity.

A few examples, taken almost at random, may help to make vivid the fact that Protestant Christianity was ceasing to be exotic and was becoming rooted in India. It was clear that Christians were more nationalistically self-conscious than formerly. Indian Christian groups had begun to meet in provincial organizations and in an All India Christian Association. In the Anglican communion autonomous diocesan councils and synods had come into being and the missions were being rapidly merged with them. Self-support was growing in the urban churches.[208] The more costly institutions, such as colleges, hospitals, and publishing houses, still depended on foreign funds, but Indians had an increasing share in their management and support.[209] In the 1930's it was reported that in spite of the severe financial depression, the economic resources of the Indian churches were steadily, although slowly mounting. It was also declared that the quality of the Indian clergy had greatly improved and that many times the numbers of Indians were sharing in supervision, teaching, and administration than had been available a generation earlier.[210] It was reported that in several different areas characterized by mass movements the totals of self-supporting congregations were rising.[211] When, in 1930, the National Missionary Society of India celebrated its twenty-fifth anniversary, it had over a hundred missionaries and helpers in forty-seven centres in eight provinces and in nine languages.[212] The Methodist Episcopal Church of Southern Asia, an outgrowth of the mission of American Methodists, increasingly achieved autonomy and initiative. In 1920 its Board of Home and Foreign Missions

---

[208] Davis, *Mission Finance Policies and the Younger Churches*, p. 14.
[209] *The Christian College in India*, pp. 55-59.
[210] Pickett, *Christian Mass Movements in India*, p. 343.
[211] Laymen's Foreign Missions Inquiry, *Fact-Finders' Reports, India-Burma*, Vol. IV, Supplementary Series, Part 2, pp. 279-292.
[212] *The International Review of Missions*, Vol. XX, p. 31. See also *The International Review of Missions*, XXV, pp. 195-205.

chose a field in Bihar for its activity.[213] In 1930 it elected an Indian, Jashwant Rao Chitamber, as bishop.[214] In 1935 the majority of the district superintendents in its North India Conference were Indians.[215] In 1938 Methodists sent a young Indian and his wife to Africa to serve among the Indians in Rhodesia.[216] The Anglicans set up an autonomous body known as the Church of the Provence of India, Burma, and Ceylon. Its provisional constitution was framed in 1922 by representatives of thirteen dioceses,[217] and in 1930 the new body was legally set free from its connexion with the state and was given freedom to become a truly Indian church.[218] The following year an Indian was elected assistant bishop of one of the dioceses, Lahore.[219] In 1935 the Baptist Missionary Society, memorable for its creator and great pioneer, William Carey, completed the transfer to Indian hands of the responsibility for all of its work except one or two union institutions.[220] In Hyderabad the Wesleyans began bringing Indians into membership in their synod.[221] The mission of the United Lutheran Church (American) was transferring more and more functions to Indians. One synod was constituted in 1917 and another in 1921.[222] Partly because of developments arising from the repatriation of German missionaries during the first of the world wars, in 1919 the Tamil Evangelical Lutheran Church was constituted.[223] As in the government, so in ecclesiastical organization, the transfer of responsibility from foreigners to Indians did not proceed rapidly enough to satisfy all the latter. Among many Indian Christians there was much criticism of missionaries from the Occident and strains developed between foreign and Indian members of the staffs.[224] Yet this was a symptom of growing pains. Here and there Indian Christians were venturing out on their own responsibility and beginning new enterprises. For instance, an Indian Christian layman had in one village a middle school, a dispensary, and a library, and helped the farmers through co-operative credit, adult education, and efforts for temper-

---

[213] Harper, *The Methodist Episcopal Church in India*, p. 158.
[214] Harper, *op. cit.*, p. 170.
[215] Harper, *op. cit.*, p. 174.
[216] *The International Review of Missions*, Vol. XXVIII, p. 31.
[217] Clarke, *Constitutional Church Government*, p. 418.
[218] Gledstone, *South India*, p. 53.
[219] *Quarterly Notes. Being the Bulletin of the International Missionary Council*, Apr., 1931, p. vi.
[220] *The International Review of Missions*, Vol. XXV, p. 38.
[221] F. Colyer Sackett, *Vision and Venture. A Record of Fifty Years in Hyderabad, 1879-1929* (London, The Cargate Press. no date, pp. 252), p. 205.
[222] Drach, *Our Church Abroad*, pp. 57-59.
[223] J. D. Asirvadam in *The National Christian Council Review*, Vol. LV, pp. 499-505.
[224] Laymen's Foreign Missions Inquiry, *Fact-Finders' Reports, India-Burma*, Vol. IV, Supplementary Series, Part 2, p. 30.

ance.[225] Another Indian Christian, an evangelist, lived for weeks under a tree that he might win the outcastes of the neighbourhood.[226] In 1932 the growing maturity of Christianity in India was dramatically demonstrated by what was known as a Mission of Fellowship from the Churches of India and Burma to the Churches of Great Britain and Ireland. At the invitation of the Conference of British Missionary Societies the National Christian Council of India sent to Great Britain a delegation representative of all branches of Indian Christianity except the Roman Catholics. It was made up of Indians. It toured Great Britain, telling of what Christ was meaning to India. It was a vivid foreshadowing of an interchange between Christians of the East and the West and of a universal Christian fellowship in which the movement of missionaries would not be one way, but in all directions.[227]

In India as through most of the world, a continuing trend in Protestant circles was towards greater co-operation among the different denominations and even towards actual ecclesiastical union. It was not new, for it had been growing before 1914.[228] It was accelerated after that year. The initiative was taken chiefly by missionaries who appreciated the anomaly of perpetuating in India denominational divisions which were in large part the result of local environments in the Occident. It was given added impetus by the impatience of some Indian Christians with differences which were Occidental in origin, an impatience which was intensified by the accentuated nationalism of the day. A large proportion of the converts through the mass movements were not conscious of denominations and were not even aware of the name of the one of which they were members. However, where more than one denomination was represented competition was sometimes keen and might even perpetuate the caste divisions. In the Telugu area, for instance, where a centuries-long feud had existed between Malas and Madigas, both depressed classes, Madigas tended to join the Baptists and Malas the Lutherans, Anglicans, or Wesleyans.[229] The sentiment for church union, while stronger in urban churches and among missionary and Indian leaders than among the rank and file of mass movement Christians, was growing in every part of India.[230]

The most comprehensive expression of co-operation was in the National Christian Council. On the eve of 1914, as an outgrowth of regional and national conferences convened under the organizing genius and vision of John

[225] Philip, *Report on a Survey of Indigenous Christian Efforts in India, Burma and Ceylon*, p. 12.
[226] Chirgwin, *Wayfaring for Christ*, p. 107.
[227] W. Paton in *The International Review of Missions*, Vol. XXII, pp. 215-224.
[228] Vol. VI, pp. 208-210.
[229] Vol. VI, p. 205; Pickett, *Christian Mass Movements in India*, pp. 323-329.
[230] Pickett, *op. cit.*, pp. 328, 329.

R. Mott in continuation of the World Missionary Conference at Edinburgh in 1910, there was formed the National Missionary Council. When, after the first of the world wars, and also as a development of the Edinburgh meeting, the International Missionary Council was constituted (1921), J. H. Oldham, a secretary of that organization, came to India to promote the next step forward in that country. Quiet, devoted, clear-minded, and with earlier missionary experience in India, Oldham had complete success. He first called a conference of Indian Christian leaders to ensure their full participation in the new body. In January, 1923, the National Missionary Council became the National Christian Council of India, Burma, and Ceylon. The change in the name from "missionary" to "Christian" was significant, for it indicated that the body was to be not a foreign importation but in the hands of nationals. While Indians were prominent in the National Missionary Council, they had been in the minority. Nationals were by express stipulation to be at least half the membership of the new body. This organization, like its predecessor, was not based directly upon denominations but upon regional councils. Two very able men were obtained as secretaries of the new venture, an Indian, K. T. Paul, who had been a leader in organizing the National Missionary Society of India, and William Paton, who had come out of the Student Christian Movement of Great Britain and Ireland and was later to bring his extraordinary talents of comprehensive planning and administration to the International Missionary Council and the World Council of Churches.[231] Under the direction of these two men, and especially of the latter, the National Christian Council became the most successful of the growing family of its sister bodies in Asia, Africa, and Latin America.

Co-operation, thus organized on a comprehensive national basis, was extended to local areas. In addition to the Ceylon Christian Council and the Burma Christian Council, eight provincial councils, all in India, sent delegates to the national body. Each of these councils embraced in its membership most of the non-Roman Catholic organizations, including churches, missions, and other Christian undertakings, within its area. The provincial councils did not have full time secretarial staffs or maintain offices, but with varying degrees of efficiency and of emphasis they laboured for the promotion of evangelism, action on social and moral issues, the production of literature, rural improvement, and the strengthening of the indigenous churches.[232]

India saw several projects for the organic union of different churches either

---

[231] *The Harvest Field,* N. S., Vol. XLIII, pp. 43, 44, 84 ff.; Fahs and Davis, *Conspectus of Coöperative Missionary Enterprises,* pp. 57-59.
[232] Fahs and Davis, *op. cit.,* pp. 59-61.

seriously and officially discussed or actually consummated. One of those achieved, the Tamil Evangelical Lutheran Church, made up of closely related groups, we mentioned a few paragraphs above.[233] This arose out of the churches connected with the Leipzig and the Church of Sweden missions. The United Church of North India came into being in 1924 as a union of Presbyterian and Congregational groups.[234] There were discussions of including in it Methodists, Baptists, the Church of the Brethren, Friends, Anglicans, and churches connected with the Evangelical Synod of North America.[235] A project which attracted more widespread attention was that for enlarging the South India United Church to embrace Wesleyans and Anglicans. The South India United Church, it will be recalled,[236] had been constituted in 1908 by bodies connected with Presbyterian, Reformed, and Congregational societies. These groups were ecclesiastically so closely related and there was back of them so much precedent for cohesion[237] that the problem of union had presented no very marked difficulty. The addition, in 1919, of churches in Malabar founded by the Basel Mission proved fairly easy.[238] Nor did the inclusion of Wesleyans appear novel, especially in view of the part of Methodists in the United Church of Canada. The bringing in of Anglicans, however, meant facing knotty and controversial issues, especially the relation to the historic episcopate and the method of ordination. Should the orders of those in the united bodies not episcopally ordained be recognized, and should elders participate, as in the Presbyterian system, in the ordination of clergy? Could these obstacles be successfully resolved, a precedent of world-wide significance would be set for the fusion of bodies holding to the historic episcopate, especially those of the Anglican fellowship, and those not of that tradition. In 1944 the union had not been completed.[239]

In many other and ecclesiastically less significant ways co-operation among Protestants multiplied. So numerous and so varied were the institutions and organizations which crossed denominational lines that we must not even

---

[233] J. D. Asirvadam in *The National Christian Council Review*, Vol. LV, pp. 499-505.

[234] Douglass, *A Decade of Objective Progress in Church Unity*, p. 47.

[235] Douglass, *op. cit.*, pp. 47-49; William Paton, mimeographed letter, Madras, Jan. 1, 1931; *The International Review of Missions*, Vol. XXIX, p. 37, Vol. XXX, p. 40.

[236] Vol. VI, p. 209.

[237] Vol. IV, pp. 70, 87, 88, 207-209.

[238] Noble, *Christian Union in South India*, p. 26.

[239] The literature is extensive. The following is a useful selection: Noble, *op. cit., passim*; E. H. Waller, *Church Union in South India: the Story of Negotiations* (London, Society for Promoting Christian Knowledge, 1929, pp. 96); W. J. Sparrow Simpson, *South Indian Schemes* (London, Society for Promoting Christian Knowledge, 1930, pp. ix, 187); *Proposed Scheme of Union* (The Christian Literature Society for India, 1942, pp. x, 101). For a summary of developments in 1943 see *International Christian Press and Information Service*, Jan., 1944.

enumerate them.[240] Ever increasingly the trend was towards bringing non-Roman Catholic Christians together for common tasks and under Indian leadership. Through the National Christian Council and by many other means, moreover, this Indian Christianity was being knitted into the world-wide Christian fellowship.

The second of the world wars brought momentous problems to the Protestant Christian forces. First and what in some respects was among the less serious was that of the German missions. Of these there were four with a personnel which was small in comparison with the total Protestant force. At the outset of the war, thirty-eight from their staffs were interned, but within a few months all but two were released. The National Christian Council sent out an appeal to the Christians of other nationalities, foreign and Indian, to come to the financial relief of the German enterprises.[241] The response was chiefly from Lutheran sources. When, in 1940, the war engulfed Denmark, Norway, and Finland, financial assistance was given from several quarters to the India missions from these lands. Added restrictions were placed by the Government of India upon German missions, but the National Christian Council attempted to have them made as light as possible.[242]

More widespread in their effects were the intensification of nationalism, the political impasse which followed the refusal of some of the nationalists to co-operate with the Government of India, the failure of the proposals brought by Sir Stafford Cripps to compose the difficulties, the demand of the Indian National Congress for the immediate and complete transfer of control of India from the British, and the internment of the Congress leaders. India was tense, the nationalistic spirit more inflamed than ever, and the tension between Hindu and Moslem acute. Under these circumstances strains between missionaries and Indian Christians developed, to no slight degree centred about the issues of the transfer of control of administrative posts and of property from foreigners to nationals. Indian Christians, too, were disturbed by the small recognition given them in the discussions of India's political future.[243] In spite of the risk entailed in the withdrawal of the British *raj* and its protection to minorities, Indian Christians supported nationalistic aspirations and in 1943 the All-India Conference of Indian Christians called upon the British Government to promise full freedom to India within two years from the end of the

---

[240] Laymen's Foreign Missions Inquiry, *Fact-Finders' Reports, India-Burma,* Vol. IV, Supplementary Series, Part 2, p. 35; Fahs and Davis, *op. cit.,* pp. 133-135, 157, 171, 179, 183, 195, 205, 209, 210, 213, 218, 219, 221, 229.

[241] *The National Christian Council Review,* Vol. LX, pp. 164-166.

[242] *The International Review of Missions,* Vol. XXX, pp. 110, 111.

[243] *The International Review of Missions,* Vol. XXXII, p. 118.

war.[244] Some Christians, foreign and Indian, attempted to reconcile the discordant elements in the seething political and social scene.[245]

When one comes to an estimate of the effect of Christianity in the three decades subsequent to 1914, one is impressed with the fact that it was essentially a continuation and, in general, an augmentation of that which had been in progress in a half century or more before that date.

It was quite clear that Christianity had grown rapidly in numerical strength. While only about 2 per cent. of the population, Christians were proportionately a more considerable part of India in 1944 than in 1914. By the official census of 1911 Christians within those portions of India controlled by Great Britain were 3,676,122, of whom about two-thirds were in British India and about one-third in the native states.[246] To these must be added those in Portuguese and French India, between a third and a half million,[247] making a total of not far from four millions. The census of 1941 seems to have given too low a figure, and careful estimates appear to show the total of Christians in that year as between 7,750,000 and 8,000,000.[248] That is to say, Christians had about doubled in thirty years. The rate of increase by decades is reported to have been, from 1901 to 1911 34 per cent., from 1911 to 1921 25 per cent., and from 1921 to 1931 32.6 per cent. Between 1921 and 1931 the population of India was augmented by 10 per cent., the Hindu total by 10.4 per cent., the Moslem community by 13 per cent., and the Sikhs by 33 per cent. Non-Roman Catholic Christians are reported to have grown by 41 per cent. In the decade 1921-1931 the section having the largest proportionate increase of Christians was Hyderabad, where the percentage of growth was 141.6. Travancore was next with 36.8 per cent., then the Central Provinces with 31.6 per cent., and the Madras Presidency with 29.9 per cent.[249] In other words, Christians were still most numerous in the South and were multiplying the most rapidly, both in gross totals and proportionately, in the Deccan and the South. They were still weakest in the Indo-Gangetic plain, the classic strongholds of the dominant faiths of India, Hinduism and Islam. It was interesting that the number of

---

[244] *The International Review of Missions,* Vol. XXXIII, p. 29.
[245] *The International Review of Missions,* Vol. XXXII, p. 18, Vol. XXXIII, pp. 29, 30.
[246] *The Statesman's Year-Book,* 1918, p. 124.
[247] Streit, *Atlas Hierarchicus,* p. 99.
[248] *The International Review of Missions,* Vol. XXXII, p. 19.
[249] Manikam, *The Christian College and the Christian Community,* p. 12; Laymen's Foreign Missions Inquiry, *Regional Reports, Commission of Appraisal,* India-Burma, Vol. I, Supplementary Series, Part 1, p. 71.

animists declined in the decade before 1931, a phenomenon said to be due to losses to Christianity and Islam.[250]

In spite of the fact that so large a proportion of the Christian converts were from the lowest economic and social strata, their death rate was lower than that of Hindus and Moslems and their percentage of literacy higher than that for India as a whole.[251] The effect of Christianity on health and education was obvious. As a result of their faith, converts from the depressed classes came to regard lying, stealing, and quarreling as sins. Drunkenness also declined.[252] Divorce and polygamy practically disappeared among Christians, together with the practice of wife-beating.[253] It was declared that in Indore, conversion to Christianity meant the lessening of superstition, the reduction of the fear of evil spirits, friendly relations with neighbours, greater literacy, and the giving up of intoxicating liquors.[254] The same must have been true in other areas. We hear of a Christian of outcaste origin who became the chairman of the municipality where he had been a boy and who when he attempted to resign was induced to retain the post on the ground that he was the one man in the city who had the confidence of both Moslems and Hindus.[255] Non-Christian neighbours felt that mass movement converts showed less use of drugs, less gambling, and more cleanliness of person and living quarters than before the adoption of the Christian faith.[256] In the course of several generations Christians of low caste or outcaste provenance tended to attain much better educational and economic status.[257] In Travancore the Syrian Christian community owned most of the tea plantations, the public transportation services, the majority of the banks, and about a third of the rubber plantations. This was said to have been largely because of the education given them over several generations in the schools maintained by the Church Missionary Society, for in the fore part of the nineteenth century the majority of the Syrian Christians in that state were day labourers and poor.[258]

Christianity clearly made for a better status for women, with a nearer approach to equality with men. Although by the census of 1921 in percentage

[250] *Fides News Service*, Oct. 19, 1935; *Social and Economic News.* Issued by the Department of Social and Industrial Research and Counsel of the International Missionary Council, Apr., 1933, pp. 6, 7.

[251] Azariah in Mackenzie, *The Christian Task in India*, pp. 27-36.

[252] Macnicol, *India in the Dark Wood*, p. 160; Winslow, *Christa Seva Sangha*, p. 26.

[253] Pickett, *Christian Mass Movements in India*, pp. 193-195.

[254] Manikam, *op. cit.*, p. 60; Wiser, *Behind Mud Walls*, pp. 57 ff.

[255] Jones, *Christ's Alternative to Communism*, p. 158.

[256] Pickett, *op. cit.*, pp. 198-212. See also Chirgwin, *Wayfaring for Christ*, pp. 90-92.

[257] Pickett, *op. cit.*, pp. 266, 271, 273.

[258] Davis. *The Economic and Social Environment of the Younger Churches*, pp. 73, 74, 81.

of literacy Christian men, while ahead of Hindus, Sikhs, and Moslems, were behind Parsees, Jains, and Buddhists, in the literacy of their women Christians were in advance of every other religious group except the Parsees[259]—and the Christians were mostly from the wild tribes and the outcastes and the Parsees had for unnumbered generations been a small, wealthy, urban minority. A large proportion of the churches gave equal voting rights to men and women, and women held many important church offices.[260]

Christianity made for the lessening of caste distinctions. Thus one of the Indian princes, when asked why he had eliminated caste regulations in his domains, said that he had caught the inspiration in one of the mission hospitals.[261] In some sections, at least in the South, Christians from the castes worshipped with those of outcaste origin and received the ministrations of pastors and teachers of outcaste provenance.[262]

It must not be thought that these achievements of Christianity were uniform. Among many who bore the Christian name the characteristic fruits of the faith were painfully lacking. The degree of Christian attainment varied from area to area, and in some was very low. There were instances of the persistence of pagan festivals and marriage customs and of Christians owning pagan shrines.[263] Caste differences tended to survive, even though weakened, and marriage across caste lines to be difficult.[264] In some places attendance at church services was very irregular and many of the children of Christians were allowed to grow up unbaptized.[265] There were sections where numbers of the village Christians possessed idols, maintained a connexion with Hindu temples and priests, and preserved the symbolic Hindu lock of hair.[266] In the Punjab some Christians gave to the Moslem holy man two to five times in wheat or cash what they contributed to the support of their own pastors.[267] In one area about half the boys and girls from Christian families married under fifteen years of age,[268] thus conforming to pre-Christian custom. There were Chris-

---

[259] Laymen's Foreign Missions Inquiry, *Fact-Finders' Reports, India-Burma,* Vol. IV, Supplementary Series, Part 2, p. 320.

[260] Laymen's Foreign Missions Inquiry, *Fact-Finders' Report, India-Burma,* Vol. IV, Supplementary Series, Part 2, p. 541.

[261] *The Missionary Herald,* Vol. CXXIX, p. 37.

[262] Azariah in *The International Review of Missions,* Vol. XXI, pp. 457-467; Pickett, *op. cit.,* p. 304.

[263] Pickett, *op. cit.,* pp. 168-197.

[264] Pickett, *op. cit.,* pp. 207, 304; Gledstone, *South India,* pp. 58, 59.

[265] Harrington and Foley, *Problems of Religious Work in Indian Villages and Cities,* pp. 12-14.

[266] Harrington and Foley, *op. cit.,* p. 45; Laymen's Foreign Missions Inquiry, *Fact-Finders' Reports, India-Burma,* Vol. IV, Supplementary Series, Part 2, pp. 224 ff.

[267] Davis, *The Economic and Social Environment of the Younger Churches,* p. 53.

[268] Harrington and Foley, *op. cit.,* p. 16.

tians who were addicted to drink.[269] Belief in lucky and unlucky days persisted among many.[270] In one village, Christian for generations, the practice of Christian virtues was on a high level, but in another Christian village, not many miles away, crass ignorance of Christian truths existed.[271] On occasion a Bible woman used the Scriptures as a charm to drive out illness.[272] One Brahmin who had become a Christian was deeply disillusioned by the sexual irregularities among Christians of outcaste background and declared them to be greater than would be tolerated among Hindus of caste status.[273] One missionary reported of some Christian communities of long standing that their faith was conventional and jealousies were cherished.[274] In India as elsewhere not all who called themselves Christians honoured their profession by their lives. Yet the general trend was towards a conformity to Christian ideals and the failures were the exceptions.

Outside circles which were professedly of that faith Christianity also made itself felt in Indian life. It continued to contribute to the modification of the status of women, for it was largely responsible for initiating education for members of that sex and it was noted that the position of widows in Hinduism was improving and that polygamy among Moslems was declining. By the 1930's the leadership in the women's movement had begun to pass to others than Christians, but Christians continued to contribute to it.[275] The fact that Lord Irwin, Viceroy during a period of tenseness between the British *raj* and the Indian nationalists, was a deeply devout Christian and fulfilled the difficult duties of his high office in that spirit is said to have contributed greatly to the peaceable adjustment of the differences which he sought to compose.[276] The movement of untouchables into Christianity stimulated some of the Hindus to seek to improve the condition of those who remained non-Christian.[277] A life of Mohammed for children showed the influence of the example of Christ.[278] Gandhi had Christians among his chief lieutenants and presumably these contributed through him to his phenomenal moulding of India.[279] It was said that the Indian term *ahimsa*, widely used by Hindus, owed to Christianity the

---

[269] Gledstone, *op. cit.*, pp. 58, 59; Manikam, *op. cit.*, p. 31; Neill, *Out of Bondage*, p. 65.
[270] Neill, *op. cit.*, p. 31.
[271] Neill, *op. cit.*, pp. 94-106.
[272] Bisbee, *Adventures with Christ in Mystic India*, p. 71.
[273] A missionary from his own experience to the author, Dec. 2, 1931.
[274] Christlieb, *Indian Neighbours*, pp. 10 ff.
[275] *The International Review of Missions*, Vol. XXI, pp. 67-69.
[276] W. Paton in *The International Review of Missions*, Vol. XX, p. 382.
[277] *The International Review of Missions*, Vol. XXVIII, p. 29.
[278] Buck, *Christianity Tested*, p. 53.
[279] F. Whittaker to the author, Oct., 1940.

alteration of its connotation from passive harmlessness or "hands off" to posi
tive and active redemptive love.[280] Although those who called themselves by
the Christian name and were baptized were largely limited to certain social
groups, Christianity itself was leavening the entire mass of Indian life.

India was increasingly placing its stamp upon Christianity. This might
mean the assimilation and denaturing of the faith, but it might also indicate
that by becoming better rooted in India and partly divesting itself of the
accretions acquired in the Occident it would have even greater vigour in
communicating its distinctive message to India. Some of the accommodation
to Indian culture was deliberate on the part of missionaries and Indian
Christians, stimulated by the heightened nationalism of the time, and part of
it was almost unconscious. Again, as so often in our pilgrimage, we can give
only a few concrete examples and trust these to be a fair sampling of what a
full account would disclose.

A few pages above we noted two of the most widespread effects—the rapid
increase of Indian leadership and responsibility in the churches, and the growing movement to transcend Western denominational divisions.

We have also seen again and again the fashion in which Indians tended to
enter the Church by their natural groupings and that the faith proved most
attractive to the depressed groups and to the tribes of animistic faith and primitive culture. In spite of the efforts of both foreign and Indian Christians,
although partly erased, caste persisted in the Church. As in many other countries Christianity arranged itself by the existing social divisions.[281]

The communal principle, adopted in the emerging political framework of
India, made of the Christians a distinct political entity and brought with it
the danger of the Church becoming a political party, segregated from the rest
of Indian society and used by ambitious men to promote their own ends. The
communal trend, too, made conversion more difficult, for the latter would be
interpreted as a political tool to strengthen the Christians at the expense of
their rivals for the control of the state.

Christianity, as in other environments, could never become fully at home in
India without losing its savour. Some features which seemed essential to its
practice were alien and even repugnant to Indians. Baptism meant a break
with the social nexus; the Lord's Supper, with its symbolism of partaking of

---

[280] A missionary in India to the author.
[281] As in Gledstone, *South India*, p. 57, and Manikam, *The Christian College and the Christian Community*, pp. 28, 33-36.

the body and blood of Christ, was repulsive to Hindus, Jains, and Buddhists; congregational rather than individual worship was strong.[282] Christianity could not well divest itself of these, for they were close to its core. Its theism, with its teaching of God as transcendent as well as immanent, was opposed to the prevailing pantheism. Its insistence upon Christ as the unique and final revelation of God antagonized the Hindus, who believed in many incarnations and in none as definitive. Accommodation to India, if it was not to be fatally denaturing, must, therefore, be largely in externals.

A number of Indian customs were adopted or adapted. Following one of these, in an outstanding Protestant church the Bible was read through continuously by a succession of readers from a Wednesday morning to a Saturday night.[283] Numbers of churches were experimenting with a Christian *mela*, or festival. Others had long had something of the kind in a harvest celebration.[284] There was an increasing use of indigenous hymns and music instead of translations and transcriptions from the Occident.[285] The singing of the Christian story in lyrics to the accompaniment of Indian musical instruments was according to a procedure followed for centuries in India and became fairly widespread, especially in the South.[286] Some of the devotional songs of Hindu *bhakti* saints were adapted for use in Christian worship.[287] Western hymns were being set to Indian tunes and metres and the Psalms were being put into Indian garb.[288] The *ashram*, a form of group community living for meditation, worship, and sharing of religious experience, was an Indian pattern which was beginning to be extensively employed.[289] It was especially associated with the name of E. Stanley Jones, a missionary of the Methodist Episcopal Church.[290] The *Christa Seva Sangha*, which may be freely translated the Society of the Servants Belonging to Christ, incorporated the *ashram* idea, embraced both Indians and Europeans, and had a community life of prayer, study and service.[291] We hear of the *Christo Samaj*, a fellowship somewhat nebulous in or-

[282] Buck, *op. cit.*, pp. 104, 105.

[283] *The Missionary Review of the World*, Vol. LXI, pp. 167-169.

[284] Neill, *Out of Bondage*, p. 69.

[285] Laymen's Foreign Missions Inquiry, *Fact-Finders' Reports, India-Burma*, Vol. IV, Supplementary Series, Part 2, p. 289.

[286] Chirgwin, *Wayfaring for Christ*, pp. 122 ff.; *The International Review of Missions*, Vol. XXI, p. 82.

[287] Niles, *Sir, We Would See Jesus*, p. 101.

[288] *Ibid.*

[289] *The World Tomorrow*, Vol. XIII, pp. 466, 467; Fleming, *Ventures in Simpler Living*, p. 136.

[290] Jones in Badley, *Indian Church Problems of Today*, pp. 44-51; *The Message of the Sat Tal Ashram, 1931* (Calcutta, Association Press, 1932, pp. vii, 300), *passim*.

[291] Jack C. Winslow, *Christa Seva Sangha* (London, Society for the Propagation of the Gospel in Foreign Parts, 1930, pp. vii, 62), *passim;* Fleming, *op. cit.*, p. 135.

ganization, with its centre at Madras, and made up of educated Indian Christians.[292] In an attempt to utilize the Indian village system, there were experiments in training the *chaudris,* or headmen, in Christian villages to lead their communities in a Christian way.[293] There were buildings for Christian purposes which employed Indian architecture,[294] Christian subjects were portrayed in paintings after the Indian fashion.[295] Here and there were those who attempted to embody Christian ideals in the guise of a *sadhu,* or Indian holy man.[296] The most famous was Sundar Singh, from a wealthy Sikh family. Tall, strikingly handsome, with the face of a mystic and saint, he made a profound impression upon those who knew him, and finally disappeared into Tibet.[297] Missionaries seriously discussed the adoption of standards and manners of living more nearly on the level with those of India,[298] and some went beyond the discussion stage in practising them.[299] E. Stanley Jones became internationally famous in using Indian methods of approach to present the Christian message.[300] Charles F. Andrews, who died in 1940, was greatly loved by Indians. Reared in the Catholic Apostolic Church (the "Irvingites"), after an interesting spiritual pilgrimage he went to India in 1904 as an Anglican clergyman in connexion with the Cambridge Mission. A celibate, he identified himself with the Indians, was a close friend of Gandhi and Rabindranath Tagore, and espoused the cause of Indians in South Africa and Fiji, endeavoring to right the wrongs which he believed were being inflicted upon them. He travelled widely, not only in India but also in much of the rest of the world, seeking to be a reconciler of races and a champion of the oppressed.[301] In him as in some others India was having its effect upon missionaries as well as upon Indian Christians.

[292] Mackenzie, *The Christian Task in India,* p. 218.

[293] R. E. Diffendorfer to the author, Nov. 30, 1934.

[294] As in S. Jesudason in *The National Christian Council Review,* Vol. LI, pp. 9-11; Niles, *op. cit.,* p. 101.

[295] Fleming, *Each with His Own Brush,* pp. 54-66.

[296] *The International Review of Missions,* Vol. XXIV, p. 40.

[297] B. H. Streeter and A. J. Appasamy, *The Sadhu* (London, Macmillan and Co., 1921, pp. xv, 264), *passim;* Charles F. Andrews, *Sadhu Sundar Singh* (London, Hodder & Stoughton, 1934, pp. 255), *passim;* C. F. Andrews in *The Christian Century,* Vol. XLVIII, pp. 1421-1424.

[298] D. A. McGavran in *The International Review of Missions,* Vol. XXII, pp. 33-49.

[299] Fleming, *Ventures in Simpler Living,* pp. 7-11.

[300] E. Stanley Jones, *The Christ of the Indian Road* (New York, The Abingdon Press, 1925, pp. 213), *passim.*

[301] Charles F. Andrews, *What I Owe to Christ* (London, Hodder & Stoughton, 1932, pp. 311); John S. Hoyland, *C. F. Andrews, Minister of Reconciliation* (London, Allenson & Co., Ltd., foreword, 1940, pp. 175).

In the stormy scene which was India after 1914, compounded of ardent and growing nationalism and many diverse inherited factors, Christianity continued to have a rapid expansion. This was partly through its oldest representative in the land, the Syrian Church and its offshoot, the Mar Thoma Church, more largely through the Roman Catholic Church, and still more prominently by the youngest of the major types of Christianity, Protestantism.

In A.D. 1944 Christianity had been in India continuously for at least a thousand years and probably very much longer and yet was still represented by only a small minority and they drawn chiefly from uninfluential portions of the population. It had won comparatively few from the religions of the majority, Hinduism and Islam. These two faiths remain dominant and apparently were not seriously shaken, either by Christianity or by any other force. In spite of its prolonged presence, Christianity had not attained the triumph which it had achieved in a much briefer period in the Roman Empire, or, somewhat more tardily, in Western Europe. Yet Christianity had made amazing strides in the nineteenth century and was still doing so in the three decades after 1914.

The chief gains of Christianity, as in the pre-1914 century, were from the underprivileged—the depressed classes and the tribes of primitive culture. They were largely by mass movements. This was partly because of the greater ease with which those of primitive culture and animistic faith adopt a higher religion, but also in large measure because of the more abundant life which the Christian Gospel offered and which those upon whom the existing social order bore heavily somewhat vaguely sensed. It was of the genius of the Christian faith to "preach good tidings to the poor, to proclaim release to the captives, and recovering of sight to the blind."

Numerically Christianity was growing much more rapidly than the population as a whole, and by 1944 was probably the third in size of the great faiths of India, although still far behind the other two.

Christianity was, too, becoming more deeply rooted in India. This was seen in the rapid growth of Indian leadership in the churches, in the improving quality of that leadership, and in the increasing willingness of the Christians, in spite of their poverty, to assume the financial support of their churches. Indian Christianity was still heavily dependent upon the Occident for continuing infusions of life, funds, and personnel, but more and more it was standing on its own feet. Some of the denominational differences transmitted from the Occident were being overpassed. Protestantism and Roman Catholicism each had an organization embracing India. Through Rome Indian Roman Catholicism was bound together with that communion throughout the earth and through various denominational contacts and the International Mission-ary Council Indian Protestantism was kept in fellowship with other Prot-estants the world around. In the 1940's Indian and Chinese Protestantism were seeking contacts with each other. In becoming better rooted in India, the Christianity of that land was not becoming denatured or ceasing to be a part of the ecumenical Church.

The effects were multiform. To thousands Christianity was bringing a richer life of the spirit and moral liberation and renovation. To the depressed classes, to the aboriginal tribes, and to women it was opening doors to educa-tion, improved economic conditions, physical cleanliness, health, and greater self respect. After the Indian pattern and because of the manner of its spread, Christianity was in danger of becoming identified with certain classes and of consenting to a place alongside Hinduism, Islam, and other faiths as a com-paratively closed community. Yet it had not succumbed to this peril. It was reaching thousands outside the outcastes and the tribes. In many ways it was, too, making an impression upon thousands and possibly millions who would never call themselves Christian. Christianity was an active and growing leaven in the new India which was in process of painful birth.

Chapter XII

SOUTH-EASTERN ASIA

CEYLON: BURMA: THE NICOBAR ISLANDS: BRITISH MALAYA: THAILAND: FRENCH INDO-CHINA

THE countries and peoples of South-eastern Asia which fringed India and were between it and China need not detain us for any great length of time. Until the Japanese invasion of the 1940's they experienced no revolutionary changes. The first of the world wars did not affect them in any basic fashion. In all of them, but in varying degrees, the spirit of nationalism was growing and, with the possible exception of the Malay Peninsula, found one of its expressions in restiveness under the control of the white man. The penetration of Occidental culture was accelerated. In each of the lands Christianity continued its expansion and became better rooted in indigenous leadership. All except Ceylon were overwhelmed by the Japanese in the 1940's. Japanese control brought the sharpest crisis which the Christianity of the region as a whole had ever known at any one time. There was little or no active persecution of Christians as such and, so far as could be learned by the end of 1944, no deliberate attempt to extirpate the faith. However, most of the British and American missionaries fled before the approach of the Japanese armies, were interned, or were repatriated. This meant the disruption of Protestant missions, for all or almost all of the missionaries of that branch of the faith were from the United States, the British Isles, or one of the British dominions. Roman Catholic missionaries were mostly French, chiefly of the Société des Missions Étrangères of Paris. Since Japan was not formally at war with France, presumably the missionaries from that country were permitted to continue much of their usual activities. However, communications with their home-land were difficult and the hardships brought to France by the war were so great that reinforcements and funds must have been all but cut off. How Christianity fared in South-eastern Asia under Japanese occupation could only be known when the curtain of war should once more lift. Undoubtedly it had been profoundly affected.

316

We have seen[1] that in the year 1911 more than one-tenth of the population of Ceylon were Christians. Of these the large majority were Roman Catholics and were chiefly descendants of those who had adopted the faith during the Portuguese occupation in the sixteenth and seventeenth centuries.[2] The Protestantism of the days of Dutch rule had mostly evaporated with the passing of that regime and the lapse of the special privileges accorded by the Dutch to adherents of that branch of the faith.[3] The Protestantism of 1914 was overwhelmingly the product of nineteenth century missions. These missions were predominantly British and were mostly Baptist, Wesleyan, and Anglican.

In post-1914 Ceylon, nationalism was associated with a resurgent Buddhism. Buddhism had long been the religion of the majority. Now, in an age of acute and growing nationalism, it was declared to be the faith of Ceylon and Christianity that of the alien conqueror. Group demonstrations were emphasized—meetings, festivals, processions, and modern types of worship partly inspired by Christian forms.[4]

Christians, both Roman Catholics and Protestants, increased in numbers between 1914 and 1944. The percentage growth of Protestants seems to have been somewhat more rapid than that of Roman Catholics, but relative to the striking multiplication of the population taken both together they had lost ground. The census of 1911 gave Ceylon a population of about 4,110,000[5] and that of 1931 5,306,000,[6] or an addition of about 29 per cent. in twenty years. Not far from 1912 Roman Catholics were said to total 345,648[7] and in 1933 417,700,[8] an increase of approximately 20 per cent. in twenty-one years. Baptized Protestants were reported to number 26,101 not far from 1910[9] and 38,445 in 1936,[10] or an increment of about 43 per cent. in twenty-six years. It will quickly be seen that Roman Catholicism had advanced much less rapidly and Protestantism slightly more rapidly than the population. Since Protestants were much fewer than Roman Catholics the total Christian growth fell proportionately behind that of the population.

[1] Vol. VI, pp. 215-224.
[2] Vol. III, pp. 285-292.
[3] Vol. VI, p. 221.
[4] D. T. Niles in *The International Review of Missions*, Vol. XXXII, pp. 258-263; Schermerhorn, *The Christian Mission in the Modern World*, p. 73.
[5] *The Statesman's Year-Book*, 1918, p. 100.
[6] *The Statesman's Year-Book*, 1943, p. 94.
[7] Streit, *Atlas Hierarchicus*, p. 99.
[8] Parker, *Interpretative Statistical Survey of the World Mission of the Christian Church*, p. 33. Figures for 1926 gave a total of 364,000.—*Catholic Directory of India, Ceylon and Burma*, 1926, pp. 12, 13. Figures for 1931 were 388,000.—*Catholic Directory of India, Burma, and Ceylon*, 1931, pp. 320-322.
[9] Dennis, Beach, and Fahs, *World Atlas of Christian Missions*, p. 91.
[10] Parker, *op. cit.*, p. 18.

The failure of the Roman Catholic community to keep abreast numerically of the population as a whole was not due to any remissness in adding to the missionary personnel and the indigenous staff. In 1912 the foreigners serving the Roman Catholics were said to total 383[11] and in 1933 633.[12] In the same years the native staff was about 355[13] and 1,121[14] respectively. Both groups had proportionately grown much more rapidly than either population or Roman Catholics. It must also be added that there had been conversions of non-Christians.[15]

Moreover, Roman Catholics undertook new enterprises. The Rosarians, a native community leading a strictly cloistered life, began a second house in the 1930's in the heart of a jungle.[16] In 1929 seven Belgians of the Congregation of the *Sœurs de Notre-Dame de Bon-Secours* arrived to take charge of a hospital for tuberculosis.[17] There were active fresh efforts to augment the production and circulation of Roman Catholic literature.[18] In 1924 Italian Jesuits began to replace those of Belgium in the Galle mission, for the Belgians had their energies absorbed in their urgent and great opportunities in Bengal and the Congo.[19] As so widely elsewhere in the non-Occidental world, the number of indigenous priests was rapidly increasing.[20]

As we saw two paragraphs above, Protestants were multiplying proportionately slightly more than the population as a whole. There was some reaching out into new territory and to the Moslems, but there was discouragement over the fact that the percentage of Christians in the population had remained

---

[11] Streit, *op. cit.*, p. 99.

[12] Parker, *op. cit.*, p. 33.

[13] Streit, *op. cit.*, p. 99.

[14] Parker, *op. cit.*, p. 33.

[15] Charles Louwers, *Les Progrès du Catholicisme à Ceylan* (Brussels, La Générale d'Imprimerie, 1924, pp. 12), pp. 4, 5; *Missionary Vatican Exposition, 1925. Trincomalie Mission (Ceylon) under the Fathers of the Society of Jesus, Province of Champagne. Assistance of France* (Trichinopoly, St. Joseph's Industrial School Press, 1924, pp. 56), p. 21.

[16] *Fides Service*, Sept. 28, 1935.

[17] Duchaussois, *Sous les Feux de Ceylan chez les Singhalais et les Tamils* (Paris, Bernard Grasset, 1929, pp. 380), p. 203.

[18] *Forward. Souvenir & Record of the First Catholic Literature Convention held in the Bonjean Memorial Hall, on Sunday, the 16th July, 1922, pp. 61, passim*; D. J. B. Kuruppu, editor, *Forward. Volume III. Souvenir and Record of the Third Conference of the Catholic Reading Circles and other Associations Engaged in the Diffusion of Catholic Literature. Held at St. Anthony's College, Kandy, on April 25th, 1926* (Colombo, "Catholic Messenger" Press, 1926, pp. 69), *passim*.

[19] *La Missione di Galle nell' isola di Ceylan (India) affidata ai Padri della Provincia di Napoli della Compagnia di Gesù* (Naples, Procura delle Missioni, 1925, pp. 36), *passim*.

[20] See a sketch of one in Charles S. Matthews, *The Story of Tarcisius* (Trichinopoly, St. Joseph's Industrial School Press, 1928, pp. 30), *passim*.

so nearly constant for three decades.[21] Progress was recorded in the deeper rooting of Protestant Christianity in indigenous leadership, control, and culture. The Baptist Missionary Society placed all its activities under the newly constituted Ceylon Baptist Council.[22] The Ceylon Christian Council was a constituent member of the National Christian Council of India, Burma, and Ceylon and had a native of Ceylon as secretary.[23] There was utilization for church purposes of indigenous architecture and art.[24] In 1942, an indication of the stress being placed on indigenous leadership, a conference was held on theological education with Roman Catholic as well as Protestant participation.[25]

In Burma, it will be recalled,[26] Christianity had made its chief gains not among the Burmese proper, for they were loyal to their hereditary Buddhism, but among the minority groups, largely folk of animistic faith and primitive or nearly primitive culture. Of these the most numerous were the Karens. In the course of the century before 1914 a large proportion of the Karens had become Christians: indeed, they had a majority of the Christians in Burma.

Although the Roman Catholic Church had been represented in Burma intermittently in the sixteenth and continuously since the seventeenth century,[27] in 1914 it was not as strong numerically as was Protestantism. The latter had been planted mainly by the American Baptists, for whom the able and devoted Adoniram Judson blazed the trail.

In the three decades after 1914 the Buddhist Burmese became more nationalistic than in the period immediately preceding that year. Nationalism had its political aspects. It also tended to rally around Buddhism, to be fiercely jealous of any encroachment on that faith of the dominant race, and to resent the progress being made by the largest minority, the Karens, under the impulse of Christianity. It also broke out in riots against the Indians, of whom many thousands had migrated to Burma. The nationalistic wave rendered the course of Christianity more difficult.[28]

[21] *International Christian Press and Information Service,* No. 38, Nov., 1942.
[22] *Visit of the B. M. S. Foreign Secretary to Ceylon and India, Nov. 1931-March, 1932,* p. 4.
[23] Fahs and Davis, *Conspectus of Cooperative Missionary Enterprises,* p. 58.
[24] Niles, *Sir, We would See Jesus,* p. 101; Shillito, *Craftsmen All,* pp. 69-79.
[25] *The International Review of Missions,* Vol. XXXIII, p. 35.
[26] Vol. VI, pp. 225-235.
[27] Vol. III, p. 293.
[28] Laymen's Foreign Missions Inquiry, *Fact-Finders' Reports, India-Burma,* Vol. IV, Supplementary Series, Part 2, pp. 617, 618; *The International Review of Missions,* Vol. XXI, p. 82, Vol. XXVIII, p. 38, Vol. XXIX, p. 44, Vol. XXXI, pp. 33, 34.

Roman Catholics came to the year 1914 with a total of something more than 84,000.[29] By 1918 this had risen to about 90,000,[30] by 1927 to approximately 100,000,[31] and by 1933 to about 121,000.[32] Unlike Ceylon, where the proportional growth of the Roman Catholics barely kept pace with that of the island as a whole, in Burma it greatly surpassed it. While between 1911 and 1931 the population increased about 25 per cent., in the slightly more than two decades between 1912 and 1933 Roman Catholics multiplied nearly 45 per cent. About half of them were among the Karens, about a fifth among the Indians, several thousand among the Anglo-Indians (Eurasians),[33] but only between 2,000 and 3,000 (in 1931) among the Burmese proper. A large proportion of the latter were descendants of the mixed Portuguese stock which had come in before the nineteenth century, and of conversions through marriages and orphanages.[34] There were conversions from various other racial groups. In the three years or so before 1935 approximately 2,000 had come from a mass movement among the Chins.[35] In a year in the mid-1930's about 500 Shan adults were baptized.[36] There was a fairly substantial growth in the indigenous clergy, from 20 in 1912[37] to 35 in 1927[38] and to 66 in 1933.[39] However, as late as 1935 the complaint was heard that the clergy were too few even to care for those already of the faith.[40] Burma was served by the normal accompaniments of the Roman Catholic Church—schools, orphanages, hospitals, dispensaries, and printing presses. These were maintained and developed.[41]

The numerical strength of Protestants was greater than that of the Roman Catholic Church. By the census of 1921 it totalled 170,384 and in 1926, by the returns from the missions themselves, it was 192,027.[42]

The largest of the missions continued to be that of the American Baptists. In the fore part of the 1930's they had three-quarters of the Protestant foreign

[29] Streit, *Atlas Hierarchicus*, p. 99.
[30] *Catholic Directory of India*, 1918.
[31] *Missiones Catholicae Cura S. Congregationis de Propaganda Fide*, 1927, pp. 84, 85.
[32] Parker, *Interpretative Statistical Survey of the World Mission of the Christian Church*, p. 33.
[33] Laymen's Foreign Missions Inquiry, *op. cit.*, Vol. IV, Supplementary Series, Part 2, p. 580.
[34] Lesourd, *L'Année Missionnaire*, 1931, p. 110.
[35] *Fides Service*, March 9, 1935.
[36] *Fides Service*, Aug. 17, 1935.
[37] Streit, *op. cit.*, p. 99.
[38] *Missiones Catholicae Cura S. Congregationis de Propaganda Fide*, 1927, pp. 76, 77.
[39] Parker, *op. cit.*, p. 33.
[40] *Fides Service*, July 6, 1935.
[41] *Missiones Catholicae Cura S. Congregationis de Propaganda Fide*, 1927, pp. 88-97.
[42] McLeish, *Christian Progress in Burma*, pp. 83, 89.

personnel.[43] After something of an advance, their staff showed a sharp decline, a reflection of the reaction from the quick expansion after the first of the world wars and of the financial depression in the United States which began in 1929. In 1911 the American Baptists had 196 missionaries in Burma, in 1924, 217, in 1930, 204,[44] and in 1938, 142.[45]

The recession in the number of foreigners was, as in so many other regions, paralleled by a growth of self-reliance on the part of the churches. Although it was declared that missionary control in the central organization of the Baptists, the Burma Baptist Missionary Convention, was still largely in evidence,[46] by 1930 only one-sixth of its committee of management were Americans.[47] Moreover, racial associations of Christians, of which the Karen Baptist Convention was the most prominent, were in indigenous hands and increasingly overshadowed the more inclusive organizations.[48] Among the Anglicans there were sporadic evidences of adaptations in architecture and methods to Burmese traditions.[49] While it was lamented that the third generation of Christians, knowing nothing intimately of the paganism out of which their grandparents had come, tended to accept the Christian faith as a matter of course and to rest in it without pressing forward to fresh achievements,[50] it was clear that Protestant Christianity was taking root in Burma.

Moreover, in spite of the decline in the foreign staffs, fresh enterprises had been undertaken. The majority group, the Burmese proper, were still comparatively untouched, by Protestants as well as by Roman Catholics, and some of the smaller animistic tribes were not yet reached.[51] However, a new organization, unrepresented before 1914, the Bible Churchmen's Missionary Society, entered the country in 1924 and found a largely virgin field among the Kachins, the Shans, and the Burmese-speaking Shans.[52] In the 1920's William

[43] Laymen's Foreign Missions Inquiry, *Fact-Finders' Reports, India-Burma,* Vol. IV, Supplementary Series, Part 2, p. 588.

[44] *Ibid.*

[45] *American Baptist Foreign Mission Society, One-Hundred and Twenty-Fourth Annual Report,* p. 51.

[46] Laymen's Foreign Missions Inquiry, *op. cit.,* Vol. IV, Supplementary Series, Part 2, p. 583.

[47] Howard, *Baptists in Burma,* p. 109.

[48] Laymen's Foreign Missions Inquiry, *op. cit.,* Vol. IV, Supplementary Series, Part 2, p. 583; C. E. Chaney, *Burma Field Secretary's Report, April, 1933—October, 1935* (mimeographed).

[49] Laymen's Foreign Missions Inquiry, *op. cit.,* Vol. IV, Supplementary Series, Part 2, p. 624.

[50] Laymen's Foreign Missions Inquiry, *op. cit.,* Vol. IV, Supplementary Series, Part 2, p. 646.

[51] Laymen's Foreign Missions Inquiry, *op. cit.,* Vol. IV, Supplementary Series, Part 2, p. 577.

[52] McLeish, *op. cit.,* pp. 30, 31.

Young, of the American Baptists, moved to the Burmo-Chinese border and there soon began to see entire villages of tribesmen of primitive culture come into the Christian faith.[53] From schools in older Christian centres in the South what were called Gospel teams, of students, went on brief trips to give the Christian message and reported over two thousand baptisms.[54] Mission schools were highly developed and wielded an influence quite out of proportion to the size of the Christian community. The Burmese nationalists were challenging their position and as time passed non-Christian schools would outstrip them, but in the fore part of the 1930's a very large proportion of the secondary and higher education was still in Christian hands.[55] Moreover, new institutions had been inaugurated, among them Judson College, with a beautiful campus dominated by an impressive chapel,[56] and a notable agricultural school opened in 1923 by Brayton C. Case.[57] In the northern part of the country a scion of pioneer missionaries, Gordon Seagrave, with marked initiative and incredible energy, demonstrated that it was still possible, in spite of dwindling financial support from the United States, by imagination, devotion, and faith to develop a medical institution which served a wide and otherwise neglected constituency and trained its own admirable nursing staff.[58]

Efforts were made for the immigrant groups, largely Indian, and the Anglo-Indians. Baptists, Methodists, and Anglicans extended their activities to them as well as to the indigenous peoples of Burma.[59]

The effects of Christianity continued to be most marked among the Karens. Not all these had become Christians. Some were being assimilated to Buddhism.[60] There was, too, a movement in the 1930's headed by Thompson Dourmay which endeavoured to lead his fellow Karens away from Christianity.[61] Yet after 1914, as in the three-quarters of a century before that year, the Karens were being assisted to self-respect, education, and a larger and more independent part in the life of Burma. Indeed, their heightened group self-

[53] Howard, *op. cit.,* pp. 88, 89.

[54] V. W. Dyer, *Christ of the Burma Road* (Rangoon, American Baptist Mission Press, 2d ed., 1931, pp. xxvii, 157), *passim.*

[55] Laymen's Foreign Missions Inquiry, *op. cit.,* Vol. IV, Supplementary Series, Part 2, pp. 653 ff.; F. W. Padelford, Letter (mimeographed), Jan. 6, 1933.

[56] Howard, *op. cit.,* pp. 11, 12.

[57] Hamlin, *Treasures of the Earth,* pp. 19-31.

[58] Gordon Stifler Seagrave, *Waste-Basket Surgery* (Philadelphia, The Judson Press, 1930, pp. 174), *passim;* Gordon Stifler Seagrave, *Tales of a Waste-Basket Surgeon* (Philadelphia, The Judson Press, 1938, pp. 265), *passim.*

[59] Howard, *op. cit.,* pp. 86, 87; McLeish, *op. cit.,* pp. 26, 29.

[60] Laymen's Foreign Missions Inquiry, *op. cit.,* Vol. IV, Supplementary Series, Part 2, pp. 620-623.

[61] John Leroy Christian, *Modern Burma* (University of California Press, 1942, pp. ix, 381), pp. 15, 16.

consciousness was something of an irritation to the quickened nationalism of the Burmese. Among the other effects of Christianity which one notes in post-1914 annals were Merlin Kingsley, a woman physician, an Anglo-Indian, whose faith led her to devote herself to the poor and who at the time of her death (1927) was esteemed the leading citizen of Rangoon;[62] the lower death rate among Christians than among Moslems, Hindus, or Buddhists,[63] presumptive evidence of greater cleanliness and better hygiene and medical care; and the higher literacy of Christian than of Buddhist women.[64]

In 1942 the storm of the Japanese invasion broke unexpectedly and brought acute problems to the Christian forces. Even after the outbreak of war between Japan and Great Britain (December, 1941), Westerners in Burma had felt secure behind the rampart of British Malaya with its Singapore naval base. Before the middle of March, 1942, the Japanese had taken Rangoon and by the end of May they were masters of practically all Burma. Presumably the Roman Catholic missionaries, since they were mainly French and Italian, citizens of lands not then at war with Japan, could remain. However, Protestant missionaries, being British and American, left precipitately rather than become prisoners. The stories of their service to the wounded before their exodus and of their escape were dramatic.[65] The Christian communities survived, but a curtain had fallen between them and the churches in the United States and the British Isles by whom the Protestants had been nourished and only hints could be obtained of what was occurring behind it.

We must not entirely pass by the Nicobar Islands. Here, as a result of the enterprise conducted by the Anglicans, in 1933 there was an ordination of the first Nicobarese to the priesthood. The translation of the New Testament was completed.[66]

We need not pause long on the Straits Settlements and the British portion of the Malay Peninsula. Roman Catholics increased from about 32,500 in

[62] Howard, *op. cit.*, pp. 97, 98.

[63] Laymen's Foreign Missions Inquiry, *op. cit.*, Vol. IV, Supplementary Series, Part 2, pp. 646, 683-699.

[64] Laymen's Foreign Missions Inquiry, *op. cit.*, Vol. IV, Supplementary Series, Part 2, p. 731.

[65] Gordon Stifler Seagrave, *Burma Surgeon* (New York, W. W. Norton & Company, 1943, pp. 295), *passim*; *Missions*, Vol. XXXIV, pp. 227, 228, 346-349.

[66] *The International Review of Missions*, Vol. XXIV, p. 49; *The Baptist Missionary Review* (official organ of the Baptist Union of India, Burma and Ceylon), Vol. L, pp. 27, 28.

1912[67] to about 67,570 in 1930.[68] Protestants were not so numerous, but proportionately seem to have grown more rapidly, from approximately 14,000 in 1923[69] to about 32,000 in 1936.[70]

The population of the region was a mixture, as we saw in an earlier volume.[71] There were small enclaves of aborigines; Malays, Moslem by religion, were about the same total as the Chinese, and these were of several dialects from different parts of South China; and there were tens of thousands of Indians and a few thousand Eurasians and Europeans. Because of its tin and its rubber, during much of the post-1914 decades the region was enormously prosperous.

Almost none of the Malays were Christians.[72] There were Christian Indians and Eurasians, and the Europeans were at least nominally of that faith, but it was among the Chinese that Christianity had its largest accessions. Here dialectical divisions made difficult the building of any inclusive corporate Christian entity. Schools, and especially those of the American Methodists, constituted a prominent phase of Christian activity.[73] It was significant of the vigour of the Batak Christianity of the neighbouring Sumatra that missionaries from that people were going to the aborigines in the Malay Peninsula.[74]

The Japanese irruption in 1942 brought fully as marked a hiatus in Occidental missions as in Burma. British and American missionaries were interned or repatriated. This meant that Protestant missions came to a standstill, although Asiatic Christians still maintained some of the church life.[75] Since a large proportion of the Roman Catholics were served by French priests of the Société des Missions Étrangères of Paris, presumably they suffered less hurt, but the Mill Hill fathers, being largely Dutch, and the Irish lay brothers were under restraint.[76]

It will be recalled that in Siam, or Thailand as the post-1914 world learned to call it, Christianity had not made much numerical progress but had had a

[67] Streit, *Atlas Hierarchicus*, p. 99.

[68] *Testo-Atlante illustrato delle Missioni*, p. 110.

[69] Beach and Fahs, *World Missionary Atlas*, p. 101.

[70] Parker, *Interpretative Statistical Survey of the World Mission of the Christian Church*, p. 53.

[71] Vol. VI, p. 236.

[72] Laurence E. Brown, *Christianity and the Malays* (London, S. P. G., S. P. C. K., 1936, pp. 78), p. 52.

[73] *The International Review of Missions*, Vol. XXI, pp. 157, 158.

[74] *The International Review of Missions*, Vol. XXX, p. 25.

[75] *The International Review of Missions*, Vol. XXXIII, p. 25.

[76] For the national composition of the missionary body see *Testo-Atlante illustrato delle Missioni*, p. 35.

large part in pioneering in Western types of schools and in medicine.[77] The Thai were too thoroughly committed to Buddhism to accept Christianity in any considerable number.

After 1914 growth continued to be slow as compared with some other areas. Roman Catholics increased approximately 50 per cent., from about 24,000 in 1912[78] to about 36,000 in 1933.[79] Foreign clergy slightly declined, but the body of native priests was augmented. In 1930 a new mission was created in the portion of the Malay Peninsula which belonged to Thailand and was entrusted to the Salesians of Don Bosco.[80] Yet when it is recalled that Thailand was the earliest field of the Société des Missions Étrangères of Paris and that the society had been there continuously since the second half of the seventeenth century, the numerical achievement was discouragingly small. One is impressed more with the faith and persistence of the enterprise than with the effect upon the country.[81]

Protestant missions were much more recent, but before 1944 they had celebrated their centenary. Numerically they had even less to show for their labours than had the Roman Catholics. In 1936 they had approximately 8,700 communicants,[82] which was only about 400 more than thirteen years earlier.[83] Yet their schools and hospitals were prominent and popular.[84] Moreover, in 1934 the Church of Christ in Siam was constituted, a union of the predominant Presbyterian bodies, Siamese and Chinese, and the Chinese Baptists.[85] Clearly Protestantism was becoming more firmly rooted. Moreover, a National Christian Council, formed in 1930, with an initial membership which was about half Thai and Chinese,[86] both brought together the Protestant forces and knit them more closely into the world-wide Protestant fellowship.

The association of Thailand with Japan in the second of the world wars was followed by domination by the Land of the Rising Sun. Thailand was drawn into belligerency with Great Britain and the United States, and American and British missionaries were interned and many church and school

[77] Vol. VI, pp. 240-246.
[78] Streit, op. cit., p. 99.
[79] Parker, op. cit., p. 33.
[80] Lesourd, L'Année Missionnaire, 1931, p. 559.
[81] For a statistical picture of the enterprise in the mid-1920's, see Missiones Catholicae Cura S. Congregationis de Propaganda Fide, 1927, pp. 116 ff.
[82] Parker, op. cit., p. 53.
[83] Beach and Fahs, World Missionary Atlas, p. 101.
[84] The Siam Outlook, Vol. VII, No. 4, National Christian Council Guide to Missions in Siam, Oct., 1931, gives a good summary view.
[85] The International Review of Missions, Vol. XXIV, p. 28.
[86] Fahs and Davis, Conspectus of Coöperative Missionary Enterprises, p. 66.

buildings were requisitioned for military purposes.[87] Roman Catholic missionaries, being chiefly French and Italian, were probably not at first placed under such close restrictions. Yet a resurgent Buddhism, associated with Thai nationalism, was putting limitations on Roman Catholic public meetings.[88]

In French Indo-China Christianity had a substantial growth in the three decades after 1914, both in numbers and in indigenous leadership. Here, it will be recalled, the Roman Catholic Church had been almost the sole representative of the faith and had had a long and sometimes stormy but on the whole a prosperous history.[89] In 1912 Roman Catholics numbered not far from 950,000,[90] or about 5 per cent. of the population. In 1933 Roman Catholics totalled about 1,400,000,[91] and in June, 1935, about 1,441,124.[92] They had, in other words, increased not far from 50 per cent. in less than a quarter of a century. The staff was overwhelmingly indigenous, with about four times as many native priests and more than fourteen times as many native as foreign sisters. Most of the foreign staff continued to be French with a substantial minority of Spaniards. To this there were added sprinklings of Canadians, Dutch, Belgians, Chinese, English, and Swiss.[93] In 1925 an Apostolic Delegation was created, for the better supervision and co-ordination of the church.[94] In 1933 an Annamese bishop, the first of his race, was consecrated,[95] and in 1935 another was added.[96] In 1934 the initial plenary council of the church in Indo-China was assembled under the presidency of the Apostolic Delegate.[97] Efforts, too, were made to improve the quality of the Christians. Growing emphasis was placed upon Christian literature and periodicals and upon youth organizations and study circles.[98] Schools numbered hundreds, and many of them were staffed by indigenous nuns, *Amantes de la Croix*, a congregation founded in the seventeenth century.[99] Indo-Chinese Christians were becoming

[87] *The International Review of Missions*, Vol. XXXIII, p. 25.
[88] *The International Review of Missions*, Vol. XXXIII, p. 84.
[89] Vol. III, pp. 296-298, Vol. VI, pp. 246-252.
[90] Streit, *op. cit.*, p. 99.
[91] *Les Missions Catholiques d'Indochine, 1933*, pp. 5, 6.
[92] *Fides News Service*, May 2, 1936.
[93] *Testo-Atlante illustrato delle Missioni*, p. 33.
[94] *Les Missions Catholiques d'Indochine, 1933*, pp. 5, 6.
[95] *Fides Service*, March 9, 1935.
[96] *Fides Service*, Apr. 6, 1935.
[97] *Fides Service*, May 26, 1934.
[98] Thompson, *French Indo-China*, p. 472.
[99] Thompson, *op. cit.*, p. 473.

more nationalistically self-conscious.[100] In common with Christianity in much of the non-European world, the faith was more firmly rooted than earlier.

An interesting development was the emergence of a politico-religious movement, Coadaism, which came into being in 1926, a compound of Buddhism, Taoism, and Roman Catholic Christianity. It had a closely knit organization, was clandestine, and was eventually outlawed by the King of Cambodia.[101]

Protestantism was represented chiefly by the Christian and Missionary Alliance. That organization achieved its first continuing foothold in the country in 1911. In spite of some opposition by the French authorities, it found the field fruitful and by 1936 had a membership of more than 8,000, with a growing body of indigenous pastors and evangelists. Indeed, it developed what next to the Congo was the most rewarding of its undertakings.[102]

The Japanese occupation which began in 1940 in theory was not a conquest, but respected the French rule. Yet it brought disturbance. Serious, too, for the French missions was the German occupation of the mother country. However, there seems to have been but little interference with the Church, and that not in the nature of overt persecution. Indeed, until at least 1943, even the Christian and Missionary Alliance, American though it was, maintained communications with its missionaries and reported that its Annamese churches had full liberty.[103]

If one may summarize the post-1914 course of Christianity in South-eastern Asia in a phrase, it would be continuing progress in numbers and rootage, retarded but not reversed by the storm of the second of the world wars.

[100] Kendel, *Educational Yearbook of the International Institute of Teachers College,* 1933, p. 594.
[101] Thompson, *op. cit.,* p. 474.
[102] E. F. Irwin, *With Christ in Indo-China. The Story of Alliance Missions in French Indo-China and Eastern Siam* (Harrisburg, Christian Publications, Inc., 1937, pp. 164), *passim; The International Review of Missions,* Vol. XXI, pp. 282-284, Vol. XXIII, p. 29, Vol. XXV, p. 30.
[103] *The International Review of Missions,* Vol. XXXIII, p. 25.

Chapter XIII

CHINA

GENERAL CONDITIONS: ROMAN CATHOLIC CHRISTIANITY: RUSSIAN ORTHODOX CHRISTIANITY: PROTESTANT CHRISTIANITY: EFFECT ON THE ENVIRONMENT: EFFECT OF THE ENVIRONMENT

IN CHINA the three decades after 1914 witnessed a more thoroughgoing revolution than in any other civilized country with the possible exception of Russia. Even Russia, large though it was, did not have as numerous a population as China nor as long a history of continuous cultural development. Here was a people, at least four hundred millions strong, with a civilization which had come down from before the time of Christ with no major break, but which now was being profoundly altered. Every phase of life, political, intellectual, social, economic, and religious, was being transformed. The process was prolonged and stability was much more slowly achieved than in Russia. It was, moreover, complicated by war and foreign invasion.

The basic cause of the change was the impact of the Occident. The pressure of the West was first acutely felt in the second quarter of the nineteenth century. Not, however, until after 1895 did the resistant structure of Chinese life begin to crumble. The process was well under way in 1914, but after that year it was accelerated. By 1944 it had by no means been completed. The disintegration of the old was still going on and the reintegration had barely begun.

The political aspect of the revolution had as its outstanding feature the abandonment of the imperial structure built upon Confucian ideals which had first come into being in the third century before Christ and the substitution for it of what was termed a republic and which took its inspiration from the Occident. The change was so abrupt and so drastic that it could not be accomplished without prolonged confusion. The Chinese had proved their political capacity by creating and operating the government which had been theirs under the empire. That achievement had been one of the most notable in the entire history of the human race. However, they were without experience with the sort of democratic republic which their leaders now essayed, and only gradually and painfully could they acquire it and adjust Western ideals and institutions to meet their needs. The immediate consequences were internal and external weakness, civil strife, and an epidemic of warlords, both regional and national. Between 1911, when the revolution which inaugurated the republic began, and 1926 the course was one of progressive disintegration, with contending armies and widespread banditry. In 1926 the armies of the Kuomintang, the party organized by Sun Yat-sen and which after his death (1925) professed to carry on his programme, began the northward march from Canton which eventually won them the mastery of most of the country. Under the leadership of Chiang Kai-shek they put the Kuomintang in power in Shanghai and Nanking. Competing warlords were either eliminated or brought to the support of the government set up by the Kuomintang. By the mid-1930's the most serious surviving rival was the Communist regime. This had its headquarters first in the Wu-han cities (Wuchang, Hankow, and Hanyang), then south of the Yangtze with a main centre in the province of Kiangsi, and finally, after a march famous for its daring and suffering, in the North, chiefly in the province of Shensi.

Intellectually the revolution meant the abandonment of the former type of education, an education based primarily upon the classics of the Confucian school and culminating in the highly competitive examinations through which admission was had to the coveted civil service. For this time-honoured educational process, a bulwark of the Confucian culture, there were substituted Western forms of education, with emphasis upon the natural sciences, engineering, and other subjects of Occidental origin, and with much less attention than formerly to the inherited Chinese philosophy, history, and literature. The ideal was adopted and progressively realized of universal primary education and of secondary and higher education of Western patterns. Thousands of Chinese youths went abroad, after 1914 chiefly to the United States and Europe, to drink of the new learning at its source. The Chinese intelligentsia, especially those of student age and status, were in ferment. Old ways were challenged and new ideas were either enthusiastically adopted or viewed critically. Literature was being produced in the vernacular, or *pai hua*, in place of the traditional classical style. What was termed the Renaissance or the New Tide was in process. Chinese youth were swept hither and yon by passionate currents of nationalism and of radical social, economic, and political theories. For years Communism had its devotees.

Social institutions and customs were being altered. The changes were chiefly in the cities and among the students, but from these they were gradually making their way into the countryside and beyond the circles of the intelligentsia. They were accelerated through the cinema, the radio, the newspaper, and many other channels by which Western culture penetrated the land. Contacts between the sexes were multiplying. Co-education was spreading. Young people were increasingly arranging their own marriages rather than consent to the accepted methods of match-making by parents and go-betweens. Old social conventions were being swept aside.

The economic phases of life were less rapidly modified than were some other aspects of culture. Industrialization had gone far at a few centres, notably in Shanghai and other cities on the lower Yangtze, and in West China after the Chinese migrations following the Japanese occupation of the coast and the lower Yangtze. Under Japanese auspices industrialization proceeded rapidly in parts of Manchuria. Foreign commerce grew and with it more foreign goods were imported. The automobile came into use and the airplane was a familiar means of transportation for the few. Yet internal political disorder discouraged extensive industrialization, railways were only slowly extended, foreign trade was very small compared with its dimensions in the Occident or in Japan, and agriculture and handicrafts went on for the majority much as they had for centuries.

Religiously the revolution was striking. Growing scepticism and organized anti-religious movements further weakened the already decadent Buddhism and Taoism. Confucianism, the main ideological basis of China's life, was dealt stunning blows by the disappearance of the Confucian state and of the educational and examination systems with which that state had been intimately associated. It was too deeply interwoven with the texture of Chinese thought, morals, and customs quickly to disappear. Yet it was seriously weakened. The assumptions and convictions on which Chinese civilization had been built were being challenged and dissolved.

China's problems were further complicated and intensified by her relations with foreign powers. She was drawn into both of the world wars. Indeed, the second of the world wars really began on her soil through the Japanese invasion of Manchuria in 1931 and the extension of that invasion to China south of the Great Wall in 1937.

The first of the world wars did not affect China as seriously as did the second. Japan took advantage of the preoccupation of Western powers with the struggle in Europe to seek to enlarge her footholds in China and, by becoming a belligerent, acquired some of the German interests in that land. In 1917 China herself technically entered the war, but had no share in the actual fighting.

In the intervals between the two world wars China's relations with foreign peoples were repeatedly strained. Nationalism, a rising tide in China as in so many other lands, was restive over restrictions on Chinese sovereignty which had been imposed by the treaties of the nineteenth and the fore part of the twentieth century.[1] Extraterritoriality, the fixing of tariffs by treaty, and the leaseholds, the concessions, and the settlements of foreign powers which dominated most of the chief ports were peculiarly irritating. There was widespread agitation against the transfer to Japan of the former German interests in Shantung. In the 1920's, beginning spectacularly in 1925, much of nationalist ire was directed against Great Britain, for that country had led in the maritime trade of China and had been in the forefront in imposing on that country what were now dubbed by patriots the "unequal treaties." Hers, too, were some of the chief concessions. Communists, encouraged by Russians, then at odds with the English, led in the anti-British activities.

Closely associated with the Communist campaign against the privileged status of foreigners was an anti-religious movement. It broke out in 1922 and was chiefly anti-Christian. It denounced Christian missions as a phase of Western imperialism. It was directed largely against Protestant, and particularly British missions, but other missions also suffered.[2]

The prelude to the second world war opened in September, 1931, with the "Mukden incident," the signal for the full occupation of Manchuria and the adjacent Jehol by the Japanese and followed by the creation of the state of Manchukuo, puppet to Japan. Japan pursued her course in defiance of the League of Nations and thereby revealed the weakness of that organization and brought it into disrepute. There was no formal war with China, but Chinese nationalists were unreconciled. An uneasy truce followed with further Japanese advances south and west of Manchuria.

Then came another "incident," in July, 1937, on the outskirts of Peking, and the curtain rose on a still more tragic act of the Chino-Japanese drama. This time hostilities between the Chinese and Japanese became general. Within a few months the Japanese had occupied Tientsin, Peking, Shanghai, Nanking, Hankow, and a number of lesser ports on the coast and the Yangtze River. By mid-1940 they had set up at Nanking what they announced to be the true Chinese government and had extended their footholds to most of the main ports along the coast and westward, up the Yangtze, as far as Ichang. Yet the Chinese did not submit. The Nationalist government moved its capital to Chungking, at the western entrance to the Yangtze gorges, where the

[1] Vol. VI, pp. 257-261.
[2] *The China Mission Year Book*, 1923, pp. 12-17; *The China Christian Year Book*, 1925, pp. 51-60, 1926, pp. 80-85, 1928, pp. 6-14.

Japanese dared to follow only by bombing planes. A migration at once pitiful and heroic took place from Japanese-occupied to "free" China. Many of the people of substance and thousands of students and their teachers took refuge in the West. Schools and universities, both Christian and government, were transferred to that area. Machinery was transported and factories were set up. Effective Japanese control was largely limited to railways—and not all of these were in Japanese hands—and to rivers and coasts, for it was only here that Japan's superior mechanized equipment could be effective. Between these thoroughfares and west of them "free China" carried on and guerrillas harassed the Japanese. In Shensi and part of Shansi the Communists maintained their stronghold. Relations between them and the Nationalist regime at Chungking remained strained, but something of a common front was presented to the invader.

The Japanese slowly drew tighter the cordon of their blockade. In 1940 they plugged the opening afforded by the railway from French Indo-China to Kunming. Within the first six months of 1942, after the outbreak of war in December, 1941, between themselves on the one hand and the British Empire and the United States on the other, they seized Hongkong and Burma, thus closing two other avenues of access from "free China" to the outer world. The only routes now open were by air over high and rugged mountains to India and along the desert roads from the North-west across Sinkiang to Russia. Inflation mounted, bearing cruelly upon the salaried classes, including missionaries and Chinese staffs of churches and Christian schools. By the end of 1944 the Japanese tide was beginning to be rolled back, but only in border countries and not in China itself. American aviation forces were coming in over "the hump" from India and were successfully disputing the hitherto unchallenged Japanese control of the air, but China was showing signs of the strain of the prolonged war and the attendant blockade.

It was in this environment that the Christian forces operated. In no other great land were there more cross-currents or was the scene more chronically turbulent. An old culture was disappearing and the birth pangs of a new were prolonged. At times the setting and general public opinion were hostile to Christianity. At others, including the years between 1914 and 1922 and the years after 1937, the trend was towards greater open-mindedness. In so stormy a scene the course of Christianity could never be easy. Always, however, there were wistful souls who in the midst of chaos were looking for sure spiritual foundations and for a reintegrating dynamic for the nation. The Confucian tradition had led them to believe that such a dynamic must be moral. Many wondered whether Christianity might not have the answer. In general, in spite of reverses brought by anti-Christian movements, scepticism, civil strife, and foreign war, Christianity made amazing progress. It gained notably in numbers, in Chinese leadership, and in influence upon the nation as a whole.

To this story we must now turn, taking up successively the **Roman Cath-olics**, the **Russian Orthodox**, and the **Protestants**.

Roman Catholic Christianity, it will be recalled, had been introduced to China in the thirteenth century,[3] and, after a lapse in the fifteenth century, had been continuously in the empire since the second half of the sixteenth century.[4] In 1914 it had not far from a million and a half baptized adherents, an increase of about six-fold in the preceding seventy years, and was being propagated chiefly by missionaries from the continent of Europe. The creation of a body of Chinese clergy had begun, but with one exception in the seven-teenth century,[5] none of the latter had been raised to the episcopate and the church was entirely under the direction of foreigners. Nor had the church been given an empire-wide organization as it had somewhat earlier in India.[6] It was still primarily an alien institution, controlled by Westerners, possessing little cohesion of a national character except its common faith and occasional regional synods, and with slight influence upon the country as a whole.

In the three decades which followed 1914, in spite of the internal disorder which plagued the country and the two world wars which hampered the European support of its missions, the Roman Catholic Church in China registered a continuing increase in numbers, an even more striking growth in Chinese leadership, both in the body of indigenous priests and the transfer of responsibility to them and to bishops from their ranks, the achievement of a national organization, and notable additions to the missionary forces from the United States. The advance made by the Roman Catholic Church in China in these thirty years was approached in magnitude only by that in equatorial Africa and the United States.

The numerical increases are quickly summarized. In 1912 the total of Roman Catholics in the empire was said to be 1,406,659,[7] in 1913, 1,535,080,[8] in 1914, 1,581,430,[9] in 1924, 2,208,880,[10] in 1929, 2,486,841,[11] in 1937, 2,934,175,[12]

---

[3] Vol. II, p. 331-333.
[4] Vol. III, pp. 336-366, Vol. VI, pp. 262-293.
[5] Vol. III, p. 346.
[6] Vol. VI, pp. 76, 99.
[7] Streit, *Atlas Hierarchicus*, p. 100.
[8] Planchet, *Les Missions de Chine et du Japon*, 1916, p. 26.
[9] Planchet, *op. cit.*, 1916, p. 28.
[10] Planchet, *op. cit.*, 1925, p. xiv.
[11] *Fides News Service*, May 18, 1940.
[12] *Fides News Service*, Apr. 9, 1938.

in 1939, 3,182,950,[13] and in 1941, 3,262,678.[14] Another set of figures for 1939 gives the total as 3,172,504.[15] In other words, Roman Catholics in China about doubled in the twenty-five years from 1914 to 1939.[16] The rate of growth had slowed down from the earlier years of the century, for in the thirteen years between 1901 and 1914, or only a little more than half the time between 1914 and 1939, the increase had been from 720,540[17] to 1,581,430,[18] or more than 100 per cent. Since in 1894 the total is said to have been 581,575,[19] the number had almost trebled in the twenty years between 1894 and 1914 as against the doubling in the twenty-five years after 1914. While the quarter of a century after 1914 had been marked by much civil war and an anti-Christian movement extending over several years, it had not seen any persecution with an attendant toll of martyrdoms even approaching the Boxer storm in the preceding period of two decades.

Roman Catholics, while still showing an amazing increment, were not multiplying as rapidly as in the years immediately after 1895. That period, however, had been the one in which resistance to Western culture had collapsed and in which the revolution of Chinese civilization and the eager learning from the Occident had set in with a rush. In the half century preceding 1894, when, in spite of the battering of defeats at the hands of Great Britain and France and the infiltration of Western commerce and missions, the structure of China's traditional life had remained almost intact, the total of Roman Catholics appears only to have doubled.[20] After 1914, even though the revolution proceeded with quickened pace, the attitude towards what was coming in from the Occident became slightly more critical.

As before 1914, the growth of Roman Catholics was most pronounced in the coastal provinces, the provinces of the Yangtze Valley east of the gorges, and in Szechwan and Inner Mongolia. There were still more Roman Catholics in Chihli (later called Hopei) than in any other province, with Kiangsu second, Shantung third, Szechwan fourth, and Inner Mongolia fifth.[21]

The staff, both foreign and Chinese, of the Roman Catholic Church in

---

[13] *Fides News Service,* May 18, 1940.

[14] *Lumen Service,* June 20, 1941.

[15] *Les Missions de Chine, Quinzième Année,* p. 450.

[16] For sets of figures which vary slightly but not greatly from the ones on which this generalization is based, see Lesourd, *L'Année Missionnaire, 1931,* p. 122, and *Revue d'Histoire des Missions,* Vol. VIII, pp. 135-137.

[17] *Missiones Catholicae Cura S. Congregationis de Propaganda Fide,* 1907, table 44.

[18] Planchet, *op. cit.,* 1916, p. 28.

[19] *Missiones Catholicae Cura S. Congregationis de Propaganda Fide,* 1895, p. 311.

[20] *Notizie Statistiche delle Missioni di Tutto il Mondo Dipendenti Dalla S. C. de Propaganda Fide,* 1844, pp. 557-572.

[21] d'Elia, *Catholic Native Episcopacy in China,* p. 64, and accompanying chart.

China was very heavily reinforced in the quarter of a century after 1914. In 1912 it embraced 1,365 foreign and 721 Chinese priests, 247 foreign and 86 Chinese lay brothers, and 743 foreign and 1,429 Chinese sisters.[22] In 1929 it included 1,975 foreign and 1,369 Chinese priests, 314 foreign and 466 Chinese lay brothers, and 1,327 foreign and 2,641 Chinese sisters.[23] In 1939 foreign priests totalled 2,979 and Chinese priests 2,026, foreign brothers 585 and Chinese brothers 677, and foreign sisters 2,281 and native sisters 3,852.[24] A little application of mathematics will show that in every category except that of sisters Chinese had increased proportionately more rapidly than foreigners and that in each classification except that of foreign priests the percentage growth in staff had been in excess of that of all Roman Catholics. Presumably this meant a somewhat greater absorption in the care of those already Christian. It ought, accordingly, to have issued in an improving quality of Christian living.

More and more responsibility was placed upon the Chinese clergy. This was in accord with a settled policy of Rome and with the general trend across the non-Occidental world. It was also in response to the growing nationalism in China with its restlessness under alien supervision. It likewise gave indication of the increasing rootage of the church in Chinese soil: the Chinese church had sufficient vigour to produce a growing proportion of those needed to give it spiritual oversight and to reach out to non-Christians. In 1923 and 1924 two prefectures apostolic were carved out of existing vicariates apostolic and entrusted entirely to Chinese clergy, the one to seculars and the other to Lazarists.[25] In 1926 a further step was taken. Six Chinese priests were raised to the episcopacy. They journeyed to Rome and there, in St. Peter's, were consecrated by the Pope himself.[26] The publicity given the event dramatically attested at once the growing maturity of the Chinese church and the determination of the Vatican to hasten the passing of her paternalistic era.

This was only the beginning. By 1932 400,000 Roman Catholics were said to be in ecclesiastical districts headed by Chinese.[27] By 1940, out of 138 vicariates apostolic, prefectures apostolic, and independent missions, at least 14 vicariates were under Chinese bishops and at least 5 prefectures were also under Chinese.[28] Nor were all these unimportant assignments. In 1936 the vicariate which included the national capital, Nanking, had a Chinese at its head.[29] In striking

[22] Streit, *op. cit.*, p. 100.
[23] *Fides News Service,* May 18, 1940.
[24] *Ibid.*
[25] Planchet, *op. cit.*, 1925, pp. 218, 498; d'Elia, *op. cit.*, pp. 80-84.
[26] d'Elia, *op. cit.*, pp. 85-88.
[27] *The Chinese Recorder,* Vol. LXIV, p. 200, citing *The Aurora,* Dec., 1932.
[28] *Les Missions de Chine, Quinzième Année, passim.*
[29] *Les Missions de Chine, Quinzième Année,* pp. 201, 202.

contrast with the temper in Roman Catholic circles in the nineteenth century, there were European priests serving under Chinese bishops.[30]

The trust confided in the Chinese seems to have been warranted. Chinese Roman Catholics displayed ability and initiative in spreading and maintaining their faith. One of the first six to be given the episcopal dignity was the organizer of a flourishing Chinese congregation, the Brothers of St. John.[31] In 1935 a new Chinese sisterhood, the Catechists of Christ the King, was established, and the following year nine of its members made their religious profession.[32] Chinese were increasing their contributions to the Society for the Propagation of the Faith.[33] In 1933 the largest number of baptisms in any one mission was in one headed by a Chinese bishop and in charge of Chinese clergy.[34] In 1934 a Chinese priest inaugurated a group of Chinese speakers and musicians who went from village to village lecturing on their faith and distributing Christian literature.[35]

Obviously more and more attention was given to the preparation of the Chinese priesthood. The Société des Missions Étrangères of Paris, which had had as one of its original purposes the raising up of an indigenous clergy and to which had been entrusted large areas, was substantially increasing the proportion of Chinese priests to the Christians under its care.[36] It was said that the necessity of acquiring Latin and of pursuing most of their studies in that language was a major handicap to the seminarians,[37] but academic standards in the seminaries were rising[38] and it was reported that the quality of the candidates for the priesthood was improving.[39]

The Roman Catholic laity also appeared to be taking a greater responsibility for the propagation of their faith and for service to their neighbours in the name of their religion. We are told of a rice-peddler who preached his faith as he travelled with his wares.[40] We hear of a large church building erected as the gift of a Roman Catholic factory owner,[41] Lo Pa Hong. Lo Pa Hong had acquired large wealth in Shanghai, in his youth had taught the catechism to the poor, was instrumental in organizing Catholic Action, gave substantial

---

[30] *Fides Service,* Dec. 11, 1937.
[31] *Fides News Service,* Dec. 26, 1936.
[32] *Fides News Service,* Feb. 13, 1937.
[33] *Fides News Service,* May 2, 1936, Apr. 3, 1937.
[34] A Roman Catholic expert on missions to the author, Apr. 21, 1934.
[35] *Fides Service,* May 25, 1935.
[36] *Revue d'Histoire des Missions,* Vol. VIII, p. 133.
[37] Devine, *The Four Churches of Peking,* p. 40.
[38] *Fides News Service,* Sep. 28, 1935.
[39] A Roman Catholic expert on missions to the author, Apr. 21, 1934.
[40] *Fides News Service,* Nov. 9, 1935.
[41] *Fides Service,* June 23, 1934.

sums to charity, founded at least one hospital, and had the custom of beginning his day with the Holy Communion and serving at the mass.[42] By its
twenty-fifth anniversary, in 1933, Catholic Action had to its credit the baptism
of about a quarter of a million, mostly infants, and the opening of twenty
churches and chapels, seventy-one lecture halls, seven schools, five hospitals,
nineteen dispensaries, two orphanages, and two homes for the aged.[43] In
Tientsin and Yenchowfu members of Catholic Action visited prisons and gave
Christian instruction to the inmates.[44] In one region where there had been few
conversions in many years, Catholic Action brought in scores of applicants for
baptism in one year.[45] In 1935 the first national congress of Catholic Action
met and was largely attended.[46]

After 1914 Rome gave to China a national organization. In 1918 it was
proposed that a papal representative be appointed to Peking, but the French
Government, still jealous of the remnants of its protectorate over Roman
Catholic missions in the empire, prevented the consummation of the plan.[47] In
1919 one of the French vicars apostolic was appointed by the Vatican as Visitor
of all the missions in China.[48] In 1922 an Apostolic Delegation was created
for China and Archbishop Celse Bénigne Louis Costantini was named the first
Apostolic Delegate.[49] Costantini gave strong leadership. There had already
been held, in preparation for a national organization, seven regional synods,
and in 1924 a general synod convened in Shanghai.[50] Out of this came a
Synodical Commission appointed by the Apostolic Delegate to deal with
matters of a general character.[51] Costantini stressed the creation of a national
church within the great Roman Catholic fellowship. He accelerated the training of Chinese clergy and the transfer of responsibility to them. He made
much, too, of the development of a Chinese art. He was instrumental in
founding a Chinese congregation, the Disciples of the Lord, whose purpose
it was to win fellow-Chinese to the faith.[52] He encouraged the formation of
youth groups in connexion with Catholic Action.[53] At first he met severe

---

[42] *Fides Service,* Aug. 5, 1935, Feb. 29, 1936, Jan. 8, 1938.
[43] *Fides Service,* Jan. 8, 1938.
[44] *Fides Service,* June 29, 1935, Sep. 7, 1935.
[45] *Fides News Service,* July 17, 1937.
[46] *Fides Service,* Sep. 21, 1935.
[47] Planchet, *Les Missions de Chine et du Japon,* 1919, p. 346.
[48] *Annals of the Propagation of the Faith,* Vol. LXXXII, p. 232; *Our Missions,* Jan.,
1921, p. 11.
[49] Planchet, *op. cit.,* 1925, pp. 5, 481, 482.
[50] Planchet, *op. cit.,* 1925, pp. 484-488.
[51] *Fides Service,* Jan. 9, 1937.
[52] *Fides News Service,* Apr., 1939; Planchet, *op. cit.,* 1929, p. 580.
[53] *Priester und Mission,* 1929, pp. 25-39.

opposition among some of the foreign clergy, but eventually he succeeded in overcoming it and winning support for his programme. By his vision, energy, and tact he hastened the transition to Chinese leadership and may thereby have forestalled a serious revolt among the indigenous staff.[54]

Although in the three decades after 1914 the Chinese staff of the Roman Catholic Church grew more rapidly than the foreign personnel, the latter, as we saw a few paragraphs back, experienced a very substantial increment. Proportionately it mounted much more strikingly than in India and approximately as much as in Africa. This seems not to have been because of any special urging from Rome, but from a general appreciation of the opportunity presented by the fluidity in the Chinese cultural scene. Although the societies and orders previously represented continued, additional ones entered and the numbers of missions and ecclesiastical territories greatly increased. Early in the 1930's the French still had more missionaries than any other foreign nationality and were almost as numerous as the two who came next to them, the Italians and the Germans, taken together. Next to the Germans were the Spaniards, then Belgians, Americans, Dutch, Canadians, and Irish, in the order named.[55] It is clear that the overwhelming majority, as before, were from the continent of Europe, but those from the United States and Canada were becoming a not inconsiderable portion of the whole.

The limitations of space do not permit the enumeration of all the organizations which now for the first time sent representatives to China. Only a few can be mentioned. In 1921 the Capuchins of the Rhenish-Westphalian province, forced out of the Caroline and Mariana Islands by the first of the world wars, were assigned a portion of Kansu.[56] Among the newly arrived societies were the Priests of the Sacred Heart of Jesus of Betharram, in Yünnan, the Passionists, in Hunan, the Picpus Fathers, in Hainan, the Conventual Franciscans, in Shensi, the Missionaries of St. Columban, in Hanyang, the Stimatini, in Paotingfu, the Missionaries of St. Francis Xavier of Quebec, in Manchuria, Canadian Franciscans, in Chefoo, Canadian Jesuits, in Kiangsu, the Swiss Missionaries of Bethlehem, in Manchuria,[57] and the Foreign Missions of Quebec and the Benedictines of St. Odile, in Manchuria.[58] Polish Dominicans undertook a mission in Szechwan.[59] Hungarian Jesuits were given charge of a portion of Hopei.[60] The monks of St. Bernard obtained permission from the

[54] A Roman Catholic expert on missions to the author, April 18, 1934.
[55] Testo-Atlante illustrato delle Missioni, p. 48.
[56] Capucins Missionnaires. Missions Françaises, p. 68.
[57] Planchet, op. cit., 1927, Part 2, pp. 59-63.
[58] Les Missions de Chine, 1938-1939, pp. 36-49.
[59] Fides News Service, Nov. 19, 1938.
[60] Fides News Service, Nov. 5, 1938.

Chinese authorities to open a hospice on the borders of Tibet, on a mountain between the valleys of the Salween and the Mekong.[61]

From the United States came Lazarists, Passionists, Dominicans, Salvatorians, Franciscan Missionaries of Mary, Sisters of Loreto, Sisters of Charity, Sisters of the Society of the Precious Blood, Franciscans, Capuchins, Benedictines, and representatives of the Chinese Mission Society of St. Columban, whose headquarters were in Maynooth, in Ireland, but who also drew from America.[62] Especially notable were the contributions of the American province of the Society of the Divine Word and of the Catholic Foreign Mission Society of America (the Maryknollers, from the headquarters of their organization). The Society of the Divine Word, of nineteenth century origin and with a constituency which was primarily German, had been represented in China since 1882.[63] During the first of the world wars financial aid came to it from the faithful in the United States and by 1921 three American priests had been sent to its Shantung mission.[64] The province in the United States grew rapidly, further assistance was given by it to the China enterprises of the society, and in 1933 *Fu Jen*, the important Catholic University of Peking, which had been begun by American Benedictines, was transferred to it.[65] More extensive were the activities of the Catholic Foreign Mission Society of America. This society, founded in 1911, sent its first contingent to China in 1918. It was headed by Thomas F. Price, the co-founder of the society, then fifty-eight years of age. Within a few months after his arrival Price died, but the enterprise went on.[66] The first assignment was in Kwangtung, and to it a second adjoining one was soon added, in Kwangsi.[67] There were other deaths,[68] but reinforcements came in a steady flow. By 1938 the Maryknollers had three vicariates apostolic and one prefecture apostolic in Kwangtung and Kwangsi and one vicariate apostolic in Manchuria.[69] By 1942 about six hundred and fifty Americans were serving in Roman Catholic missions in China, more than in any other country.[70] This was only about one-ninth of the foreign staff

[61] *Fides News Service*, Sept. 21, 1935.
[62] Latourette, *A History of Christian Missions in China*, pp. 718-720.
[63] Vol. VI, pp. 275, 276.
[64] *Our Missions*, Vol. I, p. 29.
[65] Considine, *Across a World*, pp. 153, 154; *The International Review of Missions*, Vol. XXIII, pp. 100, 101.
[66] *Father Price of Maryknoll* (Maryknoll, Catholic Foreign Mission Society of America, 1923, pp. xv, 93), *passim*.
[67] Powers, *The Maryknoll Movement*, pp. 99 ff.; Cuenot, *Kwangsi*, pp. 216 ff.
[68] Considine, *op. cit.*, pp. 172-175; James Edward Walsh, *Father McShane of Maryknoll, Missioner in South China* (New York, Dial Press, 1932, pp. xv, 227), *passim*.
[69] *Les Missions de Chine*, 1938-1939, pp. 23, 403-408.
[70] Considine, *op. cit.*, p. 177.

of the Roman Catholic Church, but it was rapidly increasing, for the total was said to have been slightly less than three hundred approximately a decade earlier, or about one-thirteenth of the foreign personnel.[71] The growth of the American contingents was the more significant in view of the rapidly mounting resources and missionary zeal of the Roman Catholics of the United States and of the impoverishment by war of Europe, heretofore the source of the overwhelming majority of the Occidental forces.

The methods of the Roman Catholic Church in China were somewhat modified after 1914. Many of the bishops disavowed any desire to influence the country as a whole as Protestants were doing and wished to devote all their energies to building the church.[72] This was still the main trend. The continued and growing emphasis upon recruiting and training a Chinese clergy and of transferring responsibility to them was part of this general programme. Efforts to win non-Christians were given major place, along with the care of those already Christian.

The approach to non-Christians varied. Some favoured assembling large numbers in catechumenates at the church's expense, a method widely employed by Lazarists, Scheutvelders, and missionaries of the Paris Society, especially in Chihli (Hopei), Manchuria, and Mongolia. Others were critical of the material inducements involved in this wholesale group instruction. Open meetings for non-Christians assisted by Catholic Action were tried in Tientsin, but they were compromised by association with anti-Japanese agitation and were discontinued.[73] In one area there were night classes for the instruction of adults.[74]

As in other years and countries, the motives which led to the acceptance of the Christian faith as represented by the Roman Catholic Church varied greatly. An entire community in Inner Mongolia asked to be received into the church because it had observed that Christian villages fought off bandits more successfully than did their non-Christian neighbours.[75] During the course of a flood of the Yangtze a bishop urged Christians to beg the protection of the Virgin Mary. When, soon afterward, the waters began to subside, non-Christians, impressed, asked for Christian instruction.[76] In an adjoining province, in time of drought masses offered and prayers said for rain were followed by a welcome downpour and many pagans, in consequence, listened respectfully

[71] *Testo-Atlante illustrato delle Missioni*, p. 48.
[72] A Roman Catholic expert on missions to the author, May 3, 1934.
[73] Berg, *Die katholische Heidenmission als Kulturträger*, Vol. I, pp. 347-350.
[74] *Fides News Service*, Feb. 13, 1937.
[75] *Fides Service*, March 2, 1933.
[76] *Fides Service*, March 23, 1935.

to Christian teaching.[77] A general, condemned to execution, had a vision of the Holy Family assuring him of release. When the vision was fulfilled he became a Christian and later joined the Trappists.[78]

Although major efforts were still put forth to reach non-Christians, more emphasis than formerly was given to education. Much of this was for the preparation of the priesthood. However, much also was for the laity. Greater stress was placed upon secondary schools and universities. Because of the demand in China for education, here was felt to be an opportunity, largely neglected by Roman Catholics, to reach the intelligentsia. Only three institutions could be classed as universities, Aurora in Shanghai, founded in 1903, *Hautes Études* in Tientsin, also of pre-1914 origin, and the Catholic University in Peking, founded in 1925 by American Benedictines, as we saw a few paragraphs above, and later transferred to the American province of the Society of the Divine Word.[79] In 1936 there were 103 colleges and middle schools, of which 15 had been opened the preceding year, and 4,283 primary schools, of which 166 had been added in the preceding three months. In 1936 the enrolment in colleges and middle schools was 18,604, of whom about two-thirds were not Roman Catholics, and that in primary schools 180,704, of whom about one-half in the higher grades and less than one-half in the lower years were non-Roman Catholics.[80] Some of the middle schools were for girls.[81] For a time in the fore part of the 1930's enrolment in the schools showed a decline,[82] but later in the decade there was a decided increase.[83] The temporary ebb seems to have been due to the reluctance of the Roman Catholic authorities to register their schools with the government and thus to be forced to comply with the official regulations which forbade religious instruction in institutions so listed. Indeed, some of the schools were closed by the local civil authorities. However, there was no objection to placing the schools in the hands of Chinese administrators, another of the demands of the state, and gradually the crisis passed.[84]

Roman Catholics had long been interested in the problems of the rural areas. They were now bringing to them added zeal and fresh devices. Vincent Lebbe founded two Chinese organizations, the Brothers of St. John Baptist and the Sisters of St. Theresa, whose members accomplished much among farmers in Hopei. Lebbe was responsible for a conference on "rural reconstruction and the

[77] *Fides Service*, Oct. 29, 1938.
[78] *Fides Service*, Apr. 2, 1938.
[79] Kandel, *Educational Yearbook*, 1933, pp. 579, 580.
[80] *Fides News Service*, Feb. 20, 1937.
[81] *Fides News Service*, July 31, 1937.
[82] *Testo-Atlante illustrato delle Missioni*, p. 48.
[83] *Fides News Service*, May 9, 1936.
[84] Kandel, *op. cit.*, p. 575; Lesourd, *L'Année Missionnaire*, 1931, pp. 491-493.

Gospel," which was held in Peking in 1935.[85] In Inner Mongolia at least one Roman Catholic village seemed better to have maintained its irrigation system in time of drought than did non-Christian ones.[86] There, indeed, the Congregation of the Immaculate Heart of Mary built irrigation canals and its missions became centres of refuge from war and banditry.[87]

As earlier, Roman Catholics paid much attention to orphans. Also as had been their custom for many years, they baptized infants in danger of death: in the year ending in June, 1926, the total of such baptisms was said to be 231,-539.[88] The number of orphanages and of orphans cared for declined from 392 and 29,198 respectively in 1912[89] to 367 and 24,793 in 1933,[90] but even the totals in the latter year were greater than in any other country in Asia and in other large geographic divisions of the non-European world were surpassed only by those of Africa south of the Sahara.

Roman Catholic dispensaries were also more numerous than in any other country in Asia and were exceeded only by those in Africa south of the Sahara. There were more Roman Catholic hospitals than in any other country of Asia or than in all of Africa.[91] Roman Catholics maintained more dispensaries in China and gave more treatments through them than did Protestants, but had only about a third as many hospitals and two-fifths as many hospital beds as the latter.[92] In 1935 the Catholic Medical Service was organized, with headquarters in Peking, to aid and co-ordinate Roman Catholic medical activities throughout China.[93]

The publishing achievements of Roman Catholics included 115 periodicals in 1937 of which 72 were wholly or partly in Chinese.[94]

In a few sections a large proportion of Roman Catholic Chinese were of old Christian stock, that is, from those who had been Christian for more than thirty years, but, thanks to the rapid growth of the church through conversions, the large majority were either first or second generation Christians.[95]

Considerably less than half the funds for the maintenance of the Roman

[85] *Fides News Service*, Dec. 14, 1935.
[86] Y. Y. Tsu in *The Chinese Recorder*, Vol. LXII, pp. 283, 284.
[87] *Agrarian China*, p. 47.
[88] *Missiones Catholicae Cura S. Congregationis de Propaganda Fide*, 1927, pp. 146-151.
[89] Streit, *Atlas Hierarchicus*, p. 100.
[90] Parker, *Interpretative Statistical Survey of the World Mission of the Christian Church*, p. 35.
[91] *Ibid.*
[92] Parker, *op. cit.*, pp. 35, 214.
[93] *Fides News Service*, Jan. 11, 1936.
[94] *Fides News Service*, March 23, 1935, Feb. 20, 1937.
[95] *Missiones Catholicae Cura S. Congregationis de Propaganda Fide*, 1927, pp. 146-151.

Catholic Church and its missions in China were from current contributions from abroad.[96] Much came from the characteristic Chinese means of the support of philanthropic undertakings, endowments in lands. The proportion of expenses met from the latter source varied greatly from mission to mission.[97] French missions had large holdings in the French concession in Shanghai.[98] We also hear of extensive possessions in farm lands.[99] Under Mussolini the Italian Government gave substantial subsidies to missions of that nationality in China.[100]

Scattered over the length and breadth of China as they were, Roman Catholic missions and the Roman Catholic Church could not but be affected by the disorders of the turbulent three decades after 1914.

During the first of the world wars about a third of the French priests, or nearly a fifth of the entire body of foreign priests in China in 1914, were summoned to the colours, most of them to Europe and some of them as reservists in the Far East. A few of the Germans were imprisoned and, after the armistice, several were repatriated. Reinforcements fell off, and the decline of gifts from Europe to the Society for the Propagation of the Faith was only partly made good by an increase of gifts to that organization from the faithful in the United States. Some schools had to be closed and others reduced and there was curtailment in the number of orphans cared for.[101]

The banditry which characterized much of the period took its toll in lives of Chinese Christians and of foreign missionaries. This was not always because Christians were singled out for persecution, but because they, like others, were victims of the general distress. At times the Communist and anti-imperialistic, anti-religious agitation vented itself on Christians, both Chinese and foreign. Between 1923 and 1932 it was said that two bishops and thirty-one priests suffered violent deaths, the maximum number being in the year 1927. In that eight year period, in the province of Hunan, where the Communist elements were especially active, thirty-four churches, seventy-one chapels, ninety-two residences, and thirty-one schools were destroyed.[102] Many priests were captured and held, some of them for ransom. It is said that in the years 1912-1933 inclusive fifty Roman Catholic missionaries were killed and three hundred and twenty-two captured. Of the Chinese clergy sixteen were killed and

[96] Devine, *The Four Churches of Peking*, pp. 126, 127.
[97] *Missiones Catholicae Cura S. Congregationis de Propaganda Fide*, 1927, pp. 160-165.
[98] *The Far Eastern Survey*, Vol. VII, pp. 221, 222.
[99] *The Chinese Recorder*, Vol. LXI, p. 802.
[100] *The North China Herald*, Vol. CXC, p. 365 (March 7, 1934).
[101] Latourette, *A History of Christian Missions in China*, pp. 705-708.
[102] *Testo-Atlante illustrato delle Missioni*, p. 47.

eighty-eight captured.[103] Much church property was occupied by troops and used for other than religious purposes.[104] Revenue was reduced by new taxes and the lowering of rents in Peking due to the removal of the capital to Nanking.[105]

However, the record was not entirely one of loss. Although in years of the most intense unrest the increase in the total number of Roman Catholics was less than in some others, so far as figures can be had there was no year which did not show a net gain.[106] In Kwangsi Maryknollers persevered in spite of civil war and banditry which became prevalent soon after they had entered that province.[107] A commemorative stele was erected to an Italian Jesuit who during civil strife served the wounded of both sides and saved a city from massacre.[108] In 1933 Roman Catholic missionaries did what they could to give medical care and alms to Communists who had been taken prisoners by the forces of Chiang Kai-shek.[109]

In the intensification of the struggle between China and Japan which commenced in July, 1937, Roman Catholics could not but share in the general toll of life and property. Yet here, too, the church performed its characteristic ministry to the sufferers. In 1937 much church property was destroyed and a Chinese priest was killed by Japanese soldiers while he was attempting to protect a school mistress.[110] Refugees were cared for in mission property and the wounded were tended.[111] The numbers of students for the priesthood declined slightly,[112] in Sinkiang because of Communism missions were almost at a standstill,[113] and from some areas there was an extensive exodus of Christians.[114] Yet there were conversions and the Roman Catholic faith gained in prestige.[115] Indeed, the number of baptisms of adults in the year 1939-1940 was over 111,000, apparently the largest on record.[116]

When, in December, 1941, the Sino-Japanese war merged with the second

[103] Paschal M. d'Elia, lecture, *When the Storm had Blown Over* (1933), *passim*. See also *Fides Service*, July 30, Nov. 26, Dec. 10, 1931. For a death in Manchuria in 1937 see John Joseph Considine, *When the Sorghum Was High* (New York, Longmans, Green and Co., 1940, pp. 177).

[104] Planchet, *Les Missions de Chine et du Japon*, 1929, pp. 580-653.

[105] Planchet, *op. cit.*, 1929, p. v.

[106] Lesourd, *L'Année Missionnaire*, 1931, p. 472.

[107] Cuenot, *Kwangsi*, pp. 226 ff.

[108] Lesourd, *op. cit.*, p. 472.

[109] *The Chinese Recorder*, Vol. LXIV, p. 198, citing *Fides Service*, Dec. 22, 1933.

[110] *Fides News Service*, Feb. 15, 1938.

[111] *Fides News Service*, Feb. 19, May 28, June 11, 1938.

[112] *Fides News Service*, Apr. 6, 1940.

[113] *Fides News Service*, March 9, 1940.

[114] *1944 Mission Annual of the Seraphic Mass Association*, Sept. 10, 1943.

[115] *Fides News Service*, Aug. 6, Nov. 19, 1938.

[116] *Lumen Service*, May 23, 1941.

of the world wars, the situation became more acute. Many missionaries in "occupied China" were interned. In consequence numbers of institutions were closed, including hospitals, dispensaries, orphanages, and schools.[117] In Hong-kong some institutions were commandeered by the Japanese forces.[118] Scores of missionaries were repatriated. Yet the church continued in both the "free" and the "occupied" parts of the country.

The sorrows of the second world cataclysm did not mark a break in the life of the Roman Catholic Church in China. In spite of them and in part because of them the church continued to grow.

For the Russian Orthodox Church in China the first of the world wars did not immediately work much change. This old mission, never important numerically, continued its quiet way.[119] However, the revolution in Russia which grew out of the war had striking effects. At first these seemed disastrous. Most of the enterprises for the Chinese, including those in the main centre, Peking, were closed.[120] Soon the influx of "White" Russians, dissidents from the "Red" Communist regime, brought large reinforcements to the church's constituency. For them the Orthodox Church was a symbol of the Russia to which they were loyal and a rallying point of their community life. The majority of the Russians were in Manchuria and in 1922 the parishes in that region were organized into the diocese of Harbin. In spite of the extension of Japanese control and the creation of Manchukuo in 1931-1932, this became and remained the most important diocese of the Russian Church in the Far East. Under the metropolitan were two additional bishops. In 1934 the first Orthodox University in the Far East was opened. There was also a theological seminary.[121] In general, the Japanese were friendly. This was to be anticipated, for they were against Communism and would encourage those Russians who might be expected to share their attitude. South of the Great Wall the Russian Orthodox were under the Archbishop of Peking. A bishop had his seat in Shanghai. There were several parishes in Sinkiang, but an attempt from Peking to provide them with episcopal supervision failed.[122]

The major form of Christianity most recently introduced to China, Protestantism, had an even more stormy course than did Roman Catholic Chris-

---

[117] *Missions and Missionaries*, Oct. 9, 1943; *N.C.W.C. News Service*, Aug. 16, 1943.
[118] *N.C.W.C. News Service*, Sept. 27, 1943.
[119] On the earlier history see Vol. III, p. 359, Vol. VI, pp. 294, 295.
[120] Y. Y. Tsu in *The China Christian Year Book*, 1926, pp. 92, 93.
[121] Bolshakoff, *The Foreign Missions of the Russian Orthodox Church*, pp. 81-83.
[122] Bolshakoff, *op. cit.*, pp. 68, 69.

tianity and only a slightly less chequered career than did the Russian Orthodox Church. The anti-Christian movement had it more directly as its objective than the other two main branches of the faith. The anti-imperialistic and Communist agitation, aimed as it was largely against Great Britain, touched it more nearly than it did the others, for a large proportion of Protestant missionaries were British. The fluctuations in financial support from the Occident bore more heavily on Protestant than on Roman Catholic missions. The foreign staff was said to be 5,750 in about the year 1914, and of these 2,862 were from the United States and Canada.[123] In 1924 it was reported to be 7,663, of whom 4,492 were from the United States and Canada.[124] In 1936 it was said to be 6,020, of whom 2,808 were from those two countries.[125] In other words, the Protestant foreign personnel, after increasing about a third in the decade following 1914, and largely because of a great influx from the United States, by 1936 had fallen to about the level of twenty-two years earlier, a decline which was chiefly attributable to the loss in the North American contingents. This advance and loss reflected the great surge in missionary giving in the United States immediately after the first of the world wars and the reaction from that transient impulse accentuated by the financial depression which had its incidence in 1929. The number of missionaries from the British Isles also dropped after 1929, but not so markedly as from North America.[126] Another set of figures gives the total Protestant missionary body in China in 1919 as 6,636, in 1926 as 8,325, in 1928 as 3,133, in 1929 as 4,728, in 1930 as 6,112, and in 1933 as 5,743.[127] The drop from 1926 to 1928 reflects the exodus, much of it temporary, due to the anti-imperialistic, Communist movement of that period.

This sharp fluctuation and lack of permanent increase was in marked contrast with the continuing growth in the Roman Catholic foreign staff. Yet Protestant communicants rose proportionately even more rapidly than did the Roman Catholic membership. In 1914 they were reported as being 257,431,[128] in 1924, 402,539,[129] and in 1936, 567,390.[130] They had, therefore, more than

[123] Beach and St. John, *World Statistics of Christian Missions*, p. 63.

[124] Beach and Fahs, *World Missionary Atlas*, p. 82. For the biography of a missionary whose life in China spanned part of the pre-1914 and post-1914 years, see Annie Jenkins Sallee, *W. Eugene Sallee, Christ's Ambassador* (Nashville, Sunday School Board, Southern Baptist Convention, 1933, pp. viii, 256).

[125] Parker, *Interpretative Statistical Survey of the World Mission of the Christian Church*, p. 20.

[126] *Conference of Missionary Societies of Great Britain and Ireland, Report of the Twenty-Second Annual Conference . . . 1933*, p. 51.

[127] C. L. Boynton in *The China Christian Year Book*, 1932-1933, pp. 212-221.

[128] Beach and St. John, *op. cit.*, p. 63.

[129] Beach and Fahs, *op. cit.*, p. 99.

[130] Parker, *op. cit.*, p. 50. The total is obtained by adding those for China and Manchuria, to make them comparable with the earlier figures.

doubled in the twenty-two years between 1914 and 1936, whereas in the twenty-five years after 1914 Roman Catholics had barely doubled. As for Roman Catholics, so for Protestants, the rate of increase slowed down after 1914 in comparison with the opening years of the century. Figures for baptized as against communicant Protestants, which would be fully comparable for those of the Roman Catholics, were defective. Probably in 1939 baptized Protestants were only between a third and a fourth as numerous as were Roman Catholics.

The Protestant figures were not the full measure of those who at one time or another had had a church connexion. There was a very substantial seepage. Some members were dropped for disciplinary reasons. Much larger numbers drifted away and all trace of them was lost by the churches with which they had once been associated.[131]

Men were more numerous than women in the Protestant churches. The proportion the country over was not quite forty women to over sixty men.[132] Although some congregations drew from a particular occupational group, and in the cities many families as a whole were members, in general conversion was not by the natural social entity, as in the mass movements in India, but by individuals.[133] In one denomination in the North, for instance, there were usually only one or two Christians in a village and the average local church had a membership of between twenty and thirty of whom only about a fifth lived in the centre where the church met.[134]

In the fore part of the period, the large majority of the Protestant Christians were in the coastal provinces, where penetration by the Occident and by missionaries had been longest in process.[135] However, more of the interior was being progressively reached and the Japanese invasion of the latter part of the 1930's led to an extensive migration of Christians, both Chinese and foreign, to the West.

A few societies entered China for the first time after 1914. However, all the bodies who continued to have major representation had been present before that year. The large majority were still from the British Empire and the United States, with a substantial minority from the continent of Europe. The first of the world wars did not work lasting injury to any of the German societies. The proportionate strength of the different societies was altered. Very notable was

---

[131] Laymen's Foreign Missions Inquiry, *Fact-Finders' Reports, China*, Vol. V, Supplementary Series, Part 2, p. 243.

[132] Laymen's Foreign Missions Inquiry, *op. cit.*, Vol. V, Supplementary Series, Part 2, pp. 243-245.

[133] *Ibid.*

[134] Laymen's Foreign Missions Inquiry, *op. cit.*, Vol. V, Supplementary Series, Part 2, p. 10.

[135] Stauffer, *The Christian Occupation of China*, pp. 283 ff.

the fact that between 1924 and 1936, when most of the larger Protestant denominations suffered a sharp curtailment in their foreign staffs, the Seventh Day Adventists and the China Inland Mission substantially augmented their forces.[136] The China Inland Mission still had more missionaries than any other society, either Roman Catholic or Protestant. In 1936 it had about 23 per cent. of all Protestant missionaries in China. Moreover, after the exodus brought by the Japanese invasion which began in 1937, a smaller proportion of its staff left than did those of most of the other major societies. To some degree, although not entirely, this was because a larger percentage of its missionaries were already in the interior, in what remained "free" China, than was true of the others, strongly entrenched as they were on the coast in the regions which the Japanese occupied. The shifting complexion of the missionary body altered the kind of Protestant Christianity propagated. It was more theologically conservative and less liberal than was true in the decade which immediately succeeded 1914.

One of the most striking developments in Protestantism after 1914 as in the Roman Catholic Church was the rapid transfer of responsibility to Chinese leadership. This, as we have seen, was a trend through most of the non-Occidental world. As elsewhere, it was in part because of the long preparation and desire of the missionaries, but it was accelerated by the nationalistic temper of the Chinese with its mounting restlessness under any form of foreign control. In the schools the process was hastened by the requirement of the government that the heads of all educational institutions be Chinese and that the official boards of control have a majority of Chinese members. This was particularly emphasized after the coming to power of the Kuomintang.[137]

Passing over the administration of schools to Chinese was not difficult, for the latter had a tradition which honoured teachers and made the recruiting of them easy. Nor was it hard to discover able Chinese executives for central boards and ecclesiastical agencies. There was much greater delay in raising up and training an ordained ministry, for nothing in the Chinese background quite corresponded to the Christian pastor.[138] More of a precedent existed for the celibate priest, for there were parallels, even though far from exact, in Buddhism, but nothing remotely corresponded to the married ministry of the Protestant churches. However, even here progress was registered.[139] A notable study heading up in a survey in 1935 by a commission led by Luther A. Weigle helped

---

[136] Compare Beach and Fahs, *op. cit.*, pp. 82, 83, with Parker, *op. cit.*, pp. 86-88.

[137] E. H. Cressy in *The China Christian Year Book*, 1929, pp. 268 ff.

[138] Laymen's Foreign Missions Inquiry, *op. cit.*, Vol. V, Supplementary Series, Part 2, pp. 283, 284.

[139] See a history of theological training in Charles Stanley Smith, *The Development of Protestant Theological Education in China* (Shanghai, Kelly and Walsh, Ltd., 1941, pp. ix, 171), *passim.*

greatly to push forward and co-ordinate Protestant theological education.[140] The number of ordained Protestant Chinese rose from 764 in 1915 to 1,305 in 1920[141] and to 2,196 in 1936.[142] This was proportionately a slightly larger increase than that of Chinese Roman Catholic priests in the same period. Actually, too, there were more Protestant ordained ministers in 1936 than Chinese Roman Catholic priests. It must be said, however, that the preparation required of the latter was longer and more exacting than it was for the majority of the former. Yet the standard of education for the Protestant clergy was rising.[143] Most of the Protestant denominations in China did not have bishops, but in such as were episcopally organized Chinese were being raised to that office and in it were giving a good account of themselves.[144]

As late as 1935, however, many missionaries were still occupied with administration.[145] Moreover, the rapid transfer of authority to the Chinese gave to some of the missionaries a feeling of insecurity. They found themselves wondering whether China offered a lifetime of service and whether the inclination to transfer posts to the Chinese and to allow Chinese to have a voice in the decision of whether a foreigner should return after furlough made their tenure hazardous.[146]

Chinese Protestants increasingly assumed responsibility for the spread of their faith and for the financial undergirding of their churches. From among them rose able leaders. To those who cherished the vision of what should be, progress towards the goal at times seemed discouragingly slow. There remained much of reliance upon the churches of the Occident both for initiative and for the budgets of Christian institutions. However, over the course of the years advance was registered and, in view of the many internal disturbances in China, of the foreign invasion, and of the difficulty of adapting methods of Western origin to Chinese conditions, one of amazing dimensions. Protestant Christianity was not yet fully rooted in China, but it was more and more drawing its support from Chinese.

[140] Chester S. Miao, editor, *Education for Service in the Christian Church in China. The Report of a Survey Commission, 1935* (Shanghai, National Committee for Christian Religious Education in China, 1935, pp. vi, 157), *passim*.

[141] Stauffer, *op. cit.*, p. xc.

[142] Parker, *op. cit.*, pp. 49, 50.

[143] *The Chinese Recorder*, Vol. LXVI, pp. 350-353.

[144] *The International Review of Missions*, Vol. XXIV, p. 21; *The Chinese Recorder*, Vol. LXVI, pp. 101 ff.; J. H. Franklin in *The Baptist*, Vol. XI, pp. 1125, 1126; Stewart, *Forward in West China*, p. 20.

[145] Maclennan, *Report to the Conference of Missionary Societies of Great Britain and Ireland on a Visit to the Far East, January-July, 1934*, p. 13.

[146] Laymen's Foreign Missions Inquiry, *op. cit.*, Vol. V, Supplementary Series, Part 2, pp. 82, 91.

Of this there were many examples. The Chinese Missionary Society, interdenominational, was organized in 1918 and by 1937 had fifteen thousand subscribing members living in twenty provinces. Its first missionaries went to Yünnan. Another enterprise was undertaken by it in the northern province of Manchuria, but because of the political situation was discontinued after 1931. In 1937 the society had thirty-seven missionaries in Yünnan, Szechwan, and Mongolia.[147] Early in the 1930's in one great port on the coast laymen led in a city-wide effort to present the Christian message to the entire population.[148] Numbers of congregations were attaining financial as well as administrative independence of foreigners.[149]

The movement towards self-support and self-government was not without its problems. The complaint was heard that the median giving of Christians to the church was less than what the poorest non-Christians paid to the pagan temples in offerings.[150] It was said that when a Chinese subscribed to a non-Christian temple or festival he would be assured a reasonable return in social recognition and in a share of the food and decorations presented to the gods, but that he could see little gain in contributing to the salary of a pastor who might have a larger income than he.[151] In one rural church over fifty years old and with prosperous members only twelve dollars was given in one year to the support of the ministry. Presumably this was not exceptional.[152] It was also declared that Chinese, in accordance with their traditions, were prepared to respond liberally to special appeals for specific objects, but were slow to establish the habit of regular gifts to continuing budgets.[153] There were instances of pastors drawing from foreign funds without holding services and of engaging in business practices palpably contrary to Christian ethics and yet escaping discipline because of clan or family ties which made such a step impossible or because some of the members shared in the spoils.[154] Here and there independent churches arose which engaged in extravagant practices.[155]

Yet these were exceptional, and against them could be set churches which

---

[147] *The Chinese Recorder*, Vol. LXVIII, p. 457.

[148] Foster, *The Chinese Church in Action*, pp. 102-104.

[149] *The International Review of Missions*, Vol. XXI, p. 50; A. R. Kepler, *Occasional Letter No. 13*. Sep. 19, 1931; *The Chinese Recorder*, Vol. LXII, p. 762.

[150] Laymen's Foreign Missions Inquiry, *Fact-Finders' Reports, China*, Vol. V, Supplementary Series, Part 2, pp. 120, 121.

[151] Davis, *The Economic and Social Environment of the Younger Churches*, p. 41.

[152] Z. S. Zia in *The Chinese Recorder*, Vol. LXVI, pp. 277-280.

[153] Letter of a missionary to the author, Feb. 26, 1934.

[154] Laymen's Foreign Missions Inquiry, *op. cit.*, Vol. V, Supplementary Series, Part 2, p. 590.

[155] Laymen's Foreign Missions Inquiry, *op. cit.*, Vol. V, Supplementary Series, Part 2, p. 12.

in the face of banditry displayed singular vitality and were developing an unpaid leadership.[156] As funds from the Occident declined because of the financial depression in the 1930's, much dismay was felt by churches confronted with sudden cuts,[157] but the difference was at least partly made up by gifts from local sources.[158]

Co-operation between denominations increased and in some instances there was ecclesiastical union. The outstanding example of co-operation was the formation and progress of the National Christian Council. The National Christian Council was largely although not entirely an outgrowth of the Edinburgh Missionary Conference of 1910 and came into being in 1922 through the National Christian Conference of that year.[159] It brought together Chinese and foreigners but was increasingly Chinese in leadership and initiative. One of its early secretaries was the English Friend, Henry T. Hodgkin. Of long and prominent Quaker lineage, of commanding physical presence, and possessed of marked intellectual and spiritual force, Hodgkin helped give to the National Christian Council a distinction which kept it from innocuous mediocrity.[160] From the outset the new organization had Chinese on its secretarial staff. Under its revised constitution of 1929, moreover, it acquired an even firmer Chinese rootage by dropping all representation by mission boards as such and basing its membership firmly upon the Chinese churches.[161] More and more it gave leadership to the Protestant Christian forces. In 1929, for instance, following the series of attacks by the anti-Christian movements and the Communists, not content with remaining on the defensive, it came forth boldly with the Five Year Movement—a comprehensive programme for enlarged evangelism, religious education, the promotion of literacy, the cultivation of the Christian home, the advance of stewardship (by which was meant increased giving by Christians), and the enlistment of youth for the Church.[162]

Co-operation multiplied across denominational lines in many kinds of enterprises, among them schools, colleges, universities,[163] the National Committee

[156] E. S. Burket in *The Chinese Recorder*, Vol. LXIII, pp. 748-755.
[157] *The International Review of Missions*, Vol. XXIII, p. 19; *The Chinese Recorder*, Vol. LXVIII, pp. 480, 481.
[158] *The Chinese Recorder*, Vol. LXV, pp. 281, 282.
[159] *The China Mission Year Book*, 1923, pp. 54-65, 1924, pp. 147-157.
[160] On Hodgkin see H. G. Wood, *Henry T. Hodgkin* (London, Student Christian Movement Press, 1937, pp. 281), especially pp. 200-243.
[161] Laymen's Foreign Missions Inquiry, *op. cit.*, Vol. V, Supplementary Series, Part 2, p. 79.
[162] *The China Christian Year Book*, 1931, pp. 126-129. For friendly strictures on the National Christian Council see Maclennan, *op. cit.*, pp. 10-13.
[163] Fahs and Davis, *Conspectus of Coöperative Missionary Enterprises*, pp. 111 ff.; Carleton Lacy in *The China Christian Year Book*, 1938-1939, pp. 123-130.

for Christian Religious Education (constituted in 1931),[164] and the closer integration of the operations of the various Bible societies on a local and national scale.[165]

The organic union of denominations made progress, although somewhat more slowly. Steps were taken to bring together into national bodies members of the same denominational families. In 1912 the Anglicans merged their branches of varying national origins into the *Chung Hua Shêng Kung Hui*.[166] In 1917 several of the Lutheran bodies joined to constitute the *Chung Hua Hsin I Hui*.[167] In 1930 the China Baptist Alliance was formed.[168] Most comprehensive of all was the Church of Christ in China (*Chung-hua Chi-tu Chiao-hui*). This was an outgrowth of the Presbyterian fellowship. In 1901 the Federal Council of the Presbyterian Church of Christ in China was constituted. Out of this came, in 1918, the first general assembly of the Presbyterian Church in China. Partly from this there arose, in 1922, the provisional assembly of the Presbyterian Church in China.[169] In 1927, a year of political chaos, the determinative step was taken in the meeting, in Shanghai, of the first general assembly of the Church of Christ in China. There were present, in addition to representatives of seven Presbyterian and two Reformed bodies, delegates from several independent churches and from groups associated with the United Church of Canada, the London Missionary Society, the American Board of Commissioners for Foreign Missions, the Swedish Evangelical Free Church, the United Brethren in Christ, and the English Baptists.[170] While, therefore, the Church of Christ in China had as its main nucleus the Presbyterian and Reformed constituencies, it also included a large proportion of the Congregationalists, some of the Baptists, the United Brethren, and those former Methodists who were in the United Church of Canada. Ecclesiastically it was the most comprehensive union which had thus far been achieved anywhere in the world. By 1934, it embraced about one-third of all non-Roman Catholic Chinese and over one-half of all non-Roman Catholic clergy and ministers.[171] The chief architect of the Church of Christ in China was its general secretary, A. R. Kepler. The outstanding indigenous leader was Chêng Ching-yi. Chêng Ching-yi was a Manchu, son of a pastor long connected with the London Missionary Society. While not yet thirty he had been one of the

[164] *The China Christian Year Book*, 1932-1933, p. 162.
[165] *The China Christian Year Book*, 1934-1935, pp. 186 ff.
[166] *The China Christian Year Book*, 1928, p. 81.
[167] *Ibid.*
[168] *The China Christian Year Book*, 1931, p. 143.
[169] A. R. Kepler in *The China Christian Year Book*, 1928, p. 76.
[170] A. R. Kepler in *ibid.*, pp. 84-89.
[171] *The International Review of Missions*. Vol. XXIV, p. 19.

few non-Occidental delegates to the World Missionary Conference in Edinburgh (1910). He there made a profound impression. It was natural that he should become a secretary of the China Continuation Committee of that body and later of the National Christian Council. As a vice-chairman of the International Missionary Council and an extensive traveller through the churches of the Occident he helped to tie Chinese Protestantism into the world-wide fellowship of that wing of the Church. Dignified, poised, possessed of a deep faith, he was an earnest of the contribution of Chinese Christianity to the Church universal.[172]

It must also be added that through the membership of the National Christian Council in the International Missionary Council and of the Church of Christ in China in the World Council of Churches, Chinese Protestantism was being integrated in the Ecumenical Movement and so was not being absorbed into Chinese nationalism.

Not all Protestants were drawn into these co-operative and union movements. Theological conservatives were numerous among the missionaries and viewed some of the trends as departures from basic Christian beliefs. In 1920 they formed the Bible Union of China, a body which held its first national gathering in 1922, immediately following the National Christian Conference of that year. To them the tendencies of the National Christian Council were alarming.[173] While the China Inland Mission, all of whose members were frankly conservative, for a time joined in the National Christian Council, it eventually withdrew. There was also an Association of the Christian Fundamentals League for China.[174] The rift between "Fundamentalists" and "Liberals" or "Modernists," which was especially pronounced in Great Britain and the United States in the years immediately following the first of the world wars, presented a greater obstacle to inclusive action by Protestants than in any other major section of the non-Occidental world with the possible exception of Latin America.

In the methods of Protestant Christianity there was persistence of most of those employed before 1914, a modification in many, and some innovations.

The active endeavour to present the Christian message and to win Chinese to the faith, or what was known as evangelism, took many forms. Sherwood Eddy, evangelist to the world and who concentrated chiefly on the intelligentsia,[175] had toured China before 1914. He visited China more than once

---

[172] Nelson Bitton in *The International Review of Missions*, Vol. XXX, pp. 513-520.

[173] *The China Mission Year Book*, 1923, pp. 95-101.

[174] *The China Fundamentalist* (1928 ff.), Vol. II, No. 2, gives the articles of the association.

[175] Vol. VI, pp. 179, 198, 242.

after 1914, addressing great audiences of students and officials and presenting Christ as the salvation from the dire chaos and weakness of the country. It was an approach which found a response in the Chinese tradition which regarded the achievement of an ideal society as the goal of philosophy and religion and which believed the foundations of social order to be moral. Thousands responded with a promise to study the Christian faith and hundreds professed themselves Christians.[176] K. L. Reichelt, a Norwegian Lutheran, inaugurated and headed a specialized mission with headquarters first in Nanking (beginning in 1922) and, commencing in 1930, in a valley on the mainland ten miles from Hongkong. He used an approach which sought points of natural contact with Buddhist terminology, ideas, and forms of worship.[177] In 1929 the China Inland Mission called for prayer for two hundred new workers in two years to reach parts of China untouched by Protestants and within a year opened about twenty new stations.[178] In an attempt to carry out the principles of Sidney James Wells Clark,[179] what were known as Clark evangelistic bands were organized in connexion with the London Missionary Society and gave the Christian message to thousands in the North who had not before heard it.[180] The example proved contagious and similar bands appeared elsewhere.[181] Jonathan Goforth, theologically a pronounced and devoted conservative, was an outstanding leader in revivals which swept much of the country.[182]

Symptomatic of the fashion in which Christianity was increasingly becoming a conscious possession of the Chinese was the initiative which many Chinese were taking, and in different ways, in spreading their faith. In Anhui not far from 1930 a group of Chinese Christians gave a week each to six market towns and the neighbouring villages, distributing literature, speaking against opium, gambling, wine-drinking, foot-binding, and pagan worship, and holding Bible classes.[183] Not far from 1930 there began in Shantung a religious movement, with deep conviction of sin, public confession, preaching

[176] Eddy, *A Pilgrimage of Ideas*, pp. 119 ff.; Sherwood Eddy, Letter from Peking, Oct. 28, 1931; Sherwood Eddy, Letter from Kiangsu, Sept. 22, 1934; *The Chinese Recorder*, Vol. LXII, p. 669, Vol. LXIII, pp. 184-186.

[177] K. L. Reichelt in *The International Review of Missions*, Vol. XXVI, pp. 160 ff.; K. L. Reichelt in *The China Christian Year Book*, 1932-1933, p. 112; *The Chinese Recorder*, Vol. LXIV, p. 331.

[178] *The Chinese Recorder*, Vol. LXI, p. 734.

[179] Vol. IV, p. 100.

[180] W. F. Rowlands in *The International Review of Missions*, Vol. XXI, pp. 272-280.

[181] Knott, *The Light Approaching*, p. 70.

[182] Rosalind Goforth, *Goforth of China* (Grand Rapids, Zondervan Publishing Company, 1931, pp. 364), *passim*.

[183] *The Chinese Recorder*, Vol. LXII, p. 263.

against hatred, covetousness, stealing and adultery,[184] and accompanied by such phenomena as speaking with tongues, the curing of demon possession, and the use of singing, usually of passages from the Bible set to Chinese tunes. This continued through much of the 1930's.[185] In the 1930's several Chinese travelled widely through the country, some of them singly, others with organized parties, some quiet and others dramatic in their methods. The Bethel Band, led by John Sung and Andrew Gih, visited a number of centres, reaching rich and poor, students, business men, coolies, and beggars and stimulating confession of sin and restitution.[186] Some Chinese preachers proclaimed the second coming of Christ as imminent.[187] Chang Chih-chiang, a general, was active in promoting Bible study, prayer bands, the winning of individuals by individuals, and efforts at bringing the Christian spirit to bear on national and international issues.[188] Here and there were companies of soldiers who professed to be Christians.[189] In some instances officers were marching their men to church every Sunday.[190] In 1938 Chiang Kai-shek ordered all hospital units to make contacts with local Christian communities and to provide facilities for preaching to the wounded.[191] On Christmas Eve, 1943, Chiang Kai-shek sent out a message by radio and newspapers to wounded and sick officers and soldiers commending Jesus to them as the saviour of the world.[192] There were efforts, not unsuccessful, by Chinese Christians to carry the Christian message to non-Chinese tribes in the West. Some of this was done even during the trying days of the Japanese invasion.[193] The "Oxford Groups," outgrowths of the Buchman movement, and composed of both Chinese and foreigners, had influence in some quarters.[194] A group, largely Chinese, inaugurated a radio broadcasting station in Shanghai for putting Christian programmes on the air.[195] These instances do not provide a complete picture,

[184] Mary K. Crawford, *The Shantung Revival* (Shanghai, The China Baptist Publication Society, 3d ed., 1933, p. 106), *passim*.

[185] A missionary in Shantung to the author, Apr. 10, 1938.

[186] *The China Christian Year Book*, 1932-1933, pp. 176-180; *The Chinese Recorder*, Vol. LXII, p. 463, Vol. LXIV, pp. 622, 623, Vol. LXV, pp. 740-742, Vol. LXVI, pp. 46-48.

[187] *The Chinese Recorder*, Vol. LXV, pp. 303-306.

[188] *The China Christian Year Book*, 1932-1933, p. 180; *The Chinese Recorder*, Vol. LXI, p. 470, Vol. LXIV, p. 398.

[189] French, Cable, and French, *A Desert Journal*, pp. 23-25.

[190] *The Chinese Recorder*, Vol. LXV, p. 139.

[191] *The International Review of Missions*, Vol. XXVIII, p. 14.

[192] See a translation of the text by F. W. Price in *The Christian Century*, Vol. LXI, pp. 331, 332.

[193] Franklin, *The Never Failing Light*, p. 24; Newton Chiang to the author, April, 1944; *The Chinese Recorder*, Vol. LXII, p. 732.

[194] *The China Christian Year Book*, 1932-1933, p. 176; *The Chinese Recorder*, Vol. LXVI, pp. 237-241, 251, 255.

[195] *The Chinese Recorder*, Vol. LXV, p. 60.

but they give some indication of the manner in which, largely in the 1930's, Chinese Protestants were spreading their faith.

We must pause for a moment to note a huge area, Sinkiang, which, while part of the Chinese Empire, was loosely attached to China Proper and was only partly Chinese in population. Across it led the ancient caravan routes from China to Western Asia and the Occident. In the nineteenth and twentieth centuries the steamship and the Trans-Siberian Railway usurped its traditional function as a main contact zone between China and the world to the west. Occidental culture and, with it, Christianity, were slow in permeating it. In the 1890's the Swedish Missionary Society established itself at Kashgar and from there reached neighbouring towns. In the first decade of the twentieth century members of the China Inland Mission traversed part of the region.[196] After 1914 the China Inland Mission increased its efforts.[197] In 1938 Russian influence forced out the Swedish missionaries and the following year the Society of the Friends of Moslems in China was also constrained to leave.[198]

Outer Mongolia, also through Russian Communist ascendency, became impossible for Christian missionaries. In 1924 Swedish missionaries were compelled to leave Urga and thereafter the only contact of the region with Christianity seems to have been through the sale of portions of the Bible to Mongol traders.[199]

Protestant Christianity was having slightly less difficulty in penetrating Tibet. From the Indian and especially from the Chinese borders of that land several societies were reaching Tibetans and journeys were even being made into Tibet itself. However, very few converts were won.[200]

Active and growing as was Protestant Christianity within China Proper, in these three traditional outlying dependencies of China neither it nor Roman Catholic Christianity was making much headway. Indeed, in Sinkiang and Outer Mongolia such slight footholds as had been gained were largely lost by 1940.

As we continue with our survey of the methods employed by Protestants we must note the use of literature. Here, as previously, chief emphasis was upon the Bible. As we hinted a few paragraphs above, a China Bible Society

[196] Cable *et alii*, *The Challenge of Central Asia*, pp. 48-52.

[197] Mildred Cable and Francesca French, *Something Happened* (London, Hodder & Stoughton, Ltd., 1934, pp. 320), *passim*; Mildred Cable and Francesca French, *The Making of a Pioneer. Percy Mather of Central Asia* (London, Hodder & Stoughton, 1935, pp. 288), *passim*.

[198] *The International Review of Missions*, Vol. XXIX, p. 48.

[199] Cable *et alii*, *The Challenge of Central Asia*, p. 72; *The International Review of Missions*, Vol. XXI, pp. 164-168.

[200] Cable *et alii*, *op. cit.*, pp. 88-103.

was formed. In 1937 a constitution was adopted and the British and Foreign Bible Society and the American Bible Society united their enterprises in the China Bible House. The National Bible Society of Scotland continued its separate activities. In the fore part of the 1930's a decline was noted in the demand for discrete portions of the Scriptures, but sales of entire Bibles and especially of New Testaments markedly rose. This trend seemed to indicate a serious reading of the Bible which was not content with single books. Now and again the Bible in whole or in part was being issued for the first time in an additional dialect.[201] As the storm of the Japanese invasion covered more and more of China, the circulation of the Bible became increasingly difficult. The Japanese blockade placed obstacles in the way of importing the Scriptures and the shortage of paper retarded their printing. Yet the demand seemed to mount and the distribution continued in an amazing fashion.[202]

Closely associated with the propagation of the faith and the production and use of Christian literature was what was technically denominated religious education. Religious education was emphasized in the United States during this period and almost inevitably some of the methods and ideals developed in that country were taken to China by missionaries and by Chinese trained in America. Indeed, one visiting American declared that the Sunday School in China reproduced quite too faithfully its American prototype, with its weaknesses as well as its strength.[203] Following American precedent,[204] daily vacation Bible schools were widely developed.[205] Early in the 1930's eighty-five groups were reported to be working in the field of religious education, there was much preparation of curriculum materials, and there were numbers of training schools for leaders.[206] In July, 1931, a National Religious Education Conference was held. Out of it came a Religious Education Fellowship and a National Committee on Religious Education.[207]

Protestant Christianity continued to have a large share in the general education of the country. It had been the chief pioneering agency in introducing schools of a Western type, especially those of secondary and higher grades. After 1914 private and state schools continued rapidly to emerge and Christian

[201] Lawrence Todnem in *The China Christian Year Book*, 1936-1937, pp. 376-388; *The North China Herald*, Vol. CLXXXI, p. 277.
[202] *American Bible Society, One Hundred and Twenty-Seventh Annual Report, 1943*, pp. 201-214.
[203] Laymen's Foreign Missions Inquiry, *Fact-Finders' Reports, China*, Vol. V, Supplementary Series, Part 2, pp. 302-310.
[204] Vol. IV, p. 378.
[205] *The Chinese Recorder*, Vol. LII, p. 65.
[206] *The Chinese Recorder*, Vol. LXIII, pp. 620 ff.
[207] F. W. Price in *The Chinese Recorder*, Vol. LXII, pp. 627-634.

schools were no longer as prominent as they had been. However, they still had an influence quite out of proportion to the numerical strength of the Protestant Christian community.

Soon after the first of the world wars, in 1921 and 1922, a comprehensive survey of Christian education was made by a distinguished commission headed by Ernest DeWitt Burton.[208] Its recommendations, while by no means followed slavishly, for many years had an important influence upon educational policies.

When, late in the 1920's, the Kuomintang consolidated its power, it adopted measures for the control of Christian institutions which were in part designed to lessen the foreign element and in part to prevent education from being employed for purposes of religious propaganda. The steps emerged from the strong nationalist feeling with its resentment against all that smacked of imperialism in whatever form. They issued, too, from the secularist temper of many in the government. To the regulations requiring Chinese rather than foreign heads of schools and a majority of Chinese on boards of control no great opposition was offered. To the stipulation that no religious instruction be included as a requirement and that attendance at religious services be optional much protest was heard: mission authorities closed some of the schools rather than acquiesce in what were deemed anti-Christian procedures.[209] However, the adjustment was made by most institutions, and in time the conviction was expressed that the Christian impact of the schools had been enhanced by the change.[210] More drastic measures considered by the government for the supervision not only of the schools but also of the churches were not carried through.[211]

From Christianity, stimulated by the first of the world wars and an obvious need in China, came an innovation in education, amazing in its daring. As we saw a few chapters above,[212] a Chinese Christian student, James Y. C. Yen, endeavouring to meet a situation among the Chinese labourers behind the lines in France, devised a method of teaching illiterates to read which he later intro-

---

[208] See the report in *Christian Education in China* (New York, Committee of Reference and Counsel of the Foreign Missions Conference of North America, 1922, pp. xv, 430). See also E. W. Wallace in *The China Mission Year Book*, 1923, pp. 155-165.

[209] E. H. Cressy in *The China Christian Year Book*, 1929, pp. 268-278; *The Chinese Recorder*, Vol. LXI, pp. 594-599, 601-603, 616-630.

[210] Miao and Price, *Religion and Character in Christian Middle Schools*, pp. 36, 37; Hodgkin, *Living Issues in China*, pp. 57,58; Foster, *The Chinese Church in Action*, p. 90.

[211] A. R. Kepler, *Occasional Letter No. 13* (mimeographed), Sept. 19, 1931.

[212] See Chap. III in this volume. Also see Y. C. James Yen in *The China Mission Year Book*, 1923, pp. 205-215; Y. C. James Yen, *The Mass Education Movement in China* (Shanghai, The Commercial Press, Ltd., 1925, pp. ii, 25); Eddy, *A Pilgrimage of Ideas*, pp. 128-131.

duced to China, first under the Young Men's Christian Association and later as the Mass Education Movement, to attempt to bring to literacy all of China's millions. The scope was eventually even further widened to embrace the economic, political, and moral remaking of Chinese society. Other Christians, Chinese and missionaries, took up the idea and in the North especially there was a notable effort at promoting literacy through the churches.[213]

In spite of protests by some of the missionaries,[214] Christian primary schools were fading into the background. They were declining in number and even Christian parents tended to send their children either to government or to non-Christian private schools.[215] Here and there, however, were notable institutions of that grade, one of them for underprivileged boys developed by a Chinese Christian[216] and some with industrial features.[217]

Christian middle schools persisted and by many were considered the most important means of reaching the student class with the Christian message. Statistics showed hundreds of baptisms in them, the total rising from 1,248 in the year 1933-1934 to 2,363 in the year 1935-1936.[218] Protestant middle schools were particularly strong in the coastal provinces.[219] In numbers they reached their peak not far from 1924. Then, in the nationalistic disturbances which followed that year, they suffered severely. They partly recovered and again multiplied.[220] Yet in later years the Christian character of many of them suffered. The proportion of Christian teachers and students declined. Because of their equipment, educational standards, and discipline Protestant middle schools had the confidence of prominent and wealthy Chinese parents. Yet because of their higher fees, unless assisted by scholarships boys and girls from financially circumscribed Christian homes could not afford to attend them.[221] The trend was aggravated by the decline in the financial resources of the boards and the consequent decrease in subsidies from them to the

[213] *The Chinese Recorder*, Vol. LII, pp. 37-40; *Foreign Missions Conference Bulletin*, No. 24, Apr. 1, 1931; Laymen's Foreign Missions Inquiry, *Regional Reports of the Commission of Appraisal, China*, Vol. II, Supplementary Series, Part 2, pp. 129-131.

[214] *The Chinese Recorder*, Vol. LXIII, pp. 615-620.

[215] Miao and Price, *op. cit.*, p. 46.

[216] *The Chinese Recorder*, Vol. LXI, p. 469.

[217] Laymen's Foreign Missions Inquiry, *Regional Reports of the Commission of Appraisal, China*, Vol. II, Supplementary Series, Part 2, p. 43; Laymen's Foreign Missions Inquiry, *Fact-Finders' Reports, China*, Vol. V, Supplementary Series, Part 2, p. 555.

[218] E. H. Cressy in *The Chinese Recorder*, Vol. LXVII, pp. 539-547.

[219] *The Chinese Recorder*, Vol. LXIV, p. 691.

[220] Laymen's Foreign Missions Inquiry, *Fact-Finders' Reports, China*, Vol. V, Supplementary Series, Part 2, p. 413.

[221] E. H. Cressy in *The Chinese Recorder*, Vol. LXVII, pp. 539-547; *The International Review of Missions*, Vol. XXIII, p. 25, Vol. XV, p. 25.

schools with the corollary of added enrolments and mounting fees to ensure balanced budgets.[222] For a time the numbers from the middle schools volunteering for service in the Church fell off,[223] but in the 1940's they seemed again to be increasing.[224]

Christian colleges and universities continued prominent in Protestant effort. The total enrolment in them moved upward, until in the year 1932-1933 it was well over five thousand.[225] On the eve of the Japanese invasion in 1937 it was over six thousand.[226] Under the stress of war and of the westward migration of most of the institutions to "free" China attendance for a time fell off. However, in the year 1941-1942 it had risen to over nine thousand.[227] The story of the trek of student bodies and teachers, who sometimes carried with them as they went libraries and laboratory equipment, is among the most amazing in educational history. The experience was one in which the Christian organizations were not alone, for government and private non-Christian universities and professional schools also moved to the West. That, however, did not make any less remarkable the achievement of the Christian foundations.

Most of the Christian colleges and universities drew from the United States the majority of their foreign staff and their financial subsidies. The trend was towards interdenominational co-operation and, in the United States, towards joint management and raising of funds.[228]

As in Protestant middle schools, so in Protestant colleges and universities, the drift was towards secularization.[229] The proportion of Christians in student bodies and faculties declined, budgetary necessity brought higher fees, young people from well-to-do homes were attracted, and those from poor homes found attendance impossible without scholarship aid.[230] Those of the graduates who were Christians often found it hard to fit into the average

[222] *The Bulletin of the National Christian Council*, No. 50, March 15, 1934, p. 5; Miao and Price, *op. cit.*, p. 46.

[223] Miao and Price, *op. cit.*, p. 107.

[224] Newton Chiang to the author, March, 1944.

[225] *The Chinese Recorder*, Vol. LXIV, p. 396.

[226] *Associated Boards for Christian Colleges in China, Annual Report,* June 30, 1943, p. 2.

[227] *Ibid.*

[228] E. H. Cressy in *The International Review of Missions*, Vol. XXII, pp. 240-250; *Leaders for China. A Call to the Colleges. Higher Education's Century of Progress in China* (New York, The Associated Boards for Christian Colleges in China, 1934, pp. 11), *passim.*

[229] Kiang Wen-han in *The Chinese Recorder*, Vol. LXVIII, pp. 302-305; Laymen's Foreign Missions Inquiry, *Fact-Finders' Reports, China*, Vol. V, Supplementary Series, Part 2, p. 355.

[230] See a very interesting autobiography of a girl who had been a student in three of the leading Christian colleges and universities in Helena Kuo, *I've Come a Long Way* (New York, D. Appleton-Century Company, 1942, pp. 369), pp. 55-165.

Protestant church.[231] Yet the institutions continued to exert a Christian influence and in them lives were transformed.[232] Government schools rapidly outstripped them in attendance,[233] but they still gave a good account of themselves.

For a time in the 1920's and the 1930's many of the ablest and most intellectual of the students of China were attracted by Communism because it seemed to promise a quick and decisive attack on the problems of the country.[234] Many of the Christian students appeared to be uncertain and uninformed on the basic tenets of their faith.[235] We hear of at least one prominent young Christian who joined the Communists on the ground that they offered a shorter road than did the Church to rescuing China from her ills.[236]

However, the Christian forces were continuing to approach students not only through schools under their auspices but also in other ways. The Young Men's Christian Association devoted much of its attention to students. As before 1914, so after that year it held summer conferences for them. Most of those in attendance were already Christians, and the experience of common worship and study strengthened their faith.[237] There were also local units of Christian students. The student Christian movement associated with the Young Men's and Young Women's Christian Associations gave much thought to the social reconstruction of China.[238]

The Young Men's and Young Women's Christian Associations, especially the former, were prominent in China, probably relatively more so than in any other large non-Occidental land. With their emphasis upon the building of character and upon education and social welfare they appealed to the better elements in China, nurtured as they had been in Confucianism.[239] Because of the reaction from the phenomenal expansion during and immediately after the first of the world wars, the Young Men's Christian Associations of the United States, which had borne the chief load of supplying the foreign staff, had greatly to curtail their commitments. The foreign personnel, therefore, declined

[231] Maclennan, *Report to the Conference of Missionary Societies of Great Britain and Ireland on a Visit to the Far East, January-July, 1934*, p. 21.

[232] Laymen's Foreign Missions Inquiry, *op. cit.*, Vol. V, Supplementary Series, Part 2, p. 400.

[233] J. L. Stuart in *The Chinese Recorder*, Vol. LXIII, p. 603.

[234] Snow, *The Battle for Asia*, p. 282; Sherwood Eddy, mimeographed letter, Shanghai, Dec. 8, 1931.

[235] W. E. Wilkinson in *The Chinese Recorder*, Vol. LXI, pp. 490-497.

[236] E. C. Lobenstine, in the presence of the author, May, 1930.

[237] *The Chinese Recorder*, Vol. LXI, p. 665, Vol. LXII, pp. 664-666.

[238] *The Bulletin of the National Christian Council.* Oct. 8, 1935; *Christ and Students of the East*, p. 38.

[239] *International Survey of the Young Men's and Young Women's Christian Associations*, pp. 185, 186.

sharply in the 1920's and 1930's.[240] However, Chinese secretaries were found in fairly large numbers.[241] Moreover, even under the stress of the war between China and Japan, new Young Men's Christian Associations were organized and budgets of several local associations were over-subscribed by Chinese.[242]

Protestants still had a large share in bringing the methods and facilities of modern Western medicine and surgery to the healing of the diseases of China and to education in public health. They had been the leading pioneers in this area of life.[243] Thanks in large part to their achievements, by 1945 Chinese Government and other secular agencies, with much larger financial resources, were forging ahead of Protestant institutions. However, in 1931 six medical schools were supported by Protestant missionary societies.[244] In addition, there was an important school which had arisen from the efforts of the Yale Mission. Moreover, the leading medical school in China, the Peking Union Medical College, was built on the foundations laid by Protestant mission boards and was financed by the China Medical Board, a creation of Rockefeller benevolence.[245] In 1931 about nine-tenths of all nurses in China were Christians,[246] vivid evidence of the place of the Christian forces in creating that profession. Public health on a local and nation-wide scale owed much of its inception to W. W. Peter who, under the Young Men's Christian Associations in the early years of the period, toured the country lecturing and organizing demonstrations for the prevention of disease.[247]

To the chronic problems of the Chinese city were added, in a number of urban centres, notably Shanghai, those which followed from industrialization. Protestants were making efforts to meet the evils which attended the growth of modern factories. We hear of projects corresponding to the "social settlements" of the Occident,[248] and of activities of the Young Men's and Young Women's Christian Associations for the labourers.[249] Here and there missions

[240] *The Chinese Recorder*, Vol. LXIII, p. 259.

[241] Gerald W. Birks, mimeographed letter, Hongkong, Feb. 16, 1931.

[242] S. C. Leung, General Secretary of the National Committee of the Young Men's Christian Associations, mimeographed letter, Oct. 16, 1939.

[243] For the autobiography of one who first came out under a missionary society and later, independently, built up a notable sanitarium in Shanghai, see Anne Walter Fearn, *My Days of Strength* (New York, Harper & Brothers, 1939, pp. xiii, 297), *passim*.

[244] Laymen's Foreign Missions Inquiry, *Fact-Finders' Reports, China*, Vol. V, Supplementary Series, Part 2, p. 437.

[245] The author was a trustee of both Yale-in-China and the China Medical Board and so wrote from personal knowledge.

[246] *Report of the Commission of Appraisal of the Laymen's Foreign Missions Inquiry*, Vol. XII, p. 15.

[247] *The China Mission Year Book*, 1916, pp. 315, 316, 1918, pp. 211-216.

[248] Emma Silver in *The Chinese Recorder*, Vol. LXII, p. 124.

[249] *The Chinese Recorder*, Vol. LXII, pp. 351-355; Laymen's Foreign Missions Inquiry, *Fact-Finders' Reports, China*, Vol. V, Supplementary Series, Part 2, pp. 512, 524.

encouraged home industries under satisfactory working conditions.[250] The National Christian Council and the Young Men's and Young Women's Christian Associations strove valiantly to alleviate the deplorable state of labour in the factories of Shanghai.[251]

Since the overwhelming majority of Chinese lived in rural areas and since the pressure of population upon subsistence was both chronic and acute, it is not strange that the efforts at improving agriculture and rural communities which characterized the Protestant missions of the period were particularly marked in China. They were numerous and varied. The College of Agriculture and Forestry of the University of Nanking, founded on Christian initiative in an attempt to prevent famines and conducted under Christian auspices, was the outstanding pioneer in bringing to bear upon the utilization of the soil the knowledge and skills accumulated in the Occident.[252] A somewhat similar department was carried on in Lingnan University.[253] Specialists in agriculture were sent as missionaries by more than one society,[254] agricultural experiment and demonstration centres were set up, and the curricula of numbers of schools were made to include subjects suitable to rural areas.[255] The North China Christian Rural Service Union sought "redemption of the whole of life through a church deeply rooted in the village."[256] One of its branches encouraged co-operative societies, agricultural extension, and the promotion of subsidiary industries for the rural population.[257] We hear of a pastor of a rural church who on a small salary managed to fit out a library and reading room for his young men, conducted a night school to teach his people to read, introduced tested rice seed, conducted a campaign for vaccination, and had a parents' education class.[258] In another rural district the Christian wife of an official established a woman's self-help institute, a nursery school, and a

[250] Hodgkin, *Living Issues in China*, p. 91.

[251] Adelaide Mary Anderson, *Humanity and Labour in China. An Industrial Visit and Its Sequel (1923 to 1926)* (London, Student Christian Movement, 1928, pp. xv, 285), pp. 102 ff.

[252] *University of Nanking Bulletin, Catalog*, Dec., 1931, pp. 18 ff.; *University of Nanking Bulletin, Report of the President, 1918-1919*, pp. 34 ff., *Report of the President and Treasurer, 1922-1923*, pp. 36 ff., *1925-26*, pp. 30 ff., Carson, *Agricultural Missions*, pp. 32-40.

[253] *Report of the Commission of Appraisal of the Laymen's Foreign Missions Inquiry*, Vol. X, p. 11.

[254] Laymen's Foreign Missions Inquiry, *Regional Reports of the Commission of Appraisal, China*, Vol. II, Supplementary Series, Part 1, p. 13. See also *The Chinese Recorder*, Vol. LXII, pp. 329-331, Vol. LXIII, pp. 518, 519.

[255] J. H. Reisner in *The China Mission Year Book*, 1919, pp. 158-172.

[256] *The Chinese Recorder*, Vol. LXIII, p. 518; *The Tungchow Rural Institute . . . Tunghsien, Hopei, China, March 20-April 3, 1935* (pp. 90), *passim*.

[257] *The Chinese Recorder*, Vol. LXV, p. 62.

[258] Felton, *The Rural Church in the Far East*, p. 22.

women's household discussion association.[259] In Kiangsi, in the 1930's, in an area formerly overrun by Communists, an American missionary with the encouragement of Chiang Kai-shek and the aid of some other Christians worked out a project for rural reconstruction.[260] Under the direction of Frank W. Price, Nanking Theological Seminary undertook a special curriculum for the training of rural ministers.[261] So successful was the experiment of agricultural fairs inaugurated in North China under the inspiration of the mission of the American Board of Commissioners for Foreign Missions that the national government ordered them to be held throughout the country.[262] The Young Men's Christian Association had a secretary who specialized on rural problems.[263] For a time it concentrated this effort on a rural area near Soochow.[264] In one mission in the North, varieties of drought resistant grain were developed to improve the production of food in that semi-arid region.[265] These examples of what was being undertaken by Protestants will give some inkling of the fashion in which that branch of the Christian movement was seeking to contribute to the rural life and the agricultural production of the country.

Protestants gave attention to the creation of distinctively Christian homes. This was the more important because their faith led Chinese Christians to abandon or modify the traditional honours to ancestors, the strongest of the bonds which held the family together, and because, under the impact of Western ideas and education, numbers of younger Chinese rejected the customs of arranging and consummating marriage which had come down from the past. Many Chinese Christians modeled their homes in part on what they saw in the homes of missionaries.[266] In the 1920's and 1930's organized efforts were made, some of them by the National Christian Council and the Young Men's Christian Association, to give education in Christian ideals of sex, marriage, and the family.[267]

[259] *The Chinese Recorder*, Vol. LXVIII, pp. 366-369.

[260] *The International Review of Missions*, Vol. XXIV, p. 27; G. W. Shepherd in *The International Review of Missions*, Vol. XXVI, pp. 167-176; Letter of Sherwood Eddy, Sept. 22, 1934.

[261] *Agricultural Mission Notes*, No. 7. July, 1933; Butterfield, *The Rural Mission of the Church in Eastern Asia*, pp. 39-43.

[262] Willard Simpson, an agricultural missionary in North China, to the author, Sept. 24, 1933.

[263] The Laymen's Foreign Missions Inquiry, *Fact-Finders' Reports, China*, Vol. V, Supplementary Series, Part 2, pp. 226-228. See also *International Survey of the Young Men's and Young Women's Christian Associations*, pp. 199, 200.

[264] Hodgkin, *Living Issues in China*, p. 92.

[265] Outerbridge in *Annals of the American Academy of Political and Social Science*, Vol. CLII, pp. 99-104.

[266] Helen Wiley Dutton in *The Chinese Recorder*, Vol. LXIV, p. 439.

[267] *The Chinese Recorder*, Vol. LXII, pp. 182, 666-668; *The Christian Century*, Vol. XLVIII, p. 1185.

In a variety of other ways Protestants sought to contribute to wholesome social movements and to the elimination of chronic evils. Chinese Protestants were active in a National Child Welfare Association.[268] Several Protestant organizations in which foreigners and Chinese joined raised and distributed funds for the relief of sufferers from floods.[269] Protestant Christians fought opium,[270] thus reinforcing the best of the Chinese conscience.[271] It must be noted that in this,[272] as in famine relief, the Roman Catholics were also active.

From what has been said in this summary fashion, it will be clear that Protestant Christianity was deliberately seeking to affect Chinese life from many angles and in numbers of its phases. Not all Protestant Christians, whether foreign or Chinese, shared the dream of bringing their faith to bear on all of Chinese life, but there were those who thought of their mission as the remaking of China in its many complex facets. Although, when compared with the vast mass of China, they were few in number, and although possessed of pitifully small resources in funds, they were venturing out with daring and faith in the endeavour to mould the nation in its day of revolution. In an age when Chinese culture was in flux they were striving to build Christian ideals into the new civilization which was slowly and painfully emerging.

Protestants could no more hope to escape the disorders through which China was passing than could Roman Catholics. Rampant nationalism, the anti-Christian movements, Communists, civil war, banditry, and the Japanese invasion all took their toll.

Chinese nationalism often looked askance at Protestant as at Roman Catholic Christianity as alien and under foreign control. As we saw a few paragraphs above, schools run by missionaries, with their influence in moulding the oncoming generation, were regarded with distrust[273] and not even the transfer of the management to Chinese hands entirely cleared them from suspicion. The special protection by their governments which missionaries, along with other foreigners, enjoyed under the treaties was a cause of complaint by Chinese. In the 1920's, when the agitation was acute, many mission-

---

[268] *The Chinese Recorder*, Vol. LXIV, p. 690; *The China Christian Year Book*, 1939, pp. 350-358.
[269] *The Chinese Recorder*, Vol. LXI, pp. 348, 349, Vol. LXII, pp. 139, 678, Vol. LXIII, pp. 461, 662, 679, 685.
[270] Hodgkin, *op. cit.*, p. 121.
[271] *The China Christian Year Book*, 1929, pp. 328-335.
[272] *The Chinese Recorder*, Vol. LXIII, p. 122.
[273] A. R. Kepler, letter, June 13, 1930; Laymen's Foreign Missions Inquiry, *Fact-Finders' Reports, China*, Vol. V, Supplementary Series, Part 2, p. 148.

aries strove to dissociate themselves from their special status and advocated the abolition of extraterritoriality.[274]

The first burst of the anti-Christian movement, in 1922, did not bring serious loss. Indeed, by attracting attention it increased the interest of many in Christianity.[275] The renewal and intensification of the anti-Christian movement in the mid-1920's, coupled with the agitation against foreign imperialism as personified in Britain, brought much greater embarrassment. Many British and American missionaries felt it necessary to leave their posts, partly because their presence placed their Chinese friends in jeopardy, and Chinese Christians, especially pastors, were derided as "running dogs of the foreigners."[276]

The Communist movement added to the difficulties. In areas controlled by the Communists missionaries either had to leave or were harshly treated. Some mission property was destroyed.[277] A few missionaries were killed.[278]

Losses from banditry and civil war were heavy. There had been a time in the fore part of the twentieth century when missionaries and Chinese Christians were to some degree immune from attack. The stern measures taken by foreign powers in behalf of their citizens who had been mishandled, especially in 1900, tended to ward off attempts on their persons and property. Some mission stations were regarded by the Chinese as havens in the storm and in their search for security numbers of Chinese became Christians. By the end of the 1920's the situation had changed. Anti-imperialist and anti-Christian propaganda and the growing reluctance of Western governments to resort to force in behalf of their nationals made missionaries and Chinese Christians rather more than less subject to attack than their non-Christian neighbours.[279] Because of the supposed wealth of foreigners, missionaries became for the bandits desirable objects of kidnapping and ransom. In the six years from 1924 to 1929 inclusive at least twelve Protestant missionaries were killed and fifty-nine kidnapped[280] and in

[274] *The Chinese Recorder*, Vol. LIV, p. 569, Vol. LVI, pp. 705-715, 769-771, 834-838; *The China Christian Year Book*, 1926, pp. 483-534.

[275] *The Chinese Recorder*, Vol. LIV, p. 3.

[276] *The China Christian Year Book*, 1928, pp. 105-119.

[277] *The Chinese Recorder*, Vol. LXI, pp. 396, 737; *The International Review of Missions*, Vol. XXV, p. 22; A. B. Lewis, *"Is Thy God . . . Able?" The story of 100 days' captivity in the hands of Communist bandits* (London, The China Inland Mission, 1931, pp. 63), *passim*; R. A. Bosshardt, *The Restraining Hand. Captivity for Christ in China* (London, Hodder and Stoughton, 1936, pp. 288), *passim*; Daniel Nelson, *The Apostle to the Chinese Communists* (Minneapolis, The Board of Foreign Missions of the Norwegian Lutheran Church of America, 1935, pp. vi, 139), *passim*; E. H. Giedt, letter, Nov. 12, 1931.

[278] Mrs. Howard Taylor, *The Triumph of John and Betty Stam* (Philadelphia, China Inland Mission, 1936, pp. 129), *passim*; Lee S. Huizenga, *John and Betty Stam—Martyrs* (Grand Rapids, Zondervan Publishing House, 1935, pp. 101), *passim*.

[279] *The Chinese Recorder*, Vol. LXII, pp. 709-713, 801.

[280] *The Chinese Recorder*, Vol. LXI, p. 475.

the succeeding five years fifteen were killed, one died in captivity, one was either killed or perished in captivity, and twenty-one were in captivity for longer or shorter periods.[281] There seem to be no available statistics of the numbers of Chinese Christians who suffered. The most spectacular of the attacks on missionaries was on March 24th, 1927, when members of a Nationalist army after taking Nanking rudely handled foreigners in that city and killed one of the most prominent of the Protestant missionaries.[282] There were a few instances of Christians turning bandit.[283] Yet there were also instances of Chinese Christians risking their lives to ward off bandits and marauding soldiers, of their going to the relief of the wounded, and of their staying by a village or town to maintain order after the local officials had fled.[284] In some of the sections most affected by the disorders, the Christian forces, too, persisted in carrying on their usual activities and even reached out to preach to non-Christians.[285] Many missionaries stuck by their posts, giving relief and protection.[286]

The Japanese invasion which began on a large scale in the occupation of Manchuria in 1931 and 1932 and the setting up of the state of Manchukuo brought problems to Protestants, as to Roman Catholics, in the affected areas.[287] On the eve of the Japanese action Protestantism in Manchuria had been displaying a revival. For several years the churches had seemed to be suffering from a falling tide. There had been losses in membership, due partly to extensive migration from the southern to the northern province.[288] There was, too, division on the issue of whether Christians should participate in political and social movements for the remaking of the country, or should cultivate a life separate from that of their environment.[289] However, by the spring of 1931 churches in several districts had experienced awakenings, baptisms were increasing, and attendance was improving.[290] The immediate effect of the Japanese occupation was far from uniform. In one large section unrest and

[281] *The Chinese Recorder*, Vol. LXVI, pp. 704-706. See instances in *The Chinese Recorder*, Vol. LXIII, pp. 120, 121; Ernst Fischle, *Sechzehn Monate in chinesischer Gefangenschaft* (Stuttgart, Evang. Missionsverlag, 1931, pp. 192), *passim*; Simkin in *West China Missionary News*, Vol. XXXII, nos. 7 and 8, pp. 11-15.
[282] W. Reginald Wheeler, *John E. Williams of Nanking* (New York, Fleming H. Revell Company, 1937, pp. 222), pp. 169 ff.; Richard H. Pousma, *An Eventful Year in the Orient* (Grand Rapids, Eerdmans Publishing Co., 1927, pp. 233), *passim*.
[283] G. W. Shepherd in *The Chinese Recorder*, Vol. LXII, p. 145.
[284] *The China Christian Year Book*, 1929, pp. 173-196.
[285] Lipphard, *Out of the Storm in China*, pp. 42-52.
[286] As in Clayton, *Heaven Below*, pp. 49-106.
[287] For one whose life in Manchuria spanned much of the period immediately preceding 1931, see Margaret Weir, *Andrew Weir of Manchuria* (London, James Clarke & Co., Ltd., no date, pp. 255).
[288] Macnaughton in *The Chinese Recorder*, Vol. LXII, pp. 454-456.
[289] Morton, *To-day in Manchuria*, pp. 25-29.
[290] Macnaughton in *The Chinese Recorder*, Vol. LXII, pp. 454-456.

banditry led to the closing of about half the Christian centres and the crowding of country folk into the cities.[291] Japanese, too, tended to view the churches with suspicion, as they did all Chinese organizations.[292] Yet for the most part the movement towards the churches continued. To many the churches and their faith seemed the only stable element in a distraught and shifting world. At Christian gatherings there were emotional scenes, with the casting out of demons, speaking with tongues, and the public confession of sins. New churches were erected, summer conferences were held, and Bible study flourished. Church membership rapidly increased.[293] Numbers of Japanese were friendly.[294] Then came an abrupt change. On October 10th, 1935, the Japanese police suddenly arrested sixty of the leading Christians. It was the Chinese "Double Tenth," the anniversary of the revolution which led to the founding of the republic. Non-Christian Chinese were also among those arrested. The step was obviously an attempt of the Japanese, not to stamp out Christianity, but to curb all Chinese organizations which might conceivably jeopardize Japanese rule. The Christians were bewildered, but no extensive apostasy occurred.[295] Pressure was brought on Christians in both church and school to do reverence in Confucian temples, for it was on the basis of this ancient Chinese cult that Japan was endeavouring to give spiritual cohesion to its puppet child.[296] After the outbreak of war on December 7th, 1941, between Japan on the one hand and the United States and the British Empire on the other, most of such Protestant missionaries as remained in Manchuria were interned and then sent to Japan to await repatriation.[297] The various types of Protestantism were forced to unite in one church, a procedure upon which the Japanese Government was insisting both in Japan Proper and in its dependencies.[298] Manchurian Christianity was facing difficult years.

The enlargement of Japan's invasion of China which began in July, 1937, brought grave and progressive dislocation to the Protestant forces. Yet this was by no means all loss. Many missionaries left the country, partly on the urgent advice of their governments. Others continued at their posts or accompanied

---

[291] *Quarterly Notes, being the Bulletin of the International Missionary Council,* July, 1933, p. iii; *The Chinese Recorder,* Vol. LXIII, p. 123.

[292] *The Chinese Recorder,* Vol. LXIII, pp. 391-393.

[293] *The Chinese Recorder,* Vol. LXIII, p. 259, Vol. LXIV, pp. 394, 395, 773-785, Vol. LXV, pp. 392, 393; Maclennan, *Report to the Conference of British Missionary Societies of Great Britain and Ireland on a Visit to the Far East, January—July, 1934,* p. 27.

[294] F. W. S. O'Neill in *The International Review of Missions,* Vol. XXIV, pp. 515-523; Morton, *op. cit.,* pp. 56-64.

[295] Morton, *op. cit.,* pp. 65 ff.

[296] *The International Review of Missions,* Vol. XXIX, p. 14.

[297] *The International Review of Missions,* Vol. XXXII, p. 9.

[298] *International Christian Press and Information Service,* Feb., 1944.

the migrants to "free China." In the months following December 7th, 1941, such British and American missionaries as remained in "occupied China" were interned and many of them were repatriated. Thousands of Protestant Christians went westward to "free China." There they greatly strengthened the Christian cause.[299] There, as in "occupied China," relief by the Christian forces was administered on an extensive scale. New churches were organized and the Young Men's Christian Association enlarged its service.[300] In "occupied China" missionaries, until interned, and their Chinese *confrères* ministered to the destitute and suffering and in numbers of instances stood, at the risk and even at the cost of their own lives, between the Japanese soldiers and their victims.[301] The example of the Christians in these times of stress made a deep impression on thousands of non-Christians. Many became Christians and in some cities the decline in church membership caused by the westward exodus was compensated by fresh accessions from the destitute who were unable to leave. At least partly on the initiative of the Japanese armed forces, Japanese Christians established relations with the Chinese churches. Under their direction, in the North the same kind of amalgamation of the Protestant churches was effected that had been brought about in Japan.[302] A somewhat similar union was effected in Central China.[303]

While exact statistics were lacking, it seemed clear that in spite of the distress through which the nation was passing and in the face of the destruction of mission and church property, Protestant Christianity was gaining in China during the war years. The withdrawal of so large a proportion of the foreign staff threw more responsibility upon the Chinese. In some places the latter cracked under the testing, but in others they rose nobly to the emergency. Moreover, in spite of the Japanese blockade, Chinese Protestantism was keeping in touch with the world-wide Church. It was ably represented, chiefly by Chinese, at the Madras meeting of the International Missionary Council in December, 1938. In 1943 and 1944 it established closer contacts with Indian Christianity.[304] By letter and by travel it maintained ties with the founding churches of the West. For Protestant Christianity in China as in so many other parts of the world, the years were ones of advance through storm.

[299] Wu Yi-fang and Frank W. Price, *China Rediscovers her West* (New York, Friendship Press, 1940, pp. xiii, 210), *passim*; Ballou, *Dangerous Opportunity*, pp. 166 ff.

[300] *Minutes of the International Board* (Ms.), Sept. 17, 1943.

[301] Ballou, *op. cit.*, pp. 132-165. See a vivid autobiographic account of one missionary in "occupied" China in Clayton, *Heaven Below*, pp. 1-11, 169-273.

[302] See Chapter XIV.

[303] *The International Review of Missions*, Vol. XXXIII, p. 24.

[304] *Overseas News Letter of the National Christian Council*, February, 1944 (mimeographed).

In the effect of Christianity upon China during the turbulent decades after 1914, two generalizations stand out: the impression of Christianity upon China was growing and in the main was a continuation of what had been begun before 1914.

From what has been recorded in earlier paragraphs it must be clear that numerically Christians were a more considerable proportion of the population in 1944 than they had been thirty years earlier. In 1914, as we saw in the preceding volume,[305] baptized Christians were approximately one and three-quarters millions, or slightly less than one-half of one per cent. of the population. In the difficult years of the 1940's accurate statistics were impossible. The latest totals obtainable, and they were obviously imperfect, gave the numbers of Roman Catholics in 1941 as slightly above three and a quarter millons,[306] of Russian Orthodox as over one hundred thousand,[307] of whom the large majority were non-Chinese, and baptized Protestants in 1936 as over six hundred thousand.[308] This made a total of about four millions or approximately one per cent. of the population. Uncounted other thousands had once considered themselves Christians or still regarded themselves as such.

More important than the statistical summary was the effect of their faith upon those who bore the Christian name. As in other lands and ages, this varied in extent and intensity from individual to individual.[309] In some a growing and striking approximation to New Testament standards was seen. In others the impress of the Christian spirit and ideals was slight. We hear of an educated Christian who slipped into gambling and opium smoking, but who, after adversity, returned to his faith, abandoned his vices, and became humble and penitent.[310] We read of others who by their faith were freed from gambling or who were reconciled after long estrangement.[311] There was also a woman who came to a Christian hospital to be cured of the opium habit, obtained the victory, and then gave herself to unselfish service to the underprivileged.[312] Christian faith usually brought emancipation from the fear of spirits which was so widespread an aspect of Chinese life.[313] Among the reprehensible characteristics attached to some Christians were said to be deracination from old attachments with only half-hearted commitment to Christian standards, the pauperizing of

[305] Vol. VI, p. 356.
[306] *Lumen Service,* June 20, 1941.
[307] Bolshakoff, *The Foreign Missions of the Russian Orthodox Church,* p. 82.
[308] Parker, *Interpretative Statistical Survey of the World Mission of the Christian Church,* p. 50.
[309] For autobiographical instances see *The Chinese Recorder,* Vol. LXVIII, pp. 216-221.
[310] Scott, *Chinese Twice Born,* pp. 13-26.
[311] Johannsen, *A Great Door,* pp. 19, 20.
[312] Hollister, *Lady Fourth, Daughter of China,* p. 33.
[313] Cressy, *Yellow Rivers,* p. 99.

groups by continued financial aid from foreign sources to churches and schools, a weaning away from Chinese culture, whether good or bad, and a clannishness which avoided association with non-Christian Chinese of good character.[314] On the other hand, Christianity made for the abandonment of vices and of concubinage, for new happiness and harmony in the home, for greater cleanliness, for the education of women, and for greater joy.[315]

The outstanding part that Christians, and especially Protestant Christians, had in the life of China in the three decades after 1914 was very striking. Of those listed in a volume labeled *Who's Who in China*, thirty-five per cent. had at one time or another been connected with Protestant schools.[316] This was partly because of the fashion in which these schools had been pioneers in the type of education which prepared their students for the new age brought by the West. It seems also and primarily to have been for deeper reasons. One Chinese prominent in education, business, and government declared that in the testing brought by war the graduates of Christian colleges were more public-spirited and less self-seeking than those who had not had that training.[317] A non-Christian foreign newspaper correspondent with opportunities for wide observation gave it as his considered judgment that Christianity had produced a special type of human being in China, more alert, more modern, more socialized in his outlook, less intensively individualistic, and more committed to the public welfare.[318] It was clear that after 1914 the Chinese who were most widely influential were Christians. We have already seen[319] that the outstanding figure in the Republic, the patron saint and national hero of the dominant Kuomintang, was Sun Yat-sen, who owed his formal education to Christian institutions and to the end of his life called himself a Christian and confessed that he had drawn many of his ideals and theories from his Christian faith.[320] The Soong family, sometimes half seriously called the Soong Dynasty, was of earnest Christian parentage. One of its sons, T. V. Soong, was the financial genius of the nationalist government. Its three daughters married Sun Yat-sen, Chiang Kai-shek, and one long a member of the cabinet, H. H. K'ung, a Chris-

[314] Laymen's Foreign Missions Inquiry, *Fact-Finders' Reports, China,* Vol. V, Supplementary Series, Part 2, pp. 167, 168.

[315] Laymen's Foreign Missions Inquiry, *op. cit.,* Vol. V, Supplementary Series, Part 2, pp. 157, 158.

[316] Laymen's Foreign Missions Inquiry, *op. cit.,* Vol. V, Supplementary Series, Part 2, p. 154.

[317] Quoted in J. L. Stuart, letter, mimeographed, Apr. 5, 1940. For examples of students in a Christian middle school seeking to "save China," see Clayton, *Heaven Below,* pp. 153-168.

[318] George E. Sokolsky, *The Tinder Box of Asia* (Garden City, Doubleday, Doran and Company, 1932, pp. x, 376), pp. 21, 22.

[319] Vol. VI, pp. 363, 364.

[320] Pascal M. d'Elia in *The Chinese Recorder,* Vol. LXII, pp. 75-88.

tian from boyhood.[321] Chiang Kai-shek became a Christian after his marriage into the Soong family and seems to have done so from conviction rather than from a desire to conform to the wishes of his new connexions. Both he and his wife gave frequent public expression of their Christian faith. It appears clear that from this faith came much of the poise, the calm courage, and the persistence which enabled Chiang to carry the country through the long and exhausting struggle with Japan.[322] Although he combined his Christian faith with what had come to him through Confucianism, Chiang seems to have been more intelligently and diligently Christian than Sun Yat-sen or some of the others who were prominent in the state. Among the other Christians were Fêng Yü-hsiang, a vigorous and picturesque war-lord, who attracted attention in the 1920's by his furthering of Christian preaching to his troops and his stern curbing among them of some of the usual camp vices;[323] Chang Chih-chiang, a general, who was baptized while in Fêng's army;[324] and descendants of Tsêng Kuo-fan (the outstanding Chinese statesman of the third quarter of the nineteenth century), one of whom, a woman, remaining unmarried, conducted a Christian school for girls.[325] The list might be multiplied to include a business man who resigned from a lucrative post in a company rather than consent to the "squeeze" which he found there,[326] the distinguished college president and national figure, Chang Po-ling, and a number of other leading educators and statesmen.

Christians were the inspiration of programmes for moral reform which were directed either to the entire nation or to particular groups. The New Life Movement, a project of Chiang Kai-shek for the renovation of the country, was one such.[327] The Officers' Moral Endeavour Association was frankly pat-

[321] Vol. VI, pp. 324, 364.

[322] As examples of the extensive literature see *The New York Times,* Apr. 26, 1937, Apr. 13, 1943; letters of an intimate friend of Chiang-Kai-shek and his wife, Frank W. Price, Nov. 10, 1930, Nov. 21, 1931; Madame Chiang Kai-shih, *My Religion (Shanghai Evening Post & Mercury,* May 14, 1934, pp. 13)); Wu I-fang to author, June 7, 1936; May-ling Soong Chiang, *This Is Our China* (New York, Harper & Brothers, pp. 312), pp. 157-182; *The Christian Century,* Vol. LIV, pp. 611, 612; J. L. Stuart, letter, mimeographed, April, 1940.

[323] *The China Mission Year Book,* 1919, pp. 281-286; Marshall Broomhall, *General Feng, a Good Soldier of Christ Jesus* (London, China Inland Mission, 1923, pp. xiii, 80), *passim*; Marcus Ch'eng, *Marshal Feng, the Man and his Work* (Shanghai, Kelly & Walsh, Ltd., 1926, pp. 107), *passim*; *The Chinese Recorder,* Vol. LXIII, p. 70.

[324] Chang Chih-chiang, in *The Chinese Recorder,* Vol. LXIV, pp. 586-591, 659-664.

[325] Galbraith, *The Dragon Sheds his Skin,* pp. 29-36, 46.

[326] Franklin, *The Never Failing Light,* p. 75.

[327] Madame Chiang Kai-shek in *The Chinese Recorder,* Vol. LXVIII, pp. 279, 280; George W. Shepherd in *op. cit.,* Vol. LXVIII, pp. 280-282; R. Y. Lo in *op. cit.,* Vol. LXVIII, pp. 283-290; C. T. Wang in *The Christian Herald,* Sept., 1937; Barnett, *The Far East in the Summer of 1940,* p. 42.

terned after the Young Men's Christian Association.[328] The San Min Chi I Youth Corps, founded by the Kuomintang to enlist and train youths for its ranks, called on Christians, both Chinese and foreign, to help inspire it with a spiritual purpose.[329]

Christians were active in the 1930's in attempting to avert the general war between China and Japan which was clearly impending. Chinese and Japanese Christians sought to cultivate friendly relations between the churches in the two countries and missionaries laboured in unobtrusive ways to ease the tension between the two nations.[330]

An experienced foreign newspaper correspondent who described his attitude towards Christianity as that of a friendly sceptic declared that Christianity had provided the impetus for most of the really constructive social work in China in the 1930's.[331]

Christianity had effects on non-Christian faiths. Several new syncretistic cults frankly sought to combine it with elements from other religions.[332] At least one of the reform movements in Buddhism adopted methods which it had seen employed by Christian missionaries.[333] One outstanding Chinese Christian who had wide contacts with students declared that when the intellectuals spoke of religion, even to denounce it, they usually meant by the term Christianity, for in their eyes the other faiths in the country were too nearly moribund to merit attention.[334] He may have been biased, but his comment seems to have had in it much of truth.

Certainly from what we have seen in this chapter it is clear that Christianity was increasingly making itself felt in many aspects of Chinese life. This was particularly the case in education, in the state, in the relief and remedying of human suffering through medical care and public health, in the easing of famine and in its prevention through improved agriculture and forestry, in the

[328] Vernon Nash in *The Christian Century*, Vol. XLVIII, p. 1184.

[329] Newton Chiang, one of the Christians associated with the corps, to the author, Feb. 27, 1944.

[330] *The China Critic*, Oct. 13, 1931; *The Chinese Recorder*, Vol. LXII, pp. 129, 534, 606, 732, Vol. LXIII, pp. 393, 394, Vol. LXIV, pp. 555-557, Vol. LXVIII, p. 473; *The New York Times*, Dec. 4, 1931; *The Chinese Christian Student*, Jan., 1932; *The International Review of Missions*, Vol. XXIII, p. 18.

[331] H. J. Timperley in *The China Quarterly*, Summer, 1936, p. 75. See an example in Hollister, *Lady Fourth, Daughter of China*, p. 42.

[332] Hodous in Stauffer, *The Christian Occupation of China*, p. 29. See an interesting one of these cults—that of "religious brethren" proclaiming the near advent of the Chinese saviour—in *Asia*, Vol. XXXV, p. 540.

[333] K. L. Reichelt in *The China Christian Year Book*, 1932-1933, p. 110; Laymen's Foreign Missions Inquiry, *Fact-Finders' Reports, China*, Vol. V, Supplementary Series, Part 2, p. 48.

[334] Kiang Wen-han in *The China Christian Year Book*, 1932-1933, p. 320.

structure of the family, in the relations between the sexes and the position of women, in various measures for social and moral reform, and in building Christian communities through which the Christian faith could find continuing embodiment in China.

More than before 1914 China was beginning to place its impress upon Christianity. Much that was Western persevered in architecture[335] and even in the observance of foreign national holidays and the honouring of foreign flags in schools.[336] There was some defection of Chinese Christians, both Roman Catholic and Protestant, to Buddhism, on the ground that the latter placed less of a straitjacket on them and better permitted an unbiased study of the deepest problems of human life.[337] However, the Chinese environment was having its effect.

Some of this was through conscious adaptation. Paintings of Christian themes were increasingly and deliberately in the Chinese manner, with virgin and child or the holy family with Chinese features and in Chinese dress.[338] Many church buildings were in Chinese style.[339] There were instances in Christian funerals of the use of incense before the picture of the deceased.[340] Chinese tunes were being adapted for Christian worship.[341] On the walls of an Anglican cathedral there were tablets with the names of those of its constituency who had died and the lists were read on every All Saints Day, a conscious substitute for the Chinese honours to ancestors.[342] In the home of at least one devout Christian a room was dedicated as a memorial to the ancestors of the family. Christian services in commemoration of the dead were held at the time of Ch'ing Ming, one of the native festivals for the ancestors.[343] Indeed, forms of honouring the dead in a Christian manner were increasing. A clan village, turned Christian, kept its ancestral hall. There were combinations of Christian with traditional wedding and funeral ceremonials.[344] On December 8th, 1939,

[335] *Fides Service*, March 7, 1936.

[336] Laymen's Foreign Missions Inquiry, *Fact-Finders' Reports, China,* Vol. V, Supplementary Series, Part 2, p. 42.

[337] K. L. Reichelt in *The Chinese Recorder,* Vol. LXV, pp. 766-768, and *The International Review of Missions,* Vol. XXVI, p. 159.

[338] Lesourd, *L'Année Missionaire,* 1931, plate XII; *Dossiers de la Commission Synodale,* May, 1932; Fleming, *Each with His Own Brush,* pp. 14-39.

[339] Laymen's Foreign Missions Inquiry, *Fact-Finders' Report, China,* Vol. V, Supplementary Series, Part 2, p. 45.

[340] *The Chinese Recorder,* Vol. LXI, pp. 711-713.

[341] *The Chinese Recorder,* Vol. LXV, pp. 107 ff.

[342] Pakenham-Walsh, *Twenty Years in China,* p. 88.

[343] *The Chinese Recorder,* Vol. LXII, pp. 680-685.

[344] Laymen's Foreign Missions Inquiry, *op. cit.,* Vol. V, Supplementary Series, Part 2, p. 45.

the Propaganda issued a new ruling on the Chinese rites, the theme of the long and stormy controversy of the seventeenth and eighteenth centuries.[345] This fresh decision permitted Christians to be present at functions in honour of Confucius, allowed the placing of likenesses of Confucius in Roman Catholic schools, and consented to Christians paying signs of respect before images or tablets of the dead if these were inscribed simply with the name of the deceased and had no phrases implying worship. Roman Catholic missionaries were no longer required to take the oath prescribed by the bull of 1742.[346] The concession concerning the ceremonies in honour of Confucius was to enable Roman Catholics to meet the requirements of the Japanese regime in Manchuria which sought to undergird the puppet state of Manchukuo with a Confucian basis. Rome was not necessarily reversing its decision of the eighteenth century, for it still did not permit what it regarded as compliance with paganism. It was, however, easing its attitude towards traditional Chinese rites.

Much of the adaptation to the Chinese environment was made unconsciously or only semiconsciously. The Confucian atmosphere which had so long been dominant could not but influence Chinese Christians. One leading Protestant scholar declared that the modern Chinese Christian was at heart a Confucianist, for he had turned Jesus into Confucius and followed him not because of his religious faith but because of his moral character.[347] This might be an exaggeration, but even if Confucianism as a cult was disappearing and as a philosophy of life was a waning force, it was still part of the warp and woof of the Chinese spirit and Christians could not easily, even if they had so desired, completely wean themselves from it. It was declared that many church buildings more suggested a village hall or a school—the latter a Confucian tradition—than they did a church.[348] The majority of Chinese peasant Christians were said to regard the Bible much as they had the Confucian classics and to treat it with a mixture of literal faithfulness and free interpretation.[349] Vegetarianism, of Buddhist provenance, was observed by at least one leading Christian.[350] Many Christians preserved their inherited belief in ghosts.[351] In ecclesiastical circles the tendency was, after the Chinese manner, to find positions for friends and relatives, to form cliques according to family divisions, and to rely upon endowments rather than regular periodical collections for the maintenance of the

[345] Vol. III, pp. 349-355.
[346] *Fides News Service,* Dec. 23, 1939.
[347] T. C. Chao in *The International Review of Missions,* Vol. XXVII, p. 585.
[348] Morton, *Life in the Chinese Church,* pp. 62, 63.
[349] *The Chinese Recorder,* Vol. LXII, p. 776.
[350] Chiang Chih-chiang in *The Chinese Recorder,* Vol. LXIV, p. 732.
[351] *The Chinese Recorder,* Vol. LXV, p. 219.

Church.[352] The Buddhist and Taoist traditions had their effect in encouraging a quietistic mood, in regarding the Christian faith as a way of escape from the ills of the present life, and, probably, in emotional revivals with their striving for the salvation of the individual through repentance of sin and the leading of a moral life. Confucianism was reflected in the emphasis upon Christianity as a means of salvation for society as a whole from the collective ills from which it was so obviously and acutely suffering and in the stress laid upon social service and reform.[353] By an interesting parallelism, the trend towards individual salvation coincided in part with the message of some of the Protestant missionaries of conservative theology, and the desire to use Christianity for the present remaking of the fabric of Chinese life was in accord with much of the social message of some phases of Anglo-Saxon Protestantism. Even though slowly and in co-operation with Occidental Christianity, Chinese types of Christianity were beginning to emerge.

We have given so large a proportion of our space to China because of the size of the country, the strategic importance of the land for the Far East, and the phenomenal gains which Christianity was making in the three decades which followed 1914.

China held about a fourth of the human race, the largest fairly homogeneous group of mankind. It was the seat of an ancient and high civilization and had long been giving its culture to the other peoples of the Far East. Because of the impact of the Occident it was in the throes of a revolution in which every phase of life was being altered. The experience was one which the Chinese had never before known. In no other area of the globe of similar dimensions in population, not even Europe, did the changes and tumults of the post-1914 years bring so sweeping and thoroughgoing a remaking of society. The transformation had begun in the closing decade of the nineteenth century and was well under way in 1914, but after that year it proceeded at an accelerated pace.

Until the structure of Chinese life had begun to disintegrate Christianity had made but slight progress. Twice in earlier centuries it had been introduced only to die out. It had now been continuously represented since the close of the sixteenth century. In spite of a small Russian mission, from late in the sixteenth until early in the nineteenth century Roman Catholic Christianity had been the only form of the faith which was actively propagated. Then had come Protes-

[352] Laymen's Foreign Missions Inquiry, *Fact-Finders' Reports, China*, Vol. V, Supplementary Series, Part 2, p. 47.
[353] *The Chinese Recorder*, Vol. LXII, pp. 70-72, Vol. LXIV, pp. 485-488.

tant missionaries and until after 1914 they had multiplied more rapidly than had Roman Catholic missionaries. They were predominantly from the British Empire and the United States, while the latter were chiefly from the continent of Europe. After the wall of Chinese resistance began to crumble, Christianity made great strides. Proportionately Protestantism grew more rapidly than Roman Catholic Christianity and had a wider effect upon the life of China. However, in 1914 the latter, because of its earlier start, had between three and five times as many adherents as did the former.

By its presence in China Christianity had contributed to the dissolution of the older culture. However, had Christianity not been propagated that dissolution would have come and at the time that it did and with the completeness which it displayed. It was primarily the result of the political and commercial impact of the Occident. By bringing in a fresh spiritual dynamic and, especially through its Protestant wing, by pioneering in the introduction of phases of Western culture, particularly education and medicine, which later proved of service to China, Christianity was helping to make the transition from the old to the new wholesome and not merely destructive.

In spite of the series of storms of civil strife, foreign war, and revolution which swept across China, in the thirty years subsequent to 1914 Christianity continued its phenomenal gains. Both Roman Catholics and Protestants enlarged their missionary staffs. Roman Catholics did so through much of the period. After initial substantial accessions, the Protestant foreign personnel, because of conditions in Great Britain, the United States, and China, remained about stationary and then, with the intensification of war after 1937, fell off. The totals of both Protestant and Roman Catholic Chinese about doubled during the period. The Russian Orthodox, never numerous, grew chiefly by immigration from Russia of dissidents from the Communist regime. Both Protestant and Roman Catholic Christianity became much more deeply rooted in China through the emergence of Chinese leadership, the progressive transfer to it of responsibility, and the development of a national structure for each of these two great branches of the Church. Christianity was more active than was any other religion. Buddhism and Taoism had long been declining, and under the impact of the revolution Confucianism was suffering. Only Christianity was growing. It was having a more striking effect upon the country than it was upon any other major land in Asia. To its contributions in education, medicine, agriculture, forestry, and social service, in some of which it was the outstanding impulse and pioneer of new methods and professions, and to its characteristic fruits in individual lives, it added influences upon the leaders who most shaped the political and ideological structure of the new China.

In India the effects of Christianity were seen mainly among the underprivileged classes, on the periphery of the life of the country. In Ceylon, Burma, Indo-China, and the Netherlands Indies it was chiefly minorities outside the main stream of the region's life which were transformed. In Japan Christians were from influential urban groups, but the currents of tradition and militarism were running too strongly to enable them to place much impress on national policies. In China Christians were a small minority, but from that minority were emerging many who were in the forefront of the nation's life. In an hour when a new China was coming to birth, they were making contributions quite out of proportion to the numerical strength of the Church. China was far from being Christian, but Christianity was a factor with which to reckon.

Christianity in China was beginning to show the effect of the environment. This was partly in ways which were superficial, but it was also in partial conformation to the traditions of Buddhism, Taoism, and especially Confucianism.

Yet by being knit into the world-wide Christian fellowship through missionaries, through the Roman Catholic Church, and through the Ecumenical Movement of Protestantism, Chinese Christianity was kept in contact with the historic stream of the faith and was being woven into the emerging global pattern of the Church's life.

Chapter XIV

THE JAPANESE EMPIRE

JAPAN PROPER (ROMAN CATHOLIC, RUSSIAN ORTHODOX, AND PROTESTANT CHRISTIANITY; EFFECT ON THE ENVIRONMENT: EFFECT OF THE ENVIRONMENT): FORMOSA: KOREA

IN THE Japanese Empire after 1914 Christianity operated in a peculiarly difficult *milieu* and faced a great challenge.

Christianity, it will be recalled, had had a chequered career in Japan[1] and Korea,[2] and had not had an easy time in Formosa.[3] In Japan it had flourished in the sixteenth century, only to be proscribed and persecuted in the seventeenth, the eighteenth, and the fore part of the nineteenth century. It was to keep out Christianity that Japan had secluded herself from the rest of the world for the two centuries which were terminated by Commodore Perry in the 1850's. Although Christianity was reintroduced late in the 1850's and early in the 1860's by Roman Catholics, Russian Orthodox, and Protestants, not until the 1870's were the edict boards against the faith removed. Christianity grew in numbers and influence, but the main ideological structure of Japanese life remained intact and the Church had little effect upon it. In Korea Christianity had been bitterly persecuted until well past the middle of the nineteenth century. However, in the thirty years prior to 1914 it had made rapid headway, especially in its Protestant form. Although it had existed fairly peacefully in Formosa, the Japanese occupation in the mid-1890's had brought it problems.

The Japanese Empire was in a state of war for most of the three decades which followed the year 1914. Japan was a participant in the first of the world wars and not until 1922 did she withdraw her forces from Siberia, where they had been stationed as an aftermath of that struggle. From the time of her operations in Manchuria in September, 1931, she was virtually at war with China (although there were intervals of comparative quiet until 1937) and was being partly ostracized by a large proportion of the rest of the world. Hers was

---

[1] Vol. III, pp. 322-335, Vol. VI, pp. 370-411.
[2] Vol. VI, pp. 412-430.
[3] Vol. III, pp. 359, 360, Vol. VI, pp. 322, 332.

increasingly a war psychology. The Japanese came to 1945 on a great adventure of foreign conquest, but in which the tide was beginning to run against them. In the nationalistic fervour which was an accompaniment of war, patriotism was reinforced by Shinto and was religious in its intensity and intolerance. In the 1930's there was a reaction against the Occident. Tension mounted with the United States, the chief source of Protestant missionaries and a growing source of the Roman Catholic staff, until, in December, 1941, it broke out into open war. During much of the period, then, and especially in the later years, the atmosphere was adverse to Christianity. There was no overt persecution in Japan Proper, but Christians were partly on the defensive. This was especially true of the form of Christianity which was numerically strongest, Protestantism, for its ties were chiefly with the United States. In the process of assimilating Korea to her culture and rule, Japan found Christianity, and notably Protestant Christianity, an obstacle. The faith, accordingly, suffered, especially after 1937. Foreigners, particularly Protestants, who would propagate their faith in Formosa found their road increasingly difficult. It was against powerful adversaries that Christianity was constrained to labour in the post-1914 decades.

Yet the challenge was great. The Japanese were a numerous and active people. The Christian Church could not ignore them. Their influence in the world and especially in the Far East counted for much. For their own sakes and for that of the rest of the world the Japanese must, so the Christian missionary forces believed, be confronted with the Christian faith.

In spite of the obstacles, Christianity made amazing progress in Japan after 1914. It did not attain the influence which it exercised in China, but it increased in numerical strength and in its rootage in the life of the nation.

In Japan Proper the Roman Catholic Church enjoyed a fairly steady but not a striking growth. In 1912 it had 66,134 members, 152 foreign priests, 33 Japanese priests, 133 lay brothers, and 232 nuns.[4] In 1933 its membership had risen to 100,491, and it had 251 foreign and 73 Japanese priests, 96 foreign and 141 Japanese lay brothers, and 423 foreign and 355 native nuns.[5] In 1936 its membership was said to have been 108,934.[6] The staff of the church, it will be seen, had grown proportionately more rapidly than had the total of Roman Catholics.

To the orders and societies represented in 1914, mainly the Société des Missions Étrangères of Paris, a few Dominicans, Jesuits, Trappists, and members

[4] Streit, *Atlas Hierarchicus,* p. 100.

[5] Parker, *Interpretative Statistical Survey of the World Mission of the Christian Church,* p. 33.

[6] *Fides News Service,* Jan. 30, 1937.

of the Society of the Divine Word, and a number of lay brotherhoods and sisterhoods, were added others. The Jesuits had been from the German province of Cologne. There now came as well Jesuits from the Spanish province of Toledo.[7] Franciscans arrived, one unit of them Canadians, and were given charge of two ecclesiastical divisions.[8] Salesians augmented the missionary staff and the Society of the Divine Word took increased responsibilities.[9] Mary-knollers were given a field centring in Kyoto.[10] The Trappist monastery on the southern peninsula of the island of Yezo, near Hakodate, prospered and did much to improve the agriculture of the area. To it in 1926 was added another, in Kyushu.[11] There were also in Japan, largely in charge of schools, but some of them in hospitals and orphanages, the Brothers of Mary, Sisters of the Sacred Heart, Sisters of St. Maur, Sisters of St. Paul of Chartres, Sisters of the Holy Child Jesus of Chauffailles, Franciscan missionaries of Mary, and Sisters of the Holy Spirit (of Steyl).[12]

Roman Catholics were reaching out in fresh ways. In 1913 Jesuits opened in Tokyo what in 1928 became a full-fledged university, Sophia, which in 1938 had over a thousand students.[13] A Japanese priest, a physician, began a sanitorium on the outskirts of Tokyo for indigent sufferers from tuberculosis and the institution so prospered that in the mid-1930's new buildings were erected for it.[14] Extensive use was made of literature in the form of books, journals, and brochures.[15] In 1937 over four hundred different works on the Roman Catholic faith were on sale.[16] Most of the Roman Catholics were from the humbler walks of life, but some were in comfortable circumstances,[17] and there were women of excellent social standing, including a daughter of the ancient and highly aristocratic Fujiwara family, who joined the Carmelites in their house in Tokyo, an institution founded in 1930.[18] The Roman Catholic Church, like the other forms of the faith, was predominantly urban[19] and in 1927 it was said that 59 per cent. of the nation were still without access to its teaching.[20]

[7] *Fides Service,* Jan. 12, 1935.
[8] *Testo-Atlante illustrato delle Missioni,* p. 116.
[9] *Ibid.*
[10] Considine, *Across a World,* p. 202.
[11] *Fides News Service,* Apr. 18, 1936.
[12] Planchet, *Les Missions de Chine et du Japon,* 1925, pp. 362 ff.
[13] *Fides News Service,* Dec. 3. 1938.
[14] *Fides News Service,* Jan. 16, 1937.
[15] Lesourd, *l'Année Missionnaire,* 1931, p. 147.
[16] *Fides News Service,* Feb. 27, 1937.
[17] *Missiones Catholicae Cura S. Congregationis de Propaganda Fide,* 1927, pp. 184, 185.
[18] *Fides Service,* May 26, 1934. In the 1930's the daughter of a former premier became a Roman Catholic.—*Fides News Service,* June 19, 1937.
[19] *Missiones Catholicae Cura S. Congregationis de Propaganda Fide,* 1927, pp. 184, 185.
[20] *Testo-Atlante illustrato delle Missioni,* p. 56.

The growing nationalism of Japan, which in its most intense forms was seeking to oust foreign cultural influences, at times was a threat. In the 1930's it was reported that the military were trying to wean from the faith thousands from the old Roman Catholic communities in Kyushu and that the army even wished to drive Roman Catholicism from Japan.[21]

However, the Roman Catholic Church was making rapid strides in becoming acclimatized. It rapidly developed a national organization and raised Japanese to the episcopate. In 1919 an Apostolic Delegation was created for the Japanese Empire.[22] In 1927 a Japanese was appointed to head the diocese of Nagasaki, in which were more than half of the Roman Catholics of Japan. The consecration was by the Pope himself,[23] an act which, as in the case of the six Chinese bishops which we noted in the last chapter, vividly demonstrated the intention of the Vatican to pass over episcopal administration as quickly as possible to the indigenous clergy. In 1937 a Japanese was made Archbishop of Tokyo.[24] In 1940 the attitude of the Japanese Government brought pressure upon all of the churches to become independent of foreign financial aid and to transfer all administrative offices to Japanese. Before 1940 the Roman Catholic Church had taken steps in this direction. It was also the first Christian body to obtain official recognition under the religious bodies law of 1939. Japanese were placed at the head of all the ecclesiastical divisions, and Archbishop Tatsuo Doi, of Tokyo, was named as the *Torisha*, or head, of the church with whom the state was to deal.[25] In September, 1940, the decision was reached to replace foreign with Japanese principals of schools.[26]

In ways other than administrative the Roman Catholic Church was also adjusting itself to the environment. As early as 1890 a council meeting at Nagasaki permitted Roman Catholics to take part in patriotic ceremonies at Shinto shrines. In the 1930's, when because of the heightened nationalism the issue became acute, Rome gave it as its mind that the faithful could be present at ceremonies which had only a purely patriotic meaning, such as respect for the imperial family and for benefactors of the country.[27] Since the government had declared that the rites of state or shrine Shinto, as distinct from sect Shinto, were purely patriotic and not religious, Roman Catholics could share in them without ecclesiastical censure and thus meet the requirements of the national-

---

[21] *Missions,* Vol. XXVI, p. 584.

[22] Lesourd, *op. cit.,* p. 146.

[23] *Fides News Service,* Dec. 26, 1936; Planchet, *op. cit.,* 1929, pp. vii, viii.

[24] *Fides Service,* Dec. 11, 1937.

[25] *The National Christian Council Bulletin* [Japan], May, 1941; Considine, *op. cit.,* pp. 202, 203.

[26] *The Japan Christian Quarterly,* Vol. XV, p. 404.

[27] *Fides News Service,* July 4, 1936. See also a statement by the Apostolic Delegate in *Fides Service,* Feb. 22, 1936.

istic regime. Indeed, in 1936 the Propaganda explicitly directed Roman Catholics to acquiesce in the official declaration that state Shinto was non-religious and to participate in ceremonies at the shrines.[28] A test case at Sophia University made clear the attitude of both the church and the state.[29] The Propaganda also allowed Roman Catholics to join in funerals, weddings, and other private ceremonies which had features of pagan origin, on the ground that in common opinion these rites had only a meaning of "urbanity and reciprocal benevolence."[30] On the anniversary of the founding of the Japanese Empire, prayers for the imperial family and the prosperity of the realm were offered in Roman Catholic churches throughout the realm.[31] There was developing a Japanese Christian art and architecture, both in painting and in church buildings.[32] To undergird the "Greater East Asia Co-prosperity Sphere," as the rapidly expanding area in the Far East brought under Japanese rule in the 1940's was euphemistically called, in April, 1943, on the Emperor's birthday, there was held in the cathedral in Tokyo the inaugural ceremony of an organization for the "friendship of Japanese and Overseas Catholics."[33] Japanese Roman Catholics believed that by these steps they were not separating themselves from the world-wide fellowship of their church but were merely, in quite permissible ways, having a loyal place in the life of their country.

For the Roman Catholic Church in Japan the second of the world wars did not have quite such striking effects as it had upon the Protestant wing of the faith. The overwhelming majority of Protestant missionaries were from the United States and the British Empire, and therefore after December 7, 1941, were enemy aliens. The majority of Roman Catholic missionaries were from France, Germany, and Spain, lands with which Japan was technically at peace. While they were largely cut off from their home constituencies, presumably they were not placed under such restrictions as were American and British missionaries. Yet the Roman Catholic Church could not but be affected by the vicissitudes of the war. Together with the nation as a whole, it was passing through a period of great testing.

In the preceding volume we saw[34] the remarkable history and growth of the Russian Orthodox Church in Japan. The founding was the work, it will be

---

[28] Holtom, *Modern Japan and Shinto Nationalism*, p. 99.
[29] *Fides News Service,* Dec. 3, 1938.
[30] *Fides News Service,* July 4, 1936.
[31] *Fides Service,* Apr. 6, 1935.
[32] *Fides Service,* June 30, 1934; *Fides News Service,* March 9, 1940; Fleming, *Each with His Own Brush,* pp. 42, 43, 45, 46, 50, 51.
[33] *Pacific Affairs,* Vol. XVI, p. 318.
[34] Vol. VI, pp. 379-381.

recalled, of Nicolai, who lived until 1912. The staff was predominantly Japanese, but much of the financial support was from Russia. After the Russo-Japanese War of 1904-1905 the numerical increase slowed down. In 1912 the total membership was said to be about thirty-two thousand.[35] The course of events in the international and national situation subsequent to 1914 still further retarded advance. The Russian revolution and the coming to power of the Communists late in 1917 brought to an end financial aid from the mother church, now itself disestablished and hard bested. This meant cutting down the staff of the Japan mission. Although the difference was in part made up by more self-support by the Japanese, the employed force remained small and accessions declined.[36] In 1937 the membership was slightly over forty thousand, but of these less than half were regarded as active.[37] Indeed, in 1939, while the grand total was placed at over forty-one thousand, the actual membership was said to be only between thirteen and fourteen thousand.[38] Until 1940 the church remained under the direction of Sergius, who was formerly suffragan to Nicolai and became archbishop in 1921 or 1923 and metropolitan in 1930.[39] Great difficulty was encountered in obtaining recruits for the priesthood: in spite of an effort to revive the theological seminary, in 1939 no candidates for that office were reported.[40] However, because of the attitude of the Japanese Government towards foreign executives of religious institutions, in 1940 Sergius resigned his see, transferred the property of the mission to the newly constituted Japanese church, and in 1941 a Japanese was consecrated, at Harbin, to Tokyo. The new bishop, Ono, had come up through the Russian Orthodox Church in Japan, and at the time of his consecration was in his early seventies.[41] The leadership was aging and the outlook was not bright.

As in 1914, so after that year, Protestantism was numerically the strongest and in many other respects the most active of the forms of Christianity represented in Japan. It was through Protestantism that in the latter part of the nineteenth and in the twentieth century Christianity chiefly made its impact upon Japan. Protestantism, as we have seen,[42] was transmitted for the most

[35] *The Christian Movement in Japan*, 1914, statistical table.
[36] *The Christian Movement in Japan, Korea, and Formosa*, 1921, pp. 192, 193.
[37] *The Japan Christian Year Book*, 1938, p. 167; Bolshakoff, *The Foreign Missions of the Russian Orthodox Church*, p. 78.
[38] *The Japan Christian Year Book*, 1940, p. 180.
[39] Bolshakoff, *op. cit.*, p. 78; *The Japan Christian Year Book*, 1938, p. 166.
[40] *The Japan Christian Year Book*, 1940, p. 188.
[41] Bolshakoff, *op. cit.*, p. 80.
[42] Vol. VI, pp. 381-407.

part by missionaries from the United States, but also to some extent from the British Empire and to a very slight degree from the continent of Europe. It was predominantly urban and drew mainly from the middle classes. By 1914 it had made marked strides towards self-government and financial self-support. However, in 1914 missionaries still had a large place and extensive subventions in funds came from the founding churches.

Numerically, the membership of Protestant churches increased both proportionately and absolutely more rapidly than did that of either the Roman Catholic or Russian Orthodox churches. In 1914 it was 102,790,[43] and in 1936 210,384, of whom all but 1,422 were communicants:[44] it had slightly more than doubled in twenty-two years. This was a much smaller rate of growth than in the fourteen years from 1900 to 1914,[45] but was considerably more rapid proportionately than in the discouraging decade of the 1890's.[46] In other words, the troubled years which succeeded 1914 were accompanied by a retardation of the growth of Protestant Christianity, but the contrast was by no means as disheartening as had been that between the mushroom expansion in the 1880's and the sharp reaction in the 1890's.

The foreign staff of Protestant Christianity displayed striking fluctuations. In 1914 or 1915 it was 1,123,[47] more than half again the size of that of 1900. A decade later it had risen to 1,253,[48] and in 1936 it had fallen to 829.[49] The proportionate decline from the peak which followed the first of the world wars was much greater than in China or India. This may have been in part because a much larger percentage of the missionaries were from the United States than was the case in India and China. For reasons which had to do with the temper and the economic contrasts in that country the variation in the personnel maintained abroad by the churches of that land was more marked than was that of the contingents sent by the British churches. The decline also reflected the rapid coming of age of the Japanese churches and the changing role of the foreigner. Leadership was rapidly passing into Japanese hands and the missionary was more the colleague and even the subordinate than the director. The intense nationalism of the 1930's and 1940's led, as with Roman Catholics and Russian Orthodox, to the abrupt transfer, in 1940 and 1941, to

[43] *The Christian Movement in Japan*, 1914, statistical table.
[44] Parker, *Interpretative Statistical Survey of the World Mission of the Christian Church*, p. 18.
[45] Vol. VI, pp. 398, 399.
[46] Vol. VI, p. 396.
[47] Beach and St. John, *World Statistics of Christian Missions*, p. 62.
[48] Beach and Fahs, *World Missionary Atlas*, p. 82.
[49] Parker, *op. cit.*, p. 84.

Japanese of such administrative posts as remained in the hands of foreigners.[50]
As the clouds of war gathered, many missionaries withdrew from Japan. Some
left after the outbreak of hostilities between Japan and China in the summer of
1937, for they found themselves embarrassed by their inability to endorse the
Japanese programme on the continent. Many more departed as the strain between Japan on the one hand and the United States and Great Britain on the
other became more intense. They did so partly on the order of their mission
boards, partly on the advice of the diplomatic officers of their governments,
partly because of the altered relations between missions and churches, and to
some degree because they felt their presence to be a handicap to their Japanese
colleagues.[51] The outbreak of war between Japan and the Anglo-Saxon powers
in December, 1941, rapidly completed the process. As enemy aliens, British and
American missionaries were restricted to their houses, interned, or imprisoned,
and the larger part of them were repatriated.

In spite of the changing and waning place of the missionary, the Protestant
churches of Japan went forward. The foundations had been so well laid, the
churches displayed such vigour, and the indigenous leadership was so strong,
that Protestant Christianity moved ahead. Much of this was with the aid of the
missionary so long as he remained in the land, but increasingly it was through
Japanese initiative.

One of the outstanding features of Protestant Christianity in Japan in the
years immediately following 1914 was the endeavour to reach the entire nation
with the Christian message. An effort towards this end took concrete form in
1928 as the Kingdom of God Movement. It enlisted most of the Protestant
forces, but had as its chief leader Toyohiko Kagawa.[52]

Kagawa was born in 1888, the son by a concubine of an ex-*samurai* father
who was headman of his community and moderately prominent in national
affairs. Adoption gave him legitimacy, but the early death of his parents put
him in an ancestral home where he was not wanted and made childhood an

---

[50] C. W. Iglehart in *The Japan Christian Quarterly,* Vol. XV, pp. 315 ff., Vol. XVI,
pp. 21 ff.

[51] *The Japan Christian Quarterly,* Vol. XVI, pp. 1-4, 34-39.

[52] Of the extensive bibliography on Kagawa and by Kagawa the most important for
the understanding of his life are William Axling, *Kagawa* (New York, Harper & Brothers,
1932, pp. x, 202), by an intimate friend and admirer and with the co-operation of Kagawa
and his wife; Toyohiko Kagawa, *Before the Dawn,* translated from the Japanese of
Across the Death Line by I. Fukumoto and T. Satchell (New York, George H. Doran
Company, 1924, pp. 398), a novel which was in part autobiographical and which had a
wide sale in its Japanese original; Toyohiko Kagawa, *Love, the Law of Life* (Philadelphia, The John C. Winston Company, 1929, pp. vii, 313); and Toyohiko Kagawa,
Meditations on the Cross (Chicago, Willett, Clark & Company, 1935, pp. 211), translated
from the Japanese by Helen F. Topping and Marion R. Draper.

acutely unhappy experience. Contact with missionaries during his school days led him to the Christian faith. His avowal of his new allegiance brought him disinheritance by his family. Yet he persevered and went on to a theological school and later to ordination to the Christian ministry. He devoted himself to the poor. He chose to live in one of the worst slums of Japan and there preached by life and word, sharing his pittance with the diseased and the criminals, and fighting the prostitution which added to the wretchedness of the district. His was an inquiring and wide-ranging mind and he read omnivorously in many fields, and that, latterly, in spite of near-blindness from trachoma contracted from one of the denizens of the slums with whom he had shared his humble abode. He espoused the cause of organized labour, thereby incurring imprisonment. He became a prolific author, and some of his books had a prodigious circulation. Eventually fame came to him, both in Japan and in Protestant Christian circles throughout much of the world. He had given himself to the way of love as he saw it in Christ and was seeking to make it effective in the lives of individuals and in the community. He organized social settlements, promoted co-operatives, and strove to better the lot of both city-dwellers and rural folk.

It was this Kagawa who became outstanding in the Kingdom of God Movement. The movement took its immediate inspiration from the Jerusalem meeting (1928) of the International Missionary Council. For a time Kagawa set for it the goal of bringing in "a million souls." He sought to make it a means of social as well as individual transformation. In spite of his emphasis upon love and upon changing collective institutions, Kagawa at times found it difficult to co-operate with the churches and the phase of the movement which he headed was not always closely integrated with that in which the churches joined. Yet the campaign brought the Christian message to many thousands and won numbers to the faith. In 1930 the effort was extended for another two years.[53] Here was a comprehensive plan in which Japanese took the chief initiative for bringing the Christian gospel to the entire nation. It was an indication of the remarkable degree to which Protestant Christianity had commanded the allegiance and won the devotion of thousands of Japanese.

There were many instances of the fashion in which the faith was spreading, partly in connexion with the Kingdom of God Movement and often inde-

---

[53] *The International Review of Missions,* Vol. XXI, pp. 19 ff., Vol. XXIII, p. 7; *The Japan Mission Year Book,* 1929, pp. 94-98, 1930, pp. 139-147; Toyohiko Kagawa in *The International Review of Missions,* Vol. XX, pp. 333-344; *The Christian Century,* Vol. L, pp. 1464, 1465; Laymen's Foreign Missions Inquiry, *Fact-Finders' Reports, Japan,* Vol. VI, Supplementary Series, Part 2, p. 165; *Quarterly Notes, being the Bulletin of the International Missionary Council,* Apr., 1933, p. iii.

pendently of it. The reading of Kagawa's widely circulated, partly autobiographical novel, *Across the Death Line*, stimulated young Christians to
inaugurate Sunday Schools in the sordid by-streets of great cities.[54] A Japanese
who while on his way to commit suicide was won through the Salvation Army
gave himself to gathering a church in a rural community and later, associating
himself with Kagawa, went to serve in a fishing village.[55] In Kyushu, largely
as the result of a station of the American Board of Commissioners for Foreign
Missions, there were twice as many churches in one province as in the other
eight of the island.[56]

Efforts, too, were made to correct the disparity between country and city in
the strength of the churches and more vigorous measures for reaching the
country were adopted. The task was difficult, partly because rural communities
were more conservative than urban ones and held more firmly to the traditional
religions.[57] Kagawa and some other Christians[58] sought through a special type
of school to do for the farmers what the folk schools in Denmark had accomplished.[59] In 1931 a conference was held to plan for rural evangelism.[60]
Although the Japanese pastor was said to engage less in community service than
his colleagues in other lands, there were reported to be in the 1930's a score of
rural pastors who gave themselves in sacrifice to the people in their areas.[61]
The Omi Mission, a quite unique enterprise, predominantly Japanese,[62] extended its activities in the rural region to which it had given itself.[63]

In spite of the war with China, evangelism continued on a large scale. In
1939, in consequence of plans made in November, 1938, by the All-Japan
Christian Conference, the Nation-wide United Evangelistic Campaign was
launched, with Kagawa prominent as a speaker.[64] It continued through 1940.[65]

The Sunday School was more employed in Japan than in China and made

[54] Mishima, *My Narrow Isle*, p. 55.
[55] H. and H. F. Topping, *Salting the Earth. A Story of Rural Reconstruction* (no date
or place of publication, pp. 38), *passim*.
[56] *News Bulletin from the Japan Mission of the American Board*, Vol. XXXIV, No. 3,
June, 1930.
[57] Laymen's Foreign Missions Inquiry, *Fact-Finders' Reports, Japan*, Vol. VI, Supplementary Series, Part 2, p. 85.
[58] Clark, *The Other Half of Japan*, p. 41; Felton, *The Rural Church in the Far East*,
p. 56.
[59] Vol. IV, p. 167.
[60] Clark, *op. cit.*, p. 121.
[61] Felton, *op. cit.*, pp. 60, 74.
[62] Vol. VI, p. 400.
[63] William Merrill Vories, *A Mustard Seed in Japan* (Omi-Hachiman, Omi Mission,
4th ed., 1922, pp. 147, vi, iv), *passim*.
[64] *The National Christian Council Bulletin* [Japan], February, March, May, 1939.
[65] *The National Christian Council Bulletin* [Japan], Dec., 1940, Jan., 1941.

so great an impression that Buddhists paid it the compliment of copying its methods to give religious education to their youth.[66]

Japanese Protestant Christians exerted themselves to follow their fellow-countrymen who went overseas. A Christian colony was established in Man-chukuo.[67] The Overseas Evangelistic Association was constituted in 1931 both to minister to Japanese abroad and to attempt to reach non-Japanese in Formosa, Manchukuo, and the mandated islands in the Pacific.[68] By 1934 it had extended its operations to the Philippines, Brazil, and Peru, countries in which there were substantial numbers of Japanese.[69] Earlier the South Sea Islands Association was organized and in 1920 its first missionaries went to the mandated islands.[70] There was a Manchurian Missionary Association which in 1938 was reorganized as the East Asia Evangelistic Association.[71] In 1940 the latter reported eighty-five workers in seventy-one centres in Manchukuo and China Proper. It declined subsidies from the government, presumably to free itself from any trace of taint of political objectives, and sought to proclaim the Christian message through Chinese lips and the Chinese language.[72]

Protestant Christianity was much stronger in Japan than the statistics of church membership would indicate. Partly because it appealed extensively to the professional and civil service groups, elements which often shifted their residence, thousands who had once been on church rolls lost touch with the Church and were dropped from membership.[73] Numbers, some of them eminent in the life of the country, who regarded themselves as Christians, did not affiliate themselves with any Christian organization.[74] This was probably in part because the religions longer in Japan did not have group organizations for the laity which in any way corresponded to the Christian Church and many Japanese Christians did not see any reason why they should identify themselves with such a body.[75]

For a people so nearly universally literate as the Japanese and with so large an element of the highly educated, the press provided a convenient and important means of presenting the Christian message and of nurturing the Christian

---

[66] R. M. Hopkins in *The International Review of Missions,* Vol. XIX, pp. 575-592.

[67] *The National Christian Council Bulletin* [Japan], July, 1941.

[68] Paton, *Christianity in the Eastern Conflicts,* p. 36.

[69] *The International Review of Missions,* Vol. XXIII, p. 8.

[70] Kozaki, *Reminiscences of Seventy Years,* pp. 280-284.

[71] *The National Christian Council Bulletin* [Japan], March, 1938.

[72] *The National Christian Council Bulletin* [Japan], Oct., 1940.

[73] Davis, *The Economic and Social Environment of the Younger Churches,* p. 38.

[74] Laymen's Foreign Missions Inquiry, *Fact-Finders' Reports, Japan,* Vol. VI, Supplementary Series, Part 2, p. 17.

[75] Laymen's Foreign Missions Inquiry, *op. cit.,* Vol. VI, Supplementary Series, Part 2, pp. 67, 157, 158.

community. "Newspaper evangelism," inaugurated before 1914, was maintained and enlarged. Through it articles on the Christian faith were inserted in the secular press and readers were invited to correspond with the central offices. For the co-ordination and direction of the enterprise and in succession to an earlier organization, in 1926 the Newspaper and Correspondence Evangelism Association was constituted. In 1929 this was followed by the Japan Christian News Agency.[76] In 1926 the Christian Literature Society of Japan was formed through a merger of two earlier bodies. It was chiefly foreign in direction and a predominantly Japanese committee called the Library of Christian Thought and Life in Japan was brought together by some who were not satisfied with the other.[77] During much of the period the sales of the Bible, largely of portions of it, showed a striking increase.[78] Translations of Occidental novels built around Christian themes sold by the hundreds of thousands.[79] Use was also made of the radio and the cinema.[80]

Schools continued to have a large part in the Protestant programme in Japan. The time had long passed when in some of the categories Christian schools were in the vanguard. It was frankly admitted that in secondary and higher education Christian institutions were distinctly the second choice of aspiring applicants. From this it followed that most of the abler youth were in non-Christian schools. Yet it was felt that the pressure for education was so great and accommodations in the government institutions were so limited that Christian schools still met a need.[81] Moreover, in spite of a fairly large proportion of non-Christians on the teaching staffs and the fact that at entrance most of the registrants were not Christians, in the Christian middle schools by the time of graduation about 30 per cent. of the students had become Christians and of these the large majority had united with some church.[82] The middle schools also helped to remove anti-Christian prejudice.[83] Here and there, too, were schools not under ecclesiastical auspices but founded and directed by earnest Japanese Christians which were outstanding in their educational methods and

[76] W. H. Murray Walton, *The Press and the Gospel* (London, Student Christian Movement Press, 1932), *passim*; Laymen's Foreign Missions Inquiry, *op. cit.*, Vol. VI, Supplementary Series, Part 2, p. 227.
[77] *Report of the Commission of Appraisal of the Laymen's Foreign Missions Inquiry*, Vol. VIII, pp. 8, 9.
[78] *The Japan Mission Year Book*, 1929, p. 172.
[79] Missionaries of the United Church of Canada, *Fruits of Christian Missions in Japan*, p. 218.
[80] *The International Review of Missions*, Vol. XX, p. 6.
[81] L. J. Shafer in *The Japan Mission Year Book*, 1930, pp. 75 ff.
[82] *Christian Education in Japan*, pp. 55, 61.
[83] *Christian Education in Japan*, p. 46.

in the creation of Christian character.[84] In some areas the Christian forces continued prominent. That was notably the case in kindergartens[85] and to a somewhat lesser and a rapidly dwindling degree in secondary and higher education for girls.[86] As in so many other parts of the world, the state could bring such overwhelmingly larger financial resources for the equipment and maintenance of schools that the churches could justify their persistence in the field only by the effect on the character of the graduates and by initiating new methods and types of education.

Outside the Christian schools were the thousands of students in the government and private institutions. For a time during the first of the world wars Christianity seemed to have easy access to them, but the disappointment of Japan over not attaining her full desires at the Paris Peace Conference and at the Washington Conference, the resentment at the attitude of the United States towards Japanese immigration, and anger at the opposition of the United States and Great Britain towards the Japanese adventure in Manchuria in the 1930's led many to turn against Christianity, for that faith was regarded as identified with these lands.[87] In the 1930's it was felt that the Christian movement had lost ground in government schools.[88]

Protestant Christianity continued to touch Japanese life from a number of angles. The complaint was heard that most churches put forth no efforts for social welfare. However, there were many exceptions.[89] Kagawa was active in promoting co-operative societies.[90] Two Christians formed a nation-wide farmers' union—which was later captured by Communists.[91] We hear of a rural church which gave counsel to the three hundred impoverished households of its community on ways of solving the problem of economic security[92] and of a rural pastor who operated a night school and, in the busiest season of the farmer, day-nurseries for the otherwise untended children.[93] This was in spite of the fact that less than in any other major land in Asia the missionaries and

[84] Laymen's Foreign Missions Inquiry, *Regional Reports of the Commission of Appraisal, Japan,* Vol. III, Supplementary Series, Part 1, pp. 104-107; Michi Kawai, *My Lantern* (Tokyo, Kyo Bun Kwan, 1939, pp. 230), pp. 178 ff.

[85] *The International Review of Missions,* Vol. XXI, p. 11.

[86] *Christian Education in Japan,* pp. 85 ff.

[87] M. S. Murao in *The Student World,* Vol. XXVI, pp. 210-216.

[88] Laymen's Foreign Missions Inquiry, *Fact-Finders' Reports, Japan,* Vol. VI, Supplementary Series, Part 2, p. 240.

[89] Laymen's Foreign Missions Inquiry, *op. cit.,* Vol. VI, Supplementary Series, Part 2, pp. 119, 123, 143.

[90] Galen M. Fisher in *The International Review of Missions,* Vol. XXVII, pp. 635-637.

[91] Missionaries of the United Church of Canada, *Fruits of Christian Missions in Japan,* pp. 147, 148.

[92] Davis, *The Economic and Social Environment of the Younger Churches,* pp. 86, 87.

[93] *Ibid.*

churches had focussed attention on the rural districts.[94] In their initial, unpopular stages, movements for the abolition of licensed prostitution were largely initiated and led by Christians.[95] An outstanding missionary, a woman, lectured widely and to many different kinds of groups on sex education.[96] Numbers of social settlements were maintained in the overcrowded and drab sections of the huge cities.[97] In 1928 more than a third of all money raised for Christian organizations was spent on social welfare. Proportionately to their membership, the Protestant churches were much more active in such matters than were non-Christian religious groups.[98] The National Christian Council undertook research in social and economic problems.[99] In one village a Japanese who had been won to Christianity while in Hawaii brought a church into being, established a nursery, organized a society to pay the salary of a resident physician and a midwife, encouraged the formation of co-operatives, and stimulated the creation of a leisure time school to occupy the farmers in their slack season when they otherwise spent the days in drinking *sake* and going to houses of ill fame.[100] One mission operated a dormitory for casual workers in a suburb of Tokyo.[101] In 1930, at the height of the economic depression, the National Christian Council called together the pastors of Tokyo to confer on the problem of unemployment.[102] Efforts begun before 1914 for the care of ex-prisoners were continued.[103] A national temperance league was organized in 1929 and within a few years had over sixteen hundred local units.[104] There were schools for the blind and hospitals for lepers.[105] St. Luke's Hospital in Tokyo, with Rudolf Bolling Teusler as its inspiring creator, built an enlarged plant and inaugurated public health stations, public school clinics, and pre-natal and post-natal clinics in that great city.[106] The Omi Brotherhood was responsible for modern housing

[94] Butterfield, *The Rural Mission of the Church in Eastern Asia*, pp. 113 ff.

[95] Missionaries of the United Church of Canada, *op. cit.*, pp. 102-106; *The International Review of Missions*, Vol. XXIII, p. 11; *The Japan Mission Year Book*, 1930, pp. 149-158.

[96] Laymen's Foreign Missions Inquiry, *Regional Reports of the Commission of Appraisal, Japan*, Vol. III, Supplementary Series, Part 1, p. 172.

[97] Laymen's Foreign Missions Inquiry, *op. cit.*, Vol. III, Supplementary Series, Part 1, pp. 45, 46; Missionaries of the United Church of Canada, *op. cit.*, p. 109.

[98] Laymen's Foreign Missions Inquiry, *Fact-Finders' Reports, Japan*, Vol. VI, Supplementary Series, Part 2, p. 31.

[99] *Social and Economic News. Issued by the Department of Social and Industrial Research and Counsel of the International Missionary Council*, Apr., 1932, p. 9.

[100] Hunnicutt and Reid, *The Story of Agricultural Missions*, pp. 79 ff.

[101] Missionaries of the United Church of Canada, *op. cit.*, p. 134.

[102] *The National Christian Council Bulletin* [Japan], Sept., 1930.

[103] *The International Review of Missions*, Vol. XXVIII, p. 103.

[104] *The Japan Mission Year Book*, 1930, pp. 87 ff.

[105] *Ibid.*

[106] Howard Chandler Robbins and George K. McNaught, *Dr. Rudolf Bolling Teusler, An Adventure in Christianity* (New York, Charles Scribner's Sons, 1942, pp. xv, 221); *The Japan Mission Year Book*, 1929, pp. 131 ff.

and a weekly rest day for several thousand workers in factories and industrial establishments.[107] In Kyushu American Lutherans founded the Colony of Mercy to rescue and redeem the geisha.[108] This list is by no means exhaustive but indicates something of the varied fashion in which Protestant Christianity was making its impress upon the life of the country.

Following 1914, as we have again and again hinted in the preceding pages of this chapter, Japanese Protestant churches made rapid strides towards independence of foreign support and control and towards union. This trend was not new, but had been present since almost the first planting of Protestant Christianity in Japan.[109] It was now greatly accelerated and in the 1940's was given added impetus by the requirements of the Japanese Government. It was in part a reflection of the environment. Japanese nationalism, long intense and in the 1930's and 1940's super-heated by developments in the domestic and international situation, could ill brook groups which might seem to be agents of foreign peoples and cultures. The state would insist upon the severance of ties which savoured of such a connexion. Japanese Christians were sensitive and wished to demonstrate their independence. The drive would be towards financial and administrative autonomy of the churches and of Christian institutions and towards a unity which would transcend the ecclesiastical divisions transmitted from the Occident. Yet the achievement would have been impossible but for an inner vitality in Japanese Protestant Christianity which produced the needed leadership, evoked the required financial support, and stimulated the devising of measures for the achievement of unity. Moreover, Japanese Protestant Christians did not by any means surrender unconditionally to nationalism. Their leaders insisted that the Christian faith and the Christian Church were supra-national and so far as war permitted maintained their ties with their fellow Christians in other lands. Consciously and by choice they were members of the emerging world-wide Christian fellowship.

The steps taken after 1914 towards independence and unity can be quickly summarized. In 1923 the National Christian Council of Japan was constituted and the Japanese federation of churches was merged with it.[110] Through the National Christian Council Japanese Protestantism had membership in the International Missionary Council. In 1935 the Federation of Christian Missions in Japan voted to transfer to the National Christian Council and to other indigenous bodies all its functions other than the nourishing of fellowship

---

[107] Vories, *The Omi Brotherhood in Nippon*, p. 84.
[108] Drach, *Our Church Abroad*, p. 89.
[109] Vol. VI, pp. 407, 408.
[110] *The International Review of Missions*, Vol. XXI, pp. 18, 19.

among missionaries.[111] In 1922 the American Board of Commissioners for Foreign Missions passed over all its evangelistic work to a body representing the *Kumiai* churches and on which were only four missionaries. In 1927 similar steps were taken with other phases of the enterprises of the American Board.[112] In the 1920's three Japanese were consecrated to the Anglican episcopate.[113] In 1929 86 per cent. of the Congregationalists (*Kumiai*), 75 per cent. of the Presbyterians, 66 per cent. of the Methodists, and 37 per cent. of the Anglicans —and these were the four largest Protestant bodies—were in self-supporting congregations.[114] Between 1924 and 1934 the number of Japanese Protestant congregations increased 45 per cent. and the number of those which were financially self-supporting 151 per cent.[115] It was held that city pastors were men of good scholarship and intellect and that some of them were commanding personalities. Many of the urban churches, moreover, had strong bodies of lay members.[116]

Beginning in 1940 the progress towards independence and unity became much more rapid. In 1939 the Imperial Diet passed a law to govern religious bodies in Japan.[117] This gave legal recognition to Christianity, placing it in that respect on a par with Buddhism and sect Shinto. It also made necessary registration and, therefore, some degree of supervision by the state. The bill took effect in April, 1940. The approval of registration for religious bodies was required to be accomplished by March 31, 1941. The progress of the war in Europe and of the hostilities in China heightened the war psychology of the realm. Feeling against British subjects and, indeed, against all foreign connexions was mounting. In the summer of 1940 the Salvation Army, partly because of its affiliation with the London headquarters, fell under official suspicion and was forced to reorganize and to sever all organic ties abroad. Because of counsel which came through friends in government ministries, Protestant leaders, to forestall probable compulsory action by the state, proceeded to transfer to Japanese such administrative posts in churches and schools as were in foreign hands, to remove foreigners in Christian schools from teach-

[111] *The International Review of Missions*, Vol. XXV, p. 10.

[112] *The International Review of Missions*, Vol. XXI, p. 21.

[113] *Ibid.; The Japan Mission Year Book*, 1929, pp. 99, 100.

[114] Laymen's Foreign Mission Inquiry, *Fact-Finders' Reports, Japan*, Vol. VI, Supplementary Series, Part 2, pp. 40, 41.

[115] Davis, *Mission Finance Policies and the Younger Churches*, p. 56.

[116] Laymen's Foreign Missions Inquiry, *Regional Reports of the Commission of Appraisal*, Vol. III, Supplementary Series, Part 1, pp. 62, 63.

[117] See a translation of the text of the bill as presented to the Diet and which was passed with some amendments in *The Japan Christian Quarterly*, Vol. XIV, pp. 35-41. See extracts from the debate on the bill in the Diet in *The Japan Christian Quarterly*, Vol. XIV, pp. 169-172.

ing positions which dealt with social, philosophical, political, or religious subjects, and to free themselves from foreign financial subsidies. As we have seen in earlier pages of this chapter, somewhat similar steps were being taken by the Roman Catholics and Russian Orthodox. For much the same reason, Japanese Protestant leaders deemed it expedient to hasten the bringing together of the various Protestant bodies into a single ecclesiastical structure. In pursuance of the latter programme a commission representing twenty-six different denominations, within a few months augmented to forty-one, set about the framing of a constitution. This was completed in March, 1941, and in May of that year received the approval of the government. In June, 1941, at a conference in Tokyo the Church of Christ in Japan, as the fusion was called, came formally into being. At the outset the Anglicans and the Seventh Day Adventists felt unable to join, but even without them the new body included more different varieties of Protestantism than ever before had been brought into an ecclesiastical whole. The leadership, it need scarcely be added, was Japanese.[118] While the religious bodies law and fear of compulsion by the state hastened the union, the achievement would have been impossible had there not been earlier movements in that direction and competent Japanese Christians to effect the consummation of the process. By the autumn of 1943 most of the Anglicans had joined the new body. Only the Seventh Day Adventists and a few congregations of other denominations remained aloof. Moreover, a larger co-operation had been effected. By the autumn of 1943 the National Christian Council had been modified to embrace both Roman Catholics and Protestants. Archbishop Doi, of the former, had become the chairman and a Protestant continued as secretary.[119]

In addition to the hastening of union and the transfer of authority from foreigners to Japanese, Protestant Christianity in a number of other ways gave evidence of the effects of the hyper-nationalism and the environment of war in the midst of which it was set. This was seen in the problem presented by state or shrine Shinto. For Protestants as for Roman Catholics the issue was whether these ceremonies were religious. If they were, a Christian could scarcely share in them. If they were not, he might participate. The problem had long been present for Christian schools. They were expected, as were all schools, to possess and revere a copy of the portrait of the Emperor, to have

[118] S. Saito in *Contemporary Japan*, Vol. IX, No. 11; C. W. Iglehart in *The International Review of Missions*, Vol. XXX, pp. 493-502; C. W. Inglehart in *The Japan Christian Quarterly*, Vol. XV, pp. 315-326, Vol. XVI, pp. 21-33; T. Miyakoda in *The Japan Christian Quarterly*, Vol. XVI, pp. 15-20.

[119] Foreign Missions Conference of North America, Committee on East Asia, mimeographed communication, Dec. 13, 1943, giving reports by missionaries repatriated from Japan.

read, with appropriate ceremonies, the imperial rescript on education, and on specified occasions to have their students go to the shrines of state Shinto. As the war fever mounted, homage at the Shinto shrines became increasingly a test of the patriotism of every Japanese subject. Japanese Christians formerly had qualms and had collectively expressed them. As the wars progressed, however, they accepted the government's declaration that the ceremonies were not religious but purely patriotic. Some missionaries held them to be clearly religious and were very unhappy over what they deemed to be the compromise of principle made by their Japanese brethren.[120] In general, moreover, Japanese Protestant Christians, while at the outset deploring the Manchurian adventure of 1931,[121] supported their government in the enlarged conflict which began in 1937. They accepted at their face value the official declarations which avowed idealistic objectives for the "new order in East Asia." They sought to establish friendly contacts with Chinese Christians and wished, probably with entire sincerity, to help relieve the suffering in China.[122]

As we summarize the effects of Christianity upon Japan in this period, we must, after what was said in the last paragraph, hasten to add that Japanese Christians did not entirely surrender to the exaggerated nationalism of the 1930's and 1940's. Several Protestant Christians resigned or were dismissed from teaching posts in government educational institutions because of their pacifism.[123] Japanese as well as Chinese Protestant leaders attempted to keep unbroken their Christian fellowship across the barriers of hostility, and deputations were exchanged between the National Christian Councils of the two countries.[124] A leading Japanese Christian endeavoured to make peace between China and Japan and was imprisoned for his pains.[125] Moreover, Protestant missionaries laboured for peace, not only between China and Japan, but also between the United States and Japan. American missionaries were outspoken in their condemnation of the legislation in their country which was discriminatory against the Japanese.[126]

[120] Holtom, *Modern Japan and Shinto Nationalism*, pp. 95-123; D. C. Holtom in *The International Review of Missions*, Vol. XXVII, pp. 158-173; W. Paton and M. Sinclair in *The International Review of Missions*, Vol. XXIX, pp. 161-188, 305-314.
[121] Mimeographed copy of a resolution adopted by the annual meeting of the National Christian Council of Japan, Nov. 11, 1931.
[122] J. W. Decker in *The International Review of Missions*, Vol. XXIX, pp. 519-532.
[123] *The Japan Christian Quarterly*, Vol. XIII, p. 70.
[124] *Quarterly Notes, Being the Bulletin of the International Missionary Council*, April, 1933, p. iii.
[125] A missionary in Japan to the author, March 7, 1941.
[126] Laymen's Foreign Missions Inquiry, *Fact-Finders' Reports, Japan*, Vol. VI, Supplementary Series, Part 2, p. 32.

Even more than before 1914, Christianity was exerting an influence upon Japan quite out of proportion to its numerical strength. Probably the churches enrolled a smaller percentage of the population in 1944 than at the close of the sixteenth century. Unquestionably the influence of Christianity was much greater in the 1930's and 1940's than it had ever been.

Some of the features of that influence were noted in the preceding volume[127] and others must have been apparent in earlier pages in this chapter. Christianity was a marked factor in social reform. A prominent Japanese social worker, probably with this in mind, declared Christianity to be the strongest religious force in Japan.[128] As additional instances, we hear of a scion of a noble family who was inspired by his faith to serve among the coal miners and to become a social radical and reformer[129] and of a Christian of considerable wealth who lived simply to devote as much as possible to the uplift of society.[130] Christian ethics had penetrated the life of the country. The effects were strikingly shown in an improved status of women, in efforts towards better social conditions, in larger emphasis upon the worth of the individual, and in the fight against licensed prostitution and intemperance.[131] Those chiefly responsible for moulding the newer social ideals were largely Christians.[132] Many of them did not continue to be affiliated with organized Christianity, but they acknowledged their debt to the faith.[133] The Christmas festival was widely observed outside as well as inside Christian circles and its celebration was becoming quite the fashion in non-Christian homes, especially of the higher classes. While it was partly commercialized, few could participate in it without learning something of its deeper meaning.[134] Many Christian songs became common property and tunes of Christian origin were used for secular words.[135] Japanese secular literature showed the effects of Christianity in a number of ways, among them a trend towards belief in the personality of God, a new value on womanhood, an altered and higher ideal of marriage and family life, an interest in the

[127] Vol. VI, pp. 404-407.

[128] Laymen's Foreign Missions Inquiry, *op. cit.,* Vol. VI, Supplementary Series, Part 2, p. 156.

[129] Baroness Shidzué Ishimoto, *Facing Two Ways* (New York, Farrar and Rinehart, 1935, pp. vi, 373), *passim.*

[130] Missionaries of the United Church of Canada, *Fruits of Christian Missions in Japan,* p. 113.

[131] Kennedy, *The Changing Fabric of Japan,* pp. 225, 226; Laymen's Foreign Missions Inquiry, *op. cit.,* Vol. VI, Supplementary Series, Part 2, p. 308.

[132] Laymen's Foreign Missions Inquiry, *op. cit.,* Vol. VI, Supplementary Series, Part 2, p. 30.

[133] Laymen's Foreign Missions Inquiry, *op. cit.,* Vol. VI, Supplementary Series, Part 2, pp. 119-121.

[134] *Contemporary Japan,* Vol. III, pp. 450-456.

[135] *Asia,* Vol. XXXV, p. 158.

depressed classes, stricter standards of sex,[136] and higher business ethics.[137] Both Buddhism and Shinto were being led towards a monotheistic conception of God.[138] Buddhist Young Men's Associations, the Buddhist Salvation Army, Buddhist Sunday Schools, and many organized Buddhist efforts for social welfare were clearly the fruit of Christian example.[139]

Christianity was having more influence in China, where the fabric of life had disintegrated more extensively than in Japan, but in the latter country it was by no means negligible.

Christianity was clearly bearing the impress of its Japanese *milieu*. Most of the main features of the effect of the environment must be obvious from what has thus far been recorded in this chapter. Conformation to the Japanese setting, already marked in 1914,[140] made rapid strides after that year. Except for the descendants of the sixteenth century Christians and a few other groups, the faith was predominantly urban in its membership. Protestantism, increasingly the major form of the faith, was mainly recruited from the middle classes, especially those of the professions and the products of Western education. The trend towards ecclesiastical autonomy and financial independence of the founding churches, already strong before 1914, was greatly accelerated, especially by developments in the international scene. By 1944 all leading administrative posts in the churches, whether Roman Catholic, Russian Orthodox, or Protestant, had been transferred to Japanese. The second of the world wars, with the hostilities between Japan on the one hand and the United States and Great Britain on the other, led to the repatriation of a large proportion of the missionary body. This was especially the case with Protestantism, for the overwhelming majority of its missionary staff were from the United States and the British Empire. At the same time, both through pressure, in large degree indirect, from the Japanese Government and through the exigencies of war, financial assistance from abroad had lapsed. It was by thinly veiled coercion by the state that the union of the various Protestant bodies had been hastened and the Church of Christ in Japan had come into being. Under the same constraint, Roman Catholics and Protestants were brought into some degree of co-operation

[136] S. H. Wainright in *The Japan Mission Year Book*, 1930, pp. 159-166.

[137] White, *A Working Faith for the World*, p. 133.

[138] A. K. Reischauer in *The International Review of Missions*, Vol. XXVI, p. 327.

[139] Laymen's Foreign Missions Inquiry, *op. cit.*, Vol. VI, Supplementary Series, Part 2, pp. 19, 32, 216-218; Kennedy, *op. cit.*, p. 227; Missionaries of the United Church of Canada, *op. cit.*, p. 107.

[140] Vol. VI, pp. 407-409.

in a reorganized National Christian Council. Both Roman Catholics and Protestants had made their peace with the intense nationalism expressed by state Shinto. There were beginnings of accommodation in art and architecture.

In more subtle ways Japanese tradition was felt. The Protestant ministry tended to conform to a Japanese conception that a teacher of religion should be a scholar rather than a man of action and for the most part was not greatly concerned with the social transformation of the country. It may have been this outlook which helped to account for the vogue which Barthianism had among the Protestant clergy.[141] The lack of precedent for a society such as the Church was probably to some degree responsible for the neglect of many who regarded themselves as Christians to associate themselves with any branch of the Church and for the ease with which numbers who had had such a connexion allowed it to lapse. Traditional religious eclecticism was partly accountable for the fraternizing of some Christians with adherents of other faiths in an interchange of experience and conviction[142] and for adaptations by Christians of the inherited veneration of deceased parents.[143]

Moreover, as war prolonged its exhausting way and more and more engrossed the nation's energies, attendance at church services and Sunday Schools fell off. Clergymen were compelled to go into the army or to engage in industries connected with the struggle. In the case of Protestants, with their married ministry, the wives undertook some of the clerical functions of their husbands,[144] but this could not entirely compensate for the loss.

However, the Christian churches by no means completely surrendered to the national temper. They maintained essential characteristics transmitted by the founding bodies. In their outlines of doctrine they were in the historic stream of the faith.[145] In the face of the pressure for conformation with the imperial cult their leaders found ways of persevering in their Christian theism. Roman Catholics through their tie with the Papal see and Protestants through their connexions with the International Missionary Council cherished their fellowship with Christians of other lands and held to the supra-national and

---

[141] On the Barthian vogue see E. Hessel in *The Japan Christian Quarterly,* Vol. XII, pp. 139 ff.

[142] Hocking, *Living Religions and a World Faith,* pp. 271-274.

[143] Letter of a missionary in Japan to the author, March 14, 1936, giving a concrete illustration.

[144] Foreign Missions Conference of North America, Committee on East Asia, mimeographed document, Dec. 13, 1943.

[145] As an example, see how much of historic Christian teaching and how little that is peculiar to Japan is contained in Toyohiko Kagawa, *Meditations on the Cross* (Chicago, Willett, Clark & Company, 1935, pp. vii, 211).

universal character of their faith. The Japanese churches were consciously part of the world-wide Church of Christ.

Formosa must not long detain us. Racially and culturally it was overwhelmingly Chinese. Although politically it had been Japanese since 1895 and the process of assimilation to Japanese language and institutions was being pushed by the government, the outcome of the second of the world wars might rejoin the island to China. The population rose from 3,612,184 in 1914[146] to 5,212,426 in 1935,[147] predominantly by an excess of births over deaths, for in the latter figure there were not quite 300,000 Japanese.

In proportion to the population Christians were slightly less numerous than in Japan Proper. In 1933 Roman Catholics, under the charge of Spanish Dominicans of the Province of the Holy Rosary as they had been long before 1914, numbered 7,193[148] and in 1936 Protestant communicants were 14,895.[149] Almost all the latter were in the Presbyterian Church of Formosa and were of Chinese ancestry. This church had arisen out of the efforts of English and Canadian Presbyterians. The united church had been constituted in 1912.[150] It was an indication of the rootage of Christianity in Formosan soil. By 1931 the Protestant churches were practically self-supporting.[151] Roman Catholics had increased from 3,469 in about the year 1915,[152] and Protestants from 6,132 communicants in 1914.[153] In other words, Christians had multiplied proportionately more rapidly than the population and Protestants more rapidly than Roman Catholics. Japanese Christian organizations were seeking to reach Japanese residents.[154] The Japanese Government forbade approach to the uncivilized aborigines, a small minority.[155]

The Japanese insistence upon participation in ceremonies at Shinto shrines, part of the process of assimilating Formosans to Japanese rule, brought problems for the Christian schools.[156] Late in the 1930's and in the 1940's diffi-

---

[146] *The Statesman's Year-Book,* 1915, p. 1107.
[147] *The Statesman's Year-Book,* 1943, p. 1066.
[148] Parker, *Interpretative Statistical Survey of the World Mission of the Christian Church,* p. 33.
[149] Parker, *op. cit.,* p. 49.
[150] Edward Band, *Barclay of Formosa* (Tokyo, Christian Literature Society, 1936, pp. 212), pp. 136-138.
[151] *The International Review of Missions,* Vol. XX, p. 11.
[152] *Los Dominicos en el Extremo Oriente,* pp. 160-162.
[153] Beach and St. John, *World Statistics of Christian Missions,* p. 62.
[154] *The International Review of Missions,* Vol. XXI, p. 26.
[155] *The International Review of Missions,* Vol. XXI, p. 25; *The Japan Christian Quarterly,* Vol. XI, p. 229.
[156] *The Japan Mission Year Book,* 1929, p. 274.

culties for the Formosan Christians multiplied. Formosan Chinese Protestants regarded their churches as the only institutions which were really their own and free from Japanese control. Probably for this reason, the Japanese eyed them with suspicion, particularly when, as the war with China deepened, the Formosans might be suspected of sympathy with fellow Chinese on the mainland. Attempts to spread the faith met obstacles from the Japanese authorities.[157] As the Japanese fear of British citizens grew, in 1940 and 1941 both English and Canadian missionaries felt it necessary to withdraw.[158] Formosan Protestants were cut off from the founding churches so long as the war between Japan and the British Empire continued.

The three decades which followed the year 1914 brought additional chapters to the stormy history of Christianity in Korea, or Chosen as the Japanese called it. We have seen[159] the fashion in which the Roman Catholic Church, the one form of Christianity represented before the 1880's, had been subjected to repeated and severe persecutions from its introduction late in the eighteenth century until treaty relations with Western powers were entered into by the rulers of Korea. We have recorded the rapid growth of Christianity after the 1880's, both Roman Catholic and Protestant, with a slight representation of the Russian Orthodox Church. Protestantism, introduced chiefly by Presbyterians and Methodists from the United States, multiplied more rapidly than Roman Catholic or Russian Orthodox Christianity, but there were marked tides in its growth.

In 1912 Roman Catholics numbered 78,850,[160] served by the Société des Missions Etrangères of Paris, and baptized Protestants in 1914 totalled at least 86,000.[161] The population of the peninsula mounted from 15,508,872 in 1914[162] to 22,800,647 in 1938.[163] In 1934 Roman Catholics had risen to 147,476[164] and in 1936 baptized Protestants were 168,477.[165] In other words, the percentage growth of Christians was much more rapid than that of the population.

Yet the years after 1914, in spite of this increase and in part because of it,

[157] *The Japan Christian Year Book,* 1940, pp. 220-231.
[158] *The International Review of Missions,* Vol. XXX, p. 13, Vol. XXXI, p. 12.
[159] Vol. VI, pp. 412-430.
[160] Streit, *Atlas Hierarchicus,* p. 100.
[161] Beach and St. John, *op. cit.,* p. 62.
[162] *The Statesman's Year-Book,* 1915, p. 1104.
[163] *The Statesman's Year-Book,* 1943, p. 1063.
[164] *Fides Service,* Jan. 19, 1935.
[165] Parker, *op. cit.,* p. 18.

were extraordinarily difficult for Christians and the 1940's were especially a time of trouble. Korea was a conquered country. The Japanese were attempting to assimilate the population. They sought this, among other ways, by promoting the use of the Japanese language and insisting upon the attendance of Koreans, particularly of the youth during their school days, at the shrines of the official Shinto. To this process the churches, especially the Protestant churches, were obstacles. They were in the hands of Koreans. With them were associated non-Japanese foreigners. Among the Protestants most of the latter were from the United States, tended to be critical of the Japanese, and in ecclesiastical matters and in general temper stood for a democracy and self-govenment which ran counter to the Japanese purpose. Churches and missionaries, especially of the Protestants, were, therefore, viewed by Japanese officialdom with jaundiced eyes.

The difficulties were aggravated by economic distress. Korea was picturesque but, to some degree for that very reason, poor. Although latterly industrialization had been promoted by the Japanese, her living came mainly from agriculture, the amount of arable land was limited, to no small extent because so much of the surface was mountainous, and the population was increasing. Some Japanese by ruthless exploitation accentuated the suffering, partly by taking over much of the land, but even the best of administrations could not completely have eliminated it.

As the years passed the tension became not less but more acute. After 1931 and increasingly after 1937 Japan was embarked upon a course of conquest. She could not tolerate possible defection in Korea and her measures to prevent it became more stringent. The Christian forces felt the pressure.

Roman Catholics appear to have been somewhat less affected than Protestants. Most of the foreign personnel was from France, a nation with which Japan was officially at peace. After the first of the world wars the dearth of staff of the Paris society was such that the Benedictines of St. Odile from Bavaria, whose first contingent had arrived in 1909, in 1920 were assigned a region in the North-east.[166] In 1922 Maryknollers were entrusted with territory in the North-west. The initial instalment of the Americans reached their field in 1923 and others followed.[167] Latterly, too, had come missionary priests of St. Columban.[168] Since these last two groups were from countries with which Japan was at war after December 7, 1941, their enterprises suffered. In 1943 we learn of the prohibition by the Japanese of instruction in the Catholic faith in one of

[166] *The Catholic Church in Korea*, p. 90; Considine, *Across a World*, pp. 242, 243.
[167] *The Catholic Church in Korea*, pp. 92, 97 ff.; Considine, *op. cit.*, p. 242.
[168] Considine, *op. cit.*, p. 242.

the minor or preparatory seminaries.[169] In accordance with what was being done in much of the rest of the non-Occidental world, in 1937 a prefecture apostolic was created in the South which was placed under the exclusive jurisdiction of Korean clergy.[170] This was the first step of its kind in Korea and was evidence that the Roman Catholic Church was beginning to be less dependent upon its foreign staff. Early in the 1930's, indeed, the percentage of Koreans in the priesthood and in the sisterhoods of Chosen was about twice that of Japanese in the priesthood and sisterhoods of Japan.[171] The Roman Catholic Church was, accordingly, in a better position than formerly to weather the storm. Moreover, the tolerance of Rome for the participation by the faithful in the rites at the shrines of state Shinto eased for Korean Roman Catholics the impact of Japanese efforts to secure their rear against sedition.

The mission of the Russian Orthodox Church, never large,[172] suffered from the disasters which overtook the mother church after 1917. In 1923 the enterprise was placed by patriarchal decree under the archdiocese of Japan. In 1934 it was said to have seven hundred Christians in Seoul and five other centres, with a church and school in Seoul and an archpriest in charge. Some Koreans had been ordained.[173] The number of Christians seems to have declined since the years before 1914.

The growth of the Protestant churches in Korea displayed marked variations. In general, the years from 1906 to 1910 had shown a rapid increase. This may have been in part because of the hope that Christianity would be able to save the country as a whole from the impending annexation by Japan. Then came approximately a decade, from 1910 through 1919, when the number of adult baptisms declined or remained nearly stationary. One reason assigned for the pause in the advance was the discouragement following the annexation by Japan: for the time being Koreans had lost hope of any corporate remaking of the country.[174] In 1919, at the end of the first of the world wars, probably stimulated by the espousal of the self-determination of peoples by President Wilson as spokesman for the victorious allies, a popular demand for independence became vocal. In it Protestant Christian pastors were prominent.[175] While the Japanese quickly suppressed the movement, reforms were made in the

---

[169] *N.C.W.C.*, Sept. 27, 1943.
[170] *Fides News Service,* Apr. 24, 1937.
[171] *Testo-Atlante illustrato delle Missioni,* p. 58.
[172] Vol. VI, pp. 427, 428.
[173] Bolshakoff, *The Foreign Missions of the Russian Orthodox Church,* pp. 74, 75.
[174] Wasson, *Church Growth in Korea,* pp. 50-97, 166; Soltau, *Korea,* p. 59.
[175] Wasson, *op. cit.,* pp. 98-101.

administration of the country. Through their leadership in the effort for in-dependence Christians gained in popularity among Korean patriots. Moreover, the large accessions to missionary staffs and to funds from the United States which followed the first of the world wars gave fresh impetus to the churches. Through 1924 baptisms of adults showed an increase.[176] The five years after 1924 witnessed another drop in the rate of accessions, a decline which was more marked for Methodists than for Presbyterians. This seems to have been due to the world-wide agricultural depression, to the embitterment of unemployed youth, and to the reduction of grants from America. The anti-Christian agita-tion in China and Russia had an adverse effect.[177] Later something of an upward trend was resumed. The distress of the late 1930's and the 1940's was a depressant which we are to note in a moment.

In Korea as in Japan the Protestant churches suffered from severe leakages of members. The reasons for this phenomenon in Korea were somewhat obscure. They were partly the high ethical standards maintained by the churches and the severity of discipline for moral lapses, and in part the migra-tions to the cities, to Japan, and to Manchuria brought about by the poverty and the growing pressure of population.[178]

Christians were most numerous in the North, where society was more fluid and less rigidly stratified than in the central regions.[179]

In spite of fluctuations in the rate of growth and the failure to hold a large proportion of their members, the Protestant churches of Korea gave evidence of marked vitality. Missions were conducted for Koreans in Japan and Man-churia. Until the Russian Government closed the churches, there were Korean congregations in Siberia. Several cities in China had Korean churches.[180] The Korean mission to the Chinese in Shantung flourished.[181] The financial self-support which had been emphasized from almost the beginning of Protestant effort led to a larger per capita giving than among the Presbyterians in any of the other "younger churches" planted by nineteenth and twentieth century missions. In 1937, of the nearly three thousand Presbyterian congregations in

[176] Wasson, *op. cit.*, pp. 101 ff., 166; Clark, *The Korean Church and the Nevius Methods,* pp. 164-167.

[177] Soltau, *op. cit.*, p. 103; Wasson, *op. cit.*, pp. 125 ff.; Van Buskirk, *Korea*, pp. 54-57, 145-161.

[178] Charles Allen Clark to A. L. Warnshuis, May, 1932; Van Buskirk, *op. cit.*, pp. 51-53.

[179] Soltau, *op. cit.*, pp. 66, 67.

[180] The secretary of the National Christian Council of Korea to the author, June, 1932; *The International Review of Missions*, Vol. XX, p. 12, Vol. XXIII, p. 15; Charles Allen Clark to A. L. Warnshuis, May, 1932; George W. McCune, mimeographed letter, Jan. 18, 1933.

[181] Clark, *The Korean Church and the Nevius Methods*, p. 162.

Korea about two-thirds fully supported their own pastors and the other phases of their programmes.[182]

Increasingly co-operation and autonomy characterized the Protestantism of the country. The formation by Methodists and Presbyterians of the General Evangelical Council in 1905 and of the Federal Council of Protestant Missions in 1912—to the latter of which the Young Men's Christian Association and the Bible societies were added—was followed, in 1919, by a federal council of the Presbyterian and Methodist churches and, in 1927, by the Korean Christian Council.[183] An independent Presbyterian Church, growing out of the efforts of the several Presbyterian missions, came into being before 1914 and in 1922 adopted a new constitution.[184] In 1930 the two Methodist bodies, the one organized in 1908 and the other in 1918, united to form the Korean Methodist Church, also autonomous, and a Korean was elected bishop.[185] Koreans were also chosen as district superintendents.[186] The churches were being prepared, all unconsciously, for the storm which would remove from them their Occidental missionaries and cut off financial aid from the West.

Protestant Christianity was continuing to touch Korean life from many angles. Much was made of the propagation of the faith by the Korean Christians and without financial subsidies from the founding churches of the West. Great emphasis was placed upon the study of the Bible.[187] Schools were maintained, from those of primary grade through colleges and theological seminaries.[188] Hospitals and clinics cared for the sick and a medical school prepared physicians.[189] Increasingly steps were being taken to turn over schools and hospitals to the Korean churches and to encourage the churches to support them.[190] More and more aware of the difficulties presented by the economic situation to a predominantly agricultural population, Protestants were paying

[182] Davis, *Mission Finance Policies and the Younger Churches*, pp. 59, 60. See also on self-support, Herbert E. Blair, *Christian Stewardship in Korea* (The Department of Social and Industrial Research, International Missionary Council, 1938, pp. 36), *passim*.

[183] Soltau, *op. cit.*, pp. 58-60; Wasson, *op. cit.*, p. 4; Clark, *op. cit.*, p. 203.

[184] Clark, *op. cit.*, p. 177.

[185] Wasson, *op. cit.*, p. 4; *The Christian Century*, Vol. XLVII, p. 1629.

[186] *The International Review of Missions*, Vol. XX, p. 12.

[187] Soltau, *op. cit.*, pp. 29-34, 38-40; Clark, *op. cit.*, p. 215; S. Kate Cooper, *Evangelism in Korea* (Nashville, Board of Missions, Methodist Episcopal Church, South, 1930, pp. 95), *passim*.

[188] James Earnest Fisher, *Democracy and Mission Education in Korea* (New York, Teachers College, Columbia University, 1928, pp. xiii, 187), *passim*; Soltau, *op. cit.*, pp. 52, 53; Van Buskirk, *op. cit.*, pp. 133, 134.

[189] For examples see W. H. Chisholm, *Vivid Experiences in Korea* (Chicago, The Bible Institute Colportage Association, 1938, pp. 136), *passim*. See also Soltau, *op. cit.*, pp. 45-47; Van Buskirk, *op. cit.*, pp. 108-113.

[190] Clark, *op. cit.*, pp. 220-227; Soltau, *op. cit.*, pp. 47-58.

attention to rural conditions. Agricultural experts were added to the staffs of missions and churches, counsel in better methods of farming was given to those who wished it, and plant and tree diseases were fought.[191]

Upon this Protestant movement in Korea, promising and growing, the darkening international scene brought dire distress. Missionaries and Korean Christians had long been scrutinized by Japanese police officers. With the intensification of hostilities between Japan and China in 1937, the Japanese authorities were increasingly watchful of Korean Christians, especially of those who had studied in the United States and so might be supposed to desire the independence of the country. They became insistent, too, that students in Christian as well as in other schools attend the ceremonies at Shinto shrines. Rather than accede to this demand, the Southern Presbyterians resolved to close their schools (1937). The Methodists decided to comply.[192] In 1938 the government ordered some of the churches to see that all their members presented themselves at the shrine of the Sun-Goddess, of the Shinto pantheon, before coming to Christian services, and that failing the presence of such a shrine in the village the church must erect one on its own premises. On the ground that this was idolatry, some pastors and lay Christians refused obedience and suffered at the hands of the police. Others submitted, presumably on the plea that the required acts were patriotic and not religious. Schisms over the issue divided the churches.[193] To relieve Korean Christians from the embarrassment of the foreign connexion, and because of differences between missionaries and Koreans over the shrine question, in 1939 and 1940 most Presbyterian missionaries engaged in what was technically known as "evangelistic work" withdrew from official positions with the Presbyterian Church of Korea, but continued unofficial relations.[194] In 1939 the Australian Presbyterian mission retired from schools in one of the provinces.[195] In 1938 the offices of the National Christian Council, the Young Men's and Young Women's Christian Associations, the Sunday School Association, and the Society of Christian Endeavour were closed by the government, presumably because of their international affiliations and because they might encourage

[191] *The International Review of Missions,* Vol. XX, p. 12; Soltau, *op. cit.,* pp. 69, 70; Felton, *The Rural Church in the Far East,* p. 181; Hamlin, *Treasures of the Earth,* pp. 3-16; Hunnicutt and Reid, *The Story of Agricultural Missions,* pp. 86-88; Van Buskirk, *op. cit.,* pp. 74-86; Helen Kiteuk Kim, *Rural Education for the Regeneration of Korea* (New York, privately printed, 1931, pp. xiii, 124), *passim.*
[192] *The International Review of Missions,* Vol. XXVII, pp. 11, 12.
[193] *The International Review of Missions,* Vol. XXVIII, p. 10.
[194] H. H. Underwood in *The Japan Christian Year Book,* 1940, pp. 204 ff.; *The International Review of Missions,* Vol. XXX, p. 12.
[195] *The International Review of Missions,* Vol. XXIX, p. 9.

Korean nationalism, and it was urged that connexions be formed with the corresponding bodies in Japan.[196] In 1940 the large majority of Protestant missionaries left the country. The reasons were partly the advice of the respective governments because of the deterioration in the relations between Japan on the one hand and the United States and the British Empire on the other, partly the unhappiness of many missionaries over the fashion in which Korean churches had submitted to the demands of the state for attendance at the Shinto shrines, and to some degree because the missionaries felt that under the existing international tensions their presence was a handicap to the Korean Christians.[197] The process was hastened of affiliating the Korean churches with those of Japan and of bringing them together in the one Church of Christ in Japan.[198] Thus the assimilation of Korea to Japan would be expedited and what to the Japanese government was the anomaly of churches in a political dependency affiliated with churches in foreign lands would be ended. While the larger proportion of the Roman Catholic missionaries remained, almost all the Protestant foreign staff had left. This was because of nationality and because the Roman Catholic Church took a more tolerant attitude towards Shinto than did the Protestant missionaries.

Japan and its empire were a storm centre through most of the tempestuous thirty years which followed 1914. Economic stress, industrial and commercial expansion, internal political upheavals, and large ambitions implemented by an aggressive army and navy made Japan a problem to herself and her neighbours.

In general, the atmosphere seemed adverse to the extension of Christianity. This was especially the case since the national traditions were unfriendly to that faith and heightened nationalism looked askance at communities having external ties with some of the powers with whom Japan was at enmity.

In spite of the difficulties and of the small numerical strength of the churches, Christianity displayed a substantial growth. The increase, as in the decades immediately preceding 1914, was chiefly in the Protestant forms of the faith. It was both numerical and an influence upon the life of the peoples as a whole. Indeed, Christianity, while by no means dominant, was the most vigorous and rapidly growing religious force in the empire—unless the state-stimulated Shinto be classed as a religion. Christianity was certainly potent far beyond the size of the churches.

[196] *The International Review of Missions*, Vol. XXVIII, p. 11.
[197] C. A. Sauer in *The Japan Christian Quarterly*, Vol. XVI, pp. 40-44.
[198] *The International Review of Missions*, Vol. XXXI, p. 11

By processes which were greatly accelerated by political conditions and pressures, the churches were passing under indigenous leadership—to Japanese in Japan proper, to Formosans in their island, and to Koreans in Chosen. Under the same stimuli, Protestant bodies were being brought together in an inclusive unity, a unity which not only embraced the various denominations but also was progressively empire-wide. There was obvious danger that this Christianity, led by Japanese and under the stress of a rampant nationalism, would conform so largely to its environment that it would lose its savour and cease to be Christian except in name. The peril was augmented by the vicissitudes of war which repatriated most of the Protestant and some of the Roman Catholic missionary staffs, thus attenuating ties with the world-wide Church. So far as could be ascertained, however, by the close of 1944 the churches had not succumbed to this trend. Some compromises there had been, but the leaders, whether Roman Catholic, Russian Orthodox, or Protestant, were seeking to conserve the supra-national ideals of their respective bodies and the consciousness that the Japanese churches were members of an ecumenical fellowship.

Chapter XV

THE FIRST THREE POST-1914 DECADES: A SUMMARY

A S ONE essays a summary of the three decades in the expansion of Christianity which were introduced by the events of the year 1914 he is painfully conscious that in 1944 the period of which they were a part was clearly incomplete. Any estimates must, therefore, be tentative and ventured upon with the frank realization that the era might be far from its conclusion. Yet before we pass to the second and, incidentally, the much briefer section of this volume, the survey and interpretation of the course of Christianity from its inception, we must pause for rapid retrospect over so much of the post-1914 years as by 1944 had become history.

The most obvious of the general characteristics was storm. The time was one of world-wide war and revolution. There had been earlier ages when portions of mankind had been as profoundly shaken. Never within recorded history, however, had all of the human race been so clearly on the march. In varying degrees, the globe over, existing patterns of culture were being broken or reshaped. The old and familiar were passing amid tempest. Through inconceivable agonies a new world was coming to birth. The revolutions were most marked in Europe, Africa, and Asia, but they were also in evidence in the Americas.

The natural supposition would be that in the period of change Christianity was a receding force. It had been intimately associated with the development of European culture. Europe was the main centre and source of the tempests which were sweeping away the old order. What more probable than that Christianity, along with the rest of the past, would be thrown into the discard or relegated to the category of remnants of the passing age? Was it not, like other survivals, to carry over, not because of inner vigour, but only by reason of inertia, or what some scholars denominated "social lag," a bit of unburied archeology? Would not a new era view it with mingled amusement, impatience, and curiosity?

That appraisal gained force from the fact that Christianity had enjoyed its greatest expansion in the century between 1815 and 1914 in association with cultural features which were now clearly passing. The comparative freedom from governmental control not only in economics but also in many another phase of life had been paralleled by the voluntary co-operation of thousands of individual Christians in the propagation of their faith. Now that the state was augmenting its functions and a period of regimentation had come, the methods by which Christianity had been spread in the nineteenth century would presumably be anachronisms. The contrast would bear particularly hard upon Protestantism, through which the expansion of Christianity had been mainly achieved in the nineteenth century, for Protestantism seemed intimately connected with the free initiative of the individual.

This conjecture was in part justified by the event. In what had long been a chief centre of their strength, the continent of Europe, churches which were the organized embodiment of Christianity suffered severe numerical losses. Huge defections, avowed or by neglect, kept from the Church millions who in an earlier age would have been her sons and daughters. Bodies of ideas supported by the most powerful states on the continent seemed in process of nullifying or extirpating the faith.

Yet Christianity, far from disappearing, in 1944 was a more potent factor in the total world scene than it had been in 1914. Indeed, the thirty years had been one of the greatest ages of the faith. Measured by the criteria of geographic extent, vigour as evidenced by new movements, and effect upon mankind as a whole, Christianity had not lost but gained.

Christianity was more nearly evenly distributed over the earth's surface in 1944 than it had been in 1914. It had lost numerically in Europe—although as a spiritual force it was probably more potent in that continent than it had been at the dawn of the era. But in proportion to the population it had gained in the United States, in the islands of the Pacific, in Africa south of the Sahara, and in the most populous countries of Asia—India, China, and the Japanese Empire. In most non-Occidental lands it still could claim only small minorities as avowed adherents—in India about two per cent., in China approximately one per cent., and in Japan barely one half of one per cent. of the whole. Yet, with the possible exception of the Japanese Empire, these percentages had about doubled in the thirty years and were still mounting. In several large sections of Latin America Christianity was clearly stronger than in 1914.

Even more significant was the fact that in 1944 Christianity was better rooted in a larger number of peoples than it had been in 1914. In 1914 among most non-Occidental tribes and nations it was being kept alive and growing by continuing transfusions of blood from the founding churches of the West. The transfusions were in the form of missionaries who headed the ecclesiastical organizations and the educational and philanthropic institutions which were expressions and channels of the faith. They were also through the financial subsidies by which these institutions were maintained. By 1945 the leadership, whether Roman Catholic or Protestant, was rapidly ceasing to be foreign and was becoming indigenous, recruited from the sons and daughters of the soil. That leadership was both young and able. Increasingly the financial support was being found locally. The missionary era was passing. The very storms which disturbed the Occident and which reduced the flow of missionaries and of funds hastened the transition. Missionaries were still going and were of service, but increasingly they were colleagues or assistants and not directors of the "native" Christians.

For the first time in its history Christianity was becoming really world-wide and not a colonial or imperial extension, ecclesiastically speaking, of an Occidental faith. Indeed, in this it was unique. No other religion had ever achieved such world-embracing dimensions. We may go further and say that no other set of ideas, not even the widely propagated Communism of the period, had ever been so extensively represented by organized groups or so rooted among so many different peoples.

It must be added that the gains of Christianity among non-European peoples in numbers and in indigenous leadership and support were not distributed with entire uniformity. They were less marked in some areas and classes than in others. They were particularly rapid among those whose culture was most disrupted by the impact of Occidental culture or who were underprivileged in the existing social structure. The advances were notable among the Indians of North America, the Negroes of the United States, the folk of primitive culture in the islands of the Pacific, including the East Indies, among the vast masses in Africa south of the Sahara who were being hurried, unprepared and bewildered, into the white man's world, among the intelligentsia in China and Japan who had been educated in Western patterns and thereby largely divorced from their inherited background, along the coasts of China, areas which had been longest subjected to the invasion of Western civilization, among the depressed classes of India, and among the racial minorities of Burma, notably the Karens. Accessions were least numerous in lands still geographically remote from contacts with the West, such as Tibet, Afghanistan, and Sinkiang, in regions dominated by religious or ideological systems thus far almost impervious to Christianity, particularly Moslem lands, Communist-controlled Siberia, and among classes, often large, which had a stake in the continuation of the existing order, notably the higher castes of Hinduism, and the Buddhist Burmese and Thai. Even with these exceptions, however, the advances deserve the sweeping generalizations of the last paragraph.

Very notable, moreover, was the fashion in which the Christians of the world were achieving a conscious world fellowship. In the structure of their church Roman Catholics already had the framework for such cohesion. The movement was most striking among what may broadly but not accurately be denominated Protestantism. By its nature and tradition Protestantism was the most fissiparous of the major branches of Christianity. Now in ways which were quite new in Christian history it was drawing together and was also, although only here and there, reaching out towards the Roman Catholics and the Eastern churches for better reciprocal understanding. There were instances, too, of Roman Catholics seeking co-operation with Protestants. Each of these great wings of Christianity was seeking to win converts from the other, but there were trends towards a fellowship which did not seek to alter ecclesiastical affiliations. Unlike the unity in the Catholic Church of the first few centuries, which was obtained within the existing political structure of the Roman Empire, a pattern which the Roman, Eastern, and Anglican bodies still partly preserved, this new movement towards Christian unity was progressing in a world which was woefuly lacking in political cohesion.

Part of the impulse towards unity was fear. Obviously the perils which confronted the faith could be better met by a united front. Self defense was, however, by no means the only or the chief propulsive force. More potent was a deep conviction that all followers of Christ should be one in love and that the mission of spreading and making effective the Christian message could best be accomplished by collective witness and joint action.

The kind of Christianity which was spreading was somewhat altered after 1914. The Eastern churches, and especially the Russian Orthodox Church, had less share than in the nineteenth century, although even then they had not been as prominent as Roman Catholicism and Protestantism. Indeed, after 1914 they lost more ground than they gained and the gains were almost entirely by migrations rather than conversions. In comparison with the years between 1800 and 1914, when expansion was much more prominently through Protestantism than through the Roman Catholic Church, the latter was now increasing its relative share in the propagation of the faith. Yet the spread of Christianity was still being achieved more through Protestants than through Roman Catholics. In some sections the latter were multiplying more rapidly than the former, but in several of the major non-European lands Protestants were proportionately increasing more rapidly than Roman Catholics. Moreover, in Latin America and the Philippines they were winning accessions from nominally Roman Catholic populations much more extensive than Roman Catholics were attracting from Protestantism anywhere in the world. Then, too, more new movements were afoot in Protestantism than in the Roman Catholic Church and non-European peoples and cultures as a whole were being more influenced by the former than the latter.

Protestant Christianity was being changed. This was partly by the theology of crisis associated with the name of Barth and by a reaction from much of the liberalism which had been strong in the latter part of the nineteenth century. There was a deeper consciousness both of sin and of the unique character of the Christian Gospel. Alteration was also by the trends towards unity. It was still more by the modifications which were being made as the faith achieved rootage in non-European peoples and cultures. For instance, in Africa prophet movements and the multiplication of sects were giving an African tinge to Protestantism, in India depressed classes were flooding into what had been regarded in much of Europe and America as associated with the middle classes, and in China the Confucian tradition was helping to shape the temper and objectives of the transmitted Christianity. Christianity, and especially Protestant Christianity, was moving in directions which in 1944 could be only dimly discerned.

Probably still more significant was a change which was taking place in all the major divisions of Christianity. More than at any time since the first three centuries, Christians, whether Orthodox, Roman Catholic, or Protestant, were tending to be self-conscious minorities set in an alien and hostile world. The trend was away from the idea of *corpus Christianum,* or Christendom, a society ostensibly and collectively Christian embracing a given geographic area in which all were baptized as a matter of convention and supposedly accepted Christian standards, even if they did not fully attain them, and towards the *corpus Christi*, into which individuals moved by their own choice and which was in the world but never fully of it.

Several factors operated to reinforce this trend. The extensive defections from the faith which had begun in the eighteenth and nineteenth centuries in what had been Christendom and which proceeded apace in the post-1914 years broke the unity in what had been professedly Christian states and communities. Some states, formerly officially Christian, became openly or actually anti-Christian. Within the churches, because of the awakenings of the eighteenth and nineteenth centuries, the tendency was to set higher standards for admission and continuing membership, a closer approximation to what was set forth in the New Testament. Moreover, in non-Western lands where the faith was being extended by the missionary movement of the nineteenth and twentieth centuries, the churches were still small although growing minorities and in general required careful instruction and clear change of life before baptism.

The movement from a state or a geographic entity collectively Christian towards churches as minorities was by no means universal or uniform. Some of the smaller European states, Protestant, Roman Catholic, or Orthodox, still regarded themselves as Christian and held membership in the Church to be co-extensive with citizenship. In the United States the direction continued to be towards mass conversion. In Canada, Australia, and New Zealand the overwhelming majority professed a preference for one or another of the churches. However, these represented a persistence of conditions and ideals from an earlier age. The general drift was in the opposite direction.

Probably more important was the fact that although the churches were minorities, Christians had not given over the ideal of transforming the entire world. This was especially true of Protestantism and particularly of much of Anglo-Saxon Protestantism. The missionary impulse would not let those who felt it rest content until the Christian message had been presented to all men. In some of its manifestations it inspired many Christians to strive to bring all human society towards the standards of life set in the Gospels. Many Christians explicitly or tacitly assumed that these standards were written in the law of the universe, that they were identical with the "law of nature," and that all men, whether or not they called themselves Christian, in their consciences recognized them as authentic. In an increasing variety of ways Christians were attempting to mould for good the life about them.

Partly in consequence of these convictions, Christianity was more widely influential in the post-1914 decades than ever before. In no state or large segment of mankind was it dominant. In some sections of what had been Christendom it appeared to be waning. However, if mankind was surveyed as a whole, Christianity was clearly a growing factor in human affairs. For this the evidences were many. Among them were the efforts to regulate and eliminate war, most of them having Christian origins even though latterly espoused by many who were not aware of their beginnings; movements for the betterment of Negroes in the United States and Africa; much of the emancipation of women; contributions to the stirrings among the depressed millions of India with their demand for better living conditions; much of the leadership which was helping to guide the Chinese people through their bewildering revolution; a large part of the medical, nursing, and public health service of the world; and many of the efforts to relieve and prevent famine. Some of the non-Christian religions and systems of thought which were governing hundreds of millions were in debt to Christianity. Hinduism and in several countries Buddhism were being modified by it. Certain phases of socialism and Russian Communism could be traced in part to it. Democracy, widely spread in spite of the reaction against it in some quarters, had the Christian faith in its rootage. In practically every land, moreover, were men and women of outstanding nobility of character who were what they were mainly because Jesus of Nazareth once walked the hills of Galilee and Judea. Never before had there been so many such in as many different peoples. Here in an age of storm was a power which, usually unnoticed and unappreciated by those whose self-appointed function it was to interpret the day by day passage of events, was quietly at work, transforming individuals and societies, and more widely potent than ever before.

Chapter XVI

A BRIEF SUMMARY OF THE COURSE THUS FAR TRAVERSED

AS WE pause at what, because of the date at which these pages are being written, must be the present end of our story, it behooves us to look back over the course thus far traversed and to attempt to summarize it. In this manner we can see in perspective the main features of the ground we have covered and be prepared for the generalizations to which the history invites us. In this survey we will not impede the onward sweep of our story by the paraphernalia of extensive footnotes. We will rely upon facts already brought out in the main body of our narrative and there supported by references to their sources.

At the outset of our journey we propounded certain questions which seemed to us the obvious ones to ask in each successive stage of our pilgrimage. Those, it will be recalled, were: what was the Christianity which spread; why did Christianity spread; why has Christianity suffered reverses and at times met with only partial successes; by what processes did Christianity spread; what effect did Christianity have upon its environment; what effect did the environment have upon Christianity; what bearing did the processes by which Christianity spread have upon the effect of Christianity on its environment and of the environment upon Christianity? To these questions we have again and again recurred, either explicitly or implicitly. To the seventh we have not devoted much direct attention, but the answers to it must have been fairly obvious from what was said in response to the two which immediately preceded it. These questions again demand our attention as we look back upon the movement of Christianity across the centuries.

From the beginning, we have endeavoured to view the expansion of Christianity against the background of the entire human race. Christianity professes to have validity for men everywhere. At the very outset of its career its leaders were impelled by a solemn commission to go into all the world and preach the Gospel to every creature. The most comprehensive and detailed form of that commission was the imperative to make disciples of all nations, baptizing them, and teaching them to observe all things that their Lord had commanded them. One of the amazing facts about this particular version is that it is in the most Jewish of the gospels, in the only one which contains the words: "I am

not sent but unto the lost sheep of the house of Israel." Clearly the inclusive
sweep of the faith had impressed itself upon the author almost in spite of himself. So, too, that same gospel contains the fullest report of the Sermon on the
Mount with its ideals so seemingly impossible of attainment that some have
held them to have been intended only for the small circle of the disciples and
for the period, presumably brief, between their pronouncement and the anticipated second coming of the Lord. Among them were exact truthfulness, complete purity of motive, love for enemies, and the perfection of God himself.
Yet the express instruction was to teach all nations the full range of what was
required of the disciples. It was a breath-taking enterprise upon which the early
Christians felt themselves constrained to embark. The achievements of Christianity must be appraised by the standards set at the very inception of the faith.
The yardsticks must be comprehensive enough to embrace the entire inhabited
world and the apparently unreachable goals held up to the first Christians as
obligations.

As one seeks to measure the degree to which the initial vision was fulfilled,
three criteria present themselves. The first, and the most obvious, is geographic,
how far those who have called themselves Christians and who presumably
have been the bearers and exponents of the Christian message have been spread
throughout the world. This, fortunately, is easily ascertained if one asks only
for the broad outlines and not for minute details. At any particular time an
approximate map can be made of the extent of Christian communities. We can
seldom know precise numbers and of some communities no traces survive, but
the broad outlines are fairly readily sketched. A second criterion is the vigour
of Christianity in any given era. This is generally best evidenced by the new
movements which emerge from it. In periods of great vitality those inspired
by the Christian faith are impelled to revive old movements or to inaugurate
new ones. These have often taken the form of monastic orders, for the monk
has been one who at his best has sought to give himself fully to the Christian
faith, and the founders of monastic orders and congregations have been those
whose devotion and radiance have proved contagious. In Protestantism new
life has expressed itself in fresh denominations or in organizations such as
the Sunday Schools, the Young Men's and Young Women's Christian Associations, and societies for the spread of the faith or for attack upon some
collective evil of mankind, and, latterly, in the striving for Christian unity.
These and other movements emerging from the Christian impulse have been
indications of vitality. When they have been numerous the Christian stream
has been flowing strongly. When they have been few the stream has been stagnant. That criterion, too, is somewhat easily applied: the rate of the emergence

of new movements or the reinvigoration of old ones can be discerned, if not with complete precision, yet for purposes of broad comparison. The third criterion is the effect of Christianity upon mankind as a whole. This is much more difficult, for one cannot always be sure of the extent or even the presence of that influence. Causative factors in human events and institutions are usually so complex that we must often confess ourselves baffled in attempts to appraise the responsibility of any one element for a particular movement or series of occurrences. Moreover, the third criterion entails the determination of the extent to which individuals have been shaped, whether by social forces stemming from Christianity or by the inner springs of life which are in part independent of these forces. How numerous and how widespread at any one time have been what may be termed distinctly Christian personalities? Exact measurements seem impossible. Even here, however, we can often be sufficiently sure of our ground to venture positive statements. We can, if with only rough approximation to the truth, discern the degree to which Christianity shaped mankind in any particular era.

As we seek to apply these criteria, it becomes apparent that the course of Christianity in the history of mankind has been somewhat like that of an incoming tide. As one stands on the shore and watches the tide sweep in, he sees that each major wave carries the waters a little higher than did its predecessor. Each retreat from a major wave carries the flood a little less farther back than did the one before it. So with Christianity. When viewed against mankind as a whole and measured by the three criteria which we have suggested, it is seen to have great periods of advance and recession. In each major advance it becomes more widely potent in human life than in the one before it, and each recession is marked by less dwindling of the impact of Christianity than the one which immediately preceded it.

The major pulses of the Christian tide, thus appraised, fall into chronological divisions. The boundary years of each cannot be exact. Losses occurred in some sections of the world in every period of advance and during each major recession in some areas the faith was moving forward. Yet when one focusses his attention upon the main course, the following emerge as the most striking outlines of the historic pattern.

At the outset was the advance of the first five centuries. Then came the longest and most disheartening of all the recessions, roughly from A.D. 500 to A.D. 950. This was succeeded by a forward push which stretched from A.D. 950 to A.D. 1350. After this ensued another retreat, briefer and not so extensive as its predecessor, from A.D. 1350 to A.D. 1500. The next surge of the tide, from A.D. 1500 to A.D. 1750, made Christianity more of a factor in human affairs than did either of the ones before it. There then came, from A.D. 1700 to A.D. 1815, what was not so much a recession as a pause in the onward sweep of Christianity, and in the two generations embraced by the period, to those who had eyes to see, Christianity was gathering momentum for another advance. That advance, from A.D. 1815 to 1914, we have termed the great century, for it was the era in which Christianity for the first time became world-wide. In the three decades which were inaugurated by 1914 progress became less rapid and severe losses were encountered. Yet the years were ones of significant gains. We have been forced to pause in our narrative at a most tantalizing time. The period which began in 1914 seems not yet to have ended. We cannot know how long it will continue or what its future course will be. The Christian story appears to be only at its inception. Yet, because our life span is at this particular time, we must essay, as best we can, to appraise what has thus far transpired. We must now, somewhat more in detail but still through inclusive generalizations, attempt to survey one by one the advances and recessions which have marked the expansion of Christianity.

Christianity appeared late in geologic time and in the development of mankind. Life seems to have been present on the planet at least a billion years ago. A creature that may be called human roamed the earth at an undetermined date between 1,200,000 and 500,000 years before Christ. Something approaching civilization may have been present from 40,000 to 20,000 years before Christ. However, metals seem not to have come into use until about 5,000 years before Christ. Compared with the vast reaches revealed by the geologist, mankind is a tardy arrival and human civilization a recent phenomenon. By that same scale, Christianity appeared only a few seconds ago. Unless some startling interruption supervenes, then, the presupposition is that in 1944 the history of civilized man was only in its early stages. Judging, too, from its past course and the fact that it had been carried forward by periodic onward impulses, Christianity was still young. To that question, however, we must recur a little later when we can have more of our summary behind us. Our main point for the moment must be that by the year 1944 Christianity's course was very brief.

Christianity appeared in a region and at a time which favoured its future extension. It emerged in the basin of the Mediterranean, the centre of what was then probably the most populous of the civilized areas of the globe. It came in an epoch when that basin was being for the first time brought under one political rule, the Roman Empire, and at the inception of the longest era of relative internal peace and of economic prosperity which that portion of the earth's surface had known. A few centuries earlier Greek trade and settlement followed by the conquests by Alexander had prepared the way for that unity and had given a basis of a common culture in Greek language, art, and thought. At the time of Christianity's birth, moreover, a religious and ethical hunger existed which would welcome a satisfying faith. That faith must have universality to match the seeming ubiquity of the Roman Empire, it must have high moral standards, it must give assurance of personal immortality, and it must be intellectually respectable.

In some respects Christianity appeared to be little likely to win acceptance. It had many competitors, several of which seemed more congenial to the Græco-Roman spirit and to be more willing to fit into the current cultural and religious environment. The old pagan cults of the city states, while lacking in intellectual and ethical content, were reinforced by tradition and the government, and through the convenient device of allegory could have their most repugnant features softened. Greek philosophic systems enjoyed wide vogue and were supported by the prestige of the dominant culture and of what seemed to be the best minds. Numbers of mystery cults through claims to the authentication of hoary antiquity and through elaborate ritual and the lure of initiation into secret rites promised happy immortality to their adherents.

Moreover, at the outset Christianity seemed most unlikely of extensive growth or long continuance. It was but one of several sects of Judaism. Its founder had had only a brief public career. He had written no book and so far as the surviving records of his teachings show had given little thought to an organization to perpetuate his influence. His life had seemed to end ignominiously and by a venture which was sheer and quite unnecessary folly: he had challenged the religious leaders of his nation at the centre of their power in such fashion as to rouse their frightened and implacable enmity and yet he had taken none of the precautions which the most common prudence would have suggested to avert the end. As one of the early Christians frankly recognized, by the Greeks the story of the cross was regarded, with amused contempt, as sheer foolishness and to the Jews was a stumbling block and an offense, an inconceivable end to God's agent for the redemption of their race. The first Christians were a small minority who had the temerity to insist that this Jesus was risen from the dead, exalted to the right hand of God, and the source of endless and abounding life to those who received him as Lord. There were many other lords and gods, as the clearest-eyed of them readily acknowledged. This particular Lord, moreover, had burdened his followers with standards quite impossible of full attainment by human beings: he had demanded of them a perfection which, however admirable in theory, was entirely beyond human capacity. What less likely than that his cult would eliminate all the others?

Even if the inconceivable happened, and this faith should achieve a nominal triumph in the Roman Empire, its victory in the world at large was far from assured. The Roman Empire was by no means the only centre of human civilization. To the east were the Persian realm, debating with Rome the control of Mesopotamia, one of the oldest seats of civilization; India, with an ancient and rich culture; and China, then not far from the middle of the Han period, when it vied with Rome as the largest in square miles of the empires of the earth and while probably less populous was in some respects quite as highly cultivated as the regions over which the Caesars presided. Beyond these civilized areas were the still more widely extended primitive and semi-primitive congeries of men, most of them entirely oblivious of even the Roman name. Nor would the Roman Empire last forever. At its birth it carried the seeds of its decay. If Christianity were to win it and could not heal its mortal illness, the Empire might carry Christianity with it to ruin.

The most thought-provoking set of facts in human history is that in spite of this seemingly absurdly inauspicious start within five centuries Christianity won the professed allegiance of the overwhelming majority of the Græco-Roman world, that it survived the demise of that world, and that within nineteen centuries, brief even as the short span of human history goes, it penetrated to practically every corner of the inhabited globe and became a moulding force in every great cultural area of mankind. It quite outstripped its parent Judaism and with one exception long outlived all the various sects of that faith with which it had started off as a contemporary. The exception was the school which became dominant in orthodox Judaism. Moreover, Judaism, while going on, remained constricted by its racial bounds and thereafter gave birth to little that was religiously new.

Christianity was fortunate in early gaining a foothold in the Hellenistic world. Through this it achieved its first extensive spread. It soon reached outside the bounds of the Greek-speaking sections of the Mediterranean basin. By the beginning of the third century, in spite of recurring and to some extent chronic persecution, it had developed an organization which next to the Roman state was the most widespread and potent in that region. The Roman Emperors felt called upon to make their peace with it and to seek to enlist its support for their rule. By the close of the fifth century its triumph organizationally seemed almost complete. Here and there it had begun to spill over beyond the boundaries of the Caesars.

Yet the movement of Christianity into the Hellenistic world was not an unmixed advantage. The partial identification with Hellenism brought handicaps. It hampered the spread into regions where Hellenism was not strong —in much of Syria, Palestine, and the northern shores of Africa, and beyond the Euphrates. The close association with Hellenism made Christianity seem Western rather than universal. Not even in the twentieth century had it fully freed itself from the Hellenistic integuments acquired in the first few generations of its course. A knowledge of Greek philosophy was still essential to an understanding of the history of Christian thought. It may well have been that the easy triumph of the Crescent over the Cross in large areas in the seventh and eighth centuries was due in large part to the fact that the chief victories of Islam were among elements in the population which had not been assimilated to the Hellenistic world.

Within the Roman Empire in these first five centuries Christianity had to its credit several new creations. It brought into being the Christian Church, Christian theology, Christian liturgy, and a vast body of literature. It was chiefly responsible for numbers of individuals of outstanding force of character and with a common likeness which could be called distinctively Christian. Paul, Origen, Ambrose, and Augustine at once come to mind as a few of the many, differing in native gifts, but lifted out of dusty mediocrity to enduring note by a faith which had made of them uncommon individuals. The *Confessions* of Augustine was the first full length autobiography of a human soul. The fact that Christianity both brought about the culmination of the spiritual experience which they recorded and stimulated their composition was evidence of a significant phase of its effect and characteristic of what it was to accomplish in later centuries in creating great personalities. Augustine, moreover, had a profound influence upon the thought of the subsequent Christianity of Western Europe. Towards the end of the period Christianity was giving rise to monasticism.

These creative achievements were in a civilization which otherwise seemed incapable of doing or saying anything basically new. Its political institutions showed development, but only that forced upon them by the logic of the initial nature of the state. Classical civilization, the embodiment of the Greek and Roman spirit, with its particular type of humanism, had attained such heights as were possible for it and, incapable of further originality, was on the downward course of a cycle which, as it saw history, was inevitable and was to be followed by a similarly Sisyphean series of eras.

Christianity, with all its inner vigour, proved powerless to save the Græco-Roman world from ultimate collapse. Although then and later there were those who declared it to be responsible for the downfall of the Roman Empire, it probably neither hastened nor retarded the disintegration. Certainly it was not a major cause. The results of the faith were chiefly in what might be described as the strictly religious phases of life, in the bringing into being of the Church, of Christian theology, of the liturgy, and of distinctively Christian literature. By its teaching and its discipline, moreover, it had marked effect upon the lives of millions of individuals. After the mass conversions of the third, fourth, and fifth centuries, however, these results were marked only in the minority of the members and in the monastic communities. By the year 500 Christianity had begun to place its impress on the laws of the realm, the family, art, amusements, and the social and economic institution of slavery. Yet this was only beginning. Moreover, the dwindling place of slavery and the end of the gladiatorial spectacles of the arena could be ascribed only in part to Christianity. Other, non-religious factors, had also been operating. Christianity had neither destroyed nor remade Græco-Roman society. That society was going to its own death in its own way. From it Christianity salvaged important features and, transmitting and transfusing them, made them part of the basis of a new culture. This, however, was a later accomplishment.

The reasons for the success of Christianity in the face of the vigorous competition of its many rivals were to be found primarily in the founder. It was true that the faith early acquired a foothold in the Hellenistic world, but in this it was by no means alone. Its universality as against the racialism of Judaism, its monotheism, its appeal to the authority of the Jewish scriptures, its high ethical demands, its assurance of immortality, its combination of adaptability and of inflexible adherence, regardless of cost, to its standards, the miracles worked in its name, the heroism of its martyrs, the enthusiasm of its adherents, the closely knit fellowship of its church, all contributed to its triumph. Ultimately these had their rise or their effective reinforcement in Jesus—in his teachings, his deeds, his crucifixion, his resurrection, and the access of power that came through him.

In its early stages Christianity seems to have spread from individual to individual and not by groups. Before many generations, however, mass movements began. Long before A.D. 500 entire communities were coming into the Church. Of this the Armenians were a notable example. On a much larger scale was the fashion in which, beginning with Constantine, the Roman Empire became Christian, so that by A.D. 500 to be a Roman citizen and a Christian were, with some exceptions, roughly identical.

In the process of its spread and of its victory, Christianity acquired forms which were to shape it through the succeeding centuries. At the outset it was varied in organization and expression. There was a major conflict between those who wished it to fit into the existing patterns of Judaism and those who would free it from its Jewish associations, and, by moving out into the Hellenistic world, realize its inherent universality. Other differences quickly developed. The many kinds of Gnosticism may at one time have enrolled a majority of the Christians. There also appeared Marcionites, Montanists, Donatists, Arians, Nestorians, and many another strain. Increasingly, however, the trend was towards uniformity. In creed, in an accepted list of books in the New Testament, and by claiming apostolic succession for its bishops, what came to be the church of the majority developed tests for what it claimed to be the true faith. Christianity in its majority form bore the imprint of several of its rivals. It derived from its Jewish parentage its Old Testament, its conception of a divinely chosen community in covenant relations with God, and some features of its worship. Its theology was thought through in the atmosphere of Greek philosophy. The popular mystery religions may have had some effect upon it. Many of the converts carried over attitudes from their pre-Christian past: they expected their new faith to accomplish for them what their old religions were supposed to do, only to do it better. In structure the Catholic Church, as it called itself, partly paralleled that of the Roman Empire. Its bishops, archbishops, and patriarchs and the ecclesiastical divisions governed by them roughly corresponded to the administrative structure of the Empire. The position which was recognized as outranking the others was that of the Bishop of Rome. While the traditional association with the name of Peter contributed to the prestige of that see, the chief source of the growing position of the Papacy was the connexion with the city which had created the Empire. It was within the existing framework of the Roman Empire and with no little assistance from the later Emperors that the Catholic Church took form and achieved dominance. There was enough truth in the clever phrase that the Catholic Church was the ghost of the Roman Empire to give barbs to the quip. The creeds, the New Testament, the form of organization, and the general outlines of the theology and the liturgies which then developed and became standard were regarded as authoritative by the majority in succeeding generations of Christians. The monasticism which took shape became for most of the churches the characteristic method for the expression of the perfect Christian life. To be sure, both contemporary and later ages saw many departures from these norms. Particularly did several of the forms of Protestantism which had large extension in the nineteenth and twentieth centuries denounce some of them. However, all but a few of the variants received as determinative several of the contributions of the Catholic Church. They at least held to the New Testament, and most of them adhered to what had come to be termed the Apostles' Creed. The Græco-Roman world placed its indelible stamp upon the Christianity to which it had given its allegiance. Christianity was victor, but in its structure it bore the marks of the vanquished.

Yet Christianity was much more than a mosaic of contributions from its environment. The whole was moulded and given its outstanding features by its own peculiar genius, a genius which was from the life, teachings, death, and resurrection of its founder.

For hundreds of years the triumph of Christianity in the Roman Empire seemed to be its undoing. By that victory Christianity had apparently become identified with a particular culture and one political order. Both of these were disintegrating and their ruin would presumably carry with them into the tomb the religion which had lately become integrated with them. For approximately four and a half centuries, from about A.D. 500 to approximately A.D. 950, this appeared to be the unhappy outlook.

The disintegration of the Græco-Roman world came, as is well known, as the result of decay within and of invasions from without. The success of the latter was made possible by the former, but the two factors interacted to spell the ruin of the Roman Empire.

The invasions commenced on a grand scale before the year 500. The battle of Adrianople, A.D. 378, is sometimes taken as marking their beginning. The capture and sack of Rome by the Goths in A.D. 410 made spectacular the weakness of the empire which to its citizens had seemed synonymous with civilization. Now for approximately five centuries wave after wave of invasion flooded the basin of the Mediterranean. Recovery from one was only partly achieved when another submerged much of what had been rebuilt.

The invasions were both from the North and from the South-east. Many of the first invaders from the North were Christians, although mostly Arians. Their successors were pagans—animists or crude polytheists. The last series of inroads, that of the Scandinavians, seemed peculiarly destructive and extended from the British Isles on the north and west to the Mediterranean on the south and to the plains of Russia and the walls of Constantinople on the east. The Church eventually won the barbarians to its faith, but in the conquest and the early stages of assimilation it suffered in the quality of its life. There was within the Church the power of self-renewal. In spite of the low ebb to which it sank, whenever the incursions paused the Church displayed revival. When they finally ceased the morale of the Church quickly rose.

Not far from A.D. 950 the Church in the West was at its nadir. This was vividly symbolized by the poor quality of the Popes of that generation. Several of the brief tenants of the see of Peter were both weak and vicious. Later ages were to see wicked pontiffs, but the worst of them were strong men who sinned on a grand scale. The poorest of those of the middle of the tenth century were such nonentities that their depravity and frivolity were beneath contempt. The corruption in the Papacy was matched by that in the monasteries and the ecclesiastical structure through much of Western Europe. In the East the tenth century was not so low a point for the Church as were several other and much later periods; indeed, the tenth century saw one of the strongest Patriarchs of Constantinople and some significant gains. No general pattern can be drawn which does not have its exceptions. In the main, however, from A.D. 500 until the middle of the tenth century the course of Christianity was downward.

Much more disastrous for Christianity than the invasions from the North were those of the Moslems from the South-east and the South. In the seventh and eighth centuries the Moslems subdued parts of the eastern and western and all the southern shore of the Mediterranean. In the ninth and tenth centuries they conquered most of Sicily and troubled Italy. Unlike the pagan conquerors of the North, whose faith crumbled under the civilizing impact of the Christianity and culture of the peoples whom they ruled, the Moslems were the bearers of a younger religion than Christianity and regarded the older faith as superseded by their own. There was little overt compulsion in the conversion of Christians to Islam, but movement in the opposite direction, from Islam to Christianity, was impossible where Moslem law prevailed. From the Lebanon to the Pyrenees and for a short period in parts of Gaul north of the Pyrenees Christians were subject peoples. In Asia and Africa Christian communities dwindled and in time became minorities. Relative to the area occupied and to its total numbers, in the era of the great recession Christianity lost more ground to Islam than it ever again did to any rival in the centuries which these volumes have covered. In all of the areas submerged in the retreat, except Sicily and the Iberian Peninsula, the Christian churches remained on the defensive, shrinking through slow attrition. Obviously their morale and the quality of their life deteriorated. The end of Christianity in most lands of Moslem princes might be long delayed but it could scarcely be averted. Even in the twentieth century the slow absorption was still in process.

Dark for Christianity though the four and a half centuries between A.D. 500 and A.D. 950 undoubtedly were, they saw some developments which from the standpoint of later ages were to be of larger significance than the staggering losses. In Western Europe peoples were being won through whom the greatest advances of Christianity were eventually to come. Some of the Teutonic peoples were being brought to the faith. These included the Frankish conquerors of Gaul and the Anglo-Saxon immigrants to Britain. Thus ground sacrificed or threatened within the former borders of the Roman Empire was retaken. Christianity was also carried beyond the erstwhile boundaries of the Empire into regions which the Roman legions had never seen, or had seen only transiently, in the Low Countries and beyond the Rhine.

At the moment these gains appeared unimportant compared with the vast and continuing losses. They were on the periphery of civilization and among peoples of seemingly little political or cultural consequence. Presumably they were poor compensation for the unwilling surrender of some of the most ancient centres of civilization. Largely because of what it accomplished among these western barbarians, however, Christianity ultimately achieved its most extensive distribution and its most widespread effects upon mankind. Indeed, what had once seemed irreparable defeat became, to some degree because of the clean sweep which that had made of the past, an advantage. Because, particularly in Britain, Roman civilization had been so nearly erased, Christianity had an opportunity to build afresh, unhampered by remnants from a culture which had given it lip service but which it had really never transformed. In so building, it was able to transfuse the new with more of its spirit.

Moreover, in the lands overrun by the Moslems, Christianity made contributions to the conquerors and to the Islamic culture which followed. In translating Greek philosophers into Arabic, as artisans and architects for Arab builders, and as physicians Christians did much to shape what the world usually ascribed to their masters. Christianity even helped to mould some of the religious expressions of Islam, notably in the respect which the latter paid to Jesus and in the groups of mystics which arose. Christianity did not have nearly so free a course in Moslem lands as it had north of the Mediterranean, but it was not without effect.

It was also during these years of enforced retreat in much of its first stronghold that Christianity was spreading up the Nile and east of the Caspian. It became important in the valley of the Nile south of Egypt and penetrated eastward as far as China. Although precise dates largely elude us, it was almost certainly well established in India in communities which continued to be Christian in the twentieth century. From Persia eastward, however, Christians then as later were minorities. By the year 950 they had died out in China Proper. No major people or state accepted the faith as their official religion.

Not far from A.D. 950 a new forward surge of the Christian tide became apparent. It continued for approximately four centuries, or until about A.D.

1350. This fresh wave of advance carried Christianity over a wider geographic area and probably made it more influential in the life of mankind as a whole than had the first one.

Between A.D. 950 and A.D. 1350 Christianity had been planted from Greenland and Scandinavia on the west and north to the China Sea on the east and it was to be found as far south as India, Nubia, and Ethiopia. It is probable that Vikings had carried it in their own persons to North America and it is possible that they may there have baptized a few of the Indians and Eskimos. Contingents were won among the tribes of Central Asia. Although the Christian communities which had sprung into being in China Proper in the seventh century had disappeared before A.D. 950, new communities arose there in the thirteenth and fourteenth centuries. The earlier Christianity persisted in India. Never before had any religion been represented over so large a proportion of the earth's surface.

For a time there seemed to be some chance that even greater success might attend the Christian faith. The Mongols had rapidly constructed an empire which stretched from Korea and the China Sea into Russia, the most extensive in area and the greatest in population which had yet appeared. The Mongols were shamanists and were fairly neutral religiously, seeking the prayers of all faiths. Their ruling house, however, had taken wives from princely stock which was Christian and some of the male offspring were baptized in infancy. Christianity had, therefore, an opportunity. Some Christians sought to enter the doors thus thrown ajar and to win the Mongols as a whole. It is interesting but fruitless to speculate what might have been the future of Christianity had they succeeded.

Several kinds of Christianity spread, but all were variants of that Catholic Church which had developed in the Roman Empire in the first five centuries. What may now begin to be called Roman Catholic Christianity had the widest extension. It was carried by adventurers, settlers, merchants, crusaders, and missionaries from America and Greenland to China. Eastern Orthodoxy, which centred in Constantinople, prevailed in its ancient strongholds in Asia Minor, continued the footholds which it had earlier won in the Balkans, including the important realm of Bulgaria, and began what proved to be its most extensive triumphs in the vast reaches which were eventually included in Russia. It was also scattered in some of the prevailingly Moslem areas in Western Asia. Nestorianism was dotted across Asia from Mesopotamia and Persia to the China Sea. Other forms of Eastern Christianity, especially the Jacobites, were active in Asia.

Widely though Christianity was now distributed, over most of the area across which it was scattered it was represented only by minorities. In some great regions, notably in China, these were enclaves of alien merchants, soldiers, or officials, possibly with small fringes of converts, and had little chance against the dominant systems, strongly entrenched in the indigenous cultures. It was not all clear that the outlook for Christianity was as good as in the fourth century, before the barbarian invasions of the Roman Empire had begun their disintegrating blows on that realm.

Where, as in much of Europe, Christianity was the faith of the nation, tribe, or community, usually it had become so through acceptance by the group as a whole. The conversion of the prince or king was generally followed by that of his subjects. This meant for the majority a very superficial knowledge of Christianity. The true genius of Christianity was only slowly apprehended and then merely by a minority. The deepening of the faith with a corresponding commitment to it went on for centuries and was never fully accomplished. The European middle ages, sometimes called the ages of faith, did not deserve that appellation. There was much of practical scepticism and still more of superstition which, although it bore the Christian name, was non-Christian in character. It is not strange that in the nineteenth and twentieth centuries widespread defections occurred. These were partly a rebellion against the superficial caricatures of Christianity which ensued from the mass conversions and were to some extent a deliberate rejection of the faith when once its full demands and its true nature were understood.

The wide extension of Christianity was in part due to new tides of life in that faith. These were most notable in Western Europe. As the incursions of barbarians subsided and the invaders were won, a process which in the year 950 was well advanced, the vigour inherent in Christianity began to show itself in efforts to improve the quality of life and to purge the Church of the most palpable departures from Christian standards. Some of this was seen in a movement associated with the monastery of Cluny, a foundation dating from A.D. 910. Recurring revivals expressed themselves through other manifestations of the monastic spirit, such as the Cistercians, and, in the thirteenth century, in the Franciscans and Dominicans. It was natural that attempts to realize the Christian ideal should seek outlet through monasticism, for it was in that guise that since the fourth century most Christians had been accustomed to regard the full demands of the Gospel as fulfilled. Later orders, notably the Franciscans and Dominicans, were, however, more aggressively missionary than the earlier ones had been and were, for that reason, a novel type of monasticism and evidence that Christianity had by no means lost its power of fresh creation. There were as well, chiefly in Western Europe, but also, to some extent, as offshoots of Orthodox Christianity, movements which the official church stigmatized as heretical, but many of which were efforts to attain the standards set up by Jesus and his Apostles. The Christianity of Europe, and especially of Western Europe, was pulsing with life. In some ways it was displaying more originality than it had since the first three hundred years of the initial stage of advance.

Moreover, Christianity was having a deeper and more inclusive effect upon the culture of Western Europe than it had had upon that of the pre-sixth century Roman Empire. In that stage, as we suggested a few pages above, Christianity bore its fruits chiefly in the more strictly religious field and did not do more than modify the other phases of Græco-Roman culture. The medieval civilization of Western Europe was in large part the creation of Christianity. Every major aspect of that culture was to some degree moulded by the faith.

Western Europe afforded Christianity an unusual opportunity. The disintegration of the structure of the Roman Empire and of Græco-Roman life was much more extensive in that area than in the Greek East. In the latter region the Roman state passed without serious break into the Byzantine stage. There the Church was kept in the traditional position which religion had been accorded in the Roman Empire and was ancillary to the state and largely subordinate to it. By their continuity, showing transition but little of sharp revolution, other phases of Græco-Roman culture persisted in the East and somewhat cramped the Christian spirit. Christianity had larger influence in the Byzantine than in the pre-sixth century Græco-Roman world, but it did not have nearly such free course as in the West.

In Western Europe the Church was the vehicle by which most of such of Græco-Roman culture as survived was transmitted. Christianity was the inspiration of the formal education and the mother of the universities. The intellectual life centred about Christian theology as the "queen of the sciences." Under the impulse to think through the faith, to see its intellectual implications, and to validate it to the thoughtful mind, a tradition was established for mental discipline which underlay much of the later scientific and philosophic achievements of Europe. Trust in the orderliness and dependability of the universe, born of a belief in the Christian God, became a characteristic of the European mind. Belief in the incarnation, in which the second person of the Trinity became man that man might be redeemed and raised into eternal fellowship with God, made for a high evaluation of the individual, the dignity of man, and confidence in man's ability, through the use of his reason, to grow in his understanding of the universe, and through the knowledge so acquired and the exercise of his will, to make himself master of much of the world about him.

All this was not immediately to come to fruition: it entered as a determinative factor into the science, the industry, the geographic discoveries, and the democracy and socialism of a later age. Medieval art was largely religious, devoted to Christian themes, whether in architecture, music, sculpture, or painting. The monastic communities combined prayer and labour as integral factors in the Christian ideal and did much for the advancement of agriculture. Agriculture owed a particular debt to the Cistercians. The foundations of capitalism go back to some phases of the Church's activities. One of the monastic orders, the Templars, hastened the development of banking. The Christian conscience sought to regulate industry and commerce. It also endeavoured to curb the chronic fighting and to bring the warrior's code into conformity with its standards. Kings were supposed to rule as responsible to God and were crowned with Christian ceremonies. At the height of its power the Church placed itself above kings and emperors. Great saints arose, cynosures of their own age and influential in later eras. Christian devotion made much of the sufferings of Jesus and meditated on the eucharist to such effect that the doctrine of transubstantiation was elaborated and the feast of *Corpus Christi* instituted. Scarcely an angle of medieval Europe but showed the influence of Christianity.

By its geographic situation, at the tip end of the European peninsula of the Euro-Asiatic continent, Western Europe was partially protected from the successive outbursts of invasion from the great reservoir of peoples in the centre of that land mass. After the Viking raids stopped, no major incursions succeeded in flooding it. Mongols and Turks were stopped short, partly by distance and natural obstacles, before they could extend their conquests to it. This also afforded Christianity an unusual opportunity.

In the total world scene of the tenth to the fourteenth centuries Western Europe counted for much less than did China, the Caliphate, or the Mongols. In population, political power, and wealth it was distinctly not in the first rank. In civilization it was certainly no higher than China, India, or the Moslem world. However, what culture it had it owed mostly to Christianity, either directly or as the means of transmission. It was by no means fully Christian. In many respects it less approached Christian standards than did Western Europe of the nineteenth century. Yet in it Christianity was a potent ferment.

For human history as a whole the contribution of Christianity to Western European peoples had its chief effect in the period which commenced late in the fifteenth century, when the expansion of Europe began to be a major phenomenon and when, within a brief four centuries, Western Europeans and their culture became dominant in the globe.

Precisely how far European peoples owed their later primacy to Christianity cannot be accurately determined. Clearly that faith was not the only factor. Clearly, too, much of the European hegemony was accompanied by developments such as African slavery and the intensification of the incidence and destructiveness of war which were quite contrary to the genius of the Christian faith. Yet it seems to be something more than a coincidence that in the region in which, beginning not far from the ninth or tenth century, Christianity had the freest course, that culture developed which by its striking attainments eventually, in the nineteenth and twentieth centuries, led the human race. If it be said that this position was due to the Græco-Roman heritage, one must recall that the Moslem world was also an heir of Greece and Rome and that from it issued no comparable achievements. The most obvious difference in the ingredients of the two was that one had Christianity and the other Islam. If it be claimed that the cause must be sought in race, one recalls how varied was Western Europe racially and how some of its greatest accomplishments were from stocks very similar to those in some of the Moslem lands and certainly not much different from those in the Byzantine East which, though officially Christian, did not give the faith as free course as did the West. If climate be put forward as the explanation, some other portions of the globe with almost the same conditions have had a vastly different cultural record. Christianity was undoubtedly a factor. It seems to have been the ingredient without which the distinctive results would not have followed. The foundations for these results were laid before A.D. 1350.

While Christianity was chiefly influential in Western Europe, it was not without effects elsewhere. They were seen mainly in Central and Eastern Europe, where Greek Orthodox Christianity was dominant. Although the Byzantine tradition, inherited from the pagan past, of the supremacy of the secular state placed greater curbs on Christianity than existed in the West, Christianity was potent. Especially was it a factor in the formation of the cultures of those barbarian peoples who were won to it. Bulgars and Slavs and notably the Russians showed the results. The Russian soul was in no small degree the creation of Christianity.

The age embraced between A.D. 950 and A.D. 1350 left its impress upon Christianity. In most of Asia the fact that Christians were minority enclaves, often on the defensive, bred characteristics in their communities which long persisted. Often better educated than their neighbours and forced to live by their wits, Christians tended to be clever, somewhat grasping, skillful as merchants, but not seeking to propagate their faith or to influence the culture about them. In the East, with its Byzantine traditions inherited from the Roman past, Christianity was somewhat passive, confined to the formalities of the cult, stressing the public services and the liturgy, finding refuge in an ascetic and quietistic monasticism. The challenge of winning and transforming the non-Christian borders on its northern fringes partly saved it from this trend, but much of the Byzantine emphasis was transmitted. In Western Europe, because of the weakness of the civil power, especially in the early stages of the period, the power of the Church was enhanced and more nearly than in the East society was a theocracy ruled by a priestly class which professed divine authority and direction. In its organization and even in its thought the Church was in part feudalized. Christianity, moreover, was more activistic than in the East. This was because the early disorganization of society impelled its leaders to take a leading part in restoring order and forming the standards of life: the Christianity of the region was more consciously and purposefully applied to all phases of life.

In the period which may be roughly bounded by A.D. 1350 and A.D. 1500 Christianity suffered a second series of reverses. Not so severe or prolonged as their great predecessor, they yet proved serious.

To the reverses there were a number of contributory factors, not necessarily causally interrelated. The break-up of the Mongol Empire made unsafe the overland routes which had connected Central and Eastern Asia with the West and so helped to cut off the small Christian minorities from their mother churches. As their realm broke into fragments, the Mongols tended to conform to the religion which chanced to be dominant in the regions which each of the succeeding groups controlled. Thus in Central Asia the Mongols became Moslems. In Mongolia, largely by contagion from the strong Buddhist region of Tibet, they became Buddhists. Timurlane, of Mongol descent and fanatically Moslem, in the early part of the period waged wars which by their destruction wasted and possibly annihilated the surviving Christian communities of Central Asia. The rise and conquests of the Ottoman Turks, Moslems, at last overwhelmed the remnants of the Byzantine Empire, sadly weakened by the blows dealt earlier by their fellow Christians, the Crusaders from Western Europe. The Ottoman Turks overran Asia Minor, which had been the first large area to be predominantly Christian. They conquered Constantinople and transformed into a mosque the cathedral of Greek Orthodox Christianity. For some time the eastern portions of the Mediterranean, long in the hands of ostensibly Christian fleets, were controlled by the Moslem Turkish sea power. Very disturbing, too, was the passing of the culture of medieval Europe. Since that culture had been so largely shaped by Christianity, Christianity had become in part intertwined with it, as it had earlier been with the Roman Empire. The transition brought with it a threat to the faith which had done much to produce that culture.

The second of the great periods of recession in Christian history was marked in part by the disappearance of the faith from wide reaches of the earth's surface. The small Christian communities in Greenland perished, a disaster due to the extinction, apparently through adverse physical surroundings, of the Scandinavian population. The western periphery of Christendom thus suffered contraction. In the East Christianity died out in China, Mongolia, and most of Central Asia. The erasure was so complete that we do not know the story of the last stages of the Christian communities or the manner and precise causes of their demise. The losses were more pronounced than in the preceding era of decline. Then, while the faith disappeared from China it continued on the fringes of that realm in what we know as Inner Mongolia and Sinkiang. It also persisted in Central Asia. Now it not only vanished in these regions but it was also weakened in the strongholds from which it had chiefly spread eastward, the Nestorian Church of Mesopotamia and Persia. Islam, too, won most of Asia Minor and established strong footholds in what for several centuries had been solidly Christian territory in the Balkan Peninsula.

However, dismaying though the territorial losses were, they were not as discouraging as had been those of the four and a half centuries which followed A.D. 500 and, like the latter, they were in part offset by gains. The contraction of the boundaries of the territory across which Christianity was disseminated, although more pronounced than in the earlier recession, was chiefly by the disappearance of what had been small minorities. The main body of what might be denominated Christendom, where Christians constituted the overwhelming majority of the population, remained substantially intact. It had suffered attrition in Asia Minor, Constantinople, and the Balkans, but the shock was in no sense comparable in severity to that which had accompanied the conquests of the Moslem Arabs in the seventh, eighth, and ninth centuries. In that earlier, tragic era almost half of its territory was torn from Christendom. Now only a small proportion was lost. Moreover, Christianity was recovering almost and perhaps quite as much from Islam as it lost to that faith. It was regaining the Iberian Peninsula. This achievement was particularly significant since through the peoples of that area Christianity had its main geographic extension in the breath-taking era of advance which followed A.D. 1500. In other words, the victories of Islam at the expense of Christianity in the century and a half which followed A.D. 1350 were ultimately more than made good from the ground regained in that very period by the Cross from the Crescent. Then, too, in that hundred and fifty years the frontiers of Christianity were still being pushed forward in Northern Europe. The Lithuanians received baptism and Russian monks were winning tribes north of Moscow for the Orthodox faith.

The period between A.D. 1350 and A.D. 1500 saw serious internal decline in at least some phases of Christianity in what had been the strongest centres of the faith, the Byzantine Empire and Western Europe. The extinction of the Byzantine Empire by the Ottoman Turks did not mean the obliteration of Christianity in the former Byzantine domains. The churches continued and the Œcumenical Patriarch still had his seat in Constantinople. However, in the Turkish territories the Orthodox Church was forced to arrive at a *modus vivendi* with Moslem rulers. The latter insisted that its executives be acceptable to them. In consequence, subservience to the state increased and corruption was rife in ecclesiastical circles. In Western Europe, the Roman Catholic Church presented a sorry spectacle. In the fore part of the fourteenth century the head-quarters of the Papacy were moved to Avignon and the nearly seventy years there, as their designation, "the Babylonian captivity," indicates, were ones of truckling to the French crown, a humiliating descent from the proud pinnacle to which Innocent III had brought the Papacy in the preceding century. Still worse was to come. Prolonged schism between the adherents of rival Popes followed. The breach had not been fully healed when the Renaissance brought a secular temper into much of the official church. Renaissance Popes embodied a worldliness which ill comported with the true spirit of the faith. With such conditions at the top, it is not surprising that much of the rest of the ecclesiastical structure was honeycombed with moral decay. A faith hampered by a negation of its ideals by the Church which was supposed to be its embodiment faced a grim future as Western Europe moved from one age to another. It seemed already foredoomed. The secularism of the new era appeared about to destroy it by capturing it.

Unquestionable as were the abuses and weaknesses, they were not all of the picture. In emerging from the Mongol domination, the Russian people developed a greater loyalty to the Church and were more permeated by Christianity than before that experience. Moscow became, so the Russians averred, the "third Rome," the successor of Rome and Constantinople as the centre of true Christianity. Moreover, in Western Europe protests and efforts at reform gave evidence that the Christian faith was spurring the consciences of sensitive and resolute souls. Wyclif, Hus, and Savonarola were only among the more eminent of the multitude who saw the inconsistency between much in the official Church and the faith of which it was the custodian and who were resolved both to live in accord with the precepts of Christ and to call others to them. In Germany a developing school of mysticism and in the Low Countries the Brethren of the

Common Life were evidence that Christianity was putting forth fresh and living shoots. Vitality was much more apparent in the Christianity of Europe than in the dark days of the ninth and the fore part of the tenth century.

Although Christianity was by no means at so low an ebb at the end of the fourteenth as it had been in the middle of the tenth century, the new age which was dawning was characterized by gigantic movements which seemed to menace whatever of life that faith might still possess. Western Europe was moving into a new world. It was not immediately clear that Christianity would thrive in the fresh environment. Although of a different nature, the threats to it were fully as great as those which had accompanied the disintegration of the Roman Empire.

Politically, in the sixteenth century Western Europe was in a new age. The endless divisions of the feudal structure held together loosely by the fading dream of unity of Church and Holy Roman Empire were being superseded by nation states governed by absolute monarchs. For several centuries feudalism had been decaying. The rise of cities in the twelfth and thirteenth centuries had dealt it severe blows. However, the coming of the autocratic kings was both facilitated by the decline and accelerated it. Western Europe was by no means fully unified. Variety had been too deeply entrenched in language, custom, and tradition to be erased by a new empire. Not every region was at once brought together. Germany and Italy especially came through the age as geographic rather than political entities. However, in France, England, Spain, and Portugal, together with Scandinavia and some of the fragments of Germany, powerful families knit hitherto loosely connected peoples into units, brought the feudal nobility into subjection, and ruled with an iron hand. They insisted that the Church also acknowledge their sway. Nominally they were Christian: indeed, some of the monarchs were ardent supporters of the faith. However, whether the Church in their domains remained part of the Papal structure or whether it broke with it, they exercised enough control over it to make sure that it should not threaten their rule. By being made ancillary to the state official Christianity might easily and almost unobserved lose its savour. In Russia, which remained largely aloof from Western Europe and was still the main stronghold of the Orthodox Church, the crown was becoming absolute and eventually dominated the Church more effectively than in any major state of Western Europe. Among these absolute monarchies war was customary and chronic. The jockeying for power entailed practices which were the negation of Christian ethics.

Intellectually Western Europe seemed to be moving away from Christianity. The humanism nourished by the Renaissance had a confidence in the human mind which, while usually paying lip service to Christianity, had little or no room for the independent act of God in the Self-revelation which was the central conviction of the Christian faith. The humanism was in part a return to the temper of pre-Christian classical Greek and Roman times. It was not merely that, however. The Western European mind had too recently been through the discipline of the theological discussions of the Christian schoolmen and was too largely the product of Christianity quickly to revert to a pure paganism. Many of the outstanding humanists were convinced Christians. Their confidence in the powers of the human intellect stemmed in large measure from their conviction of the enhancement of man's native gifts by the transformation wrought by God's redemption of sinful man through Christ. Yet among many humanists the trend was away from Christianity.

A commercial revolution was destroying much of the economic pattern with which the support and the life of the Church had been associated. It was presenting Christianity with fresh problems. The type of industry and commerce for which the Christian conscience had developed rules was passing. Could the Christian temper regulate the new?

More serious was the rapid expansion of European peoples. Near the end of the fifteenth century Europeans crossed the Atlantic and, rounding the Cape of Good Hope, reached India by a new route. These geographic achievements were followed quickly by others and by the subjugation of large sections of the Americas. Trading posts were established in Southern and Eastern Asia and along the shores of Africa. The export of African slaves to the Americas began a new chapter in human misery. Russians made their way across Northern Asia to the Pacific. Never before had any one group of peoples penetrated and mastered so large a proportion of the surface of the globe. Could Christianity accompany these voyages, conquests, and settlements? Could it soften the impact of European upon non-European races? The outlook was not promising. Although the initial voyages were usually undertaken in the name of Christ, the first discoveries were made when Christianity was at a low ebb in Europe and the initial conquests were marked by wanton cruelties which augured ill for the future.

In the face of the seeming weakness of Christianity and the apparent impossibility of rising to the challenge of the new age, awakenings came which made Christianity more effective in the affairs of mankind as a whole than ever it had been. They broke out early in the sixteenth century. In general they took two forms. One was what in its most inclusive sense can be called the Protestant Reformation. It had many expressions, but it had in common the repudiation of much of the heritage which had come through the Roman

Catholic Church and positive emphasis upon salvation by faith and the priest-hood of all believers. Through it much of North-western Europe broke away from the church in which it had been nurtured but which it deemed to have perverted Christian faith and life. The other main expression of the awakening in the Christianity of Western Europe was within the old church. It sought to purge that church of its moral abuses, to inspire and equip it better to fulfil its mission, and to enable it to win back the territory lost to Protestantism. It was both a reformation and a counter-reformation. It was embodied in new reli-gious orders, the chief of which was the Society of Jesus, and in revivals in old orders and congregations. Through it the Roman Catholic Church held most of South-western Europe and much of Central Europe, and regained some of the regions which at first had departed from it. Somewhat later new move-ments appeared in the Russian Orthodox Church. They, too, were evidence of revival, but in different forms and of not quite the same vigour as those in Western Europe.

Under the impulse of the renewed and enhanced life, in the two and a half centuries after A.D. 1500 Christianity had a phenomenal expansion. Earnest missionaries accompanied or followed European explorers, merchants, con-querors, and settlers wherever they went. Often they preceded them and in some vast areas they went where the others did not. Moreover, Western Euro-peans who made their homes in the lands thus opened to them and formed the nuclei of new nations of European stock did not adopt the religions of the subject peoples but retained allegiance, although often very nominal, to Christianity.

Through these missions and migrations Christianity became far more widely distributed geographically than it had been in either of the two preceding ages of advance. It regained only a small part of the ground which had been lost in the times of the great recessions. Save for the still dwindling remnants of pre-Moslem churches, the southern and eastern shores of the Mediterranean remained loyal to Islam, and almost no Christians were to be found in the heart of Asia where Christian minorities had once been generously sprinkled. However, Christianity was renewed in a few areas where it had disappeared or had been weakened and was now planted for the first time in vast reaches of the land surface of the globe which never before had known it. Even more than in the fore part of the fourteenth century it became by far the most widely represented of the faiths of mankind.

A brief enumeration of the areas now partly recovered or claimed for the first time will make concrete the generalization of the preceding paragraph. In Asia and the islands which fringed that continent, Christianity was represented in most of the major and in many of the minor areas. It penetrated more of India than ever before. It had never died out in that land, but it had long been confined to small enclaves of Syrian Christians in the South. It was now carried to much of the interior. It was firmly planted in Ceylon, from which it seems earlier to have disappeared. It was introduced to Burma, the Malay Peninsula, Siam, Cambodia, Annam, the East Indies, and the Philippines. Heroic missionaries brought it fleetingly into Tibet. It was reintroduced to China and for the first time was taken to Japan. It was scattered across Siberia. In only a few of the smaller lands, Ceylon, the Philippines, and some of the lesser islands of the East Indies, did Christians constitute a large proportion of the population. In India they were mostly in the communities of the Syrian Christians and in the ports held by the Portuguese. In Burma, Siam, Cambodia, and Annam they were almost infinitesimal minorities. By A.D. 1750 practically all the provinces of China held some of them, but they formed only about one-twentieth of one per cent. of the population. In Japan, after a brief period of prosperity they were driven into hiding. In Northern Asia they were only a few widely scattered Russian trappers, traders, officials, and missionaries, with small groups of converts. Yet the larger part of Asia was now dotted with Christian communities as never before. Christianity was planted at intervals along the fringes of Africa south of the Sahara. Here, so far as we know, it had never before been present. It was only on the coast and was not carried far inland. Nor did it win any large numbers of Africans. The chief gains of Christianity were in the Americas. There, except for possible contacts through the Northmen, the faith had never before been known. In the two and a half centuries after A.D. 1500 the main centres of pre-Columbian civilization, in the Mexican and Andean highlands, became professedly Christian and main strongholds of the faith. Christianity also spread widely among the uncivilized Indians, especially in Central and South America. The white elements in Latin America were professedly Christian. In the English colonies on the Atlantic seaboard of North America, while only a small minority of the population had formal church membership, Christianity was vigorous.

It must be noted, however, that this phenomenal spread of Christianity was predominantly by migrations of peoples who were already Christian and by conversions from peoples of primitive or near-primitive cultures. Christianity made almost no headway among the adherents of the advanced religions and cultures. Islam, Hinduism, and Buddhism were practically untouched by it and in the ancient seats of high civilization in Asia embraced in the Ottoman

Empire, Persia, India, China, and Japan, Christians still constituted small minorities which were of slight importance socially or politically.

The kind of Christianity which had this phenomenal expansion was mainly Roman Catholic. In Eastern Europe and Northern Asia it was Russian Orthodoxy which spread, but only small numbers were involved. Protestantism was dominant in the English colonies in North America and was growing in the British West Indies and the Dutch colonial possessions in the West Indies, Ceylon, and the East Indies. It also had footholds in the Danish West Indies and through the Danish, British, and Dutch trading posts in India. Yet it was the Roman Catholic form of the faith which was most widely propagated. This was because the major explorations and conquests were by Spain and Portugal. Both these powers were solidly Roman Catholic and early felt the effects of the Catholic reformation. Their support made possible most of the phenomenal territorial advance of Christianity during the years of their might.

More than in any other period, whether earlier or later, the expansion of Christianity between A.D. 1500 and A.D. 1750 was under the direction of the state and of commercial companies. Since the age was one in which absolute monarchies dominated the Church in Europe, and nowhere more emphatically than in Spain and Portugal, this was to be expected. Especially did the crown dominate the Church and finance and direct its extension in Spanish America and the Philippines. If the Portuguese kings were somewhat less in control in their spheres of influence, that was not from any lack of intention but because Portugal was smaller than Spain and its authority was effective only on the coasts of Brazil and in limited although widely scattered posts in Africa, Asia, and the East Indies. The East India companies of the Protestant English and Dutch were as autocratic in their direction of the Church in such ports and islands as they controlled as were Roman Catholic Spain and Portugal. The Tsar's government was even more responsible for the initiation and direction of the spread of Christianity in the Russian domains. There was little of overt force in this propagation of the faith. Very few were given the alternative of death or the baptismal font. The active teaching of the faith was by missionaries who were moved by inward conviction and not by the commands of king or company. Yet it was the state or the chartered, monopolistic company which told the missionaries where they might go, licensed them, and assisted or fully supported them financially.

The leading role of the autocratic monarch or commercial company in the expansion of the faith is probably accountable for the passive nature of the Christianity thus planted. Whether in the Spanish or the Portuguese colonial domains or in the areas under the British and Dutch East India companies, the churches which arose showed little zeal for winning converts. There were exceptions, but they were few. In Ceylon, when Dutch rule disappeared almost all the Protestant Christians reverted to their earlier religion, whether that was pagan or Roman Catholic. In most of the other areas, Roman Catholic, Protestant, or Russian Orthodox, where it had been propagated in this paternalistic fashion, the faith remained anæmic. It was only in the British colonies in North America that it displayed vigour and spread by an inward momentum. In most of these colonies very little direction or assistance was given by the mother state: the churches were dependent upon the support of the colonists or, for a time in their early stages, upon aid from Europe little of which was through governments.

If its effect upon mankind be surveyed as a whole, Christianity was more potent between A.D. 1500 and A.D. 1750 than at any earlier era. This was partly, but by no means entirely, because of its broader geographic extension. It greatly ameliorated the impact of the European conquerors upon the non-European subject peoples. During the first stages of exploration and conquest in the Americas atrocities were numerous. Soon, however, the Christian conscience impelled protests. Measures were enacted, notably sections in the Spanish Laws of the Indies, which sought to protect the natives. Although they were not always strictly enforced, many missionaries and civil officials appealed to them and they were of very considerable benefit. Such schools and universities as existed in the European colonies, whether for the immigrant Europeans or the non-Europeans, were initiated and maintained by the Church. The spiritual and ethical foundations of the incipient nations which were beginning to arise from European settlements, especially in what was soon to be the United States of America, were largely Christian: American idealism had Christian rootage.

To no inconsiderable extent Christianity was responsible for the geographic discoveries of these years. It was more than a coincidence that the peoples of Western Europe, the ones of all those of the earth among whom Christianity had had the freest course, were also the ones who dared to explore the remotest corners of the globe, to seek the North and South Poles, and to climb the highest and most dangerous mountains. Prince Henry the Navigator, the master spirit back of the early Portuguese ventures, was to no small degree moved by a purpose to extend the Catholic religion. Columbus was far from being an ideal Christian, but he saw significance in his baptismal name, Christopher, and regarded himself as commissioned to bear Christ to peoples as yet untouched by the faith. The increment of courage and perseverance which was his through his religious convictions was an important source of his dreams of discovery and of the resolution which sustained him in making them real. Much the same was true of other less notable explorers. Christianity was not the only cause, but it may have been the determinative one without which the others would not have been operative.

We must add that if Christianity was even in some measure accountable for the geographic discoveries of this and later periods, it must share the responsibility for the evils as well as the blessings which attended and followed these exploits. Out of them came such enormities as the cruelties of the *conquistadores* in the New World and Negro slavery. Christianity, by nature and intention beneficent, became contributory to untold bestiality and suffering. It proved to have released a dangerous force which, like the scientific method and attitude of which it was also a source, could be a means of immeasurable blessings, but through ignorance or ill will could also work man's infinite hurt.

In Europe, Christianity, far from being ushered out by the transition from one age to another, profoundly moulded the new era. This it did in part through what had already been woven into the warp and woof of European life by the Christian faith in ethical principles, spiritual standards, the discipline of intellect, and motifs of art and architecture. It also made important fresh contributions. The law which was developed to regulate the relations between the states, both in peace and in war, an attempt to bring order into the anarchy of European international relations, owed its initial impulse to men of Christian faith and conscience. The first pure democracies, unless the monasteries and some of the heretical groups of the Middle Ages were such, were radical Protestant groups. It was mainly through Christianity, both Protestant and Roman Catholic, but chiefly the former, that democratic ideals began to be realized in the state. With its emphasis upon salvation by faith, the priesthood of all believers, and the right and the duty of individual judgment, Protestantism in its most extreme forms was a major source of democracy. Most of the new methods in education and the fresh types of schools had their birth in deeply devout souls and in religious movements, some of them Roman Catholic and some Protestant. Much of the greatest literature was built around Christian themes and much of the best art and most of the greatest music came from Christian devotion and were inspired by Christian subjects. Untold thousands showed in their lives the fruits of the inner impulse of the Christian spirit. Many emerged from Orthodox, Roman Catholic, and Protestant ranks who by their contemporaries and later generations were esteemed embodiments of the power of the Christian faith, saints who were both to be honoured and emulated. Some of these gave themselves unstintedly to the poor. Some, in the Roman Catholic Church, founded new orders and congregations for service to the underprivileged. The appearance and the popularity of *The Pilgrim's Progress* and of books, both Protestant and Roman Catholic, for the cultivation of the life of the spirit gave evidence of the quickening in Christianity and the broadening and deepening interest among clergy and laity in appropriating the riches of that faith in personal experience. Liturgies and forms of service were developed to guide Christians in their collective worship. Although much was left to be desired, probably the rank and file of lay folk in Western Europe and perhaps in Russia were more intelligent on matters of their inherited faith than at any earlier time: the descendants of the mass converts were better instructed than before in what had come down to them. The religion adopted for the masses by their rulers was beginning to be understood by the majority and to win from many of the humbler classes their conscious and intelligent loyalty.

Christianity was profoundly shaped by the events and the environment of the two hundred and fifty years from A.D. 1500 to A.D. 1750. The Christianity of Western Europe acquired some of the main features which it was to display down into the nineteenth and twentieth centuries. The major division between the Roman Catholic and Protestant wings of what had been Latin Christianity then appeared. All but a few of the chief denominational families of Protestantism emerged—Lutherans, Reformed, Anabaptists and Baptists, and Socinians. The Roman Catholic Church tightened its organization and more closely defined its distinctive tenets. The political, cultural, and national divisions of Western Europe placed their stamp on Christianity much more than in the thousand years between A.D. 500 and A.D. 1500. Roman Christianity became chiefly the faith of the Latin South-west, the portion of Europe which had been most assimilated to Roman rule. Protestantism was the faith primarily of the non-Latinized peoples, mainly Teutonic, of North-western Europe. The division between Latin and Greek Christianity had become final before A.D. 1500, but Russian Orthodoxy was now more self-conscious and distinct. Emerging nationalism, in part but not entirely under autocratic dynasties, helped to shape various strains of Christianity, notably those of Russia, England, Scotland, Holland, Scandinavia, and Germany. The Thirty Years War put its impress upon German Lutheranism, to some extent in providing the setting for the rise and growth of Pietism. Even the Roman Catholic Church, more compact doctrinally and in temper because of the Protestant secession, showed national patterns, especially in France and Spain. The Christianity of A.D. 1750 was different from that of A.D. 1500. Its continuity was unbroken and it held loyally to its founder, but it had undergone striking alterations.

In the second half of the eighteenth century what seemed to be another major recession of the Christian tide set in which was to continue until about A.D. 1815. However, it proved to be more a pause in the advance than a significant retreat.

Several factors contributed to the retardation. Spain and Portugal, with whom most of the territorial gains of the preceding two and a half centuries had been associated, were now in decay. The Society of Jesus, which had provided a large proportion of the missionaries for the Roman Catholic gains since the middle of the sixteenth century, was expelled from Spanish, Portuguese, and French territories and was then (1773) dissolved, or, in effect, suspended by the Pope. A series of general European wars engrossed the energies of most of the continent which was the stronghold of Christianity. They culminated in the French Revolution and the wars of Napoleon. The upheavals in Europe were paralleled by others in the Americas. Through the latter the Thirteen Colonies became the United States of America and all but small fragments of Latin America became independent of Spain and Portugal. Much of the eighteenth century rationalism which contributed to these revolutions and sought through them to usher in a new society was inimical to Christianity. Many hastily assumed that through it the Christian faith would be ushered out of European civilization. In China long continued persecution kept the faith stationary in numbers and slowly sapped the morale of the Christian communities.

In spite of these adverse factors, there was little or no loss of territory. In some areas the Church was dealt severe blows, but it suffered from no such inward corruption as had threatened it in the preceding ages of retreat and, while on most of its frontiers it ceased to move forward, it was forced to surrender almost none of the ground won earlier.

Moreover, in Protestantism awakenings were in progress which soon were to make that branch of the faith the leader in the Christian advance and which were to usher in the greatest century in the history of the expansion of Christianity. In the Thirteen Colonies the Great Awakening brought a deepening of Christian conviction and life. It had repercussions in the British Isles, especially in Scotland and some of the Nonconformist circles in England. After a lull brought by the war of independence the revivals again broke out and with even greater power in what was now the United States. In England the Evangelical revival began and gained headway. It spread to the Thirteen Colonies, there reinforcing what had come out of the Great Awakening. Its chief figures were John Wesley and George Whitefield, but it was by no means confined to them. It gave rise to Methodism in its various branches, but much of it remained within the Church of England and reinvigorated that body. Out of the Great Awakening and the revivals which followed it near the turn of the century and from the Evangelical revival and kindred movements in the British Isles came societies for the spread of the faith. Unnoticed or scorned at the time by all but a few, in the nineteenth century they were to attain large dimensions. They appeared first in the United States and Great Britain but before 1815 were beginning to emerge, by contagion, on the continent of Europe. Even in the midst of the pause and threatened recession in the Christian advance, the wave was rising and was gaining momentum which soon was to carry the Christian tide to a new highwatermark.

Between A.D. 1815 and A.D. 1914 Christianity moved forward so rapidly and became potent over so much of the earth's surface that the designation "the great century" seems the most appropriate designation for the era. Whether some later age will outstrip it and take its title from it the cautious historian ought not to predict. He might venture the prophecy that its success in that period presaged even greater achievement at some later time, but he could not hope to live long enough to see that prediction either proved or disproved by the event.

In several ways the hundred years which followed A.D. 1815 favoured the spread of Christianity. The era was one of relative peace. No wars of the dimensions of those of the two centuries which preceded A.D. 1815 engrossed the attention and wasted the energies of European peoples. Outside of Europe no major wars, except the four-year civil conflict in the United States, the T'ai P'ing Rebellion in China, and the brief struggle of 1904-1905 between Japan and Russia, disturbed the peace of mankind. Within Europe a few conflicts between some of the larger powers threatened that peace, but they were brief and did not become general. There were wars on the periphery of the expansion of Europe, but none of them brought exhaustion to the combatants. The age was also one of growing prosperity and wealth in the Occident. Developing science, rapidly mounting invention, the multiplication of new machines, and the quickening of transportation and communication combined with the relative peace to increase the wealth, the power, and the populations of European nations to a degree without precedent in history. The expansion of European peoples which had begun in the twelfth, thirteenth, and fourteenth centuries and had been renewed in the fifteenth century went on with accelerated pace. By A.D. 1914 Europeans had brought most of the earth's surface under their control. Some of this was through extensive migration, mainly in the temperate zones in the Americas and in Australia, New Zealand, South Africa, and Siberia. Much of it was by conquest, notably in Africa, India, and the Islands of the Pacific. A large part of it was by commerce. Both in lands which were dominated politically by Europeans and in those which retained their independence Western culture made headway. Indeed, those nations which preserved their political autonomy did so only by sacrificing their cultural integrity and adopting in large measure the appliances and ideas of the Occident. Since Christianity was so closely associated with European civilization as to seem to non-European peoples an integral part of it, the dominance of European peoples and the acceptance of their culture opened wide the doors for the Christian missionary and predisposed some of his hearers to accept his message.

However, the atmosphere of the nineteenth century was by no means entirely favourable to the spread of the faith. In the Occident in the very seats of its traditional strength Christianity was more openly challenged than it had been at any time since the conversion of the Northern European peoples. Much of the science of the period seemed to be undercutting not only details but also the basic postulates of the Christian faith. For many the secularism and the prosperity of the era appeared to render Christianity irrelevant: by millions the faith was not so much openly denied as tacitly ignored. What men esteemed the goods of life, those objectives for which they most earnestly strove, were, so they felt, not to be obtained through Christianity. Vast movements of population to the new lands in the Americas and the Pacific and from the rural districts to the rapidly growing cities removed millions from hereditary associations of which the Church was an accepted part. The Church would need to put forth unprecedented exertion if it were to follow them, hold their allegiance, and make itself and its message an essential feature in their new environments. As they established contacts with non-Western peoples, merchants and sailors tended to cast off Christianity and its moral standards and restraints. It was not only west of Suez that the ten commandments were ignored, but also wherever Occidentals came in touch with non-Occidental folk. Christian missionaries were looked upon with ill-concealed hostility or contempt by the majority of their fellow-countrymen in trade, diplomacy, and colonial officialdom, and the lives of the latter often seemed to non-Occidentals to belie the message of the emissaries of the Church. Moreover, many non-Occidentals, even while adopting the mechanical appliances of the West, scorned the religion that came from that region and insisted that their own spiritual and moral heritage was superior. Consciously or unconsciously they sought to compensate for the sacrifice of self-respect entailed in going to school to the Occident in matters material by vehemently maintaining that in things spiritual they were far superior to the West.

The main cause of the phenomenal expansion of Christianity in the nineteenth century in the face of these obstacles was not to be found in friendly features of the environment but in the inward vitality of the faith. This vitality showed itself in an enhancement of the awakenings which had begun in the eighteenth century and in the reinforcement of these by additional revivals and fresh movements.

That there was a connexion between the fresh burst of life in Christianity and the abounding vigour in other phases of Western culture is obvious. The religious awakenings were the most marked among those peoples which led in scientific, industrial, and commercial advance and in the building of empires. How far one was the cause of the other and to what extent, if any, they arose from a common cause it would be impossible to measure with precision. Christianity was certainly a contributory factor. As we have said more than once in this chapter, through the discipline, the daring, and the endurance which it had given the European mind and spirit, particularly in the western part of that continent, it undoubtedly shared in the achievements of the era. Other elements entered, among them the Græco-Roman heritage, geographic position, and natural resources. Yet Christianity may have been the factor without which the others would not have issued in the startling developments of the age.

The Christianity which spread was both like and unlike that of earlier periods. It was almost entirely Russian Orthodox, Roman Catholic, and Protestant. Each of these main divisions of Christianity was a continuation of what had gone before: it was not a new faith which was being propagated. However, the relative participation of the three was altered. The most rapid expansion was through Protestantism, with the Roman Catholic Church second and the Russian Orthodox far in the rear.

The change in proportion was in part due to the fact that in contrast with the preceding three centuries the most active colonial and commercial powers were not Roman Catholic but predominantly Protestant. The major expansion of European peoples in the nineteenth century was from the British Isles and in the United States of America, in both of which Protestants were in the large majority and in which the traditions were prevailingly Protestant. France, Germany, Russia, Holland, Belgium, and Italy either acquired colonial territories for the first time or added to those which were already theirs. France especially was building an empire, and France was preponderatingly Roman Catholic. Portugal, Belgium, and Italy tended to favour Roman Catholic missions, but Holland was chiefly Protestant and from Germany issued both Protestant and Roman Catholic missions. Russia was the only power which supported the expansion of an Eastern communion and there was little of this outside her own vast territories. It was clear, therefore, that in the vigour of the peoples from which the missionaries came Protestantism had the advantage. How far these peoples owed their position to Protestantism would be impossible to determine with accuracy. Protestantism was contributory, for it encouraged the thrift and the individual initiative which lay back of much of the enterprise of the peoples of Great Britain and the United States. It was not, however, the only cause.

The leading position of Protestantism was not due entirely to the preeminence of the British Empire and the United States in the expansion of the century. It was also because of the burst of new life within Protestantism itself. Largely a continuation of that of the eighteenth century, the renewed vigour was mainly in British and American Protestantism, the wing of the movement from which the chief expansion was achieved. It was seen as well on the continent of Europe and in the new nations of British stock (and, in South Africa, likewise of Dutch stock) which were rising in Canada, Australia, New Zealand, and South Africa. The new life expressed itself partly through such movements as the Young Men's and Young Women's Christian Associations, the Sunday School, the Young People's Society for Christian Endeavour, and student Christian movements, especially the Student Volunteer Movement for Foreign Missions. It was also seen in the Oxford movement in the Church of England, in the creation of the Free Church of Scotland, in the rapid growth of Methodism and the Baptist churches, and in the emergence of such new denominations and fellowships as the Disciples of Christ and the Plymouth Brethren. It displayed itself in many missionary, Bible, and Christian literature societies and in societies for moral and social reform. Because of this new life the main current of Christianity was beginning to flow through Protestantism.

Moreover, Protestantism itself was being altered. The Evangelical awakening and the many revivals were enlarging those sections of Protestantism which were nourished by them. It was predominantly the Protestantism of these movements which propagated itself on new frontiers. Expanding Protestantism was by no means entirely of these schools. The Anglo-Catholic revival in the Church of England gave rise to missions, and the Lutheranism and the Reformed churches of the continent of Europe had a share. Among the Lutherans and the Reformed, however, the elements responsible for missions were chiefly those which had been affected by Pietism or the revivals which had come by contagion from the British Isles. Although displaying many varieties, the Protestantism which spread was largely that which emphasized the conversion of the individual and in varying degrees laboured for moral reform and the application of Christian principles to the entire life of man.

The Roman Catholic Church was also being modified. It, too, was experiencing revivals, but these were expressing themselves largely in the traditional way of new celibate orders and congregations. More of these arose between A.D. 1815 and A.D. 1914 than in any preceding century. As against defections from its ranks and the anti-clericalism directed against it by liberals in Latin lands, the Roman Catholic Church stressed the distinction between itself and the secular currents of the age, and encouraged the laity to more conscious allegiance and to more active practice of religious rites. The national particularisms within its ranks waned and more and more it was centralized under the Papacy. It was a symptom of the times that the doctrine of the infallibility of the Pope was first formally promulgated in the nineteenth century. The trend was in the direction of a self-conscious, closely integrated ecclesiastical structure intent upon witnessing to its faith in a world which was increasingly alien and even hostile. In its temper and to some extent in its organization, the supposedly changeless Roman Catholic Church was being altered.

Eastern Christianity was little if any different from the preceding age. Within the Moslem world the remnants of the pre-Islamic Christianity were still on the defensive, clinging resolutely to what had come down from the past in an effort to save themselves from final extinction. As Greece and the Balkans emerged above the receding Turkish tide, autocephalous Orthodox churches were set up which were largely co-extensive with the new states, both bulwarks of nationality and sustained by it. They had no expansion except by migration to the Americas. Russia was still the main champion of Orthodoxy and within its borders the Orthodox Church continued to be bound hand and foot to the state. Such expansion as it experienced was in close association with Russian imperialism.

The methods of the spread of Christianity in the nineteenth century were strikingly different from those of the preceding three hundred years and, indeed, from those of any earlier age. Christianity expanded largely through voluntary missionary societies organized and maintained without assistance from governments. There were some exceptions. Russian missions were usually in close association with the state; the French Government gave Roman Catholic missions protection to further its prestige abroad and as an excuse for annexation of territory; and the British Government often subsidized mission schools in its colonial possessions. None of this, however, was on the scale seen in the preceding three centuries in Spanish and Portuguese domains, the British grants-in-aid were given because the mission institutions assisted were schools and not because they were Christian, and French colonial administrations were often anti-clerical and cool or opposed to missions. As never before in its history, unless possibly in the first three centuries, the expansion of Christianity was not left to small professional monastic groups through the initiative of princes, but was by the support of large elements in the rank and file of its lay adherents. This was especially the case among Protestants, but only to a slightly less degree it was characteristic of Roman Catholic missions, and it was seen, although faintly, in the Russian Orthodox Church. Never since its earliest age had the spread of the faith been so much the recognized responsibility of the entire body of Christians, and even in the first centuries no such elaborate organizations had been developed for that purpose.

For both Protestants and Roman Catholics the trend was towards the conversion of individuals rather than of groups. Group movements into the faith there still were, but not since the first centuries had the decision to become a Christian been so extensively a matter for the individual rather than an existing social unit—a family, a village, or a tribe. In general, too, higher standards for admission to the Church were insisted upon than earlier. This tended to make the emerging Christian communities, especially in the larger nations of Asia, small minority enclaves recruited member by member from a hostile society about them. The trend paralleled one in the Occident, in which large scale defections from the Church, together with the Church's emphasis upon a high standard of Christian living, set the Church in conscious opposition to the world. However, this was to some degree offset by the sense of mission on the part of Christians to present their faith to every human being, "the evangelization of the world in this generation" as a Protestant slogan had it. Christians could not rest content until they had given to all men the opportunity to accept their faith. That had now for the first time become possible. They sought to rise to the challenge. They endeavoured as well to relieve physical suffering wherever they found it and many strove to remove the basic social and economic causes for that suffering. Christians also furthered education and literacy.

Never before, not even in the preceding three centuries, had Christians come so near the goal of reaching all men with their message. Missionaries penetrated to almost every corner of every continent and to the overwhelming majority of the islands of the sea. To make the Bible available to all, they reduced more languages to writing than had been given written form in all the preceding centuries of human history. By A.D. 1914 there were few tribes or peoples in which at least a few Christians were not found.

In Europe advances were registered among the remaining pagans in the eastern parts of Russia, and in Western Europe numbers of Jews became converts. The faith was still spreading, although slowly, among those minorities who had no ancestral attachment to it. More important were the efforts to hold to the faith those with a Christian background but whom the vicissitudes of the changing age had swept from their customary church connexions. Here success was far from complete: hundreds of thousands of labourers in the new industries drifted away and their children grew to maturity with no religious instruction. Yet the story was by no means entirely one of failure. Thousands of church buildings were erected in the great cities and in the manufacturing and mining towns and were staffed by clergy. Fresh methods and organizations were developed. Of these the Young Men's Christian Associations, the Sunday Schools, the Salvation Army, and the Salesians of Don Bosco stood out but were only more prominent examples of a multiplicity of new undertakings. Moreover, from the effort of a German pastor to meet the physical and spiritual needs of his parishioners came the most significant of the beginnings of a nursing profession which was eventually to become worldwide. Out of the Christian impulse, too, there arose, on the continent of Europe, the Red Cross, using the Christian symbol for organized ministry for the relief of human suffering. Traceable to Christian origins were multitudes of reform movements, mainly stemming from Great Britain, with such objectives as the abolition of slavery, the curbing of the excessive use of alcoholic beverages, and the achievement of international peace.

Numerically the greatest expansion of Christianity in the nineteenth century was in the United States of America. Here was developing what in the twentieth century was to be one of the three or four most powerful nations on the planet. If it could become important in its life Christianity would have greatly augmented its place in the total world scene. Yet the problems which that growing country presented to Christianity during the course of the nineteenth century were so difficult and on so large a scale that at the outset the outcome was by no means assured. At the beginning of that century, although the background of the new nation was Christian and in some of the older sections attendance at religious services was a social convention, less than one-tenth of the population were church members. Such remnants of financial support of the churches by the state as survived the colonial period were ended while the century was still young. For that method of maintaining the Church, traditional in the lands from which the ancestors of most of the population came, voluntary support by individuals had to be substituted, and this required more personal conviction than did the other. Nor could the Church expect much aid from the state in the religious education of youth. Increasingly the state schools adopted what was called religious neutrality. This in effect, except in some where the Bible was read without comment and the Lord's Prayer was said, left religion out of the programme. Forced to face their task without the aids on which centuries of precedent had taught them to rely, the churches were confronted with the multiple problem of accompanying the westward moving frontiers and making themselves an integral part of the new communities which were rapidly coming into being, of holding to the faith the millions of immigrants who were pouring in from Europe, of winning the Negroes and the Indians, and of adjusting themselves to the rapidly shifting conditions in the older states and the spectacular growth of the urban centres.

It is one of the outstanding achievements of an amazing era that the churches addressed themselves to all of these challenges and with remarkable success. Except for retrogression during the period of the Civil War and reconstruction, the percentage of the population having church membership rose continuously and in the year 1914 was more than four times as large as it had been a hundred years earlier. Progress was registered in solving each of the major problems. The frontier was followed so effectively that eventually the churches had some of their strongest centres in the Mississippi Valley, a region which at the opening of the nineteenth century seemed religiously destitute. The large majority of the immigrants and their children were held to the churches of their fathers, whether Roman Catholic, Protestant, or Orthodox. By A.D. 1914 the percentages of Negroes and Indians who had church membership were not far from that of the whites. Of the urban population, early in the twentieth century a slightly larger proportion were attached to the churches than of the rural population. This does not mean that complete success had attended the efforts of the churches: it had not. Yet distinct progress had been made.

Christianity, moreover, was having profound effects upon various aspects of the life of the United States. It set the moral standards and largely shaped the ideals of the nation. From it came the impulses which freed the Negroes, sought the protection of the Indians, brought better care for the insane, eventually wrote prohibition into the constitutions and laws of several of the states and of the United States, founded the large majority of the colleges and universities of the country, encouraged in several states the systems of public education, brought into being the numerous parochial schools, provided better educational facilities for the Negroes, and founded hundreds of hospitals and orphanages. Christianity was the chief inspiration of American democracy.

Mainly in consequence of this successful expansion of the faith, the Christianity of the United States was the most varied that any country had thus far seen. The Roman Catholic Church and almost all of the larger and many of the smaller of the Eastern and Protestant bodies were represented through immigrants and their children who maintained their traditional religious allegiance. In general the denominational alignment was by the strains of immigration: the standard denominations of Great Britain became the religious home of settlers from England, Scotland, and Northern Ireland; German Lutherans who arrived in the nineteenth century largely went into synods distinct from those of the seventeenth and eighteenth century German settlers; Lutherans from Scandinavia grouped themselves into predominantly Swedish, Norwegian, Danish, or Icelandic synods; Celtic Irish were enthusiastic Roman Catholics; immigrants from Greece, the Balkans, and Russia formed the basis of the Orthodox fold; and other nationalities grouped themselves ecclesiastically in similar fashion. In the first and second generations there was comparatively little passing from the denomination of one's ancestry to another.

However, the Christianity of the United States was not simply a reproduction of that of Europe. As between denominations the advantage lay with Protestantism and with those bodies which were of British background and, in general, of the radical wing of Protestantism. The country was prevailingly Protestant in affiliation and atmosphere. The Negroes were attracted chiefly to the Baptists and Methodists, the leading denominations among the lower income levels of the older white stock. Most of the denominations, moreover, acquired in the American environment a flavour different from that of the parent bodies in the old world. The Roman Catholic Church achieved a national structure in which the national lines inherited from Europe were superseded and progressively dimmed.

Since all churches were equal in the eyes of the law, none had social or political pre-eminence over the others. There was a rough stratification by social levels. For instance, Presbyterians and Episcopalians, presumably because they were related to the state churches of Scotland and England respectively, the countries which were the chief sources of the older white stock, tended to attract the educated and well-to-do of the nation, a position which was shared with the Congregationalists (both Trinitarian and Unitarian) because the latter had formerly enjoyed the support of the state in New England. Roman Catholics, recruited mainly from the newer immigration and from the economically depressed groups of Ireland and Europe, were predominantly in the lower social strata. The trend was towards greater co-operation, especially between those Protestant bodies which had been longest in the country.

In the United States a new kind of Christianity was arising. It had its roots in the past, but it was more variegated than any which had yet been seen, more intent upon the transformation of society, and progressively more inclined to transcend inherited ecclesiastical divisions than was that of the old world. The trend was to be accelerated after 1914.

In Canada some of the same problems faced the Church as in the United States. Here, too, were the westward moving frontier, immigration from across the Atlantic, Indians, and growing cities. However, the immigration was predominantly from the British Isles and mainly Protestant, and Negroes were few. There was, too, a rapidly increasing enclave of French Canadians which antedated British rule and was solidly and tenaciously Roman Catholic. The churches were even more successful than in the United States and all but a very small minority of the population either had formal membership in some church or professed a preference for one. Newfoundland was prevailingly Christian in allegiance and the sparse population on Greenland had mostly been won.

In the British, Dutch, and Danish West Indies the Negroes who constituted so large an element were more and more being drawn to the Church, chiefly in one or another of its Protestant forms. Only slowly were they brought to an approximation to Christian standards. The family and sex mores were particularly slow to be moulded by their new faith.

Latin America constituted a peculiar problem. At the dawn of the century the only form of Christianity represented was the Roman Catholic Church. The white and mestizo elements all belonged to it and the majority of the Indians were at least nominal adherents. In the political upheavals which accompanied the achievement of independence, the church suffered severely. Only slowly did it recover. The Christianity of the region, always passive, continued so, and the Roman Catholic Church tended to be associated with those elements which perpetuated something of the order of colonial days: it found its chief support in the landed proprietors. The more liberal elements looked askance at it and sought to curb it. With the coming of political independence, partial religious toleration was introduced. Protestantism entered through immigration and missionaries. The latter were mainly from the United States, but some were from the British Isles. By A.D. 1914 Protestantism had gained a foothold in all of the republics, but its strength varied greatly from country to country and was most marked in Brazil and Mexico. A few Orthodox entered as immigrants, but made little or no attempt to propagate their faith.

Australia was only sparsely settled in A.D. 1815. To the scattering aborigines had been added a few whites, largely convicts, from the British Isles. In the course of the ensuing century immigration, now voluntary and not convict, poured in, mainly from the British Isles. The aborigines dwindled. Through personnel and funds from Britain and the efforts of the colonists themselves the churches were firmly planted and the overwhelming majority were affiliated with them. Protestants, chiefly of standard British denominations, Anglican, Presbyterian, and Methodist, predominated, but there was a large Roman Catholic minority, mostly Irish. A few of the aborigines were won. Christianity was clearly an integral part of the life of the new nation.

Christianity was even stronger in New Zealand than in Australia. Active missions won most of the Maoris, the Polynesian people who preceded the whites by several centuries. Some of the earliest white immigration was centred about religion, one group Anglican and another Presbyterian. The immigration was even more Anglo-Saxon than that of Australia.

From the churches of both Australia and New Zealand missionaries were sent to many of the islands of the Pacific and to some of the countries of Asia.

Before A.D. 1815 few of the islands of the Pacific had been touched by either the white man or Christianity. It was only in the last quarter of the eighteenth century that the first extensive voyages of discovery were made and the first Protestant missionaries came. In the late decades of the eighteenth and the early decades of the nineteenth century traders, sealers, and whalers touched most of the islands and in the course of the nineteenth century all the islands were claimed by one or another of the white nations. Most of the islands became British, some went to the French, a few to the Germans, and Hawaii, Guam, and part of the Samoan group to the United States. Missionaries made their way to most of the islands. The majority were Protestants, mainly British but Americans in Hawaii and some of the northern groups. A substantial minority were Roman Catholics, largely French. On the easternmost of the islands, predominantly Polynesian by race, Christianity became the prevailing faith. In A.D. 1914 it was making rapid progress in the western islands, where the population was chiefly Melanesian, Micronesian, and Papuan. Here numbers of the missionaries were from the islands earlier won to the faith. Through the missionaries languages were reduced to writing, the Bible was translated, and systems of schools were developed. Through the missionary, too, the vices of the non-missionary whites were fought and the natives, plunged, bewildered, into the white man's world, were assisted in making their adjustment to it.

At the dawn of the nineteenth century most of the Filipinos were Roman Catholics. Animists were still to be found in the mountains and Moslems in the South. During the course of the century the frontiers of Roman Catholic Christianity were pushed slowly forward against animism. The substitution of American for Spanish rule in the closing years of the century brought striking changes. Under nationalistic fervour, several hundreds of thousands of Filipinos broke away from the Roman Catholic fold into a church staffed by their own clergy. Protestantism was introduced and won many of the Roman Catholics. The Roman Catholic Church was in part reinvigorated by the coming of non-Spanish leadership.

The East Indies became predominantly Dutch in political control, but with a small remnant of Portuguese rule and, on Borneo, large British enclaves. In the Dutch domains Protestant Christianity registered marked progress, chiefly through Dutch and German missions and among animistic tribes. Few of the Moslems, who constituted the majority of the population, were won. Roman Catholic missions, while growing, were in the minority. Protestant missions, mainly Anglican, were inaugurated in British territory.

In Madagascar, Christianity, in spite of severe persecution early in its career, made remarkable strides among the Hòva, the most energetic of the tribal groups. By the year 1914 it was planted among several of the other peoples. Protestantism led, especially among the Hòva, but Roman Catholic missionaries were also having phenomenal success. The coming of French rule, in the 1890's, brought embarrassment and necessitated readjustments but was not followed by permanent reverses.

On most of the various smaller islands which fringed the African coast or lay between that continent and India Christianity was firmly planted.

Africa south of the Sahara was beginning to experience a series of revolutions. Especially in the second half of the nineteenth century Europeans penetrated the remotest recesses. By the close of the century almost all of the area had been partitioned among European powers. Great Britain had the lion's share, but extensive sections were held by France, Portugal, and Germany, and most of the basin of the Congo was administered in a fashion which was soon to make it a possession of Belgium. The Africans, largely primitive in culture and animistic in religion, were being hurried into the white man's world and were in the initial throes of the disintegration of their old life and institutions.

It was under these circumstances that Christianity had a very rapid expansion. Often its missionaries were ahead of secular explorers. Indeed, the greatest of the pioneers in revealing the interior to the white man was a missionary, David Livingstone. Henry M. Stanley, who was next to him in geographic exploits, although not professionally a missionary, was drawn to Africa through Livingstone. Missionaries of lesser fame were also among the explorers. To the large majority of the missionaries exploration was incidental or entirely absent as a motive. They were primarily interested in planting their faith. Because of them, by the year 1914 every political division had growing Christian communities. In general, Protestants were more prominent in British and Roman Catholics in French, Portuguese, and Belgian territories, but there were very few of the colonial possessions where both great wings of the faith were not represented. Protestant missionaries were mostly from the British Isles, but there were large contingents from the continent of Europe and the United States. The distribution of the Christian communities was somewhat spotty. Christianity, chiefly Protestant, was spreading especially in what by 1914 was the Union of South Africa and related British protectorates. In Uganda both Protestantism and Roman Catholicism had a rapid growth, after an early chequered and stormy course. Nyasaland was the scene of particularly prosperous missions, mainly of Scottish Presbyterians, Anglicans, and Dutch Reformed from South Africa.

Christianity was already making major contributions to the life of Africa. Scores of languages were reduced to writing, and the Bible, in whole or in part, was translated into them. Most of the schools which prepared the African in the learning of the white man were begun and conducted by missionaries, or, if taught by Africans, were supervised by missionaries. Much of such modern medical care as was given was by missionaries. The Christian forces, chiefly in Great Britain, had all but brought to an end the African slave trade. Churches were arising and in their members the characteristic fruits of the Christian faith were beginning to be apparent. Here was a positive moral and spiritual force which was assisting in the disintegration of the older patterns of African life, but which also, and more significantly, for the old would have passed without it, was beginning the reconstruction of the life of the region.

On the north shores of Africa and in Western Asia Christianity made relatively much slighter progress than in many other regions. Here was the main centre of Islam and large numerical gains from that faith were as yet out of the question. Moslem law and public opinion made them impossible. In Algeria and Tunisia large influxes of settlers from Europe, chiefly from France and Italy, gave rise to extensive Christian communities, predominantly Roman Catholic. Missionaries, both Roman Catholic and Protestant, multiplied and established residences and institutions in every country except Afghanistan. In a few areas the Russian Orthodox were active. However, the accessions through these missions were almost exclusively from the existing communities of Eastern Christians. Through schools, hospitals, and literature a leaven was penetrating Islam, but the latter remained intact.

India was the scene of a great advance of Christianity. Not far from the middle of the nineteenth century the British conquest of India was completed. British rule was accompanied by profound internal peace, order, improved facilities of transportation and communication, and protection for all religions, including those of minorities. It also brought Western civilization and built up a system of education which was predominantly Occidental.

Under these favouring circumstances missionaries came in ever increasing numbers. They were both Roman Catholic and Protestant, but the latter were the more prominent. The Protestants were from other portions of the British Empire, mainly the British Isles themselves, and from the United States and the continent of Europe. Proportionately Protestantism, although the more recent arrival, grew more rapidly than did the Roman Catholic Church. The latter was hampered by the remnants of control exercised by the Portuguese state and the majority of its staff were engrossed in the care of those already Christian. Both great wings of the Church reached out into most of the administrative divisions and the native states. The Roman Catholics were especially numerous among those claiming Portuguese nationality. In the nineteenth century both Protestants and Roman Catholics drew most of their converts from the depressed classes and the animistic tribes of the hills. These came largely by mass movements. Christians of all the major divisions of the Church, Syrian (the oldest Christian community in India), Roman Catholic, and Protestant, were most numerous in the South.

Through Christianity hundreds of thousands of the hereditarily underprivileged were finding a door of hope, with education for their children, freedom from degrading vices, and greater self-respect. The Christian forces were having a large part in the schools through which Western learning was being mediated to India. In a variety of ways Christianity was touching Indian life. It was, too, having effects upon the other religions of India.

In Ceylon a substantial percentage of the population had become Roman Catholic Christians under the Portuguese rule of an earlier period. During the succeeding Dutch rule most of these had, perforce, become Protestants. Because of the material inducements offered, some Buddhists had also accepted baptism. Soon after the Dutch were supplanted by the English, one of the consequences of the Napoleonic wars, practically all the Protestants reverted to their earlier faith, whether Roman Catholic or Buddhist. Because of this fact, in the nineteenth century Roman Catholics were much more numerous than Protestants. However, British societies and one American organization entered and through them new Protestant communities came into being.

In Burma, in contrast with Ceylon, in the nineteenth century Protestants outnumbered Roman Catholics. They were largely the product of an American Baptist mission and were chiefly from the Karens. At the beginning of the century these were folk of nearly primitive culture. Through the Christian faith and Christian schools they made rapid strides in civilization. Converts were also won from most of the other peoples of Burma, but among the dominant race, the Burmese proper, they were not numerous.

Siam, like Burma and Ceylon prevailingly Buddhist in religion, was hospitable to the schools and hospitals maintained by missions and aided by them was assimilating Western culture. Although both Protestantism and Roman Catholicism were ably represented, only a few thousand of the peoples of the land accepted Christianity.

The Malay population of the Malay Peninsula and the Straits Settlements, solidly Moslem, although in the nineteenth century under British rule or protection, was but little affected by Christian missions. The Chinese who entered by the hundreds of thousands were more susceptible and there were also Christians among the thousands of Indian immigrants.

In what at the close of the nineteenth century was French Indo-China Roman Catholic missionaries, largely French but secondarily Spanish, had been vigorously at work since the sixteenth century. It was as a protector of French missionaries that the French Government established its first footholds in the land. Although in the latter part of the century the colonial administrators were at times anti-clerical, Roman Catholic missions flourished and Roman Catholics constituted a larger proportion of the population than in any other land in the Asiatic world except Syria, Ceylon, and the Philippines. Protestantism had very scant representation and that not until late.

At the outset of the nineteenth century China was near to being hermetically sealed against the Occident. Only in Canton and the adjacent Portuguese Macao were Western merchants allowed. There was a small Russian ecclesiastical-diplomatic mission in Peking. Thanks to footholds established in less restrictive days, there were Roman Catholics in all the eighteen provinces of China proper, with possibly one exception, and in several of the outlying dependencies. However, they were subject to recurring persecution and were probably dwindling rather than growing in numbers. The first Protestant missionary did not arrive until 1807.

The mounting pressure of the Occident did not make its first breaches in Chinese isolation until the 1840's, and it was not until after 1895 that the wall of Chinese resistance to Westernization crumbled. From that time on, except for a brief reaction from 1898 through 1900, the Occidental flood poured in. China was in revolution as it had never before been in all its long history. The Confucian monarchy fell and the system of education based upon Confucianism was swept aside. Every phase of Chinese life was being altered. Conditions were opportune, especially after 1900, for the growth of Christianity: the traditional obstacles had been weakened and the faith, bringing with it some of the features of the Occident which were most desired, could gain a hearing.

All three major branches of Christianity, Russian Orthodox, Roman Catholic, and Protestant, enlarged their forces. The latter two had by far the greatest expansion, for Russian Orthodoxy did not reinforce its staff as extensively as did the others and remained the movement of a very small minority. Protestant missionaries were from the British Empire, the United States, and the continent of Europe, but mainly from the first two. All the major varieties of Protestantism were represented. The Roman Catholic Church held the advantage over Protestantism in having been longer in the empire and in counting at the outset of the nineteenth century, when Protestantism had not yet begun to be propagated, about two hundred thousand members. In A.D. 1914 it was still the larger numerically. However, it had not increased proportionately as rapidly as had Protestantism. Moreover, Protestants were touching actively more phases of the nation's life. They were pioneering in Western types of schools, especially of secondary and higher grades, they were creating the new medical and nursing professions, and they were introducing improved methods of agriculture and forestry, education in public health, and, through their schools, were training some of the leaders who were becoming outstanding in guiding China through her difficult transition. Christianity was attaining prominence and influence and was the source of some of the most hopeful of the movements which were making for the regeneration of the nation.

At the beginning of the nineteenth century Japan was even more nearly sealed against the outside world than was China. She was, moreover, somewhat later than China in allowing her door to be pushed ajar. However, when once she had decided upon that step she took it with less hesitation than did the latter. In A.D. 1914 the basic structure of Japanese life was less altered than was that of China, but superficially the process of Westernization had proceeded much further.

Christian missionaries re-entered Japan late in the 1850's. Roman Catholic Christians who had conserved their faith in secret came out into the open, but were met with fresh persecution. It was not until the 1870's that the anti-Christian edict boards which had been part of the programme of exclusion were removed. Christianity was represented by Roman Catholic, Russian Orthodox, and Protestant missionaries. Protestant missionaries were more numerous than the others and were chiefly from the United States. In spite of the several thousands of Roman Catholics, the fruits of an earlier age of missions, with whom the revived Christianity began, Protestants eventually outstripped the other branches of the Church in numbers of converts and in influence. Christians were predominantly in the cities and were largely from the elements in the population which were most committed to Western ways: they included many products of the new schools and were especially prominent in the learned professions. Numbers, too, were from the *samurai*, the lesser military aristocracy of the old regime, who, having been cast adrift by the passing of the order which had supported them, found it necessary to make painful readjustments. Uprooted and by tradition educated, they became a leading source of supply of the new professions, and many of them were more responsive to the message of a faith which came by way of the Occident than were the rank and file of the nation. In proportion to the population, by A.D. 1914 Christians were less numerous than in China, but the Protestant churches had made greater progress towards self-support and self-government than in the latter country. The faith, too, was having effects upon the life of the country much more extensive than its statistics of membership would have led one to expect.

Except for fleeting contacts not far from A.D. 1600, Christianity seems not to have been introduced into Korea until late in the eighteenth century. It then came from China and in its Roman Catholic form. Until the nineteenth century was two-thirds over, persecutions from time to time reduced the size of the Christian communities and deprived them of their foreign pastors. In the 1880's Korea entered into treaty relations with Western governments and open opposition by the state ceased. Protestantism then began to be propagated, mainly by missionaries from the United States. As in Japan, it grew more rapidly than did the Roman Catholic Church. Russian Orthodox were also active, but less prominently than in Japan. Missionaries, especially Protestant missionaries, had a large share in inaugurating education and medical practice of Occidental patterns. The stormy political course of Korea in the quarter of a century which preceded A.D. 1914 was reflected in the spurts and pauses in the advance of the churches. By that year, however, Christianity seemed firmly rooted in the peninsula.

The huge portion of Asia under Russian control was but sparsely settled. Across much of it Christianity enjoyed a rapid growth in the nineteenth century through immigration from European Russia. For obvious reasons this was mostly by members of the Russian Orthodox Church, but there were also some Roman Catholics and a few Protestants. Russian Orthodox missions made converts among several of the primitive tribes of the region. As elsewhere, the Moslem populations were impervious to the Christian appeal.

From this brief summary of the advance between A.D. 1815 and A.D. 1914 it will be clear that Christianity had been more widely propagated in that period than in any preceding era. Never had any other set of ideas, religious or secular, been spread so extensively over the earth's surface by agents who were giving their full time to the enterprise. Although merchants and diplomatic and colonial officials from the West far outnumbered missionaries, the latter had made their way even beyond the boundaries of the others' efforts. The achieve-ment was amazing.

More than any other impulse in the history of mankind, moreover, in these brief decades Christianity furthered the intellectual progress of the race. In reducing languages to writing it had no equal. In inaugurating and conducting schools on the enlarging frontiers of the settlement of Western peoples in America, Australia, New Zealand, and South Africa and among non-Occi-dental peoples in the Americas, the islands of the Pacific, Africa, and most of the lands of Asia, it was also without a peer. In several countries, notably China, it began the creation of a new medical profession. It was the main source of the nursing profession in both the Occident and the rest of the world. It fought intemperance, opium, prostitution, and chattel slavery. It strove to protect weaker peoples against exploitation. It endeavoured both to relieve and to prevent famines. It contributed to the ideals of the new nations which were emerging from European settlements. To untold millions of individuals it brought larger vistas of the possibilities of human life and the power to press towards their attainment. Never had Christianity or any other religion been so potent in the affairs of mankind as a whole.

At first sight the era which began in A.D. 1914 seems to be another of the ebbs in the Christian tide to which our story has accustomed us. It was a time of wars of unprecedented magnitude which had their beginnings in what had long been the geographic centre of the strength of Christianity. Social and political revolutions shook the fabric of Europe. The chief of them were anti-Christian and by their victory appeared to be dealing fatal blows to the faith. The blows were most severe in Russia and Germany, the two largest states on the continent. Outside the Occident, peoples who in the nineteenth century had been brought into subjection by Western powers were attempting to shake off the white man's yoke. They resented the control by missionaries of churches in their midst almost and perhaps quite as keenly as they did political admin-istration by white colonial officials. In most of these churches in A.D. 1914 the transition from white to indigenous administration had either not begun or was only in its initial stages. The rapid expansion of Christianity in the preced-ing century had been, almost inevitably, by a kind of ecclesiastical imperialism. The feeling against it was only less hot than it was against political imperial-ism. Financial stringency in the Occident rendered more difficult the raising of funds for missions. The swing towards state initiative and control appeared to make anachronistic the private initiative through which Christianity had been propagated in the pre-1914 decades. Rampant secularism and non-theistic humanism challenged by their temper as well as their basic assumptions the convictions central to Christian faith. The shock of war, especially the second of the world wars, uprooted millions in Europe from their accustomed associations, including the Church. European peoples were on the march culturally. Again an old order was dying and a new one coming to painful birth. Because of its close relations with the old, Christianity was once more threatened. Recession was to be expected.

However, in the portion of the period embraced in the three decades between A.D. 1914 and A.D. 1944 what was seen was not recession but a continuation of advance. The advance was of a somewhat different kind than that of the nineteenth century. Here and there, notably in Europe, there were numerical losses. Yet in A.D. 1944 Christianity was more firmly planted among more different peoples and was more potent in the affairs of man as a whole than it had been thirty years earlier.

The advance was seen in three main ways. In the first place, Christianity and its influence were more nearly evenly distributed across the face of the earth in A.D. 1944 than in A.D. 1914. The percentage of Christians among non-Occidental peoples had approximately doubled in the thirty years. In some regions, notably in equatorial Africa, it had more than doubled. In India and China, which together comprised more than half the population of the globe, it had about doubled. In some large lands, notably Africa south of the Sahara, India, and China, Christianity was clearly more influential in A.D. 1944 than in A.D. 1914. As a spiritual and moral force, Christianity was probably at least as influential in Europe and the Americas in A.D. 1944 as it had been a generation earlier.

In the second place, Christianity was more deeply rooted among non-Occidental peoples in A.D. 1944 than it had been in A.D. 1914. Leadership in the churches outside the Occident was passing from foreigners to those sprung from the soil. This was true of both Roman Catholics and Protestants. More of the financial support was coming from the members and less from the founding churches. The process was hastened by the reduction of assistance from the Occident in personnel and money. Except in lands from which the second of the world wars had cut it off, this aid was in general somewhat larger in the latter than in the earlier year, but because of war and economic crises it had been subject to violent fluctuations and had not mounted as rapidly as in the prosperous and peaceful decades immediately preceding A.D. 1914. The cutting down of aid from the West only hastened a process which was already under way: the "younger" churches were coming of age. The main strength of Christianity was still in the Occident, but the process of making the faith universal in its spread and influence, which had been so striking in the nineteenth century, continued.

In the third place, Christians were being knit more consciously into a world-wide fellowship than had been the case since the first three centuries when the Catholic Church was coming into being. The movement was most marked among Protestants, but here and there Protestants and Roman Catholics and Protestants and Eastern Christians were making common cause against the evils of the day. The trend towards Christian unity had only begun. Great historic rifts remained unhealed. The process might be interrupted. However, remarkable advance had been achieved in the thirty years subsequent to A.D. 1914 and the movement was gaining momentum.

The Christianity which was spreading after A.D. 1914 was much the same as that of the century before that year. Proportionately Protestantism was still the most active wing of the faith and the majority of the new undertakings were in it or from it. Relatively the Roman Catholic Church was more prominent and active than in the preceding hundred years. The Eastern churches had suffered severely. Probably a more significant change was the fashion in which non-Western peoples were increasing their participation in both the Protestant and the Roman Catholic fellowships. Christians, too, were more consciously a minority in a hostile world than in A.D. 1914, but they had by no means given over the hope of the transformation of that world and the coming of the City of God.

After what has been said earlier in this volume and especially after the summary in the preceding chapter, we need not here recapitulate the advance region by region or country by country as we have that of the nineteenth century. We need only remind ourselves of the outstanding features of the years. In Europe the faith, while numerically weakened by losses, was probably more vigorous because of the testing which had stimulated the inner vitality of the Church to resistance and fresh expression. In the Americas the advances of the preceding period continued. The same was true in the islands of the Pacific, including the East Indies and the Philippines. In much of Africa the gains had been peculiarly rapid and spectacular. Losses in numbers had been suffered in parts of the northern shores of Africa and Western Asia. However, in the largest populations of Asia, India and China, progress had been notable, although as between these two countries it was in ways which were not precisely similar. In Japan, too, there had been gains. The year 1944 presented to the Christian forces a sobering and complex situation, but it was more in the nature of a challenge than a dismaying menace whose gloomy outcome was foreshadowed by losses. The outlook was not the bleak one which had faced Christianity in the two great recessions of A.D. 500 to A.D. 950 and A.D. 1350 to A.D. 1500.

As, in A.D. 1944, the historian looked back over the course of Christianity from the beginning, he was conscious that as by successive pulses of a great tide the faith had gained in the affairs of men. It had by no means brought mankind into full conformity to the Sermon on the Mount. Indeed, some of the chronic evils which plagued mankind, notably war and Negro slavery, had reached their most colossal dimensions among peoples which had been long under its influence. Nor had Christianity always survived in lands where it had acquired promising footholds. In some vast areas the forces against it had been too powerful for it and it had disappeared or had for centuries been in slow decline. Moreover, in spite of its wide distribution in the nearly four and a half centuries after A.D. 1500, the faith still had its chief strength where it had been since at least the eighth century, among European peoples and their descendants. Its fate seemed to be tied up with theirs. However, as a force in the human race as a whole, Christianity had clearly advanced. So far as could be foreseen, its course had only begun. More than any other religion in human history it was becoming universal. Its history had demonstrated that it appealed to individuals in all races, nations, and stages of culture and that among those who accepted it specific fruits appeared which were clearly recognizable. Each major forward wave had carried the faith into additional portions of the earth's surface. Each recession had been less marked than its predecessor. In the advances of the post-A.D. 1500 periods Christianity had become world-wide to an extent attained by no other religion. Especially after A.D. 1815 it had been planted among practically all peoples and tribes and after A.D. 1914 was becoming firmly rooted in the texture of their cultures.

The historian could not prove that this course would continue. The brief nineteen centuries in which Christianity had been spreading were only a small fragment of human history. Yet no other religion had had a similar record, and so far as the past constituted a basis for prophecy the advance would continue.

Chapter XVII

A COMPARISON WITH THE RECORDS OF OTHER RELIGIONS

W E MAY find additional perspective in appraising the expansion of
Christianity, the outlook for the future, and the significance of Christianity in history if we can see the record of that faith against the background
of the course of the other religions which have long been a part of the human
scene and have had wide extension. Obviously we cannot enter upon a detailed comparison. Clearly, too, here more than in almost any other phase of
our enterprise we must be aware of our bias and must seek to safeguard our
judgments from being warped by it. We cannot, moreover, include all religions, but must restrict ourselves to those which have displayed viability over
centuries and have given some proof in experience to a claim to universal
validity. However, in spite of its palpable dangers and limitations, the attempt
at comparison should yield useful generalizations.

We are not here to concern ourselves with the philosophic aspects or the
intellectual validity of the several religions. These would extend our study to
unwieldy dimensions and take us into an area which has been repeatedly
covered. Our concern is rather with the historical record of spread, of decline,
and of interaction with the environment—subjects which have had our attention in our pilgrimage with Christianity.

As we enter upon our venture, we must remind ourselves that the time span
covered by the other religions as well as Christianity is, when contrasted with
the total life of mankind on the planet, very brief. Judaism and Hinduism are
probably the most ancient of the high religions which we shall consider, and
at the longest they are scarcely more than four thousand years old. The Buddha
and Confucius were less than six centuries before Christ. While the systems
which look back to these two as their founders were, like Christianity, indebted to a long tradition which preceded them, in their most distinctive
aspects they dated from those whose names popular nomenclature has attached to them. Mohammed was approximately six hundred years younger
than Christ. The sceptic might say that even the four or five thousand years
of the oldest living religions may be only a short chapter in the long journey
of the human race, a phase which from the vantage of a hundred thousand

years hence will be seen to have been relatively brief, and that religion as we have historically known it is an experience which mankind puts behind it as a stage in its development. To this question we must later recur. Dissent from the sceptic, however, must not blind us to the relative brevity of the time embraced in this chapter. From the standpoint of the life of an individual it is long. It also covers the larger part of the period embraced by recorded history. Yet when set against the measure of the days which man has thus far had it is short.

We here need not concern ourselves at length with the vast family of religions embraced under the categories of animism and polytheism. Elements from these faiths usually persist, more or less thinly disguised, in the customs and beliefs of peoples who have supposedly discarded them for what are generally esteemed more advanced systems. We find them associated with Confucianism and as integral parts of Hinduism and Buddhism. In spite of its stern monotheism, Islam in practice makes room for animism. Popular Christianity has not always escaped animism and polytheism. Yet as he advances in civilization and towards intellectual and spiritual maturity, man finds both these protean forms of religion untenable. However old they may be, they disintegrate under the impact of Christianity and its associated cultures. Any return to them is viewed as a recession in civilization, a recrudescence of an outworn era. As rivals of Christianity they cannot justify claims to universal validity. In each of them Christians find some conceptions akin to their own faith, but at best as imperfect gropings for what is more clearly discerned in Christianity. They and the cultures of which they have been a part have never succeeded in standing permanently against Christianity. In some areas elements from them have persisted under a Christian mask, but more often it has been attitudes and expectations which they have expressed and nourished which have carried over. In becoming Christians their adherents have expected the new faith to do for them what they demanded of the old, only more effectively. It is the conceptions of the nature and function of religion contained in animism and polytheism, many of them contradictions of Christian convictions, which have longest endured and which Christianity has found most difficult to supplant.

We need pay no attention to Shinto, for that is a mixture of animism and polytheism which has owed its survival to association with Japanese nationalism, and, clearly, has no future as a universal faith. The religion of the Sikhs and that of the Parsees have been too much circumscribed by identification with limited racial or social groups or to one cultural environment to give any promise of wide acceptance. Much the same is true of the Jains. Manichæism, once widespread in Asia, Africa, and Europe, so completely disappeared that we can only guess at the reasons for its former prosperity and its eventual demise. Taoism as a cult seems never to have expanded beyond China, was always a minority faith, and in later centuries has been clearly moribund, with insufficient inner vigour to give hope of revival.

Judaism has never been a formidable competitor with Christianity for the allegiance of the human race. By conviction it is monotheistic and ethical and to it Christianity has been indebted in a multitude of ways. However, it has not been able to escape from its tribal origin. Through the centuries it has been peculiar to a particular people. Racial cohesion has been essential to it. Christianity sprang from it, but it is significant that since giving birth to that faith Judaism has never made further new or original contributions to the religious life of man. In the Christian era Jews have added greatly to mankind's store of art, music, philosophy, social theory, and letters, but after the emergence of Christianity no other great religious movement has issued from them. It is provocative of thought, moreover, that of all the varieties and schools of Judaism which were contemporary with Christianity in its first century the sole survivor was that which crystallized in orthodox Judaism. Christianity is the only faith to spring from the parent stock of Judaism which endured and spread. Moreover, in the nineteenth and especially the twentieth century Judaism seemed peculiarly vulnerable to the corrosion of the secular spirit. This was particularly noticeable in a land like the United States where Jews were not confined to ghettos but tended to be absorbed into the life of the country. The religious tie seemed associated with existence as a distinct social and cultural enclave, but when the racial element was weakened it did not have enough vitality to persist, except in anæmic and diminished forms of liberalism. Christianity took over all the universal elements of the Hebrew tradition and interpreted and transfigured them in what it found in Jesus and in its own experience. So obvious is it that it need scarcely be said that the differences between Judaism and Christianity have centred in Jesus. Judaism, if it has honoured him at all—and to many Jews he has been anathema—have regarded him simply as one of its prophets. Christians have insisted that he was much more than a prophet, that he was the fulfilment of the hope and the crown of the Hebrew religious development, and that in him mankind had a new beginning. It has been Jesus and the place accorded him which have constituted the essential difference between Judaism and Christianity. In him is to be found the basic source of the contrast between the course of the two faiths and of their respective effects on mankind.

Christianity was never reabsorbed into Judaism as was Buddhism in India by the Brahminism from which that religion came and against which it was in part a protest. Nor was Christianity so nearly supplanted by Islam as it had earlier, for the Gentile world, superseded Judaism. Islam, while honouring Jesus, claimed to have a later revelation, much as Christianity, while revering the Jewish scriptures, saw them as fulfilled in Christ. However, while Christianity outstripped Judaism, Islam, although in the first eight centuries of its course winning millions of Christians, did not stop the growth of Christianity. Indeed, Christianity eventually covered far more territory than did Islam.

For centuries Islam was Christianity's most dangerous and formidable rival. Like Christianity, it was monotheistic, ethical, and claimed universality. Its moral demands were not so exacting or so impossible of full achievement this side of the grave as were those of Christianity. Being younger, it could give plausible reasons for its assertion that it had a later word from God which was final and complete. It won from Christianity a larger proportion of the latter's territory than did any other competitor. Moreover, it usually held the ground so won. Only in the Iberian Peninsula and Sicily did Christianity regain substantial portions of the populations among whom Islam had once supplanted it. In the nineteenth and twentieth centuries, the age in which Christianity most nearly made good its claim to being the universal faith, Islam was, of all religions, the most resistant to it. In the areas dominated by Islam in that era Christianity lost more in numbers than it gained. The fraternity proclaimed by Islam for all followers of the Prophet, while never fully realized, was more nearly attained than was that brotherhood which its rival held to be a distinguishing feature of those who had Christ as their master. Moreover, Islam did not have the vast fluctuations which the Christian tide displayed. At some periods it was more vigorous than in others, but, unlike Christianity, which more than once disappeared from territories over which it had been widely disseminated, Islam almost never surrendered a people or a region which it had once entered. Its most notable losses were to Christianity and these, as we have said, were extensive only in Sicily and in what became Spain and Portugal, Islam was extremely tenacious. Christianity and Buddhism all but died out in the lands of their birth. In some of the lands where once it had been strongest Christianity was erased or reduced to encysted minorities. Islam continued dominant in the country and among the people of its origin, so much so that Christianity was never able to re-establish there more than the most tenuous of holds.

On the opposite side of the scale must be placed other facts. Islam did not spread as widely as did Christianity. It was much more nearly identified with one culture, that of the Arabic world, than was Christianity with that of the

Occident. Arabic was so much the language of the Koran that in orthodox circles translation into some other was regarded with suspicion: the Koran was translated into only a fraction of the number of tongues into which the Christian Bible was put. No other volume was so nearly universal in its speech as was the latter. It was literally the book of a thousand tongues. Moreover, after less than its first thousand years Islam ceased to gain much ground. Its chief territorial advances were in the first two centuries of its life. It had other important geographic extensions in the eighth, ninth, and tenth centuries of its career. Thereafter it made few large gains. The rate of the emergence of new religious movements from within it also slowed down. Not even at its height did it produce the highly organized and extensive missionary activity which Christianity displayed. The latter, indeed, mounted and was never so striking or extensive as in the nineteenth and twentieth centuries, the latest which, because of the portion of time in which our lot is cast, we are able to record. The expansion of both Christianity and Islam was closely associated with the conquests and the commerce of their adherents. However, the spread of Christianity was more often apart from or ahead of these than was that of Islam. Professional Christian missionaries penetrated to many areas which were reached only later, if at all, by Christian merchants, soldiers, or government officials. Islam seldom if ever went ahead of Moslem rulers and merchants. There was no equal in Islam to David Livingstone.

The contrasts in the effects upon culture between Islam and Christianity were even more striking and significant than were those in the geographic extension of the two faiths.

Islam was an integral part of a great civilization, that of the Arab world. It entered it as a constituent and an inspiration much as Christianity became a moulding element of the civilization of Europe. Both civilizations were heirs of the Græco-Roman world. Into each went contributions from Greek philosophy, from the Hebrew religious and ethical heritage, and, less directly, from the ancient cultures of the valleys of the Nile and of the Tigris and Euphrates. In some ways Islam seemed to have an advantage over Christianity as the creative force in a new culture. It found strong Christian communities which had preceded it and on which it drew heavily. It was Christian scholars who first put into Arabic some of the great classics of Greek thought and Christian artisans who helped form the distinctive patterns of Arab architecture. Moslems made a somewhat similar contribution to European thought, for it was through translations into Arabic that Western Christians of the middle ages were first brought in contact with some of the works of Aristotle. The Moslem Averroes contributed to the quickening of philosophical thought in the Christian West.

However, Moslems did not have as large a part in stimulating Western European culture as Christians had in the formative stages of Arab culture.

Yet eventually Moslem culture became stagnant while the culture of which Christianity was so prominent a part displayed a continuing dynamic. After a few centuries nothing new came out of the one while from the other fresh creations of the mind and spirit poured forth in ever increasing abundance. The essential difference seems to be that in the one Islam was the dominant religious factor and in the other Christianity. It may be more than a coincidence that as the Christian communities in the Moslem world dwindled the rate at which new cultural achievements appeared in that cultural zone also declined. The parallel suggests the hypothesis that the presence of Christianity, so stimulating to Europeans, had much to do with the activity of the Arab mind and spirit.

As we have again and again reminded ourselves, the dynamic in Western European civilization worked for both man's woe and weal. It was in Christendom that some of the chronic evils of mankind, especially war and the assertion of the will of one group over that of another to the exploitation of the weaker, reached their most formidable dimensions. Obviously Christianity was not directly the source of these evils, but if it was in any way accountable for the vigour in European civilization it must share some responsibility for them. Yet clearly traceable to Christianity were the impulses that inspired the struggle against man's ills and sins. Movement after movement for reform owed its inception and the persistence which carried it to successful completion to consciences sensitized and wills and hopes made strong by Christian teaching and Christian faith. Even more demonstrably from Christian sources were the many philanthropic undertakings—hospitals, orphanages, and famine relief—far more extensive than anything known in Islam. Nor did Islam inspire such movements for the restraint of exploitation of one people by another as did Christianity. Islam had no Las Casas, Claver, Penn, or Wilberforce. Less palpably arising from Christianity were the achievements which could be employed for either bane or blessing, among them the scientific method and the related mechanical inventions and machines. However, as we have repeatedly noted, they, too, appear to have had Christianity as at least one of their sources. A Christian origin for such social and political ideals as democracy and socialism is somewhat easier to prove, although it was obviously not the only or always the major cause.

From that world separated geographically from Europe by only the Mediterranean, joint heritor with it of the Græco-Roman and Hebrew traditions, and strikingly distinguished from it by the fact that the major religious ingredient of one was Islam and of the other Christianity, came much less of science, invention, geographic exploration, social reform, and political and social innovation. In Europe the rate of creative output continued to mount, but that in the Moslem world, while not reaching the vanishing point, declined.

If the differences here outlined between Christianity and Islam are valid, the question inevitably emerges: What feature or features absent in the one and present in the other are responsible for them? Here again facile generalization is dangerous. May one venture to suggest that the major contrast is in the fact that Islam postulates a vast gulf between God and man which is spanned, on the divine initiative, by revelation through prophets, of whom Jesus was one but Mohammed was the greatest: whereas Christianity, also recognizing the gulf, declares it to have been bridged, partly by prophets but also and chiefly by the incarnation? The Koran denies that God can have a son. Christians have insisted that in Christ God became man that man might become God. The disciples were to set as the goal of their calling moral likeness to God. They were to be filled unto all the fulness of God. The difference between Islam and Christianity was not that one denied and the other affirmed the Self-revelation of God. Both were emphatic that it had occurred. The two were at opposite poles in the method and the goal of that revelation. To the Moslem, revelation did not lift man to God (although Sufis, influenced by Christianity and Hinduism, sought that experience). To the Christian, God had redeemed man through His incarnation in Christ, the cross, the resurrection, and the giving of His spirit. Through that redemption it was possible for man, if he availed himself of God's free gift, to be born anew and to begin an endless life in which the divine likeness would be progressively perfected. The enhancement of personality and the infinite dignity accorded man by the Christian faith go far to account for the creative vigour in a civilization which had that faith as a prominent constituent.

Related to this contrast between Islam and Christianity was another. The Moslem, in stressing the power of God and the gulf between God and man, believed so strongly in the omnipotence and the "otherness" of God that he made the will of God both determinative and inscrutable. Man did not have free will, but could simply submit to God's predetermined decree. Christians were divided as to whether man had free will, but they tended to believe that he had at least enough of option to accept or reject God's offer of salvation. They left more room for human initiative, and once the choice had been made and the new birth had occurred, the individual's powers were amazingly heightened. Here was a conception which might, through a corrupt will, be twisted to man's hurt. It may help to account for the gigantic dimensions attained by some social evils in lands where Christianity was potent. Christendom had been only partially Christianized and to some degree the dynamic released by the Christian faith had opened a Pandora's box. Yet that dynamic, when directed towards man's advancement, had contributed to the greatest achievements of Western civilization.

Confucianism was long the dominant philosophy of the Chinese. Its outlook was that of a universal faith. Like other religions and philosophies claiming cosmic validity, it had developed in connexion with one of the cultural traditions of mankind. It had striking success in the area of its civilization. Here it was the chief basis of a comprehensive unity which so amalgamated the diverse racial and cultural elements that the Chinese became the largest most nearly homogeneous group of mankind. They regarded their culture as the norm for all civilized human beings. Actually it was so closely associated with the Chinese Empire that with one exception it did not spread to peoples which were not at one time or another brought within the political structure of that realm. The exception was Japan, and there Confucianism, although influential, was made to fit into the inherited Japanese patterns. The Japanese took it because it was a part of the only high civilization which they then knew well, while they were adopting and adapting other phases of that civilization. Korea and Annam more nearly conformed to Confucianism, but they were among the lands which over long periods were integral parts of the Chinese domains.

Within the area in which it was dominant, Confucianism displayed remarkable persistence. It survived the long period of political division between the second and the seventh centuries of the Christian era. In spite of the fact that Buddhism was then making rapid headway and establishing itself firmly in China, it continued and eventually again became supreme.

Yet while in theory it was sceptical of much that is currently called religion and at times its spokesmen denounced all other systems, in practice Confucianism did not erase its rivals. Animism, polytheism, Taoism, Buddhism, and Islam all survived in the Confucian *milieu*. Christianity had more difficulty and twice died out, but after its third introduction, in the sixteenth century, it also continued. In other words, Confucianism was vigorous enough to persist under adverse circumstances, but was not sufficiently potent fully to eliminate its rivals. This was not because of a convinced tolerance. Again and again Confucianists instituted persecutions against other faiths. It may have been that Confucianism was so thoroughly humanist, so much a philosophy, and so agnostic as to much that is generally termed the supernatural that it could not satisfy some of mankind's most deeply felt needs, and systems which were more clearly religious lived because they appeared to be filling the vacuum.

In the twentieth century Confucianism appeared to be losing ground. As never before in its history, the order with which it was intimately associated was disintegrating. Two of its traditional chief bulwarks, the political organization and the system of education based upon it, were thrown into the discard. This was the kind of experience through which Christianity had more than once passed and which it had survived. It was not certain that Confucianism would not display similar resilience. So much of the very essence of the traditional Chinese attitude towards man, nature, and society was associated with Confucianism that it seemed clear that the latter would not immediately disappear. In a sense, Confucianism was a misnomer, for Confucius was only the most prominent figure in a way of thinking and acting which was much older than he and of which he was acknowledged to be even more a transmitter than a creator. It appeared unlikely that what for at least two thousand years had been the dominant note in Chinese life and which had probably been only somewhat less than dominant for hundreds of years earlier would quickly pass. It was too deeply imbedded in the social patterns and ethical judgments of a great people easily to be dislodged. It might well, however, be henceforth a waning, even though a slowly waning force. It most certainly gave no indication of spreading beyond the Chinese cultural circle.

In their relative effects upon their environments, Confucianism and Christianity had similarities and differences. Both held to the conviction that the morals which govern the relations of man to man are of the essence of the structure of the universe. Both tended towards a social order which had the physical well-being and the cultivation of man's moral nature among its objectives. However, Confucianism had as its chief goal what it deemed an ideal human society this side of the grave. It inculcated reverence for ancestors but was largely agnostic as to their state. Christianity held up an ideal which could never be fully attained in this life and, while giving rise to much more active movements than did Confucianism for the creation of a better society here and now, taught that the perfect social order could not be achieved within history but must be consummated beyond history. Through much of its course, Confucianism displayed a strain of agnosticism and was uncertain in its theism. Its primary loyalties were to the family. Christianity was centred about God as revealed in Christ and its loyalties were primarily to Him. To it sin was primarily against a holy and righteous God, a note but hesitatingly struck in Confucianism, and it also stressed redemption and the transformation of believers into a growing likeness to that God, an aspect which Confucianism lacked. Christianity, therefore, cherished a different conception of the possibilities of man and a higher goal for human faith and striving. It made for a type of democracy which Confucianism did not know and gave rise to a religious experience which was alien to that system.

Hinduism, another strong competitor of Christianity, was circumscribed by Indian culture. Through Buddhism it reached outside the Indian culture circle, much as through Christianity and Islam the Hebraic tradition was carried beyond the limits of the Jewish community. Ideas from it affected some aspects of Greek philosophy and Manichæism, and in the nineteenth and twentieth centuries, chiefly through theosophy, it placed its impress upon widely scattered minorities in Europe and America. In its full expression as a cult and a philosophy, however, Hinduism was almost entirely confined to India and Indian colonies. Through the latter it exerted for centuries a profound influence in much of South-eastern Asia and the East Indies. As these colonies disappeared and with them the commerce and the states which were associated with them, Hinduism also largely vanished. Only on one of the smaller of the East Indies, the island of Bali, did it persist in a fairly unadulterated form. Elsewhere it was superseded by Buddhism or a syncretistic form of Brahminism and Buddhism. Hinduism was unable to win or to hold even all of India. In spite of its hospitality to numerous gods and beliefs and of the fact that many of India's peoples and cults were assimilated to it, millions of animists remained outside it or were only slightly touched by it, and other millions of the depressed classes were so imperfectly assimilated as really not to be of it. Moreover, Islam made great advances at its expense, millions separated from it to form the Sikh community, and the Jains were never fully reabsorbed into it. So closely connected was it with a particular social structure, caste and especially the Brahmin caste, that an alternative name for it was Brahminism and it was not at all clear that it could flourish apart from that form of society. It had not proved that it could, like Christianity, survive a culture with which it had once seemed to be identified.

In its effects, Hinduism gave rise to many schools of mysticism and from within it came much profound philosophic thought. It would be difficult to prove, however, that in either of these aspects it was richer or more fertile than was Christianity. Moreover, little of the activism, the striving for the transformation of society, could be ascribed to it that was prominent in the effects of Christianity. The seeming chief exception, Gandhi and the movements which he led, while indubitably Hindu, were also almost as clearly due to the stimulus given by contact with Christianity. The theoretical respect of Hinduism for all life was bound up with its convictions of the reality of the transmigration of souls and of the closely related karma. The goal of human life was almost the opposite from that of Christianity. For Hinduism it was the ultimate extinction of the individual through absorption into the impersonal universe (although here Hinduism wavered and in some of its expressions sought to salvage personality in man and in God). For Christianity the goal was eternal life for the individual in growing fellowship with the eternal God and of other, similarly transformed souls. Hinduism was basically pantheistic, finding God in all, both good and evil. Christianity, in contrast, held to the transcendence as well as the immanence of God and revered Him as personal. The social consequences of these contrasting beliefs were quite different. For instance, in some of its phases Hinduism encouraged temple prostitutes and other sexual practices which were abhorrent to the Christian. Hinduism had had aspects, indeed, which included animal and even human sacrifice, neither of which could be viewed by Christians with equanimity.

Along with Christianity and Islam, Buddhism had wide geographic expansion. Like Christianity and Islam, it appealed to men and women of many different races and customs. It began in India as an offshoot of Brahminism and took as axiomatic such basic assumptions of the latter as reincarnation and karma. Yet it gained wide followings among peoples to whom, before its arrival, such beliefs were entirely alien. This was notably the case in China, where it won a lasting place in a civilization which had very different fundamental convictions. It is true that in China it found a point of approach in the somewhat kindred Taoism, but the dominant philosophy, Confucianism, was remote from it. Moreover, in contrast with both Islam and Christianity, much of the geographic extension of Buddhism was independent of commerce, colonization, or political conquest. To be sure, Buddhism owed its first great extension in India and its introduction to Ceylon to Asoka, the most powerful monarch in the India of his day, and its prosperity in the North-west of India and in Central Asia was closely associated with the Kushan dynasty and especially with Kanishka, of that line. In much of South-eastern Asia and the East Indies the way was opened by Indian commerce, conquest, and Brahminism. In most of Central Asia and Tibet, however, none of these, unless it may have been commerce, appears to have paved the way for Buddhism, and commerce seems not to have been important. Missionaries were the chief agents and the superiority of the associated Indian culture gave prestige. The connexion with a higher culture clearly was a factor in the initial popularity of Buddhism in Japan. In China even this advantage was largely lacking. Buddhism seems to have spread there primarily through missionaries and mainly because it appeared to meet deeply felt human needs which the indigenous philosophies and religions could not satisfy. Like Christianity, Buddhism won numbers of peoples of primitive culture and was repeatedly the vehicle by which a higher civilization was transmitted. From it, as from Christianity, came impulses to a rich art, to a voluminous literature, to much personal religious experience, to moral transformation of men and of groups, and to profound philosophies.

On the other hand, certain striking contrasts must be pointed out between the spread of Christianity and that of Buddhism. Buddhism was never carried to as much of the earth's surface as was Christianity. In India it was reabsorbed into the Brahminism from which it had arisen as Christianity never was in any area by its parent Judaism. Buddhism, too, was far more nearly eliminated from India, the land and the civilization in which its first great triumphs were won, than ever Christianity was from the basin of the Mediterranean, the region which first submitted to it. In other words, Buddhism did not seem to have as much persistence and as much ability to hold its own as did Christianity. It lost out in India in part because of the massacre of many of its monks by Moslem invaders, but more significant was the fact that it became corrupt and did not seem to have within itself the power of reform and inner renewal which has been so characteristic of Christianity. The Christian Church has more than once seemed to fall to fully as low a level as has Buddhism, and yet, to a far greater degree than in Buddhism, from within it issued, as part of its inner genius, springs of revival which carried it on to ever greater achievements. No great new movements came from Buddhism after the fourteenth century or the fore part of the fifteenth century. This seems to indicate that after about nineteen centuries of life the force of Buddhism was spent and fell into irreparable decline. Indeed, the decay had begun to be obvious several centuries earlier. Christianity, in contrast, in its nineteenth century most displayed its amazing vigour and had its greatest geographic extension and in its nineteenth and twentieth centuries its effects on mankind as a whole attained unprecedented proportions. It was still moving forward. Moreover, Buddhism never fully won even the nominal allegiance of a highly civilized people as did Christianity that of the Græco-Roman world and most of the Europeans. India was never so nearly entirely Buddhist as was the Roman Empire Christian. In China, although that realm was profoundly influenced by it, Buddhism was never as dominant as was Christianity among European peoples. For several centuries it seemed to have submerged Confucianism, but the fashion in which the latter reasserted itself was ample evidence that it had never been eliminated. In the Confucian renaissance in the eleventh and twelfth centuries of the Christian era, Buddhism placed its stamp on its successful rival, but it continued to be a waning factor in Chinese life. Contrast this with the Renaissance in Europe, where Græco-Roman polytheism was never renewed, where Græco-Roman humanistic philosophy was in theory always kept subordinate to Christianity, and where humanism contributed to the fresh outburst of life in Christianity which we call the Reformation. In China Buddhism was in progressive decay after the revival of Confucianism and never recovered. In Europe much of the most vigorous life in Christianity came after the Renaissance. Buddhism, like Christianity, was the main vehicle for the civilizing of a number of folk of primitive and near-primitive cultures. However, none of those transformed by Buddhism attained the place in the world occupied by the peoples of Northern Europe, whose culture was so largely the fruit of Christianity. Moreover, in spite of its wide missionary activities, Buddhism did not inspire nearly as extensive a spread of the faith as did Christianity.

In comparing the effects of Buddhism with those of Christianity, it must be noted that, in spite of its regard for all living beings and its prohibition of the taking of life, Buddhism did not prevent some of its outstanding exponents from engaging in war. Indeed, Japan, where it was peculiarly vigorous, became the most persistently militaristic of the peoples of the Far East. The development in Japan of the military class and of the attendant military feudalism took place after the introduction of Buddhism and one form of Buddhism, Zen, became especially popular with members of that class. From Buddhism issued no organized movements for the prevention of war. These came primarily from Christianity. Although Buddhism inspired some philanthropy and some care for animals, in the extent of institutions and organizations for the relief of suffering of both men and animals and especially in movements for the elimination of such ills, Christianity far surpassed it. The difference seems to stem from a contrast in basic convictions. Buddhism inculcated pity for living creatures and their sufferings, but to it life and suffering were inseparable and so long as the one continued the other would also be found. In their vision of the New Jerusalem, however, Christians declared that there would be no more pain. There was that in their faith which inspired them hopefully to strive to eliminate collective evils, no matter how colossal, within history as well as to expect that the holy city beyond history would know neither death nor sorrow.

As one attempts to draw generalizations from this all too brief and cursory comparison of the spread of the various other religions with that of Christianity, several conclusions emerge.

It seems clear, in the first place, that no religion obtained an extensive following and long persisted unless somewhat early in its history it succeeded in winning the collective allegiance of a fairly large and highly civilized centre of mankind. It was from the Roman Empire and through the peoples of Europe that Christianity had its greatest expansion. Islam was all but identified with

Arabic culture, Judaism with the Jews, Confucianism with China, and Hinduism and Buddhism with India. In some instances each was the chief inspiration of the culture with which it was associated. In every instance it powerfully affected it, and it was from such a base that it spread. One reason for the complete disappearance of Manichæism, a faith once disseminated from the Mediterranean to the China Sea, seems to have been the lack of support by a powerful racial and cultural group. For a time the Uighurs, potent in Central Asia and in the north-western portion of China, appeared to be an exception and it was largely through them that Manichæism gained its foothold in China, the land where it longest endured. The Uighurs, however, did not create a strong, unified, and distinct culture and were politically important for only a few centuries. Even they may never have been entirely Manichæan. There was a time, we know, when Nestorian Christianity had adherents among them.

It is also obvious, as a second generalization, that no religion, not even Christianity with all its extensive spread, ever succeeded in fully divorcing itself from the culture in connexion with which it achieved its widest geographic extension. This was in part because this culture to some degree was an expression of its genius. No religion could be long the professed faith of any group of people without placing its stamp upon them. They might not fully attain its ideals, but in their civilization they would give evidence of its presence. Moreover, in becoming the faith of a culture and a people, a religion soon bore the impress of its environment. That impress it carried with it as it spread.

As a corollary there followed that, at least into the twentieth century of the Christian era, no religion had become universal in the sense of eliminating all its rivals and being acknowledged as the faith of mankind as a whole. None of what may be called the high religions which were associated with a powerful people and culture had been completely eliminated. Some of the varieties of animistic or polytheistic cults had vanished, notably those of ancient Babylonia, Egypt, Greece, and Rome. They, however, could scarcely be included in the category of high religion. Some which could claim a place in that category but which had not established such a relation with a strong people or culture had also vanished. The others survived. Even the ancient Zoroastrianism, all but supplanted by Islam, persisted among the Parsees, attenuated but wealthy remnants of the great Iranian constituency which was once its stronghold.

Obviously these two last generalizations meant, as well, that by the fore part of its twentieth century Christianity had as yet neither become fully universal nor had succeeded in eliminating the other religious systems. It was still largely identified with the culture of Europe, and its geographic spread had been chiefly at the expense of polytheism and animism. It had supplanted the polytheisms of the Græco-Roman world, of the peoples of Northern Europe, and of the pre-Columbian civilizations of the western hemisphere, and it had gained against the animism of the primitive peoples of the Americas, Africa, and the Pacific and in the enclaves of primitive cultures in Asia left unassimilated by Islam, Hinduism, and Buddhism. Although numbers had come to it from Confucianism, it had made relatively few converts from Islam, Hinduism, and Buddhism.

In several significant ways, however, it must be said as a fifth generalization, in the record of its expansion and of its effect upon mankind Christianity, as compared with other religons, was unique. Geographically it had spread much more widely than had any other faith. Beginning with the latter part of the fifteenth century this had been almost entirely through peoples of European stock. In the preceding fifteen hundred years, however, much of the extension had been through those of other races and cultures. Although it had as yet won only minorities from Islam, Hinduism, and Buddhism, by 1944 there was almost no people or civilization where Christianity was not represented and among whom it had not won converts. It had demonstrated by experience that its appeal was not limited by race or culture but was effective among some from all classes, tribes, nations, and cultural levels. More than any other religion in the history of mankind, it had survived the death of cultures with which it had been intimately associated. It had lost territory, in its first and second major periods of recession to such a degree that its future appeared dark. Some of the ground then surrendered, especially to Islam in the seventh and eighth centuries, it never regained. At times its inner light burned low and seemed about to be quenched. Yet, to a greater degree than any other religion, it displayed the power of inward renewal and of winning and moulding new cultures. It gave evidence of universality not only in geography but also in years. It was not identified solely with one era in the development of mankind but was timeless in its appeal. Its greatest period of expansion and the era of its largest influence upon mankind as a whole was the latest which we have been able to record. Even in the stresses of the post-1914 decades it was being more widely disseminated and more deeply rooted among more peoples than ever before. This was in large part through its association with Europeans, but the qualities in the civilization of the Occident which led to the wide extension and revolutionary effects of Western culture were, as we have repeatedly seen, at least partly from Christianity. More than any other religion, or, indeed, than any other element in human experience, Christianity had made for the intellectual advance of man in reducing languages to writing, creating literatures, promoting education from primary grades through institutions of university level, and stimulating the human mind and spirit to fresh explorations into the unknown. It had been the largest single factor in combating, on a world-wide scale, such ancient foes of man as war, disease, famine, and the exploitation of one race by another. More than any other religion it had made for the dignity of human personality. This it had done by a power inherent within it of lifting lives from selfishness, spiritual mediocrity, and moral defeat and disintegration to unselfish achievement and contagious moral and spiritual power. It had also accomplished it by the high value which it set upon every human soul through the possibilities which it held out of endless growth in fellowship with the eternal God.

Whether Christianity would eventually eliminate other religions and become accepted by all mankind the historian, on the basis of the past experience which it was his function to record, could not confidently either deny or affirm. It seemed so probable as to be almost certain that in A.D. 1914 Christianity was only at the beginning of its history. It was clearly continuing to spread. The other religions were not giving evidence of as much vigour as they had formerly displayed and some of them, notably Buddhism and Confucianism, had either long been in decline or stagnant. All were suffering from the corrosion of the secularism of the nineteenth and twentieth centuries. This secularism in its intensified form had come from the Occident, the stronghold of Christianity. Although Christianity had taken severe blows from it and at times had reeled under the impact, it was giving evidence of an inward vitality which augured well for its future.

The age was one which desperately required spiritual and moral unity. Science and mechanical appliances had made all mankind a neighbourhood. It was, however, an extremely quarrelsome neighbourhood which was in imminent danger of destroying itself through internecine strife. It was in dire need of a unifying faith which would help it transcend its divisions, resolve its conflicts, and knit it into a co-operating community. Because of its inherent qualities, its growing universality, its past achievements, and the fashion in which the Christians of the world were coming together, Christianity appeared to offer more hope of providing the healing tie than did any other religion or cultural force. That it could succeed was as yet by no means assured. Success, if it came, would not be quickly achieved, or, to judge from past experience, complete or unqualified. Yet it might be nearly enough attained to prevent the collapse of civilization.

It seemed clear that if Christianity met the challenge and became the dominant religion of the world, it would not be by absorbing the other religions and making from them a new synthesis. Although it had been modified by each new age and culture into which it had moved, the Christianity which had shown sufficient vigour to propagate itself had always held to the uniqueness of Jesus Christ and had insisted that through him God had supremely revealed Himself and had wrought for the redemption and transformation of man. Types of Christianity which had failed to stress the centrality of Jesus as God's Christ had not shown the power to reproduce themselves through many centuries. The continuing vitality of Christianity was intimately bound with this conviction. So far as the historian could be sure of anything about the future of Christianity it was this: if the Christian faith triumphed it would be through uncompromising loyalty to him through whom it had come to birth and who in all its ages had been the acknowledged master of its most flaming spirits. As the most discerning of the disciples of its first century had seen: "In him was life and the life was the light of men." In the first century that had been an assertion of faith. By the twentieth century experience had made it demonstrated fact.

Chapter XVIII

THE CONCLUSION OF THE WHOLE MATTER

AS WE come to the end of our undertaking, almost inevitably we seek an appraisal, even though brief, of the larger implications of the story which we have endeavoured to relate. We ask ourselves whether inclusive answers can be given to the questions with which we introduced our narrative: What was it that spread? Why did it spread? Why at times did it not spread but lose ground? By what processes did it spread? What effect did it have? What were the effects upon it of the environment? To these questions we have again and again recurred. To them we have given answers which hold for special periods and countries. We must here set ourselves to see what reply can be made to them one by one and over the entire course of Christianity.

We must go beyond this. We must venture upon more difficult tasks and into areas where conclusions are even more highly debatable. We must enquire what the past record seems to presage for the future. Is Christianity to continue to expand and is it to bring all men and all human society to the high standards set before the disciples in the Sermon on the Mount? Does the experience of these nineteen centuries warrant the hope that at some time, no matter how distant, the disciples will have taught all men to observe all that their master commanded the original group? Will human society, as the environment of the faith, through progressive pulsations of the Christian tide be gradually brought to full conformity with the ideals of Christianity? Can our story answer the age-old query as to whether human history has a meaning, and, if so, wrest from it some inkling of that meaning? Can we draw any legitimate inferences concerning the nature of man, of the universe, and of the universe's dealings with man?

As we approach all these questions, and especially those in the last paragraph, we must frankly recognize our limitations. The history of Christianity is by no means completed. If our appraisal of its course is correct, it appears to be only a short distance removed from its beginning. Yet even of that we cannot be sure. Deep religious convictions colour our conclusions. Faith becomes important and determinative, and faith is not fully demonstrable or it would not be faith. Yet faith must be placed alongside ascertained fact, where fact can be had, and submitted to reason. Fact and reason cannot tell all, but they must be invoked in any such queries as we have dared to propound. Nor can we enter upon a full discussion of the questions which we have raised. To do that would require at least another volume. They have to do with issues which have engaged the attention of the greatest minds and noblest spirits of the race. In view of their nature, we must be modest, and modesty enjoins brevity.

The essentials of the story of the expansion of Christianity to A.D. 1945 have been covered in the volumes to which our narrative has stretched. They stand, even though the inferences we may here seek to draw from them be later modified by the event or even be proved to be in error. No one, however, unless he be quite heedless, can have followed the narrative from its inception to the point where we have been compelled to pause without asking the questions which we have here formulated. Even though he may feel constrained to challenge them, he has the right to hear the answers which have framed themselves in the author's mind. We have suggested that they are the conclusion of the whole matter. In a certain sense they cannot be that, for, if we are right in the prophecy that the story has only begun, by far the larger part of "the whole matter" is still ahead in the history which is still to be made. They may, however, have some value, even though subject to later review.

The kind of Christianity which spread varied from age to age and from region to region. No one branch was responsible for all the expansion of the faith. The strain apparently chiefly accountable in the first two centuries was that connected with the name of Paul, but Gnostics obviously had a large part, and even the Ebionites had a share. From the third through the eighteenth century, what we think of as Catholic Christianity bore the major load, either in its western or Latin form (the Roman Catholic Church) or in its eastern section (the Greek Orthodox Church). Yet the Goths and the Vandals were originally mainly the converts of Arian Christianity, Jacobites had extensive missions in the Nile valley, Ethiopia, and Western Asia, and Nestorians planted Christian communities across almost the entire breadth of Asia. In the seventeenth and eighteenth centuries Protestant Christianity in one or another of its forms began to be carried by migration or missions to areas which had not before known Christianity, and in the nineteenth and twentieth centuries it and Roman Catholic Christianity had the greatest expansion. Indeed, the former increased much more rapidly than did the latter.

Although the kinds of Christianity which spread were not always the same, the ones which had the largest continuing share were, as we said at the close of the last chapter, those which found their centre in Jesus and declared that in him God had once for all bridged the gulf between Himself and man, that he was fully man and yet that in him God was incarnated. Those, like the Gnostics, who minimized the historical Jesus or, like the Jacobites, exalted his divinity above his humanity, flourished for a time, but had no long continuing place in the expansion of the faith. Those who, like the Arians, tended to stress his humanity and to make him something less than of the very essence of the eternal God also had no persistent part in the spread of the faith. The more extreme representatives of this view, the Socinians and Unitarians, had scarcely even a fleeting share in the expansion. Precisely how far what came to be the majority view of Jesus was such because of this conviction we ought not here to attempt to say, for other factors entered to complicate the issue. However, the connexion was clearly more than a coincidence.

The reasons for the spread of Christianity were both varied and constant. Sometimes, as among the Saxons, along the Baltic, and in Mexico and Peru, conversion followed political conquest and was either required or encouraged by the conquerors. In some places, chiefly in Russia, the government offered such material inducements as lower taxes and freedom from military service to those who received baptism. In many areas Christianity came in association with what appeared to be a higher culture and was accepted along with other aspects of that civilization. Often a people whose inherited culture, including their religion, was disintegrating under the impact of a civilization of which Christianity seemed to be a part, turned to that faith for guidance and assurance in their spiritual uncertainty. Many accepted Christianity because they believed it more potent than their former cults to fulfil for them what they conceived to be the function of religion. In doing so they either imperfectly apprehended or completely failed to grasp the essential nature of Christianity. For instance, they regarded its rites as magic through which healing could be had for the diseases of their crops, their animals, or themselves. Only slowly if at all did the masses, led by some of their rarer, more sensitive spirits, comprehend the true genius of the faith.

Amid all this mixture of factors, however, there was one which was persistent. In Christianity was a vigour which impelled some of its choicest and most understanding exponents to go forth as missionaries and proclaim their faith by word and deed. Even where crass force was invoked to bring non-Christians to the baptismal font—and this was against the teaching of the Church—the actual instruction in the faith was by missionaries. The overwhelming majority of missionaries were from the minority who had committed themselves fully to Christ. Among Roman Catholics, Anglo-Catholics, and the Eastern churches they were usually members of monastic orders and congregations or of societies which in their spirit were in the monastic tradition. Although Protestants disavowed monasticism, most of their missionaries were those who had consecrated themselves as completely as had the others to what they believed to be the requirements of their faith. The Christian ideal was such that few if any fully attained it, but the missionaries were from those who had determined to give themselves to it. Here was a factor present in the expansion of Christianity on all its geographic and cultural frontiers.

Christianity did not always expand. It failed to take advantage of what appeared to be some of its greatest opportunities. Of this the Mongols in their broad conquests were an outstanding example. Sometimes its geographic boundaries contracted and it surrendered ground where it had advance stations or which it seemed safely to have won. Of this the disappearance of the widely extended outposts of Nestorian Christianity in Asia and the loss to Islam of approximately half of the littoral of the Mediterranean were conspicuous instances. In the nineteenth and twentieth centuries millions of European stock whose ancestors had been Christian were no longer of that faith.

The reasons for the losses, like those for the gains, were many. Overt persecution was seldom a major factor. The most famous of the official persecutions were those instituted by the authorities of the Roman Empire and those, less frankly anti-Christian, by National Socialism in Germany and the Communists in Russia. Yet none of these succeeded in obliterating the faith. Persecution was probably in part accountable for the elimination of Christianity in China in the ninth or tenth and in the fourteenth or fifteenth century. Here, however, another and probably more important factor was the disappearance, for other reasons, of the foreign enclaves which were the nuclei of the Christian communities in the first two eras of its presence in that empire. In the eighteenth century persecution contributed to the slow recession of Christianity in China. It drove Christianity underground in Japan from early in the seventeenth until the third quarter of the nineteenth century. Taken by itself, however, it seems seldom to have succeeded in erasing Christianity. The vast losses to Islam were not through prohibition of Christianity but were partly through social and economic disabilities from which Christians suffered in Moslem lands, partly because of the prestige which accrued to Islam through its political success, partly through the compulsory rearing as Moslems of some of the children of the Christians, and to no small degree because, while permitting conversion to Islam, apostasy from that faith was countered by death. The wastage of war seems to have been responsible for the demise of some of the Christian minorities which were once scattered across much of Asia. The defections in Europe and the Americas in the eighteenth, nineteenth, and twentieth centuries arose to some degree from a reasoned scepticism, but they were more from the secularism of the age and still more from vast shifts of population which carried millions away from their hereditary ecclesiastical connexions. In some ages the organized expressions of Christianity suffered from inner decay. This was often and perhaps usually because these had become sufficiently wealthy and politically influential to attract men who wished power or ease and captured them for their selfish ends.

It was clear that the nature of the faith did not ensure the persistence of Christianity among peoples who had once known it. It seemed also borne out by experience that open persecution was seldom if ever solely accountable for the elimination of the faith. Nor were the attacks of a scepticism which appealed to reason much if any more successful. The most dangerous foes were more subtle—the social or political prestige of a rival religion, slow attrition by weaning away the rising generations, a secularism which held that the most desirable goods of life were not those most esteemed by Christianity but were to be obtained in other ways than through that faith, and movements of population which took millions from environments in which the outward observances of the Church were a normal part of the social conventions.

We must here also note a striking power of renewal. Again and again when Christianity seemed moribund revivals broke out within it. This was not true in every region. In some areas it disappeared and had no recurrence. However, from every major period of general decline there came a resurgence which made Christianity more potent in the affairs of men than ever before. Almost always the first signs of the quickening became apparent while the ebb was still in process and in quite unexpected regions—some of them areas where great losses had been encountered. Thus the fresh advance after A.D. 950 was largely from Western Europe, where the faith had suffered from the centuries of invasions from the North and East. Pietism, early stirrings of the life which swelled to the great movements in nineteenth and twentieth century Protestantism, arose in Germany soon after that land had been wasted by the Thirty Years War. The Evangelical awakening and the great revivals in American Protestantism were in their incipient stages during the eighteenth century recession and when rationalism capped by the French Revolution appeared to be spelling the doom of Christianity. Christianity possessed amazing vitality.

The processes by which Christianity spread were no more uniform than were the reasons for its expansion and its recessions. Much was through the conversion of entire groups. This was the usual way in which religions had spread. Much was also through the conversion of individuals. Probably the latter was more prominent in the first two and in the nineteenth and twentieth centuries than in the intervening sixteen hundred years. A large proportion of the extension was with assistance from princes and the state. The support of the emperors in the fourth and fifth centuries facilitated the completion of the conversion of the Græco-Roman world. In Europe among people after people the espousal of Christianity by the king gave the needed impetus for the acceptance of the Christian name by his subjects. A similar phenomenon was seen in several of the Pacific islands in the nineteenth century. In more than one instance a king used the Church to extend or consolidate his power over nobles or rival chiefs. In the sixteenth, seventeenth, and eighteenth centuries most of the expansion of Christianity was under the direction and by the financial support of the absolute monarchies and the almost equally absolute chartered commercial companies of that era. The Spanish, Portuguese, and Russian monarchies and the Dutch East India Company were the outstanding examples.

Had it been only by these means that Christianity spread, very little vigour could have been anticipated in the resulting churches. Initiative by princes, mass compliance, and the direction of the state were alien to the genius of the faith. Indeed, in regions and among groups where these were most prominent, notably in Latin America and in the state church in the Netherlands East Indies, the Christianity so transmitted was distressingly anæmic. Moreover, some of the most palpable weaknesses of the Christianity of Europe, including the striking contradiction between the Christian profession of the region and the denial or ignoring of Christian standards in much of the collective and individual living of European peoples, stemmed from the processes by which the faith had first been accepted.

However, as we suggested a few paragraphs above, those who did the actual teaching of Christianity were they who in theory and very largely in practice had given themselves fully to the Christian faith. Beginning in the fourth century, most of the missionaries of all except the Protestant wing of the faith were either those who in one form or another had taken the monastic vows or who were members of fellowships, like the Société des Missions Étrangères of Paris which, while technically made up of secular priests, in their temper required the thoroughgoing commitment to Christ which were of the essence of monasticism. Although with somewhat different outward expressions, among them the absence of the vow to abstain from matrimony, Protestant missionaries were also from those who had given themselves unreservedly to the full requirements of the faith. In the nineteenth and twentieth centuries missionaries, both Roman Catholic and Protestant, were supported mainly not by subsidies from governments, but by the voluntarily offered gifts of millions of Christians through societies and other organizations which were dependent for their existence upon the religious convictions of their members. Probably never in Christian history and certainly not since the first three centuries had the propagation of the faith been the concern of so large a proportion of those who regarded themselves as Christians.

Since the essence of Christianity spreads best by contagion from spirits who have given themselves fully to it and experienced its power, the fact that the active missionaries, and, in the nineteenth and twentieth centuries, their supporters, were from this devoted core of the churches augured well for the vitality of the faith so transmitted.

Indeed, in the nineteenth and twentieth centuries in both the founding and the younger churches the trend was towards the status of a minority made up · of those consciously and fully devoted to the Christian way in a world which was antagonistic to much for which they stood. The tendency was one to which there were many exceptions. Moreover, Christians, while recognizing the contradiction between their ideals and the practice of mankind at large, insisted that the standards towards which they strove were of the very structure of the universe and sought to present them to all men, together with the power in the Christian Gospel to progress towards the seemingly unattainable. Yet the opposition remained.

As we come to the effects of Christianity, we must again remind ourselves that what from the standpoint of Christian faith are the most important escape the historian's art. The Christian declares that only a small segment of his life is lived within history and that the most significant fruitage is in the infinitely longer period beyond the grave and time. Even for that fragment spent within the dimensions of time the historian often encounters insuperable difficulty in devising and applying exact measurements.

It is clear that from the standpoint both of the Christian and of the historian the most important effects of Christianity are in human beings. The precise extent of the changes cannot be determined. We do know, however, that Christianity has issued in transformations in millions of lives in many ages, races, and climes. There has been within it attraction to the standards which it sets up and power for growth towards those ideals. The degree of attainment has varied with the individual. Often it has been inconsiderable. Often, however, it has been striking. Sometimes the transformation has been by almost imperceptible stages. At others it has been by dramatic conversion. Even an abrupt transition has been succeeded by long and usually gradual development. From its first century, Christian history has been marked by sudden changes from moral impotence and inner conflict to moral and spiritual power. Saul of Tarsus became Paul the Apostle. Augustine, from a brilliant but admittedly frustrated teacher of rhetoric, became one of the towering intellectual and moral figures of the Western world. From an unhappy, inwardly tormented monk, Luther was made over into one of the greatest religious leaders of Europe. Ignatius Loyola, a crippled soldier of no great importance, was transformed into the most potent single individual in bringing the needed new life into the Roman Catholic Church in the sixteenth century. From a strait-laced, rather humour-lacking Anglican priest, John Wesley grew to be the most contagious spirit of eighteenth century England. Through nineteenth and twentieth century missions thousands besotted with drink and drugs were led into victorious lives. These were spectacular. Less striking but not less characteristic were those reared as Christians who knew no sudden wrench from a downward to an upward path, but whose growth was by quiet decision and unheralded inner struggle. Nor are there full records of the millions who through their Christian faith faced family and personal tragedies and came through with lives made radiant. The historian can know of only a few of the millions who because of the Christian commitment have spent themselves unselfishly in the home and the community and for whom those about them were ever the richer.

We know that out of Christianity have come the Church in all its many branches and the liturgies, hymns, and forms of worship through which the churches have expressed their devotion and brought their members into transforming fellowship with the unseen. The historian has available hundreds of books for the guidance of the soul in the life of the spirit and other hundreds which record the experiences of the Christian mystics. These are clearly among the most potent effects of Christianity. We have said little of them in the course of our long narrative. Clearly, however, they are among the most significant of the results of Christianity.

It is, then, in the field of religion that the impact of Christianity has been the most marked. Christianity has become the most widely spread of all religions and has had effects, sometimes very striking, upon other religious systems. To those who have accepted it with honest hearts and minds it has given meaning to life, with a height and a depth which have been unique.

We have, and properly, had much to say of the effects of Christianity upon the collective life of communities, nations, and mankind as a whole. Here has been the most potent force which mankind has known for the dispelling of illiteracy, for the creation of schools, and for the emergence of new types of education. From Christianity have issued impulses for daring intellectual and geographic adventure. The universities, centres for pushing forward the boundaries of human knowledge, were at the outset largely Christian creations. Many of the most courageous of the explorers of the earth's surface were to no small degree impelled by the Christian faith. Music, architecture, painting, poetry, and philosophy have owed some of their greatest achievements to Christianity. Democracy as it was known in the nineteenth and twentieth centuries was in large part the outgrowth of Christian teaching. The abolition of Negro slavery was due chiefly to Christianity. So, too, were the measures taken to protect the Indians against the exploitation of the whites. The most hopeful movements for the regulation of war, for the mitigation of the sufferings entailed by war, and for the eventual abolition of war owed their inception chiefly to the Christian faith. The nursing profession of the nineteenth century had the same origin and the extension of Western methods of surgery and medicine to much of the non-Occidental world in that and the twentieth century was chiefly through the Christian missionary enterprise. The elevation of the status of women owed an incalculable debt to Christianity. Christian ideals made for monogamy and for a special kind of family life. No other single force has been so widely potent for the relief of suffering brought by famine and for the creation of hospitals and orphanages.

Christianity was an important creative factor in many cultures. This was most prominently seen in those of European peoples. It was also witnessed among several non-European peoples as they passed through the revolution of the nineteenth and twentieth century impact of the Occident. Through Christianity some of the peoples of the islands of the Pacific found reintegration and the faith was obviously a constituent of the cultures which were beginning to emerge in China and Africa. There was that in Christianity which was disturbing to cultures. None under its influence could long remain static. It also assisted in the successive stages of the cultural development which arose from its influence. It was both destructive and constructive. It could never be content with less than its ideal and it kept impelling those moved by it to the attainment of the impossible. Faith and hope characterized it as well as love.

Christianity was inevitably moulded by its environment. To some degree it reflected every culture, age, and social and political structure into which it moved. It bore the indelible impress of its Hebrew heritage and Jewish origin. This was seen in its basic beliefs about God, its ethics, its sacred writings, its forms of worship, and its organization. Its theology carried the mark of the philosophies of the Greeks. This was true not only during its formative centuries but throughout its later history. Augustine did not fully escape from his Platonic stage. Thomas Aquinas and numbers of other Christian schoolmen of the European Middle Ages thought through their conceptions of their faith in an atmosphere in which Aristotle was important. The sixteenth and even the twentieth century had their Christian Platonists. Down as far as our narrative has taken us the large majority of Christians were in churches whose organization reflected the administrative pattern of the empire in which the Church first developed, and the largest of the churches had its headquarters at Rome and incorporated many of the traditions of the state of which that city had been the capital and the symbol. The various national churches both shaped the peoples who held to them and were modified by them. For example, the Church of England moulded the English character and was moulded by it, and the Church of Scotland was in large degree both the creator and the creature of the Scottish spirit. Russia could not be understood apart from the Russian Orthodox Church and the latter was obviously to no small extent the product of Russian history. The Roman Catholic Church prided itself on its universality in time and space, but in each country or region it reflected its environment. Creedally and in its theoretical allegiance to the Pope it was the same, but its temper varied from land to land and from age to age. For instance, the Roman Catholicism of Latin America differed greatly from that of the United States, and in the nineteenth and twentieth centuries the Pope could make his will effective throughout the entire church to a much greater degree than in the preceding three centuries. Protestantism displayed even greater variations from nation to nation and from century to century. The churches, too, incorporated the class and racial divisions of their environment. In the United States denominations reproduced in part the economic and racial stratifications of society and the countries of origin of their constituencies.

However, in spite of the diversification brought by its environment, Christianity through all ages and lands preserved a remarkable continuity and family likeness. Those forms which conformed so much to the environment that they sacrificed this timeless and placeless identity died out with the passing of the age, the society, and the climate of opinion to which they had adjusted themselves. This was true of Gnosticism and Arianism and of many less widely popular variations. The central core of the uniqueness of Jesus, of fidelity to his birth, life, teachings, death, and resurrection as events in history, and of belief in God's working through him for the revelation of Himself and the redemption of man proved essential to continuing life. It was no accident that the religion which arose from Jesus was called Christianity and his followers Christians. In the designation, the Christ, which implied his humanity and his divinity, was the symbol of the secret of the persistent life and growing power of the faith. Not always was loyalty to him a warrant of life. Many groups which had it died out. However, only those who cherished that loyalty continued through the centuries.

We must now address ourselves to the problem of the future of Christianity.

Is Christianity a passing phase of the history of mankind? In the preceding chapter we saw that religions tend to display a cycle of birth, rapid growth marked by vigorous new movements and geographic expansion, the slowing down of expansion and of the emergence of fresh offshoots, and eventual decay. The cycle may cover millenniums and the final demise may be long delayed. A faith may, indeed, persist almost indefinitely because of its association with a given people or culture and send forth an occasional new shoot even after geographic extension has all but ceased and hope of becoming universal has died. That seems to be true of Hinduism and Islam. Yet even for them the course appears to be downward. Is Christianity foredoomed to conform to that pattern? Or is it, on the contrary, to continue to spread, to be ever more potent in the affairs of men, and eventually to bring all men and all of human society to its standards? May there be still another possibility? May not Christianity continue to spread and to increase in its influence upon mankind as a whole but never bring all of the human race into full conformity? May not the wheat and the tares both grow, possibly for thousands, perhaps only for hundreds or scores of years, until some cosmic event brings a sudden interruption and the end of history? That seems to have been the expectation of at least some of the New Testament writers. Any answer involves prophecy and prophecies are notoriously fallible: "Whether there be prophecies they shall fail." Yet on the basis of the record on so much of the scroll of history as has thus far been unrolled we may venture a guess which may not be entirely disproved by the event. The details we cannot hope to know. Even the main outlines may be inscrutable. The ability to forecast the future accurately in all its phases implies a determinism which is contradicted by the element of free will which, no matter how circumscribed, seems to be present in human affairs. Yet we can know trends thus far apparent. We can also know the characteristics of Christianity. On the basis of these facts the role of prophet may not be entirely incompatible with that of the historian.

The record of as much of the course of Christianity as has thus far become history seems to presage a continued expansion in the area covered and in the effect upon human-kind as a whole. Christianity has now been present for over nineteen centuries and through its Hebrew rootage, which Christians have claimed as an integral part of the process of which Jesus was the culmination, it is approximately two thousand years older. It is thus among the most ancient of the religions of mankind. Yet, in contrast with these others, all of which, even the youngest, Islam, have slowed down in a fashion which gives no promise of marked revival, in the past hundred and fifty years Christianity has had its greatest geographic extension and its widest influence upon mankind.

Throughout its history it has gone forward by major pulsations. Each advance has carried it further than the one before it. Of the alternating recessions, each has been briefer and less marked than the one which preceded it. This has been the case by whichever of the criteria the advance and recession have been measured—geographic extent, the new movements issuing from Christianity, or the influence upon the human race.

In the area covered, the progress is fairly obvious. Never had any faith been so rooted among so many peoples as was Christianity in A.D. 1944. It was still in part tied to a particular culture, as had been all other religions, but it was more nearly emancipated from that exclusive association than it or any other religion had even been.

Vitality as measured by the new movements issuing from the faith is more difficult to establish, partly because it is not easy to count the innovations but more because no statistical enumeration would suffice. One would need to know the relative significance of the items listed. If one gauges them by the degree to which the entire body of Christians was affected and by progress towards standards set up in the New Testament, the same scale of advance also probably holds true. In no age were those who bore the name Christian collectively worthy of that name. In the processes of mass conversion by which the majority had assumed that designation the degree of change wrought initially was usually slight. The bringing of even the conception of the nature and function of religion into accord with that seen in the life, teachings, and death of Jesus and in the greatest of his early disciples was only slowly and imperfectly accomplished. In A.D. 1944 it was far from being attained. Yet it was then more nearly approached by larger numbers of people and possibly by a higher proportion of professing Christians than in any other age. Certainly the trend was in that direction. It was a concomitant of the tendency we have repeatedly noted in the nineteenth and twentieth centuries to sharpen the distinction between Christians and the world about them and to place greater emphasis upon a thoroughgoing commitment to the Christian faith and its demands upon the great rank and file of Christians.

In the effect upon the environment the very fact of the progressively wider extension of Christianity made for an increasing influence. Certainly in A.D. 1944 Christianity was affecting more deeply more different nations and cultures than ever before. If its influence had declined in some, it had begun or increased in others, and the latter outnumbered the former.

In some aspects of the life of the race the effect of Christianity had demonstrably increased through the centuries. Fairly obviously this was true in the area of religion. The geographically broadening impact of Christianity in itself brought this about. Late in the nineteenth and in the twentieth century almost no people or cult remained untouched by the Christian faith. Some cults were unable to stand under the joint impact of Occidental civilization and Christianity and disintegrated. Segments in a few religions responded with movements inspired by the purpose of countering the Christian advance or of taking over and adapting some of the methods of the churches. The Arya Samaj was an example of the one, and some of the new methods of Japanese Buddhism were illustrations of the other. Numbers of movements arose which were compounded of pre-Christian and Christian impulses. Of these the T'ai P'ings in China in the mid-nineteenth century and some of the African prophets of the post-1914 years were outstanding examples. Certainly in A.D. 1944 Christianity was moulding the religious life of mankind as never before.

In education and the intellectual life of man the effect of Christianity was more widely extended in the twentieth century than in any earlier era. This was seen in the reduction of languages to writing, in the creation of the beginnings of literatures in these tongues, in efforts to teach the illiterate masses to read, especially in China, in pioneering in new methods of education in various lands, and in introducing schools of a Western type among non-Occidental peoples in every continent. By A.D. 1944 the state was beginning to take over more of the burden and the direction of the systems of schools inaugurated by the churches, but the latter had led the way. Back of all the efforts towards literacy and education was something more than the desire to equip all men with some of the technique of civilization. There was even more a respect for human personality and the longing to see it develop which arose from the value attached by the Christian faith to every individual as a potential child of the God and Father of Jesus Christ. Since from the standpoint of Christian faith all those who had entered upon the new life made possible through God in Jesus were heirs of God and joint heirs with Christ, earnest Christians wished to have men, women, and children here and now enter some of that heritage and regarded education, rightly conceived and ordered, as a means towards that end.

It was this value placed upon human beings which was largely accountable for the increasing success of Christianity in opposing the selfish exploitation of man by man. In the first five centuries Christianity lightened the lot of many slaves within the Roman Empire and was one of the forces making for the reduction of the prevalence of slavery in that part of the earth. In the succeeding thousand years voices of individual Christians were raised against the wholesale cruelties of conquest, and there were many efforts to better the condition of the poor. In lands in Europe which called themselves Christian the conviction was widespread that Christ was on the side of the poor and the oppressed against the rich and the powerful who ground them down. Much more extensive and better organized were the efforts inspired by the Christian conscience in the sixteenth, seventeenth, and eighteenth centuries to mitigate and if possible eliminate the cruelties and the heartless forced labour which attended the conquests, chiefly in the Americas, of non-European peoples by Europeans. Even more widespread and effective were the measures in the nineteenth and twentieth centuries arising from the Christian conscience and inspired by Christian faith to deal with the impact of Europeans upon non-Europeans. The most spectacular of these attempts was the successful campaign against the African slave trade and Negro slavery. There were also other movements to protect folk of primitive culture in many different parts of the world. The insistence that the colonial rule of the white governments should have as their goal the welfare and the eventual autonomy of the subject peoples which achieved prominence and effectiveness in the latter part of the nineteenth and in the twentieth century was mainly from Christian sources. In counteracting man's inhumanity to man Christianity was a growing force.

In political ideals and in government Christianity's effect was mounting. For centuries Christians largely acquiesced in the forms of government under which they lived and even accorded to them the support of divine sanction. With the seventeenth century, however, democracy began to emerge. Some of it went back to Stoic theory, but Christianity, and especially the radical forms of Protestant Christianity, by emphasizing the worth of the individual and both his dignity and his responsibility, made the major contribution. The extensive development and spread of democracy in the nineteenth and twentieth centuries greatly increased that particular effect of Christianity. This is not to say that democracy and Christianity were inseparable. Clearly they were not. Many Christians supported undemocratic states and in democracy was much of un-Christian selfish individualism. Yet through its contribution to democracy Christianity's influence was growing. Moreover, in its influence upon such Chinese leaders as Sun Yat-sen and Chiang Kai-shek and, to a less extent, upon Gandhi, Christianity was placing its impress upon the political features of Chinese and Indian life and was extending the range of its political impact outside the Occident.

It may seem strange and a palpable disregard of the facts to declare that Christianity was increasingly effective in the relations between nations. Had not Europe, the continent of its longest continuing influence, been chronically racked by war? Had not the twentieth century witnessed the two most extensive wars, both centred in so-called Christendom? Yet by a strange paradox that statement was precisely true. In the paradox, moreover, was much food for thought. In the first centuries of the faith many Christians held that their faith and participation in war were incompatible. That, indeed, was their majority opinion. Yet their attitude did not affect the policies of the Roman Empire. Christians were a seemingly inconsequential minority and were from elements in the population from which came few recruits for the legions. Besides, there were no Christians in most of the other great contemporary realms and the policies of the latter were even more unaffected by the faith. Beginning with Constantine, Christians largely acquiesced in the foreign policies of the Roman Empire. When, as that empire waned, war became the accustomed profession of the aristocracy of the successor states and principalities into which Western Europe disintegrated, the Christian conscience impelled an occasional voice to speak out in criticism of some particularly outrageous act in war. In time, as the Middle Ages proceeded, that Christian conscience began to find collective voice and to seek to regulate war through the Peace of God, the Truce of God, and the canons of chivalry. Popes, too, attempted to apply Christian principles to the relations between princes. Yet, while some progress was made, the Christian portions of Europe counted for little in the total world scene—much less than had the Roman Empire in its prime. As the modern age came on and divided Europe imperfectly coalesced into nation states ruled by absolute and ambitious monarchs, wars continued to be chronic and were on a larger scale. Its professed faith had not cured Europe of its inherited pre-Christian barbarism. Now, however, the Christian conscience sought to formulate and win acceptance for a law of nations to regulate the relations between the states and to put some bounds to war. For precedent appeal was made to principles of pre-Christian Græco-Roman pagan philosophy and for forms recourse was had to Roman law, but the faith and the determination which first sought to apply them to the international relations of "Christian" Europe were those of spirits quickened and sustained by Christianity. In the nineteenth century, when by what later seemed an historical accident Europe was given a near century of freedom from a general war, proposals multiplied for the substitution of peaceful law, compromise, and arbitration for the arbitrament of war. Peace societies became numerous. At their inception most of such devices and organizations were sprung from the vision and the faith of earnest Christian souls. So, too, the League of Nations, the World Court, and all the associated machinery by which men hopefully attempted to secure peace after the spasm of the first of the world wars, had their original source and their initial chief backers from the same spring of idealism. Futile though these seemed to be in the catastrophe of the second of the world wars, Christian faith, undaunted, strove to build better. Only now, in the twentieth century, that faith was compelled, by the shrinking of the globe, to think and act in planetary terms. No longer could peace machinery be regional and limited to "Christendom." It must be universal. In China and India as well as in the Occident Christians, some of them in high position, were seeking to place the relations between nations on the basis of a moral law which they believed to be of the structure of the universe and identical with the Christian ethic. Christianity had not yet subdued to itself the realm of world politics and world economics. Far from it. But more widely than ever before it was felt in these phases of the affairs of men. As the dangers of war to world-wide civilization became more urgent, from within Christianity more than from any other source there issued the faith and the will to find some other means than war to ease the frictions between peoples and states and to achieve just as well as lasting peace.

It was clear that if righteous and enduring peace were to be obtained, it must be on the basis of moral principles generally accepted by the rank and file of mankind. Because of the nature of its principles, of the hope, the unselfish devotion, and the resolution which it inspired, and of its world-wide spread Christianity seemed the most likely source of this indispensable common ethos. Now, moreover, Christians were drawing together in a world-wide fellowship. This was, in A.D. 1944, only in its inception. Many deep divisions still rent the seamless robe of Christ. Yet amazing progress was being made towards that fellowship. It was, too, not within a pre-existing structure of political and cultural unity such as that within which the Catholic Church of the Roman Empire had been formed centuries ago. It was ahead of that unity, possibly foreshadowing it and laying for it the necessary foundations.

With the background of this summary, all of it a repetition of what we have previously said, we recur to the question: what hope is there that Christianity will ultimately bring the entire human race to its standards? Is there warrant in history for confidence in the dogma of progress, so fondly cherished by many in the nineteenth century? Is mankind, perhaps by painful and slow stages, but still surely, to attain within the historic process collective and individual perfection as defined by Jesus?

It may well be that in the course of the centuries Christianity will become the professed faith of all mankind. If this comes, presumably it will be only after a vast reach of time. In A.D. 1944 such major non-Christian religions as Islam, Hinduism, and Buddhism, while long comparatively static, were substantially intact. Moreover, in what had been termed Christendom millions had openly or tacitly abandoned the faith of their fathers and unfriendly political systems made difficult the work of the Church. The outlook was bright for the continued growth of Christianity. The great non-Christian systems were subject to the corrosion of the same acids of modernity and secularism which Christianity had known but were without the record of survival and added vigour which past experience had shown the latter to display as one age and culture with which it had been associated gave way to another. It may well be that in the twentieth century some such conflict among religions and philosophies has been in process on a global scale as the Græco-Roman world saw in its limited portion of the earth's surface in the first five centuries of the Christian era and that out of it as from the earlier struggle Christianity will emerge triumphant. However, progress, even in numerical extension, will presumably be measured in centuries and possibly millenniums rather than decades.

A basis for hope for the continued growth of the influence of Christianity upon mankind is to be found not only in the past record but also in the nature of the faith. In the Sermon on the Mount and elsewhere the New Testament sets before men standards which are at once alluring and impossible of full attainment within the bounds of time. Yet Christianity is far more than a set of ethical principles. The name given it in the New Testament is not Christianity but Gospel, Good News. It proclaims its standards as the demand of God upon men, but with this demand it couples, inseparably, the assurance of power to progress towards them. Because of these qualities, which are of the very essence of the faith, Christianity contains the dynamic for continuing growth. It can never be fully at home in any culture or age, and none can ever be fully conformed to it. So long as time lasts it will always be a disturbing element, luring men onward by the goal of better ends and inspiring the confidence that progress can be made towards the ideal. It is no accident that so many cultures with which Christianity has been intimately connected have passed and that Christianity has displayed a phenomenal capacity not only for survival but also for moulding the new. It has not been the only cause of the demise of the old nor the only factor in the creation of the new, but by its nature it has contributed to both. Presumably this will continue to be the record of Christianity. The natural expectation is that as one stage of civilization succeeds another Christianity will have a part in the destruction of each and in inspiring and shaping its successor and that in each new age it will be more potent than in what was being displaced.

Yet two facts forbid the confident expectation that eventually, in the slow

processes of history, all men on the planet will be brought into full conformity to the Christian pattern.

One is in the very essence of that pattern. It is forever beckoning man on and
appealing to him as both a duty placed on him by his nature and as a hope,
yet it is unattainable within time. Within the span of history none, not even
the greatest of Christian saints, can expect to be perfect as God is perfect or to
be filled unto all the fullness of God. Through the power inherent in the
Gospel outstanding Christians can achieve such progress towards it as to be
the inspiration and the despair of their fellows. Yet each forward step makes
them more conscious of the distance between themselves and the ideal set
in Christ. If that is true of the choicest human spirits, how much more is it
true of the rank and file of men and of society as a whole!

Moreover, the historical record reveals the fact that in lands longest under
strong Christian influence not only has striking advance been registered towards the Christian ideal, but also some of the chronic sins of mankind have
swelled to gigantic proportions. This was true of chattel slavery. It has also
been true of war. Christianity has within it curative forces which sooner
or later have operated against these evils more effectively than any other known
to man. However, when one evil has been eliminated another has emerged.
Thus after the Christian conscience had abolished Negro slavery, it found
itself confronted in the United States and South Africa with other phases of
the race issue, in some respects rendered more acute by emancipation, in the
West Indies by a problem of poverty and illegitimacy, and in the United
States by a faulty method of tenancy, the aftermath of the plantation system
under slavery, which has borne with heart-breaking weight upon the masses
of the rural population, both black and white, in areas where slavery was most
prevalent. Emancipation was not the cause of these problems. They had been
present, the fruit of the slave system, but emancipation did not at once solve
them.

A Christian conviction, deeply imbedded in the New Testament and held
with varying degrees of emphasis in the later centuries, is not surprised by
these phenomena. It expects evil and good to go on together throughout the
span with which historians concern themselves and it maintains that sooner or
later the historical process will be terminated by the act of God. God's will is
to be done fully in a new society, but that is to be beyond the realms of time.
Obviously the historian can neither confirm nor deny the validity of that expectation, for its fulfilment is outside the areas with which he deals. In his
capacity as a Christian he may affirm his accord with that faith, but in a land

where avowedly time is to be no more his historical equipment cannot be employed.

All this does not indicate that the historian sees the human process as static or going by cycles which forever and with discouraging monotony repeat themselves. It does not mean that Christianity teaches that for the consummation of the hopes which it arouses men must wait entirely for a world beyond history. Within the bounds of time and space, so experience has shown, the Christian Gospel is potent in shaping men's lives, in building in both individuals and society character of the kind which it envisages, and in reducing and even eliminating many of the evils which beset man's rough road. It does mean, however, that the Christian ideal and the historical process are each such that perfection, as the Christian judges perfection, will not be attained within time. Yet here is no futility within history. Here is no downing of one giant to have two more take his place. Within history struggle continues, but those whom the Christian recognizes as saints emerge in more and more peoples and increasingly human civilization displays the fruitage of the Christian faith in transformed lives, in growing value upon human personality as seen in the light of the Christian dream, and in social institutions which further the realization of that dream.

There remains the final question: What light does the story we have surveyed shed upon the nature of man, the nature of the universe in which man finds himself, and the fashion in which the universe deals with man?

Here more than elsewhere we must be brief. That is partly because we must content ourselves with affirmations. The affirmations find support in the history which we have recounted but some of the most important of them cannot be fully validated by it. To no small degree they are statements of faith, the faith of the historian who has penned these pages, and, he believes, in its essentials, that of the majority of thoughtful Christians through the centuries.

Man finds himself in a universe in which he is restless. He is not content to accept it without reflection. He does not fully understand it. He is not entirely happy in it nor completely adjusted to it.

Within himself man finds conflicting trends. He is a civil war. On the one hand he is capable of great cruelty to his fellows and to other living beings. He is filthy, disorderly, the victim of his physical appetites, stupid, self-assertive, self-centred. Yet he is never content with himself in these roles. He feels that in them he has sunk lower than the beasts. He believes that he is called to self-forgetfulness, self-control, kindness, love, joy, and an inner peace in which the struggle is resolved in the victory of his higher qualities. He is stirred by an impulse to reverence and worship. When he sees these qualities in one of his fellows he may affect to scorn them and he may be so angered that he seeks to do away with the one who embodies them, but his conscience is troubled by them. His very wrath is evidence that he is disquieted.

It appears clear that the universe is against the degrading features of man's practice and that they are a sin against it. The universe permits them—why man does not know, although he has long wrestled with the problem. Yet the universe is such that "the wages of sin are death." The evil features in himself with which man contends will, if they are not held in leash, destroy, physically and spiritually, both the individual and human society.

Man seeks a meaning for himself, the universe, and the paradox which he senses within himself. There is that which compels him to continue the struggle and not to succumb to the hostile elements in his environment or to what he is persuaded are temptations to baseness and degradation. Always the warfare is on, but, except for a few thoroughgoing sceptics who for a time may convince some of their fellows, the trend in mankind is not to surrender. Man bows in awe and even in terror before the world about him, but in general he believes that it is a universe, orderly, and not confused anarchy, and that he can win through to enough understanding of it to maintain himself in it. He feels insecure and uncertain but, even though dimly, he believes that the inner conflict can be so waged that the higher impulses in himself will triumph and that he can accomplish enough of control of his environment or establish a sufficient accord with it to bring to him and his fellows a degree of security, happiness, and peace.

From the effort various systems arise, some of them philosophies, some religions, some political and economic patterns, and almost all of them a mixture of all these elements. Among them are those which the men who hold to them claim to be the achievements of themselves and their fellows, unaided by the universe. The latter, they declare, is indifferent to their fate. Others are conceived by their adherents as being solely from the initiative of the universe or of Him who governs it, with man as a passive recipient. Still others are regarded as the result of effort from both directions, of the universe stimulating man to undertake and persevere in his quest, and of man, responding, beginning and pursuing the quest. All such systems, if they win many followers and persist, have in them elements of profound conviction and dogmatism. They may inculcate tolerance, but even the tolerance is itself conviction and, in its way, dogmatism.

Numerous though these systems are, and although many men, weary of the debate and the variety, become agnostic as to the possibility of determining the relative truth or falsity of each, yet mankind as a whole will not abandon the conviction that truth either has been revealed or discovered or can be attained and that man can either find salvation in his age-long struggle or make progress towards it. Fully to yield to agnosticism or to despair would mean death, for both the individual and the race. Presumably there is that in the universe which impels man to maintain the fight and persuades him that life can be worth living.

In this world of men, with its aspirations and its struggles and its many philosophies and religions, there appeared one, born of woman and in the stream of one of these traditions. To most of such of his contemporaries as knew him he seemed a failure. His brief public career was terminated by an apparently futile death. His followers, unorganized, except for a small, informal inner circle of close friends, included few whom the nation or the world counted influential. One of the inner circle betrayed him.

Yet no life ever lived on this planet has been so influential in the affairs of men. From it has grown the most nearly universal fellowship, the Christian Church, that man has known. That Church is to be found among almost all tribes and peoples, on all the continents, and on the large majority of the islands of the sea, even some of the most lonely and remote. In A.D. 1944 it was more widely spread and more deeply rooted among more peoples than at any earlier time. Although divided into many branches, in A.D. 1944 it seemed to be drawing together as never before. As its members met in the central and crowning service of Christian worship which reproduced in its symbolism the once presumably futile and needless sacrifice of its Lord's death, they could know that that very day millions from all but a few remote and small tribes and tongues had gathered or were to gather in similar fashion, although under differing rites, and that they were part of a growing company whom no man could number who across more than nineteen centuries had also been gathering because of that same sacrifice.

From that brief life and its apparent frustration has flowed a more powerful force for the triumphal waging of man's long battle than any other ever known by the human race. Through it millions have had their inner conflicts resolved in progressive victory over their baser impulses. By it millions have been sustained in the greatest tragedies of life and have come through radiant. Through it hundreds of millions have been lifted from illiteracy and ignorance and have been placed upon the road of growing intellectual freedom and of control over their physical environment. It has done more to allay the physical ills of disease and famine than any other impulse known to man. It has emancipated millions from chattel slavery and millions of others from thraldom to vice. It has protected tens of millions from exploitation by their fellows. It has been the most fruitful source of movements to lessen the horrors of war and to put the relations of men and nations on the basis of justice and peace.

Seldom if ever has the triumph been clear cut and complete. The greatest saints are aware that they have not fully attained. The Church is divided by jealousies and strife. In its great forward surges the faith has been closely associated with movements in economics, statecraft, and international, inter-racial, and inter-class contention which are contrary to its aspirations. Again and again, even within the Church itself, the elements appear dominant which bound Jesus to his cross and he seems crucified afresh. Some of the hereditary evils of the race attain their most colossal dimensions among the peoples and cultures in which the faith which stemmed from Jesus has been longest represented. Always the faith seems dying, yet it lives. Culture after culture with which the faith has been intimately associated has passed into history, seemingly to carry it also into oblivion. Yet the faith spreads ever more widely and moulds more and more peoples.

To millions who have been counted wise by their fellows and in their own eyes, the story of the cross has seemed foolishness. Yet never has Jesus been as widely potent in shaping history as in A.D. 1944, when in many ways he and what he stood for have appeared the most obviously defeated.

These are facts, some of them possibly debatable and most of them challenged, but still facts and within the realm with which the historian can deal.

On the basis of these facts—and others which have been recorded in these volumes and still others which there has been no space to include—the Christian boldly affirms his faith. He declares that in Jesus, so far as they concern man, the heart and the meaning of the universe are revealed. He builds his life upon the conviction that in Jesus he sees God. He holds that a universe which could produce Jesus must be as good as he, that Jesus is "very God of very God," that creating and controlling the universe, infilling it yet never fully contained in it, is One who, although He may be more, is at least personal in the sense in which Jesus is personal, and that His essence is seen in the teachings and life of Jesus. The Christian insists that in the birth, life, and death of Jesus is revealed the fashion in which God deals with man. Always, for some reason which no one yet completely understands, there is evil, and at times evil seems triumphant. Always, however, God is striving with men, partly by the pressure in judgment of inexorable law which He has decreed, but also partly by the power of His sacrificial love seen in Jesus and his cross. Man's freedom is far from complete, but God has given to man enough ability to choose to permit him to decide whether he will cast in his lot with or against His Christ.

It is of the very core of the Christian's faith that the God and Father of his Lord, Jesus Christ, will not be defeated. The Christian holds the resurrection of Jesus also to be fact. The life of Jesus, so he confidently maintains, did not end on the cross. Nor was it continued merely through the growing influence of Jesus, amazing though that has been. The Christian is bold to declare that through the resurrection Jesus entered into a fresh stage of life, glorified, endless, and inconceivably rich in love and power. He holds that in the resurrection God was working, bringing out of the evil of man's rejection of Jesus a good far greater than could have been possible without that defeat. The Christian affirms that through Jesus God makes possible for all who will receive Him a similar endless life of growing and glorified fellowship with Himself. He declares that through His spirit, the spirit which "proceedeth from the Father and the Son," God is even now in history. At times the Christian is staggered by the all too obvious and clamant evil in his own heart and in the world about him, but in what he believes to be his moments of clearest insight he is certain that God and His Christ will triumph. He knows that if not within the long span which men call history, itself but a moment against the background of sidereal time, then beyond history, God's purpose for man will be fully realized. Not always have God's thoughts been man's thoughts, nor God's ways man's ways. Yet God's word, so the Christian when he is most Christian knows, shall not return unto Him void but shall accomplish that which He pleases and prosper in the thing whereto He sent it.   .

The Christian is certain that Jesus is central in human history. His confident faith is that in those who give themselves to God as they see Him in Jesus there is working the power of endless life and that from them God will build, to be consummated beyond time, the heavenly city, the ideal community, in which will be realized fully the possibilities of the children of God. This eternal life and this ideal community are, in the last analysis, not the fruit of man's striving, but the gift of a love which man does not deserve, and are from the quite unmerited grace of God.

BIBLIOGRAPHY

As in the preceding four volumes, only those titles are listed in the bibliography which have been cited more than once in the footnotes. For those cited only once, and these are fully as many as the others, the necessary data are given with the citation.

Abel, Theodore, *Protestant Home Missions to Catholic Immigrants* (New York, Institute of Social and Religious Research, 1933, pp. xi, 143). Scholarly, careful, based largely upon field work.

Addison, James Thayer, *The Christian Approach to the Moslem. A Historical Study* (New York, Columbia University Press, 1942, pp. x, 365). Scholarly and readable.

Agrarian China. Selected Source Materials from Chinese Authors. Compiled and translated by the Research Staff of the Secretariat, Institute of Pacific Relations. With an Introduction by R. H. Tawney (University of Chicago Press, pp. xviii, 258).

Agricultural Mission Notes. Published Quarterly by the Agricultural Missions Foundation. Edited by John H. Reisner (New York, Jan. 1932 ff.).

Allen, Devere, *The Fight for Peace* (New York, The Macmillan Company, 1930, pp. xi, 740). In large part a history of the peace movement, especially in the United States, based upon laborious research in original sources. The author's bias, that of an earnest pacifist, is apparent.

Allen, Henry Elisha, *The Turkish Transformation. A Study in Social and Religious Development* (The University of Chicago Press, 1935, pp. ix, 251). Careful, sympathetic with Turkey.

Anderson, Paul B., *People, Church and State in Modern Russia* (New York, The Macmillan Company, 1944, pp. vii, 240). Valuable for its competent summary and for its extensive excerpts, translated, from documents.

Annals of the Propagation of the Faith (New York, Society for the Propagation of the Faith, 1838-1923. Then continued with *Catholic Missions* to form *Catholic Missions and Annals of the Propagation of the Faith*).

Anuario Católico Argentino 1932. Publicacion de la Junta Nacional de la Accion Católica Argentina (Buenos Aires, 1932, pp. 583).

Anuario Católico Argentino 1933. Publicacion de la Junta Nacional de la Accion Católica Argentina (Buenos Aires, 1933, pp. 737).

Arens, Bernard, *Handbuch der katholischen Missionen* (Freiburg im Breisgau, Herder & Co., 1920, pp. xix, 418).

Arens, Bernard, *Handbuch der katholischen Missionen* (Freiburg im Breisgau, Herder & Co., 1925, pp. xix, 510).

Asia (New York, 1901 ff.). A monthly magazine for a popular constituency.

Attwater, Donald, *The Catholic Eastern Churches* (Milwaukee, The Bruce Publishing Co., 1935, pp. xx, 308). By a Roman Catholic. Contains excellent bibliographies.

Australia Facing the Non-Christian World. Report of Australian Missionary Conference . . . April, 1926 (Melbourne, Alpha Printing Company, pp. 139).

Ayyar, Rao Bahadur L. K. Anantakrishna, *Anthropology of the Syrian Christians* (Ernakulam, Cochin Government Press, 1926, pp. xvii, 338). The author, among other posts, has held that of superintendent of ethnography in the Cochin state, and has been lecturer and reader on ethnography or anthropology at two Indian universities. Is often uncritical.

Badley, Brenton Thoburn, editor, *Indian Church Problems of Today* (Madras, Methodist Publishing House, 1930, pp. 311). The volume is by a number of authors, mostly if not all members of the Methodist Episcopal Church.

Ballou, Earle H., *Dangerous Opportunity* (New York, Friendship Press, 1940, pp. xi, 206). Well written, by a Protestant missionary of wide and long experience.

The Baptist (Chicago, 1920-1933). An official publication of the Northern Baptist Convention.

Barnett, Eugene E., *The Far East in the Summer of 1940* (Mimeographed, New York, 1940, pp. 145). By the general secretary of the International Committee of the Young Men's Christian Associations.

Barton, James L., *Story of Near East Relief (1915-1930), an Interpretation* (New York, The Macmillan Co., 1930, pp. xxii, 479). The official history of the enterprise. The author, a secretary of the American Board of Commissioners for Foreign Missions and an expert on the Near East, as Chairman of the Board of Trustees of Near East Relief throughout its history had intimate relations with the undertaking.

Bates, M. Searle, *Data on the Distribution of the Missionary Enterprise* (New York, International Missionary Council, 1943, pp. 15). A painstaking, comprehensive statistical study, with important comparative totals.

Beach, Harlan P., and Fahs, Charles H., *World Missionary Atlas* (New York, Institute of Social and Religious Research, 1925, pp. 251). The standard survey of Protestant missions of its time.

Beach, Harlan P., and St. John, Burton, editors, *World Statistics of Christian Missions* (New York, The Committee of Reference and Counsel of the Foreign Missions Conference of North America, 1916, pp. 148). Authoritative.

Becker, C., *Im Stromtal des Brahmaputra* (Munich, Salvator-Verlag, pp. xxix, 512). (Second edition, Aachen, Aachener Missionsdruckerei, A.-G. 1927, pp. xx, 584).

Berdyaev, Nicolas, *The Origin of Russian Communism*. Translated from the Russian by R. M. French (London, Geoffrey Bles, 1937, pp. 239). Strongly anti-Communist.

Berg, Ludwig, *Die katholische Heidenmission als Kulturträger* (Second edition, Aachen, Aachener Missionsdruckerei, 3 vols., 1927). Carefully supported by references to authorities, which as a rule are standard German experts and missionary periodicals. Warmly pro-Roman Catholic and critical of Protestants,

Binchy, D. A., *Church and State in Fascist Italy* (Oxford University Press, 1941, pp. ix, 774). Excellent. Carefully documented.

Bisbee, Royal D., *Adventures with Christ in Mystic India* (Madras, Methodist Publishing House, 1931, pp. xvi, 323). By an American Methodist missionary in India. The book recounts his experiences.

Blumit, Oswald A., *Sentenced to Siberia. The Story of the Ministry, Persecution, Imprisonment and God's Wonderful Deliverance of Pastor Basil Malof, "Apostle of Russia"* (Berne, Ind., Mayflower Press, 1940, pp. 201).

Bolshakoff, Serge, *The Christian Church and the Soviet State* (London, Society for Promoting Christian Knowledge, 1942, pp. ix, 75). A popularly written account.

Bolshakoff, Serge, *The Foreign Missions of the Russian Orthodox Church* (London, Society for Promoting Christian Knowledge, 1943, pp. 120). A good summary, but something of an *apologia*.

Bouniol, S. (editor), *The White Fathers and Their Missions* (London, Sands and Co., 1929, pp. 334). A popular account, not especially scholarly.

Braga, Erasmo, and Grubb, Kenneth G., *The Republic of Brazil. A Survey of the Religious Situation* (London and New York, World Dominion Press, 1932, pp. 184). Braga was executive secretary of the Committee on Co-operation in Brazil and probably the leading Protestant in the country. Grubb spent a good deal of time there to collect information.

Brian-Chaninov, Nicolas, *The Russian Church*. Translated from the French by A. B. Wells (New York, The Macmillan Company, 1930, pp. xi, 210). Scholarly, under a Roman Catholic imprimatur.

Brookes, Edgar H., *The Colour Problems of South Africa* (Lovedale Press, 1934, pp. viii, 237). A set of lectures at the University of Cape Town.

Brookes, Edgar H., *Native Education in South Africa* (Pretoria, J. L. van Schaik, Ltd., 1930, pp. 138). A small handbook based on standard books and reports.

Brown, William Adams, *A Teacher and His Times* (New York, Charles Scribner's Sons, 1940, pp. xiv, 391). An autobiography.

Browning, Webster E., Ritchie, John, and Grubb, Kenneth G., *The West Coast Republics of South America. Chile, Peru and Bolivia* (London, World Dominion Press, 1930, pp. vi, 183). An excellent survey, especially of Protestant missions. Browning was long a missionary in Chile, Ritchie long lived in Peru, and Grubb writes of Bolivia.

Brunner, Edmund de S., *Immigrant Farmers and Their Children* (Garden City, New York, Doubleday, Doran & Co., 1929, pp. xvii, 277). Carefully done.

Brunner, Edmund de S., Hughes, Gwendolyn S., and Patten, Marjorie, *American Agricultural Villages* (New York, George H. Doran Company, 1927, pp. 326).

Buck, Oscar MacMillan, *Christianity Tested. Its Significance for Modern Missions* (Cincinnati, The Abingdon Press, 1934, pp. 257). A statement of the contemporary missionary situation by an American professor of missions who knew India well and wrote largely from that viewpoint.

Burton, J. W., *Missionary Survey of the Pacific Islands* (London, World Dominion Press, 1930, pp. v, 124). The author was general secretary of the Methodist Missionary Society of Australasia.

Burton, Margaret E., compiler, *World Cooperation of the Young Women's Chris-

tian Associations of the United States of America. A Record of the Foreign Work of the American Associations, 1930-1935 (Multigraphed by the Y.W.C.A., Dec., 1935, pp. 91).

Butterfield, Kenyon L., *The Rural Mission of the Church in Eastern Asia. Report and Recommendations* (New York, The International Missionary Council, 1931, pp. 222). The author, formerly president of the Massachusetts Agricultural College and the Michigan Agricultural College, here reported on an extended trip made for the International Missionary Council.

Cable, Mildred, Houghton, F., Kilgour, R., McLeish, A., Sturt, R. W., and Wyon, Olive, *The Challenge of Central Asia. A Brief Survey of Tibet and its Borderlands, Mongolia, North-West Kansu, Chinese Turkistan, and Russian Central Asia* (London, World Dominion Press, 1929, pp. iv, 136).

Callcott, Wilfrid Hardy, *Liberalism in Mexico, 1857-1929* (Stanford University Press, 1931, pp. xiii, 410). A careful piece of work.

Camargo, G. Baez, and Grubb, Kenneth G., *Religion in the Republic of Mexico* (London, World Dominion Press, 1935, pp. 166). Pro-Protestant.

Le Canada Ecclésiastique. Annuaire du Clergé Rédigé par L.-J.-A. Derome. Pour l'Année 1921. Trente-Cinquième Année (Montreal, Librairie Beauchemin, 1921, pp. xxx, 533).

Le Canada Ecclésiastique. Annuaire du Clergé. Fondé par feu L.-J.-A. Derome. Pour l'Année 1932. Quarante-Sixième Année (Montreal, Librairie Beauchemin, 1932, pp. 963).

The Capuchin Mission Unit (C.S.M.C.), Cumberland, Maryland, *India and Its Missions* (New York, The Macmillan Co., 1923, pp. xxi, 315). Prepared over a period of four years of study by the theological students of the Capuchin monastery of SS. Peter and Paul, Cumberland, Md. A fairly careful piece of work, usually based upon excellent authorities.

Capuchins Missionnaires. Missions Françaises. Notes Historiques et Statistiques (Paris, Société et Librairie Coopératives St. François, 1926, pp. iv, 86). No author given. A popular summary.

Carson, Arthur L., *Agricultural Missions, A Study Based upon the Experience of 236 Missionaries and Other Rural Workers* (New York, Institute of Social and Religious Research, 1933, pp. 110). A condensed form of a thesis presented to the Graduate School of Cornell University.

The Catholic Church in Korea (Hongkong, Imprimerie de la Société des Missions-Étrangères, 1924, pp. 108).

Catholic Directory of India, 1918. 68th Annual Issue of the Madras Catholic Directory and Annual General Register (Madras, The Catholic Supply Society, pp. 579).

Catholic Directory of India, Ceylon and Burma. 76th Annual Issue, 1926 (Madras, The Madras Catholic Supply Co., pp. 554).

Catholic Directory of India, Burma and Ceylon. 81st Annual Issue, 1931 (Madras, The "Good Pastor" Press, 1931, pp. ii, 434).

The Catholic Encyclopedia (New York, 16 vols., 1907-1913). Written for informative and apologetic purposes.

The Catholic Laymen's Directory of India, 1933 (Mangalore, C. J. Varkey, Secretary All-India Catholic League, 1933, pp. xvi, 512).

The China Christian Year Book (Shanghai, Christian Literature Society, 1926, 1928, 1929, 1931, 1934, 1935, 1937, 1939). Successor to *The China Mission Year Book*.

The China Critic (Shanghai, 1928-1940).

The China Fundamentalist (Published by the Christian Fundamentals League for China, Shanghai, 1928 ff.).

The China Mission Year Book (Shanghai, Christian Literature Society, 1910-1919, 1923-1925). A Protestant publication.

The China Quarterly (Shanghai, 1935 ff.).

The Chinese Christian Student (New York, The Chinese Students' Christian Association in North America, 1909 ff.).

The Chinese Recorder (Published at Foochow, 1867, as *The Missionary Recorder*, at Foochow, 1868-1872, as *The Chinese Recorder and Missionary Journal,* and at Shanghai 1874-1941. Beginning about 1911 the title was shortened to *The Chinese Recorder*). The standard interdenominational Protestant missionary journal of China.

Chirgwin, A. M., *An African Pilgrimage* (London, Student Christian Movement Press, 1932, pp. 158). An enthusiastic account of a tour in 1930 among stations of the London Missionary Society.

Chirgwin, A. M., *Wayfaring for Christ* (London, Edinburgh House Press, 1932, pp. 160). The author, a secretary of the London Missionary Society, drew some of his material from an extended visit to the stations of his society in Africa and Madagascar.

Christ and Students of the East. The Report of the Java Conference of the World's Student Christian Federation, Tjiteureup, Java, September 6-14, 1933 (pp. 140).

Christendom. A Quarterly Review (Chicago, later New York, 1935 ff.).

The Christian Century (Chicago, 1894 ff.).

The Christian College in India. The Report of the Commission on Christian Higher Education in India (Oxford University Press, 1931, pp. xiii, 388). The Commission was constituted by the International Missionary Council, was headed by A. D. Lindsay, and visited India in 1930-1931.

Christian Education in Japan. A Study. Being the Report of a Commission on Christian Education in Japan Representing the National Christian Council of Japan, the National Christian Education Association of Japan, the Foreign Missions Conference of North America and the International Missionary Council (New York, The International Missionary Council, 1932, pp. xi, 247).

The Christian Family (Techny, Ill., The Mission Press, 1906 ff.). Beginning in 1931, *The Christian Family and Our Missions*. An organ of the American province of the Society of the Divine Word.

The Christian Herald (New York, 1878 ff.).

The Christian Movement in Japan (Yokohama, 1903-1904, Tokyo, various publishers, 1905-1940). Varying titles. See under *The Japan Christian Year Book*.

The Christian News-Letter. Edited by J. H. Oldham (London, 1939 ff.).

Christian Work in Latin America (New York, The Missionary Education Movement, 3 vols., 1917). (Back title, *Panama Congress, 1916*).

Christian World Facts (New York, Foreign Missions Conference of North America, 1920 ff.). An annual publication.

Christianity and Crisis. A Bi-Weekly Journal of Christian Opinion (New York, 1941 ff.).

Christlieb, M[arie] L[ouise], *Indian Neighbours* (London, Student Christian Movement Press, 1930, pp. 96). All the occurrences narrated happened in one part of an Indian district. They are all facts—although names of places and persons have been changed and the name of the missionary is not given.

The Church Missionary Review (London, Church Missionary Society, 1850-1927). Begun as *The Church Missionary Intelligencer*.

[Back title] *C.M.S. Mass Movement Survey, India 1927*. Six pamphlet studies of as many different areas are bound in this volume.

Cinquant' Anni a Mangalore sulla Costa Occidentale dell' India (1878-1928) (Venice, "Le Missioni della Compagnia di Gesù," 1929, pp. 96).

Clark, Charles Allen, *The Korean Church and the Nevius Methods* (New York, Fleming H. Revell Co., 1930, pp. 278). A doctoral dissertation by a Presbyterian missionary who had lived in Korea for the preceding twenty-seven years. The study is confined to the Presbyterian church in Korea.

Clark, Edward M., *The Other Half of Japan: a Rural Perspective* (Harrisburg, The Evangelical Press, 1934, pp. 220). By a missionary in Japan.

Clarke, Henry Lowther, *Constitutional Church Government in the Dominions Beyond the Seas and in Other Parts of the Anglican Communion* (London, S.P.C.K., 1924, pp. xvi, 543). Containing a large number of documents; by a former Archbishop of Melbourne.

Clayton, E. H., *Heaven Below* (New York, Prentice-Hall, Inc., 1944, pp. v, 282). A vivid autobiographical account by a missionary of life in Hangchow, especially in the 1920's, 1930's, and 1940's.

Clinchy, Everett R., *All in the Name of God* (New York, The John Day Company, 1934, pp. 194). By the originator and general secretary of the National Conference of Christians and Jews.

Considine, John J., *Across a World* (New York, Longmans, Green & Company, 1942, pp. xvi, 400). A well written, well informed travelogue embracing Roman Catholic missions in a number of parts of the world.

Contemporary Japan. A Review of Japanese Affairs (Tokyo, The Foreign Affairs Association of Japan, 1932 ff.).

Cooksey, J. J., *The Land of the Vanished Church. A Survey of North Africa* (London, World Dominion Press, pp. 107).

Cooksey, J. J., and McLeish, Alexander, *Religion and Civilization in West Africa. A Missionary Survey of French, British, Spanish and Portuguese West Africa, with Liberia* (London, World Dominion Press, 1931, pp. 277).

Coste, Pierre, *La Congrégation de la Mission Dite de Saint-Lazare* (Paris, Librairie Lecoffre, J. Gabalda et Fils, 1927, pp. viii, 231). By a Lazarist; based upon standard authorities.

Cressy, Earl Herbert, *Yellow Rivers. Adventures in a Chinese Parish* (New York, Harper & Brothers, 1932, pp. xiii, 153). A popularly written account by an

American Baptist missionary; a realistic picture of actual experiences, largely showing the difficulties of the missionary's life.

Cuenot, Joseph, *Kwangsi. Land of the Black Banners*. Translated by George F. Wiseman (St. Louis, B. Herder Book Co., 1942, pp. xvii, 279).

Culshaw, W. J., *A Missionary Looks at His Job* (London, Student Christian Movement Press, 1937, pp. 144). By a young missionary to India.

Curtis, Lionel, *Civitas Dei* (London, Macmillan and Co., Ltd., 1934, pp. xxiii, 297). An interesting survey of human history, stressing a belief that an ideal human society is one which is built upon the concept of Jesus, the brotherhood of man.

Curtiss, John Shelton, *Church and State in Russia—The Last Years of the Empire—1900-1917* (Columbia University Press, 1940, pp. ix, 442).

Davis, Helen Clarkson Miller, *Some Aspects of Religious Liberty of Nationals in the Near East. A Collection of Documents* (New York, Harper & Brothers, 1938, pp. xviii, 182). Admirable.

Davis, J. Merle, *The Church in the New Jamaica* (New York, International Missionary Council, 1942, pp. x, 100). By a careful, sympathetic, objective observer.

Davis, J. Merle, *The Cuban Church in a Sugar Economy* (New York, The International Missionary Council, 1942, pp. 144). By a careful observer, objective and sympathetic.

Davis, J. Merle, *The Economic and Social Environment of the Younger Churches* (Calcutta, Baptist Mission Press, 1938, pp. xiii, 211). Based upon careful research.

Davis, J. Merle, *The Economic Basis of the Evangelical Church in Mexico* (London, International Missionary Council, 1940, pp. 133).

Davis J. Merle, *Mission Finance Policies and the Younger Churches* (Bangalore, Scripture Literature Press, 1938, pp. 104). Carefully done.

Davis, J. Merle, *Modern Industry and the African* (London, Macmillan and Company, 1933, pp. xviii, 425). The result of a commission of inquiry, under the auspices of the Department of Social and Industrial Research and Counsel of the International Missionary Council.

Dennis, James S., Beach, Harlan P., and Fahs, Charles H., *World Atlas of Christian Missions* (New York, Student Volunteer Movement for Foreign Missions, 1911, pp. 172).

Descamps, Baron, *Histoire Générale Comparée des Missions* (Paris, Librairie Plon, 1932, pp. viii, 760). Seven other writers have contributed. A standard survey, by Roman Catholic scholars, of Roman Catholic mission history from the beginning, together with chapters on the spread of Protestantism and of some other religions.

Detweiler, Charles S., *The Waiting Isles. Baptist Missions in the Caribbean* (Philadelphia, The Judson Press, 1930, pp. 167). By a secretary of the American Baptist Home Mission Society.

Devine, W., *The Four Churches of Peking* (London, Burns, Oats and Washbourne, Ltd., 1930, pp. 225). A popular account, published with Roman Catholic ecclesiastical permission, telling the story, not only of the four churches, but also of Catholic missions in Peking. It draws heavily from standard works.

Diffendorfer, Ralph E., *A Voyage of Discovery. Being a Report of a Secretarial Visit to the Work of the Methodist Episcopal Church in South America, 1934* (New York, Board of Foreign Missions, Methodist Episcopal Church, pp. 104).

Los Dominicos en el Extremo Oriente. Provincia del Santísimo Rosario de Filipinas. Relaciones publicadas con motivo del Séptimo Centenario de la confirmación de la Sagrada Orden de Predicadores (no date or place of publication, pp. 391). Done by a Commission. No names of authors given.

Dossiers de la Commission Synodale, Digest of the Synodal Commission. Volumen 5, Numerus 5. L'Art Chretien Chinois (Peiping, Commissio Synodalis in Sinis, May, 1932, pp. 403-524). Contains a number of articles by various authors.

Douglass, H. Paul, *Church Unity Movements in the United States* (New York, Institute of Social and Religious Research, 1934, pp. xxxviii, 576). A careful study based upon extensive research.

Douglass, H. Paul, *A Decade of Objective Progress in Church Unity, 1927-1936* (New York, Harper & Brothers, 1937, pp. xxii, 140). Contains many documents and excerpts from documents.

Douglass, Paul F., *God among the Germans* (Philadelphia, University of Pennsylvania Press, 1935, pp. xiii, 325). Carefully done.

Drach, George, editor, *Our Church Abroad. The Foreign Missions of the Lutheran Church in America* (Philadelphia, The United Lutheran Publication House, 1926, pp. 277). An official description of the missions of the various Lutheran bodies of the United States.

Dubois, Henri, *La Répertoire Africain Conference des Missions Catholiques d'Afrique* (Rome, Sodalité de S. Pierre Claver, 1932, pp. xvii, 400). Represents Roman Catholic thought on mission methods in Africa.

Duncan-Jones, A. S., *The Struggle for Religious Freedom in Germany* (London, Victor Gollancz, 1938, pp. 319). By the (Anglican) Dean of Chichester.

Eckhardt, Carl Conrad, *The Papacy and World-Affairs as Reflected in the Secularization of Politics* (University of Chicago Press, 1937, pp. xiv, 310).

Eddy, Sherwood, *A Pilgrimage of Ideas or the Re-education of Sherwood Eddy* (New York, Farrar and Rinehart, 1934, pp. xiii, 336). An autobiography.

The Education of American Ministers (New York, Institute of Social and Religious Research, 4 vols., 1934). By various authors. The standard survey of the education of the Protestant clergy of the United States and Canada.

Elder, John Rawson, *The History of the Presbyterian Church of New Zealand 1840-1940* (Christchurch, Presbyterian Bookroom, no date, pp. xv, 464). Carefully done, but without footnote references to the sources.

d'Elia, Pascal M., *Catholic Native Episcopacy in China. Being an Outline of the Formation and Growth of the Chinese Catholic Clergy, 1300-1926* (Shanghai, T'usewei Printing Press, 1927, pp. v, 107). By a competent Jesuit scholar.

Emhardt, William Chauncy, *Religion in Soviet Russia. Anarchy* (Milwaukee, Morehouse Publishing Co., 1929, pp. xix, 386). By an American Episcopalian. Controversial, but valuable for its many excerpts from documents.

Evangelical Handbook of Latin America, 1937 Edition (New York, Committee on Co-operation in Latin America, pp. 119).

Fahs, Charles H., and Davis, Helen E., *Conspectus of Coöperative Missionary Enterprises* (New York, International Missionary Council, 1935, pp. v, 252). Carefully done.

Far Eastern Survey (New York, 1932 ff.). A publication of the American Council, Institute of Pacific Relations.

Federal Council Bulletin (New York, The Federal Council of the Churches of Christ in America, 1918 ff.).

Feeney, Thomas J., S.J., *The Padre of the Press. Recollections of Rev. John J. Monohan, S.J.* (New York, Jesuit Mission Press, 1931, pp. 161).

Fellowship (New York, 1935 ff.). The Journal of the Fellowship of Reconciliation.

Felton, Ralph H., *The Rural Church in the Far East* (Calcutta, Baptist Mission Press, 1938, pp. x, 215, xxxii). By an American expert on the rural church.

Fides News Service (Rome, c. 1926 ff.). A mimeographed set of news release notes on current happenings in Roman Catholic missions. Compiled in close co-operation with the Association for the Propagation of the Faith. The title is sometimes merely *Fides Service*.

Fisher, Frederick B., and Foley, Walter Brooks, *Building the Indian Church. A Book of Experimental Methods* (Calcutta, The Albin Press, 1930, pp. 151). The volume was prepared as a methods book for the Calcutta Area of the Methodist Episcopal Church and is based on a book, *The Way to Win,* written by Bishop Fisher a decade before for American churches.

Fleming, Daniel Johnson, *Christian Symbols in a World Community* (New York, Friendship Press, 1940, pp. 150). By an outstanding authority in Christian missions.

Fleming, Daniel Johnson, *Devolution in Mission Administration As Exemplified by the Legislative History of Five American Missionary Societies in India* (Chicago, Fleming H. Revell Co., 1916, pp. 310). A standard, pioneer work.

Fleming, Daniel Johnson, *Each with his own Brush. Contemporary Christian Art in Asia and Africa* (New York, Friendship Press, 1938, pp. 85). Excellently selected, well reproduced paintings.

Fleming, Daniel Johnson, *Ethical Issues Confronting World Christians* (New York, The International Missionary Council, 1935, pp. vii, 280). A penetrating discussion of contemporary problems.

Fleming, Daniel Johnson, *Heritage of Beauty: Pictorial Studies of Modern Christian Architecture in Asia and Africa. Illustrating the Influence of Indigenous Cultures* (New York, Friendship Press, 1937, pp. 95).

Fleming, Daniel Johnson, *Ventures in Simpler Living* (Privately printed, New York, 1933, pp. 169). An able discussion of the problem of missionary standards of living.

Fleming, Daniel Johnson, *The World at One in Prayer* (New York, Harper & Brothers, 1942, pp. xi, 204). A collection of prayers, largely contemporary, from many peoples.

Foreign Affairs (New York, Council on Foreign Relations, 1922 ff.).

Foster, John, *The Chinese Church in Action* (London, Edinburgh House Press, 1933, pp. 144). Popularly written, by a missionary in South China.

Franklin, James H., *The Never Failing Light* (New York, Missionary Education

Movement of the United States and Canada, 1933, pp. 207). By a secretary of the American Baptist Foreign Mission Society, and based in large part on the author's experiences in other lands.

Fraser, Agnes R., *Donald Fraser of Livingstonia* (London, Hodder and Stoughton, 1934, pp. ix, 325). A charmingly written biography by the widow.

French, Evangeline, Cable, Mildred, and French, Francesca, *A Desert Journal. Letters from Central Asia* (London, Constable & Company, 1934, pp. ix, 261). By members of the China Inland Mission, from June, 1928, to June, 1932.

Frey, Arthur, *Cross and Swastika. The Ordeal of the German Church* (London, Student Christian Movement Press, 1938, pp. 224). By a Swiss and endorsed by Karl Barth.

Fry, C. Luther, *Diagnosing the Rural Church* (New York, Gearge H. Doran Company, 1924, pp. 234).

Fry, C. Luther, *The U. S. Looks at Its Churches* (New York, Institute of Social and Religious Research, 1930, pp. xiv, 183).

Galbraith, Winifred, *The Dragon Sheds His Skin* (London, Jonathan Cape, 1928, pp. 221). Chiefly an account of the author's experiences as a teacher in a school in Changsha, China.

Gamio, Manuel, *The Mexican Immigrant. His Life-Story. Autobiographic Documents Collected by Manuel Gamio* (University of Chicago Press, 1931, pp. xiii, 285). Scholarly.

Garrison, Winfred Ernest, *Religion Follows the Frontier. A History of the Disciples of Christ* (New York, Harper & Brothers, 1931, pp. xiv, 317). A well written, scholarly book by a Disciple.

Gill, Everett, *Europe and the Gospel* (Richmond, Va., Educational Department, Foreign Mission Board, Southern Baptist Convention, 1931, pp. 174). By a European representative of the Foreign Mission Board of the Southern Baptist Convention.

Gillard, John T., *The Catholic Church and the American Negro* (Baltimore, St. Joseph's Society Press, 1929, pp. xv, 324). A careful survey written from the Roman Catholic standpoint.

Gillard, John T., *Colored Catholics in the United States* (Baltimore, The Josephite Press, 1941, pp. x, 298).

Gledstone, Frederick F., *South India* (Westminster, The Society for the Propagation of the Gospel in Foreign Parts, 1930, pp. 83). By a missionary in the diocese of Dornakal.

Goodman, Fred S., *Glimpses of the Story of the Waldensians* (New York, The American Waldensian Society, 1928, pp. 20). A popular pamphlet.

Guilday, Peter, editor, *The Catholic Church in Contemporary Europe, 1919-1931. Papers of the American Catholic Historical Association,* Vol. II (New York, P. J. Kenedy and Sons, 1932, pp. xiv, 354).

Hagspiel, Bruno, *Along the Mission Trail* (Techny, Mission Press, S.V.D., 5 vols., 1925-1927). A travelogue by a priest of the Society of the Divine Word.

Hailey, Lord, *An African Survey. A Study of Problems Arising in Africa South of the Sahara* (Oxford University Press, 1938, pp. xxviii, 1837). A standard work.

Halich, Wasyl, *Ukrainians in the United States* (The University of Chicago Press, 1937, pp. xiii, 174). Based upon fairly extensive research and personal knowledge.

Hamlin, Fred, *Treasures in the Earth* (New York, The Friendship Press, 1931, pp. 160). A mission study text for young people, made up of incidents from various lands, partly from first hand observations of the author.

d'Harcourt, Robert, *The German Catholics* (London, Burns, Oates & Washbourne, Ltd., 1939, pp. xiii, 274). Translated by R. J. Dingle. By a French Roman Catholic cleric.

Harper, Marvin Henry, *The Methodist Episcopal Church in India. A Study of Ecclesiastical Organization and Administration* (Lucknow, The Lucknow Publishing House, 1936, pp. vii, 222). Carefully done. A doctoral dissertation by a Methodist missionary.

Harrington, B. C., and Foley, W. B., *Problems of Religious Work in Indian Villages and Cities (A Survey of Families). The Calcutta Area Survey of the Methodist Episcopal Church, 1930* (Calcutta, 1931, pp. xvii, 100). An excellent survey according to good statistical standards. Includes Methodist work in Lucknow, Central Provinces, Bengal, and Burma.

Hartenstein, Karl, *Anibue. Die "Neue Zeit" auf der Goldküste und unsere Missionsaufgabe* (Stuttgart and Basel, Evang. Missionsverlag, 1932, pp. 126). The popular report of a trip by the Director of the Basel Mission.

The Harvest Field (New Series, 1880 ff., comprehending all Protestant activity in India and contin ed by *The National Christian Council Review*. The original series began in 1861).

Hatch, D. Spencer, *Up from Poverty in Rural India* (Calcutta, Oxford University Press, 1932, pp. vii, 208). By a secretary in charge of the rural work of the Y.M.C.A. in one district in South India.

Hayden, Joseph Ralston, *The Philippines. A Study in National Development* (New York, The Macmillan Company, 1942, pp. xxvi, 984). By a former American official in the islands.

Hayes, Carlton J. H., *France. A Nation of Patriots* (New York, 1930).

Hecker, Julius F., *Religion under the Soviets* (New York, The Vanguard Press, 1927, pp. xv, 207).

Herman, Stewart W., *It's Your Souls We Want* (New York, Harper & Brothers, 1943, pp. xv, 315). A description of the religious situation in Germany by a young American who had served as pastor of an American church in Berlin.

Herring, Hubert, *Good Neighbors. Argentina, Brazil and Seventeen Other Countries* (Yale University Press, 1941, pp. 381). Popularly written, by an expert.

Hitler, Adolf, *Mein Kampf. Complete and Unabridged* (New York, Reynal & Hitchcock, 1940, pp. xxxvi, 1003). Edited by a group which contained some distinguished scholars. Anti-Nazi in its annotations.

Hocking, William Ernest, Chairman, the Commission of Appraisal, *Re-thinking Missions. A Laymen's Inquiry after One Hundred Years* (New York, Harper & Brothers, 1932, pp. xv, 349). A much debated, influential book, of composite authorship.

Hocking, William Ernest, *Living Religions and a World Faith* (New York, The Macmillan Company, 1940, pp. 291).

Hodgkin, Henry T., *Living Issues in China* (New York, The Friendship Press, 1932, pp. viii, 215). A mission study text book, by a former Friends missionary to China and a secretary of the National Christian Council of China.

Hollister, Mary Brewster, *Lady Fourth, Daughter of China, Sharer of Life* (Cambridge, The Central Committee on the United Study of Foreign Missions, 1931, pp. 237). A mission study text, by a missionary born in China of missionary parents.

Horton, Walter Marshall, *Contemporary Continental Theology. An Interpretation for Anglo-Saxons* (New York, Harper & Brothers, 1938, pp. xxi, 246). A useful summary.

Horton, Walter Marshall, *Contemporary English Theology. An American Interpretation* (New York, Harper & Brothers, 1936, pp. xix, 186). A useful summary.

Howard, Randolph L., *Baptisms in Burma* (Philadelphia, The Judson Press, 1931, pp. 168). The author was for fourteen years a missionary in Burma under the American Baptist Foreign Mission Society.

Hull, Ernest R., *Bombay Mission-History with a Special Study of the Padroado Question* (Bombay, Examiner Press, no date, Vol. I, 1534-1858, pp. vii, 493, xi, Vol. II, 1858-1929, pp. xiv, 521). By a Jesuit, with an expressed purpose of objectivity on the padroado question, and incorporating many documents, given in English translation.

Hunnicutt, Benjamin H., and Reid, William Watkins, *The Story of Agricultural Missions* (New York, Missionary Education Movement of the United States and Canada, 1931, pp. ix, 180). A study book for adults. Hunnicutt was an agricultural missionary in Brazil and Reid was active in the International Association of Agricultural Missions.

Hunting, Harold B., *The Adventures of Mr. Friend* (New York, Friendship Press, 1931, pp. viii, 130). A popular book for young people made up of incidents from American church life.

Hutchison, John A., *We are not Divided. A Critical and Historical Study of The Federal Council of the Churches of Christ in America* (New York, Round Table Press, 1941, pp. xi, 336). Well documented.

Indisch Verslag, 1931. II. Statistisch Jaaroverzicht van Nederlandsch-Indië over het Jaar 1930 (Batavia, Landsdrukkerij, 1931, pp. xxxvii, 536).

Information Service (New York, Department of Research and Education, Federal Council of the Churches of Christ in America, 1922 ff.).

International Christian Press and Information Service. Information Series (Geneva, 1940 ff.).

The International Review of Missions (London, 1912 ff.). The standard Protestant journal on foreign missions.

International Survey of the Young Men's and Young Women's Christian Associations (New York, The International Survey Committee, 1932, pp. vi, 425). A careful, objective study.

Iswolsky, Helen, *Light before Dusk. A Russian Catholic in France, 1923-1941* (New York, Longmans, Green and Co., 1942, pp. ix, 253). Autobiographical.

The Japan Christian Quarterly (Tokyo, The Federation of Christian Missions, and later, The Christian Literature Society of Japan, 1926-1941). An interdenominational Protestant journal.

The Japan Christian Year Book (Yokohama, 1903-1904, Tokyo, 1905-1940). The title varies: 1906-1914, *The Christian Movement in Japan*; 1915-1920, *The Christian Movement in the Japanese Empire*; 1921-1926, *The Christian Movement in Japan, Korea and Formosa*; 1927-1931, *The Japan Mission Year Book*; 1932-1940, *The Japan Christian Year Book*.

Johannsen, Anna Magdalena, *A Great Door* (London, The China Inland Mission, 1930, pp. ix, 86). For children, by a woman long a missionary to China, and with many concrete instances from China.

Johnson, Charles S., *The Negro in American Civilization. A Study of Negro Life and Race Relations in the Light of Social Research* (New York, Henry Holt and Co., 1930, pp. xiv, 538). The synthesis of many studies presented to a national interracial conference of agencies for social work among Negroes and the improvement of the relationships between white and coloured.

Jones, E. Stanley, *Christ's Alternative to Communism* (Cincinnati, The Abingdon Press, 1935, pp. 302).

Jones, Thomas Jesse, *Education in East Africa. A Study of East, Central and South Africa by the Second African Education Commission under the Auspices of the Phelps-Stokes Fund, in Coöperation with the International Education Board* (New York, Phelps-Stokes Fund, London, Edinburgh House Press, no date, pp. xxxiii, 416). The commission was in Africa in 1924.

Josson, H., *La Mission du Bengale Occidental ou Archidiocèse de Calcutta. Province Belge de la Compagnie de Jésus* (Bruges, Imprimerie Sainte-Catherine, 2 vols., 1921). Based on careful research, by a Jesuit.

Kandel, I. L., editor, *Educational Yearbook of the International Institute of Teachers College Columbia University, 1933* (Bureau of Publications, Teachers College, Columbia University, 1933, pp. xvi, 642). Articles, chiefly on education by Protestant missions, of various types and in various countries, and one chapter on Roman Catholic education.

De Katholieke Missie in Nederlandsch Oost-Indië Jaarboek 1933 (Batavia, Centraal Missie Bureau, Dec., 1933, pp. xxxiv, 374).

Keay, F. E., *A History of the Syrian Church in India* (London, Society for Promoting Christian Knowledge, 1938, pp. 124). A careful and inclusive summary.

Keesing, Felix M., *The Changing Maori* (New Plymouth, N. Z., Thomas Avery and Sons, 1928, pp. xvi, 198). *Memoirs of the Board of Maori Ethnological Research*, Vol. IV. Written in popular style and without many footnotes. It has, however, a bibliography and apparently is based on sound scholarship. Its attitude is one of sympathy for the Maori.

Keller, Adolf, *Christian Europe Today* (New York, Harper & Brothers, 1942, pp. x, 310). By a Swiss Protestant with wide contacts.

Keller, Adolf, and Stewart, George, *Protestant Europe: Its Crisis and Outlook* (New York, George H. Doran Company, 1927, pp. xv, 385). Based upon wide and intimate knowledge.

Kennedy, A. M., *The Changing Fabric of Japan* (New York, Richard R. Smith, Inc., 1931, pp. vii, 282). An interesting account by a careful observer.

Knott, Margaret C., *The Light Approaching. China and the L.M.S.* (Westminster, Livingstone Press, Foreword, 1928, pp. 142). A textbook on the work of the London Missionary Society in China. Written by the wife of a missionary in Central China.

Kolb, J. H., and Brunner, E. deS., *A Study of Rural Society. Its Organization and Changes* (Boston, Houghton Mifflin Co., 1935, pp. xiv, 642). Objective, scholarly.

Kozaki, Hiromichi, *Reminiscences of Seventy Years. The Autobiography of a Japanese Pastor.* Translated by Nariaki Kozaki (Tokyo, Christian Literature Society of Japan, 1933, pp. iv, 406). The author was a member of the Kumamoto Band, second president of the Doshisha, and long a pastor in Tokyo.

Kraemer, H., *De Huidige Stand van het Christendom in Nederlandsch-Indië* (The Hague, 1937, pp. 89). By an outstanding Dutch missionary to the Netherlands Indies.

Kügelgen, Carlo von, *The Whited Sepulchre. An Authentic Account of Church Persecution in Russia.* Translated by L. M. Stalker (London, The Lutterworth Press, 1935, pp. 119). An autobiographical account of the sufferings of a German pastor.

Landis, Benson Y., editor, *1941 Yearbook of American Churches* (Jackson Heights, N. Y., Yearbook of American Churches Press, 1941, pp. x, 213). Under the auspices of The Federal Council of the Churches of Christ in America.

Latourette, Kenneth Scott, *A History of Christian Missions in China* (New York, The Macmillan Co., 1929, pp. xii, 930).

Report of the Commission of Appraisal of the Laymen's Foreign Missions Inquiry (New York, 1932, pp. viii, 417). References are not to the printed report but to a reproduction of a mimeographed copy.

Laymen's Foreign Missions Inquiry (New York, Harper & Brothers, 7 vols., 1933).

Lemmens, Leonhard, *Geschichte der Franziskanermissionen* (Münster i. W., Aschendorffschen Verlagsbuchhandlung, 1929, pp. xx, 376). Carefully done, by a Franciscan.

Lennox, John, *The Story of Our Missions. South Africa* (Edinburgh, Offices of the United Free Church of Scotland, 1911, pp. 87).

Lesourd, Paul, editor, *L'Année Missionnaire 1931* (Paris, Desclée de Brouwer et Cie, pp. 667).

Light and Darkness in East Africa. A Missionary Survey of Uganda, Anglo-Egyptian Sudan, Abyssinia, Eritrea, and the Three Somalilands (London, World Dominion Press, preface 1927, pp. 206). By various authors.

Lipphard, William B., *Out of the Storm in China. A Review of Recent Developments in Baptist Mission Fields* (Philadelphia, The Judson Press, 1932, pp. 201).

Loram, C. T., and McIlwraith, T. F., editors, *The North American Indian Today. University of Toronto—Yale University Seminar Conference, Toronto, September 4-16, 1939* (Toronto, The University of Toronto Press, 1943, pp. xi, 361).

Lynd, Robert S., and Lynd, Helen Merrill, *Middletown. A Study in Contemporary American Culture* (New York, Harcourt, Brace and Company, 1929, pp. x, 550).

Lynd, Robert S., and Lynd, Helen Merrill, *Middletown in Transition* (New York, Harcourt, Brace and Company, 1937, pp. xviii, 604).

McCullagh, Francis, *The Bolshevik Persecution of Christianity* (London, John Murray, 1924, pp. xxi, 401).

Macdonald, Aeneas, *One Hundred Years of Presbyterianism in Victoria* (Melbourne, Robertson & Mullens, Ltd., p. 190). Carefully done.

Macfarland, Charles S., *Chaos in Mexico. The Conflict of Church and State* (New York, Harper & Brothers, 1935, pp. 284). Objective; by an eminent Protestant after six weeks of intensive study in Mexico.

Macfarland, Charles S., *The New Church and the New Germany. A Study of Church and State* (New York, The Macmillan Company, 1934, pp. xii, 209). Contains important documents in its appendices.

Mackay, John A., *The Other Spanish Christ. A Study in the Spiritual History of Spain and South America* (London, Student Movement Press, 1932, pp. xv, 288). By a scholarly Protestant missionary executive, long a missionary in Peru.

McKee, William S., *New Schools for Young India. A Survey of Educational, Economic, and Social Conditions in India with Special Reference to More Effective Education* (The University of North Carolina Press, 1930, pp. xxi, 435). The author was the creator and principal of a famous village teachers' training school in Moga.

Mackenzie, John, editor, *The Christian Task in India* (London, Macmillan and Company, 1929, pp. xvii, 297). By various authors.

McLeish, Alexander, *Christian Progress in Burma* (London, World Dominion Press, 1929, pp. 100). A careful survey of Protestant effort.

McLeish, Alexander, Part II of *"Europe in Transition," Churches under Trial* (London, World Dominion Press, no date, pp. 47). An excellent summary.

Maclennan, Kenneth, *Report to the Conference of Missionary Societies in Great Britain and Ireland on a Visit to the Far East, January-July, 1934* (London, Edinburgh House, 1934, pp. 30).

Macmillan, William Miller, *Complex South Africa. An Economic Foot-note to History* (London, Faber and Faber, Ltd., 1930, pp. 293). A somewhat controversial volume based on long observation and research.

Macnicol, Nicol, *India in the Dark Wood* (London, Edinburgh House Press, 1930, pp. 224). A popularly written book by an authority on India and missions in India.

"The Madras Series," Presenting Papers Based upon the Meeting of the International Missionary Council, at Tambaram, Madras, India, December 12th to 29th, 1938 (New York and London, International Missionary Council, 7 vols., 1939).

Manikam, Rajah B., *The Christian College and the Christian Community. A report based on recent research studies by certain Christian colleges in India* (Madras, The Diocesan Press, 1938, pp. 144).

Mann, Cecil W., *Education in Fiji* (Melbourne University Press, 1935, pp. 138).

From a special visit for the Methodist Missionary Society of Australasia by a lecturer at the Teachers' College, Sydney.

Martin, Paul R., *The First Cardinal of the West. The Story of the Church in the Archdiocese of Chicago under the Administration of His Eminence, George Cardinal Mundelein, Third Archbishop of Chicago and First Cardinal of the West* (The New World Publishing Co., 1934, pp. 215).

Martindale, C. C., *African Angelus. Episodes and Impressions* (London, Sheed & Ward, 1932, pp. xvi, 436).

Maryknoll, The Field Afar. An official organ of the Catholic Foreign Mission Society of America.

Mathews, Basil, *John R. Mott, World Citizen* (New York, Harper & Brothers, 1934, pp. xiii, 469). A warmly appreciative biography by a personal friend, based upon careful research and upon data provided by Mott.

Mays, Benjamin Elijah, and Nicholson, Joseph William, *The Negro's Church* (New York, Institute of Social and Religious Research, 1933, pp. xiii, 321). Scholarly.

Means, Paul Banwell, *Things that are Caesar's: The Genesis of the German Church Conflict* (New York, Round Table Press, 1935, pp. 288).

Meriam, Lewis, and Hinman, George W., *Facing the Future in Indian Missions* (New York, Council of Women for Home Missions and Missionary Education Movement, 1932, pp. xv, 224). A mission study text book.

Miao, Chester S., and Price, Frank W., *Religion and Character in Christian Middle Schools. A Study of Religious Education in Christian Private Middle Schools in China* (Shanghai, 1929, pp. x, 240). Gathered largely by travel of the authors in 1928-1929. Very well done.

Micklem, Nathaniel, *National Socialism and the Roman Catholic Church* (Oxford University Press, 1939, pp. xi, 243). By an English Protestant scholar.

Miller, Janet, *Jungles Preferred* (Boston, Houghton Mifflin Co., 1931, pp. 321). A racily written story of about three years of medical missionary life in the Belgian Congo—an autobiography and diary combined.

Mishima, Sumie Seo, *My Narrow Isle. The Story of a Modern Woman of Japan* (New York, The John Day Co., 1941, pp. 280). Autobiographical.

1944 Mission Annual of the Seraphic Mass Association (Yonkers, N. Y., edited by Capuchins).

Missionaries of the United Church of Canada, *Fruits of Christian Missions in Japan* (Toronto, The Woman's Missionary Society of the United Church of Canada, no date, pp. x, 260). No separate authors are given.

The Missionary Herald (Boston, 1821 ff.). An official organ of the American Board of Commissioners for Foreign Missions.

The Missionary Review of the World (Princeton, later New York, 1878-1939). Earlier, *The Missionary Review.*

Missiones Catholicae cura S. Congregationis de Propaganda Fide Descriptae in Annum MDCCCXCII (Rome, S.C. de Propaganda Fide, 1892, pp. xxxvi, 682).

Missiones Catholicae cura S. Congregationis de Propaganda Fide Descriptae Statistica. Data Statistica Referunter ad diem 30 Juni 1927 (Rome, Typis Polyglottis Vaticanis, 1930, pp. xiv, 534). Official and full figures and summary descriptions.

Missions (New York, 1910 ff.). An organ of American Northern Baptists.

Les Missions de Chine. A continuation of Planchet, *Les Missions de Chine et du Japon* (Peking, Lazaristes du Peit'ang, and Shanghai, 1935-1940).

Les Missions Franciscaines (Quebec, 1923 ff.).

Moore, John F., *Will America Become Catholic?* (New York, Harper & Brothers, 1931, pp. x, 252). Objective; by a Protestant.

Moreira, Eduardo, *Portuguese East Africa. A Study of its Religious Needs* (London, World Dominion Press, 1936, pp. 104).

Morse, Hermann N., editor, *Home Missions Today and Tomorrow. A Review and Forecast* (New York, Home Missions Council, 1934, pp. xvi, 419). An official study by the Home Missions Council.

Morton, T. Ralph, *Life in the Chinese Church* (London, Student Christian Movement Press, 1931, pp. 94). A short sketch, vivid, accurate, and sane, by a young missionary of the Presbyterian Church of Ireland in Manchuria.

Morton, T. Ralph, *To-Day in Manchuria. The Young Church in Crisis* (London, Student Christian Movement Press, 1939, pp. 128). Well written, by a missionary recently in Manchuria.

Moyer, Elgin S., *Missions in the Church of the Brethren. Their Development and Effect upon the Denomination* (Elgin, Ill., Brethren Publishing House, 1931, pp. 301). Scholarly.

The National Christian Council Bulletin (Tokyo, The Christian Council of Japan).

National Christian Council of China. The Bulletin (Shanghai, 1922-1937).

The National Christian Council Review (Formerly the Harvest Field). The organ of the National Christian Council of India, Burma and Ceylon. *The Harvest Field* began in 1861 and the *New Series* in 1880.

The Navajo Indian Problem: An Inquiry Sponsored by the Phelps-Stokes Fund (New York, 1939, pp. xvi, 127).

Neill, Stephen, *Out of Bondage: Christ and the Indian Villager* (London, Edinburgh House Press, 1930, pp. 143). By a brilliant young missionary, later an Anglican bishop, who writes from first hand experience, chiefly of South India.

Niles, D. T., *Sir, We Would See Jesus. A Study in Evangelism* (London, Student Christian Movement Press, 1938, pp. 128). By a young Ceylonese Christian.

North, Eric M., *The Book of a Thousand Tongues. Being Some Account of the Translation and Publication of All or Part of the Holy Scriptures into more than a Thousand Languages and Dialects, with Over 1100 Examples from the Text* (New York, Harper & Brothers, 1938, pp. 386). By a secretary of the American Bible Society.

The North-China Herald (Shanghai, 1850-1941). The weekly edition of *The North-China Daily News.*

Noble, W. J., *Christian Union in South India. An Adventure in Fellowship* (London, Student Christian Movement Press, 1936, pp. 94).

Noble, W. J., *The Black Trek. From Village to Mine in Africa* (London, Edinburgh House Press, 1931, pp. 143).

Notizie Statistiche delle Missioni di Tutto il Mondo Dipendenti dalla S.C. de Propaganda Fide (Rome, Coi Tipi della S.C. de Propaganda Fide, 1844).

Nygren, Anders, *The Church Controversy in Germany. The Position of the Evan-*

gelical Church in the Third Empire. Translated by G. C. Richards (London, Student Christian Movement Press, 1934, pp. ix, 115). By a distinguished Swedish theologian.

O'Brien, John A., *The Priesthood in a Changing World* (New York, P. J. Kenedy & Sons, 1936, pp. xx, 314). By a Roman Catholic priest.

The Official Catholic Directory, 1940 (New York, P. J. Kenedy & Sons, pp. xx, 1107, 157, 107).

Ohm, Thomas, *Indien und Gott. Religions- und Missionskundliche Streifzüge durch Ceylon und Vorderindien* (Salzburg, Anton Pustet, 1931, pp. 276). By a Benedictine.

Oldham, J. H., and Gibson, B. D., *The Remaking of Man in Africa* (Oxford University Press, 1931, pp. 185). By secretaries of the International Missionary Council.

Our Missions. See *The Christian Family and Our Missions.*

Pacific Affairs (New York, 1928 ff.). An organ of the Institute of Pacific Relations.

Pakenham-Walsh, W. S., *Twenty Years in China* (Cambridge, W. Heffer & Sons, 1935, pp. x, 127). Impressions of an English missionary in Fukien.

Parker, Joseph I., editor, *Directory of World Missions* (New York, International Missionary Council, 1938, pp. xi, 255).

Parker, Joseph I., editor, *Interpretative Statistical Survey of the World Mission of the Christian Church* (New York, International Missionary Council, 1928, pp. 323). Standard.

Parsons, Wilfrid, *Mexican Martyrdom* (New York, The Macmillan Company, 1936, pp. vi, 304). By a Jesuit with experience in Mexico.

Paton, William, *Christianity in the Eastern Conflicts. A Study of Christianity, Nationalism and Communism in Asia* (Chicago, Willett Clark & Co., 1937, pp. 224). By a secretary of the International Missionary Council, arising from a trip through Asia in 1935-1936.

The Persecution of the Catholic Church in the Third Reich. Facts and Documents translated from the German (New York, Longmans, Green & Co., 1942, pp. x, 565).

Philip, P. O., *Report on a Survey of Indigenous Christian Efforts in India, Burma and Ceylon* (Poona, Scottish Mission Industries Co., 1928, pp. 14).

Phillips, Ray E., *The Bantu are Coming. Phases of South Africa's Race Problem* (London, Student Christian Movement Press, 1930, pp. 238). By an American missionary in Johannesburg.

Phillips, Ray E., *The Bantu in the City* (The Lovedale Press, no date, pp. xxix, 452). Completed about 1938; by a distinguished American missionary in Johannesburg.

Philp, Horace R. A., *A New Day in Kenya* (London, World Dominion Press, 1936, pp. vi, 188). By a missionary of the Church of Scotland with long experience in Kenya.

Pickett, J. Waskom, *Christian Mass Movements in India. A Study with Recommendations* (Cincinnati, The Abingdon Press, 1933, pp. 382). Based upon a careful, objective study reaching over some years.

Pinfold, James T., *Fifty Years in Maoriland* (London, The Epworth Press, 1930, pp. 200). Chatty, not very well organized, made up in part of reminiscences but chiefly of notes concerning the history of New Zealand.

Planchet, J-M., *Les Missions de Chine et du Japon* (Peking, Imprimerie des Lazaristes, 15 vols., 1916-1940). An annual. Beginning in 1935 not under Planchet's name, but continuing as a Lazarist publication. Later issued from Shanghai.

Platt, W. J., *An African Prophet. The Ivory Coast Movement and What Came of It* (London, Student Christian Movement Press, 1934, pp. 157).

Platt, William J., *From Fetish to Faith* (London, Edinburgh House Press, 1936, pp. 159). An account of Protestant missions in West Africa by a missionary to that region.

Power, Michael, *Religion in the Reich* (London, Longmans, Green and Co., 1939, pp. viii, 240). Based largely upon visits to Germany; attempting to be objective but in general critical of the Nazis.

Powers, George C., *The Maryknoll Movement* (Maryknoll, Catholic Foreign Mission Society of America, 1920, pp. xix, 167). By a member of the society.

Priester und Mission. Jahrbuch der Unio Cleri pro Missionibus in den Ländern, deutscher Zunge. Herausgegeben von der Unio Cleri pro Missionibus in Deutschland, Österreich, Schweiz, Tschechoslowakei (Aachen, Unio Cleri pro Missionibus, 1917 ff.).

Proceedings of the Church Missionary Society for Africa and the East (London, 1801 ff.).

Proceedings of the Congress of Catholic Action, held at Karachi, October 18th to 21st, 1931. Pp. 181.

Prokhanoff, I. S., *In the Cauldron of Russia 1869-1933. Autobiography* (New York, All-Russian Evangelical Christian Union, 1933, pp. 270).

Quarterly Notes. Being the Bulletin of the International Missionary Council (London and New York, 1924 ff.).

Rauws, Joh., Kraemer, H., Van Hasselt, F.J.F., and Slotemaker de Brüine, N.A.C., *The Netherlands Indies* (London, World Dominion Press, 1935, pp. 186). Authoritative survey of missions.

Religion in Life. A Christian Quarterly (New York, Abingdon-Cokesbury Press, 1932 ff.).

Revista de la Exposición Misional Española, Barcelona, 1929 (Barcelona, 1928-1930).

Revue d'Histoire des Missions (Paris, 1924 ff.).

Rice, Esmé Ritchie, *Eclipse in Ethiopia and Its Corona Glory* (London, Marshall, Morgan & Scott, Ltd., no date, pp. 125). An account of the Sudan Interior Mission in Ethiopia.

Richards, J. R., *The Open Road in Persia* (London, Church Missionary Society, 1933, pp. ix, 68).

Richter, Julius, *Die evangelische Mission in Fern- und Südost-Asien, Australien, Amerika* (Gütersloh, C. Bertelsmann, 1932, pp. xii, 488). Readable. Few footnote references to sources, but occasional bibliographies.

Richter, Julius, *Die evangelische Mission in Niederländisch-Indien* (Gütersloh, C. Bertelsmann, 1931, pp. 167). The only general history, except in Dutch, of missions in the Netherlands East Indies. Somewhat lacking in footnote references to the sources.

Richter, Julius, *Geschichte der evangelischen Mission in Afrika* (Gütersloh, C. Bertelsmann, 1922, pp. 813). The standard account of the history of Protestant missions in Africa. The book suffers somewhat from a paucity of footnote references to authorities. The author had decided convictions which occasionally make themselves manifest. His German nationality and sympathies are at times obvious.

Richter, Julius, *Indische Missionsgeschichte* (Gütersloh, C. Bertelsmann, 2d ed., 1924, pp. vi, 570). The standard history of Protestant missions in India. There is an English translation of an earlier edition.

Richter, Julius, *Tanganyika and Its Future* (London, World Dominion Press, 1934, pp. 112).

De R. K. Kerk in Nederlandsch Indië. Missie almanak 1929 (Djokjakarta, Canisius, 1929, pp. 249).

Rockwell, William Walter, *The Pitiful Plight of the Assyrian Christians in Persia and Kurdistan* (New York, American Committee for Armenian and Syrian Relief, 1916, pp. 72). Largely from the accounts of eye witnesses.

Ross, Edward Alsworth, *The Social Revolution in Mexico* (New York, The Century Co., 1923, pp. 176). By a distinguished sociologist.

Ross, Emory, *Building the Church in Congo Belge, with Special Reference to the Use of Foreign Money* (Mimeographed. New York, International Missionary Council, 1934, pp. 15).

Ruppin, Arthur, *The Jews in the Modern World* (London, Macmillan and Co., 1934, pp. xxx, 423). By a Jewish scholar; comprehensive, objective.

Rusillon, H., *Une Enigme Missionnaire. Les Destinées de l'Église Chrétienne dans l'Afrique du Nord* (Paris, Société des Missions Évangeliques, 1931, pp. 166). A resume, partly historical, from a Protestant point of view.

Rycroft, W. Stanley, *On This Foundation. The Evangelical Witness in Latin America* (New York, Friendship Press, 1942, pp. xiii, 210). By a secretary of the Committee on Co-operation in Latin America.

Schapera, I., editor, *Western Civilization and the Natives of South Africa. Studies in Culture Contact* (London, George Routledge and Sons, 1934, pp. xiv, 312). By various authors.

Schermerhorn, William David, *The Christian Mission in the Modern World* (Cincinnati, The Abingdon Press, 1933, pp. 360). A survey, historical and contemporary, of missions, especially Protestant missions, around the world.

Schmidlin, Joseph, *Das Deutsche Missionswerk der Gegenwart* (Munster in Westfalen, 1929). Carefully done; detailed.

Schonfield, Hugh J., *The History of Jewish Christianity. From the First to the Twentieth Century* (London, Duckworth, 1936, pp. 256). Moderately objective, rather pro-Jewish Christian, sketchy, with many omissions.

Schulze, Adolf, *200 Jahre Brüdermission. II Band, Das Zweite Missionsjahrhundert* (Herrnhut, Verlag der Missionsbuchhandlung, 1932, pp. xii, 715). Well documented.

ɔcott, Charles Ernest, *Chinese Twice-Born: Kingdom Trophies in the Orient* (New York, Fleming H. Revell Company, 1931, pp. 159). Accounts of some Chinese Christians whom the author, a missionary, knew.

Scott-Craig, Thomas Stevenson Kirkpatrick, translator, *Germany's New Religion: the German Faith Movement*, by Wilhelm Hauer, Karl Heim, and Karl Adam (New York, The Abingdon Press, 1937, pp. 168).

Sequeira, Rosario D., *My Ramble through the Missions of the Diocese of Mangalore* (Mangalore, Codialbail Press, 1929, pp. 97). By a missionary.

Shaw, Mabel, *God's Candlelights, an Educational Venture in Northern Rhodesia* (London, Edinburgh House Press, 1932, pp. 196). By the originator of the venture.

Shillito, Edward, *Craftsmen All. Fellow-workers in the Younger Churches* (London, Edinburgh House Press, 1932, pp. 142). A popularly written book by a secretary of the London Missionary Society.

Shuster, George N., *Like a Mighty Army. Hitler versus Established Religion* (New York, D. Appleton-Century Company, 1935, pp. vii, 286). By an American Roman Catholic layman, scholar, and educator.

The Siam Outlook. Published quarterly by the National Christian Council of Siam. Vol. VII, No. 4, Oct., 1931, is called *National Christian Council Guide to Missions in Siam.*

Silcox, Claris Edwin, *Church Union in Canada. Its Causes and Consequences* (New York, Institute of Social and Religious Research, 1933, pp. xvii, 493). Carefully done.

Singha, Shoran S., and Shepherd, Arthur P., *More Yarns on India* (London, Edinburgh House Press, 1930, pp. 80).

Slosser, Gaius Jackson, *Christian Unity. Its History and Challenge in All Communions, in All Lands* (New York, E. P. Dutton and Co., 1929, pp. xix, 425). A comprehensive account, with the chief emphasis upon the nineteenth and twentieth centuries.

Smith, Edwin W., *The Way of the White Fields in Rhodesia. A Survey of Christian Enterprise in Northern and Southern Rhodesia* (London, World Dominion Press, 1928, pp. 172). By a competent scholar who had been a missionary in that area.

Smith, G. W., *Conquests of Christ in the West Indies. A Short History of Evangelical Missions* (Browns Town, Jamaica, The Evangelical Book Room, preface 1939, pp. 128). By a missionary to Jamaica.

Snow, Edgar, *The Battle for Asia* (New York, Random House, 1941, pp. xii, 431).

Soltau, T. Stanley, *Korea, the Hermit Nation and Its Response to Christianity* (London, World Dominion Press, 1932, pp. 123). By a member of the American Presbyterian Mission, North.

Spinka, Matthew, *Christianity Confronts Communism* (New York, Harper & Brothers, 1936, pp. xii, 221). By a competent Protestant specialist on the history of Eastern Christianity.

The Spiritual Issues of the War (London, Religious Division, Ministry of Information). British propaganda, but much of it dependable.

The Statesman's Year-Book (London, Macmillan and Co., 1864 ff.).

Stauffer, Milton T., *The Christian Occupation of China* (Shanghai, China Continuation Committee, 1922). A very careful, comprehensive survey, by Protestants.

Stelzle, Charles, editor, *The New Handbook of the Churches* (New York, J. E. Stohlmann, 1930, pp. 304). Published by the Federal Council of the Churches of Christ in America.

Stimson, Henry L., *The Far Eastern Crisis. Recollections and Observations* (New York, Harper & Brothers, 1936, pp. xii, 293). By the American Secretary of State who dealt with the Manchurian issue in 1931-1933.

Stonelake, Alfred R., *Congo Past and Present* (London, World Dominion Press, 1937, pp. 202).

Storm, W. Harold, *Whither Arabia? A Survey of Missionary Opportunity* (London, World Dominion Press, 1938, pp. xvi, 132). By a former Protestant missionary in Arabia.

Streit, Carolus, *Atlas Hierarchicus* (Paderborn, Typographia Bonifaciana, 1913, pp. 128, 37, 35). A standard book of reference.

Streit, F. C., *Catholic World Atlas* (Germany, St. Boniface Press, 1929, pp. 37, xlvii, 37, xi). An official publication, by Papal command, of the Society for the Propagation of the Faith.

Streit, Robert, *Catholic Missions in Figures and Symbols Based on the Vatican Missionary Exhibition* (New York, Society for the Propagation of the Faith, 1927, pp. xii, 172). A book for a popular audience by a recognized authority on the statistics of Catholic missions.

Strong, Esther Boorman, and Warnshuis, A. L., editors, *Directory of Foreign Missions. Missionary Boards, Societies, Colleges, Coöperative Councils, and Other Agencies of the Protestant Churches of the World* (New York, International Missionary Council, 1933, pp. xii, 278).

The Student World (New York, 1908 ff.). The organ of the World's Student Christian Federation.

Survey of Service. Organizations Represented in International Convention of Disciples of Christ (St. Louis, Christian Board of Publication, 1928, pp. 723). Various authors have contributed, writing from first hand knowledge describing the work of the denomination.

Tatlow, Tissington, *The Story of the Student Christian Movement* (London, Student Christian Movement Press, 1933, pp. xv, 944). By one of the most important past secretaries of the movement.

Teeling, William, *Crisis for Christianity* (London, John Gifford, 1939, pp. 320). The Roman Catholics and the Nazis.

Testo-Atlante illustrato delle Missioni. Compilato a cura dell' Agenzia Internazionale "Fides" con i dati Cartografici e Statistici dell' Archivio della S. Congregazione di Propaganda Fide (Rome, Istituto Geografico de Agostini, 1932, maps 53, illustrations 60, text pp. 160). Authoritative maps and statistics.

Theile, F. Otto, *One Hundred Years of the Lutheran Church in Queensland* (Publication Committee of the Queensland District United Evangelical Lutheran Church in Australia, 1938, pp. 290).

Thompson, Virginia, *French Indo-China* (New York, The Macmillan Co., 1937, pp. 517). Based upon extensive reading.

Timasheff, N. S., *Religion in Soviet Russia, 1917-1942* (New York, Sheed & Ward, 1942, pp. xii, 171). From a Roman Catholic standpoint. Well documented and, in general, objective.

Tinling, Christine I., *Hope for the Leper. The Present-Day Solution of an Ancient Problem* (New York, Fleming H. Revell Company, 1932, pp. 57). A popularly written account of the Mission to the Lepers; a semi-official document.

Tragella, P. G. B., *Pio XI, Papa Missionario Ricordo del Guibileo Sacerdotale del S. Padre* (Milan, Pont. Istituto delle Missioni Estere, 1930, pp. 187). Laudatory of the Pope. Contains Papal documents, in Italian.

Tucker, John T., *Angola. The Land of the Blacksmith Prince* (London, World Dominion Press, 1933, pp. viii, 180). By an experienced missionary in Angola.

The Tungchow Rural Institute. A Report of the North China Institute for Supervisors of Rural Work Held under the Auspices of the North China Christian Rural Service Union at the Lu Ho Rural Service Center (Tunghsien, March 20-April 3, 1935, pp. 90).

Union of South Africa, Union Office of Census and Statistics, *Official Year Book of the Union and of Basutoland, Bechuanaland Protectorate, and Swaziland, No. 9, 1926-1927* (Pretoria, The Government Printing and Stationery Office, 1928, pp. xix, 1157).

Union of South Africa, *Report of Native Churches Commission* (Cape Town, Cape Times, 1925, pp. 38).

United States Department of Commerce, Bureau of the Census, *Religious Bodies: 1936* (Washington, United States Government Printing Office, 1941, 2 vols. [Vol. II in two parts]). Criticized for incompleteness.

Van Buskirk, James Dale, *Korea, Land of the Dawn* (New York, Missionary Education Movement, 1931, pp. xii, 200). A study and reading book for church circles by a Methodist medical missionary in Seoul.

Van Dusen, Henry P., *For the Healing of the Nations. Impressions of Christianity around the World* (New York, Charles Scribners' Sons, 1940, pp. xx, 227). Sympathetic, discerning.

Van Dusen, Henry P., *What IS the Church Doing?* (New York, Charles Scribners' Sons, 1943, pp. xii, 194). Based in large part on first hand sources.

Van Kirk, Walter W., *Religion Renounces War* (Chicago, Willett, Clark & Company, 1934, pp. vi, 262). By a secretary of the Federal Council of Churches; listing, in an optimistic way, the recent pronouncements of churches, chiefly American, on the subject of war.

Visser 't Hooft, W. A., *Anglo-Catholicism and Orthodoxy. A Protestant View* (London, Student Christian Movement Press, 1933, pp. 175).

Vories, Wm. Merrell, *The Omi Brotherhood in Nippon* (Omi-Hachiman, Nippon, The Omi Brotherhood Book Department, pp. x, 180). By the founder.

Vories, Wm. Merrell, *A Mustard-Seed in Japan* (Omi-Hachiman, Omi Mission, 4th ed., 1922, pp. 147, vi, iv).

Walker, F. Deaville, *The Romance of the Black River. The Story of the C.M.S. Nigeria Mission* (London, Church Missionary Society, 1930, pp. xvi, 267). A popular account, without footnote references to authorities, but based upon several earlier books and on articles in the C.M.S. magazines.

Walsh, James Edward, *Father McShane of Maryknoll, Missioner in South China* (New York, Dial Press, 1932, pp. xv, 227).

Wasson, Alfred W., *Church Growth in Korea* (New York, International Missionary Council, 1934, pp. xii, 175). A scholarly study, chiefly of the part of the Korean church related to the Methodist Episcopal Church, South.

Watthé, Henry, *La Belle Vie du Missionnaire en Chine. Récits et Croquis* (Vichy, Maison du Missionnaire, no date, 2 vols., pp. xiv, 194, 223). By a Lazarist; giving a popular account of mission work in Kiangsi, largely from his own experience.

Weber, Herman C., *1933 Edition Yearbook of American Churches* (New York, Round Table Press, 1933, pp. 400).

Wenger, John C., *History of the Mennonites of the Franconia Conference* (Telford, Penn., The Franconia Mennonite Historical Society, 1937, pp. xvi, 523). Based upon careful and extensive research.

West China Missionary News (Chengtu, 1911-1941).

White, Hugh Vernon, *A Working Faith for the World* (New York, Harper & Brothers, 1938, pp. x, 213). Thoughtful.

Williams, Michael, with the collaboration of Julia Kernan, *The Catholic Church in Action* (New York, The Macmillan Co., 1934, pp. 358). By a Roman Catholic.

Wilson, Roland, *Official Year Book of the Commonwealth of Australia, No. 32, 1939* (Canberra, L. F. Johnston, 1940, pp. xxxii, 990).

Winslow, Jack C., *Christa Seva Sangha* (London, Society for the Propagation of the Gospel in Foreign Parts, 1930, pp. vii, 62). By the head of the group described.

Wiser, Charlotte Viall, and Wiser, William H., *Behind Mud Walls* (New York, Richard R. Smith, Inc., 1930, pp. x, 180). A popular description of a fairly typical village in North India, by Presbyterian missionaries; based upon a careful and scientific survey.

Work, Monroe N., editor, *Negro Year Book. An Annual Encyclopedia of the Negro* (Tuskegee Institute, The Negro Year Book Publishing Co., 1914 ff.).

The World Council Courier (New York, American headquarters World Council of Churches, 1941 ff.).

World Dominion. A Quarterly International Review of Christian Progress (London, World Dominion Press, 1923 ff.).

The World Tomorrow (New York, 1917-1934).

Wright, Edward Needles, *Conscientious Objectors in the Civil War* (University of Pennsylvania Press, 1931, pp. vii, 274). A scholarly study, unbiased and well documented.

Wrong, Margaret, *Africa and the Making of Books. Being a Survey of Africa's Need of Literature* (London, International Committee on Christian Literature for Africa, 1934, pp. 56). By the secretary of the International Committee on Christian Literature for Africa.

Yoder, Sanford Calvin, *For Conscience Sake. A Study of Mennonite Migrations Resulting from the World War* (Goshen, The Mennonite Historical Society, 1940, pp. xix, 300).

Young, Miriam, *Seen and Heard in a Punjab Village* (London, Student Christian Movement Press, 1931, pp. ix, 227). An account of personal experiences of a missionary.

Zeitschrift für Missionswissenschaft (Münster i.W., 1911 ff.).

INDEX

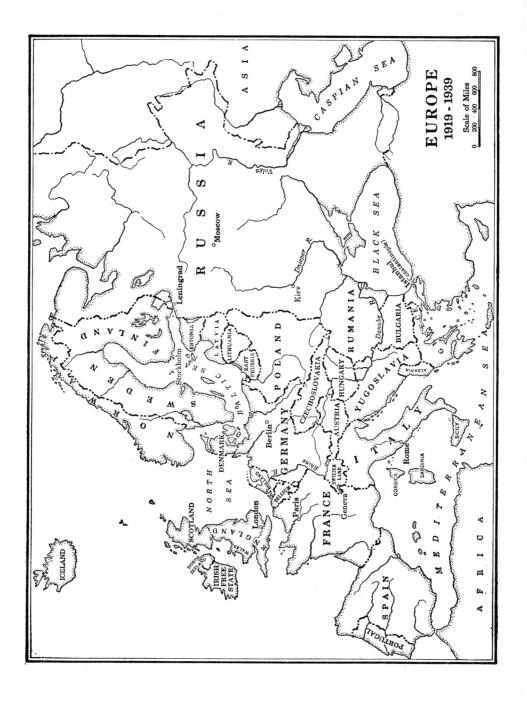

EUROPE
1919 - 1939

Scale of Miles
0   200   400   600   800

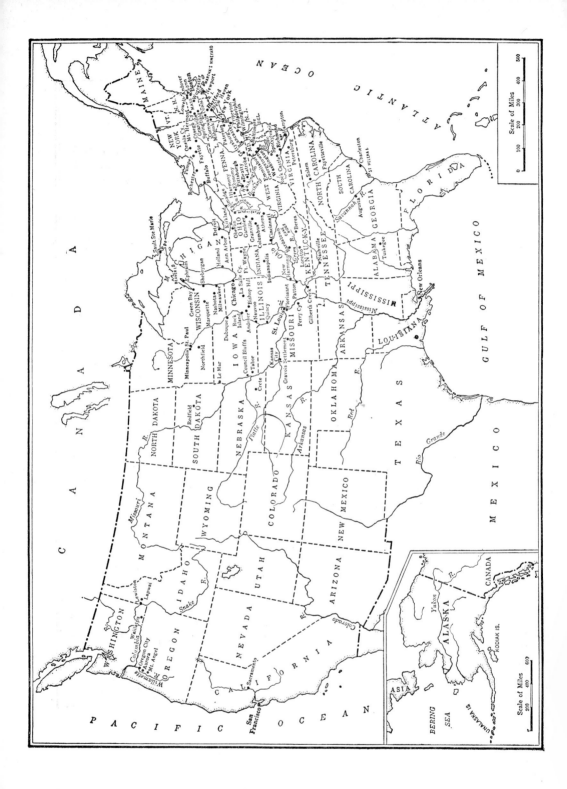

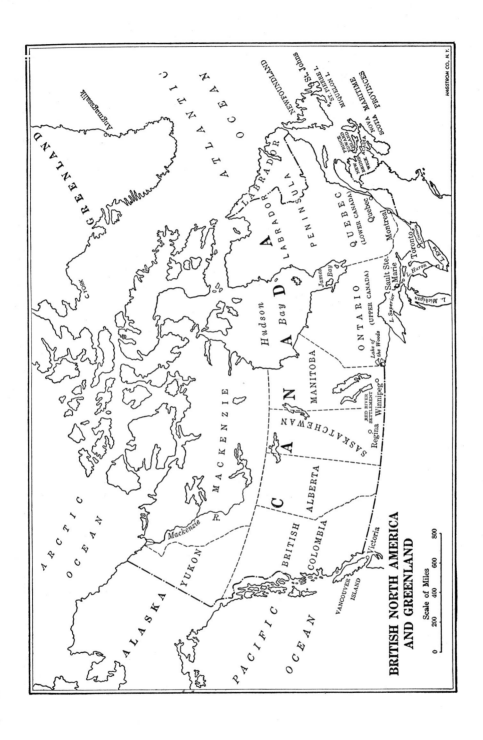

BRITISH NORTH AMERICA
AND GREENLAND

Scale of Miles

0   200   400   600   800

HAGSTROM CO., N. Y.

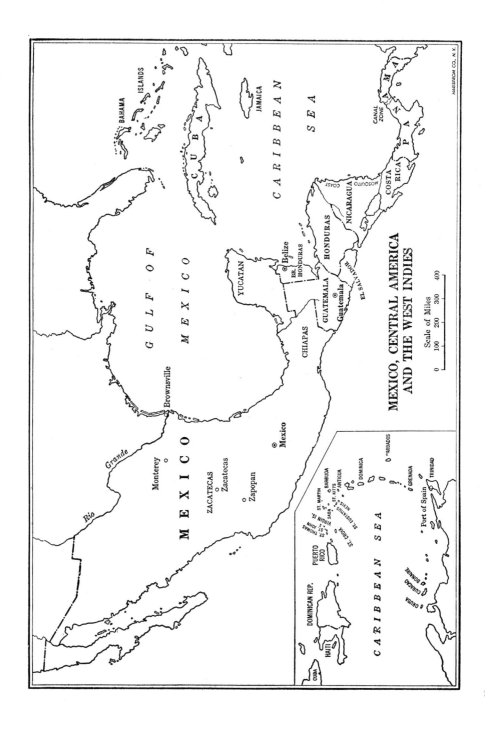

MEXICO, CENTRAL AMERICA
AND THE WEST INDIES

Scale of Miles

0   100   200   300   400

SOUTH AMERICA

Scale of Miles

0   200   400   600   800   1000

HAGSTROM CO., N.Y.

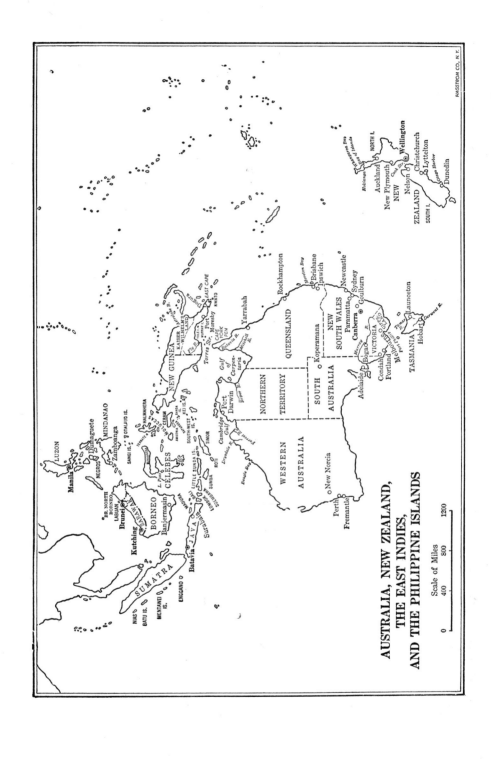

AUSTRALIA, NEW ZEALAND,
THE EAST INDIES,
AND THE PHILIPPINE ISLANDS

Scale of Miles

0   400   800   1200

HAGSTROM CO., N. Y.

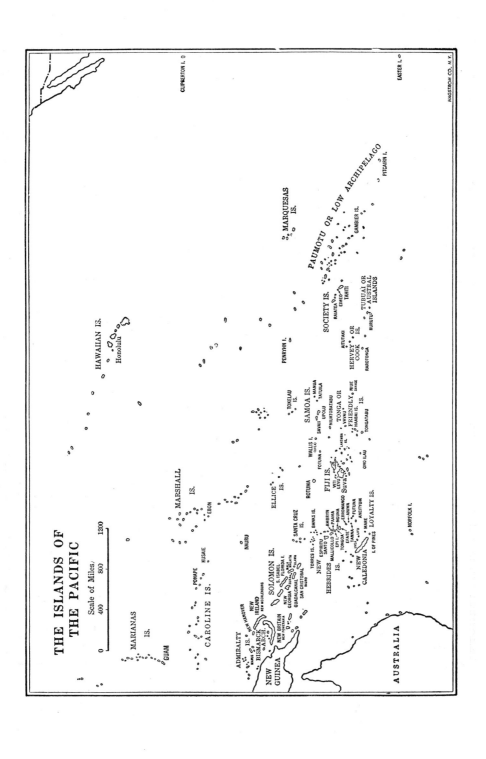

THE ISLANDS OF
THE PACIFIC

Scale of Miles
0   400   800   1200

MARIANAS IS.

GUAM

CAROLINE IS.

PONAPE
KUSAIE

MARSHALL IS.

EBON

NAURU

HAWAIIAN IS.
Honolulu

ADMIRALTY IS.
NEW HANOVER
NEW IRELAND
NEW MECKLENBURG
NEW BRITAIN
NEW POMERANIA
BISMARCK ARCH.
NEW GUINEA

SOLOMON IS.
S. ISABEL
NEW GEORGIA
GUADALCANAL
MALAITA
SAN CRISTOBAL
FLORIDA I.
GUADALCANAR

SANTA CRUZ IS.

BANKS IS.

TORRES IS.
NEW HEBRIDES IS.
ESPIRITU SANTO
MALLICOLLO
AMBRYM
PAAMA
EPI
API
TONGOA
EROMANGO
FUTUNA
EFATE
TANNA
ANIWA
ANEITYUM

NEW CALEDONIA
LOYALTY IS.
MARE
LIFU
I. OF PINES

NORFOLK I.

ROTUMA

FIJI IS.
WTI
LEVU
VTI LEVU
LAKEMBA
KANDAVU I.
Suva
ONO ILAU

WALLIS I.
FOTUNA

ELLICE IS.

TOKELAU IS.

SAMOA IS.
SAVAII
UPOLU
TATUILA
MANUA

TONGA OR FRIENDLY IS.
NIUATOBATABU
VAVAU
NIUE SAVAGE
HAABAI IS.
TONGATABU

PENRHYN I.

SOCIETY IS.
RAIATEA
EIMEO
TAHITI

MARQUESAS IS.

PAUMOTU OR LOW ARCHIPELAGO

GAMBIER IS.

PITCAIRN I.

HERVEY OR COOK IS.
AITUTAKI
RAROTONGA

TUBUAI OR AUSTRAL ISLANDS
RURUTU

CLIPPERTON I. 0

EASTER I. 0

AUSTRALIA

HAGSTROM CO., N. Y.

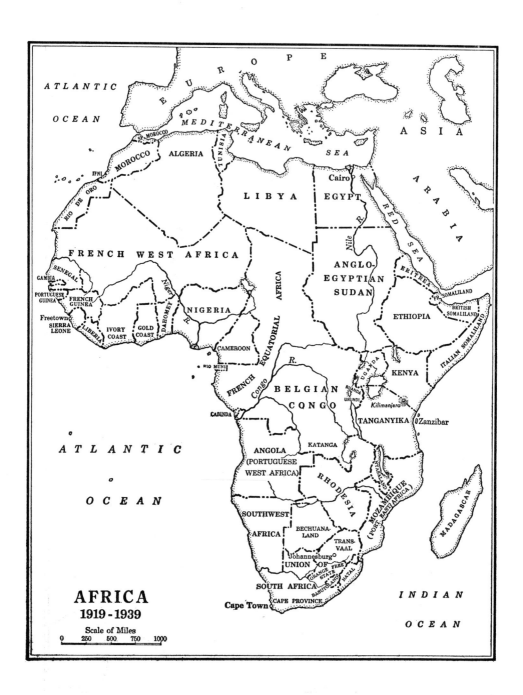

AFRICA
1919-1939

Scale of Miles
0   250   500   750   1000

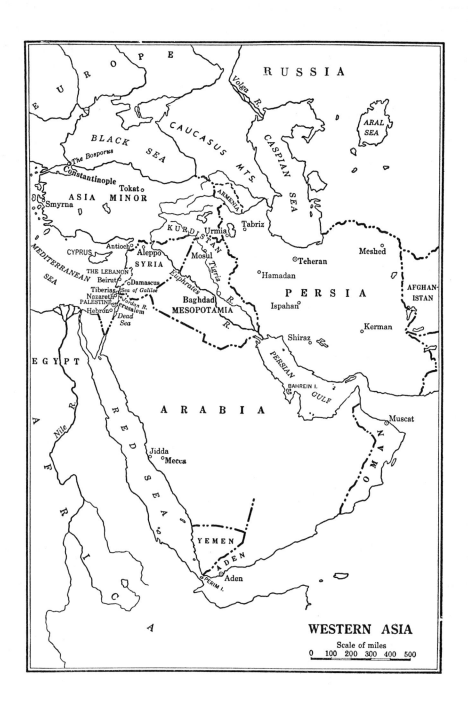

RUSSIA

Volga R.

ARAL
SEA

BLACK SEA

CAUCASUS MTS.

CASPIAN SEA

The Bosporus

Constantinople

Tokat

ASIA MINOR

Smyrna

ARMENIA

KURDISTAN

Urmia

Tabriz

Meshed

CYPRUS

Antioch

Aleppo

SYRIA

Mosul

Teheran

AFGHAN-
ISTAN

MEDITERRANEAN SEA

THE LEBANON

Beirut

Damascus

Euphrates

Tigris R.

Hamadan

PERSIA

Tiberias

Sea of Galilee

Nazareth

PALESTINE

Jordan R.

Jerusalem

Hebron

Dead
Sea

Baghdad

MESOPOTAMIA

R.

Ispahan

Kerman

EGYPT

Shiraz

PERSIAN

Nile R.

RED SEA

ARABIA

GULF

BAHREIN I.

Muscat

A F R I C A

Jidda

Mecca

OMAN

YEMEN

ADEN

PERIM I.

Aden

WESTERN ASIA

Scale of miles
0   100   200   300   400   500

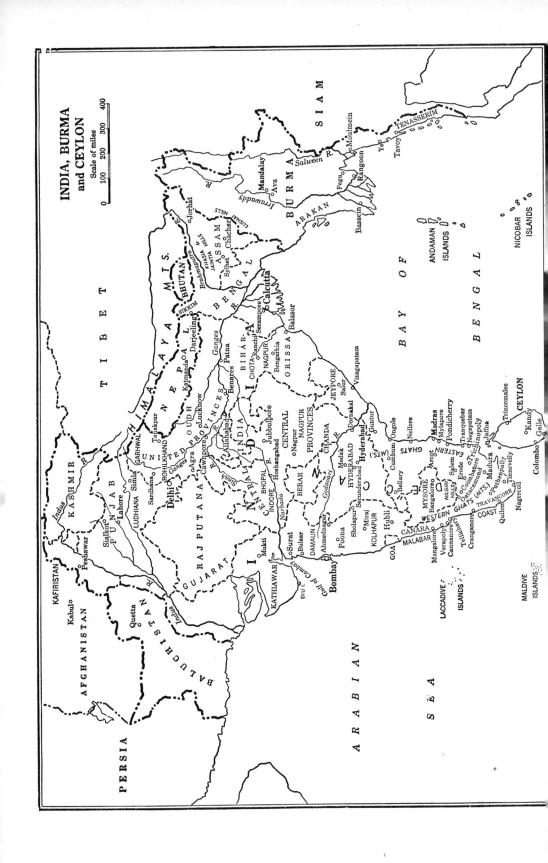

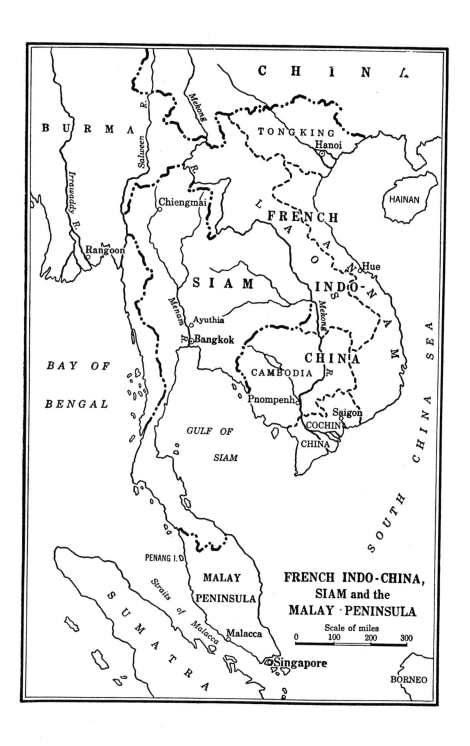

FRENCH INDO-CHINA,
SIAM and the
MALAY · PENINSULA

Scale of miles

0   100   200   300

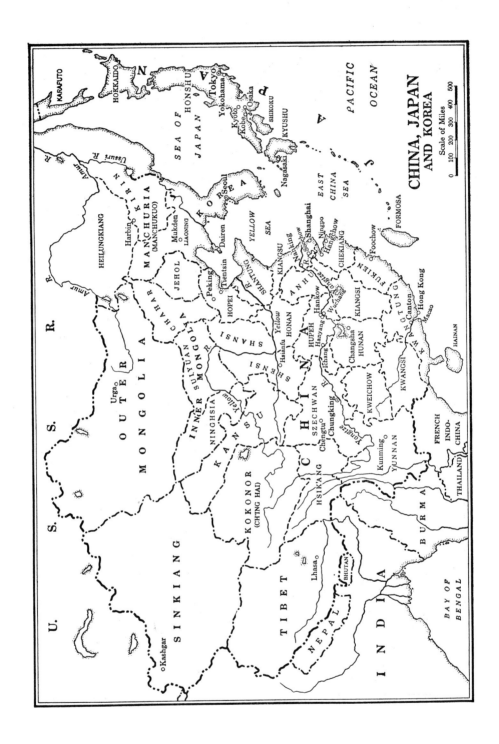

CHINA, JAPAN
AND KOREA

Scale of Miles

0   100 200 300 400 500